California
Wildlife

California Wildlife

A Practical Guide

FIRST EDITION

Tom Stienstra

FOGHORN ◢◣ OUTDOORS

California Wildlife

FIRST EDITION

Please send all comments to:

California Wildlife
First Edition
FOGHORN OUTDOORS
AVALON TRAVEL PUBLISHING, INC.
5855 Beaudry Street.
Emeryville, CA 94608, USA
e-mail: info@travelmatters.com
www.travelmatters.com

Printing History
1st edition—June 2000
5 4 3 2 1 0

All illustrations by Paul B. Johnson/California
Department of Fish and Game unless otherwise noted.

Front cover photo: sea otter *(Enhydra lutris)* © Gerry Ellis/ENP Images

Editors: Jeannie Trizzino, Valerie Sellers Blanton
Design and Production: David Hurst, Karen McKinley
Cartography: Colby Barr, Mike Morgenfeld
Index: Sondra Nation

ISBN: 1-57354-087-0
Library of Congress Cataloging-In-Publication Data has been applied for.

Published by
Avalon Travel Publishing, Inc.
5855 Beaudry St.
Emeryville, CA 94608, USA

Printed in the U.S.A.

Distributed in the United States and Canada by Publishers Group West

For Jeremy and Kris

Credits

Paul B. Johnson, artist

The late Paul Johnson was a renowned artist and wildlife specialist. He worked as an artist and draftsman for the then State Division of Architecture, and as his talents became recognized, started creating artwork for the Department of Fish and Game on commission. His artwork later became a trademark in the magazine *California Outdoors*. Unlike many of the top artists of the past century, Johnson did not kill any wildlife, including birds, in order to sketch or paint them. He painted California's first seven duck stamps, then donated the designs to Ducks Unlimited to raise conservation funds to protect wetland habitat.

George Seymour

George Seymour conducted many of the draft interviews with scientists that appear under the heading, "Biologists' Notes." Seymour, an avid wildlife lover, worked for the Department of Fish and Game as a conservation education consultant.

Janet Connaughton

Research editor Janet Connaughton worked with Tom Stienstra to network with hundreds of scientists and field scouts in the process of coordinating the location information in this book, including fact-checking all listings. She is credited as research editor in eight of Tom Stienstra's current books.

The following scientists, staffers and field scouts provided research assistance in this project.

Department of Fish and Game

Ray Alley, Bill Asserson, Angie Barlow, Joyce Bigham, Sam Blankenship, Vern Bleich, L.B. Boydstun, Tim Burton, Rich Callas, Roy Cameron, Lyann Comrack, Mark Crossland, Chanelle Davis, Angie DeFrancesco, Jack Edwards, John Fisher, Gene Fleming, Barry Garrison, Gordon Gould, Nathan Graveline, Bill Grenfell, John Gustafson, Debra Hamilton, Doyle Hannon, Kevin Hill, Terry Hodges, Bill Holtz, Kevin Hunting, Nancy Hutchins, Brian Hunter, Wendell Jones, Ron Jurek, Randolph O. Kelly, Cris Langner, Greg Laret, Terry Mansfield, John Massie, Ken Mayer, Russell Mohr, Debbie Petersen, Andy Pauli, Steve Parmeter, Bruce Reno, Alexia Retallack, Mike Rode, Ron Schlorff, Jackie Smith, Jerry Spratt, Bob Stafford, Steve Torres, Diana L. Watters, Dave Walker, Paul Wertz, Dave Zezulak

U.S. Department of Fish and Wildlife

Karl Benz, Dick Hardt, Michelle Hester, Tim Keldsen, Anne Marie LaRosa, Dave Peretka, Ron Ryno, Tom Vanderburg, Dave Vogel

Additional Assistance

Bruce Babbitt, Secretary, U.S. Department of Interior; Joe Cordaro, National Marine Fisheries Service; Joe DiDonato, East Bay Regional Park District; Mike Dombeck, Chief, U.S. Forest Service; Tom Gardali, Palomarin Field Station, Point Reyes Bird Observatory; Pat Garrahan, Klamath National Forest; Ned MacKay, East Bay Regional Park District; Matt Mathes, U.S. Forest Service Regional Headquarters; Carol McCall, Smith River National Recreation Area; John McCosker, Steinhart Aquarium; Diana McDonell, Cosumnes River Preserve; Micki Mitchell, Six Rivers National Forest; Bob Richards, Tahoe Research Lab; Debby Shelby, Shasta-Trinity National Forest; Hugh Vicker, Washington D.C. headquarters, Department of Interior

Field Scouts

Dan Bacher, Dusty Baker, Bill Beebe, Elvin Bishop, Jack Brown, Rob Brown, Pete Cafone, Barry Canevaro, George Carl, Paul Chinn, Dave Dayton, Cy Donaldson, Jacqueline Douglas, Ed Dunckel, Steve Dunckel, Andy Eldridge, Doc Eldridge, Neal Eldridge, Clancy Enlow, Rich Fletcher, Phil Ford, Keith Fraser, Michael Furniss, Mike Gaddis, Billy Gianquinto, Ron Gribble, Steve Griffin, John Hamilton, Tom Hampson, Chuck Harrison, Will Hearst, John Higley, Joe Hiss, Waylon Jennings, Bill Karr, Rob Keck, Jim Klinger, Terry Knight, John Korb, Hippo Lau, Jonah Li, Dave Lyon, Ned MacKay, Doug McConnell, Jim McDaniel, Gary Miralles, Bob Moore, Kathie Morgan, Mike Moropoulos, Dick Murdock, Jim Niemiec, Peter Ottesen, Galen Onizuka, Jeffrey Patty, Brett Pauly, Dick Pool, Tom Randall, John Reginato, Ed Rice, Brian Riley, Bob Robb, Kurt Rogers, Tom Rooney, Ray Rychnovsky, Donna Sager, Rick Sager, Robyn Schlueter, Glenn Schwarz, George Seifert, Jim Sevrens, Bob Simms, Wayne Smith, Eleanor Stienstra, Robert Stienstra, Sr., Robert Stienstra, Jr., Stephani Stienstra, Craig Stone, David Strege, Bill Sunderland, Pete Thomas, Roger Thomas, Jeannie Trizzino, Don Vachini, Jim "Meatball" Williams, Lance Williams, Rolla Williams, Toby "Cloud Dancer" Williams, Larry Yant, Gus Zimmer

Contents

Introduction

ONE EVENING WHILE WORKING ON THIS BOOK, I asked my family, "If you could choose to be any animal—bird, fish, or reptile—what would you be?"

Kris, 8, answered "bald eagle," and then explained why: "Because they can fly high and fast, they're smart and have great eyesight, and they're illegal to shoot." His brother, Jeremy, 11, said he would prefer being a duck, a drake mallard in particular. "Because they can do it all—fly, swim, dive, and walk," he explained, "and plus they're pretty, with their shiny heads." My wife, Stephani, said she would like to be an owl. "They are gifted flyers, silent at night, and they are majestic birds especially at sunset, and they get a lot of respect from people and other animals."

All my family's favorites share a common trait—they are once again abundant after being nearly wiped out early last century. In fact, in an analysis of the state's wildlife history, you will discover that many species are at population highs. There are more ducks, geese, elk, mountain lions, sea lions, white sharks, largemouth bass, turkeys, pelicans, raccoons, sandhill cranes, sea otters, squirrels, swans, wild pigs, sturgeon, whales, and many other creatures than at any time in the past 100 years. It is a testimonial that we are back on the right track, though there are still threats.

It wasn't always this way. After people nearly annihilated many species by 1900, a relatively new public consciousness has evolved in California since the 1960s, bringing with it a wildlife ethic that has allowed many species to again thrive.

From the gold rush in 1849 until the laws banning DDT in the 1960s and protecting marine mammals in the 1970s, many species were nearly wiped out in California from a combination of habitat loss, market hunting, trapping, poisoning, and poaching. The wildlife put at severe risk include the California condor, curlew, bald eagle, golden eagle, falcon, hawk, heron, pelican, sandhill crane, swan, beaver, mink, otter, elk, and whale. Two that didn't make it to the 21st century were grizzly bears and wolves, which have been extirpated in California.

It is largely to the credit of the Department of Fish and Game, the California legislature, Congress, and the federal U.S. Fish and Wildlife Service that these species have been brought back all the way from the brink of destruction. We are a nation of laws: Congress and the California legislature write the wildlife laws, and the Department of Fish and Game and the U.S. Fish and Wildlife Service enforce them, despite being constantly undermined politically in many arenas. The difficulties include a shortage of game wardens, very little support for wildlife laws, and very little punishment for those breaking them in cities and urban areas, and appointed resource department executives whose decisions are often politicized—that is, their decisions are made with primary regard to political paybacks and little regard to the final effect to wildlife.

As the 21st century arrives, the biggest threats to wildlife are only somewhat different than in the past—losses to habitat and overharvest (excessive commercial fishing). Now, as other animals are on the way to recovery (such as the elk, peregrine falcon, and bald eagle) aquatic and desert wildlife have become the most vulnerable.

In the coming century, the single biggest threat to natural resources in California are massive water projects and the manipulation of water resources that go with them, often schemed with little regard to natural aquatic systems and effects on fisheries. Water projects have already caused massive declines in many fish populations in California, yet more are being planned. These water projects are often treated as above the law, rendering useless the Endangered Species Act: In 25 years, more than 500 aquatic species have been listed as endangered in America, typically victimized by water manipulation, and yet the National Marine Fisheries Service has been unable to recover and de-list a single aquatic species. That's zero-for-500, a "perfect" record.

The second biggest threat is overharvest of fish at sea by commercial mother ships, including boats from other countries, most notably Japan. By using lines miles long with 5,000 or more hooks, as well as massive vacuum cleaner-like driftnets, these fishing techniques are simply killing too many fish and marine mammals, including a huge, wasted by-catch of non-target species. To protest this horrendous loss of life, I support the vote by the International Game Fish Association for a worldwide boycott on the purchase and consumption of swordfish, which are taken commercially by both longlines and driftnets.

Lastly, a handful of slow-growing desert creatures, most notably the desert tortoise and horned lizard, could be wiped out by commercial poachers who supply an illegal, underground market at L.A.-area pet stores. This simply must be stopped. Just as the market hunters killed all but the last two elk in California more than 100 years ago, poachers would happily take the last existing tortoise in exchange for cash, then go on to something else. To stop this, or any other illegal wildlife activity, if you have information, call the state's toll-free poacher hotline at 888-DFG-CAL-TIP (888-334-2258 or 916-327-9953).

The truth is, I believe the public will win all of these battles to protect wildlife resources, just as has been done before with so many species. Remember that a century ago, there were catastrophic declines with dozens of wildlife species and that many of these are now returning to their most abundant numbers in 100 years.

You see, I believe that deep in the core of public consciousness there is something good, and that given a choice between good or evil, mankind as a collective will always choose good. Such are the choices with the critters we love so much.

This book was written with the intent that it will quickly become your bible for California wildlife, to learn about the most vital wildlife species in California, their unique habits, and how to see them and make them a part of your life. (I've also included a few prime wildlife viewing spots along the California border—the Klamath Basin National Wildlife Refuges Complex and the Kalmiopsis Wilderness.) Enjoy California's great natural resources. I have learned that when people learn to love something is when they are most apt to protect it.

The outdoors is good for the soul. An adventure can refresh the spirit, especially while sharing the world of your favorite wildlife, whether it be elk, eagle, bear, salmon, tortoise—or who knows, maybe Bigfoot!

See you out there!

—*Tom Stienstra*

How to Use This Guide

Species: The scientific name of each animal is listed. Where a number of species are discussed, only the genus is given.

Type: Each animal has been classified generally as fish, bird, mammal, or other (insect, crustacean, reptile, or amphibian).

ANIMAL	Deer, Mule
SPECIES	*Odocoileus hemionus*
TYPE	mammal
STATUS	OK
SEE ALSO	Bighorn, Elk, Pronghorn

Status: The status given for each animal reflects the most critical state or federal classification that animal has received. For example, the bald eagle has been delisted under the federal Endangered Species Act, but as of this writing, it is still listed as an endangered species in California under the California Endangered Species Act. Thus, I have listed its status as endangered, though its status will probably be reviewed and changed in the future.

In cases where one species or genus described in the text is endangered or introduced and others are not, all the symbols will appear on the status line, and the text will make it clear which species or varieties are either stable, endangered, threatened, or introduced. The status ratings are based solely on California and federal endangered species classifications. If the status is listed as **OK**, the population is stable or possibly growing. This is the highest rating possible. Many of the animals listed here as stable may be declining or extremely limited in their distribution, but simply haven't completed the federal or state review process (and let's hope they haven't disappeared before the process can be finished!).

See Also: Animals that are in the same family or that are closely related in behavior are listed here by their common names.

About the Maps

The maps in this book show the general range of each animal in the state of California based on range maps provided by state and federal agencies. The gray areas represent areas where the animal can be seen. White areas represent areas where the animal is not typically found.

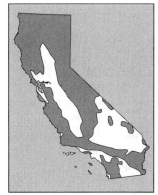

About the Wildlife Viewing Locations

These locations represent the best places to view California wildlife based on recommendations from state wildlife biologists and includes a few excellent Oregon locations that are along the California border. The listing of primary sightings that follows the site description is merely a starting point and is keyed directly to the text. Some animals, like the marten, are difficult to find, but the sites listed for the pine marten represent accessible marten habitats. Viewing wild animals in their native surroundings is not like seeing animals in a zoo; it requires patience and practice, but when you do spot an animal you've never seen before, the experience is unforgettable and will last a lifetime.

About the Wildlife Checklist

The index doubles as a handy wildlife viewing checklist. Place a check next to each animal and make a note of the date and location where you first saw the animal. You might find this information useful in planning future wildlife viewing expeditions.

Anchovy

WHO WOULD THINK THAT A SIX-INCH FISH COULD determine the course on which fortunes turn? Or even define the abundance of the Pacific Ocean?

Those who grasp how the little anchovy is the linchpin of the marine food chain also understand the risks that men of the sea have taken to catch unbelievable tons of them, the battles on the docks over their value, and how in the end nearly every creature of the sea along the Pacific Coast is at least partially dependent on them.

The first time I realized the impact the anchovy has on California marine resources

ANIMAL	Northern Anchovy
SPECIES	*Engraulis mordax*
TYPE	fish
STATUS	OK

—and the people who fish for them—was one morning on the docks many years ago, when I boarded a fishing boat called the *Buccaneer* with a commercial fisherman known as "Meatball." His real name was Jimmy Williams, but when I introduced myself, he stuck his hand out and said, "Hi, I'm Meatball." Meatball explained how uncertain and risky it was to be a commercial fisherman. "It can be dangerous out here," he said as we cruised out of port. "Most of the time it's fine for us, but every once in a while we get caught in marginal conditions."

He was half-complaining, half-bragging: complaining about dealing with the weather and hazardous seas, fish migrations and fluctuations, politics and permits, overhead costs and market forces—but also bragging because, despite those factors, he was making a fortune. In 10 years, he had become a millionaire. Then, in 1998, his seemingly casual words about "danger" rang in my mind when the news came that Williams had been killed at sea in a boating accident while netting anchovy.

While Williams was on the deck of a friend's commercial fishing boat (that is, supervising the net operation, not piloting the boat), the *Vaya con Dios*, it apparently struck a pinnacle. It suddenly had a gash in the bottom and was going down amid a tangle of net. The tragedy came quickly. In the end, four men died. Close friends said that Williams, who spent most of his life on the open sea, had never learned how to swim. The Coast Guard later reported that rescuers on the scene discovered the net had not been cut free and was still attached to the boat, survival suits were unworn, and an assist boat and

anchovy

life raft were all floating. Ironically, *Vaya con Dios* means "Go with God" in Spanish.

The lure of big money quick is why there is always a line for the commercial permits to net anchovy. Few have quarrels over the relatively small number caught for use as bait or for human consumption as canned, frozen, or fresh-caught fish, but that is just the beginning of the real saga on the docks: Anchovy are also caught by the metric ton and ground up to make animal feed and fertilizer in a process known as "reduction."

Many believe that taking such huge numbers of anchovy for reduction into fish meal is a waste of a vital resource. Because of the huge amount of money at stake, those with permits at times appear to stop at nothing in their quest to vacuum the ocean as they gather in purse seine nets full of anchovy. Federal and state authorities are in the delicate position of determining a quota for the annual catch—balancing the welfare of the anchovy against the welfare of the commercial fishing industry. However, this sector of the commercial fishing lobby is an extremely wealthy and powerful political force, and it is set on protecting its own interests.

About 65% of the anchovy population dies each year naturally as forage for other species.

The pressure from that self-interest, in turn, has weakened the scientific focus of the management of this fishery. Many marine mammals and fish appear to be dependent on the anchovy as their primary food source on the Pacific coastal marine food chain. Yet it is also true that the populations of these marine species cycle up and down without a direct parallel to the number of anchovy; hence, it is an imperfect science. But the obvious conclusion is: Catch too many anchovy and you put the marine food chain at risk.

Hence this little six-inch fish holds the fate of much of the Pacific.

The day I joined Meatball on the *Buccaneer,* he said he planned to head out to sea and then along the coast to a favorite spot of his, though it meant fishing a bit shallow, close to the ocean breakers. But on the way out, a few hundred yards out of the harbor, Meatball flicked on his electronic fish-finding equipment, just to demonstrate it to me, and was stunned to discover that we were right over the top of a huge school of anchovy.

In the next half hour, Meatball orchestrated the setting of the purse seine around the school, and in minutes had them in the boat—a giant haul. Seagulls were everywhere, and the sea air was filled with their harsh squawks.

Back at the dock, huge scoops of anchovy were lifted out of the boat, and Meatball smiled at each one.

"This was incredible today," he said. "Can you believe we got them within two minutes of the dock?"

Then he paused, and smiled again.

"It isn't always this easy."

Biologists' Notes

Although small in size, the Northern anchovy is one of the most valuable fishery resources along the western shore of North America.

The Northern anchovy *(Engraulis mordax)* is a small, slender-bodied fish. It may attain a maximum length of nine inches but is usually less than seven, and often four to six inches. It has only one dorsal fin, and there is no lateral line along the sides. The color is metallic blue-green on the back, and the sides and belly are silver.

Anchovy occur in vast numbers and can be spread over thousands of square miles of coastal waters off the Queen Charlotte Islands, British Columbia, to Cabo San Lucas, Baja California.

The Northern anchovy is a schooling fish and is the most abundant species in the California current. It ranges up to 200 miles out from shore, with eggs and larvae found 300 miles out from Cape Mendocino, California, to Cabo San Lucas, Baja California, in some years; however, most schools occur within 100 miles offshore. The schools are generally near the surface at night and move deeper in the water during the day.

Studies investigating genetic characteristics of anchovy in different areas indicate there are three subpopulations in California and Baja California waters. The northern stock occurs off northern California, Oregon, and Washington. The central stock, which is the most abundant, extend south from San Francisco to Punta Baja, Baja California. The southern stock is found from Punta Baja to Cabo San Lucas.

Egg and larva surveys have been the primary means of determining the size of the spawning portion of the populations, which fluctuates from year to year. Natural environmental changes are believed responsible for the changes in the numbers of anchovy produced annually.

Northern anchovy are primarily filter feeders, straining tiny food particles from the water as they passes over their gills. Sometimes, as they grow larger, they become predatory. Fish remains up to an inch and a half long have been found in the stomachs of five-inch-long anchovy.

Most anchovy reach sexual maturity at the end of their first year and spawn when they are four and a half to five inches long. Almost all mature in two years. When they are six to eight inches long, the females may contain from 4,000 to 20,000 oval-shaped eggs in various stages of development. When conditions are right, anchovy may spawn many times a year in small batches. The major spawning occurs in the early spring months.

The anchovy is an important forage fish. Many marine mammals, birds, and fish include anchovy in their diets. As with most forage fish, they have a high reproductive potential and a short lifespan. About 65% of the population dies each year naturally as forage for other species. Few anchovy reach extended ages although a few may live up to seven years.

The oval shape helps distinguish anchovy eggs from the round eggs of other pelagic fishes. Recent analysis of anchovy spawning and larval success has shown that the larval survival depends heavily on the timing and duration of the coast upwelling relative to the time of anchovy spawning. Upwelling along the coast brings up nutrients that nurture the production of food that is available to the anchovy larvae, after the egg sac is absorbed. This is crucial to the larvae's survival.

Where to see anchovy

ANACAPA ISLAND, CHANNEL ISLANDS, OFFSHORE FROM VENTURA COUNTY

FISHERMAN'S WHARF, IN SAN FRANCISCO

PACIFICA PIER, IN SAN MATEO COUNTY

SAN PEDRO LANDING, IN LOS ANGELES COUNTY

UNDERWATER WORLD, IN SAN FRANCISCO

Besides its importance as a forage fish, the anchovy also supports an important commercial fishery. Some of the catch is canned, frozen, or sold fresh for human consumption, and a share is canned for pet food. In addition, huge quantities of the fish are reduced into fish meal, which is used as a protein additive to livestock and poultry foods.

Anchovy are also important to the recreational fisherman in California. Sport anglers are aware that the anchovy is the principal forage of many fish of interest to them, and many use anchovy as bait for ocean game fish.

Because of its ecological importance as well as its commercial and recreational value, the use imposed on the central stock of the Northern anchovy by the United States and Mexico has been the center of a spirited controversy. The controversy involves the appropriate use of the resource and the allocation of the resource to different user groups.

The anchovy resource is presently managed under state and federal regulations. These regulations establish minimum size limits and annual catch quotas on the fisheries. A major protective measure has been the establishment of a one-million-ton reserve to provide protection for the long-term existence and productivity of the resource, and forage for the dependent marine species.

Badger

The real world isn't a sanctuary for most animals. It's a war zone. One reason for that is the badger. There are some animals you just plain don't mess with, whether you are a dog, gopher, or person—the badger is one of those animals.

I remember one evening when I was hiking across some coastal foothill grasslands with my old companion, Rebel, my canine buddy for 17 years. Rebel usually shadowed my every move, but he also had hunting instincts. This evening he suddenly picked up a scent and in a few minutes had led me to a hole in the ground that was about the size of a lunch plate. Rebel stalked that hole, and then when inches away, suddenly jumped backwards in mid-air, like a gymnast in the Dog Olympics, landing five feet away.

ANIMAL	Badger
SPECIES	*Taxidea/taxus*
TYPE	mammal
STATUS	OK
SEE ALSO	fisher, marten, mink, otters, raccoon, skunks

A moment later, a badger stuck his nose about one inch out of that hole, his small dark eyes like laser beams, white stripes jetting back across the sides of his dark broad head. The badger then bared his teeth and uttered the fiercest growl in all of nature. It was a sound that was frightening, electrifying, and paralyzing all at once. Rebel, the smartest dog in the vicinity (and also the *only* dog in the vicinity), backed off slowly, as if he had confronted a grizzly bear.

As we walked across the foothills at dusk, I realized that I had seen a rare, full-on glimpse of what makes the badger like no other animal in the wild.

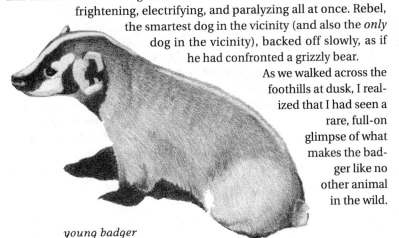

young badger

Of course, they are unmistakable on sight, with those white stripes across a dark head and eyes that seem as black as the eyeholes of a skull. They weigh only about 10 to 15 pounds, but pound-for-pound, might be the most ferocious of all creatures when provoked. If they grew to the size of grizzly bear (about 800 pounds), they would rule the world like *T. rex.*

Fortunately their primary diet is rodents, especially mice and gophers, and can also include marmots in the high country, ground squirrels in the alpine zone, and just about anything dumb enough to stick its nose in its hole, or sett. Their claws are made for digging, and they seem to enjoy digging gophers or anything else out of the ground. That is how they hunt, digging for burrowing animals.

El tejon is Spanish for badger, which lends its name to the Tejon Pass between the Central Valley and Southern California.

After a meal, they will return to their own sett and mind their own business. At that point, they tend not to bother any other animals about anything. But you know something? What the badger hates more than anything is when something uninvited goes poking a nose into its hole. Then out comes the growl and the bared fangs—if the intruder is still within short range, it's big trouble ahead. Many curious young dogs that get too close can be savagely clawed, and if the dog tries to fight back, it can be torn to shreds.

About the only thing the badger can't fight is encroachment by high numbers of people, especially by rural subdivisions. Badgers don't like being crowded, and they will leave if pushed by development, never to return. In the long run, this is their only real threat.

A Native American friend, Dancing Water, once told me that many of the most successful people are blessed with what is called "badger medicine"—the ability able to withdraw into their hole for long periods of time and sustain and nurture their natural passions into projects—but if anybody violates the sanctity of the den, they get their heads bitten off. She also said I had a lot of badger medicine, and by the way, was I working on a book? Yes? "See you later."

Most people have only seen badgers in wildlife museums, small zoos, and on TV in nature film clips. In a lifetime in the field, I've only seen three.

In each case, I felt an unexpected sense of awe, just by the look on its face. I've felt similar sensations with mountain lion, great horned owl, white shark, and grizzly bear. Of those, it was the badger that sent the deepest shivers through me.

Biologists' Notes

The badger, *Taxidea taxus*, is a short-legged, powerfully built animal that weighs from 10 to 20 pounds. It is classified in the same family as weasels and wolverines (Mustelidae). Its front legs are bowed and the tail is stubby, only four or five inches in length. Loose fur hangs down on the sides, giving the animal a low, squat appearance.

The badger's overall color is a grizzled yellowish gray. The flat, broad head is dark brown to black and strikingly marked with white stripes along the sides and top of its face. Its ears are short and rounded and black on the back side—its markings are so distinctive that it cannot be mistaken for any other native California mammal.

The badger is noted for being a tenacious fighter. When cornered or backed into his den, the badger's fierce growls and explosive hissing intimidate most predators. If caught out in the open, its thick fur and loose, tough skin protect it from nearly all attackers except the mountain lion and man.

Unlike the fox and coyote, which capture their prey by fleet pursuit or by stealth, the badger digs its prey out of the ground. It is obvious that its short, powerful legs and long claws are adapted for this purpose and not for running. Sometimes in high mountain meadows or on the grassy benches of the low rolling foothills, there will be evidence of profuse digging, especially in colonies of gophers or picket pin ground squirrels, which are the badger's favorite prey. This usually indicates a badger's presence and perhaps a nearby den. Although most of their hunting and digging is done at night, they can be observed near these areas usually in late afternoon. They lie flat on the ground or, if disturbed, they run to their den.

The badger is still found all over California, from the floors of the great valleys to the red fir belt at six or seven thousand feet. It has been seen on the floor of Death Valley and on top of the White Mountains at 13,000 feet. However, it is localized and found in the greatest abundance on flats and grasslands where there are numerous burrowing rodents on which it preys. During from spring to summer, the badger will have a larger territory than during the winter when it will have a smaller territory and possibly go into a semi-hibernation state, though badgers are not true hibernators.

When digging out a gopher or a ground squirrel the badger's actions are methodical and seem almost leisurely. As it progresses into the earth the soil is thrown back by the front feet and kicked out of the hole by the hind feet in a slow, constant stream. Apparently the badger can sense or feel

Where to see badger

BUTTE VALLEY NATIONAL GRASSLANDS, IN SISKIYOU COUNTY

KYBURZ MARSH, NEAR SIERRAVILLE, IN SIERRA COUNTY

LIVING DESERT, NEAR PALM DESERT, IN RIVERSIDE COUNTY

SHASTA VALLEY STATE WILDLIFE AREA, IN SISKIYOU COUNTY

TOPANGA STATE PARK, SOUTH OF SANTA MONICA, IN LOS ANGELES COUNTY

approaching footsteps, for if a human nears the hole there is a sudden flurry of digging and in seconds it literally digs itself out of sight. All at once the sand ceases to spurt out of the hole, and the growls and snarling of the disturbed badger become barely audible as he plugs up the hole behind him.

It digs its own den by burrowing underground. The den's opening is readily recognized since it is 10 to 12 inches wide and oval-shaped horizontally instead of vertically like other burrowing animals.

The badger's young are born in April and May. The mother has one litter a year of two to four babies. Occasionally, the young can be seen from a distance sunning themselves near the entrance to their den. Even as babies they are almost exact duplicates of the adults in color and markings. As juveniles, they enjoy digging.

In an area where there is an abundance of burrowing rodents, there will be many badger holes and much digging, for even the young practice digging as they learn from their parents the things a young badger should know. Apparently they are attentive students, and, like their parents, develop a keen sense of smell, for by the time they are a few months old they are soon in pursuit of a hapless mouse or gopher and, like their parents, dig with fierce intent.

Bass, Largemouth

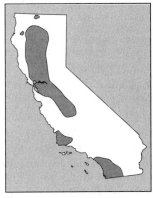

On a warm, sunny afternoon at a farm pond, a largemouth bass stretched the possibilities of what is possible on this planet of ours.

We were out for a picnic mostly, having received permission to fish this pond on private property, said to be filled with little bluegill. Occasionally we'd even catch one, between throwing a stick in the water for a golden retriever to fetch.

At one point, I had hooked this little bluegill and was letting it tussle about for a bit, just letting it swim around, not reeling it in right away, enjoying the moment. Right then, in full view and to my complete shock,

ANIMAL	Bass, Largemouth
SPECIES	*Micropterus salmoides*
TYPE	fish
STATUS	OK

this 12-pound bass came up from behind that bluegill, opened his mouth, and swam forward, inhaling that bluegill like a starship taking in a shuttle-craft in *Star Trek*.

largemouth bass

With the bluegill inside its mouth, the bass then disappeared to the bottom of the lake. Figuring I had just hooked the biggest bass of my life by accident, I tried to set the hook. A moment later, the little bluegill popped to the surface and played dead. For a moment I was crestfallen. But then the giant bass was right back, suspended just under it, and when I twitched the bluegill, it came back to life, and just like that, the bass inhaled it again.

This time I waited several minutes, hoping the bass would eat the bluegill. Finally, I set the hook, and just like before, the bluegill popped free, and came to the surface. I waited about five minutes, but this time the bass was gone, apparently spooked. I finally let the bluegill go, and as it swam off, the bass charged out of the depths and obliterated that bluegill, consuming it in one, ferocious attack.

In 1959 a southern strain of largemouth bass was airlifted from Florida and planted in some southern California lakes. Under ideal conditions, this strain can attain much greater weights than the northern types, and about 100 bass weighing 10 pounds or more are caught annually.

It is memories like these that inspire a cult-like following for bass among anglers. Almost everybody who chases bass has a story like this.

Of course, it is illegal to intentionally use bluegill for bait, just as it is illegal to use rainbow trout for bait. But this encounter shows how in California, memories are being made every year, not just looked up in the record books.

The most famous of all is a 22-pound bass caught and released at Lake Castaic by Bob Crupi. It was the biggest bass ever photographed in the world, and the largest caught in California history. In addition, it was just four ounces shy of the all-time world record, a legend among legends: That fish weighed 22 pounds, four ounces, and was caught in 1932 in Georgia by a postal worker named George Perry, who after documenting the fish's weight at the post office scale, then took it home, cut it up, cooked it, and with the help of his family, ate it.

But like I said, there are many such stories. Between three Southern California lakes, there are a half dozen world records: four line-class world records at Lake Castaic, one line-class record at Lake Casitas, and the largest 5-fish limit at Lower Otay Lake.

Because bass can stretch the imagination, and the pursuit often so passionate that in the choice between bass or spouse, some anglers have chosen bass. Fishing for bass is fun at all stages, whether fishing ponds for scads of 10-inchers, coves of lakes for 2-pounders, or deepwater reservoirs for the big ones, the 10-pounders and up.

They strike hard, fight hard, and yet are easily released to fight again another day. In the freshwater world of fish, they are natural-born predators. Bass love eating, nightcrawlers, minnows, and other small fish. As they get bigger, they will expand their diet to small trout, shad, shiners, and small crawdads. As they grow and get huge, they will consider all of the above, plus 12-inch rainbow trout and on a lucky day, maybe a baby duck. Lures are even sold that simulate 10-inch trout and ducklings.

You never know what is going to happen next with these fellows, and that's what makes them so exciting.

One time my late friend, Clyde Gibbs, had built a miniature motor boat, about a foot long, complete with tiny gas engine, and took it to a pond to give it a test drive. Unfortunately, the engine quit about 60 feet offshore. To retrieve it, he pulled out a fishing rod, tied a bolt on for a weight, and cast right over the top of the boat and snagged it. Clyde then started reeling in his boat. Get this: Right then a giant bass rammed that boat and blasted it two feet out of the water.

Let me tell you, you've never seen a guy go running home for his tackle box faster than ol' Clyde at that exact moment.

Biologists' Notes

The largemouth bass *(Micropterus salmoides)* is one of the most popular of the warm water fish in California. It lives in nearly all suitable lakes, sloughs, and slow-moving rivers across the state.

It is uncertain just when the largemouth was introduced, but it is believed to have been in 1879 when 22 native largemouth were brought from the east and planted in Crystal Springs Reservoir, San Mateo County. The progeny of these early plants have been distributed widely over the state. It is generally accepted that the early strains were known as Northern bass. In general, largemouth bass of three and four pounds are considered good-sized fish.

In 1959 a southern strain of largemouths was airlifted from Florida and planted in some southern California lakes. This strain is native to the southeastern states and under ideal conditions, they reach a much greater weight than the northern strain. It is now typical that about 100 bass weighing 10 pounds or more are caught each year.

The southern strain of largemouths soon began to hybridize with the northern strain. Eventually, after much study, the southern strain was introduced in several places in central California. This is consistent with the original intent of introducing the Florida bass, which were reported to grow

Where to see largemouth bass

CLEAR LAKE, IN LAKE COUNTY

EASTMAN LAKE, IN MADERA COUNTY

FOLSOM LAKE STATE RECREATION AREA, IN SACRAMENTO COUNTY

LAKE CASITAS, IN VENTURA COUNTY

LAKE CASTAIC, IN LOS ANGELES COUNTY

LAKE SONOMA RECREATION AREA, IN SONOMA COUNTY

LOWER OTAY LAKE, IN SAN DIEGO COUNTY

SAN VICENTE LAKE, IN SAN DIEGO COUNTY

SHASTA LAKE NATIONAL RECREATION AREA, IN SHASTA COUNTY

SHASTA LAKE, SHASTA-TRINITY NATIONAL FOREST, IN SHASTA COUNTY

faster, live longer, spawn earlier and be more difficult to catch than the northern strain.

Largemouth bass are easily distinguished from the other black basses. The upper jaw extends past a vertical line drawn through the rear margin of the eye. Largemouth bass prefer warm waters, around 80°F. They lose their appetite when the water reaches 50°F and go into deep water for much of the winter. As the water warms, they move into the shallows, and when the temperature rises to about 65°F in the spring they begin to spawn.

The bass, like other members of the sunfish family, are nesting fish. The male scoops out a depression or nest in which one or more females deposit their eggs. A female may lay from 2,000 to 40,000 eggs, depending on her size. The male then guards the eggs and newly hatched young for several days. Under normal conditions the eggs hatch in two to six days, depending on water temperature.

By fall, the young fish may be from two to eight inches in length and within a year the more advanced individuals may be 10 inches in length. Under highly favorable conditions, they may mature and spawn when one year old, but more often they do not reach maturity until they are two or three years old.

The young feed on minute organisms at first and later upon larger insects and aquatic animals. As the largemouth continue to grow they live mostly on smaller fishes. Their rate of growth is dependent on the amount of food available and water temperature. In southern climates, the active feeding season can be as long as nine months.

Bass, Striped

Memories can have a way of eating at your mind.

One of the earliest memories tucked away in the back of my thoughts dates back to the late 1950s when an excited 5-year-old caught the first fish of his life, a small striped bass. That kid was in such a frenzy that his father, grandfather and brother practically had to rope that little maniac to a tree to keep him from self-destructing. I remember this well because that wild 5-year-old was me.

Since then, I've found that you can chase striped bass across thousands of miles of waterways, try all manner of strategies, and after years of effort, find yourself being just what you were when you started: a prisoner of hope.

ANIMAL	Bass, Striped
SPECIES	*Morone saxatilis*
TYPE	fish
STATUS	Introduced

Let me explain. Striped bass not only get big, but they are also school fish, so when you hit it right, you have the chance to catch a lot of big fish in a short period of time. This experience can change your perspective on the world, where, hey, as far as I know, this planet of ours is still the best one around.

To recapture the feeling over and over, you may even start chasing the fish on their migratory pathway, in the ocean, through San Francisco Bay and the Delta. To reservoirs, Pyramid Lake, New Hogan and others, and the canals, the California Aqueduct, and Colorado River lakes.

But this fishery has always been a paradox, a rugged fish yet one that is suffering cataclysmic declines at the hands of the state of California.

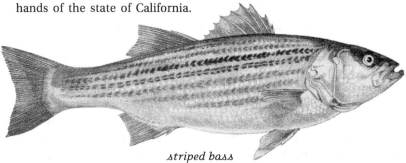

striped bass

The pumping station for the California Aqueduct in southern Delta, best known as the Delta Pumps, takes 70 million gallons of water per second and ships it to points south, and with that water go unbelievable millions of baby striped bass and unhatched eggs during the spring spawn. Many are simply killed and ground up in the pumps.

The age of a striped bass is recorded in the yearly growth rings on its scales, but in general a one-year-old fish is about four inches long; a two-year-old fish, 10 inches; a three-year-old fish, 15 inches. By the end of the fourth year, it is 19 inches long. Striped bass may live for 20 years, attain a length of four feet, and weigh 50 pounds or more. The first introduction of striped bass into California was made in 1879, when 132 small bass were brought by rail from New Jersey and released near Martinez.

The reason the fish are so vulnerable is because they spawn in midwater and the eggs remained suspended in the water column for roughly two days before hatching. The Delta Pumps are so powerful that they can reverse tide action—the eggs and tiny juveniles simply get sucked right down the hole.

Like I said, memories have a way of eating at your mind.

But there is hope for the future. A small percentage of fish, about 3%, are being salvaged at the screens at the Delta Pumps, then placed in submerged net pens, where they are fed and grown until large enough to swim against the suction power of the pumps. It is a fantastic program, one that is straight forward, relatively inexpensive and could become the savior to a troubled fishery.

At peak years, as many as 30 and 40 million baby striped bass were lost at the Delta pumps. Even with a modest recovery, 5 million to 10 million could still be salvaged, providing wild fish to jump-start what could again be one of the greatest fisheries anywhere in America.

Of course, they could just shut the pumps down, eh?

Maybe people could start making new memories again, instead of recalling the old ones.

Biologists' Notes

The first introduction of striped bass (Morone saxatilis) into California was made in 1879 when 132 small bass were brought by rail from New Jersey and released near Martinez. In 1882 a second planting of about 300 young fish was made in lower Suisun Bay.

Ten years after the first release, stripers were being sold in San Francisco markets, and in another ten years the catch by commercial netters was averaging over 1 million pounds a year. Since being introduced into the

San Francisco Bay-Delta complex, stripers have been taken from Vancouver Island, Canada, to a scattered few 25 miles south of the Mexican Border. In 1935, all commercial netting of stripers was stopped by law and since then only anglers have been permitted to fish for them.

They have established populations in Coos Bay and in some Oregon streams, and relatively small numbers have been taken in Tomales Bay and the Russian River. However, since they spawn in large rivers that empty directly into the sea the bulk of the stripers abound in San Francisco Bay and nearby ocean waters. They have also been stocked in several lakes, as well as being pumped south in the California Aqueduct and reaching storage reservoirs.

Striped bass are beautiful fish, steel blue to olive green above, shading down the sides to a silvery white on the belly. They have a series of seven or eight horizontal blackish stripes along their sides. There is a faint brassy reflection from the large scales. They grow large. Although the record sport-caught striper in California weighed 65 pounds, the average fish caught weighs less than 10 pounds.

Stripers are anadromous, living a part of their life in the sea and returning each season to spawn in the waters of the Delta and the Sacramento and San Joaquin Rivers. In California the stripers spawn in April, May and June. They do not dig nests in the gravel like trout and salmon, but choose shallow, slow-moving waters and lay their eggs near the surface. Hundreds of fish, both males and females, in small groups of 10 to 30, mill around near the surface until the eggs are expelled and fertilized.

Where to see striped bass

Brannan Island State Recreation Area, in Sacramento County

Pacifica Pier, in San Mateo County

San Francisco Bay, out of Emeryville, in Alameda County

San Joaquin Delta, in San Joaquin County

San Pablo Bay, Loch Lomond Marina, in Marin County

Suisun Bay, Martinez Pier, in Contra Costa County

Other places to see striped bass

Lake Havasu, in San Bernardino County and Arizona

New Hogan Lake, in Calaveras County

Sacramento River at Colusa, in Colusa County

A five-pound female spawns the first time in her fourth or fifth year. She may lay as many as 250,000 tiny eggs the first year, and later, when she weighs 10 or 12 pounds, she may lay as many as 1 million eggs each year. The males may reach sexual maturity when they are two years old and only 11 inches long. After the eggs are fertilized by the sperm of the male, they increase rapidly in size and settle slowly to the bottom. The current carries them slowly back and forth for two days before the babies hatch. If the eggs hit bottom they will often die.

After hatching, if the fish can avoid being destroyed by the Delta pumps, they will use Suisun and San Pablo bays and nearby sloughs as nursery areas.

The striper's age, like other fish, is recorded by the yearly growth rings on its scales. A one-year-old fish is about four inches long, a two-year-old fish 10 inches, a three-year-old fish 15 inches and, by the end of the fourth year, it is 19 inches long. They may live for 20 years, attain a length of four feet and weigh up to 40 or 50 pounds, and sometimes more.

California's striped bass fishery is a valuable resource from both a recreational and an economic standpoint. It has been estimated that the fishermen spend nearly $20 million annually fishing for stripers.

Hence, the fishery's decline because of the Delta pumps, where cheap water is provided to grow subsidized crops in the Central Valley, is an example where one business, farming, is profiting at the expense of another, fishing. The pumps have also proven to be a crime against nature, causing not only declines in the striped bass, but annihilating many other species, including putting the endangered winter-run salmon and the Delta smelt on the edge of extinction.

Bats

Near dark, when most all have gone home, out come the bats, diving, swirling and taking bugs in a series of dipsy-doos. They don't emerge until it's near dark, and then they are difficult to see, often appearing as nothing more than a black flash as they streak by. Under a full moon you can get a better look at them, and they appear the most acrobatic of all flyers.

ANIMAL	Bat, Pallid
SPECIES	*Antrozous pallidus*
TYPE	mammal
STATUS	OK

I like to fish the mountain trout lakes until the last moment of light because the biggest trout, particularly the giant browns, will wait for this time of day before coming out to feed. I have experienced many a warm summer evening in my canoe, trolling slowly amid the rising pools of trout, feeling little "tick-ticks" on my fishing line. No, it's not from fish. It's from bats, hitting the near-invisible fishing line as they grab bugs. I call them "bat bites."

pallid bat

I've caught many of my biggest trout when the bats are out. After all, no bats means no bugs, and no bugs means no fish. It's always an exciting moment when the bats emerge from their caves, bridge underpinnings, and other hiding places for the day, and then dart about in their night dance. Yet whenever I mention this, many of my companions grimace and say things like, "Have you been bitten? You can get rabies from them, right? Oh no, let's go in fast!"

Bats? The Native Americans revered them as a symbol of rebirth, as night must pass to day. They seem to scare the heck out of everybody else.

Because most species do not fly during the day, few get good glimpses of them. Fewer still even try. Yet they have a huge range across California, from the foothills on up through the alpine zone. They seem most abundant in the mother lode country of the foothills and Sierra Nevada where gold was discovered, possibly because they can use abandoned mine shafts for roosting.

Many bats use echolocation to locate food while flying and for orientation while in flight, crawling, or motionless. A bat calls out high-pitched sound waves that bounce off flying insects, walls, or other objects and return to the bat as reflected waves.

I have explored two such caves and found bats roosting, a bizarre sight for newcomers, as this odd-looking half-mouse, half-bird creature hangs upside down, sleeping off the day. In both cases, I was shown these caves with the promise that I would not reveal their locations; not that most people would jump with eagerness at the opportunity to find bats in the belfry.

As the biologists point out, bats aren't immune to rabies; if they have the rabies virus, they can transmit it before dying from it. However, they also don't go out of their way to bite people, a common misconception. Why would they, unless you picked one up or disturbed its roost? After all, a human hardly resembles a gnat, a piece of fruit, or a Jerusalem cricket, all favorite dinner items for different species. Vampire bats are not found wild in California, but 23 other species are, from Townsend's big-eared bat to the California leaf-nosed bat, not one of which features blood or humans in its regular diet.

Night sky, silent flight—the bat is one of the least understood of nature's creatures, and with talents that make it among the most exceptional.

Biologists' notes

Mention the word "bat" and many people immediately think of a winged animal with spooky, if not evil, tendencies.

Actually, bats are very interesting mammals responsible for many delicious and useful items. Nectar-eating bats and some fruit bats pollinate more than 130 different kinds of tropical and sub-tropical trees and shrubs. Bananas, peaches, mangoes, avocados, cashews, and dates come from bat-adapted plants. Bat guano has been used to manufacture gunpowder and in some countries is an important source of fertilizer.

Bats are mammals, meaning that they nurse their young, and are classified in the order Chiroptera, meaning "hand wing." The struts of a bat's wing are modified finger bones, so bats essentially fly with their hands. Bats are found all over the world and range in size from flying foxes that have a wingspan of up to six feet to Kitti's hog-nosed bat, or bumblebee bat, of Thailand that weighs about two grams (under one-tenth of an ounce), which at just over one inch long is probably the world's smallest mammal.

Depending on the species, bats may eat pollen, nectar, fruit, insects, fish or frogs. Trees, caves, storm sewers, or tunnels are among the roosting sites of bats. Bats are not adapted for active foraging during cold weather, so they either migrate or hibernate in colonies when winter comes. Interestingly, bats do not have the ability to lower their body temperature and go into torpor like a true hibernator—instead those species that do not migrate put on a layer of body fat during the summer and fall and then roost in a colony for the winter, sharing body heat with their fellow bats.

California is home to 23 species of bats. One of the most common species is the pallid bat. The pallid bat's scientific name, *Antrozous pallidus,* comes from the Latin words *antron,* meaning cave, and *zoos,* meaning alive or living within. *Pallidus* is another Latin word, describing the bats' pale coloration. Thus the Latin name means "pale cave dweller," an apt name.

Pallid bats live in most counties in the state and may be found in barns, houses, mines, caves, rock crevices and trees. Its habitat can range from sandy deserts to oak and pine forests. The bats are fairly common at lower elevations but are uncommon above 6,000 feet.

The pallid bat is large, as California bats go, weighing as much as an ounce and having a wingspan of up to 14 or 15 inches. The females are larger than the males. Both sexes have broad wings, big ears, and large eyes. Large scent glands on the muzzle give these bats a distinctive odor. The fur is light yellow on the back and creamy or almost white on the underparts.

Many bats use echolocation to locate food while flying and for orientation while in flight, crawling, or motionless. A bat calls out high-pitched sound waves that bounce off flying insects, walls, or other objects and return to the bat as reflected waves. The bat's sensitive ears pick up these waves and automatically analyze them for direction and size information. Bats that feed on flying insects, such as the little brown myotis, get most of their food this way. In most species, including the pallid bat, these echolocation calls are too high-pitched for humans to hear, though many bats have lower-pitched, audible social calls that they use when they are roosting.

Pallid bats use echolocation for orientation but rarely use it to capture food while in flight. Pallid bats instead listen for the low frequency mechanical, or rustling, sounds made by ground-dwelling insects to zero in on a meal. The bat's rather large eyes and ability to fly low may also be adaptations for ground feeding.

Pallid bats are primarily insectivorous, favoring large insects. The list of entrees is long and includes Jerusalem crickets, scorpions, june bugs, potato beetles, grasshoppers, and ground crickets. Pallid bats thoroughly chew their food before swallowing. They have been observed feeding in trees and in the flowers of agave, a spiny desert plant. The bats were probably "chowing down" on insects in both cases.

Bats are social animals and roost in colonies of up to 100 bats. When pallid bats are active during the summer, they have separate day and night roosts. Day-roosting sites are chosen so the bats can retreat out of sight and wedge themselves in tight crevices. The day roost is often a barn, hollow tree, attic or rock crevice, and the bats retire there to spend the day resting. The night roosts are generally in more open places where flight in and out is easy. Humans may notice bats at night, since preferred night roosts include porches, garages and open buildings as well as roofs, shallow caves, mines, and bridges. Pallid bats use night roosts as a place to rest and eat freshly-captured food.

Among pallid bats, breeding begins in October and probably occurs sporadically through February. The gestation period is 53-71 days, but most young are born during the first half of June. The breeding, gestation period, and birth dates do not directly correspond because the female pallid bat can retain live sperm in her uterus over the winter. The stored sperm fertilize the female's eggs when she ovulates the following spring.

Twinning is common in the pallid bat, but single births occur about 20% of the time. Yearling females generally produce only one baby. During birth, the mother hangs upright and delivers the baby into a basket formed by a membrane between her legs and includes the tail. The young bat is born rump- and tail-first and, as soon as its feet are out, it assists in the birth by pushing against the mother. The baby weighs just a few grams. After birth, the baby climbs up the mother's side and attaches itself to a mammary gland. The mother bat will fly to another roost carrying her babies, but probably does not take them with her on feeding flights.

Female pallid bats form nursery colonies during early April and segregate themselves from the male bats until after the young are born. The male pallid bats may roost in a different part of the same area. While the young are still nursing, lactating females make quick, night-feeding flights. The nursery colony begins to break up well after the young bats are able to live independently. By late August, the male bats are mingling with the adult females and immature bats, by fall it is difficult to distinguish the young from the adult bats.

Bat biologists presume that pallid bats hibernate in winter, unlike other bat species that migrate south to warmer climates. The summer colonies break up into small groups by mid-October and retreat to rock crevices and other secluded spots.

Like most bats, pallid bats have few natural enemies. Their nocturnal habits protect them from birds that hunt by sight during daylight. If pallid bats are disturbed and forced to leave the day roost, they may be attacked by

---

Where to see bats

ANDERSON MARSH STATE HISTORIC PARK, IN LAKE COUNTY

BIZZ-JOHNSON TRAIL/SUSAN RIVER, IN LASSEN COUNTY

CHINA FLAT/SILVER FORKS CAMPGROUNDS, EL DORADO NATIONAL FOREST, IN EL DORADO COUNTY

DEATH VALLEY NATIONAL PARK, IN INYO COUNTY

JOSHUA TREE NATIONAL PARK, IN RIVERSIDE AND SAN BERNARDINO COUNTIES

KYBURZ MARSH, IN SIERRA COUNTY

LAKE DAVIS, IN PLUMAS COUNTY

MOUNT SAN JACINTO STATE PARK AND STATE WILDERNESS, IN RIVERSIDE COUNTY

PICACHO STATE RECREATION AREA, ON THE COLORADO RIVER, IN IMPERIAL COUNTY

POINT MUGU STATE PARK, IN LOS ANGELES COUNTY

POINT REYES NATIONAL SEASHORE, IN MARIN COUNTY

PROVIDENCE MOUNTAINS STATE RECREATION AREA, IN SAN BERNARDINO COUNTY

SILVERWOOD LAKE STATE RECREATION AREA, IN SAN BERNARDINO COUNTY

small hawks. Kestrels and sharp-shinned hawks harass and sometimes capture pallid bats under these conditions. At night, when the bats are flying abroad, they may be caught by owls. Snakes also have been seen capturing and eating pallid bats. A bat's low flight and occasional landing on the ground when hunting may bring it within range of an alert snake. These bats are most vulnerable to destruction of suitable nursery colony locations; as is so often the case, loss of habitat is the most serious threat these creatures face, even though they have otherwise adapted well to the increasing numbers of humans within their range by using buildings and bridges as roosts. Humans, however, have not been as flexible in their attitudes towards bats. Although pallid bats eat scorpions and other pest insects, many misinformed homeowners often don't want bats on their property.

Bear, Black

A strange noise woke Steve Williams of Mount Shasta from a deep sleep. "It sounded like a burglar was in the house," he recalled. He climbed out of bed, went to his bedroom door, and in the darkness found himself nose to nose with a large bear that was standing at the doorway, breathing in his face. "I almost had a heart attack," Williams gasped.

But the bear was apparently just as shocked, because it grunted, whirled around, and hurtled through the living room, and eventually flung itself out an open window to disappear into the forest. It

ANIMAL	Bear, Black
SPECIES	*Ursus americanus*
TYPE	mammal
STATUS	OK
SEE ALSO	Bear, Grizzly

took my buddy Steve nearly an hour to compose himself enough to explore the damage. He came to feel that the bear had been just as scared as he was, and discovered that among other things it had actually peed right on the living room floor.

These are the stories that make bears the lovable bums that are so famous in California.

At a cabin near Lake Tahoe, a bear crept through a window, headed into the kitchen, opened the refrigerator, and snatched a pound of bacon. It

black bear

then marched upstairs to the guest bedroom, climbed up on the bed, and ate the bacon. The owners of the cabin were not only in shock, but in their report to the Department of Fish and Game they noted that "the bear slobbered all over everything" and that "such behavior would not be tolerated in a human."

In national forests, the highest numbers of bears documented by the Department of Fish and Game are in the Ukonom Basin of the Marble Mountain Wilderness and the McCloud Flats on the southeast side of Mt. Shasta, with 40 bears in 10 square miles.

Before the dump was closed at Happy Camp near the Klamath River, landfill owner George Chandler had counted as many as 40 bears in the pit at one time. At Dorst Campground in Sequoia National Park, food raids in the summer season have become so common that rangers post a running weekly score on a placard, with as many 75 incidents recorded in one two-month period. At Shasta Lake, a bear swam out into the lake, and then, remarkably, boarded a houseboat.

The number of bear-human encounters is increasing rapidly, with more and more incidents every summer involving campers, backpackers, and owners of homes and vacation cabins (not to mention the odd houseboat)

Bear Attacks in California

Bear attacks in California are so rare that there are far more reports of Bigfoot sightings, according to the Department of Fish and Game. Never in history has anyone been killed in an attack by a California black bear. In fact, a search of state records by Department of Fish and Game bear experts Bob Stafford and Cris Langner showed only a handful of bear attacks documented in the past 20 years.

Here is a synopsis of the bear attacks documented in the past 20 years in California:

May 1986, Trinity County: A man camping in a tent in the Trinity Alps Wilderness was caught in the middle of a fight between two bears when one of the bears attacked him, biting him in the shoulder and swatting him once in the back of the head. When the man hit the bear with a tent pole, the bear retreated and fought with the other bear, then both bears left.

September 1986, Siskiyou County: A man who had been feeding bears at his house for 30 years was cuffed up, but otherwise uninjured.

September 1989, Kings Canyon Wilderness: A backpacker 38 miles from the trailhead used his food bag as a pillow, and in the middle of the night, had his face scratched.

August 1991, Siskiyou County: In the Marble Mountain Wilderness a man was trying to photograph a bear at very close range when he suddenly noticed it was a female with two cubs. The bear charged him and bit him around the shoulders.

May 1993, Shasta County: A man camping at Shasta Lake, with garbage littering the campsite, woke up to a bear drooling on him. When the man sat up, the bear swatted him on the head, then ran off. The man received a small gash that required three stitches.

August 1993, San Bernardino County: Two separate incidents occurred within three days of each other. In each case, a bear grabbed a sleeping 13-year-old boy and tried to drag him away. Though scared out of their wits, the boys suffered only minor injuries. Residents in the area believed that the same two bears had been

in bear country. In California thousands of episodes are reported each summer to rangers at national parks and forests, as well as to state game wardens and wildlife experts with the Department of Fish and Game. Virtually all of the incidents involve food raids, and occasionally these result in injuries to humans.

The backlash of these encounters is that many problem bears have been destroyed as rangers try to deal with emboldened bears inspired by a

observed with a female bear (possibly their mother) the previous summer feeding on garbage and handouts.

July 1995, Lake Tahoe: A bizarre encounter where a bear apparently in search of food in the middle of the night reached out and gashed a 13-year-old boy, leaving him with scrape wounds and a headache.

August 1996, Yosemite National Park: A group of adults cornered and taunted a timid bear at the Curry Village housekeeping cabins, until the bear finally swung and scratched one of the adults in the arm.

July 1996, Mammoth Lakes: A man was working on his car in his driveway, bent over the engine, when a bear emerged out of the neighboring forest and bit him in the butt. It is one of the few unprovoked injuries ever documented in California.

July 1998, Nevada County: A man was picking up pinecones around his house when he was surprised to see a 30- to 40-pound bear emerge from under his house. The bear ran into him, but the man said he didn't feel the event was a true charge, though he did get a scratch on his cheek.

July 1998, Tulare County: At conservation camp, an inmate sitting at a picnic table drinking iced tea was approached by a bear, which scratched him lightly on the arm. The bear was recognized as a repeat offender that had been fed by inmates at this site in the past.

August 1998, Kern County: In Bodfish Canyon in the Paiute Mountains, two campers in a single sleeping bag woke up to find a sow with cubs staring them in the face. When the man got up, the cubs ran off, but the sow bit him in the arms and also scratched him; his female companion received a black eye and superficial cuts on her leg.

July 1999, Humboldt County: In a remote mountain area, a Forest Service employee spotted a bear. She shouted at the bear, which then came at her and knocked her down. She had no scratches or bruises, and investigating game wardens wrote in the incident report that they were not confident of the reliability of the narrative.

prodigious hankering for human food. The only solution, rangers say, is to keep the bears from learning about human food in the first place.

"Bears are being killed as a result of the fact that they recognize free easy meals being available," said Bob Stafford, the state's leading bear expert with the Department of Fish and Game. "The bears learn from experiences with careless, negligent campers in their past." He said people who feed bears or allow them to raid their food could be giving the bear a death sentence at a later date, and possibly endangering another human being.

"A lot of people who live in the city think of bears as cute and cuddly things, a curiosity to watch," said Department of Fish and Game Warden John Dawson. He said some will actually leave food out in hopes of taking a photograph or carelessly leave their food and garbage within easy reach of a bear.

Once a bear develops a taste for human food, it will not only become extremely bold in its attempts to get human food, but the cubs will learn to do the same. There is ample opportunity for bears to meet campers—there's no shortage of either in California. The Department of Fish and Game estimates that there are between 20,000-24,000 black bears across 46 million acres of bear habitat, and that there are an estimated 12 million hikers, campers and fishermen who frequent that habitat. The encounters that result can almost defy belief.

"I was up at Onion Valley [north of Mt. Whitney] for a bear study, and I was sleeping in the camper of my truck," Department of Fish and Game bear expert Stafford said. "Suddenly my partner and me woke up when the truck started rocking back and forth—I mean it was more than an earthquake. I looked out the window and saw that a large bear was trying to move the truck to reach an ice chest that we'd hidden underneath the truck."

Near Callahan in the Shasta-Trinity National Forest, a bear broke the window of a camper trailer, climbed inside, then ripped the cupboards off the wall and tore the refrigerator door off. "The bear proceeded to scrounge butter, crackers, ice cream—everything—spreading food everywhere," said Warden Dawson, "then [it] climbed out the window and left."

At a luxury home in Monrovia, east of Los Angeles, near the Angeles National Forest, a bear made a habit one summer of leaving the forest, entering the backyard, and then jumping in the owner's hot tub. The owner responded by putting up a sign that said, "No Bears Allowed." The bear, nicknamed Samson, is now in the Orange County Zoo.

In Yosemite, my brother Rambob and I were camped at Emeric Lake, located in the wilderness near Vogelsang Pass. At 11 p.m., while we were faking sleep, we had not one, but three bears in our camp at once. Few things are more fun, or more worthy of concern, than having a bear in camp, and it's a rare thrill to sit up in your snug sleeping bag, say "Hi, Yogi!" and watch the bear, or bears, sprint off in panic.

Except before we could say a word, a woman at a camp across the lake started banging on a pot, shouting, "Get away, bear!" Let me tell you, those three bears in our camp jumped up and *galloped* around the lake to get there. You see, banging on the pot was like ringing a dinner bell. In 15 minutes, the woman was still banging on the pot, and she had called in about a dozen bears to her camp—all going through giant ice chests full of steaks and other goodies, which had been brought in by horseback.

Bear-Proof Food Hang

Making a bear-proof food hang is the best way to safeguard yourself from bears in search of a snack. If you suspend all of your food double-wrapped in heavy-duty plastic garbage bags, the bears will merely inspect your camp and hopefully move on to more suitable food. Above treeline, using a bear-proof food canister is a must.

Food hangs can be accomplished two ways, either with your food in a single bag, or by counter-balancing two bags. The former is accomplished by tying a rock to a rope, then throwing it over a high but sturdy tree limb. Next tie your food bag to the rope and hoist it in the air. This is often best accomplished by having one camper "throw" the bag into the air while another hoists the rope, which will raise the food bag well out of bear range. Then tie the end of the rope to another tree. Be certain the bag is not too close to the tree trunk; bears will climb and swing at the bag as if it is a piñata. In addition, never tie the rope to the same tree; the bears can climb the tree, start banging on the rope to get the bag to swing, then whack it when it swings within their range.

If you can find a perfect limb, or a hang wire, such as is provided in the backcountry of many national parks, the best system is to create a counterbalanced food hang by dividing your food in two separate bags of equal weight. To accomplish this, find a good limb, and use the same system as described above: Tie a rock to a rope, throw the rock over the limb, tie on a food bag, and hoist it up. With the other loose end of the rope, tie off your other food bag—leaving a large fixed loop at the knot. Using a long stick, lift the bag with the fixed loop. As you raise the bag, the other bag, now high in the air, will then descend. By using a long stick, you can raise the bag so both are high in the air, counterbalanced, and well out of reach of bears and other critters.

The reason for using a fixed loop to raise the bag with a stick is simple. If you try to raise the bag without a stick, you won't get it high enough. If you try to raise the bag with a stick and no loop, you can poke a hole in the bag. And with a loop, it is easy to retrieve your food by simply reaching up with the stick, putting it in the loop, then pulling down the bag.

The key advantage of the counterbalanced system over the single rope system is that there is no rope tied to a tree available for tree-climbing bears to reach and try to whack.

Problem bears are no longer relocated, as is commonly believed, but are instead often shot by professionals. Studies showed that relocating bears just shifted the problem to a different location, that it created competition problems for resident bears, and that the relocated bear would often return anyway, even if it meant traveling great distances.

"It's a sad thing, but what else is there?" Stafford said. "You can't move them because all you're doing is creating a problem for somebody else. You can't train them. So this is the only alternative."

Given proper precautions, bears are nothing to fear in California. They want your food, not you, and they are experts at getting it. Typically they slink in sometime in the night, as quietly as possible so as not to wake you, make their rounds around a camp, searching for an easy food grab, and then when finding none, they head off to the next camp, in stealth mode. The last thing in the world they want to do is wake you up. Then you'd just get up and scare them off, right?

Of course, **never** intentionally bait in bear, **never** leave your food out, and **never** sleep with your food. After all, at the spots to see bears, they will likely be coming anyway to take a look.

At national parks in bear country, signs are posted at each campground warning of food-raiding bears, and bear-proof metal food boxes and garbage cans are available. Before receiving wilderness permits, back-packers often receive a refresher course for bearproofing food, and in the most notorious spots, such as at Lyell Fork in Yosemite, hang wires are available at several campsites. Forest Service district offices in national forests provide literature that detail how to keep food and garbage from bears. When provided, a metal bear-proof food locker is virtually foolproof. If you go fishing, burn the fish entrails, heads, and tails; never leave fish out overnight for breakfast; and *never* wipe your hands on your pants.

Even the slightest sweet scent can inspire a hungry bear. In a memo-rable incident at Sequoia, a bear bashed out the windows of a car and ripped the door open, then tore out the back seat in order to get into the trunk of the car—where there was a single bottle of body lotion. That's all. No food. Just some sweet-smelling body lotion.

There are many such stories. One of the craziest was at Wawona in south-ern Yosemite, where a group of European tourists thought their rental car had been bombed by terrorists; rangers later discovered the "powder residue" from the "bomb" was actually pancake mix and that paw prints were all over the back seat.

It wasn't always like this in California. Historically, black bears have always been shy, and it is one of the reasons why they have survived despite the presence of 34 million people in the state. When confronted, instead of taking a stand and fighting it out, that is, kill or be killed, they are more apt to run, hide, or climb a tree.

Black bears prefer the alpine coniferous zone of the mountains. Though they come in a variety of colors, primarily black, brown, cinnamon, silver-tipped and combinations of these, they are all considered the same species.

The black bear population is not only healthy, but it is expanding in several areas. Their ability to travel up to 20 miles per day has occasionally put them in unlikely locations, such as the one spotted at the Grizzly Island Wildlife Area near Fairfield. That bear likely traveled south from the Cache Creek Wildlife Area southeast of Clear Lake. That was the first documented bear sighting in the Bay Area in decades. Another was sighted near Woodland, north of Sacramento, in the Central Valley, another anomaly.

In national parks near campgrounds, there can be as many as four or five bears living in a one-mile radius, such as at White Wolf, Little Yosemite, and Tuolumne Meadows in Yosemite National Park, Dorst in Sequoia, and at Manzanita Lake at Lassen. In national forests, the highest numbers of bears documented by the Department of Fish and Game are in the Ukonom Basin of the Marble Mountain Wilderness and the McCloud Flats on the southeast side of Mt. Shasta, with 40 bears in 10 square miles.

At the Happy Camp dump, there were so many that the Department of Fish and Game started calling it a different species, the "North American Landfill Bear," according to Paul Wertz of the Department of Fish and Game.

At the wilderness of Sequoia National Park bear expert Stafford received the kind of lesson they don't teach in universities. He was hiking and backpacking with some companions along the High Sierra Trail, a 40-mile hike from Mt. Whitney on down the Kern River to Crescent Meadows.

"It was late afternoon, and it was muggy and warm, and we thought we might get a thunderstorm," Stafford said. "We were setting up our campsite, and I looked up and saw a female bear and a cub approaching, about 30 or 40 yards away. One of the guys started yelling at them, but they kept coming, and the female started swatting the ground with her paws.

"The female sauntered off a little, but then the cub, about 40 pounds, came running right at me, making huffing noises, and then pulled up 10 or 15 feet from me. It was a false charge by a cub. I was in disbelief."

What Stafford had just experienced was a lesson in how a mother bear was teaching her cub how to scare campers and raid food . . . and the cycle continues.

Biologists' notes

The American black bear *(Ursus americanus)* is found throughout the United States, with an estimated 20,000-24,000 black bears in California, compared to an estimated 4,000-5,000 elk, 5,000-6,000 mountain lions, and one million deer. Despite its common name, the American black bear can be black, brown, cinnamon, blond, or combinations of all, with location playing a role in color. There are two races of black bear in California. One is the northwestern black bear, which is found in California's northwestern counties and almost always has a black coat of fur. The other is the Sierra Nevada black bear. It lives in the Sierra Nevada mountains, and its range extends south to Kern County and then west into parts of the Coastal Ranges. The Sierra Nevada black bear generally has a brown coat. Though a member of the order Carnivora, the black bear has adapted to a largely vegetarian diet, unlike its cousins, the polar bear and the grizzly bear.

The black bear weighs about eight ounces at birth, 75 pounds at one year, 150 pounds at four years (and females don't get much bigger). Most males weigh about 350 pounds at eight years and are between 35-40 inches tall at the shoulder and 4.5-6 feet long from nose-tip to tail—though weight and size vary widely, depending on availability of food and climate. The biggest bear ever documented in California weighed 690 pounds. They reach sexual maturity at four years and have been known to reach 25 years or more in the wild. The oldest documented wild black bear in California was 28 years old.

They can appear rather clumsy because of their flat-footed shuffling gait but can move rapidly if the occasion demands. They climb trees readily, and the smaller bears usually seek safety in trees if danger threatens. They are called plantigrade animals, meaning that, like humans, they walk on the entire foot, from toe to heel.

Bears are omnivorous animals—meaning they will eat just about anything. Meat is a relatively small portion of their diet, with insects supplying a relatively high percentage of protein and fruits and berries providing a significant percentage of calories. After emerging from hibernation in early spring, the first food the hungry bears seek out are sprouting grasses and emerging leaves—early in the season these food sources have a relatively high proportion of protein and have not become bitter, as they will later in the season. They will also become opportunistic carrion-eaters, eating fawns and other animals that perished in the winter or spring. In summer, they switch to berries, and in fall, they look for manzanita berries and

Where to *see* black bear

BIG BEAR LAKE, IN SAN BERNARDINO COUNTY

CALAVERAS BIG TREES STATE PARK, IN CALAVERAS COUNTY

DEVILS POSTPILE NATIONAL MONUMENT, IN MADERA COUNTY

DORST CAMP, SEQUOIA NATIONAL PARK, IN TULARE COUNTY

LASSEN VOLCANIC NATIONAL PARK, IN LASSEN COUNTY

ONION VALLEY CAMPGROUND, INYO NATIONAL FOREST, IN INYO COUNTY

SEQUOIA AND KINGS CANYON NATIONAL PARKS, IN TULARE AND FRESNO COUNTIES

TUOLUMNE MEADOWS, YOSEMITE NATIONAL PARK, IN TUOLUMNE COUNTY

UKONOM BASIN, MARBLE MOUNTAIN WILDERNESS, IN SISKIYOU COUNTY

acorns. Throughout the year, about 10% of their diet is insects, such as ants, termites, and yellowjackets.

Bears who have acquired a taste for human food will pursue it at every opportunity, especially when taught by parents or during bad crops for their normal food groups. The black bear occupies a rather small range in the forest, but it does wander with the seasons as different food becomes available. Males have a about 20-square-mile home range but have been documented to travel 20 miles in a day. Females travel far less. Normally, the black bear does not prey on game or domestic livestock. However, because they are opportunistic carrion eaters, they may be seen eating the remains of an animal that died of other causes. As a result they are sometimes falsely accused. In areas where bears are overabundant and normal food supplies short they may also turn to eating the inner bark of trees, thus doing some damage to second-growth timber.

Bears tend to be nocturnal, even though they sometimes move around in daylight hours. Tagging studies by the Department of Fish and Game in Trinity County showed that the study area had a summer density of more than two bears per square mile. In spite of this relatively high density, bears were seldom seen in the area in the day time.

In winter in the southern parts of the state and at lower elevations in the mountains, the weather is so mild that some bears do not go into winter-sleep. In colder areas and at higher elevations, they do den up and hibernate for long periods of time. During hibernation bears slow down their breathing and metabolism by half; their body temeperature also drops slightly, but not as much as in hibernating rodents. The young are born during this dormant period, usually in January. They are very small, weighing only six or eight ounces, and are blind and helpless for 30 or 40 days. They grow slowly at first, but by the time the mother is ready to leave the den in May they are usually well developed and are about 18 inches long. The first young of a three-year-old female is usually a single cub, but twins and triplets are common after that. Females breed every other year, usually in the early summer, depending on the climate (the colder the climate, the later the breeding season). By a process known as delayed implantation, the fertilized egg or eggs will not begin to develop until the female dens up for the winter.

The males do not parent the cubs in any way, and in fact, if possible, they will kill the cubs. The cubs will stay with the female for a little more than a year, at least through the following winter, during which time they are taught survival skills. Wildlife biologists estimate that roughly 3,000 cubs are born each spring. Young bears are very appealing as babies, but no attempt should be made to capture them. First, it is illegal, and second, a mother bear with cubs is dangerous and will fight savagely to defend them. Female bears are extremely protective of their young and hikers and campers face a threat from bear injury when they stand between a mother bear and her cubs.

Bear, Grizzly

The last grizzly bear in California is on the state flag. Though extinct, the grizzly bear will always be a vital piece of California history.

What few realize, however, is that their natural habitat was not in the high Sierra Nevada, Shasta-Cascade or Trinity Alps mountain ranges, but primarily in the lowlands in the vicinity of what is now the Los Angeles foothills, San Francisco Bay Area and the Central Valley and nearby foothills. In fact, California black bears did not historically live in the Bay Area or L.A. because the grizzly bears would drive them out.

Dates of the last recorded grizzly bear for representative counties of California are:

ANIMAL	Bear, Grizzly
SPECIES	*Ursus arctos*
TYPE	mammal
STATUS	Extinct in California
SEE ALSO	Bear, Black

grizzly bear

Monterey and Santa Cruz counties 1886, Marin County 1888, Kern County 1898, San Diego County 1908 and Fresno County 1922. The last California grizzly bear

The last verified California grizzly bear was killed in 1922 in Fresno County.

was reported to have been seen in 1924 in Tulare County, but some question exists as to whether the sighted bear was actually a grizzly. The 1922 Fresno County bear was the last verified grizzly bear in California.

The primary reasons the grizzly was exiled to extinction was because population growth in Los Angeles, the Bay Area, and Sacramento resulted in the loss of habitat—and their own fearless nature. When sheep ranchers tried to establish herds in grizzly bear habitat, for instance, the bears loved the free, easy meals they could obtain, but the ranchers would then shoot or poison them, hoping to kill every last one. Market hunters also shot every one they could find.

When wildlife habitat is eliminated by development, it leaves wildlife without homes, and forces them to search elsewhere. But in the case of grizzly bears, I've learned from over 200 grizzly encounters in Alaska, is that they don't run. Hence, the arrival of people can create forced showdowns between mankind and bear. With the advent of the rifle in the 1840s in California, they started losing those showdowns for the first time in their evolution.

But even as late as the 1870s, L.A. residents were reluctant to hike in the San Gabriel Mountains because of the chance of running into a big griz.

The changes started early in the nineteenth century with the arrival of the rifle. There were no game laws then; in fact, what was called the "State Division of Fish and Game" was not established until more than 100 years later, in 1927. In the meantime, locals made their own laws, and in the process, grizzlies were shot to extinction, and elk and antelope were annihilated. Beavers and otters were virtually eliminated by trapping, and anything that flew was a target. Most of the remaining wildlife was then pushed out by encroachment from pioneer settlers.

Malcolm Margolin was able to unearth the original diaries from the first explorers to California, and the accounts of the grizzly bears are incredible.

In Father Pedro Font's diary, for instance, he writes: "[Grizzly bears] are horrible, fierce, large and fat. Several Indians are badly scarred by the bites and scratches of these animals." Imagine that, just 200 years ago.

There are accounts of grizzly bears bounding down the beach, then tearing their jaws into the flesh of the whale that had washed up in the surf.

Along the waterfront of Los Angeles and San Francisco, this was what it was like some 200 years ago, when so many whales were in the ocean they would spout every 30 seconds "within a pistol shot" of boats and "countless troops" of grizzly bears roamed the land.

A few years ago, a desk-bound executive for the Mountain Lion Foundation suggested that grizzly bears be reintroduced in California in the Trinity Alps. Guess what? They never lived there to begin with. To reintroduce grizzly bears, it was explained, you'd have to start by reclaiming their natural habitat. To accomplish that, all the people in the L.A. region and the Bay Area would have to move out to make room.

Maybe that's not such a bad idea after all, hah!

Biologists' Notes

Grizzly bears were once abundant in California. These big animals were at the top of the food chain, that is, they could out-compete the other native animals and had first choice of food available. No wild animal, including the coyote and the mountain lion, hunted and killed grizzly bears for food.

The grizzly held the topmost position until another mammal, the human, became so abundant in California that the grizzly was forced into extinction.

Ursus arctos californicus was larger than the black bear currently living in the state. The males weighed up to 1,200 pounds and had a maximum length of about seven feet. Females were somewhat smaller than the males and weighed up to about 650 pounds dressed. Both sexes had long claws. In males, the claws were five or six inches long. A hump, formed from the underlying muscles, was located over the shoulders. The coat color varied from black or brown to yellow brown, with the tip of the hairs lighter in color than the rest of the hair, giving a "grizzled," or silver-tipped effect. The face was dish-shaped, the ears about three inches long and the tail only two inches long.

California grizzlies probably first bred at the age of three years. Twin or triplet cubs were the most common, but one or four cubs was also possible. The cubs were born in the winter, nursed through their first summer and then began eating solid food. Cubs stayed with their mother until the third summer when they left and began living on their own. Grizzlies were long-lived, over 26 years.

Grizzlies had some habits that might be considered unbear-like today. They were good swimmers, a fact noted in the 1840s by the pioneer Bidwell, who saw a bear swim across a Sacramento Valley stream, and James Capen "Grizzly" Adams, whose pet grizzly "Lady Washington" swam after his raft on the Columbia River in 1853. In 1827, a boat near Angel Island encountered a bear swimming in San Francisco Bay. Soldiers shot and killed the bear when it attempted to climb aboard.

The big bears liked shallow water too, and would wallow in pools during hot weather to cool off and to escape insects. Paso Robles Hot Springs in San Luis Obispo County was an attraction to grizzlies. One bear visited the springs at night and, once in the water, would grab onto an overhanging cottonwood branch and bounce up and down in the water.

Grizzly bears don't climb trees. This fact was used to advantage by a "Yankee visitor" to California in the 1870s who attempted to rope a bear in the style of the Spanish settlers. The visitor set out on horseback and when he found his bear he lassoed it with his reata. He stopped the horse and expected the bear to have fallen flat on the ground, but when the visitor turned to look, the grizzly was seated and pulling the rope in paw over paw. The man stayed mounted until he saw the rope go taut and the horse coming closer and closer to the bear. He finally decided to let the horse cash in its chips while he high-tailed it up the nearest tall tree.

The commonness of the bears can also be seen by noting the numerous locations named after them: Grizzly Island (Solano County), Canada de los

Osos (San Luis Obispo County), Bear Valley in the San Bernardino Mountains, Grizzly Peak (Alameda County) and others. California has at least 22 Grizzly Creeks.

Grizzly bears ate both plant and animal foods. Among the plant materials they consumed were clover, different kinds of berries, tule roots, wild cherries, grapes, wild oats, brodiea bulbs, grasses and nuts. Almost any animal caught live or found dead was eaten. These critters included ground squirrels, lizards, frogs, deer, fish, whales, mice, grubs, gophers and yellow jacket nests. Honey was eagerly sought and quickly devoured.

The free-flowing, undammed rivers found in California until recently provided a large supply of fish for the bears to feed on. The runs of salmon were particularly important. These fish are hatched in streams but migrate downstream to the ocean where they mature and live for up to three years. When the salmon are ready to reproduce they head upstream to the area where they were hatched. The females build nests in the gravel and lay their eggs after mating with the males. After the eggs are laid, both sexes die and the carcasses and dying salmon float around in the shallow water. The bears could walk the streams' shores or wade in, pick up the fish and sit down to a salmon dinner.

Whales were a plentiful food source for coastal grizzlies. Ocean waves would wash whales up on the California beaches, and the bears would come down to the water to feed. The whaling ships of the 1850s and later years used Monterey as a base for rendering whale fat, and local grizzlies would feed on the offal that washed ashore. This food was shared by as many as 15 bears at one feeding time.

The attitudes of the settlers toward grizzlies changed rapidly. By 1837, grizzlies no longer provided a welcome, appreciated food source to starving travelers, but were seen as a challenge to the experienced hunter. Grizzlies provided an awesome target against which the sportsman could test his nerve, marksmanship and courage. One man bragged that in 1837 alone he shot 45 bears near San Luis Obispo and that he had probably shot over 200 bears in his travels up and down the California coast. The meat and hides were not taken as there was no market for them at the time.

The 1849 gold rush and the resulting influx of humans into California brought a new perspective on the grizzly resource. Fresh meat was in demand in the cities and the miners in the gold camps wanted dried meat as it kept for long periods of time. Market-hunting of grizzlies became big business; the fatter, tastier bear jerky often sold for twice as much as deer meat. The bear hunting industry continued through the late 1880s.

Where to see grizzly bear

Although no grizzly bears remain in California, they still live in relative abundance elsewhere in North America:

KATMAI NATIONAL PARK AND PRESERVE

P.O. BOX 7, KING SALMON MALL, KING SALMON, AK 99613. FOR A BROCHURE DETAILING FISHING LODGES IN KATMAI NATIONAL PARK, WRITE KATMAILAND, 4550 AIRCRAFT DRIVE, ANCHORAGE, AK 99502.

KODIAK ISLAND CHAMBER OF COMMERCE

P.O. BOX 1485, KODIAK, AK 99615, TEL. (907) 486-5557 OR FAX (907) 486-7605; E-MAIL: CHAMBER@KODIAK.ORG. KODIAK ISLAND CONVENTION AND VISITORS BUREAU, 100 MARINE WAY, KODIAK, AK 99615, TEL. (907) 486-4782 OR FAX (907) 486-6545; E-MAIL: KICVB@PTIALASKA.NET.

YELLOWSTONE NATIONAL PARK

P.O. BOX 168, YELLOWSTONE NATIONAL PARK, WY 82190-0168, TEL. (307) 344-7381, WEBSITE: WWW.NPS.GOV/YELL/.

BOB MARSHALL WILDERNESS, BOB MARSHALL FOUNDATION

P.O. BOX 1052, KALISPELL, MT 59903, TEL. (406) 758-5237.

GLACIER NATIONAL PARK

P.O. BOX 128, WEST GLACIER, MT 59936, TEL. (406) 888-7800 OR FAX (406) 888-7808.

Bull and bear fights were a popular pastime of the Spanish settlers. These fights were first held in Spain between bulls and bears from the Pyrenees. The abundant grizzly bear supply in California was a boon opportunity to continue this tradition.

Habitat loss caused the bears to be crowded out of their home territories by humans and the ever-expanding livestock ranges. One estimate is that each grizzly bear needed almost 20 square miles of territory in which to forage. The bears couldn't survive being densely packed together. Intentional poisoning with strychnine by sheep herders and general harassment by many settlers also contributed to the loss of California's largest land animal. The massive exploitation of grizzly bears, including sport hunting, market hunting and deaths caused by provoked fighting, led them to extinction.

The grizzly bear has been an important symbol to the people of California for the last 150 years. The bear was the symbol of the California settlers who proclaimed the territory's independence from Mexico in 1846. In 1849, when California became one of the United States, the bear found a place on the state seal and the bear flag of the California Republic became the California state flag. The grizzly bear was proclaimed the official state animal in 1953 by the California Legislature.

Beaver

I've never been fooled so much as by a beaver. It was a bright, full-moon night at a wilderness lake on the flank of the Sierra Nevada. I drifted off to sleep amid dreams of golden trout, when suddenly I heard this giant trout splash as if somebody had thrown a brick into the lake.

The next morning, I was up at daybreak, trying to catch that giant trout. For a week, taking breaks to hike to nearby mountain peaks, explore streams, check out other camps and lakes, I kept coming back to that one spot, dawn and dusk, figuring it was just

ANIMAL	Beaver
SPECIES	*Castor canadensis*
TYPE	mammal
STATUS	OK

a matter of time before that giant trout bit my lure—perhaps it would even be a world-record fish. The sound of its splash resonated in my thoughts.

The last day, I still had not caught that monster fish, though I knew it was there; after all, I had heard it. That night, my last at the lake, I was just about to drift off to sleep when again, I heard it: WHAP! It was a tremendous splash. The fish had to weigh 15 or 20 pounds to make a sound like that. I immediately jumped out of my sleeping bag, tip-toed to lake's edge, and waited to see the creature that could make such a sound.

Suddenly, it happened again: WHAP! I looked over, and there, to my surprise, was about a 30-pound beaver swimming along near the surface. When he saw me, he did it again, whapping the surface with its paddle-like tail. Turns out that I'd been fooled all along.

Beavers can fool a lot of people, whapping the surface like that. The tail smack is actually a warning to the other beavers in the area that a human, or perhaps a predator, is in the area.

This is how most people see their first beaver. They hear them first, then see them. Since beavers work mainly at night, you only occasionally can see them by accident by day. And only the lucky few will surprise a beaver in the act for which they are most famous, gnawing around a tree with those gigantic buck teeth, skillfully cutting it down, then dragging it to build a dam along a small stream, or building their den with all matter of wood debris.

When most see their first beaver, many are surprised at their size. They seem to average about 40 pounds, and I've seen some whoppers, with a rolling layer of fat and giant paddle-like tails. Yet they are smooth, silent, graceful swimmers. There seems little wasted motion. The big ones do not appear to be swimming fast, yet if you take your eyes off them, they can seemingly disappear with an ability to not only swim quickly, but to dive and hide when in stealth mode.

The beaver is the largest member of the rodent family in North America. It is the only wild animal that dramatically changes its environment to suit its needs.

Beaver can really do a number on an aspen grove or in lower elevations, alder. I have seen stretches of forest where it appeared that a logger with a dull chainsaw had gone through on a maniacal spree, leaving stubble-like remains of small stumps behind. They tend to go for the younger trees, which are easier to chew on and cut down, and then easier to drag to the dam site.

On one scout trip, I came upon an area of high wild grass along a stream where it appeared several bears had steamrolled the grass in a four-foot swath. I've always enjoyed seeing bears so I followed this swath. It led to a massive beaver dam, and the

beaver

swath in the grass was not from bears, but from beavers dragging young trees to their dam site.

Many often wonder what it must have been like when the first trailblazers came to California. Many of the first trailblazers were beaver trappers, such as Joe Walker, a hero of mine (among other things, he was the first trailblazer to see Yosemite, discovering it by accident in 1833), and Jedediah Smith (he is the trailblazer known for the first multiple trips into California, both across the Sierra and the Mojave Desert—he discovered what is now known as Ebbetts Pass in 1827), and they walked virgin streams. Beaver must have been everywhere. Because of the lure of wild—and the ability for trappers to pay for their explorations with beaver pelts—three native strains of American beaver were virtually trapped out across California, as well as the rest of the West.

Now the first sighting of a beaver for most people is in a cartoon. For many, sadly, it is also often the last, and the prospect of finding a live beaver is not even given a passing thought.

They are seen primarily in wildlands, and in the midst of a wilderness trek, the prospects of finding beaver is often not considered likely. In beaver country, though, it is always an adventure to keep your wildlife detector on, looking for signs. Being alert in this way can be like traveling in a time machine, imagining how Joe Walker, the greatest trailblazer of them all, approached his trips, where finding beaver would determine the success or failure of the day. While modern explorers don't have the pressure that Walker did, we can replace dead pelts with living memories, and money with priceless adventures.

Where to see beaver

ANTELOPE LAKE, PLUMAS NATIONAL FOREST, IN PLUMAS COUNTY

HONEY LAKE WILDLIFE AREA, EAST OF SUSANVILLE, IN LASSEN COUNTY

JOE DOMECQ WILDLIFE AREA, IN STANISLAUS COUNTY

LAKE SOLANO COUNTY PARK, IN SOLANO COUNTY

OROVILLE WILDLIFE AREA, IN BUTTE COUNTY

PICACHO STATE RECREATION AREA, IN IMPERIAL COUNTY

SACRAMENTO RIVER NATIONAL WILDLIFE REFUGE (LLANO SECO UNIT), IN BUTTE COUNTY

SAND POND, TAHOE NATIONAL FOREST, IN SIERRA COUNTY

Biologists' notes

The beaver *(Castor canadensis)* is the largest rodent in North America. It is the only wild animal that dramatically changes its environment to suit its needs. It cuts trees, both large and small and builds dams to impound water in which to live. It also digs canals to transport food and building materials when the supply of trees near water is exhausted.

The beaver is a large animal. Adults average from 30 to 40 pounds each, with some individuals bigger. Its head is massive and its large, orange-colored incisors are well suited to gnawing. Its eyes are small and its little ears are nearly hidden in its dense fur. The beaver's body is plump and covered uniformly with rich, brown fur. Its large hind feet are webbed and it has a large, flat, hairless, paddle-shaped tail.

The beaver is semiaquatic and needs a continuous supply of water in which to live, with available food nearby. Water several feet deep is required for escape to safety. Whenever a beaver chooses to live near shallow water, it builds dams to impound the water and increase its depth. Some dams may be 200 or 300 feet long and 8 feet high. They are built of limbs, mud, tules, cornstalks and other easily available materials and are constantly repaired and maintained.

Along deep rivers and sloughs, the beavers prefer to live in dens they dig themselves in the banks along the water. In small rocky streams or shallow waters, they sometimes build homes or lodges. A beaver lodge may be 15 feet across and 6 to 8 feet high. The lodge is built of the same types of material as the dam. The beaver always provides for its home an underwater entrance which leads up to a chamber above water level.

The beaver feeds on the bark and tender twigs of water-loving trees like willow, cottonwood and aspen, and it also likes roots, bulbs, grasses and tules.

Beavers do not hibernate, but in cold weather they stay in their homes for days, subsisting on food which they have stored. A beaver may come out in daylight, but for the most part, cutting and building is done at night. Each lodge contains a family of beavers, the young of the year and the juveniles from the previous year. When the juveniles are approaching their second year, they are driven out to start a colony of their own. This is nature's way of dispersing this species.

The mating season commences in February and most litters are born in April and May. The mother has only one litter a year and there is an average of four kits to the litter.

Although there is only one species of beaver, there were three geographical variations in California: the Sonora beaver along the Colorado River, the Golden beaver in Sacramento and San Joaquin Valleys, and the Shasta beaver in Northern California. They were trapped nearly to extinction by the end of the 19th century. In 1911, the season was entirely closed and for the next 35 years trapping of beaver was limited to areas where they were interfering with agriculture.

From 1945 to 1955, the Department of Fish and Game transplanted 3,000 beavers into all the suitable waters in California. Today beaver may be found in suitable waters throughout the state and up to 9,000 feet elevation in the Sierra.

Bigfoot

The snowfield stretched out before us for a hundred yards, and though reflected sunlight made us shield our eyes, the huge footprints could not be mistaken: 17 inches long! Six inches wide! Bigfoot? Or fakes?

We were silent, just standing there, staring at them. Each of these massive prints plunged 10 inches deep into the snow, and where each one bottomed out, the snow was rock hard from being packed down. Whatever made these prints, it was big and heavy—but it was not a bear. The steps followed in an even one-two, one-two pattern through the snow, the trail from a two-legged creature.

ANIMAL	Bigfoot
SPECIES	Not yet classified
TYPE	mammal
STATUS	?

We're talking about a human-like beast (or beasts) who stands eight feet tall and weighs 800 pounds, who leaves little trace save giant footprints, and who has confounded explorers for thousands of years in remote areas around the world.

The Bigfoot Expedition, sponsored by the Hearst Corporation, entailed more than six months of extensive research and a month in the field, had led us to the Klamath Mountains northeast of Eureka, and now to these footprints. Imagine that: I got paid to look for Bigfoot.

And now this, 17-inch footprints. My first feeling was, "If this gets out, there goes my career." As we looked closer, I remembered what Grover Kranz, an anthropology professor at the University of Washington and Bigfoot specialist, said about a set of footprints that provides the best evidence yet for the existence of Bigfoot. "We've got over 1,000 cases of sightings and plaster casts of prints," Kranz said. "But now we have ones with dermal ridges and that's what sets them apart. The intricate pattern of skin ridges would be almost impossible even for the best hieroglyphics expert to fake. I am convinced Bigfoot exists."

We were searching for Bigfoot. My partners were both wilderness explorers: photographer Jeffrey Patty and U.S. Forest Service scientist Michael Furniss. The three of us traveled light and quick over some of the most rugged and remote terrain in California and Oregon, exploring key areas where Bigfoot sightings and tracks had been most prevalent. We hiked mountain rims, bushwhacked into dense wilderness, crossed through streams chilled by glacial melt and, at times, even crawled on hands and knees on animal trails to reach areas rarely, if ever, visited by any modern humans.

Our first trip was mapped to take us into the Siskiyou Wilderness, a diverse habitat filled with firs, pines, spruces, and cedars, and cut by a vast spiderweb of mountain streams. After traveling via four-wheel drive on a logging road to the Bear Basin Saddle at 4,900 feet, we found the road blocked by snow.

Bigfoot

"Mr. Jack Dover, one of our most trustworthy citizens saw an object standing 150 yards from him picking berries or tender shoots from the bushes. The thing was of gigantic size 'about seven feet high' with a bulldog head, short ears and long hair. He aimed his gun at the animal, or whatever it was, several times, but because it was so human, would not shoot."
—*Del Norte Record,* January 2, 1886

BOB KAGE

"This is where we start doing some thumpin' and gruntin'," said Patty, gazing to the north at the Siskiyou Backbone, a long series of jagged mountain crests, all covered by snow. "Maybe it's time for me to start using the Bigfoot call I've been working on."

Furniss and I looked at him as if he had antlers growing out of his head.

"Let's hear it," I said.

Patty put his hands to his mouth, then shouted across the canyon, "Here Bigfoot, Bigfoot. Heeere Bigfoot."

When we crossed the first snowfield, the unbroken surface told us just what we wanted to know. "This area has not been open to vehicular traffic all winter," said Furniss. "There are no footprints at all in the snow, so that means we are the first people to walk into this part of the wilderness area in months, maybe in half a year, maybe more."

That was a critical factor in our trip, and why we had been so secretive about the areas we intended to explore—we didn't want to get duped by a hoax. Like the mysteries of UFOs, ghosts, and the Bermuda Triangle, a mystique surrounds Bigfoot's existence as well. It can set people off in the woods wearing gorilla costumes, using stamps to make footprints. Bigfoot can lead to bizarre tales.

For instance, an Oregon man who would not allow the use of his name said that he watched Bigfoot get out of a spaceship and then talked to him. "I also saw the Little People," he said, dead serious. A commercial fisherman at Moss Landing—who also wouldn't provide his name—said he knew why no Bigfoot remains had ever been found. "The Bigfoot go to sea to die," he said. "I just saw one swimming in Monterey Bay." Well, the Bigfoot we were looking for did not have a zipper running down his back.

Yeah, surrrrrrre! Heh, heh, heh.

In our case, only Terry Moyles, the primate specialist at the San Francisco Zoo, had knowledge of the areas we were exploring. Having heard of our expedition, Moyles called us and suggested two areas. Remarkably, those were two of the five areas we had already targeted after six months of research. Other than Moyles, no one else knew where we were.

It was Patty's idea to occasionally retrace our trail to see if, indeed, Bigfoot would be tracking us instead of the other way around. So after three days of wilderness travel, we decided to hike back to inspect a series of snowfields. If anything was following us, it would show up in the snow.

It was an all-day pull on a warm June day where snow can melt rapidly. Late in the afternoon, we broke through some trees and found the snowfield. What we saw was hard to believe. Here were these giant footprints staring at us, carving an icy trail around the bend. They seemed awesome, and the blinding reflection of light off the snow added to the mystery. I measured one—17 inches long!

Furniss, the scientist, looked at me with apprehension and said, "Nobody's going to believe this."

The trip was just three days old. Were we already close to Mr. Bigfoot? We kept staring and measuring, but something seemed amiss. We all sensed it at once.

"I don't think this is Bigfoot," Patty said. "The footprints don't seem far

Bigfoot Sightings

One of the earliest documented Bigfoot sightings occurred on January 2, 1886, and was reported in the now defunct *Del Norte Record:* "Mr. Jack Dover, one of our most trustworthy citizens," the account reads, "saw an object standing 150 yards from him picking berries or tender shoots from the bushes. The thing was of gigantic size—about seven feet high—with a bulldog head, short ears and long hair. He aimed his gun at the animal, or whatever it was, several times, but because it was so human, would not shoot."

This episode was recorded in 1890 in the little-known book, *The Hermit of Siskiyou,* in which a bizarre tale was reported from a logging camp: "One morning, our guards failed to come in for breakfast," the account reads. "That ain't like a logging man. We went out to look. The poor souls had been picked up like firewood and slammed against those big tree trunks. We armed ourselves and followed the tracks. We had no doubt that old Bigfoot had murdered them. We followed his trail far into the Siskiyou Mountains, and finally lost it in some volcanic rocks."

In August of 1958 near Bluff Creek in Klamath National Forest, a timber operation was invading the wilderness with the construction of a logging road. Supposedly, an unknown visitor made a late-night appearance at the road builders' camp. An oil drum was carried up a slope and tossed into a ravine. An 800-pound tire and wheel were lifted from an earth mover and dumped 50 yards away. The only clue to the prowler's identity were huge footprints found around the equipment. Plaster casts of the footprints made by archaeologists have never been proven to be fakes.

Joe Eudemiller, a former restaurant and lodge owner, was wide-eyed when he provided this account: "We [Joe and his wife] were driving across Alaska and one night we were in the trailer and heard this terrible scream, this incredibly frightful scream like nothing we had ever heard in the world. Whatever it was, it came up to my trailer and shook it, violently. We were afraid for our lives. Then we heard it again, many times through the night. It was a piercing cry. After daylight, I went outside and found these huge crimps in the top of the trailer—[which was made of] thick steel—where the thing had gripped it when it shook us."

enough apart." Sure enough, the distance between them was only 17 or 18 inches. That is about the stride of a man who is 6-foot-1. Well, that's how tall I am. Then I tried walking in the footprints. Perfect match, except for the outrageous size.

Then it hit us. The footprints were our own, created on our way in when each of us stepped in the same spot to ease the travel across soft snow. But 17 inches? Figure it: The hot early days of summer had melted the snow on the edge of the footprints, turning the print of a 13-inch hiking boot into a 17-inch Bigfoot print.

That's right, Bigfoot was me!

That night, in our sleeping bags at camp, we were watching the stars, talking about the day's episode. Saturn, the Big Dipper, and Polaris patrolled the sky. Even for scientists trained in logic, we noted, there are things for which there is no rational explanation. Could Bigfoot fall into that territory? Perhaps.

Logic gives us what we need, but magic gives us what we crave.

Biologists' Notes

In the 1930s Dutch geologist Ral von Koenigswald came across a number of unusual human-like teeth for sale in a Chinese apothecary shop, one of which was a lower molar that was twice the size of the corresponding tooth in an adult gorilla. This find led to more exploration, and eventually these teeth were determined to be the fossil remains of a large apelike species dating back some 400,000 years to the Pleistocene era. Paleontologists have named this species *Gigantopithecus blacki*.

Later finds include an unusual jawbone found in China by Dr. Pei Wen-Chung. He identified it as belonging to a descendant of *Gigantopithecus*.

The alleged descendant of *Gigantopithecus* has been called by many names: the Abominable Snowman of Mt. Everest, the Yeti of China, the Sasquatch of British Columbia, the Mono Grande of the Andes and Russia's Agachikishi. In the Klamath Mountains, the Hupa Indians call the creature Ohmahah, which means Wild Man of the Woods. In the past century, trailblazers and loggers have used the name Bigfoot, and the name has stuck.

The scream of Bigfoot is allegedly an intense, cackling shriek that cannot be imitated without electronic equipment.

Many Native Americans have their observations and beliefs about Bigfoot. Jimmy Jackson, a tribal elder of the Hupa tribe in Northern California and a personal adviser on my Bigfoot expedition, provided the following: "You will never see him. You will only see his footprints. And if you do not make peace with the mountain, you will be led to danger. The mountains there do not know you." He continued, "Do not do anything wrong, wherever you are; otherwise the mountains will punish you."

There are many Native American legends of Bigfoot. The Yurok Indians, who live downstream from the Hupa on the Klamath River, call Bigfoot the "Indian Devil." Most of the Hupa, however, believe Bigfoot is a spirit and that you will never see Bigfoot, but find only footprints. They also tell of the legend of Tan (pronounced "Tawn"), the immortal ruler of the woods, and Kishwish—the Little People—two-and-a-half-foot tall creatures who live like moles in the earth.

Tan takes care of the woods and all its creatures and is to be feared and respected, according to the Hupa. Louise Jackson, a Hupa, said that the Indians would go to the mountains and put out big bowls filled with fish and acorns as an offering. "Two weeks later, they would go back and find articles in trade in the bowls," said Minnie McWilliams, the daughter of Louise Jackson. "This was up in Blue Creek, where nobody goes."

"If you kill a deer, you leave the entrails for Tan," said Jimmy Jackson, who then reached into his pocket and extracted a root, which he said was magic. "When you hike, put medicine on your stick."

Where to try to see Bigfoot

As with any wildlife, the key is the habitat. The Klamath and Siskiyou ranges have a remarkable variety of trees and plants, which in turn support a wide variety of animals. *The Klamath Knot* by David Raines is an aptly titled book that describes the delightfully tangled ecosystem in this area. Among other things, this area has the greatest density of conifers in one place compared to anywhere in the world. The area also has the food, water, and remoteness Bigfoot would demand. Any place that supports a large bear population, yet is dense enough to hide wildlife and remote enough to make entry extremely difficult might be a prospect.

BLUE CREEK HEADWATERS, IN SISKIYOU COUNTY

CLEAR CREEK HEADWATERS, IN SISKIYOU COUNTY

FISH LAKE, IN HUMBOLDT COUNTY

KALMIOPSIS WILDERNESS, IN SOUTHWEST OREGON

Bighorn Sheep

Only the most rugged and skilled mountaineers are lucky enough to see bighorn sheep in the high country. After all, what animal, if not the Sierra bighorn or its cousins, could be considered king of the mountains?

To see one, you not only have to join bighorn sheep in their kingdom, but also have a lot of time to explore and plenty of luck in your favor.

The desert bighorn is more abundant than the Sierra bighorn, and much easier to track down and get a sighting. For that reason the five best places listed below are all destinations to see desert bighorns.

ANIMAL	Bighorn Sheep
SPECIES	*Ovis canadensis*
TYPE	mammal
STATUS	Endangered
SEE ALSO	Deer, Elk, Pronghorn

In the desert, the addition of "guzzlers" has given the desert bighorn a tremendous boost. Guzzlers trap water during infrequent rains and are constructed to minimize loss from evaporation. During periods of drought, guzzlers provide water for many kinds of wildlife, including bighorns. This has been vital for expanding the population of bighorn sheep in the desert. During times of intense drought, guzzlers can also be filled from water trucks driven into the area.

In the Sierra high country, there aren't many bighorn left (and we'll get to that), but their summer range in the high Sierra north of Mt. Whitney is one of California's most remote, quiet, and untouched wilderness areas. To explore it, you need a little of the bighorn in you. The high plateau country, generally from Tawny Point and beyond into a seeming infinity, is all above tree line, where from afar it seems a mountain wasteland of rocks and ice. But close up it comes to life, filled with tiny wildflowers. In some places there are so many violet lupines that John Muir wrote that it "radiates like a giant bee garden."

Only a scant few trekkers will go off-trail here, that is, leaving the John Muir Trail, and explore this stark and awesome country, most of which ranges from 11,000 to 14,000 feet in elevation. Spring arrives in July here, and until the first big snows of late October or early November, it can be possible to spot the remnants of a once great herd of bighorn. Another herd, the Lee Vining herd, located generally in the vicinity of the Sierra Crest on the Yosemite border, has been in severe decline.

Even if you do everything possible—complete all your detective work, get your body in excellent condition, have your gear in perfect working order, and then take weeks to explore the wilderness—it can *still* be an elusive task to add bighorn to your life list of wildlife sightings. If this is an absolute must, the best place to see bighorn sheep in the high mountains is in the Canadian Rockies, roughly northwest of the town of Hope near the border of British Columbia and Washington.

The once plentiful herds of bighorn were first decimated from a disease blight introduced by domestic sheep; the fact that grazing is still allowed and encouraged by Congress in wilderness is a crime against nature. In more recent times, attempts at population recovery have been ruined by mountain lion kills—because the bighorn populations are so small, the loss of any individual bighorn is critical. In fact, if mountain lions could read and obey hunting laws, then the evolving crisis over the Sierra bighorn would be solved. But they can't read and they obey only their hunger and their instinct, hence the continuing kills of endangered Sierra bighorns by protected mountain lions has turned into a paradox in which there is no easy way out.

A well-curled ram's horn may measure over 36 inches on the outside circumference and 14 inches around at the base. Growth rings indicate the animal's age. The head and horns of an adult ram may weigh more than 30 pounds.

bighorn sheep

The Lee Vining herd of Sierra bighorns has been down to as low as just five ewes, and the entire population of Sierra bighorns down to the vicinity of 100 animals, primarily due to long-term predation by mountain lions. In Yosemite, bighorns have adapted to their adversaries by never descending below 10,000 feet and into mountain lion range, according to park scientists. That hasn't worked. The lack of food and the deep snowpack at high elevations has put the remaining bighorns in a weakened state, and when they ultimately descend to lower elevations for food, they become easy prey.

In the short run, a consortium of wildlife organizations is working with the Department of Fish and Game to take emergency action. They are building a series of secure facilities to hold a small number of captive Sierra bighorns to protect them from mountain lions and other threats. In turn, a breeding herd of bighorns can be established, a technique that has proved successful with the California condor. From that base, wild populations can be augmented, providing that mountain lion kills can eventually be controlled, or the herds grow big enough to sustain mountain lion predation.

The Sierra bighorn in its classic high-country habitat represents something you don't see much of in California: True wildness. To see one, even from a great distance, is an experience that captures some of that wildness and infuses it in your veins.

Biologists' Notes

The bighorn sheep *(Ovis canadensis)*, or mountain sheep as they were called by the early settlers, dwell in hot arid deserts and the snow-capped Sierra Nevada range, from below sea level to over 14,000 feet. They are classified as a true sheep but are only distantly related to domestic sheep. It is speculated that the bighorn came to this continent from Asia when a land bridge existed in the area of the Bering Sea. Bighorn are closely related to the Dall and stone sheep (thinhorn sheep) of Alaska.

There are several subspecies of bighorns found in California: the Nelson bighorn *(Ovis canadensis nelsoni)*, the Peninsular bighorn *(O.c. cremnobates)*, and the California bighorn *(O.c. calforniana)*. The first two are often called desert bighorn. California bighorn, also known as Sierra bighorn, are found in the southern Sierra Nevada range and were also found in northeastern California until recent times. The California and peninsular subspecies are both federally listed endangered species. Biologists are in the process of revising the classification of the subspecies, though this will not change their endangered status.

The most impressive feature of bighorn rams is their horns. A well curled ram's horn may measure over 36 inches on the outside circumference and 14 inches around at the base. Growth rings on the horns indicate the animal's age. The head and horns of an adult ram may weigh more than 30 pounds. A true horn, these magnificent adornments are never shed and continue growing for the life of the animal. The female bighorn has horns that are flat, slightly curved, and only 8 to 10 inches long. With increasing age, bighorn sheep tend to rub the horn ends to a blunt tip. The coat of a bighorn is not woolly, but is more the texture and color of deer hair.

Bighorn separate and live in sex-specific bands most of the year, but they gather together during the breeding season, which in California extends from August to December depending on the location. Male desert bighorns weigh between 150 to 200 pounds, while female desert bighorns weight between 100 to 125 pounds. Mountain bighorns are larger, bulkier animals.

During the breeding season, the rams fight to determine which will be the dominant animal and do most of the breeding. A fight between two adult rams is a spectacle not soon forgotten. Facing each other, sometimes 20 or 30 feet apart, they rear and charge in an almost stately jousting match, crashing their massive horns together time after time until one or the other retires.

The females breed at 18 months and the single lambs are born in 180 days. The lambs start tasting different things in a few days, and are completely weaned in four or five months. Bighorn sheep feed on various kinds of grasses, leafy weeds, and shrubs and they are able to utilize the moisture from their food. If the food has considerable moisture, the animals may range as far as 20 miles from water. In the hot, dry months they come to water twice a week; more often if water is near.

Bobcat

Many people's most treasured moments in the great outdoors have come by complete accident. And so it is with bobcat—the few I have seen. I'm one of the lucky ones, I guess, because most people never see them. But on a magic day on the remote dirt access road to the Ah-Di-Nah campground on the lower McCloud River, heading out for a fishing trip, there came a scene that was like out of a wildlife fantasy.

ANIMAL	Bobcat
SPECIES	*Lynx rufus*
TYPE	mammal
STATUS	OK
SEE ALSO	Mountain Lion

There on the side of the road, playing in the dust in the shade on a hot afternoon, was not one bobcat, but a mother with three kits. The little kits were so small that you could have held them in your palm. Even as I watched, they were rolling around in the dust, playing, creating a little ruckus, as if taking a dirt bath, ignoring me. Even the mother paid no attention; of course, I had kept my distance.

It was another reminder that sometimes when you're out poking around in wildlands, you might think you're out to go for a hike, fish a stream, or find a picnic site. Then the unexpected occurs along the way, and you discover that the outdoor experience is best defined by the exhilaration in the moment. It is always like this with bobcat. You *never* will see them by simple desire. It always seems to be an accident. I've seen five other adults, twice in the dead of winter near a mountain cabin during a hard freeze in sub-zero weather, where there was very

bobcat

little snow around. In each case, they went scampering across a frozen meadow, their hind quarters bounding as if their body were a miniature teeter-totter—the classic romp of a bobcat—then disappearing into the woods as fast as they had arrived.

At first sighting, such as mine, bobcats seem almost like a pet cat. They are relatively small and look like they might purr if you rubbed them behind their ears. Wrong! They are quickly identified by their sharp ears, muscular shoulders, and bobbed tail. If they show their teeth, you will discover a set of chompers designed to bite, rip, and tear.

A few times, while camping at night, I have heard their screams, a howling, piercing wail that will petrify most anyone. They sometimes fight among themselves over territory, and the howls in the night from those fights are frightening to all that hear them. Bobcat are quick to ward off competitors (in Canada they have displaced the larger lynx in some parts of its range—mostly because the bobcat has a more adaptable diet than the lynx, which specializes in rabbits and hares), and their howls are part of their non-lethal arsenal. It is a quick reminder that the bobcat is a fierce, wild animal, possessing enough teeth, claws, and speed to represent a threat to almost any non-predator.

At first sighting, such as mine, bobcats seem almost like a pet cat. They are relatively small and look like they might purr if you rubbed them behind their ears. Wrong!

They are quickly identified by their sharp ears, muscular shoulders, and bobbed tail.

They are efficient hunters, and an unsuspecting rabbit, squirrel, gopher, vole, or rat is easy prey. But they often do not have it easy, especially in winter. Because of the cyclical nature of populations of rabbits, squirrels, and other prey, and as well as their own population cycles, there are times when bobcats find a meal difficult to come by. For people who live in rural areas, when a pet cat suddenly comes up missing—well, it's often likely that a bobcat nabbed it (an event I have witnessed). This occurs especially in winter when food is difficult to locate.

Bobcat that cannot hunt and kill regularly for food will quickly encounter difficulty. On one hike with Michael Hodgson at Grant County Park, east of San Jose, I was scanning a map at an unsigned trail junction, when suddenly a bobcat appeared about 20 feet away. It was obvious that the animal was sick and emaciated, moving slowly through the high grass, weaving, probably weighing less 10 pounds (rather than a healthy 15 or 20 pounds). While we considered contacting a ranger to arrange a wildlife rescue, the bobcat slinked into the brush and disappeared.

Though I have been involved in several wildlife rescues, this time we weighed the logic that perhaps it is best for nature's way to take control, that is, the law of the wildlands: The strong go on, living free, hunting the weak, and in time, they will pass on their genetic strengths, the best of the breed, to live on through their progeny.

In this way, nature always knows and does what is right: The bobcat, evolved over the eons into a compact and fierce hunter, seems the perfect example.

Biologists' Notes

The name "bobcat" originated from its short tail, which is only six or seven inches long, on a two to three foot long body, not including the tail. The end of its tail is always black on top tipped with white, which distinguishes the bobcat from its larger northern cousin, the lynx, whose tail is tipped solid black all the way around.

Although there is only one species of bobcat *(Lynx rufus)*, geographic variations have some effect on their color and size. Those found in timber and heavy brush fields are darker with rust-colored tones, while those found in the Great Basin area of northeastern California are generally a paler tawny-gray, often with a complete absence of spots on the back and less distinct markings. In winter their coats are dense and beautiful. Bobcat that live in Canada, at the far north of its global range, are generally larger than those that live in the south—as far south as Mexico. A large bobcat in California can weigh up to 30 pounds, but the average bobcat is only 15 to 20 pounds. The bobcat has long legs and large paws—though its thick coat and stocky torso tends to mask the length of the legs.

Despite its pussycat appearance, when seen in repose the bobcat is quite fierce and is equipped to kill animals as large as deer. However, food habit studies have shown most bobcats subsist on a diet of rabbits, ground squirrels, mice, pocket gophers, and wood rats.

The bobcat roams freely at night and is frequently abroad during the day except on the warmest of days. It does not dig its own den. If a crevice or a cave is not available, it will den in a dense thicket of brush or sometimes choose a hollow in a log or a tree. Bobcats occupy ranges from one-quarter of a square mile to as much as 25 square miles depending on the habitat and sex of the bobcat. Female bobcats occupy smaller areas than males and normally do not associate with other female bobcats. Males roam more widely than females, and while they are not particularly tolerant of other males, the home ranges of males will overlap the home range of other males

Where to see bobcat

ANDREW MOLERA STATE PARK, IN MONTEREY COUNTY

CALAVERAS BIG TREES STATE PARK, IN CALAVERAS COUNTY

CHINA FLAT/SILVER FORKS CAMPGROUNDS, EL DORADO NATIONAL FOREST,
IN EL DORADO COUNTY

HAWK HILL, GOLDEN GATE NATIONAL RECREATION AREA, IN MARIN COUNTY

HOPE VALLEY WILDLIFE AREA, IN ALPINE COUNTY

JOSHUA TREE NATIONAL PARK, IN RIVERSIDE AND SAN BERNARDINO COUNTIES

MOUNT SAN JACINTO STATE PARK AND STATE WILDERNESS, IN RIVERSIDE COUNTY

PICACHO STATE RECREATION AREA, IN IMPERIAL COUNTY

SHASTA VALLEY STATE WILDLIFE AREA, IN SISKIYOU COUNTY

SUCCESS LAKE, IN TULARE COUNTY

Other likely places to see bobcat

COACHELLA VALLEY PRESERVE, IN RIVERSIDE COUNTY

CUYAMACA RANCHO STATE PARK, IN SAN DIEGO COUNTY

DEVIL'S PUNCHBOWL NATURAL AREA, IN LOS ANGELES COUNTY

EASTMAN LAKE, IN MADERA COUNTY

LOPEZ LAKE, IN SAN LUIS OBISPO COUNTY

MILLERTON LAKE STATE RECREATION AREA, IN FRESNO COUNTY

MONTANA DE ORO STATE PARK, IN SAN LUIS OBISPO COUNTY

MOUNT DIABLO STATE PARK, IN CONTRA COSTA COUNTY

PIRU CREEK, IN LOS ANGELES AND VENTURA COUNTIES

PISMO STATE BEACH, IN SAN LUIS OBISPO COUNTY

SALT POINT STATE PARK, IN SONOMA COUNTY

SANTA ROSA PLATEAU ECOLOGICAL PRESERVE, IN RIVERSIDE COUNTY

TORREY PINES STATE PARK, IN SAN DIEGO COUNTY

as well as females, though the ranges of females generally do not overlap. In the winter, ranges of males and females shrink dramatically.

The bobcat's growls and snarls are so deep and fearsome, particularly when hidden from view, that one gets the illusion it must be a mountain lion. Its mating behavior is similar to a house cat's. Usually young are born any time in spring or summer, with most litters arriving in April and May, although litters may be born during almost any month except December and January. Litters average three kittens. The kittens are born blind and are completely dependent on their mother for several months. Young bobcats appear as lovable as domestic kittens, but it must be remembered that bobcats are wild animals. Because of this and the bobcat's ability to inflict injury on humans, it is illegal to keep bobcats as pets.

The bobcat has the widest and most continuous range of any carnivore in California and is found in all counties except San Francisco County. Except for metropolitan areas, bobcats are found in almost all habitat types, especially in California's mountains and even in desert areas where there is water. The bobcat has a preference for rocky, brushy hillsides in which to live and hunt.

Catfish

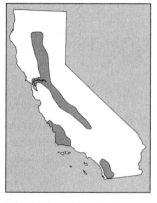

The catfish may not represent the crown jewel of California wildlife, but just like a lovable mutt, you know that inside beats a heart of gold that will never betray you.

Of the 20 or so prominent species of sportfish in California, the catfish scarcely merits respect among many anglers. A fly-fishing steelhead angler who has developed his skill into an art, for instance, wouldn't get caught dead baitdunking at a lake for catfish. But a lot more people eat hamburgers than caviar, and a lot more people are in love with the catfish than are trying to turn fishing into art. Only trout and panfish are more popular among California fisheries.

ANIMAL	Catfish
SPECIES	*Ictalurus* spp. *Ameiurus* spp.
TYPE	fish
STATUS	Introduced

That's because there's something about catfish that speaks to people, especially in an era where nobody seems to have much free time for recreation. In the middle of a traffic jam on a city highway, the catfish can reach out and grab some people's thoughts: It goes back to Tom Sawyer, Jim, and Huck Finn, the idea that you can just chuck everything, go to a lake, cast out

white catfish

your bait, and maybe catch some catfish. It's simple, fun and peaceful, and it seems the folks I know who like catfish are about the happiest, non-stressed folks I've ever met. For anybody who has undergone psychotherapy for overwork, I would suggest a better doctor's prescription would be just to go catfishing.

> It seems the folks I know who like catfish are about the happiest, non-stressed folks I've ever met.

The best lessons I ever received about catfish were from an old gent named George Powers. In fact, he was known as "Mr. Catfish," and, believe it or not, he would catch 4,000 to 5,000 catfish per year. When I heard about him, I was able to track him down and then arrange to spend a day in his boat with him. We caught 27 catfish between noon and 2 p.m. and then went home because George made a cast and didn't catch a fish. Over the several years that I fished with him, it always went like this. He was a generous, kind, talented, but eccentric fellow right up to the day he died at age 77.

George didn't even start fishing for catfish until he was in his 60s, and then, like most people, just caught one or two, or if he was lucky that day, a few more. So at age 63, this small, friendly but somewhat cantankerous fellow borrowed some scuba gear and went diving.

"I couldn't believe what I saw," he said. "The catfish were right on the bottom all right, but every one of them was lying perfectly still on the shady side of the little mud dobs, the little hills on the bottom of the lake. I never saw a fish on the sunny side of those mud dobs. That told me something. That is when I started to figure it all out."

You see, Powers explained, at night catfish spread out "all over creation," searching for something to eat. That's why so many people fish for catfish only at night. As a result, "You never really know where to fish, and you are just picking up strays," he said. But in the day, the catfish will always be on the bottom on the shaded side of those hills.

Seeing was believing, and now I understood the logic behind George's ability. The angler should always cast directly toward the sun and retrieve slowly so the bait tumbles over the hills on the lake bottom and falls gently into the shady side, right into the lair of a catfish. Hungry or not, the fish cannot resist your bait.

"Since I knew where the catfish were, I figured if I could come up with a way to get my bait right in front of them, I could catch 'em all day long."

Some catfish get huge, of course. The record for blue catfish in California is 85 pounds, caught at Lower Otay Lake near San Diego; for channel catfish, it's 52 pounds for a fish caught at Santa Ana River Lakes near Los Angeles; for flathead catfish, it's 60 pounds for a fish caught on the Colorado River at the California-Arizona border; and for white catfish, it's 22 pounds for a fish caught at William Land Park Pond. All of these are fairly recent catches from the 1990s. Big catfishes like these have heads as big as salad bowls, can eat a duck whole, and can break your will as well as your tackle.

More common are the 2 to 5-pound squaretail or yellow catfish, and the occasional 10-pound channel, which are so abundant in many lakes and ponds.

Those are the ones that speak to so many people, whether it be trying the "Mr. Catfish" method, or spending the night out at a lake with your best pal, talking about the defining moments on which fortunes turn, hoping for a bite along the way. It's still one of the best ways I know to live in a time machine, turn back the clock, and at least for a few hours, relive the days of Huckleberry Finn.

Biologists' Notes

The catfish (*Ictalurus* and *Ameiurus* spp.) in California are freshwater game fishes that have been introduced into most of the state's warm inland waters and many cold lakes as well. They are distinguished from other fish by their smooth scaleless bodies, the sharp slightly poisonous spine in the fins on their back and sides, and the eight long whiskers, or feelers, around their mouth.

Five of the seven species now found in California were introduced from eastern and midwestern waters in the 1870s. They are the white and channel catfish, and the brown, black and yellow bullhead. The flathead catfish was planted in the Colorado River in 1962. It has spread upstream in the Colorado River to the Blythe area and has moved into the entire Imperial Valley canal system. The most recent introduction, the blue catfish, was planted in Lake Jennings, San Diego County, in 1969. Since then it has been stocked in other southern California waters, and is a common fish in reservoirs throughout the Central Valley, San Francisco Bay Area, and Sierra foothills.

Catfish live in many types of aquatic habitats, waters that are clear and fast or slow and muddy, and some dwell in small lakes and reservoirs. They are normally secretive and less active in midday. They prefer to move around and feed from dusk to dawn. All are omnivorous in their feeding habits and gorge themselves on all manner of living and dead material. Besides crayfish, snails, clams, worms, and fish, at certain times of the year their stomachs have been found packed with wild grapes and weed seeds that have fallen into the water from overhanging shrubs and vines.

Catfish spawn in late spring and summer. White catfish and bullheads make a nest in sand, mud, or gravel in open water. The male white catfish moves in to protect the nest as soon as the female has deposited her eggs. In the case of bullheads, either parent or both care for the eggs. By fanning the egg mass with its fins, the adult cleans and aerates the eggs. Hatching takes place in 6 to 10 days, depending on water temperature. The young are tiny things. Thousands of them move around in what looks like a tight black cloud in the water. They are closely guarded for several weeks before the school breaks up and the fish go their separate ways.

The channel catfish is quite selective in its spawning habits and likes to use holes in rocky ledges, old hollow logs, muskrat burrows, and even old pieces of tile or pipe that are in the stream or lake. The male channel catfish builds the nest and as soon as the female has finished depositing the eggs he drives her away and takes over the hatching and rearing of the young.

The white catfish is the most abundant catfish in California and is found in most of the suitable waters in the Central Valley. About 95% of the catfish taken in the Sacramento-San Joaquin Delta are white catfish. In color, they are bluish to black on top, silvery underneath, and the tail is slightly forked. They reach weights of 12 pounds but seldom exceed eight. They seem to prefer slow, large rivers in both fresh and brackish waters. They are also abundant in Clear Lake, Lake County.

The channel catfish can be confused with the blue and white catfish. The best way to tell these species apart is to count the number of rays (supporting elements of flexible bones) in the anal fin. The channel catfish has 24 to 29, as compared with 30 to 35 for the blue catfish and 19 to 23 for the white catfish. Also, the more deeply forked tail and irregular spots of the channel catfish distinguish it from the white catfish.

The channel catfish is the most abundant catfish in the Colorado River. It also occurs in the Sacramento River drainage but in substantial numbers

Where to see catfish

CLEAR LAKE, IN LAKE COUNTY

COLORADO RIVER, YUMA-WINTERHAVEN AREA, IN IMPERIAL COUNTY AND ARIZONA
NOTE: The area below Imperial Dam on Martinez Lake is a particularly good spot for catfish.

LAKE IRVINE, IN LOS ANGELES COUNTY

LAKE KAWEAH, IN TULARE COUNTY

SAN PABLO RESERVOIR, IN CONTRA COSTA COUNTY

SUCCESS LAKE, IN TULARE COUNTY

Other places to see catfish

DEL VALLE RESERVOIR AND REGIONAL PARK, IN ALAMEDA COUNTY

FOLSOM LAKE RECREATION AREA, IN SACRAMENTO COUNTY

LAKE CASITAS, IN VENTURA COUNTY

LAKE CASTAIC, IN LOS ANGELES COUNTY

LAKE HAVASU, IN SAN BERNARDINO COUNTY AND ARIZONA

LAKE SONOMA, IN SONOMA COUNTY

LOWER OTAY RESERVOIR, IN SAN DIEGO COUNTY

SANTA ANA RIVER LAKE, IN SAN BERNARDINO COUNTY

SHASTA LAKE, IN SHASTA COUNTY

only in a roughly triangular area bound by Colusa on the Sacramento River, Marysville on the Feather River, and to the south to the confluence of these two rivers. It occurs in greatest abundance in the Sutter Bypass. It has thrived also in some large reservoirs in southern California.

The brown bullhead is the most widely distributed member of the catfish family. It has a dark brown back with a yellowish to gray belly. The sides may be slightly mottled. The tail is nearly square. It seems to prefer the deep, quiet waters of lakes and slow rivers and is usually the first catfish taken in early spring. They grow to about two pounds in weight. The black bullhead is usually found in small, shallow ponds, lakes and sloughs; it is also found in the shallow sluggish back waters of creeks and rivers. In appearance it is similar to the brown bullhead except that its color is not mottled.

The yellow bullhead is more restricted in distribution. It is found mostly in the shallower portions of the Colorado River and in some of the shallow bays of large reservoirs. It prefers clear water where there is an abundance of underwater vegetation. Its color is variable. The back is usually brownish to black, the belly yellow, and the tail is rounded instead of forked or square. The chin barbels or feelers are whitish. It is perhaps the least important as a sportfish, since it remains small and is so sparsely distributed.

The flathead catfish may reach 100 pounds in weight in the Midwest, where it is native. The flathead is recognized by the dark brown mottling on its back and upper sides, its broad, flattened head, and the fact that its lower jaw is longer than the upper. The tail is squarish, and the anal fin has from 14 to 17 rays.

The blue catfish, largest of the American catfishes, may reach weights over 100 pounds. It can be distinguished from the other catfishes by the presence of 30 to 35 rays in the anal fin. This fin is about one-third the length of the body. The blue catfish occurs mainly in San Diego County reservoirs: Lake Matthews, Sutherland Reservoir, El Capitan Reservoir and Lake Jennings.

Chipmunks

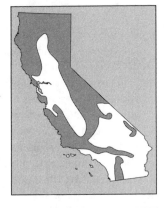

The chipmunk capital of the world is D.L. Bliss State Park on the southwest shore of Lake Tahoe. From here you walk on the Rubicon Trail, one of the prettiest easy hikes in North America, walking a pretty trail aside the cobalt blue waters of Tahoe. Many stop along the way for a picnic, and take in the remarkable panorama of beauty.

And that's when this story gets interesting.

Because you see, when you stop for a picnic lunch on the Rubicon Trail, you will discover that there are chipmunks everywhere. I think it was where chipmunks became the favorite animal of them all for my wife, Stephani.

ANIMAL	Chipmunk
SPECIES	*Eutamias* spp.
TYPE	mammal
STATUS	OK
SEE ALSO	Squirrels, Marmot

We ran into this fellow here from San Diego, on vacation with his wife, and he explained that they had stopped for a little picnic here, when the chipmunks suddenly appeared as if arriving from the far corners of the earth. Sure enough, they were irresistible, so cute, so toy-like, that he started pitching them crackers and nuts from a small bag of trail mix.

Later, done with lunch, the vacationing couple were ready to head back to the car, but first decided to get a close-up photograph. One problem: out of trail mix. No problem, he announced, and then told his wife to be ready with the camera. He kneeled, reached forward with his hand, and then jingled his car keys, immediately attracting the curiosity of several of the feisty little fellows.

"OK honey, here comes one, get ready for the picture," he barked, as a chipmunk came within a few feet.

Right then, that chipmunk darted toward the guy in a sudden burst, grabbed his keys, and just as fast, darted away and into his hole.

"My keys are gone," the guy muttered. "My keys are gone."

chipmunk

"I got a good picture, honey," she answered.

Chipmunks, you see, are mischievous little fellows. Cute? They rate a 100 on the cute scale. They also seem to be wherever people have picnics, campsites or snacks while hiking, right, just tons of the little chippies are out there. My wife has fed them by hand while they sat on her stomach; not advised, of course, but for many, it is irresistible.

Because thus they become trained to prefer snacks from people, rather than food nature has provided.

That is why if you leave food unattended, they can sneak into your daypack, sneak into your backpack, and sneak into your tent. Every time we break camp, we always conduct a search of the area, to clean up any refuse items, any litter we may have overlooked, just as all good campers will do. You typically bet that you will be joined in your search by a chipmunk or two, scouring the area for even the slightest tidbit. Finding a whole Cornut for a chipmunk is like striking gold.

The chipmunk capital of the world is D.L. Bliss State Park on the southwest shore of Lake Tahoe. It is a classic habitat where chipmunks find an abundance of food in seeds, berries, nuts, and buds, which they are busy storing all summer— stuffing the pouches inside their cheeks to carry their food to a hiding place.

But sometimes chipmunks do better than that.

We saw this one chubby woman seated in a short-legged lawn chair at a picnic site, reading a book, with a large cookie in her right hand. She had been there only a few minutes and here come the chipmunks. Cute, she thought, so she broke off a small piece of her cookie and flipped it to one of them, and it scurried away to enjoy its treasure. Then she returned to reading her book, lost in the plot, the cookie dangling a bit in her right hand. Just like that, another chipmunk jumped up and snatched that whole cookie right out of right hand, and was off with it.

She just kind of stared at her empty hand, then muttered, "My cookie's gone."

At a campfire talk, a ranger told me that there was actually more to the story.

"That night, she returned to her campsite, where she had an entire case of those cookies," the ranger explained. "The next morning, we found her tied down on a picnic table, with all the cookies gone.

"The chipmunks did it," she said. "They got all my cookies."

"I was skeptical when I first heard this story, of course," said the ranger, "but apparently with so many cookies at stake, they decided to work together, and wait until she was asleep, and then tied her down like the Lilliputians in Gulliver's Travels."

Such is the lore of campfire tales. But I tell ya, there's also a lesson there, that those cute little chipmunks are trickier than they look.

Biologists' Notes

The chipmunks (*Eutamias* spp.) are close relatives of the tree squirrels, but unlike their cousins, the chipmunks live mainly on the ground. They are found in abundance throughout the forested mountains and desert regions of California. Of all the small wild animals, they are perhaps the best known and most liked by everyone who has observed these delightful little creatures.

There are 13 recognized species in California. The largest and darkest in color inhabit the north coastal areas, while the smaller and paler in color chipmunks are found on the east side of the Sierra and in the deserts of southern California. The gap between the small, pale-colored chipmunks and the larger ones is bridged by a wide variation in color and size. However, all of them may be identified by the four light stripes, separated by dark stripes, running down the back. All of them have stripes on the sides of the head.

The chipmunks are widely known for their grace and sprightly ways and for their beautifully marked reddish to grayish coats.

The golden-mantled ground squirrel is often mistaken for a chipmunk, but note that there are no stripes on the head and only two along the back.

Anyone visiting the mountains will observe with pleasure the alert and attractive manner of these little squirrel-like animals, and if encouraged, they will accept you as neighbors. They learn to recognize a friend and will come right into camp to receive food. Like all the members of the squirrel family, they are very curious. At the appearance of anything unusual, but not too alarming, they will seek a vantage point and peer nervously with great interest.

To these small creatures, the world is full of enemies such as cats, dogs, weasels, hawks, owls, snakes, and many boys. This may account for their cautious, halting run and low, chirping call that is accompanied by slow undulations of the tail. The call note of the chipmunk, when it is extremely alarmed, is a high-pitched chirp repeated so rapidly that the syllables almost run together. This call indicates unrestrained terror.

It is a classic habitat where chipmunks find an abundance of food in seeds, berries, nuts, and buds, which they are busy storing all summer—stuffing the pouches inside their cheeks to carry their food to a hiding place. Some of it is stored in little holes in the forest floor, which are then carefully covered with dirt. Some food is taken to small storerooms in their den or nest to be used as little snacks during the long winter months.

For the most part, chipmunks make their nest underground, burrowing under a log or into a rocky ledge. Occasionally one will use the abandoned nest of a woodpecker high in a tree. In the northern part of their range, they usually retire to their dens in late September, and if it is cold, remain there until the following March or April. Some kinds of chipmunks are only partial hibernators, and their winter activities are governed by the severity of the weather.

They mate soon after coming out from the long winter sleep. The young, two to six in number, are born about one month later. By August, young chipmunks are out with their parents. The short summers in the northern part of their range only allow time for one litter to be raised. However, in the southern part of their range, where they do not hibernate, they may raise more than one litter, as do some other small mammals.

There is another beautifully marked little animal found on the floors of most of California's pine and fir covered mountains except in the Coastal Ranges south of San Francisco. It is commonly accepted as a chipmunk, yet it is the golden-mantled ground squirrel, a little larger and more brightly colored than the chipmunk. Close examination makes it easy to distinguish from chipmunks as it has a yellowish or copper-colored head with no stripes, and it has only two light stripes on its back.

The habits of the golden-mantled ground squirrel *(Spermophilus lateralis)*, to the casual observer, are much the same as those of the chipmunk, except that the golden-mantled ground squirrel seldom climbs trees. It has the same endearing qualities around a camp or cabin, and the woods are surely brightened, for the young and old alike, by these small but friendly animals.

Chukar

It can take many hours to find and see a chukar in their remote desert range. But chukar's call, hurtling flight and unique method of assembling in a covey make it worth the trek.

But like I said, get one thing straight. You typically have to hike for hours on end to have any chance of finding them. The best time is in the fall, when the high desert has been cooled by the flow of northern air, and where it can seem there is no other soul within miles, just you, out there hiking, looking for chukar.

ANIMAL	Chukar
SPECIES	*Alectoris chukar*
TYPE	bird
STATUS	Introduced

Chukar is pronounced "chuck-her," and not "choo-car," and is best known as the preeminent game bird in the west among upland game. Although the non-native bird was originally released in many habitats, they live in California only in the high desert of

chukar

northeastern California, in the most remote and forsaken country in the West. They are big, roughly three times the size of a quail, yet extremely clever and fast. They are difficult to find, and when flushed to another hiding place they seem even more difficult to find again, even if you carefully spot their touchdown. Many cannot find chukar without the aid of skilled bird dogs. I have a cousin, Andy Eldridge, who thinks nothing of hiking 10 hours on back-to-back days on a weekend inspired only by the *hope* of seeing chukar.

The birds seem to prefer rough terrain. This, combined with the high elevation and thin desert air, leaves many flatlanders gasping for breath as they clamber around through rocks and brush in pursuit of the birds. When a covey is flushed, they burst from the ground on fast powerful wings. That's when the fun starts. They go every whichaway, alighting in a scattered formation; some will turn to run uphill, others might seek cover in jumbles of rocks and brush, or they might also often fly along the side of a hill for as far as a mile.

After they have scattered, do not consider your mission complete. The adventure, for those who know this bird, is only starting. First, listen close, and second, watch close, scanning everywhere, ideally from a hidden perch with an overlook: Chukar will begin to call in a clear ringing note that can be heard a long distance in the quiet desert air. What this is, you will discover, is an assembly call. Over the course of an hour, sometimes longer, the chukar will "talk" to each other, and then when they reach a certain comfort level, will start to move back together into a large covey. Try imitating the call, and if you're good at it, and you may be able to draw the chukar out of their hiding places.

My favorite chukar story involves an outdoor writer with a large-circulation newspaper in the western U.S.

The chukar was introduced into California in 1932 from stock purchased in India. From 1932 until 1955, over 52,000 chukars were released from state game farms in different parts of the state, but it was only in the high desert country of eastern and south central California that the chukar flourished.

who got involved in a scam where he received a lakeside cabin at Lake Shastina and was paid for each time he mentioned the words "Lake Shastina" in his column. His editors finally told him to quit writing about Lake Shastina, and in a panic that he might lose his cabin, he called the producers of the once famous television show, *The American Sportsman,* and convinced them to bring their film crew to Lake Shastina to hunt chukar.

But there was one little problem. You know what it was? Lake Shastina does not have chukar. So the guy went to another state, bought 100 domesticated chukar, then planted them amid rocks and sagebrush—and the TV show was actually filmed and aired nationally, *Hunting Chukar at Lake Shastina.*

Now get this: In a few months, when stories about Lake Shastina stopped being printed in the guy's newspaper column, the real estate developer at Shastina took away the fellow's cabin anyway. The writer then filed a lawsuit, and the scam became public. When it became known that a newspaper writer had accepted a cabin and been paid for plugging a resort, he was fired on the spot for unethical behavior, a story that was printed all over the country. See? Some stories have great endings, after all.

Biologists' Notes

The chukar *(Alectoris chukar)* is a member of the red-legged partridge family and is native to countries around the Mediterranean Sea and most of the southern half of Asia. An Indian strain of chukar was introduced into California in 1932 from stock purchased in India. From 1932 until 1955 over 52,000 chukars were released from state game farms in different parts of the state, but it was only in the high desert country of eastern and south central California that the chukar flourished.

The chukar is a plump, large bird with distinctive markings. The male and female look alike—both have a white throat patch edged in black and sides barred with black and white. The sides contrast sharply with the pale brownish gray of the breast and back. The beak and legs of the mature bird are bright red.

The chukar roosts and nests on the ground, living in large flocks or coveys. Wintering coveys break up and pair in February and the nesting season lasts from May until August. The hen lays 7-16 fairly sharp-pointed eggs that vary in color from yellowish-white to brownish-cream and are speckled with purplish- to reddish-brown spots. The young are ready to leave the

Where to see chukar

BISCAR WILDLIFE AREA, IN LASSEN COUNTY

GOOSE LAKE, NEAR DAVIS CREEK, IN MODOC COUNTY

LAUREL PONDS, IN MONO COUNTY

LITTLE PANOCHE WILDLIFE AREA, SOUTH OF LOS BANOS IN FRESNO COUNTY

PINNACLES NATIONAL MONUMENT, IN SAN BENITO COUNTY

Other places to see chukar

DEATH VALLEY NATIONAL PARK, IN INYO COUNTY

DESERT TORTOISE NATURAL AREA, IN KERN COUNTY

KELLY RESERVOIR, IN MODOC COUNTY

MODOC NATIONAL WILDLIFE REFUGE, IN MODOC COUNTY

RED BLUFF RECREATION AREA, IN TEHAMA COUNTY

nest as soon as the last chick hatched is dry, but the young are not capable of flight until they are two weeks old. During this period if the young are endangered the mother pretends injury and flutters away crying in a piteous manner to decoy the danger away from her brood.

The young birds eat numerous insects. As they grow older they eat the seeds, leaves and stems of grasses and plants as well as the seeds and fruits of some shrubs.

Chukars are limited in their range by the availability of water. During hot, dry summer months they are seldom found more than a mile from water. However, as soon as the annual rains start, the coveys scatter over a wide area. There is no need then for them to concentrate near springs, for they are able to get water caught in cups in the rocks and moisture from the fresh growth of green vegetation.

Condor, California

It could be that the California condor has embodied the mystery of flight.

With up to a 10-foot wingspan, tip to tip, they fly like a top-secret military aircraft, quiet, black, and huge. Their plumage is trimmed in white, the adults with bare, reddish-orange heads and necks, and red eyes like Darth Maul from *Star Wars*.

ANIMAL	California Condor
SPECIES	*Gymnogyps californianus*
TYPE	bird
STATUS	Endangered

Their extraordinary wingspan allows them to soar very high and for long distances. They have been observed flying more than a mile high, ranging more than 350 miles from their roosts or nests. As they glide and scan the earth below, their keen eyes are in search of food—carrion, that is, dead animals. It's not the most pleasing meal in the world, but as vultures, this is their place in nature's grand ways. And after years of living in zoos, they are again finding their place in nature.

The California condor is one of the largest flying birds in the world. When it soars, the wings spread more than nine feet from tip to tip, and can reach 10 feet. It is capable of flying more than a mile high, traveling some 350 miles from its nest or roost at up to 55 mph, and gliding for hours without beating its wings.

The giant birds have become famous across America not only for their size, but because of the U.S. Fish and Wildlife Service and Department of Fish and Game program to bring them back from the brink of extinction. It has been well documented how the condor has been saved, from the initial controversy when the last remaining free-flying condors were captured and then placed in zoos in a cooperative captive breeding program (the Los Angeles Zoo and the San Diego Zoo and Wild Animal Park are notable in their efforts to develop programs to keep the *wild* in captive-bred birds). Their progeny are now being returned to the wild, establishing new colonies of one of the most dramatic bird species in history.

One area chosen for the releases is at Marble Peak Ranch in Monterey County, 2,500 feet above the Big Sur coast, adjacent to the Ventana Wilderness. It is a new beginning for the condor.

There are so few condor in the wild that the chance of making a trip to see one is an extreme long shot. But long shots do come in, and if you become one of the lucky few, the sight of this gigantic, black bird silhouetted against the sky will be like a trip to a real Jurassic Park. Some who have seen the condor releases call it a defining moment in their lives, when somehow they understood something new about nature and its power and influence.

Scientists have secured tiny transmitters to the condors' wings so they can monitor the birds, and also leave food out for them. In 1998, seven condors were released and doing well, taking up home in a redwood grove near the Big Sur Lodge. Another seven were released nearby in 1999. This is an excellent region for condor, with a huge range of habitat in the Ventana Wilderness along the Monterey County coast. That brings the number of condors in the wild to more than 50 in California and Arizona, with another 100 in zoos as part of the captive breeding program.

The release program has been successful because scientists make certain that each bird spends time with an adult condor as a mentor before release. It's like a training program with a surrogate parent.

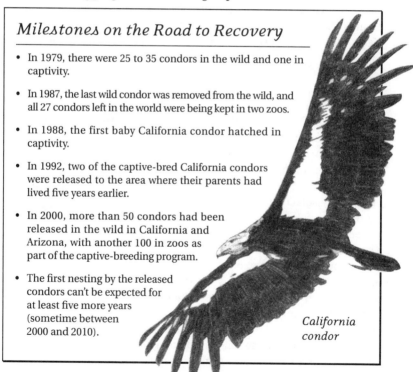

Milestones on the Road to Recovery

- In 1979, there were 25 to 35 condors in the wild and one in captivity.

- In 1987, the last wild condor was removed from the wild, and all 27 condors left in the world were being kept in two zoos.

- In 1988, the first baby California condor hatched in captivity.

- In 1992, two of the captive-bred California condors were released to the area where their parents had lived five years earlier.

- In 2000, more than 50 condors had been released in the wild in California and Arizona, with another 100 in zoos as part of the captive-breeding program.

- The first nesting by the released condors can't be expected for at least five more years (sometime between 2000 and 2010).

California condor

It is also well chronicled that the birds were shot, poisoned, and electrocuted to the very brink of extinction during an era when wildlife was simply something to be used, and when predators (even carrion-eaters) were automatically wiped out, not treasured. This is not a recent phenomenon. Most of the condors were wiped out in the 1800s, and by the 1930s, there were fewer than 100 condors left in the world, most in the Sespe Mountains of Ventura County, which had been established as a wild reserve for these birds.

Now the condors again fly above the Ventana. Each dawn brings with it the magic of flight of the bird with the 10-foot wingspan.

Biologists' Notes

The California condor (*Gymnogyps californianus*) is the one of the largest flying birds in the world. When it soars, the wings spread more than nine feet from tip to tip, and can reach 10 feet. Condors may weigh more than 20 pounds. The Andean condor (*Vultur gryphus*) of South America is even bigger than our California condor and has been listed as an endangered species since 1970. The California condor has been protected as an endangered species by federal law since 1967 and by California state law since 1971.

Condors can soar and glide for hours without beating their wings. After rising thousands of feet overhead on air currents, California condors will glide long distances, sometimes at more than 55 miles per hour. From the air, they search for dead animals, like deer or cattle. They feed only on carrion (dead animals that they find) and several birds will often dine on a large carcass, aggressively warding off interlopers, such as a golden eagle or the much smaller turkey vulture.

Condor nest sites are in cliff caves in the mountains. Some condors have nested in large cavities in the trunks of giant redwood trees. Condors form a long-term pair bond and usually nest only every other year, but they have been known to nest annually. Nesting condors raise only one chick at a time. The four-inch long egg is laid in late winter or spring, and it takes two months to hatch. It takes more than a year from the time the egg is laid until the young bird learns to live on its own. They don't reach reproductive maturity until they are six or seven years old and can live for 40 years or more, much longer than most other birds, except parrots. They do not migrate, but remain in the same range year-round.

Thousands of years ago, California condors lived in many parts of North America, from California and other Pacific states to Texas, Florida, and New York. In recent centuries, this large vulture was found by early explorers and settlers from British Columbia in Canada to Baja California in Mexico. As people settled the west, they often shot, poisoned, captured, and disturbed the condors, collected their eggs, and reduced their food supply of dead antelope, elk, and other large wild animals. Eventually, condors could no longer survive in most places. The remaining individuals were limited to the mountainous parts of southern California, where they fed on dead cattle, sheep, and deer.

Most causes of death in the past two centuries have been from human activities. For nearly 100 years it has been illegal for anyone to kill California condors, but illegal killing was not the only problem that these birds faced. Lead poisoning from unrecovered animals shot by hunters killed many. Accidents, such as collisions with power lines, are another threat. There have been so many problems facing the condor for so long that the species was not going to survive in the wild without help from people.

In the 1970s, biologists found that only a few dozen condors remained in the wild. So, in 1980 a major conservation project was started to try to keep the birds from becoming extinct. Many special studies were made. Radio transmitters were placed on the wings of some of the condors. Wild eggs were collected and hatched at zoos, and this helped to increase the population. A few birds were taken to zoos to build up captive breeding programs.

But this help came too late to stop the decline in the wild condor population, so in the mid-1980s all of the remaining condors in the wild were captured and taken to zoos. It was hoped that by raising young condors in captivity and releasing them to the wild, the species would be given another chance. But nobody knew for sure whether captive breeding would be successful. It didn't take long to find out.

The first condor chick hatched out in 1988. Within a few years, it was clear that captive breeding was working, in terms of successfully raising chicks. The captive condors laid more than 100 eggs by 1994. Nearly 20 chicks hatch each year at the three captive breeding centers. The total population grew from 27 birds in 1987 to 134 birds by mid-1997.

The first captive-bred condors were released to the wild in southern California in 1992, and more condors have been released to northern California, and also Arizona. More will be released each year in the future. The condor's numbers have increased, and some of its past threats have been

Where to *see* California condor

BITTER CREEK NATIONAL WILDLIFE REFUGE, IN KERN COUNTY
NOTE: The refuge is one of the focal areas of research activities addressing recovery of the California condor. The refuge itself is closed to the public, but the area can be viewed from county roads. Watch for condors along the high ridgelines en route to foraging and roosting areas.

MOUNT PINOS OBSERVATION POINT, IN VENTURA COUNTY

PIRU CREEK, IN LOS ANGELES AND VENTURA COUNTIES

VENTANA WILDERNESS, IN MONTEREY COUNTY

eliminated, but some of the underlying conditions that pushed the species to the brink of extinction still persist, especially habitat encroachment. The condors can only be released in places where they are not likely to encounter contaminated carcasses or other unavoidable hazards, such as powerlines, and where humans can actively supply carcasses when necessary. Even with all these obstacles taken care of, the species faces yet another hurdle—the loss of genetic variability and the threat of inbreeding. Part of the long-term management efforts for this species includes carefully releasing and tracking the birds in the wild to avoid sister-brother or parent-offspring pairing. Even then, the effects of genetic inbreeding among a small population will be hard to determine in the long run, given the long lifespans of the California condor.

Corvina

The story of the corvina and the Salton Sea is one of the strangest wildlife tales in California history.

When you first lay eyes on the Salton Sea, this huge but shallow saltwater lake appears to be a desolate, godforsaken wasteland. The lake is 35 miles long but has an average depth of just 30 feet, and is surrounded by nothingness seemingly into infinity. It is the largest inland body of water in California.

Located in southeastern California, it lies in a basin called the Salton Sink, 273 feet below sea level. The sink extends 15 or 20 miles into Mexico. The Colorado River flows into the Gulf of California, but in 1905 the

ANIMAL	Corvina
SPECIES	*Cynoscion xanthulus*
TYPE	fish
STATUS	Introduced

corvina

river broke through the irrigation headworks, turned north and flowed into the sink. In the two years it took to divert the river back into its regular channel the Salton Sea was formed. By then, this body of water became roughly 45 miles long north to south, 17 miles wide and 85 feet deep.

In the beginning the fish fauna of the Salton Sea came from the Colorado River, of course, rainbow trout and striped mullet, along with carp, several minnows and desert pupfish. But then this lake began a bizarre evolution: The waters became saline from minerals leached into the lake by rains, as well as return water from irrigation, all of which depleted the original freshwater fish.

In 1934, in an effort to reestablish freshwater sport fisheries, a program of transplanting fish into the sea was started. For instance, 15,000 silver salmon were planted in the sea, never to be seen again. The place was becoming a fiasco, and then in 1948, with salinity nearly matching the ocean, the Department of Fish and Game began to seine fish from the Gulf of California near San Felipe and transport them to the Salton Sea. Most of the plants that were made from 1948 to 1956 were wild shots in the dark, and in the end some two dozen fish species were planted without any biological study. Of the 25 species that were introduced, three survived: the orangemouth corvina, the sargo, and the bairdiella, or the gulf croaker.

The only inland water in North America where corvina are found is the Salton Sea. In 1948, the Department of Fish and Game seined 25 fish species from the Pacific Ocean and planted them in the Salton Sea. Only three species survived: the orangemouth corvina, the sargo, and the bairdiella, hence the creation of a one-of-a-kind fishery.

From May 1950 until May 1956, department biologists relocated as many as 250 orangemouth corvina from the Gulf of California to the Salton Sea. During the same period they also introduced 67 bairdiella or gulf croaker and 65 sargo, both of which provide food for the corvina. Most important of these food fish was the bairdiella. Relatively free of predators for a time, this small fish exploded in numbers, feeding on a diet of pileworms, copepods and other marine organisms in the Salton Sea.

With its own food supply assured, the corvina population also expanded rapidly. By the 1960s, a significant self-sustaining sport fishery had become established at the Salton Sea, and the orangemouth corvina had earned its ranking as one of California's top game fishes.

A continuing mystery at the Salton Sea is why the orangemouth corvina's close relatives, the scalyfin corvina, the shortfin corvina, and the totuava, also introduced during this period, failed to establish themselves.

My own experiences here are as sparse as the surrounding landscape. I learned quickly at the Salton Sea that some people pray for love, and some people pray for riches, but at the Salton Sea, you pray for the wind not to blow in the spring and for the weather not to be too hot in the summer and fall. When the wind blows, there's nothing to slow it down, so it can howl across the water, whipping up large waves that are dangerous to boaters.

Fishing is best from March to July and again in October and November. Boaters quickly discover what a strange place it is, with underwater barnacles occasionally severing fishing lines, along with all manner of structures from old fences, trees, and even signs that are now submerged.

So there you have it, a 100-year history of mistakes, flukes, and luck—and a one-of-a-kind fish, the corvina, in a place like no other on the planet.

Biologists' Notes

The chief fish in the Salton Sea is the orangemouth corvina.

The corvina is a long racy fish with a bluish tan back and silvery flanks. It is easily distinguished from the other fish in the sea by the two spines in the anal fin. The long dorsal fin is separated into two fins. The large mouth is orange-colored. The center rays of the yellowish tail are longer.

The orangemouth corvina *(Cynoscion xanthulus)* is a member of the croaker, or drum, family, so-called because the males have a special muscle that lies along the air bladder, enabling them to force air in and out of the bladder, causing a croaking or drumming noise. The seasonal peak of sound production for the orangemouth corvina coincides with its breeding season, which begins as the waters warm in the late spring.

Corvina appear to grow slowly at first, then rapidly, reaching a weight of approximately 4 to 5 pounds by the time they are 4 years old. Feeding habits appear to vary depending upon size. Corvina to about one inch feed on microscopic animal life (zooplankton) and immature barnacles. At from one to two inches, their diet is almost exclusively pileworms, and at about three inches in length they switch to eating other fish, such as bairdiella and longjaw mudsucker. The threadfin shad is also an important forage fish. Corvina usually travel in schools.

Little is known about reproduction and spawning habits of the corvina

---

Where to see corvina

SALTON SEA, IN IMPERIAL AND RIVERSIDE COUNTIES

---

other than that they appear ready to spawn in April and May. Early studies of the Salton Sea population indicated the number of eggs per female at from 400,000 to 1 million.

The only dark cloud on the future of the Salton Sea corvina fishery is the steady increase in the sea's salinity, which now is higher than that of the ocean. Biologists fear that a further increase in saline content may lead to stress and lack of reproduction.

Coyote

The coyote is the wild dog of the woods, the "little wolf" who spends its life roaming the country side, playing tricks on other coyotes, dogs, and wildlife.

On a quiet night the song of the "little wolf" may still be heard in most parts of California. Its howling *yip-yip-yiiiiiiip* can often be heard for miles across the countryside, whether in a valley, on the edge of a desert, or down a mountain canyon. It is part yip of a dog, part howl of a wolf. On camping trips, the sound of it brings back something of the heritage of the West: the

ANIMAL	Coyote
SPECIES	*Canis latrans*
TYPE	mammal
STATUS	OK
SEE ALSO	Fox

old cowboys, the campouts, and the mountain song of the coyote. Sometimes, the listener may experience a tingling fear of primitive danger, but to the seasoned outdoorsman the howl of the coyote is truly a song of the West.

There have been many times camping with my fluffball, bear-like dog, Bart, when in the middle of the night, we have been awakened by the distant call of the coyotes. Bart always sits up, then huffs a kind of a muffled bark, as only chows do—it's as if in his mind, he is talking back to the coyotes in his own language. No dog can ignore the call of a coyote.

One of the most amazing tales I ever heard was about a dog and a coyote. My longtime friend Steve Dunckel was traveling on the Pacific Crest Trail on horseback with his dog, Mouie, when one night in Plumas National Forest, 350 miles from his starting point at Sonora Pass, the coyotes started calling in the distance. Mouie put its nose to the sky and howled back for 20 minutes, then up and ran off, never to return. Steve was devastated and ended his trip, heading into Quincy, selling his horse, and then heading back to his dad's wilderness cabin near Sierra Village. Well, get this: 10 days later, Mouie comes trotting down the wilderness road to the cabin, just as Steve is arriving; the dog covered the entire 350 miles on foot to return to the starting point. It all started with the call of a coyote.

From roaming myself for so many years, I've learned that you can always tell a city person from a country person by how you pronounce coyote. City people pronounce it "ky-yo-tee," but country folk pronounce it "ky-yote." On trips afield, it can affect how the locals in rural areas treat you; for them, you are either an insider or an outsider, and this can be a tip-off for them.

The coyote is found throughout all life zones in California, from the low deserts and valleys to the crest of the highest mountains. It has adapted readily to the changes caused by human occupation of the land and its range includes all counties except San Francisco County.

One of the most astonishing facts about the life of a coyote is how little they can subsist on, as well as their daily trickery that seems to make life entertaining for them.

Coyotes don't hibernate, so they must figure out a way to make it through winter. They do it with wile and sometimes a little bit of thievery. They eat whatever they can find, dead or alive, and their scrawny bodies attest to a rough life. Occasionally they have been known to raid ranches, especially to get chickens—as a result they are held in general disdain by ranchers.

Coyotes will often trick the dogs in charge of ranch security. Working in teams, coyotes will howl and yip, drawing a dog away, while others will sometimes then circle in from the other side and try to pop a few chickens.

coyote

Only rarely are coyotes disciplined enough to stick to the plan, however. The thought of a luscious chicken is too much for the coyotes who are supposed to be the decoys, and eventually they break off, move in, and try to get one for themselves. What inevitably happens is that the rancher, alerted by his barking dogs, comes out with his shotgun and gets a glimpse of coyotes running off; that's why a lot of coyotes end up with a load of buckshot in their rear ends.

I've seen coyotes nearly everywhere but the extreme high country and isolated deserts. I've spotted solo cruisers in the alpine zone at the edge of the snowline in the middle of winter, hunting mice in a field. I've seen packs roaming the Central Valley ranchlands in fall. I've watched them in the coastal grasslands in the spring, on the edge of the high desert in winter, and in high wilderness in summer.

Somehow, against tremendous odds, they always seem to make it.

Biologists' Notes

The coyote *(Canis latrans)* is found throughout all life zones in California from the low deserts and valleys to the crest of the highest mountains. It has adapted readily to the changes caused by human occupation of the land and its range extends into all counties except San Francisco County.

At one time biologists listed three subspecies common to California—the mountain, desert, and valley coyotes. But biologists questioned this classification and suggested that mixing of populations has occurred in recent times.

The coyote is a member of the dog family. In size and shape, the coyote is like a medium-sized shepherd dog, but its tail is round and bushy and is carried straight out and below the level of its back. Coyotes found in low deserts and valleys are a grayish tawny brown with a black tip on the tail. At high elevations and on the east side of the Sierra, their color is more gray and the underparts are nearly white, with some specimens having a white tip on the tail. Coyotes of the higher elevations average a little larger in size than those in the valley. In winter their coats become long and silky.

The coyote is one of the few wild animals whose voice is commonly heard. Coyotes howl at night. The sound is both a high quivering cry and a crazy, high-pitched yapping.

Although the coyote usually digs its own den, sometimes it will enlarge an old badger hole or perhaps fix up a natural hole in a rocky ledge to suit its

Where to see coyote

BIG MORONGO CANYON PRESERVE, IN SAN BERNARDINO COUNTY

HOPE VALLEY WILDLIFE AREA, IN ALPINE COUNTY

MERCED NATIONAL WILDLIFE REFUGE, IN MERCED COUNTY

MONO LAKE, IN INYO NATIONAL FOREST, IN MONO COUNTY

MONTANA DE ORO STATE PARK, IN SAN LUIS OBISPO COUNTY

MOUNT SAN JACINTO STATE PARK AND STATE WILDERNESS, IN RIVERSIDE COUNTY

PROVIDENCE MOUNTAINS STATE RECREATION AREA, IN SAN BERNARDINO COUNTY

TIJUANA SLOUGH NATIONAL WILDLIFE REFUGE, IN SAN DIEGO COUNTY

TULE ELK STATE RESERVE, IN KERN COUNTY

Other places to see coyote

ANZA-BORREGO DESERT STATE PARK, IN SAN DIEGO COUNTY

BUTANO STATE PARK, IN SAN MATEO COUNTY

CASWELL MEMORIAL STATE PARK, IN SAN JOAQUIN COUNTY

CHAW'SE INDIAN GRINDING ROCK STATE PARK, IN AMADOR COUNTY

CUYAMACA RANCHO STATE PARK, IN SAN DIEGO COUNTY

D.L. BLISS STATE PARK, IN EL DORADO COUNTY

DESERT TORTOISE NATURAL AREA, IN KERN COUNTY

EASTMAN LAKE, IN MADERA COUNTY

FOLSOM LAKE STATE RECREATION AREA, IN SACRAMENTO COUNTY

KYBURZ MARSH, IN SIERRA COUNTY

LIVING DESERT, IN RIVERSIDE COUNTY

MALIBU CREEK STATE PARK AND LAGOON, IN LOS ANGELES COUNTY

MOUNT DIABLO STATE PARK, IN CONTRA COSTA COUNTY

NEW HOGAN LAKE, IN CALAVERAS COUNTY

PICACHO STATE RECREATION AREA, IN IMPERIAL COUNTY

PISMO BEACH STATE PARK, IN SAN LUIS OBISPO COUNTY

REDWOOD NATIONAL AND STATE PARKS, IN DEL NORTE COUNTY

SANTA ROSA PLATEAU ECOLOGICAL RESERVE, IN RIVERSIDE COUNTY

SILVERWOOD LAKE STATE RECREATION AREA, IN SAN BERNARDINO COUNTY

SKYLINE RIDGE OPEN SPACE PRESERVE, IN SANTA CLARA COUNTY

TOPANGA STATE PARK, IN LOS ANGELES COUNTY

own needs. Dens are usually hidden from view, but they are fairly easy to locate because of the trails that lead away from the den.

Mother coyote has one litter of three to nine puppies a year, usually in April or May. The gestation period is from 63 to 65 days. While the male does little to support the family, he will bring food fairly close, but the mother does not allow him to come all the way to the den. The pups live in the den and play near the entrance until they are about 10 weeks old. Then the mother starts taking them out hunting in a group. The family gradually disbands, and by fall the pups are usually hunting alone.

Some studies have indicated that in the valley and low foothills, coyotes occupy a range of no more than 10 or 12 square miles. In mountainous areas they probably have both a summer and winter range, as heavy snows drive them to lower elevations.

The coyote does not hibernate. It travels over its range and hunts both day and night, running swiftly, and catching its prey easily. It has a varied diet and seems able to exist on whatever the area offers in the way of food. Although it has been observed killing sheep, poultry and other livestock, it does not live on domestic animals. Food habit studies show that its principal diet is made up of deer, rabbits, ground squirrels, other small rodents, insects, even reptiles, and fruits and berries of wild plants.

Coyotes have a good sense of smell, vision and hearing which, coupled with evasiveness, enables them to survive both in the wild and occasionally in the suburban areas of some of California's largest cities. They are common in most rural areas, but because of their secretive nature, few are seen.

Efforts to control or exterminate the coyote by predator control agents seem to have produced an animal that is extremely alert and wary and well able to maintain itself. Coyotes have long been one of the most controversial of all nongame animals. Agricultural interests have urged its control by whatever means necessary so that actual and potential livestock losses may be eliminated. Since 1891, when the first programs aimed at control were begun in California, nearly 500,000 coyotes have been reported destroyed at a cost of an estimated $30 million of the taxpayers' money.

Environmentalists firmly believe that the coyotes are necessary to preserve the balance of nature. Biologists agree that individual animals preying on livestock and poultry should be destroyed, but that the species as a whole is not necessarily harmful, because much of its diet is made up of destructive rodents. Biologists also agree that coyote populations have no lasting effects on other wildlife populations. So the controversy rages on.

Crane, Sandhill

Watching a long skein of sandhill cranes across the valley sky can feel as if you have been transported in a time machine to a prehistoric era.

These birds have huge wingspans, typically six to seven feet, and they line up across the sky nearly wingtip to wingtip, flapping slowly with their long, labored strokes. It looks like something right out of Jurassic Park. When sandhill cranes fly, they seem graceful and slow, like a sky ballet.

On one morning in the San Joaquin Valley with waterfowl expert Robert Brown, it was one of those perfect windless moments

ANIMAL	Crane, Sandhill
SPECIES	*Grus canadensis*
TYPE	bird
STATUS	Threatened

where there was scarcely a ripple across the marsh, the kind of dawn where sound can travel for miles. Off in the distance, as the hues of yellow and orange refracted across the valley, you could hear this series of wild-sounding squawks. We scanned the horizon, and there, still miles off, was this line of birds with vast wingspans.

First we thought they were Canada geese, but as they neared, you could hear their call was more of a squawk than a honk. Then, as they moved closer still, we figured they were swans, judging by the deliberate slow wingbeat of their flying style. Finally, they were close enough to hear clearly, and there was no mistaking their one-of-a-kind trumpet-like calls and then their unique form in flight: long, pointed beak, head outstretched, streamlined gray body, giant flapping wings. It could only be sandhill crane. It was a lucky sighting. And, yep, it did feel like going back in time.

sandhill crane

Unless you spend a lot of time on a marsh, where in the course of a season you are apt to see uncounted dozens of migratory species, you often have to make it a mission to see sandhill crane.

The best spot I know is at Soda Lake at the remote Carrizo Plain in the foothills west of Bakersfield, one of California's most unique habitats. In winter, the sandhill cranes can practically fill the sky at Soda Lake, one of the few places anywhere where this can occur. One of the reasons is because the sandhill crane is a shy bird, and it avoids large population centers. The Carrizo, on the other hand, is one of the most remote habitats in the state, and by far the most isolated region in Central California. The best reason to come here is to see the sandhill cranes. Some say it's the only reason.

The eggs of the sandhill crane are laid several days apart and both parents help to incubate the eggs. Incubation starts with the first egg; consequently, one chick is hatched a day or so before the second. The parents keep the young 15 to 50 feet apart for several weeks so the older chick cannot assault the younger and smaller bird.

But on their migratory track, sandhill cranes are apt to stop at federal and state wildlife areas all through the Sacramento and San Joaquin valleys. In fact, sandhill cranes may provide the best weather forecast of any bird for those who fly this migratory journey. The key spot is the Sacramento Wildlife Refuge. If they arrive here in late September or early October, you can plan on a long, severe winter to follow. After that, for every week later they arrive, you can figure a parallel for the weather, with a shorter and less intense winter incrementally for each week. Long-range weather predictions lack reliability among scientists, but the sandhill cranes have developed their own science.

Up close the sandhill crane is not a physically imposing creature. Though they are tall, their long legs and thin gray bodies make them look uncoordinated. They walk slowly, "craning" their necks.

They hardly look like the same creature in flight, huge and majestic, filling their air with squawks, heralding the changing of the seasons.

Biologists' Notes

There are about 20 species of cranes in the world, three of which are found on this continent. The species that occurs in California is the sandhill crane *(Grus canadensis)*. This crane is gray, except for its red cap. It is a cousin of the extremely rare whooping crane that is found in the United States only along the west side of the Mississippi River Valley. The greater sandhill crane *(G.c. tabida)*, a subspecies of the sandhill crane, has been considered a state threatened species since 1983.

Market hunting nearly doomed the cranes to extinction. But now, under complete protection, about 15,000 of these stately birds annually winter in California, arriving in northern California as early as September. Their wild-sounding, trumpet-like calls can be heard at great distances as different groups assemble at their favorite wintering spots.

From 3,000 to 6,000 converge and remain in the delta of the Sacramento and San Joaquin Rivers. Other smaller flocks of a few hundred each are found from the Butte Sink in Colusa County to as far south as the Carrizo Plain west of Bakersfield.

In late winter and early spring one can witness the "dance of the cranes," which is performed in an almost ritualistic pattern. There is a clamor of calls; they leap into the air, flap their wings, and cavort in what may be a courtship display.

The cranes are extremely wary, so caution must be used when approaching them, for at any time a sharp-eyed sentinel may voice an alarm and the great birds will leap into the air and be gone.

The cranes remain on the winter grounds until February. Then, overpowered by the restless urge to return to the breeding grounds, they take to the skies. Some flocks will spiral up and up until almost out of sight, with only the lingering sound of their strange guttural calls to proclaim their departure.

There are some scattered nesting sites in northeastern California, but most of them go farther north. The nests are constructed by both the male and female, and some nests are large enough to support the crane if high water should rise and cause them to float. Most nests are located so that the birds have a clear, unobstructed view.

Egg laying commences in mid-April. There are two and rarely three large, pale, olive-colored eggs, marked by spots of buff-brown. The eggs are laid several days apart, and both parents help to incubate the eggs. Incubation starts with the first egg; consequently, one chick is hatched a day or so

---

Where to see sandhill crane

CARRIZO PLAIN NATURAL AREA, IN KERN COUNTY

COSUMNES RIVER PRESERVE, IN SACRAMENTO COUNTY

MERCED NATIONAL WILDLIFE REFUGE, IN MERCED COUNTY

MODOC NATIONAL WILDLIFE REFUGE, IN MODOC COUNTY

SACRAMENTO RIVER NATIONAL WILDLIFE REFUGE (LLANO SECO UNIT), IN BUTTE COUNTY

SHASTA VALLEY STATE WILDLIFE AREA, IN SISKIYOU COUNTY

before the second. They leave the nest as soon as the second chick is dry.

The parents keep the young 15 to 50 feet apart for several weeks so the older chick cannot assault the younger and smaller bird. The young stay with the parents and are fed by regurgitation for several months. They do not fly until they are nearly as large as the adult birds but walk long distances and run and hide to escape their enemies.

Crayfish

Their real name may be "crayfish," but everybody except scientists calls them "crawdads," and at times perhaps a few other choice words.

It all depends on how you're introduced to them, or that is, which end you become intimate with. If you meet Mr. Crawdad tail first, he's a mighty fine, tasty fellow, kind of like a junior lobster. If you meet him pincher first, well, you might try a date with the Ayatollah.

I've had plenty of both. On a fishing trip at Lake Casitas, we were using crawdads for bait. Only problem was my partner, Bob Robb, had brought them in a two-gallon lemonade thermos, the big fat kind with the small opening on top. I reached into that small opening, and just like that, felt like a blind man poking his stick at a busy traffic intersection. I could feel the little buggers

ANIMAL	Crayfish
SPECIES	*Pacificastus* spp. *Procambaris* spp.
TYPE	crustacean
STATUS	Endangered/ Introduced
SEE ALSO	Lobster

crawling around down there, and then figured, "might as well," and tried to pick one up, in the blind, so to speak. Well, Mr. Crawdad did not like that. In fact, Mr. Crawdad nabbed me right on the ring finger of my right hand.

"Yeeeeeoooooooooow!" I shouted, jerking my hand out of that thermos, with that little crawdad still hanging on to my finger. Did it hurt? Is a frog water repellent?

Then there are the other times. In waters loaded with crawdads, such as the Sacramento River near Grimes, Lake Tulloch in the foothills of the Cen-

crayfish

tral Valley, or the hundreds of other places in lakes and creeks where crawdads are abundant, they are easy to catch and easier to eat.

The eyes of the crayfish are mounted on short movable stalks that can be turned in any direction. Just behind the eyes are two feelers, which are more than half the length of the body. When the crayfish is undisturbed, these feelers are continuously moving.

You can boil them just like lobsters, dip the tails into a simple lemon-butter mix, and eat them just like lobsters.

The area most heavily populated with crawdads is the Sacramento River, from below Colusa all the way to Sacramento, in sections of river where the banks have been rip-rapped, that is, reinforced with large boulders and rock to alleviate erosion. The crawdads live in the rocks in huge numbers. There are many commercial crawdad operations here, with little floats marking crawdad traps about every 50 yards for miles on end.

To catch crawdads, I've always used a simple cane pole with a big hook, then use bacon or chicken necks for bait. The crawdads will grab the bait, start chomping down, and you just pull 'em out—they won't let go. I usually keep a 5-gallon bucket handy, and just drop them in with a thunk.

Crawdads also make a great live bait for giant bass. At Otay Lake near San Diego, we always have a large cardboard flat with about a dozen of them, then wave a hand over them. First one that moves is elected for the job. Forget that lemonade thermos idea.

They can be picked up by clasping them quickly with your thumb and forefinger, just behind the base of the pincher arms. Once you figure this out, you won't have any problems. In fact, 10-year-olds who know how to pick up crawdads love few things better than taunting their brothers or moms. Guess how I know?

Many people have wondered what it feels like to get grabbed by one of their little pinchers. From someone who has had the experience, let me explain:

The feeling is kind of like grabbing somebody's top lip with a pair of pliers and then pulling it right over the top of his head.

Biologists' Notes

Many of the fresh and brackish waters of California are inhabited by crayfish: small crustaceans seldom over five or six inches long and resembling little lobsters.

Several different types of crayfish (*Pacificastus* and *Procambaris* spp.) occur in California, occupying a wide variety of habitats. Many species have been introduced from out of state.

A species known as the signal crayfish was introduced from Oregon into the Lake Tahoe region around 1900, as forage for game fish. The distribution of the signal crayfish increased tremendously, and today it is found at high and low elevations in lakes in the Sierra Nevada, or in fast-flowing rivers and small coastal streams. It is most abundant in the Sacramento-San Joaquin River system and is found even in the brackish waters of the Delta. It is nonburrowing and prefers rocky areas that provide it with ample hiding places. The signal crayfish is identified by its smooth outer shell, its large size, rarely even up to seven or eight inches, and by a pale white spot near the hinge of the pincer. This variety has been fished commercially, primarily for export to Sweden.

Another species, the red swamp crayfish, is native to the southeastern United States. Another non-native, it was introduced into Los Angeles County in 1924. Today, this crayfish is the most widespread species in California and is found in most counties south of Colusa County. Its bright colors make it quite visible in the rice fields of central California for, as the rice fields are drained, it crawls out on land.

The swamp crayfish is quite hardy. In streams or rice fields that are dry for part of the year, this species will dig a two-inch wide burrow in the mud, some 20 to 40 inches deep, seal itself in, and wait out the dry period in a column of stagnant water. The swamp crayfish is identified by its rough, dumpy, outer shell and the red coloring of its claws and outer shell.

Still another crayfish introduction, this one from the Midwest, occurred in 1940 when individuals escaped from holding ponds in Butte County. In

1979 this crayfish was found as far south as San Diego County and north to Shasta County. It now competes with and threatens rare native crayfish in the Pit River drainage; the Shasta crayfish *(Pacificastus fortis)* is a federally endangered species partly due to competition from introduced crayfish. The introduced species also has a bumpy outer shell but lacks the bright color of the swamp crayfish.

Although the life histories of the crayfish found in California vary considerably, certain aspects are common to all crayfish. Unlike most animals whose hard parts of the skeleton are on the inside, the hard parts of the crayfish skeleton are on the outside, which is called the exoskeleton. A crayfish can grow only by shedding the exoskeleton and laying down a new, larger covering.

The younger, smaller crayfish molt most often. About a week is needed for the new shell to harden. During this soft-shell period, the crayfish remains hidden, for it is vulnerable to predation and cannibalism.

If a number of crayfish of about the same size are compared, it will be obvious that some have narrow tails and some have broad tails. The ones with the broader tails are females. Beneath the hinged tail are tiny limbs called swimmerettes. In female crayfish these serve as an aid to swimming and to hold the eggs and young. The abdominal appendages of the male are larger and stiffer and are folded up between the last pair of walking legs.

When the young are hatched they are barely a quarter inch long, but they are almost exact replicas of the mother. They remain attached to the mother for about a week before they venture out on their own.

The crayfish grows rapidly when young, but more slowly as it ages. By the end of a year it may be nearly one and one-half inches in length, at two years about two and one-half inches and at five years about five inches. They continue growing until, in exceptional cases, they may attain a length of seven or eight inches. Male crayfish are commonly larger than females of the same age. In ideal conditions, they may live 15 or 20 years.

Crayfish may be seen walking along the bottom in clear shallow water by means of four pairs of jointed legs. If disturbed or alarmed, crayfish dart backwards with rapid jerks. They propel themselves by strokes of the broad fan-shaped flipper on the end of the jointed tail.

The eyes of the crayfish are mounted on short movable stalks which can be turned in any direction. Just behind the eyes are two feelers which are more than half the length of the body. When the crayfish is undisturbed, these feelers are continuously moving, as though exploring the area around the body of the crayfish.

Where to see crayfish

SACRAMENTO RIVER, NEAR GRIMES AND KNIGHTS LANDING, IN COLUSA COUNTY

TULLOCH RESERVOIR, IN CALAVERAS AND TUOLUMNE COUNTY

Other places to see crayfish

NOTE: Crayfish live in hundreds of creeks, most so small that if they were listed, populations could be impacted by anglers.

Crayfish are intolerant of much heat or sunshine, so they are more active in the evening and at night. During the day they seek shelter under rocks, logs, overhanging banks, or in burrows which they dig themselves. Crayfish are less active during very cold weather.

Although it hunts primarily at night, even in daylight the crayfish will lie at the mouth of a hiding place, barring the entrance with its great claws. It's feelers are usually extended as it keeps a careful watch for any unsuspecting insects, larvae, tadpoles, or small frogs that pass by. If food comes within reach, it is suddenly seized and devoured.

Curlew, Long-Billed

Most creatures are built for the job. Owls are built to raid mice on night runs, osprey almost never miss when they dive for trout, and falcons can pop a dove in mid-air at 175 mph.

While the long-billed curlew may not be the marquee bird of California, it too has special abilities. As for how curlews feed, their form seems a creation of perfection, and there are other qualities that set this bird apart from all others.

The first thing you will notice is that its long, down-curved bill seems perfectly crafted for the job at hand, poking and probing about for food. That's because it is.

ANIMAL	Curlew, Long-Billed
SPECIES	*Numenius americanus*
TYPE	bird
STATUS	OK

That is why they are abundant in San Francisco Bay and environs during the winter. Curlews will search for food during minus low tides, when bay waters roll back and unveil miles of mud flats filled with tiny marine life. Curlews can also be found in large numbers

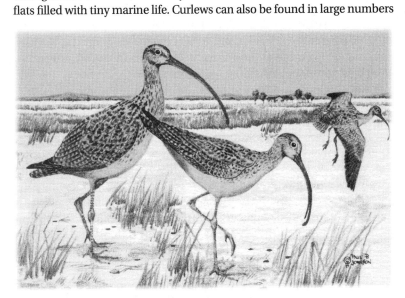

long-billed curlew

in the Central Valley and in Southern California in Imperial Valley—extremely unusual for a shorebird.

Most mud-poking marine birds are found only on coastal marshes and on tidal flats, yet the curlew can be found in the Central Valley on open grazing lands, plowed fields, and irrigated pastures where they both feed and roost. When feeding, they walk gracefully and swiftly, stopping to probe each crack and soft spot they find in the ground. Food items consist of insects, crustaceans, worms, mollusks, small berries, and seeds.

Of 35 significant shore birds regularly found in California, the long-billed curlew is the largest. While extremely shy, they can easily be found by those approaching quietly, then viewing with binoculars. Its clear, prolonged whistling notes is one of the big-time hit songs.

When landing they drop nearly to the ground, make a graceful upward sweep, and check their speed with a flash of their cinnamon wings. For aspiring pilots, I believe only the blue heron offers a more perfect example of how to flare off speed on final en route to a soft touchdown.

The long, down-curved bill of the curlew is perfectly crafted for the job of poking and probing about for food.

A typical habitat where curlew can be seen in winter is the San Francisco Bay National Wildlife Refuge, located at the eastern foot of the Dumbarton Bridge, as well as at the adjacent diked-off salt ponds. Large roosting flocks typically form here at dusk, spending the night together on the levees and bars. When a flock has gathered, whether to feed or sleep, one or more birds usually stand as sentinels against any predator—at their cry of warning the whole flock will awake, raise their wings, and take off.

Biologists' Notes

There are three species of curlews in North America outside Alaska: the Eskimo curlew *Numenius borealis*, the whimbrel *(N. phaeopus)*, and the long-billed curlew *(N. americanus)*.

During the winter months the long-billed curlew is commonly seen from San Francisco southward and in the interior valleys of central California. It breeds in southern Canada and in the American northwest, including northeastern California. The Eskimo curlew in the early days occurred in great numbers east of the Rocky Mountains, but it is now thought to be nearly extinct; occasional reports of sightings along the west coast of the Gulf of Mexico indicate there may be a remaining few. The whimbrel, which was formerly called the Hudsonian curlew, winters along the coast and also winters in great numbers in the Imperial Valley.

The curlew is exceedingly wary, however, it will stand its ground when in breeding areas, where they are concerned for the welfare of their eggs and young. Their flight is a bit erratic at first, but when under way it is strong and steady. When traveling long distances they often fly high in the air in wedge-shaped flocks. Their occasional loud whistling notes help distinguish them at a distance from a flock of smaller dark geese.

In California they arrive from their breeding grounds starting about mid-July. The migration to the wintering areas reaches a peak from August to October.

They spend the winter primarily in the southern part of Sacramento, San Joaquin, and the Imperial Valleys. Along the coast they winter from San Francisco southward. The spring migration back to the breeding grounds commences in late March, and peaks in April. Upon their arrival at the breeding ground they become preoccupied with choosing a mate, building their nests, and rearing their young.

Long-billed curlews nest on the dry ground of open grasslands. On the plateaus of northeastern California they nest in bunchgrass grazing lands, saltgrass, dry meadows, and irrigated hay fields. They prefer to be near water and are often found in the vicinity of nesting willets. Cows seem to avoid the nests but grazing sheep trample them.

Both the male and the female assist in the incubating of eggs and in the rearing of young. The nest is a simple affair, a slight hollow in the ground, thinly lined with grasses. Sometimes the nest is a substantial platform of grass, slightly elevated and hollowed to contain the eggs. There is an average of four or five eggs in each clutch. The eggs are colored from buff to olive, but all are evenly spotted with a dark rich brown. Incubation is thought to be about 30 days. The hen, on the nest, is at times quite conspicuous as she lies with eyes closed, her head and neck stretched out on the ground, looking much like a dead chicken. The male is quite attentive and noisily defends the nest. He may dive at an intruder even though several hundred feet from the nest.

The young are wobbly on their feet when first hatched. They soon become adept at hiding, for in the open areas in which they prefer to live, they are subject to heavy predation by hawks, owls, and coyotes. The young grow rapidly and as soon as the parents have taught them how to probe for food and catch grasshoppers, the breeding population is able to band together, and by midsummer they start their migration to the wintering grounds.

Unrestricted market hunting for curlews continued until 1905 when the first seasons and bag limits were placed on shore birds. It was too late, however, for the Eskimo curlew, for unrestricted hunting on the breeding grounds in Alaska, on the wintering grounds in South America and on the migratory routes in the United States depleted their numbers to a point from where they have been unable to recover.

Deer

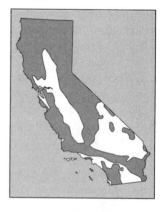

We were tracking a clear game trail and wondered: How close could the deer be? How big? How many points on the antlers?

Deer migrations in the mountains are always set off by the first snows, usually arriving in mid- to late October. Once all food sources are covered with a layer of snow, the deer will head to lower elevations below the snowline, where they can again find reliable food sources. Positioning yourself along these migration routes after the first heavy snow in the high country is one of the best ways to see high numbers of deer. This winter habitat is also critical to the health of California's deer population.

The game trail led us first through a forest of mixed cedars and ponderosa pines,

ANIMAL	Deer, Mule
SPECIES	*Odocoileus hemionus*
TYPE	mammal
STATUS	OK
SEE ALSO	Bighorn, Elk, Pronghorn

where we found fresh droppings—so the deer could not be far off. The route then fed us down to a small creek, apparently their watering hole, and after crossing, we followed the trail to a nearby clearing, a wild meadow bordered on three sides by high brush.

Here, the wild grass was three feet high but mashed right down to the ground in a 25-foot circle. We could sense that this was the spot where a small deer herd had been bedding down, a perfect spot, with plenty of food, protection, and nearby water. We hid nearby, then waited. Nothing.

The number of points in the antlers of a buck deer is not an indicator of age. The quality and quantity of good food govern the number of antler points as well as the size of the antlers. A yearling deer on good feed may have three-point antlers, while a three-year-old on poor feed may only have one point or spike on each side.

Finally we gave up this strategy and retraced our steps, enjoying the evening. We were gazing at some bubble-like cumulus building on the ridge to the west, when suddenly, to our left, four deer emerged in a clearing. They froze for a moment, one buck among them, and then went bounding off into forest.

We had done everything right, yet when we finally found the deer, it had been an accident. Lucky? So much of enjoying the great outdoors is just being out there, using your best woodsmanship skills, then seeing what happens.

In turn, being able to track deer, to see the world on their terms, can make for very satisfying moments in the great outdoors. After a long stalk, you feel closer to the natural world, more a part of the earth, and it can be an exhilarating finish that stays with you for a long time.

What I like to do is hike into the mountains and look for transitions in habitat, such as where forest gives way to a meadow, and the meadow gives way to a stream. That is where you will find wildlife: meadow for food, stream for water, forest nearby for cover.

black-tailed deer

By tracing the edge of the meadows, you can often find active game trails. You can tell if they are active or not by searching for fresh droppings, either along the trail or in meadows where the grass is mashed down, a sure sign that the deer have bedded down there.

Then I like to climb off trail up the slope of a canyon wall, so I am positioned perfectly to watch that game trail with binoculars. Often, in the last hour of daylight, I have spotted deer walking down their trail, heading for the meadow and stream. The experience is like lighting a long fuse to a stick of dynamite. It is exciting, captivating, and rewarding.

In contrast, a number of hunters in California will just drive around on Forest Service roads in their trucks or ATVs with rifles. I call this "deer trolling," and it is about as appealing to me as driving on Interstate 5 in L.A. at 5 p.m. on Friday. By being in a vehicle, you are disconnected from nature and all the more intimate sounds, smells, and feelings that come with being in the wild.

The primary diet components of deer are acorns from oak trees in the winter; newly sprouted grass, plants, and budding hardwoods in spring (as it arrives along migration routes from low to high elevations from March through July); and berries, apples, and flowers in mid- to late summer. In fact, if you hang out near an apple tree in early October, pretty soon the deer will be coming on by.

The key to the future of deer in California is making sure they have sufficient food available to support healthy animals and growth.

After you become proficient at finding deer in the wild, you will then discover that many of them, particularly the black-tailed deer, are quite small. I've had days where I've stalked and spotted 200 deer, once more than 500, and they all seemed to be very small, with very few antlers, as if they were all stunted. Many were under a hundred pounds. I saw one spindly, forked-horned buck that looked like a great Dane with little horns.

A natural forest provides such tremendous diversity that there is plenty of food for deer and other wildlife. From truffles (a mushroom-like fungus) to sprouting plants to budding hardwoods, a diverse habitat is like a grocery store for wildlife. But when logging operations cut down a forest, eliminate the diversity, and replace it with a tree farm, especially a pine monoculture, you eliminate much of the ability of the habitat to provide food for deer and wildlife. After all, a deer can't eat a pine tree. So with no food, there are few deer, and those few are small with poor horn growth.

This connection was best documented when the Department of Fish and Game conducted a deer nutrition study. It started when five mule deer fawns, two black-tailed mule deer and three Rocky Mountain mule deer, were captured in the remote Warner Mountains of Modoc County, then raised in captivity, kept in a pen and fed a high-nutrition diet, primarily Purina high-protein deer chow mixed with alfalfa. After two and a half years, the black-tailed deer averaged 185 pounds and the Rocky Mountain mule deer averaged 260 pounds, the biggest with four-by-four antlers that measured 22 inches long with a 4.25-inch circumference at the base. Compare these numbers to the puny 90-pounders with spike horns that homogenous pine forests support.

I think if I were sitting on a mountain slope and saw a deer like one of these come around the bend, I'd fall right off my rock.

Biologists' Notes

Native deer are all mule deer *(Odocoileus hemionus)* and the abundant black-tailed deer are a subspecies of mule deer. The species name is derived from the large size of their ears.

Deer are primarily browsing animals that eat the twigs, buds, and leaves of shrubs and trees. They also rely on acorns in some areas, and in the spring and fall they graze on green grasses and leafy plants. Deer that summer in mountainous areas migrate to lower elevations in the winter, typically not heading down to the foothills until snow forces them down. In other locations, deer are resident in a relatively limited area and become accustomed to contact with people who live in these areas.

The deer's keenest sense is its hearing. It has rather poor vision for stationary objects but is quick to catch motion.

Both the bucks and does have reddish coats in the summer, which are replaced with gray in the fall as the long hairs grow out to form their winter coats.

Bucks alone have antlers, which are shed each year in midwinter, and they remain bareheaded until a new set starts to grow in the spring. The antlers grow rapidly and while growing are covered with a velvet-like skin that is rubbed off as soon as the antlers harden in the fall. Normally a mature buck has four points on each antler. Contrary to some beliefs, the number of points is not an indicator of age, for the quality and quantity of good food govern the number of antler points as well as the size of the antlers. A yearling deer on good feed may have three-point antlers, while a three-year-old on poor feed may only have one point or spike on each side.

Where to see deer

FORT TEJON STATE HISTORIC PARK, IN KERN COUNTY

HAIWEE DEER WINTER RANGE, IN INYO COUNTY
NOTE: The best viewing season is December through February.

SUNOL/OHLONE REGIONAL WILDERNESS, IN ALAMEDA AND SANTA CLARA COUNTIES

SUCCESS LAKE, IN TULARE COUNTY

TIMBER MOUNTAIN, MODOC NATIONAL FOREST, IN MODOC COUNTY

Mule deer may interbreed where the ranges of subspecies coincide. Thus, variations in markings and in size may be noted in some deer where ranges overlap. The breeding season varies with elevation and latitude and occurs from mid-September through January. It is generally timed so that the fawns are born when green, leafy plants will be available for the young deer.

The doe carries the young fawn for about seven months. Fawning season varies throughout the state, from early April in parts of coastal California to the end of July in areas of the Sierra Nevada. Fawns are born with spotted coats but lose their spots at about the time they are weaned, usually 60 to 90 days after birth. However, they continue to run with their mothers until fall, some for a full year.

Early California records show that deer were plentiful in the valleys and foothills in the days of the pioneers. But deer populations, like those of other forms of wildlife, are dynamic, rising and falling with the quality of the habitat.

After the gold rush ran its course, deer populations began to decline. The use of meat and hides by settlers was unrestricted, and free grazing on public lands caused a livestock buildup that resulted in severe overgrazing by domesticated animals. These factors, together with the bitter cold winters at the turn of the century, brought the deer population to its lowest numbers ever. The cycle changed when protective laws were established.

A healthy doe on good food normally has twin fawns, one buck, one doe, so a deer herd is capable of doubling itself each year.

The demands of a growing human population have seen land use become a major factor in maintaining deer populations. In the past 50 years, reduction in deer range has continued because of urban development, subdivisions, conversion of wildlands to agriculture, spraying of sagebrush, highway and reservoir construction, and improved techniques in fire suppression, which has allowed brush on large tracts to mature past the point of providing nutritious forage for deer. In addition, second-growth timber is now maturing and gradually crowding out the much-needed browse plants.

All of these factors have caused a reduction in the quality and quantity of the deer range in California. In some areas the deer are eating up the nat-

Other places to see deer

BATTLE CREEK WILDLIFE AREA, IN TEHAMA COUNTY

BUTANO STATE PARK, IN SAN MATEO COUNTY

CACHUMA LAKE RECREATION AREA, IN SANTA BARBARA COUNTY

CHAW'SE INDIAN GRINDING ROCK STATE HISTORIC PARK, IN AMADOR COUNTY

COYOTE HILLS REGIONAL PARK, IN ALAMEDA COUNTY

DEL VALLE RESERVOIR AND REGIONAL PARK, IN ALAMEDA COUNTY

EATON CANYON NATURAL AREA, IN LOS ANGELES COUNTY

GRAY LODGE WILDLIFE AREA, IN BUTTE COUNTY

JOE DOMECQ WILDLIFE AREA, IN STANISLAUS COUNTY

LAKE SOLANO COUNTY PARK, IN SOLANO COUNTY

LAKE SONOMA RECREATION AREA, IN SONOMA COUNTY

LOPEZ LAKE, IN SAN LUIS OBISPO COUNTY

MOUNT DIABLO STATE PARK, IN CONTRA COSTA COUNTY

MOUNT TAMALPAIS STATE PARK, IN MARIN COUNTY

NEW HOGAN LAKE, IN CALAVERAS COUNTY

PALOMAR MOUNTAIN STATE PARK, IN SAN DIEGO COUNTY

PAYNES CREEK WETLANDS, IN TEHAMA COUNTY

POINT MUGU STATE PARK, IN LOS ANGELES COUNTY

SACRAMENTO NATIONAL WILDLIFE REFUGES COMPLEX, COLUSA, GLENN, SUTTER, AND TEHAMA COUNTIES

SANTA ROSA PLATEAU ECOLOGICAL RESERVE, IN RIVERSIDE COUNTY

SHASTA LAKE NATIONAL RECREATION AREA, IN SHASTA COUNTY

SKYLINE RIDGE OPEN SPACE PRESERVE, IN SANTA CLARA COUNTY

TOPANGA STATE PARK, IN LOS ANGELES COUNTY

WADDELL CREEK, IN SANTA CRUZ COUNTY

ural forage faster than it can replenish itself. In these areas malnutrition takes a toll in the form of decreased fawn production and survival and in disheartening winter kills.

Emphasis is now being directed toward habitat improvement on the remaining deer ranges. Programs are being developed for use in wildfire and controlled burns, chaparral manipulations, and logging practices, which will improve deer ranges.

Dolphins and Porpoises

Of all the creatures in the wild kingdom of earth, the happiest must be the dolphins. As they cavort, jump, and show off, they even seem to have smiles on their faces, always eager to please.

Now explain to me: How do you teach people to act like this?

The best way to see dolphins in action for yourself is to take the boat cruise from Oxnard by Island Packers out to the Channel Islands, to Santa Cruz (the closest), Anacapa, or Santa Rosa Island, or the more distant San Miguel or Santa Barbara Islands. In Northern California, dolphins frequent the Gulf of the Farallones from mid-July through fall and often can be seen on Farallon nature

ANIMAL	Dolphins and Porpoises
SPECIES	Family *Delphinidae* and *Phoconidae*
TYPE	mammal
STATUS	OK
SEE ALSO	Whales

cruises, offered by the Oceanic Society out of San Francisco.

On one trip to Santa Cruz Island, we departed Oxnard on a cool, foggy day, and as the boat left the harbor, we just sat down and dug in for the trip, hoping the two hours wouldn't go too slowly. But as we ventured out to sea, the extraordinary occurred.

First there was one dolphin jumping alongside the boat. We went to the railing and watched, and it was as if the dolphin was trying to cheer us up. Then there were two, jumping in tandem, like a commercial for Marine World USA. In minutes, a dozen had joined, keeping pace with the boat, hurdling like greyhounds over the bow wake, others alongside.

It was the darnedest thing you've ever seen. Suddenly, on this damp, dreary day on the Southern California coast, everybody on board the boat had smiles on their faces.

But there was more. Within 20 minutes, there seemed to be about 75 dolphins keeping pace with the boat. Everybody aboard was astonished. Now get this: One time on a fishing trip out of Cabo San Lucas, my boat was surrounded by what seemed to be thousands of them, acres of dolphins jumping on the surface.

I wish all the folks stuck in traffic just a few miles away on the highways of L.A. could have been transported in spirit to this moment and savored the feeling as we were savoring it. It gave us a light, happy sensation that stayed with us for weeks.

Dolphins are famous for many skills. At different times, they have been documented working in schools to fight off sharks to protect their young, they have demonstrated the ability to communicate with each other, and they use a sonar system to locate food and avoid striking objects in water with poor visibility. The lone sad note in their history is that they will occasionally beach themselves to die, and they are sometimes drowned in commercial fishing nets. The latter is an intolerable crime against one of nature's kindest creatures; all fishing nets in the ocean should be banned because of the incredible waste from the inevitable non-desired "bycatch"— and the threat from overharvest that netting creates for marine resources.

The ocean dolphin is actually a small, toothed whale, in the same family as the killer whale. They communicate with other dolphins through sounds made by air-filled sacs connected to the blowhole. From an organ on top of the head, they also make a series of whistle and click sounds, which serve as echolocation devices.

On one trip to the Farallon Islands out of San Francisco, we spotted 18 to 20 blue whales, 24 to 26 humpbacks, 45 to 55 dolphins, one minke whale and 23 species of birds. But what do you think stole the show?

Why, it was the dolphin, of course, parading along the boat, escorting us out to the whales, jumping, smiling, even laughing with us. Sure, the blue whale is the biggest air-breathing creature ever to inhabit the earth. But what set this trip apart were the dolphins. They have a way of giving you a good feeling inside, and it stays.

Biologists' Notes

Dolphins, porpoises, and whales belong to the order Cetacea, having in common the fact they are carnivorous, aquatic mammals. Unlike fish, cetaceans have lungs and breathe air, are warm-blooded, produce milk for their offspring, and have flat tails called flukes that move up and down rather than sideways. The characteristic blowhole on the top of the head is a nostril, which is sealed by powerful muscles when the animal is submerged. Another characteristic of cetaceans is their ability to use sound for communication and for echolocation, a kind of bio-sonar.

The ocean dolphin is actually a small, toothed whale belonging to the family Delphinidae, which has 18 species in North America. Ten of these are known to be present in California waters (common dolphin, short-finned pilot whale, Northern right whale dolphin, Risso's dolphin, Pacific white-sided dolphin, killer whale, false killer whale, striped dolphin, rough-toothed dolphin, and the bottle-nosed dolphin). The species of dolphin that provides the circus-like shows is the common dolphin, *Delphinus delphis*.

Porpoises are generally classified as members of the Phoconidae family, of which there are two species in North America, both found in California waters (harbor and Dall porpoises). Porpoises are smaller than dolphins and rather than the typical dolphin beak have a rounded, blunt head, which perhaps explains the name; porpoise is derived from the Latin meaning "pig fish." There remains some controversy among zoologists as to whether or not porpoises belong in a classification apart from dolphins. The justification for a separate classification is based upon skull and teeth differences. Delphinidae skulls twist to the left, while Phoconidae skulls are symmetrical and have smaller teeth. To the casual observer, there is little difference between them, though the porpoise is among the smallest species of cetaceans, seldom reaching lengths beyond six feet, while true dolphins are generally in the eight-foot range. One species, however, the killer whale, has been known to reach 30 feet.

Dolphins are equipped for ease and speed in the water, being torpedo-shaped, with flippers; powerful tail fins, or flukes; and a mid-line dorsal fin for balance. The skin is rubbery and smooth over a layer of blubber, which serves not only to keep the dolphin warm and to store nutrition, but also helps maintain buoyancy.

The gestation period for most dolphin species begins in spring or summer and lasts 10 to 12 months, resulting in a single calf about half the length of its mother. The calf is nursed and protected for more than a year by the mother; the father dolphin plays no role in caring for the young.

Dolphins typically live 25 years or more, but pilot whales have been known to live twice that long. The lifespan can be cut short by sharks, one of the dolphin's natural enemies, and humans, the other. Thousands of dol-

Where to see dolphins and porpoises

ABALONE COVE ECOLOGICAL RESERVE, IN LOS ANGELES COUNTY

CATALINA ISLAND, OFFSHORE FROM LOS ANGELES

CHANNEL ISLANDS, OFFSHORE FROM VENTURA COUNTY

CRYSTAL COVE STATE PARK, IN ORANGE COUNTY

FARALLON NATIONAL WILDLIFE REFUGE, OFFSHORE OF SAN FRANCISCO
NOTE: The refuge is about 30 miles offshore of San Francisco and is closed to
the public; however, it is possible to view a large variety of wildlife on and
near the islands via educational boat tours conducted from June through
November by the Oceanic Society.

GORDA OVERLOOK, IN MONTEREY COUNTY

KING RANGE NATIONAL CONSERVATION AREA, IN HUMBOLDT COUNTY

POINT LOBOS STATE RESERVE, IN MONTEREY COUNTY

POINT MUGU STATE PARK, IN LOS ANGELES COUNTY

TORREY PINES STATE RESERVE / LOS PENAQUITOS MARSH, IN SAN DIEGO COUNTY

Other places to see dolphins and porpoises

CABRILLO NATIONAL MONUMENT, IN SAN DIEGO COUNTY

DANA POINT HARBOR, IN ORANGE COUNTY

MONTANA DE ORO STATE PARK, IN SAN LUIS OBISPO COUNTY

POINT VICENTE, IN LOS ANGELES COUNTY

SAN MATEO POINT, NORTH OF SAN ONOFRE STATE BEACH, IN SAN DIEGO COUNTY

phins are killed annually offshore of Japan and China for meat and oil, and
sometimes unintentionally, as in the tuna fishing industry, where they are
often caught in nets. In the United States, laws limiting the number of dolphins that can be taken annually in tuna nets and improved fishing techniques have greatly reduced the number of dolphins unintentionally killed.

Scientists believe that dolphins have good vision and keen senses of
hearing and touch, but have no sense of smell and little or no sense of taste.
There is considerable interest among the scientific community in the
sound-making ability of the dolphin, in regard both to communication
and its natural sonar. Through a series of whistles and clicks that emanate
from an organ on top of the dolphin's head, called a melon, sound vibrations are transmitted throughout the surrounding area. The dolphin's keen

hearing picks up and translates the echoes into remarkably detailed distance, form, and even substance information. Another group of sounds called phonations, resemble the whistles and clicks used in echolocation, but these vibrations are made in air-filled sacs connected to the blowhole and are used in communication with other dolphins.

Man and dolphin have a history of friendly society going back to ancient times. Dolphins are depicted in ancient Greek and Roman art and appear in early mythology, the dolphin being considered sacred by the god Apollo. Even today, sailors consider the presence of dolphins alongside a ship good luck. In modern times, efforts are being made to develop the dolphin's ability to serve man, using its natural sonar to find underwater hazards and locate fish schools and using its communicative abilities to relay other information.

Dolphins' high intelligence and trainability have made them potential partners in commerce and safety, and also popular entertainers. In marine parks throughout California, they draw affectionate crowds awed by their ability to leap great distances, follow human commands, and exhibit a profound joy in play.

Doves

On many still dawns, I have been gently wakened by the soft *coo-coo-coooo* sound that at times settles across the land. It is the call of the dove, yearning for a mate, one of the prettiest songs nature has to offer.

It always makes me smile, a call that is soft yet clear, like a familiar chord of music, creating a moment of gentleness in a wild kingdom that is so often harsh to its residents. It rates with the mating call of an owl or a meadowlark as among the most compelling songs in the wild.

Dove are mercurial flyers, either solo or in giant flocks. They are best known for their immense flocks, occasional but stunning. At these times, they can appear to fill the sky, not so much as an amorphous horde, but like a massive single living being, with each bird pulsing its own heartbeat. Each bird has an extraordinary ability to dart, zig-zag, soar, and plummet, yet in the big flocks, they somehow are able to synchronize these patterns as if telepathically connected. Who knows? Maybe they are.

ANIMAL	Doves
SPECIES	Mourning - *Zenaida macroura* Ring-Necked - *Streptopelia decaocto* Chinese Spotted - *Streptopelia chinensis* White-Winged - *Zenaida asiatica*
TYPE	bird
STATUS	OK/Introduced
SEE ALSO	Band-Tailed Pigeon

The smaller groups are much more common, threes and fours. I've occasionally seen doubles and singles as well, though, typically, where there is one dove, there will be more.

Like many who track doves, I like watching them fly, listening to them call, and tracking their migration from the Oregon border all the way down to Mexico. They are among the earliest of migrants. An early fall storm hits in late September and off they will go, heading down the Central Valley, occasionally stopping to feed along farmers' fields. Because they eat seed, not insects, a recently harvested field with leftover seed can be like a magnet for large numbers of dove.

The bird itself seems fragile to many, soft-feathered and smooth-crowned, and it represents the bird of peace around the world. Yet in nature a dove's life offers a scant amount of harmony. That is because it is a favorite

mourning dove

The ring-necked and Chinese doves were imported from Asia as early as 1921, and quickly escaped into the wilds around Los Angeles. Since then, they have spread out into the surrounding suburban areas. Doves feed primarily on weed seeds and grains. Insects make up less than 1% of their diet.

prey for many raptors, especially the golden eagle, hawk, and falcon. Hawks enjoy slamming them in midflight, an amazing demonstration of speed and deftness, since the dove is an elusive and skilled flyer.

Another truth is that a small segment of poachers treat dove as something to simply be used for their own enjoyment, killing all they can shoot, wasting most. Some will illegally place large piles of grain to bait the dove, then treat the flyers as if in a shooting gallery. As a migratory bird, the dove is protected by the U.S. Fish and Wildlife Service, as well as the Department of Fish and Game, and every few years, the agencies will inevitably bust a group of poachers who are shooting over grain. It is even worse in Mexico, where there are many stories of gringos with shotguns gunning down hundreds of doves, baited with grain.

This book is filled with examples where uncontrolled shooting, trapping, egg-raiding, and poisoning nearly wiped out many species. Why would anyone yearn to repeat any of these low points in California's history?

But this conflict is not how most define the dove and its place in California's wildlife scheme. It is best defined by its natural grace, its skilled flight, and, for those who often wake up within earshot, its soft, cooing mating call.

Biologists' Notes

There are four kinds of doves found in the state: the mourning dove *(Zenaida macroura)*, white-winged dove *(Zenaida asiatica)*, ring-necked dove *(Streptopelia decaocto)*, and Chinese spotted dove *(Streptopelia chinensis)*.

The ring-necked dove and Chinese spotted doves were imported from Asia as early as 1921. They escaped into the wild in the Los Angeles area and have spread out into the surrounding suburban areas.

The white-winged dove is native to southeastern California and is found in the Imperial Valley and along the Colorado River. The mourning dove is the most numerous and is found in every state in the United States and in every county in California. The only place it is not common is in the dense evergreen forests and in alpine areas at high elevations.

The mourning dove looks like a sleek pigeon, only a little smaller. The color of the male is a delicately beautiful, soft bluish gray, with buff underparts. The sides of the neck gleam lightly with coppery iridescence. The bill is black and the legs and feet are pale red. The female looks like the male except the colors are somewhat duller.

The dove does not live in dense forests or marshes but rather prefers farm and orchard lands. It is equally at home in open woodlands and in arid semi-desert type areas. It feeds primarily on weed seeds and uses some cereal grains. Insects make up less than 1% of its diet.

The male dove selects the nesting place. The female is attracted there by the male's cooing. Doves are easily pleased when it comes to nesting sites. They nest in trees and shrubs, on the ground and even in old buildings. They are not very careful in their nest-building, consequently some eggs and young are easily dislodged from the flimsy nest and lost. However, doves re-nest two to five times throughout the year. The long breeding period allows them to raise five or six young annually.

The dove normally lays two pure white eggs. Both the male and female sit on the nest to hatch the eggs and help care for the young. The eggs are hatched in 14 days, and the young are cared for in the nest for 10 to 15 days. Within a week after the youngsters leave the nest, the parents ignore them and begin with another clutch of eggs. The male dove's cooing is of course an indication of nesting activity, and the cooing is followed by a nuptial flight. The male flies up in a steep climb for several hundred feet, sets his wings, and sails back on rigid wings to the nest, in a sweeping arc.

The dove is a migratory bird. Peak populations occur in the northern parts of the state in August, and as cooler weather commences the birds start their southern migration. Banding studies have revealed that some California doves travel far south to a favorite wintering ground near Jalisco in central Mexico.

Ducks
Canvasback
Green-Winged Teal
Mallard
Northern Pintail
Northern Shoveler
American Wigeon

Watching a marsh come alive at dawn, with dozens of species of birds flying in all directions, calling, swooping and landing, is one of the most gratifying moments in all the great outdoors. Even Elmer Fudd could rhapsodize over the wonders of it all.

And there are times when this experience can be magnified a hundred-fold by the sheer number of waterfowl. Everybody should know the elation of experiencing this at least once.

On one such dawn, at first light on the marsh, just after the first birds began to fly, off in the distance, you could hear a roar across the wetlands that sounded like the Blue Angels in formation. But the roar was not fighter jets ripping overhead at 500 mph, but rather a quarter million ducks lifting off to fly against the reddish sunrise, a reverberating wave of beating wings. The sound carried for miles, and against that crimson horizon, you could see the silhouettes of thousands of ducks, an event even a duck hunter might see only once in a lifetime.

The most passionate waterfowl supporter I know is Peter Ottesen of Stockton, a duck hunter who has contributed unbelievable hours and thousands of dollars to support habitat projects and restore waterfowl populations.

He has had moments in his blind where so many birds were flying overhead that he put his shotgun away, then sat back and just watched, listened, and absorbed the magic of a waking marsh.

"It is almost spiritual and euphoric in quality because there can be so many ducks," Ottesen said. "Sometimes I just lay there in my duck blind, scanning the sky. I remember one morning when they just came and came. I looked up, and there'd be thousands of them all around us in the pond. They were everywhere. In 40 years of chasing these things around, I've never seen so many. The resource has rebounded; the ducks are back."

The U.S. Fish and Wildlife Service has documented the increase with its fall flight forecast and population census for waterfowl. Scientists have documented that 100 million ducks are migrating across North America each fall, with 25% of those wintering in the Central Valley of California, the highest numbers since the 1960s. Every species of duck but pintail has greater population numbers than their long-term averages, which date back to 1955, when biologists started collecting waterfowl statistics. Pintail, the only major waterfowl species under the curve, is also on a big comeback.

The best place to see this rejuvenation for yourself is at the 20 state and federal wildlife areas and refuges. Note that they are open for duck hunting generally on Wednesdays and weekends from roughly late October through early January. Most are great for birdwatching the rest of the time. The Grasslands provides the best opportunity to see the huge influx of waterfowl, not only ducks, but ibis, swans, and others, with huge V-wedges of geese typically arriving in late November. Though privately owned, the

Grasslands is open to the public for birdwatching, with excellent do-it-yourself driving tours available.

Although only 1 in 600 California residents is a duck hunter, they took much personal responsibility for bringing back the ducks. Though the end of the drought in 1992 played the largest role, for years duck hunters agreed to short seasons and extremely tight limits, and they contributed huge amounts of money for water and the protection of duck habitat, an average of $150 to $3,000 for most hunters.

This is how it works:

The bottom line: How many fish or animals that exist in nature is determined by what is called the "carrying capacity" of a habitat. Carrying capacity is determined by the amount of water, food, and protective cover that is available, minus any negative "limiting factors." A negative limiting factor, for example, would be a wetland converted to a housing development, in which the waterfowl habitat was destroyed.

The effects of hunting and fishing: Game laws are designed as if scientists are managing a lucrative bank account, where the wildlife is the capital and sportsmen are the investors. Hunting and fishing is allowed to skim the annual interest, about 8 to 15%, depending on the species, but never to cut into the capital. Hence, with a flourishing habitat, you can have active hunting or fishing programs while wildlife populations are experiencing record population growth at the same time.

Paying for habitat: The key to wildlife populations is the amount of habitat available, and the reality is that somebody has to pay for it. In California, the average taxpayer pays only 11 cents to support the Department of Fish and Game, compared to an average $100 to $3,000 paid by duck hunters in the form of licenses, tags, access fees, and special excise taxes on their equipment, as well as contributions to Ducks Unlimited and California Waterfowl Association, and purchases of water for privately owned wetlands. So until state and federal wildlife agencies are able to collect more money from the non-hunting taxpayer, the agencies must rely on duck hunters to pay for habitat protection.

Because without habitat, there is very little wildlife, and that should matter to everyone.

But most people who contribute to support wetlands don't learn their waterfowl science in schools. They learn it on the marsh at a wildlife refuge. Those who have experienced the magic of dawn—watching a marsh come to life—have earned the prized masters degree from the University of Nature.

Biologists' Notes

CANVASBACK *(Aythya valisineria)*
The canvasback is the largest duck in California. The distinguishing features of the canvasback are the long, black, tapering bill and the sloping forehead. The drake in full winter plumage is a handsome fellow. The dark chestnut-brown head and neck are in sharp contrast to the white body with its black breast and tail.

ANIMAL	Duck, Canvasback
SPECIES	*Aythya valisineria*
TYPE	bird
STATUS	OK
SEE ALSO	Wood Duck

The canvasback is the fastest-flying duck. They have been known to fly at speeds of 70 miles per hour. In full flight, the wingbeat is rapid and the flight is direct. They often fly in a wedge formation. When using large bodies of water, such as bays and estuaries, they prefer to fly around projecting points of land rather than cross over them.

The canvasback has a rather wide distribution over the United States and Mexico. In central California, wintering "cans" congregate in the greatest numbers in the San Pablo Bay area of San Francisco Bay. They prefer large bodies of water near the coasts, to feed and rest in the brackish or alkaline waters, where preferred foods, principally clams, thrive. In mid-winter, when farmlands are flooded, they range out from San Francisco Bay as far as the Sacramento Valley to feed in the flooded areas.

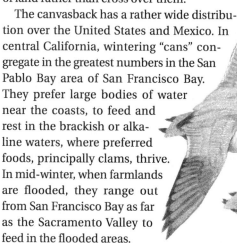

canvasbacks in flight

With the approach of spring, canvasback males undertake courtship displays to attract a mate. There may be some pairing of older birds in the winter months but most posturing consists of neck stretching, head throwing, and low guttural grunting sounds. Several drakes may surround a small band of females during this display until a mate is chosen.

Upon arrival at the breeding grounds, often the Yukon or Alaska, the pair selects a nesting site. Nest sites are widely dispersed, usually no more than one or two pair to several square miles. The male constructs the nest. It is a rather bulky affair built above the water line and is located in shallow water no more than three feet deep. Canvasbacks seldom nest on dry ground. Sometimes an old muskrat house is utilized.

The female commences to lay eggs even before the nest is completed. After a few eggs have been laid the female begins to line the nest with down which she plucks from her breast. The female lays from six to nine grayish drab green eggs before she begins to incubate them. Occasionally a redhead duck will slip in and deposit an egg in the canvasback's nest. It takes from 23 to 29 days for the eggs to hatch.

The canvasback is the fastest flying duck. They have been known to fly at speeds of 70 miles per hour.

During the egg laying and incubation period, the male waits in nearby waters. But as soon as the eggs are ready to hatch, he departs to join other males in a molting migration. The drake's molting migration may be as much as several hundred miles from the nest. This leaves the hen the full responsibility of rearing the family. The drakes band together on large bodies of water while shedding their old flight feathers. For several weeks they are unable to fly, but the new feathers grow quickly and by late summer they are ready for the long trip back down to their winter range.

The female broods her young in the nest for a few hours, longer if the weather is bad. As soon as the young are dry, they commence to preen and oil themselves for they can swim as soon as they are dry. The female takes them into the water to teach them where and what to eat. Soon they are far from the nest foraging for themselves. They spend most of their time on open water.

After several weeks and before they can fly, the mother abandons them to join other females in the molting process. The young ducks soon join the flightless mothers and they remain in small family groups until and during the migration south. Canvasbacks are gregarious, and although they associate with other diving ducks such as redheads and lesser scaup during migration, they seldom join with other ducks in flight.

Although "cans" are not numerous as in the past, those who travel around San Francisco Bay, especially during stormy or windy weather, can still see literally hundreds of them, seeking protection from the weather in the quieter waters near the shoreline.

GREEN-WINGED TEAL (Anas crecca)

The drake green-winged teal, the smallest of California waterfowl, is second in beauty only to the gorgeous wood duck.

There are four teal found in North America. The green-winged and cinnamon teal (*Anas cyanoptera*) are most familiar to California hunters.

The green-winged is the smallest of the teals, seldom weighing over 12 ounces. Because it is also the hardiest of the teals, the green-wing continues to occur in the greatest numbers.

The drake is easily recognized by the dark-brown head striped with a glossy bright-green face patch. The wings are grayish brown with a metallic-green wing patch banded with a buff-colored bar. The females are a mottled brown with white underparts and also have the metallic-green patch on the wings.

ANIMAL	Duck, Green-WingedTeal
SPECIES	*Anas crecca*
TYPE	bird
STATUS	OK
SEE ALSO	Wood Duck

Very few green-winged teals nest in California. In the spring, almost immediately following the mallard and pintail ducks, the green-wings migrate farther north to breed, nesting mainly in Canada and Alaska.

green-winged teals in flight

An elaborate courtship is conducted by the males during the leisurely migration north, so that many of the birds are paired before arriving at the breeding grounds. The courtship consists of stately displays of their handsome colors and much strutting in slow cadence on the water before the females.

The nest of the green-winged teal is difficult to find, for it may be as far as a quarter mile from water. It is usually constructed in a hollow on dry ground. The hollow is first lined with soft grasses and weeds, and as the eggs are laid the mother covers them each day with layers of soft down plucked from her own breast.

There may be as many as 18 eggs with an average of 10 or 12. The eggs are white or very pale olive buff in color, and they appear almost identical to those of the blue-winged teal. The male disappears as soon as the eggs are laid and leaves the entire burden of hatching and rearing the family to the female. It takes her from 21 to 23 days to hatch the eggs.

The young hatch within a few hours, and as soon as they are dry she leads them on their sometimes perilous journey to water. Like other ducks, they need no food for a few hours, so the mother has time to teach them to feed on insects and other soft little animals they can find in the water around the edges of ponds and among the aquatic vegetation. During this time the babies also learn to hide and obey instantly mother's warning cries when danger threatens. A mother teal surrounded by eight or 10 tiny balls of down bobbing around on the water is a charming sight.

The green-winged teal is the smallest of the teals, seldom weighing over 12 ounces.

The green-winged teal has a varied diet. In their summer homes the ducks dabble around in the shallow waters of sloughs and ponds and along creeks rather than the big open waters of lakes. Imitating the mother, the young tip up with their bodies half submerged and little feet kicking in the air, searching for aquatic insects, worms, and even tadpoles. After the ducklings learn to fly they range out into harvested grain fields, picking up grains of wheat, rice, corn, and a variety of the ripened seeds of other vegetation.

Quite at home on the ground, sometimes whole flocks will travel some distance, walking easily and gracefully in their search for food. Unlike most surface-feeding ducks, the teal is an excellent diver and can and does swim long distances under water to reach protective cover.

The fall migration begins with the first early season storms, but the teal linger along their way wherever they can find ample feeding grounds. Then when the cold weather and ice really set in, they continue south to winter in the mild climate and open waters from central California all the way down into Mexico.

MALLARD *(Anas platyrhynchos)*

Of all ducks, the species most familiar to mankind is unquestionably the mallard. It is large and well formed. The drake has distinctive markings: His head and neck are bright green, and the white collar, the chestnut-colored breast, and silver-gray body are in sharp contrast to the yellow bill and orange-red feet and legs. It is nearly impossible to confuse it with any other species.

ANIMAL	Duck, Mallard
SPECIES	*Anas platyrhynchos*
TYPE	bird
STATUS	OK
SEE ALSO	Wood Duck

Because the mallard was easily domesticated, it is as common today in the barnyard as it is in the wild. As a domestic breed the mallard is tame and easily managed, and for hundreds of years it has supplied man with vast quantities of eggs, flesh, and feathers.

The green-head mallard inhabits nearly all of the northern hemisphere but is most abundant in the United States west of the Mississippi Valley. It is California's most important breeding duck. Thousands are resident birds that nest and raise their young in central and northern California. In winter these numbers are increased by migrants from the northern breeding grounds in Canada and Alaska. Some of the birds from the northern breeding ground linger, on their way south, as long as the waters remain free of ice. A few even stay all winter along

mallards in flight

the Alaskan and Aleutian coastal waters and at the outlets of rivers and lakes. They are spoken of locally as ice birds or ice breakers.

Because of the late appearance of the mallards to the southern wintering areas, some hunters think of these late arrivals as a separate subspecies of the mallard and point to the large size, brilliant plumage, and bright orange legs; in fact they are the same, only more mature and in full adult plumage.

In January and early February the nuptial flights commence, and over the marshes one can observe several drakes flying in dogged pursuit of a female. Eventually, after much courting, she chooses one mate.

The mallards generally build their nests on or near the edges of water where the ground is dry or only slightly marshy. Occasionally they nest some distance from water. Nests have been found in trees and in haystacks and even in the lofts of old isolated barns. When this occurs it means a long and sometimes hazardous journey to water, for the ducklings at this period are subject to predation by many birds and animals. The nests are generally well concealed. The hen lays from six to 15 eggs, with an average clutch being eight to 10. The hen does not start to brood the eggs until she finishes laying them all. It takes from 23 to 29 days (usually 26) for the eggs to hatch. The female hatches the eggs unassisted, for by this time the drake has joined other breeding drakes and has gone into seclusion for the summer to molt his feathers.

During the molt the drakes are secretive and evasive, almost as though ashamed of their drab and flightless condition. This is only a temporary state, and they soon emerge to fly once more. By early December they are resplendent in their bright new feathers.

In the meantime, the unmated drakes have not molted and are seen flying around searching for a hen whose nesting efforts failed. She will pair up with one of the bachelors and re-nest. Then that breeding drake, in which nature has triggered a release of hormones, will retire to molt. If the second attempt to nest is successful, when the ducklings are a few weeks old the female molts. All ducks thus unable to fly are known as "floppers."

The mallard can be easily tamed and managed, and for hundreds of years it has supplied man with vast quantities of eggs, flesh, and feathers.

As soon as the ducklings hatch, they are ready to leave the nest. The female mallard is most attentive and courageous in defense of her babies. When danger threatens she gives a warning quack that sends the young scurrying into hiding, either on land or in the water. The old duck then feigns injury or makes such a fuss that it distracts the offender, man or beast, so the young nearly always escape. The ducklings are instinctive swimmers, riding high on the water like little yellow balls of down. Mother

pintails

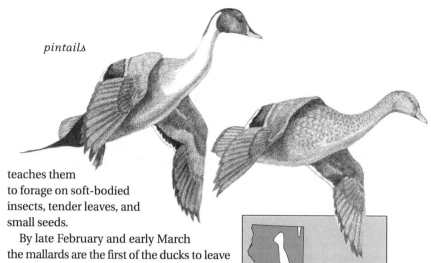

teaches them to forage on soft-bodied insects, tender leaves, and small seeds.

By late February and early March the mallards are the first of the ducks to leave the wintering grounds for the nesting areas. As many as 30,000 remain to nest throughout central and northeastern California. Others go all the way to Alaska.

If the food and water are plentiful they grow rapidly. By September they are fully feathered, hens and drakes alike in appearance. Then in an almost continuous stage of molting they assume their distinctive male and female coats of feathers.

NORTHERN PINTAIL *(Anas acuta)*

The pintail, or sprig as it is commonly called in the west, is one of the most numerous and best loved ducks on this continent. They are beautiful birds, typically with a gray body, dark brown head, long white neck, and pointed tail.

ANIMAL	Duck, Northern Pintail
SPECIES	*Anas acuta*
TYPE	bird
STATUS	OK
SEE ALSO	Wood Duck

The pintail has the widest breeding range of all ducks. Each fall millions of waterfowl migrate into California to spend the winter. They rest and feed on the chain of state and federally operated wildlife areas and refuges, as well as the flooded ponds and marshes of duck clubs, lakes, reservoirs, and wetlands that extend south through California to Mexico.

In late winter, they disperse throughout the valleys in ever-changing bands, moving from time to time with the storms through the rich agricultural lands to newly found feeding grounds.

Of the fall migrants, pintails are the first ducks to arrive in the fall, usually in August, and leave for the breeding grounds in the spring, usually in late March and April. They nest in the greatest numbers on the Canadian prairie potholes, in the Yukon and Northwest Territories, and in Alaska.

The nest of the pintail, unlike many waterfowl, is almost always on dry ground and may be as much as a half mile from water. The nest is usually made in a depression and lined with coarse grasses and sparse down, to which more materials are added each day. The pintail raises only one brood each year. She does not lay as many eggs as most surface-feeding ducks. The clutch averages from six to 12 eggs, usually less than 10. The eggs are a very pale olive green in color. Since the nest and eggs are similar in appearance to other ducks, positive identification is difficult unless the hen pintail is seen on the nest or flushed from it.

The pintail has the widest breeding range of all ducks. Its nest, unlike many waterfowl, is almost always on dry ground and may be as much as a half mile from water.

The hen does not start to incubate the eggs until the set is complete. The incubation period is 22 to 23 days, and the hen alone sits on the eggs. As soon as the eggs hatch and the ducklings are dry, the mother leads them on a sometimes hazardous trip to water, teaching them to feed on soft insects and green vegetation. The drake may help some in rearing the young, but in most cases he leaves to join other males as they molt their feathers and take on a new plumage. The pintail mother seems to be more courageous than any other duck in care and defense of her young. She also molts her feathers as she carries on her parental duties.

Most of the young are hatched in May and early June. Through the various stages of plumage change, both the male and female ducklings look similar to the mother. In September the young drake commences to "color up," and by December he becomes quite distinctive in his coat of beautifully blended brown, white, and gray.

NORTHERN SHOVELER
(Spoony) *(Anas clypeata)*

The little shoveler, which is commonly called spoonbill or spoony, is one of the best known and most widely distributed ducks in the world. It is common in North America, Europe, Asia, South America, Africa, and Australia.

The spoony is a small duck, only a little larger than a teal. It is easily recognized by the large spoon-shaped bill and by the striking color pattern of the drake. The species found in California is essentially a fresh water duck, rarely found in coastal waters unless forced there by fierce storms or scarcity of preferred habitat. It seems to prefer shallow ponds or freshly flooded agricultural lands, where it can search for food without diving.

ANIMAL	Duck, Northern Shoveler
SPECIES	*Anas clypeata*
TYPE	bird
STATUS	OK
SEE ALSO	Wood Duck

Northern shovelers have readily apparent field marks. On the water the males show more white than any other pond ducks. The large bill is held in a downward slope, and the entire bird sits low in the water. They rise from the water in a quick upward bound and alight almost vertically with hardly a splash. In the air they fly in small flocks. When startled, their movements change from a slow, steady progress to an erratic flight with sudden downward plunges.

When seen flying overhead the color markings of the males are quite distinctive: dark head, white chest, dark breast, white belt, and dark under the tail coverts. Although the female is more drab

Northern shovelers

in overall colors, they both show bright blue on the leading edge of the wings. In silhouette the thick head, short neck, and huge bill of both sexes are easily noted.

The drake is a strikingly handsome and beautifully marked bird. However, the disproportionately large bill gives it a somewhat top-heavy and ungraceful appearance.

No other duck has a bill like the shoveler. It is exceptionally large, being almost three inches in length and widens from five-eighths of an inch at the base to one and a quarter inches near the tip. All ducks' bills have short serrations or "teeth" on the edges, but on the shoveler these teeth reach the greatest degree of development and become almost comb-like. This makes it the most practical surface feeder of any of the other dabbling ducks.

No other duck has a bill like the shoveler. It is easily recognized by the large spoon-shaped bill which is about two and three-quarters inches in length and widens from five-eighths of an inch at the base to an inch and a quarter near the tip.

When feeding they paddle quickly along, sometimes several following each other with their heads half submerged, their chattering bills taking into their mouths the tiny particles kicked up by the ducks in front. They also scoop up mud from the bottom, retaining the edible matter and rejecting the remainder. Minute animal matter and insects make up about one-third of their diets; the rest is seeds and the tender shoots of many grasses and pond weeds found in western waters.

Shovelers are more conspicuous than other ducks in the practice of polyandry. That is, the female indulges in the luxury of two husbands. The second husband usually shows up after two adult shovelers have paired. He is usually a young male and still in incomplete plumage. Females of his generation do not pair until the following year. The older drake does not seem to object to this younger male hanging around while he and his mate go about the business of nesting.

The nest of the shoveler may be near or quite some distance from the water. It is usually carefully hidden in deep grass and consists of just a shallow depression in the ground, well lined with grass and some feathers and down, which the female plucks from her breast. The female lays 10 to 12 eggs. The eggs' color varies from a pale olive to greenish gray, and the eggs are smaller than mallard or pintail eggs. After the female finishes egg laying, incubation is started. It takes from 21 to 23 days for the eggs to hatch. The female alone sits on the eggs and rears the young by herself. Before the eggs are hatched, the drakes leave and bunch together for a period of molting. They do not rejoin the flocks until the young are fully feathered.

After the eggs are hatched the female leads the babies to the nearest water. It is sometimes a perilous journey for there are many predators, but the mother, even though small, guards the ducklings fiercely.

The young are excellent swimmers and can dive well. They soon learn from their mother to feed on seeds and soft animal and vegetable matter.

The shovelers love warm weather, so as soon as the first frost appears on their breeding grounds they begin their migration south; by October they are on their wintering grounds. They are the first of all duck species to start the migratory flight.

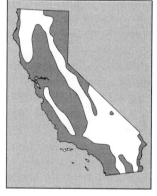

AMERICAN WIGEON (Anas americana)

Worldwide there are three species of wigeon: one in South America, the chiloe wigeon; one in Eurasia, the Eurasian wigeon; and one in North America, the American wigeon.

The chiloe or South American wigeon does not occur in North America. Although the European wigeon does not breed in North America, a small number are regular visitors to both the Pacific and Atlantic coasts. It is most often found as a lone bird in the company of a flock of American wigeons and more rarely with mallards or pintails. The drake's bright russet head, topped with a cream stripe, and its gray back and sides distinguish the Eurasian wigeon from its American cousin.

ANIMAL	Duck, American Wigeon
SPECIES	*Anas americana*
TYPE	bird
STATUS	OK
SEE ALSO	Wood Duck

The American wigeon nests across much of Canada and Alaska and winters in all four North American flyways. On the wintering grounds of California, the wigeon is also plentiful.

When the drake is at rest, the white crown of the full-plumaged bird is distinctive, giving the bird its common name of baldpate or "baldy." A green band extends from the eye to the back of the head. The rest of the head and neck is buff-colored, speckled with black. The body is mainly a pinkish brown with white underparts, and the bill and feet are bluish gray. The forepart of the wing is white with a metallic green speculum or patch in the center of the trailing edge of the wing.

American wigeons in flight

The wigeon has been observed waiting patiently for other diving birds to bring up bits of aquatic plants, which it then takes for itself.

The female is grayish brown with white underparts, the head and neck are grayish white speckled with black. The forepart of the wing is grayish white.

Wigeons fly rapidly with a fairly deep wingbeat, in compact flocks. Their flight is more erratic than other surface-feeding ducks, except the teal. The most distinctive features of the wigeon in flight are the white shoulder patch and the frequent calls of the drake. The call is composed of three whistling notes, *whee whee whew,* the middle note higher than the others. Only the pintail has a similar call, but it is briefer and more evenly pitched.

Next to the pintail and blue-winged teal, the wigeon is the duck to migrate southward earliest. They reach their peak in numbers in California by early December.

Most surface-feeding or dabbling ducks feed primarily on the seeds of grains, grasses, and aquatic plants. However, the wigeon has until recent years shown a preference for the stems and leafy parts of green vegetation. It has been observed feeding where redheads and mudhens are diving for the succulent foliage of aquatic plants. The wigeon, being a surface feeder, waits patiently, then grabs bits of the green brought up by one of the diving birds.

With the gradual but steady diminishing of marshland habitat, the wigeon is adapting to other feeding habits and is frequently found now with the mallard and pintail, gleaning the harvested fields of rice, yellow corn, and milo. After the winter rains start and green feed begins to grow, wigeons can also graze on pasture grasses and some cultivated crops.

Some of the wigeons begin to form pair bonds on the wintering areas as early as December, but most of them wait until they are near or on the nesting areas. A few pairs nest in northeastern California, but the major population goes on north to the Canadian provinces and on up into Alaska. Nesting is in full swing by the end of May. A nest site may be chosen near water or as much as several hundred yards from it. The nest is usually in a slight depression and lined with down from the mother's breast. The nests are so cleverly concealed that they are

---

Where to see ducks

BRANNAN ISLAND STATE RECREATION AREA, IN SACRAMENTO COUNTY

DELEVAN NATIONAL WILDLIFE REFUGE, IN COLUSA COUNTY

GRASSLAND RESOURCE CONSERVATION DISTRICT, IN MERCED COUNTY
NOTE: November, February, and March are peak months for waterfowl. There is limited access to some areas during hunting season (September through January).

GRIZZLY ISLAND WILDLIFE AREA, IN SOLANO COUNTY

HUMBOLDT BAY NATIONAL WILDLIFE REFUGE, IN HUMBOLDT COUNTY

MORRO BAY STATE PARK, SAN LUIS OBISPO COUNTY

PAYNES CREEK WETLANDS, IN TEHAMA COUNTY

TIJUANA SLOUGH NATIONAL WILDLIFE REFUGE, IN SAN DIEGO COUNTY

YOLO BYPASS WILDLIFE AREA, IN YOLO COUNTY

Other places to see ducks

BOLSA CHICA ECOLOGICAL RESERVE, IN ORANGE COUNTY

HARPER LAKE, IN MARIN COUNTY

SAN PABLO BAY NATIONAL WILDLIFE REFUGE, IN MARIN COUNTY

SALTON SEA NATIONAL WILDLIFE REFUGE, IN IMPERIAL AND RIVERSIDE COUNTIES

SUTTER NATIONAL WILDLIFE REFUGE, IN SUTTER COUNTY

extremely difficult to find. The eggs are creamy white and average about eight to each nest.

Wigeon eggs hatch in 23 or 24 days. The hen wigeon is a good mother and remains with the brood until they are full grown or nearly so. Even though she is quite protective of the nest, and later her young, a considerable number are lost to predators. In one study area, crows, skunks, and ground squirrels were responsible for most of the nest destruction.

After the eggs are laid and incubation begins, the drakes desert the hen and return to the larger marshes to shed or molt their feathers. They are unable to fly for several weeks thereafter. During this period large flocks of drakes may be seen together.

Duck, Wood

Few things are as satisfying as providing a home for wildlife, especially for wood ducks. It is possible to build a small box that is perfect for wood duck nesting. The Department of Fish and Game even offers a pamphlet on how to build such a box, complete with a drawing and all the measurements.

To understand how easy, fun, and rewarding this can be, I visited my old friend Phil Ford, the longtime outdoors writer who has always shared with me the value of enjoying birds, identifying them, and watching their unique habits. Ford has built several wood duck boxes near his home and explained how anybody can do

ANIMAL	Wood Duck
SPECIES	*Aix sponsa*
TYPE	bird
STATUS	OK
SEE ALSO	Ducks

this with success. Ducks will use them as long as water is within walking distance.

Ford made his wood duck boxes out of cedar fence, that is, the face boards, so the boxes are attractive and rustic looking. But you can make them out of almost any kind of wood, even plywood. Many people who build wood duck boxes place just one box on a pole, but Ford discovered that you can place two or three boxes per pole to attract more ducks.

"I face the holes in different directions because I think it reduces their stress when the chicks are born," Ford said.

Once you get the box built and posted, that's when the fun starts. As Ford pointed out, one day you'll see a wood duck sitting up in a tree. Then one day you'll see two, a hen and a drake, and pretty soon they'll be sitting on top of the flat lid on the box, and the courtship has started. The hen will cackle at the drake and wiggle her tail, and the drake will wiggle his tail in response. If she's still interested, she will eventually lean over and stretch her neck to look in the box.

wood duck

This goes on for a few days. And then, suddenly, the hen will fly out away from the box, then reverse direction and return, then grab on to the entrance of the box and peer in. She'll do this several times, then she'll disappear right into the box. She won't stay in there very long, often just a matter of seconds, then jump back out to the top of the box, and it's back to the tail wiggling. They like that tail wiggling, you know. Drives the drakes crazy.

The male wood duck is one of the most beautiful of North American birds. The rich greens, blues, and burgundy body colors are sharply contrasted by bold white markings. The head is crested with iridescent greens and purples, and the red eyes and red-orange bill are further accented by white patches on the throat. Their population has been boosted by a public nesting box program sponsored by the Department of Fish and Game.

Eventually, she'll start pulling down feathers out of her breast, from which she can make a small nest in the box. It's amazing how much down they can pull out without any difference in the appearance of the hen. Once the nest is ready, she will lay her eggs.

It takes about three weeks for the eggs to hatch. In the meantime, you can almost set your watch by the time the hen and drake will leave, feed, and water. At Ford's house, the hen would leave at 7:30 every morning, then return at 9 a.m., then again depart at 6:30 p.m. and back at about 8. Upon return, she would always swing in a wide circle, checking out the area, making certain there were no predators in the area.

Suddenly one day, the baby ducks will hatch. And they seem ready for the world quite quickly. When the babies decide to leave the box, it's a one-shot deal. The hen calls them out, and the babies crawl up to the hole and drop right to the ground. They don't fly out of the nest. Some times they drop 20 feet. They look like little fuzzballs.

"One thing I learned to help the little guys get out is to put a little ramp inside the box," Ford said. "Then when it comes time to crawl out, they can make it. You don't want them trapped inside."

Once they hit the ground, the ducklings will walk to the nearby water and float around a bit, following momma's lead. It looks like a little parade, and there is nothing more charming in nature.

And if you have provided the nesting box, as Phil Ford has discovered, there are few things in nature more satisfying. After visiting Ford and watching this scene, I've decided that in the future I'm going to build a few of the nesting boxes myself.

Biologists' Notes

The wood duck (Aix sponsa), unlike most other ducks, does not seek open water in which to live. It prefers wooded lakes and streams, and it builds its nest in cavities in the limbs and trunks of trees, rather than on the ground. It seems to prefer trees that are near the water, although it does nest as much as a mile from water. It readily uses artificial nesting boxes if they have been suitably placed.

The male wood duck is one of the most beautiful of North American birds. The rich greens, blues, and burgundy body colors are sharply contrasted by bold white markings. The head is crested with iridescent greens and purples, and the red eyes and red orange bill are further accented by white patches on the throat. The hen is a little smaller than the drake; her plumage, although brighter than other hen ducks, is not as colorful as the drake's.

The hen and drake search for a nest site together. If a likely looking cavity is found, the drake will roost nearby while the hen inspects it as a possible nest. Everything must be just so, and she may spend from five minutes to an hour before she decides if the cavity will be suitable.

The hen does not carry any materials for nest building. She merely hollows out a depression in the bottom of the cavity and commences to lay her eggs. After several days, she starts to cover the eggs with down and soft feathers, which she plucks from her breast. In a normal nest the hen lays from 10 to 15 smooth white eggs. Sometimes, if nesting sites are scarce, more than one hen will lay in the same nest. As many as 43 eggs have been found. These are called dump nests and are seldom successful.

After a clutch of eggs has been laid, the hen starts to incubate the eggs. It takes from 28 to 31 days for the eggs to hatch. The hen only leaves the nest for an hour or so at dawn and again at dusk. The time is spent with the drake, which stays nearby until the last few days before the eggs hatch. The drake then deserts the area, and the hen has the full responsibility of rearing the brood.

The morning after all the eggs have hatched, the mother flies down to the water or to the ground and after checking carefully to see that there is no danger, calls the young from the nest. The baby wood ducks have very sharp toenails that enable them to clamber up the straight sides of the nest cavity, sometimes several feet, and without hesitation fling themselves into the air to fall to the ground or the water. When the hen is certain no more babies are coming, she collects them with a soft call and starts for water.

Once on the water, the ducklings are fairly safe. It takes them nearly two months to grow large enough to fly. When they are small they live on insects and the tender leaves found at the water's edge, but as they grow older

---

Where to see wood duck

ANTELOPE LAKE/INDIAN CREEK, IN PLUMAS COUNTY

CLEAR LAKE, IN LAKE COUNTY

COSUMNES RIVER PRESERVE, IN SACRAMENTO COUNTY

LEWISTON LAKE, IN TRINITY COUNTY

PAYNES CREEK WETLANDS, IN TEHAMA COUNTY

WHITTIER NARROWS NATURE CENTER, IN LOS ANGELES COUNTY

Other places to see wood duck

CASWELL MEMORIAL STATE PARK, IN SAN JOAQUIN COUNTY

LAKE SAN ANTONIO, LOS PADRES NATIONAL FOREST, IN MONTEREY COUNTY

RUTH LAKE, IN TRINITY COUNTY

---

and learn to fly, they go inland for berries, grapes, and acorns, which they swallow whole. They eat a great variety of vegetable matter.

The wood duck rests in open pools at night, flying out to feed by day. After they have fed, they seek out quiet stretches of wooded streams or canals and roost along the banks and on the limbs of trees. The day is spent visiting and preening themselves, seemingly content but always alert to danger. If alarmed, they burst into the air with a distinctive squealing cry of danger.

The summer wood duck population is distributed sparsely over most of the state north of the Tehachapi Mountains. The winter migrations of the resident population amount to a shift out of the higher elevations into the central valleys and adjoining foothills, where they are joined by the bulk of the wood ducks in the Pacific flyway that migrate from Oregon, Washington, and British Columbia to winter in California.

The wood duck has probably suffered more from the effects of civilization than other ducks. The draining of marshes and cutting of the oak, sycamore, and willow trees along the rivers and streams greatly depleted nesting habitat. Artificial nesting boxes have contributed to nesting success.

Eagle, Bald

About an hour before dusk, we were paddling our canoe out of a quiet cove on a lake when an osprey suddenly appeared overhead. We watched as it plunged into the lake with a giant splash and emerged quickly with a rainbow trout in its talons.

"There's the best trout fisherman of them all," said my fishing partner and wildlife mentor, Ed Dunckel.

As the osprey headed off with the trout, two bald eagles suddenly appeared from above, diving on the osprey. The eagles let out these piercing screeches, and then one after another made warp-speed attacks on the osprey, approaching and passing like starfighters in *Star Wars*. The osprey, under attack and panicked, dropped the trout in

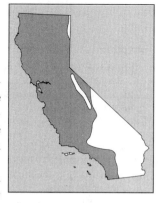

ANIMAL	Eagle, Bald
SPECIES	*Haliaeetus leucocephalus*
TYPE	bird
STATUS	Endangered
SEE ALSO	Eagle (Golden), Falcon (Peregrine), Hawks, Osprey

bald eagle

Identifying Eagles

The bald eagle *(Haliaeetus leucocephalus)* is strictly a North American species that often nests near water, especially lakes and reservoirs. The American race of the golden eagle, *Aquila chrysaetos,* is now restricted almost entirely to the mountainous regions of the west.

Identification of eagles less than three years old is sometimes confusing. The bald eagle appears the same in size and color as the golden eagle until it reaches three years of age. The golden eagle, however, shows a sharply defined white area at the base of its black-tipped tail. Immature bald

bald eagle

golden eagle

eagles can show some white at the base of the tail, but it is not sharply defined. Another noticeable difference is that the golden eagle's legs are feathered right down to the toes, while the lower legs of the bald eagle are bare. At three years of age the bald eagle's head, neck, and tail feathers turn white. At a distance this gives an impression of baldness, hence the common name, bald eagle. In 1782, Congress chose the bald eagle as our national emblem. However, the golden eagle is more widespread, found throughout the northern hemisphere.

order to free its talons to defend itself, or maybe it decided it just wasn't worth the hassle and dropped the fish anyway.

While one of the bald eagles continued to drive the osprey away, the other descended in a headlong power dive toward the lake, then abruptly turned upside down, its talons pointed upwards, and caught that trout in mid-air. Just as quickly, the eagle righted itself and flew off, joined by its mate to split up the spoils.

It was another rare glimpse into the world of nature. Of course, it's always special to see a bald eagle, no matter what tricks it might be up to.

The power from just a few wingbeats can propel a bald eagle hundreds of yards, gliding on a six-foot wingspan while keeping a razor-sharp watch for prey. Refracted sunlight at dawn and dusk can make its white head and tail feathers glisten. It's the kind of scene that stirs your spirit.

But it is not exactly a rare scene in California. While there are hundreds of resident eagles that live in different locales of California year-round, when winter arrives and the jet stream sends cold fronts from Alaska into Canada and the Pacific Northwest, the eagles head south, with more wintering here than anywhere else in the lower 48 states.

The bald eagle is second only to the California condor in size among raptors in California, with a wingspan of six to eight feet. Pairs mate for life.

They have their favorite spots, providing many opportunities to be seen by the public. The best time of year to see eagles is from December through March. The best places to see them are the Klamath Basin National Wildlife Refuge in the northeastern part of the state and Lake San Antonio in Monterey County. There are usually about 1,000 eagles in the Klamath Basin each winter, often feeding on ducks and geese, and about 60 at Lake San Antonio, enough for eagle-watching trips to be among the most successful winter nature adventures in the state.

Eagles are also commonly spotted at Eagle Lake near Susanville, Shasta Lake north of Redding, and Trinity Lake near Weaverville. There are also resident eagle families at many lakes across Northern California, such as the pairs at Lake Britton and Iron Canyon Reservoir in Shasta County. In the Bay Area foothills, the remote parklands governed by the East Bay Regional Park District in Alameda and Contra Costa Counties provide enough habitat and open space for a few resident bald eagles, though sightings are very uncommon and always special.

Dark sky, silent flight. If you ever forget what a wonder it is to be on this planet, then you are in dire need of the sight of a bald eagle lifting off at dawn from a treetop. In nature, that moment is the paramount definition of true greatness.

Biologists' Notes

Next to the California condor, the bald eagle *(Haliaeetus leucocephalus)* is the largest raptor in California. It is a soaring bird that measures from 30 to 43 inches in length, with a wingspan of six to eight feet. As with most raptors, the female is larger than the male. Adults are a brownish-black with a white head and tail and large hooked beak and talons. Unlike the golden eagle, the bald eagle's legs are not feathered to the feet.

Immature birds may be mistaken for golden eagles, for they are entirely brownish black with grayish wing linings. When molting, the immature birds may show white patches of body feathers. They do not obtain full adult plumage with characteristic white head and tail until about the fourth or fifth year.

Courtship occurs in mid-winter when two or three eagles may be seen chasing each other in rapid flight. When a mate is chosen, they commence to build or reconstruct an old nest. Bald eagles mate for life, but if one of a pair dies or is killed, the other will choose another mate.

Nests are massive structures, four or five feet in diameter, and are used year after year. Fresh, good-sized sticks are added each year until a nest is five or six feet high. Occasionally, the winds or the great weight of an old nest will topple it from a tree.

In California, all the currently known nesting pairs have nests constructed in pine trees 20 to 90 feet from the ground and near rivers or large bodies of water. Historically, in California and other parts of the bald eagle's range, nests are sometimes built on cliffs and rocky promontories.

One to three white eggs, usually two, are laid from mid-February to April 1, most in the first two weeks of March. Both sexes share the responsibility of incubating and caring for the young, which hatch in 35 days. One egg hatches several days before the other, and, oddly enough, the first hatched is usually a female. The larger of the brood gets first choice of food brought to the nest. The smaller chick suffers much abuse in the nest from the larger eaglet. This, coupled with parental indifference, causes the weaker of the eaglets to die. Biologists have termed this behavior "obligate siblicide" and theorize that the second chick is biological insurance, a replacement in case the older chick dies, not necessarily an opportunity for the parents to raise two or more chicks.

If all goes well, in eight or 10 weeks the eaglets are feathered out, then there is much play and exercising of wings in preparation for the day they fledge. After they have learned to hop and to soar a little above the nest, the adults lure them into flight.

During the first summer, much time is spent with the parent birds, learning how to catch and find food. They may return to use the nest as a roosting place but are eventually driven away to make a life of their own. The adults never allow their young to establish a nesting area near the parental range. Bald eagles occur throughout California, but during the winter months the resident population swells with the arrival of migrant birds from the north.

In 1974, only 21 pairs of bald eagles were known to nest in California. The reasons for the decline include removal of nest trees, irresponsible shooting, human encroachment into nesting and feeding areas, and con-

Where to see bald eagle

DEL VALLE RESERVOIR AND REGIONAL PARK, IN ALAMEDA COUNTY

EAGLE LAKE, LASSEN NATIONAL FOREST, IN LASSEN COUNTY

KLAMATH BASIN NATIONAL WILDLIFE REFUGES COMPLEX, IN SISKIYOU COUNTY
NOTE: While eagles can be seen throughout the Klamath Basin complex, the greatest numbers roost in the Bear Valley Refuge, which is located in Oregon, just over the California border. The best viewing opportunities are from December through mid-March. The Bear Valley Refuge itself is closed during this time to avoid disturbing the birds (not just bald eagles, but a number of other migratory birds that winter on the refuge), but their early morning fly-outs can be viewed just before sunrise from a site located about 13 miles south of Klamath Falls, Oregon.

For up-close viewing, opportunities are best in the Lower Klamath Wildlife Refuge, during the same months. A self-guided, interpretive Lower Klamath auto tour, which makes a 10-mile loop off Highway 161 in Oregon, is available.

LAKE SAN ANTONIO, IN LOS PADRES NATIONAL FOREST, IN MONTEREY COUNTY
NOTE: Eagle tours are available through the Monterey County Parks Department. For information, write Eagle Tours, Monterey County Parks, P.O. Box 5279, Salinas, CA 93915-5279, tel. (831) 755-4899.

SHASTA LAKE NATIONAL RECREATION AREA, IN SHASTA COUNTY

SHASTA LAKE, SHASTA-TRINITY NATIONAL FOREST, IN SHASTA COUNTY
NOTE: Eagles here are best viewed by boat, along the Pit River Arm. To access a public boat ramp at the Pit River Arm confluence with the Squaw Valley Creek Arm, exit Interstate 5 three miles north of Redding at Oasis Road and follow the signs to the Jones Valley ramp.

tamination of the food chain with chlorinated hydrocarbons (primarily DDT). But the bald eagle, the national bird of the United States, is now protected by state and federal laws, and conservation efforts have resulted in a four- to five-fold increase in nesting pairs over the past several decades. Restoration efforts and dramatic population increases of the species mark one of the few high points of the Endangered Species Act. In 1967 the bald eagle was placed on the federal list of endangered species; in 1994 its status was downgraded from endangered to threatened; in 1999 the bald eagle was proposed for delisting as a federal endangered species, and its state endangered status is under revision.

Eagle, Golden

It seems that destiny has relegated the golden eagle to junior status under its big brother, the bald eagle. But after watching them both for many years, I believe goldens often outshine bald eagles in many ways, a statement that might surprise some wildlife lovers.

Golden eagles are fierce predators, with a huge variety of smaller mammals for prey. To get an idea of what is possible, consider this story from the high Sierra just south of Yosemite.

An endangered Sierra bighorn ewe gave birth to several lambs, and in an effort to monitor and protect this progeny from predatory mountain lions, biologists equipped the mother bighorn with a radio tracking collar.

ANIMAL	Eagle, Golden
SPECIES	*Aquila chrysaetos*
TYPE	bird
STATUS	OK
SEE ALSO	Eagle (Bald), Falcon (Peregrine), Hawks, Osprey

A mountain lion did get ahold of one of the baby bighorns, but get this: A golden swooped down and grabbed one of the others for itself.

Can you imagine that? A golden eagle nabbing a baby Sierra bighorn?

You know what that means? It means that 90% of the critters that walk, fly, or swim are potential lunch meat for a golden. When a golden eagle shows up, mothers hide their sons and daughters, and fathers head for the timber. Golden eagles are physically imposing, beautiful in flight, and powerfully quick in the kill. Watching one take a rabbit reveals a perfect combination of grace and deadly force.

Yet it is bald eagles that have their pictures on the backs of quarters, and not goldens. It's true that watching an adult bald eagle simply gliding overhead in flight is an awe-inspiring moment and that the bald eagle is the second-largest raptor in the state (the California condor is the largest). But it's also true that the golden eagle might just be the toughest kid on the block.

Bald eagles often scavenge dying ducks in wildlife refuges and can steal trout from osprey rather than always catching the fish themselves. At the Klamath Wildlife Refuge in winter, I've seen bald eagles often just sit on the ice like wooden penguins, waiting for a sick duck to fall over. You'd never catch a golden eagle doing that. In addition, immature bald eagles often are mistaken for goldens, since a bald eagle will not gain its white head and tail feathers until it is four or five years old, so perhaps some people are judging the behavior of what they think is a golden eagle based on the actions of a juvenile bald eagle.

What golden eagles do best is hunt like an Apache helicopter in attack mode. I've seen them operate in tandem on ranch land, speeding overhead, then circling quickly in silence as they spot and identify prey, and then, if it suits them, making a headlong dive—for whatever critter is down below, not suspecting a thing, well, that's the end of the music. I've seen evidence where golden eagles have taken not only mice, rabbits, ducks, and trout, the typical fare, but also muskrats, squirrels, opossum, and remnants of wolverine-type mammals (not enough for identification, but perhaps mink).

Golden eagles can fly with prey that weighs as much as four pounds; they have been documented snatching the lambs of Sierra bighorn sheep.

golden eagle

Waylon Jennings once produced a song called "The Eagle," which had a symbolic lyric about American might when provoked . . . "Something's gonna go to ground, when the eagle flies." When it comes to the golden eagle, however, no provocation—other than the prospects of its next meal—is required to inspire it to action.

Biologists' Notes

Eagles are among the largest and most powerful birds of prey in the world. The two species that inhabit North America are the bald eagle, *Haliaeetus leucocephalus,* and golden eagle, *Aquila chrysaetos.* Two other species, the gray sea eagle and Steller's sea eagle, are casual residents of North America.

The golden eagle is a large bird, weighing up to 12 pounds, with a wingspan of more than seven feet. The body color is dark brown, with the head and neck a lighter golden brown. The body color of immature birds is darker and the golden tones of the head and neck are less pronounced. These young birds have white at the base of the tail and irregular white patches may be seen under the wings during flight. This white plumage is molted and is not visible in adult birds. The golden eagle has a varied diet consisting of a number of species of small- and medium-sized mammals, some birds, and occasionally reptiles. Prey are killed with the bird's long sharp talons and torn into bite-sized bits with its strong hooked beak. The golden eagle's prey may weigh as much as four pounds. Research on captured wild eagles indicates that it is unable to lift and fly with a 5.5-pound weight attached to its legs.

In the foothill grasslands, ground squirrels make up 70-80% of a golden eagle's diet. A moderate level of cattle grazing on grasslands actually helps increase golden eagle populations. The reason is that moderate grazing provides improved habitat for ground squirrels—too much grazing, which mows wild grasses down to stubble, or no grazing, which allows wild grasses to grow too high, results in fewer squirrels. In turn, fewer squirrels means fewer golden eagles. Historically, much of the native habitat for golden eagles was always grazed, not by cattle but by huge roaming herds of tule elk.

Because of the superb flight abilities and the efficiency with which eagles hunt and kill their prey, they have captured the imagination of man since early times. The use of golden eagles for falconry dates back to medieval times. Throughout history the eagle has been emblazoned on the coins of numerous countries and used on coats of arms. It has been chosen as the national emblem of Germany and Mexico.

Golden eagles are abundant in the coastal mountain ranges of California from San Francisco to San Diego. Smaller populations of eagles are found in the Sierra Nevada, the inner north Coastal Ranges, and in northeastern California. There is evidence of limited migratory movement. However, in more southerly areas, the birds seem to remain in the vicinity of the nesting territory throughout the year. The densest population of golden eagles anywhere in the world is within a 40-mile radius of Mount Diablo in Alameda and Contra Costa Counties, where there are 60 to 100 nesting sites.

The nest sites of the golden eagle are known as eyries. Eyries may be found in a variety of locations throughout the state. The eagle's preference for nesting ranges from trees at low elevations to ledges under overhanging cliffs at high elevations. Nests vary in size but usually are platforms about five feet wide and one to three feet deep. Nest materials generally consist of various-sized dead sticks. The nest usually is lined with shredded bark, pine needles, newspapers, and similar materials. Eagles returning to existing nests do some clean-up and add some materials, especially if wind and other forces have caused damage. Occasionally, severe winds or the sheer weight of the nest cause it to crash to the ground.

A pair of eagles will establish and defend a territory around the nest. In California egg-laying begins as early as January. Courtship, including breathtaking aerial acrobatics, always precedes nesting and also may continue through the entire nesting season.

The female usually lays two or sometimes three large smooth eggs. Eggs vary in size and also in color, from snow white to a soft cream, splotched with russet brown spots. It usually takes about 35 days for the eggs to hatch. Golden eagles are shy and wary of humans, and the female may even desert a nest of eggs if molested. The young are seldom abandoned entirely, but constant human disturbance keeps parents away and can be lethal to nestlings, because their feedings are delayed and they are exposed to heat, cold, and predators.

Young eagle hatchlings are so weak they can hardly hold up their heads. The young are covered with a thick white down, which keeps them warm. The down is replaced by feathers at eight weeks, and by 11 or 12 weeks the young are fully grown. The golden eagle feeds its young a wide variety of birds and mammals. Both living creatures and dead are included in their diets. The parents are especially busy hunting during the nesting season, when they must meet the demands of their rapidly growing young. Rabbits and ground squirrels form the staple diet of the golden eagle, particularly for feeding the young.

At 12 weeks of age the young practice flapping their wings and bound up from the nest to hang suspended by gusts of wind for increasingly longer periods of time. After a few days of practice, if the young don't take flight, the mother will push nestlings from the nest to force them to fly. One clumsy youngster was observed to fall nearly 100 feet before the mother swooped underneath and spread her wings so he could land on her back. She then soared back up with him to another location and the process was repeated.

Even after the young learn to fly and hunt for themselves, the nest is the center of their activity until fall, at which time they venture farther and farther until one day they just don't return.

Where to see golden eagle

ANCIENT BRISTLECONE PINE FOREST, IN INYO COUNTY

BUTTE VALLEY WILDLIFE AREA, IN SISKIYOU COUNTY

CACHUMA LAKE RECREATION AREA, IN SANTA BARBARA COUNTY

CLEAR LAKE STATE PARK, IN LAKE COUNTY

CUYAMACA RANCHO STATE PARK, IN SAN DIEGO COUNTY

DEL VALLE RESERVOIR AND REGIONAL PARK, IN ALAMEDA COUNTY

GRIZZLY ISLAND WILDLIFE AREA, IN SOLANO COUNTY

HARPER LAKE, IN SAN BERNARDINO COUNTY

KELLY RESERVOIR, IN MODOC COUNTY

LAUREL PONDS, IN MONO COUNTY

LOON LAKE/CRYSTAL BASIN RECREATION AREA, IN EL DORADO COUNTY

MOUNT SAN JACINTO STATE PARK AND STATE WILDERNESS, IN RIVERSIDE COUNTY

PALM TO PINES SCENIC BYWAY TOUR, IN RIVERSIDE COUNTY

PICACHO STATE RECREATION AREA, IN IMPERIAL COUNTY

SAN LUIS DAM AND RESERVOIR, IN MERCED COUNTY

SANTA MARGARITA LAKE, IN SAN LUIS OBISPO COUNTY

SANTA ROSA PLATEAU ECOLOGICAL RESERVE, IN RIVERSIDE COUNTY

SHASTA LAKE NATIONAL RECREATION AREA, IN SHASTA COUNTY

SILVERWOOD LAKE STATE RECREATION AREA, IN SAN BERNARDINO COUNTY

Elk

Elk are often described as California's most magnificent animal, a typical male standing five feet at the shoulder with antlers that practically poke holes in the clouds. They are easy to find, watch, and photograph, by far the easiest and most fun of the state's big game mammals to track.

Historically, elk were known among Native Americans as *wapiti,* which means "white rump."

Tule elk are abundant in many locations, most prominently at Point Reyes National Seashore, Grizzly Island Wildlife Area, Cache Creek Wildlife Area, Tule Elk State Reserve, and at Tinemaha Reservoir in the Owens Valley.

ANIMAL	Elk
SPECIES	*Cervus elaphus*
TYPE	mammal
STATUS	OK
SEE ALSO	Bighorn, Deer, Pronghorn

elk

At Prairie Creek Redwoods State Park, Roosevelt elk often wander about in herds as if in an outdoor zoo. Roosevelt elk are also becoming established in smaller numbers in the Marble Mountain Wilderness and other wildlands.

Rocky Mountain elk can be found in the North Warner Mountains and also in Shasta-Trinity National Forest from the Pit River Arm of Shasta Lake on northeast about 35 miles toward the town of Fall River Mills.

Finding elk is so much fun that Doug McConnell and I even taped an episode out at Point Reyes National Seashore for his TV show, *Bay Area Backroads*. We crawled around the brush, stalking, to get close without being detected, just for fun. But it's so easy to find elk that often all you have to do is just drive to the parking lot at Pierce Ranch near Tomales Point, where the elk typically are hanging out within viewing range. You can add an easy hike to it and keep count of the number of elk you spot, with 25 to 100 being fairly typical. If you want a full workout, hiking four to eight miles and exploring further on game trails, you might see 200, along with deer, fox, rabbits, and hawks.

The elk herd is no secret, and the parking lot at Pierce Ranch is often full by midday on weekends. To avoid most other people, come during the week or try before 10 a.m. or after 4 p.m. on weekends. But even when there are a lot of other elk watchers, the elk don't hardly mind at all. They are far from tame—don't get too close unless you want to get turned into elk shiskabob—but they are definitely adapted to accommodating lots of daily viewers.

The best way to see the most elk is to start by hiking the Tomales Point Trail, then after 20 to 40 minutes, veering off to the right on one of the game trails and tromping to a good lookout at the ridge. From here, you can see down into a valley to the north, where there is a watering hole where elk often congregate. I've found that the elk also herd up in two meadows adjacent to deep coves near the shore of Tomales Point.

The strange, warbled, bugling sound—the mating call of an elk—is likely a sound like nothing you've ever heard. And for many, the elk making these sounds are like nothing you've ever seen. While the growing herds of elk in California are becoming well known, what is still a surprise to many is the fall mating rituals that take place, including their bugling mating calls, sparring, collecting harems, and, if you're especially lucky, you might even see them Do It. For youngsters reading this book, that is how big elkies make little elkies.

The big elkies have mastered this ability, kind of like hamsters. At Point Reyes National Seashore, for instance, what started as a small herd of about

25 from the Grizzly Island Wildlife Area near Fairfield now numbers over 550.

Once tule elk roamed California like the buffalo ranged across the Great Plains, but they were shot to near extinction by market hunters and also had their primary habitat converted to farmland in the Central Valley. At the turn of the century, only two animals were believed to remain in California, both protected by a rancher in the Owens Valley. Those two elk became the seed for the present abundant populations. As herds have been protected, the young have been transplanted to start new herds in areas of historic habitat.

Elk were known to Native Americans as *wapiti,* which means "white rump." The tule elk was originally a valley animal, found only in California. Reduced to only a single breeding pair in the late 1800s, about 8,000 wild and free-roaming elk live in California today.

At Prairie Creek Redwoods, the elk have also adapted easily to being viewed and having their pictures taken, including right along the park's access road and the road to Fern Canyon. But some people still have not figured out why binoculars and long-range camera lenses were invented.

In one episode at Prairie Creek Redwoods, a vacationer with a point-and-shoot camera decided to take a close-up shot of a huge bull elk with a massive rack. Mr. Elk did not like this. First Mr. Elk grunted, but the guy just kept coming closer. So then Mr. Elk charged, and the vacationer did the only logical thing, quickly scampering up a nearby tree.

For several hours, the elk stomped around at the bottom of that tree, snorted now and then, and occasionally looked up at the guy.

As far as I know, he's still up there.

Biologists' Notes

The elk, *Cervus elaphus,* next to the moose, is the largest member of the North American deer family. There are three races of elk now present in California. They are the tule, Roosevelt, and Rocky Mountain.

When the early settlers first came to California, they found elk in great numbers in the San Joaquin Valley and in the foothills on either side of the valley. They named them tule elk, after the giant tule marsh grasses. The tule elk looks generally like other elk in size and shape. It is not quite as large as the Roosevelt elk, which weighs more than 1,000 pounds. A big bull tule elk may weigh 900 pounds.

The tule elk was originally a valley animal, found only in California. It did not migrate to the mountains in summer like other elk, although in the rainy winter months it would move into the low foothills on either side of the lush Central Valley.

The explorers also found a larger elk in California, which was named the Roosevelt elk. It lived and is still found in the north coast counties and in Oregon and Washington. Roosevelt elk are inhabitants of the rainforest and coastal area from Mendocino County northward to Vancouver Island and the mainland of British Columbia. These animals reach greater size than the other elk races. A large bull may weigh between 1,000 and 1,200 pounds. The Roosevelt elk appears equally at home in the mountains or the lowlands and may or may not be migratory, depending on the climate and severity of the weather.

Rocky Mountain elk range in size between tule and Roosevelt elk. The mature bulls weigh from 600 to 1,000 pounds and the females from 500 to 550 pounds. These elk are primarily mountain dwellers. Like the mule deer, they are migratory, spending the winter concentrated in the foothills or adjacent plains but moving up to scatter widely over the mountains during the summer period. Rocky Mountain elk were transplanted in 1916 from Yellowstone, and the progeny from those elk still live in national forest from the Pit River arm at Shasta Lake and range northeast for about 35 miles toward the town of Fall River Mills. Technically, then, Rocky Mountain elk are *not* a species native to California. Or are they? In recent years, Rocky Mountain elk have been documented in the North Warner Mountains, animals that migrated there from Oregon on their own. Thus, a debate has ensued in the scientific world—since the elk in the North Warners were *not* planted, their progeny could now be considered a native subspecies.

All races of elk have common characteristics. The males alone, perhaps the most stately of American deer, have beautiful antlers. Antlers of the Rocky Mountain elk have been recorded up to 66 inches along the main beam. The antlers are similar to those of the deer in structure, shedding, and growth, but not in shape. A typical set of antlers has six points on each side, but this may be exceeded. By March these antlers are shed and by September are fully grown again, and the bull is in his full glory.

Both bulls and cows have reddish summer coats with darker head and legs. The rump patch has a tawny appearance. In winter the long winter coat appears brown, varying from gray on the sides to very dark on the head and legs. The tule elk's coat is paler both winter and summer than the other races of elk.

In September, as soon as the antlers are fully developed, the mating season occurs. The bull makes his presence known by "bugling," a clear

Where to see elk

Grizzly Island Wildlife Area, in Solano County (Tule Elk)

Owens Valley, Tinemaha Reservoir, in Inyo County (Tule Elk)

Point Reyes National Seashore, in Marin County (Tule Elk)

Prairie Creek Redwoods State Park, in Humboldt County (Roosevelt Elk)

Tule Elk State Reserve, in Kern County

Other places to see elk

Off Highway 299, south of Burney in Shasta County (Rocky Mountain Elk)
Directions: From the town of Burney, drive south on Highway 299. Rocky Mountain Elk have been observed off of Highway 299 spur roads, (such as Fenders Ferry Road near the town of Montgomery Creek), from Burney to the town of Ingot south of Shasta Lake.
Contact: Department of Fish & Game, Region 1, 601 Locust Street, Redding, CA 96001, tel. (530) 225-2300 or fax (530) 225-2381.

Shasta Lake National Recreation Area, in Shasta County (Rocky Mountain Elk)

musical whistle that calls the cows to him. Each bull, by his dominance, holds the cows together in a harem band. Cows carry their young about eight and a half months; a single calf is born in May or June of the following year. The calf is spotted when born and is eating green vegetation by the time it is a month old. The calf can take care of itself by fall but may stay with its mother through the winter.

All subspecies of elk can interbreed. This may account for some mixing in areas where ranges overlap. It is estimated that there are about wild and free-roaming 8,000 elk living in California today.

In early times, the growing towns and increasing populations made a ready market for meat and hides. The great herds of elk, which seemed like an inexhaustible resource, dwindled to such a point that in 1873 a law was passed making the killing of an elk a felony punishable by imprisonment up to two years.

Under complete protection the elk survived. But, as more and more people moved to California and more land was developed, the tule elk was displaced from San Joaquin Valley. A remnant of the San Joaquin Valley herd is maintained in a state park at Tupman, near Bakersfield.

Falcon, Peregrine

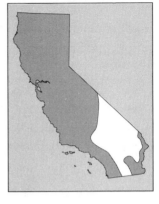

The peregrine falcon is the fastest creature alive, capable of reaching 200 mph to snatch its is prey out of the sky. How would you like to be a barn pigeon or a starling trying to get away? That's when you would find out why the falcon might just be the crown jewel of raptors, few in number but spectacular in flight, particularly in the hunt.

But it is difficult to say what is more dramatic, their fantastic speed or their recovery as an endangered species.

The peregrine falcon is one of three critters in this book that I have not personally seen; the others are Bigfoot and the California Condor. But I have seen a trained kestrel (also known as a sparrow hawk) used in

ANIMAL	Falcon, Peregrine
SPECIES	*Falco peregrinus*
TYPE	bird
STATUS	Endangered
SEE ALSO	Eagles, Hawks, Osprey

hunting at Grizzly Island Wildlife Area to get a similar picture of their skills. It is a thrilling, shocking sight. They seem to fly with little effort, dart-like, even at 50 or 60 mph. It is nothing for them to soar up, roll, and then plunge toward their prey, with the ability to turn on these amazing afterburners for a rocket-like boost in their downward plunge. They can spin in loop-to-loops, chandelles, and figure eights in a flight that looks more like a dance.

What do peregrine falcons hunt? Anything they want to. Other birds with lesser flying skills are easy targets, and falcons will knock them right out of the air. Unsuspecting squirrels and rabbits have scarcely a chance. Wherever falcons fly, they are master of the sky. They lack only significant size, being roughly the size of a crow, and large population numbers, to become renowned like the bald eagle.

In 1970 only 39 breeding pairs could be found across North America. As the year 2000 arrived, the U.S. Fish and Wildlife Service counted 1,650 pairs, including 167 breeding pairs in California. They are in a variety of spots, including even in cities where they live in office towers and building ledges, munching pigeons whenever they want. In 1999 the American peregrine falcon was officially taken off the federal endangered species list, though in California it remains an endangered species under state law.

Like the pelican, bald eagle, and so many other birds, the peregrine falcon was victimized from 1946 to 1968 by farmers' use of the pesticide

DDT. As has been so well chronicled, the poison did not break down quickly after being placed on fields but washed into streams and eventually into lakes with each winter storm. Eventually, food sources used by many birds, such as fish, would ingest the poison. When birds consumed those food sources, they too became contaminated. In turn, the DDT caused the birds' eggs to be so thin that they would often break from the weight of the parent bird sitting on them. In time, with no successful breeding, several bird populations were nearly wiped out.

The peregrine falcon, widespread across North America but never highly populated, was just about exterminated, another testimonial to the ability of mankind to screw up a good thing. Now that man is out of the way, their return is an example of the power of nature.

Biologists' Notes

The peregrine falcon, *Falco peregrinus,* is a striking bird, regal and fierce in appearance. The color of the upper parts is bluish gray, darkest on the head and cheeks, which are nearly black. The underparts are nearly white to pinkish buff on the belly. The breast and belly are sparsely spotted or streaked and the flanks are barred with black. As with most raptors, the female is nearly one-third larger than the male. The long pointed wings and long tail easily separate it from all other hawks, except other falcons from which it differs in size. The peregrine is much darker colored than the prairie falcon, and the head markings easily distinguish it from the much larger gyrfalcon. The American kestrel is the smallest of the falcons, and it is discussed under hawks.

The peregrine falcon is the fastest creature alive, capable of reaching 200 mph. As with most raptors, the female is nearly one-third larger than the male.

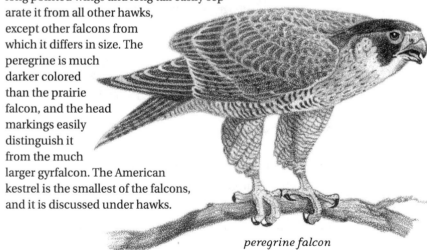

peregrine falcon

The peregrine falcon, or duck hawk as it is sometimes called in the United States, has never been abundant but is found worldwide on nearly every continent and most of the principal islands. Some 20-odd subspecies or races have been described, three of which breed in North America. The peregrine falcon was perhaps best known in Europe, where, in medieval times, it was used by kings and other royalty to hunt game birds for sport. Down through the centuries, many of the large raptorial birds have been trained and used in falconry, but the peregrine is the king of them all (though it may be described as the king, it is the female who is larger than the male).

The peregrine primarily preys on birds ranging in size from a mallard duck down to small warblers and nuthatches. It wants live game and prefers to catch it on the wing. It is the swiftest of our birds of prey, easily overtaking the fastest flying birds. If the bird is light enough to carry, the peregrine dashes alongside or underneath the quarry, seizes it with its talons, and flies away with it. The larger birds are struck with terrific force, usually killing or severely wounding them in midair. The peregrine follows the tumbling body to the ground, where it is plucked and eaten or taken to a favorite perch.

Peregrine falcons prefer to nest on a ledge or potholes in cliffs and high promontories in remote areas. Nesting sites are often used for many years.

The male falcon's days are spent feeding and calling for his mate. Eventually she arrives, and, perching nearby, watches while he performs a dazzling display of aerial acrobatics above and along the face of the cliff. Regardless of his choice of ledges, she makes the final choice of where the

---

Where to see peregrine falcon

BOLSA CHICA STATE BEACH TO NEWPORT BAY, ON THE ORANGE COUNTY COAST

DEL VALLE RESERVOIR AND REGIONAL PARK, IN ALAMEDA COUNTY
NOTE: Del Valle Reservoir is a good location to see the prairie falcon.

HUMBOLDT BAY NATIONAL WILDLIFE REFUGE, IN HUMBOLDT COUNTY

MORRO BAY STATE PARK, IN SAN LUIS OBISPO COUNTY

REDWOOD NATIONAL AND STATE PARKS, IN DEL NORTE COUNTY

SALINAS RIVER NATIONAL WILDLIFE REFUGE, IN MONTEREY COUNTY

SALTON SEA NATIONAL WILDLIFE REFUGE, IN IMPERIAL COUNTY

---

nest will be and in a few days has scratched out a shallow basin in which she lays two to four and rarely six or seven creamy white eggs. The eggs are heavily dotted and splashed with rich browns and reds. It takes from 31 to 35 days for the eggs to hatch. The female broods the eggs closely for about two weeks, taking food from the male in midair as he brings it to the nest. The last half of the incubation period is performed mostly by the female, with help from the male when she is away hunting more and more frequently.

After the young are hatched, both parents are busy hunting and bringing food to the nest, where it is fed in small pieces to the ever-hungry babies. There is considerable fighting over the food, and it is not uncommon for the weaker or smaller birds to perish.

When the young birds are about 30 to 35 days old, the parents try to lure them to take wing by flying close to the nest with food just out of reach. After much exercising at the nest edge, the strongest will leap to grab the proffered food and before he knows it, he is flying. The baby learns to strike the bird hanging from the parent's talons from the side, much in the manner it will attack its own prey. By the sixth or seventh week, young falcons are making short hunts for food on their own under the watchful eye of their parents.

Fisher

Many people think that a "fisher" is a bird, perhaps short for the inshore marine bird, kingfisher. A few others think it is a nickname for a rare ocean fish.

Fisher is actually a small predator in the weasel family, solitary always, vicious on attack. There are more alleged sightings of Bigfoot than fisher, but this little guy is the genuine article.

I have seen only one, and I don't mind revealing exactly where because the odds that the sighting could be duplicated are extremely low. It was at Upper Deadfall Lake, a mountain pond of a lake on the east side of Mount Eddy in the Trinity Divide country, where a trail to the Eddy Summit (9,025 feet) cuts off from the Pacific Crest

ANIMAL	Fisher
SPECIES	*Martes pennanti*
TYPE	mammal
STATUS	OK
SEE ALSO	Badger, Marten, Mink, Otters, Raccoon, Skunks

Trail and is routed three miles with a 2,000-foot climb to the top. The view is so beautiful that it is electrifying as you gain the top, look across to Mount Shasta, beyond to the east of Mount Lassen, to the north of Mount McGlaughlin, and to the west of the Trinity Alps, Marble Mountains, and Preston Peak. But it is seeing that fisher that was the most memorable moment that day.

My wife, Stephani, and I were hiking here, starting the climb from Middle Deadfall Lake to the summit. The lake is set at the edge of tree line amid a mix of ancient Ponderosa pines and cedars, with a sprinkling of boulders and small meadows breaking up the forest. We were within 100 yards of Upper Deadfall Lake, when suddenly something caught my eye. I turned to the left and there it was—a fisher, watching us from a crevice under a boulder.

It was about two and a half feet long, colored rich brown with sleek, healthy fur. Its legs were short but appeared powerful. But what is better remembered is the piercing stare from its dark eyes. From 40 feet away, we played staredown for maybe 20 seconds, then I blinked, and poof, it disappeared into its hiding place in a small boulder field. Later, to confirm the sighting, I talked to a Department of Fish and Game biologist, who verified that three fishers live in that habitat, but they are almost never seen.

Fisher are an extremely significant part of California's ecology. They are hardy hunters and can be successful even when many other predators fail. The best example is that they are among the few animals that can attack and kill a porcupine successfully. Even bears can't do that. During encounters with porcupines, the fisher can acquire some quills, but the quills seldom cause injury to them. The quills often go through the fisher's outer hide without piercing the second layer of skin. Instead the quills turn flat and work their way out with very little festering or inflammation. On extremely rare occasions, fishers have been found dying of starvation with their faces studded with quills, which prevent them from attacking and eating.

Ironically, fishers almost never eat fish—their prey features small mammals. At Mount Eddy, for instance, the habitat is absolutely loaded with chipmunk, so there is never a food shortage all summer long. Because they feed in daylight, unlike many members of the weasel family, it is easy for them to locate, stalk, and then surprise chipmunks and squirrels. Dawn and dusk is when this activity is most likely to occur.

It is still another reason to be out in the field at

Many people think that a fisher is a bird, perhaps short for the kingfisher, an inland marine bird. It is actually a member of the weasel family, solitary always—there are more alleged sightings of Bigfoot than fisher. The fisher is an extremely significant predator in California ecology. They are hardy hunters and are among the few animals that can attack and kill a porcupine successfully. Ironically, fishers almost never eat fish—their prey features small mammals.

fisher

sunrise and sunset, that magic time when so many types of wildlife, from trout to owls to fisher, come out to feed.

Biologists' Notes

The fisher is known to successfully prey on porcupines, and that makes it extremely unusual.

Yet the fisher, *Martes pennanti,* is unique in many other ways. In size, it is among the larger members of the weasel family. The average male is a little over three feet long, nearly twice as large as the female. Their shape resembles that of a large, dark house cat with short, powerful legs. Their fur color ranges from light to a dark rich brown. The head and shoulders are grayish brown, with the pale fur sometimes extending part way down the back. The legs and feet are black and the long, fully furred tail tapers from the body to the tip. Irregular white spots may occur on the throat or chest, with a white patch on the belly between the hind legs. The fur is long and soft, mixed with glossy black guard hairs. The whitish hairs on the inside of the short rounded ears and the white claws mark the pelt with distinction.

The fisher is a solitary animal with a relatively large home range. Like other members of the weasel family, it is an efficient and relentless hunter. Except when preying on beaver in mountain meadows and spring bogs, the fisher prefers to hunt in Douglas fir and mixed coniferous forests.

The fisher is not strictly nocturnal in its habits and often hunts during daylight hours when hungry. Because of this, the fisher finds gray and pine squirrels easy prey. Fishers have a variety of preferred prey, including rabbits, marmots, chipmunks, wood rats, mice, and spawned-out dead or dying fish.

Both the male and female make their dens in hollows in fallen or standing trees and in holes in rocky ledges.

Where to see fisher

LASSEN VOLCANIC NATIONAL PARK, IN LASSEN COUNTY

MARBLE MOUNTAIN WILDERNESS, KLAMATH NATIONAL FOREST, IN SISKIYOU COUNTY

PAYNES CREEK WETLANDS, IN TEHAMA COUNTY

SEQUOIA NATIONAL FOREST, IN FRESNO AND TULARE COUNTIES

Fishers generally mate in April, possibly as late as May. The young are born about 11 months later. This very long gestation period results from what is termed "discontinuous development." The growth of the embryo is halted at an early stage and does not resume until months later. The litter size is from one to four young. After about a week following the birth of the young, the female has to leave her blind and helpless young and hurry to find a new mate, for she remains receptive to mating for only a few days.

The young remain blind and helpless for seven weeks and demand much parental care. However, they grow rapidly and by the following winter they are nearly as large as their parents. They stay with the mother all summer to learn what they need to know to survive and then they go their separate ways.

In the early days of California the fisher was found in the northwestern counties from Oregon south to Marin County, and in the Cascade Mountains in Siskiyou County south along the western slopes of the Sierra Nevada to the Greenhorn Mountains in Kern County. Fishers are most abundant at the 2,000- to 7,000-foot elevation range, which is just below the main range of the pine marten.

By the early 1900s the fisher had nearly disappeared from most of its former range, being trapped out for its fur. However, there was still a sparse but stable population in the more remote areas of Trinity, Tuolumne, and Tulare Counties. By the mid-1930s the fisher was placed on the protected list and is no longer hunted.

Foxes

You won't see many foxes in the outdoors. That doesn't mean they aren't out there. They are crafty fellows, and showing off in front of people like a circus dog is not one of their hobbies.

Spend enough time out hiking and exploring, however, and in time you will see them. Always one at a time. Usually when you least expect it.

My most recent sighting occurred when taking a break from writing this book, a typical accident, while out hiking in the mountain foothill country. I was tromping across a meadow, intending to explore the headwaters of a small river set at the foot of a mountain in national forest, and in the process discovered a sprinkling of about a dozen giant stumps across about 100 acres of meadow, evidence of an ancient forest fire. I was enjoying the hike, and my dog Bart was sniffing everything he could find—you know, so many smells, so little time—

ANIMAL	Foxes
SPECIES	Red Fox - *Vulpes vulpes* Gray Fox - *Urocyon cinereoargenteus* Kit Fox - *Vulpes velox* Island Gray Fox - *Urocyon littoralis*
TYPE	mammal
STATUS	OK/Introduced/Endangered
SEE ALSO	Coyote

when a fox suddenly jumped out from one of those stumps. It froze for an instant at the top of the stump, staring at me, then jumped down and scurried off through the high grass. In seconds it was gone, down into a ravine with a small creek.

I investigated the stump and found that it was partially hollowed out. Apparently the fox had been living here, occasionally nabbing mice and pocket gophers from the field, perhaps even a chipmunk now and then, if one mistakenly decided to explore the stump. Meanwhile, Bart was still sniffing. Never saw a thing.

Another time, in the San Joaquin Valley on a remote county road, I spotted a fox sprinting at top speed across a succession of farm fields. Never seen anything like it. It had to be running at 25 to 30 mph, for at least a mile, until it too vanished, probably a once-in-a-lifetime sighting.

On several occasions, I've also seen fox on the edges of wetlands in the Central Valley, such as adjacent to Delevan, for instance, perhaps hoping to raid a duck nest. Most of the time with foxes, it is a surprise appearance, a flash. They disappear so quickly it is as if they have evaporated.

They are smaller than most think, yet the tail is large and bushy. That bushy tail on a small body is the fastest giveaway that you have seen a fox.

I have also seen fox that have been ill, and these are the only ones that will accept being in proximity to humans in the wild. They seem to hang around, if only in the hope of getting food. In these situations, I have seen the uninformed attempt to feed a fox by hand, as if it was a small dog. But foxes are not small dogs. They are wild animals. And in that animal's mouth are a series of small, triangular teeth built to mesh and rip flesh, and you don't want to be anywhere near that mouth.

A fox always chooses to be secretive, hunting at night, at its best under a full moon competing with great horned owls for mice. Their greatest asset is their virtually invisible presence. They're out there, but you don't see them.

It's like that fox I discovered in the hollowed-out stump. If the fox hadn't flushed, I never would have known it as there. Meanwhile, Bart never even had a clue.

I'm keeping the location of that stump my own little secret. That fox is happy out there, secretive and quiet, always relying on himself.

The gray fox uses its flattened tail as a rudder when in chase, allowing it to quickly turn and catch its prey with ease. A fox can also climb slightly leaning trees as nimbly as a cat. Island foxes are a variety of gray fox inhabiting the Channel Islands along the south central coast of California. The island fox is listed as a threatened animal in the state of California.

Biologists' Notes

There are four distinct species of foxes in California, the red fox *(Vulpes vulpes)*, common gray fox *(Urocyon cinereoargenteus)*, kit fox *(Vulpes velox)*, and island gray fox *(Urocyon littoralis)*.

The kit fox, common gray fox, and island gray fox reproduce true to color and form.

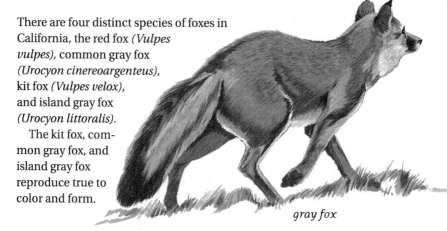

gray fox

However, in the red fox, occasional mutation occurs, resulting in four color phases: red, black, cross, and silver.

The common gray is, in fact, the most common fox in California. It is about the size of a small slender shepherd dog and has a long bushy tail. Its color is steel gray on its back and sides with varying amounts of yellowish-red fur on its underparts and legs. The black-tipped guard hairs on the back make a dark line from the shoulders to the tip of its tail. The tail, which is flattened vertically, always has a black tip. These characteristic markings readily distinguish the common gray from the other foxes.

Not strictly nocturnal, the common gray fox hunts at night when rodents are most active, but it also hunts in daylight hours. It likes to live in and near the dense brush fields found in the low mountainous country. It rarely, if ever, digs its own den. It prefers crevices in rocks and the hollows in both fallen and standing trees, and it can climb slightly leaning trees as nimbly as a cat. It does not sleep in its den like the kit fox but curls up near the den on a log, stump, or shelf of rock.

The common gray fox is omnivorous. It eats a great many insects and rodents and is an excellent hunter. Using its flattened tail as a rudder, it can turn quickly to catch gophers, mice, ground squirrels, and rabbits with ease. It also takes some birds and eggs during nesting season, but unlike the Eastern red fox it rarely takes domestic poultry. Many fruits and berries are included in its diet.

The mating season commences in early spring. The gestation period is 63 days with from three to five kits born to the litter. The male helps tend the young by bringing food, and the family lives and hunts together during the first summer.

The common gray fox is found over most of California, except in the humid coastal belt from Humboldt County north and in the northeastern parts of California. It occurs from sea level to 6,000 feet but is most abundant in the dense chaparral-covered hills from 1,000- to 3,000-foot elevations.

There are six islands along the south central coast of California inhabited by a species of gray fox. Each fox is given the name of the island on which it is found. Although they are smaller than the mainland gray fox, the variation in color is minor. They are commonly referred to as island gray foxes and they are an endangered species in the state of California.

The red fox is one of the most handsome animals inhabiting the high mountain country of California. Despite its showy coat and the fact that it hunts by day as well as by night, it is so wary of man that few are observed in the wild. A little larger than the common gray fox, the red fox is marked with distinction. Its yellowish-red coat, white underparts, black legs, and

Where to see foxes

Anza-Borrego Desert State Park, in San Diego County

Carrizo Plain Natural Area, in Kern County

Joshua Tree National Park, in Riverside and San Bernardino Counties

Lake Solano County Park, in Solano County

Lassen Volcanic National Park, in Lassen County

Pinnacles National Monument, in San Benito County

Point Mugu State Park, in Los Angeles County

San Luis Dam and Reservoir, in Merced County

Other places to see foxes

Andrew Molera State Park, in Monterey County

Battle Creek Wildlife Area, in Tehama County

Bidwell Park, in Butte County

Cabrillo National Monument, in San Diego County

Coyote Hills Regional Park, in Alameda County

Desert Tortoise Natural Area, in Kern County

Kern National Wildlife Refuge, in Kern County

Lopez Lake, in San Luis Obispo County

Malibu Creek State Park, in Los Angeles County

Mount Tamalpais State Park, in Marin County

Paynes Creek Wetlands, in Tehama County

Providence Mountains State Recreation Area, in San Bernardino County

Sinkyone Wilderness State Park, in Humboldt County

Success Lake, in Tulare County

Yosemite National Park, in Mariposa County

bushy white-tipped tail make it readily distinguishable from the gray-colored coyotes that live in the same area.

The Sierra red fox restricts itself both in summer and winter to the high timbered peaks of the Sierra Cascade range and is rarely found below 5,000 feet. Although it does not hibernate, during the worst storms it probably holes up until the storm subsides. It preys easily on mice, wood rats, squirrels, snowshoe rabbits, and carrion.

The red fox does not dig its own den but prefers the rock slides where crevices and holes offer a many-room choice of living quarters. The mating season commences in January and February, and the gestation period is 54 days with litters of five or six kits. Most litters are born in late May and June. Like the common gray fox, the male red fox helps rear the young, and the family stays together during the first summer.

The Sierra Nevada red fox was never numerous and is only found in relative abundance in three areas: the Mt. Shasta-Mt. Lassen area, the Sierra west of Mono Lake and on the western slopes of Mt. Whitney. The extreme southern range was established by a report of two being killed in the Paiute Mountains south of the Kern Gap. The Sierra Nevada red fox is a state-listed threatened species.

A population of red foxes of unknown origin is gradually extending its range along the floor of the Sacramento Valley. Because of its pale coloring and larger size, this fox is thought to be the Eastern red fox, which was imported into California for the purpose of fur farming as early as 1885. Fur farming became unprofitable in the 1930s. It is possible that as pens deteriorated, the foxes either escaped or were deliberately released into the wild near the Sutter Buttes.

This fox is now being found from Tehama County south to Yolo County, primarily west of the Sacramento River, where it has adapted itself in close proximity to ranches and cultivated crop lands.

The graceful little kit fox is the smallest of the three foxes on the California mainland. It is a slender, almost dainty animal, with large ears and a round, bushy, black-tipped tail; its color is a grayish yellow with white underparts. It is noted for its incredible bursts of speed over short distances, hence the nickname "swift fox."

Unlike the red or common gray foxes, the kit fox prefers to live in open, arid, sandy ground inhabited by the kangaroo rats and pocket mice on which it depends for food. It lives in burrows that it digs itself, and occasionally several foxes will be found with their dens close together. Mating season for the kit foxes is early. Its young are born in burrows in February and March, with four or five young to the litter.

The desert kit fox occurs in the Colorado and Mojave desert regions, and the San Joaquin kit fox is found in southern San Joaquin Valley and surrounding foothills. Because so much wildlife habitat has been destroyed by giant farming operations in the San Joaquin Valley, San Joaquin kit fox populations have plummeted and are now federally listed as an endangered species.

Frogs

Almost every youngster has a personal story about a frog. Boys everywhere have a universal fascination with the little fellows, whether it be watching them as polliwogs, searching for them along the edges of ponds and marshes, watching them jump, or listening to them croak.

My best story is about my dad's favorite frog, which lived in this small creek and pond in his backyard in northern California. It was a big bullfrog, and my dad, Bob Stienstra, Sr., loved this frog, as well as all the other creatures in the pond. He always allowed the neighborhood youngsters to play there, and in time, they too became fas-

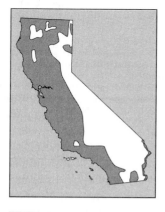

ANIMAL	Frogs
SPECIES	*Rana* spp.
TYPE	amphibian
STATUS	Endangered/ Introduced

cinated with the frogs as they progressed through their various stages from spring to summer to fall. But at one point, my dad became worried that the youngsters might take his favorite bullfrog home; it would never survive, of course, without a proper habitat of year-round water.

"Now you can play all you want here," he told them one day. "You can watch the frogs all you want, too, but don't do anything to those frogs. Don't take them home. Always protect them here."

Well, as fate would have it, there came a time when my parents decided to move to a new home. On the last day of moving out, there was a knock on the door, and my dad, a bit stressed from the packing, opened

American bullfrog

All frogs require permanent water in which to live and reproduce. They hibernate in deep mud in winter and emerge in the spring when the air temperature reaches the high 60s. It may take seven or eight years for the bullfrog to reach its full size.

it quickly without a thought, and there at the door were three little boys, looking up at him.

"We're sorry you're leaving," one said.

"I'm sorry, too," my dad answered, "I'll miss seeing you boys play."

"Before you go, we want you to know that we'll take care of your frogs when you're gone," said another.

Right then, the boy opened his hands, and sitting there was my dad's favorite bullfrog, the big one.

"We named him 'Mr. Stienstra,'" he said. ""Don't worry. We'll always make sure nothing happens to him."

It is one of the touching moments in my dad's life. And as far as I know, to this day Mr. Stienstra is still jumping around that pond.

But kids and frogs can do that to you. After all, nearly every kid knows about the legend of the bullfrog's revenge, about how if you pick one up and they pee on you, you'll get a wart.

It is always a thrill for a youngster to explore along the shore of a marsh or tule-ringed pond or lake, then find bullfrogs hiding in the shallows. Often they will surprise you, suddenly jumping nearly at your feet, and you can become more startled than the frog.

With year-round water and at least a resemblance of a marsh, frogs can breed in prolific numbers, and provide the setting for all kinds of wondrous experiences for youngsters. That goes whether it be watching polliwogs swim en masse, then observing them lose their tails as warm weather arrives, or in summer, surprising a big bullfrog and watching it jump about a foot.

On summer nights, I still enjoy the sound of happy bullfrogs croaking away. I've learned that the louder they croak, the better the weather will be the next day.

One rueful note is that there is a worldwide decline in frogs and other amphibians. In California, the red-legged frog, which lives primarily in high Sierra lakes, is listed as threatened. In part this is due to the introduction of the bullfrog, an east coast native, into California waters. It is a very aggressive predator that preys on both polliwogs and adult frogs and other amphibians, though it's not clear if the bullfrog is the main reason for the decline in the red-legged frog. The decline may also be due to a fungus that the frogs have difficulty fighting off. But why? Some scientists theorize that the depletion of the ozone layer has exposed red-legged frogs and other amphibians to a greater than normal amount of ultraviolet rays, which has somehow weakened their immune systems and made them vulnerable to infection. Whether the damaging exposure occurs at the egg, larva or adult stage is unknown, but amphibians are particularly vulnerable in the egg stage, since many species lay unshelled eggs in water.

Biologists' Notes

There are 22 species of frogs and toads in California, some of which have been introduced from other regions in the United States. Frogs and toads are easy to tell apart—frogs have smooth skins and are adapted for aquatic life; toads have rougher, drier skin, and are adapted for drier habitats. The frog's front toes are unwebbed and distinct, the hind toes are webbed, and the back legs are long and well developed for jumping, whereas toads move more by walking or short hops. The frog's eardrums, which are set behind and below the eyes, are relatively more pronounced than those of the toad. All frogs and toads are in the amphibian class.

The California red-legged frog *(Rana aurora draytoni)* is the largest native frog, attaining a total head and body length of about 4.5 inches. It is currently federally listed as a threatened species, having been exterminated over most of its former range. The yellow-legged frogs, *Rana boylii* and *R. muscosa,* (for foothill and mountain species, respectively) are between 1.5 and 3.25 inches long and are species that are being carefully watched for population decline. The California mountain yellow-legged frog is a candidate for federal endangered status.

The red- and yellow-legged frogs are found in suitable waters west of the Sierra Nevada and Cascade Mountains. They may be identified by the color on the inside of their hind legs. The leopard frog *(Rana pipiens)*, named because of its profuse spotting, is found on the east side of the Sierra in Surprise Valley (Modoc County), around Lake Tahoe, and along the Colorado River. The American bullfrog *(Rana catesbiana)* has been widely introduced in the Sacramento and San Joaquin Valleys and in streams and isolated ponds in the foothills of the coastal and Sierra Nevada mountains, and in some desert areas in Southern California. Though a native species common east of the Rockies, some speculate that the bullfrog was introduced into California as a food source after native frog numbers had been reduced after the Gold Rush.

The American bullfrog can be distinguished by its extra large ear drums and by its size, for it grows to a head and body length of nearly eight inches and to weights of more than one pound. The skin in adults becomes rough,

Where to see frogs

ASH CREEK WILDLIFE AREA, IN MODOC AND LASSEN COUNTIES

GRAY LODGE STATE WILDLIFE AREA, IN BUTTE COUNTY

GRIZZLY ISLAND WILDLIFE AREA, IN SOLANO COUNTY

JENKINSON LAKE/SLY PARK RECREATION AREA, IN EL DORADO COUNTY

LOS BANOS STATE WILDLIFE AREA, IN FRESNO COUNTY

PICACHO STATE RECREATION AREA, IN IMPERIAL COUNTY

SACRAMENTO NATIONAL WILDLIFE REFUGES COMPLEX, IN GLENN COUNTY

SALTON SEA NATIONAL WILDLIFE REFUGE, IN IMPERIAL COUNTY

the upper surface is green with a brownish overcolor and has occasional distinct spotting. The undersides are nearly white with some pale yellow. The male's eardrum is larger than its eye and considerably larger than the female's eardrum.

All frogs require permanent water in which to live and reproduce. They hibernate in deep mud in winter and emerge in the spring when the air temperature reaches the high 60s. Their moist skin allows them to absorb oxygen when they are underwater. The deep booming voice of the bullfrog has been heard as early as February in the Sacramento and San Joaquin Valleys—the voice of the bullfrog is the loudest of any of the frogs. They do not sing in a chorus; the call is isolated and the pitch of the deep notes differs with individual frogs.

By midsummer the female bullfrog deposits her eggs in still water. The tapioca-like egg mass is disc-shaped and covers an area of about 10 inches across and may have up to 25,000 eggs. The eggs hatch into tadpoles, which have gills and live underwater. Over the course of two years the tadpoles develop into frogs. The hind legs emerge first, then the front legs, and toward the end of the second summer the gills and the rudder-like tail disappear. The frog can then leave the water.

It may take seven or eight years for the bullfrog to reach its full size. It has a voracious appetite and during its maturation, it will have eaten a dozen times its own weight in insects, other frogs, small fish, ducklings, and even small snakes. This tremendous appetite is probably why there are no ponds or drainages in California where you will find both the red-legged frog and the American bullfrog. It is successful as a non-native species because there are no natural predators to control its population size.

Goose, Canada

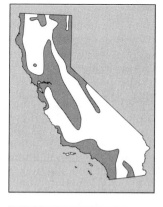

From egg to adult, from wetlands to sky, it is the Canada goose that best captures the magic of the marsh.

They are the birds of the classic V-shaped wedge across the sky, the legends of fall flights and distant honking-like squawks, of close-up grace as they pattern for landing, and the natural beauty of a 10-pound bird cut in sharp, black-and-white features.

But for many who watch and love the marsh, season after season, what is most compelling is that the Canada goose mates for life.

As mates, they live in harmonic parallel. When one calls, the other answers. When

ANIMAL	Goose, Canada
SPECIES	*Branta canadensis*
TYPE	bird
STATUS	OK/Threatened
SEE ALSO	Swans

one locks its wings and glides down to a pond, the other follows. Unlike so many other creatures, they both tend their young. They are a team. They fly together, eat together, drink together, sleep together, and nest together.

What is most compelling is encountering the bird up close and personal. I have come upon Canada geese by accident in my canoe, paddling around a point, finding just a half dozen or so within 20 or 30 yards, and then watched in wonder to have them lift off in perfect sequence above my bow. It is these snapshot moments that can be relived for years.

After studying them, I have also learned that the local California

Canada goose

The Canada goose mates for life, and a mated pair lives in harmonic parallel. When one calls, the other answers. When one locks its wings and glides down to a pond, the other follows. When one calls, the other answers. They both tend their young. They are a team. They fly together, eat together, drink together, sleep together, and nest together.

residents, that is, the non-migrants of the species, are creatures of dedicated habit. I have tracked them as they fly from feeding ground to marsh, and from pond to pond, and found that their short local trips are often timed. At this one pond, for instance, I found a resident flock of a dozen Canada geese that would fly two miles north to another pond every evening of the summer, a half hour before sunset. For a month, it was like clockwork. Many have similar habits in many phases of their lives.

By the way, many people misidentify them as "Canadian" geese. That is incorrect. A "Canadian" goose would mean it is from Canada, and that is often not the case. It is rather a species known as Canada goose, and thousands nest in America, especially northern California, Oregon, and Washington. Of course, many do come from Canada, notably in the prairie lands of Alberta, as well as British Columbia and Alaska, but the name refers to a species, rather than a description of their point of origin.

The migratory flights of thousands of Canadas is a true spectacle, with rafts of V-wedges moving as if synchronized. As they near, you can hear their squawks for miles across a still morning, and if they're flying low and close, you can even hear the powerful flaps of their wings, like a low drum roll across the marsh.

Michael Furniss, one of the preeminent hydrologists in the nation, also has a fascination with geese and told me that a study had finally been completed involving the flying patterns of Canadas.

"When Canada geese are flying in V-formation, you know why one side is longer than the other?" he asked.

"No, I don't," I answered, "I've always wondered that."

"They finally figured it out. More geese."

Biologists' Notes

Canada geese *(Branta canadensis)* are a major part of the California waterfowl scene, for within their numerous subspecies are found the largest and smallest members of the goose family.

Four Canada goose subspecies may be found in California: the Great Basin Canada goose, the lesser Canada, the western Canada, and the cackling goose. They all have a long, thin black neck, a black head with white cheek patches, and a black bill and feet. While the general appearance is the same as to color and markings, the main difference is in their size. Because of their distinct honking squawk, the two biggest geese are often called Canadian honkers.

The largest Canada goose subspecies, the Great Basin, is the only goose that breeds and lives in northeastern California, normally spending the winters in the valleys of central California. Different populations of the Great Basin Canada winter in the Imperial Valley, migrating down the east side of the Sierra from their breeding grounds in the other western states and Canada. The Great Basin Canada goose is a large bird, weighing from 8 to 14 pounds with a wingspread of 5 to 6 feet.

The other three subspecies migrate to California from Canadian and Alaskan breeding grounds. The western Canada goose, a little smaller than the Great Basin, enters California along the west coast as far south as Del Norte and Humboldt counties. The lesser Canada, which weighs from 5 to 6 pounds, and the cackling goose, or cackler, which only weighs from 2.5 to 3.5 pounds, both winter in great numbers in the central California valleys. The little cackler is the only Canada goose that winters exclusively in California.

Larger forms are easily recognized by their great size and their voices. Their call is a clear, resonant *ah-honk* with a break between the syllables. The smaller geese have a higher pitched voice and call much faster in a cackling manner. All Canadas have a variety of conversational notes or "goose talk" both in the air and on the ground. When traveling far they fly extremely fast with regular, measured wingbeats, calling frequently in a trumpeting, clangorous voice that has stirred excitement in man since early times.

Canada goose graze in open fields and are normally day feeders. They walk and swim without effort, showing more preference for water during breeding season.

The first signs of spring fill the wild geese with a restless urge for flight. They congregate in flocks and express their uneasiness with much gabbling and honking as though discussing the long trip ahead. The big honkers are the first to leave the wintering grounds.

Some of the Great Basin Canadas, on their return north, stay in northeastern California marshes and reservoirs. They build their large, rather bulky nests near water in a variety of places—on banks and little islands, on top of muskrat houses and haystacks, and in the tops of old dead trees.

Where to see Canada goose

CACHUMA LAKE RECREATION AREA, IN SANTA BARBARA COUNTY

GRASSLAND RESOURCE CONSERVATION DISTRICT, IN MERCED COUNTY
NOTE: November, February and March are peak months for waterfowl.

HONEY LAKE WILDLIFE AREA, IN LASSEN COUNTY
NOTE: The wildlife area is open to the public except Saturdays, Sundays and
Wednesdays during waterfowl hunting season (October through mid-
January). There is limited access to some areas during hunting season
(September through January).

KELLY RESERVOIR, IN MODOC COUNTY

LAKE EARL WILDLIFE AREA, IN DEL NORTE COUNTY

LOWER KLAMATH NATIONAL WILDLIFE REFUGE, IN SISKIYOU COUNTY
NOTE: Best viewing months are May through August, along Highway 161
between Highway 97 and Hill Road along the way to the visitor center. For
current sightings information, check the website: www.klamathnwr.org.

MILLERTON LAKE STATE RECREATION AREA, IN FRESNO COUNTY

PALM TO PINES SCENIC BYWAY TOUR, IN RIVERSIDE COUNTY

SACRAMENTO NATIONAL WILDLIFE REFUGES COMPLEX, IN BUTTE, COLUSA, GLENN,
SUTTER, AND TEHAMA COUNTIES

SALTON SEA NATIONAL WILDLIFE AREA, IN IMPERIAL COUNTY

Other places to see Canada goose

ANTELOPE LAKE/INDIAN CREEK, IN PLUMAS COUNTY

EMERALD BAY STATE PARK/D.L. BLISS STATE PARK, IN EL DORADO COUNTY

FOLSOM LAKE STATE RECREATION AREA, IN SACRAMENTO COUNTY

LASSEN VOLCANIC NATIONAL PARK, IN LASSEN COUNTY

LOON LAKE/CRYSTAL BASIN RECREATION AREA, IN EL DORADO COUNTY

OROVILLE WILDLIFE AREA, IN BUTTE COUNTY

Some of the geese readily accept artificial nesting platforms installed by
the Department of Fish and Game.

The goose lays from 4 to 10 (usually 5 or 6) creamy white eggs that hatch
in 25 to 30 days. While it is doubtful that the gander ever sits on the eggs, he
does remain in close attendance, ready to protect the nest from danger.

Baby geese are called goslings, and they are guarded carefully by both the goose and the gander after hatching. The family almost immediately seeks cover at the water's edge at this time for protection. Soon after the young are hatched, the annual molt of the adults occurs, leaving them flightless for several weeks. Most families of geese congregate at this time. The goose family is close-knit and remains together for the goslings' first year.

Geese are long-lived; there are records of geese nearly 50 years old that breed regularly, though this is a maximum age. The oldest recorded age of a Canada goose in the wild is 23 years. Great ability is shown by some of the older birds in leading the flocks on the long route to and from the wintering grounds.

Grouse, Blue

The grouse arrived in a maelstrom of ruffled feathers, loud and quick. It swooped down from a fir tree, then trotted up and sat next to me. It was as if the grouse thought it was my old dog. It was such a rare event and so sudden that it shocked me back into the moment. You see, I had created a little camp out in the woods and had been sitting on a log for hours. I was reliving the best times of my life with my dog, Rebel, who'd gone to doggy heaven a few days before when he finally couldn't go on anymore at age 17.

Sitting there within arm's reach, the grouse just looked at me for several minutes, tilting its head from side to side. Then it reached out with both wings, scooping up

ANIMAL	Grouse, Blue
SPECIES	*Dendragapus obscurus*
TYPE	bird
STATUS	OK
SEE ALSO	Grouse, Sage

dirt with each wing, and flipped the dirt so it landed right atop itself. In the next five minutes, this was repeated several times, until this wild blue grouse was completely covered in dirt, as happy as could be to be sitting next to me, out in the middle of nowhere.

Well, we sat there for more than an hour, grouse and me. It was the first time I'd stopped hurting in days. This was a fine May day, and though it

blue grouse

The blue grouse is the largest of the wood grouse found in North America. The low-pitched booming of the male blue grouse has a ventriloquist-like quality, seemingly as loud at a distance as when heard close at hand.

can be rare to see wild blue grouse, and some hikers go a lifetime without encountering a single one, in the next year I had dozens of episodes with them. Some of them were bizarre, but all were memorable.

"Whenever you have a particular animal that keeps appearing in your life, it is a message to you," said my Native American friend, Cloud Dancer. "That animal is bringing its medicine to you."

At my mountain cabin, I started getting these daily morning visits from a grouse. I'd walk out and the grouse would swoop down, then come trotting right up to me. One time while I was sitting outside talking about climbing Mt. Shasta with author and research editor Robyn Brewer, the grouse trotted up and plopped down on its side next to me, her feathered legs sticking out as if sunbathing.

"This is incredible," Brewer said. "I've never seen or heard of anything like this in my entire life. That grouse thinks it's a dog."

Another time, after loading for a trip, the grouse sat under the wheels of my truck for hours so I couldn't leave. On another day, with my canoe loaded atop my camper, the grouse flew up and perched on the canoe, stalling me; later, when I left, it chased my truck down the road. When I mowed the lawn, the grouse followed me around like my old dog used to.

Other people began to witness this phenomenon. Anybody driving up would get a greeting, then a personal escort to the front door. I started calling the bird "Grousey," and people in town would ask, "How's Grousey?"

When some renovation work was done to the cabin, the grouse shadowed every move of the work crew. When new crew members arrived at the job, the contractor, Dave Bonner, would take them aside and straighten them out. "Now listen," he'd order, "watch out for that grouse. If you're working away and step back to look at your work, look where you're stepping because Grousey is bound to be right behind you and we don't want you stepping on her. I almost stepped on her myself yesterday."

Then one hot summer day, she disappeared, likely gone to the high country in search of cooler climes. It wasn't long before I and my wilderness partner, Michael Furniss, ventured off too, hiking into remote wildlands.

On the last day of our trip, we were emerging from the Marble Mountain Wilderness, taking a cutoff trail from the headwaters of Wooley Creek, when we suddenly were confronted by a mother grouse with a dozen freshly hatched chicks. The grouse was standing erect, right in the middle of the trail, her chest puffed out, her wings shielding and corralling her little grouse chicks, all about the size of tangerines. "I've never seen anything like this," Furniss said. "We'll have to go around."

But while scrambling upslope off the trail, Furniss planted his hand on a buried beehive and got nailed immediately. He let out a yell and scampered down and away from the bees; we've both been swarmed, and it isn't fun. But in fleeing the bees, he ran headlong into mother grouse, which rose up, her chicks scurrying everywhere, and took two swooping dives at Furniss's head. He managed to duck the attack then advance to safety, while the grouse retreated and again corralled all her little chicks. It was the darnedest thing I'd ever seen.

Until, that is, a month later. I drove back up to the cabin from the Bay Area, and while hiking about and looking at the first sprouts of spring, I was startled by a loud cyclone of rattling feathers. This time it was a male grouse, marked by the red slashes over each eye, and he marched right up to me and sat down, as if guarding me.

Crazy, I thought, but the saga continued. In the next week, this grouse defended my cabin, hiding out under a bush, then attacking all visitors. One friend, Chief Thunderhead, was cornered by the grouse pecking at his tires; he needed to fend off the bird with a broom to get by. Tom Allen, a chimney sweep, practically got chased up his ladder.

Meanwhile, the grouse followed me around like a puppy. "You've got the only attack guard grouse in history," said a Fish and Game warden.

After a few weeks in the Bay Area, I made the drive back into the mountains, spotted Cloud Dancer's small truck parked on a side road in the forest, and pulled over. "How's the grouse?" I asked. Cloud Dancer looked me straight in the face. "The grouse learned you can't go attacking cars like that. Got hit and killed. I found the grouse and took care of it."

Then Cloud Dancer raised a hand. "Grouse symbolize the sacred spiral. Grouse medicine means your spiritual growth is accelerating, spiraling up to the creator. Everybody gets these signs from animals, but not everybody realizes it."

Well, as I drove through the rain late in the week back to the Bay Area, I thought about how I missed that bird. But I know every time I walk in the woods, I'll keep an ear out for the ruffling of feathers and think of the lessons I have learned from my animal friends in the wild.

Biologists' Notes

The blue grouse *(Dendragapus obscurus)* is the largest of the wood grouse found in North America. It is a bird of the western mountains and lives generally at some distance from centers of human population. In California it is found in the north coastal counties, in the Warner Mountains in Modoc County, and the Sierra Nevada range south through the Tehachapis. The latter area requires hiking into deep wilderness (Evolution Valley in John Muir Wilderness and the remote headwaters of Kings River, west of the Dusy Basin). Although it is widespread in distribution, it is not abundant anywhere in its range. All grouse populations fluctuate with weather and feed conditions.

There are minor geographical variations in the colors of the blue grouse, but generally the male is a mottled dark gray bird. The tail is blackish with a light gray band at the tip. It has a red or red-orange naked patch above and below the eye. The female is similar to the male except the upper parts are more brownish in appearance and the female's stomach feathers are white mixed with gray.

The blue grouse is next in size to the sage grouse and weighs from two and a half to three and a half pounds. It measures from 15 to 19 inches long, the male being larger than the female. It is variously called blue grouse, hooter, sooty grouse, and Sierra grouse.

This big grouse may be distinguished at some distance from the sage grouse by its round tail plus the fact that it is seldom, if ever, found in the same habitat as the sage grouse, which lives in open sagebrush country.

In summer the blue grouse lives in fairly open pine and fir forests, along streams near aspen, alder, and willow thickets. In winter they move up to ridge tops at higher elevations to seek dense stands of virgin or second-growth fir timber that affords protection from severe winter storms. Unlike the mountain quail, they do *not* migrate downslope to winter below snowline. In the spring and early summer, usually toward the end of May when most of the snow is gone, the male claims a territory consisting of several acres, which he defends by giving a hooting call to warn off all intruders. He takes a solitary position on a limb 50 or 60 feet up in a pine tree, standing close to the trunk.

He will hold such a position continuously for hours, from one day to another, at intervals producing a deep booming, a sound like someone striking a water-logged tub: *boont, boont, boont.* The low-pitched booming has a ventriloquist-like quality, seemingly as loud at a distance as when heard close at hand. On certain days several birds may be heard simultaneously. Each bird has a unique voice and tone and it requires considerable patience and a sharp eye to locate one in a tree.

Once the male has established his territory, his constant booming and hooting can attract many females. It's quite common for a male to mate with more than one female, as no permanent pair bond is formed. When actually wooing a mate, he struts about with his tail erect and wings drooping. At this time the fiery wattle patches above his eyes are distended and he will inflate the air sac in his throat and neck, emitting a deep resonant boom, boom, booming sound.

Alone, the female builds her nest in a shallow depression on the ground and lines it with dry grass, leaves, twigs, and feathers. The nest is usually under the protective cover of a bush, log, or rock. She lays from five to seven pale buff-colored, two-inch-long eggs speckled with reddish-brown spots

---

Where to see blue grouse

HOPE VALLEY WILDLIFE AREA, IN ALPINE COUNTY

LOON LAKE/CRYSTAL BASIN RECREATION AREA, IN EL DORADO COUNTY

SMITH RIVER NATIONAL RECREATION AREA, SIX RIVERS NATIONAL FOREST, IN DEL NORTE COUNTY

SOUTH WARNER WILDERNESS, IN MODOC COUNTY

---

and broods them for 24 days. As the time approaches for the eggs to hatch, she is so attentive to the nest that you can nearly touch her before she slips to one side.

When the eggs hatch and as soon as the chicks are dry, the hen leads them away, proud as a peacock, and shows them where to find the little bugs and leafy things that baby grouse need to eat. The young grouse need the mother grouse for shelter and defense against predators, but not to provide nourishment. The male takes no part in the incubation or care of the young.

While the chicks are small the female prefers to keep them in and near meadows where the ground cover of leafy weeds and grasses is at least 10 inches tall and usually near water. Later, when the chicks are able to fly, they expand their range to find a diet of insects, fruits, berries, and tender leaves. In winter they can subsist for weeks in a grove of fir trees, feeding entirely on the tips of fir needles.

Grouse, Sage

Like many species of wildlife, many people only see sage grouse as stuffed mounts at visitor centers. But searching out and finding sage grouse is an exciting and satisfying adventure in some of California's most remote regions.

They are located, for the most part, in the high sagebrush of eastern Modoc, Lassen, Mono and Inyo Counties. So right off, venturing out to find sage grouse will require a long drive for most residents. The first reward will come with exploring primitive country that attracts few visitors, the kind of place many forget exists in the Golden State.

The lucky few might find sage grouse in 30 minutes. But the majority spends a lot of time walking across volcanic rocks and through sagebrush in order to get a glimpse.

ANIMAL	Grouse, Sage
SPECIES	*Centrocercus urophasianus*
TYPE	bird
STATUS	OK
SEE ALSO	Grouse, Blue

sage grouse

Savvy explorers will concentrate along the crest of ridges and small shelves in the hills. That's where the grouse tend to be found, as these locations offer vantage points for the birds to spy approaching predators, including humans. Other draws include locations with heavy sage and not far from water. If the water is muddy, look for big tracks that indicate the birds have been there. These areas feature lots of loose, ankle-turning lava rocks, so you should wear a sturdy pair of boots.

The sage grouse is the largest member of North America's grouse family. The adult males, nearly twice as large as the hens, are almost as large as a hen turkey. The sage grouse does not have a gizzard but takes food directly into its stomach. Older birds eat insects, green plants, and grasses in spring and summer, but in fall and winter they eat only the leaves of the big sage.

A lot of drinking water and a good supply of snacks, along with a spare tire, jack, and shovel, also could be handy and prevent folks from being stuck in remote locations. Think I've never been stuck out there? The advice comes from experience.

Don't be surprised when the birds flush well out of range. Sage grouse can be quite spooky, sometimes flushing a hundred or more yards ahead of your approach. When this happens, the only hope is searching the area thoroughly for "sleepers" that may linger.

Marking and following a flushed bird is another sound strategy, provided, that is, that the bird doesn't fly off and leave the country, which sage grouse are prone to do.

On my first trip to find sage grouse, I was enjoying hiking and exploring the landscape so much that for a while I forgot I was on a search mission. Suddenly, this sage grouse popped up 40 yards off, then flew off 200 yards, before hiding again. Guess what happened? You probably guessed right: I spotted his touchdown spot, stalked it, then 40 yards off, off he went again, another 200 yards. This went on for about an hour, and finally, I realized I was being led off into Nevada, and I'd best turn around and try a different bird. But no, I had to try one more time. This time, when he lifted off, he just kept on going, disappearing into an infinity of sagebrush.

When that happens, about the only thing to do is take a sip of water, adjust your hat, and trudge onward. No one said finding sage grouse was easy.

Biologists' Notes

The sage grouse, (*Centrocercus urophasianus*) or sagehen as it is commonly called, is the largest member of North America's grouse family. The adult males, nearly twice as large as the hens, are almost as large as a hen turkey. The male and female are similar in appearance, strikingly marked with gray, buff, brown, and black.

The underparts are white, and a large black belly patch distinguishes them from other grouse. Both have long, sharp-pointed tails.

The colors blend so well with the soft grays and browns of the sagebrush that it is startling when a flock of these big birds bursts into flight. The wingbeat is heavy, but they gather speed rapidly and sometimes fly for as much as a mile with an alternating series of flappings and gently rising and falling glides on stiff-set wings.

In later winter and spring all the male birds from an area of several square miles gather at dawn on habitual strutting grounds and perform one of the most unusual and spectacular courtship displays of all game birds. The full season of activity may extend up to two or three months, ending usually in May.

The male starts to strut by arching his spiked tail in full spread. The patches of white feathers on each side of the breast are raised to frame his proud black head. Turning this way and that, he partially inflates the air sacs on his neck. The wings droop stiffly and air is inhaled in gulps to complete the inflation of the sacs, and he then runs forward with mincing steps. The wings scrape with a swishing noise.

This action is repeated several times, the whole air sac region bounces, and the deflation of the sacs is accompanied by a plopping sound. This may occur 10 or 15 times a minute as he shows off to attract a mate. This display, if undisturbed, may continue from dawn for as much as two hours. The females visit the spot daily toward the end of the strutting period until they have all been chosen as a mate.

The female makes a shallow nest under sagebrush and lays seven or eight grayish or greenish drab-colored eggs dotted rather thickly with reddish brown. The eggs hatch in 25 days and the young are ready to leave the nest when the last one hatched is dry.

The hen takes complete care of the nest and chicks, teaching them feeding habits and how to escape danger when she calls a warning. If she can't distract the enemy by pretending injury, she will sometimes attack by flying at the intruder with loud cackling and hissing noises.

Young birds eat insects at first but quickly start on the diet of the older birds. The sage grouse does not have a gizzard but takes the food directly into its stomach. Older birds eat insects and green plants and grasses in spring and early summer, but in fall and winter they eat only the leaves of the big sage. This specialized diet confines the sage grouse exclusively to the Great Basin sagebrush-type country.

In California the sage grouse is found only in the northeastern counties and down the easterly side of the Sierra Nevada to northern Inyo County. Lassen and Mono Counties have the most stable populations. They are found where there is a combination of sagebrush, grassy meadows, and water.

Sage grouse have been receiving a lot of attention by state and federal biologists as a key bird species within the Great Basin sagebrush habitat.

Where to see sage grouse

ASH CREEK WILDLIFE AREA, MODOC AND LASSEN COUNTIES

BISCAR WILDLIFE AREA, IN LASSEN COUNTY

CLEAR LAKE NATIONAL WILDLIFE REFUGE, IN SISKIYOU COUNTY

KELLY RESERVOIR, IN MODOC COUNTY

LAUREL PONDS, IN MONO COUNTY

Populations have declined throughout much of their range in the western United States and southwestern Canada. Habitat loss, degradation, and fragmentation have all been identified as factors in the reduction of the species range. A consortium of agencies is working cooperatively to conserve and manage the sagebrush habitats for the benefit of sage grouse and other dependent species.

Gulls

Visiting the nesting grounds for the Western gull was like getting a glimpse into a rare and fantastic world where few are allowed entry.

I took a few cautious steps on a walkway called Marine Terrace, surrounded by gulls, chicks, and active nests. The collective squawks from the mothers and chicks were deafening. Imagine this: Surrounding me in a 250-yard radius were over 10,000 gulls, so many that it seemed as if they were taking over the planet.

ANIMAL	Gulls
SPECIES	*Larus* spp.
TYPE	bird
STATUS	OK

And here, they were. This was at the Farallon Island National Wildlife Refuge, a marine sanctuary that is off limits to the public, located 25 miles out to sea off San Francisco. Haunted 100 years ago by egg raiders and seal poachers, the Farallon Islands are now the crown jewel of U.S. Fish and Wildlife Refuges.

Other major breeding areas for gulls are at Mono Lake near Lee Vining, a moon-like area with tufa spires, set on the edge of the desert along US 395 east of Yosemite, with pockets of breeding success at the Channel Islands 25 miles offshore from Oxnard and the L.A. waterfront.

Outside of Alaska, the Farallon Islands is home to the largest nesting colony of seabirds in America, 150,000 birds in all, a living science lab for wildlife and natural history.

Almost no one has set foot on the islands. The public is allowed to view the Farallon Islands only from a distance, with nature cruises offered by the Oceanic Society out of San Francisco the most popular venue. Permits for non-scientists to visit the island are nearly impossible to obtain. It took me more than a month of phone calls and faxes, including a request to a well-connected insider at the Interior Department, to finally get the cherished permit.

Upon landing, the noise was unbelievable, a cacophony of squawks from acres of nesting gulls, murres, and auklets. At the foot of the crane were three just-hatched gulls, their cracked-open eggshells sitting beside them, while their mother squawked and hovered, darting up and down, once trying to grab a staff member's baseball cap by the bill.

"The hardest thing for volunteers is the noise," said biologist Michelle Hester, explaining the never-ending background of squawking gulls, barking sea lions and elephant seals, pounding waves, and whistling winds. "One guy couldn't handle the gulls. They just drove him batty, and he had to catch a boat back to the mainland."

The Western gull, romanticized as *Jonathan Livingston Seagull,* is year-round the most common and abundant of all the sea birds in California. Outside of Alaska, the Farallon Islands is home to the largest nesting colony of seabirds in America.

Western gull

Hester is the lead biologist for the Point Reyes Bird Observatory, which runs a cooperative program with the U.S. Fish and Wildlife Service stewards of the island, to monitor and protect wildlife here, including the mammoth population of breeding gulls.

We hiked on a marked walkway, surrounded on both sides by wall-to-wall gulls, the newly hatched chicks always in groups of three, their mother nearby at guard. We turned right and walked past an acre of 500 hatch boxes, positioned to help nesting auklets, then scanned offshore and spotted both puffins and tube-nose albatross patrolling along the rocks.

Hester said she loses a baseball cap about three or four times a year, the gulls snapping it by the bill, right off her head. Hats are critical wherever there are tons of gulls. And don't be too quick to look up, either. I saw one biologist, first day on the job, who made that mistake—splat, right on her face.

Regardless, it's an extraordinary scene to share in the world of nesting gulls, whether it be at the Farallones, Mono Lake, or the Channel Islands.

The sheer numbers of them is one of the most astonishing theaters I have ever seen in all of nature. And then I thought how ironic it was, how just 25 miles away, so few are aware that such a scenario even exists.

While millions of people on the mainland chase their schedules, the remote nursery areas for Western gulls run on their own time.

Biologists' Notes

The two most commonly seen gulls in California are the Western gull, *Larus occidentalis,* which inhabits the entire Pacific coastline from Washington south to Baja California, nesting primarily on offshore islands; and the California gull, *Larus californicus,* which is essentially a bird of the inland plains that nests on the islands and rocky shores of some of the lakes in the Great Basin between the Sierra Nevada and the Rockies. The California gull is common enough along the coast in winter, but the Western gull year-round is the most common and abundant of all the sea birds. It is the one romanticized in the book and motion picture as *Jonathan Livingston Seagull.*

Seeing these beautiful black and white birds sailing in the wind against a clear blue sky, or walking over the clean sandy beaches, it is hard to associate them with the struggling screaming hordes that, at other times, can be seen fighting for and gorging themselves on refuse from sewers and garbage dumps. Despite its untidy feeding habits, the adult bird manages to keep its snow-white plumage spotlessly clean.

In spring, its migration is more like a partial withdrawal to its breeding grounds along the rocky shoreline and to the islands along the coast. The nesting period begins as early as March in the southerly part of its range in lower California. It is progressively later farther north along the Washington coastline.

The best known breeding ground of the Western gull is the Farallon Islands, where it begins building new or repairing old nests about the first of May. Some nest sites are chosen on the face of cliffs, but the gull seems to favor grassy knolls in the open. The nests, like those of so many of the sea birds, are crude, bulky structures and are built of native grasses and twigs. They are about 12 or 13 inches across. The nest cavity is eight inches wide and four inches deep. The female lays from two to four eggs. If the first nest is destroyed, the second nest rarely contains more than two eggs. The Western gull's eggs are similar in size, shape, and color to those of other gulls of the same size. The egg's color ranges from buffy brown to olive and is heavily splotched with tan or brown markings.

Incubation begins as soon as the last egg is laid. Both parents assist in sitting on the eggs. The bird that is off duty usually stands nearby guarding the nest, slipping onto the nest when the sitting bird leaves. The young are hatched in 24 days and are brooded by both parents, who are very bold and devoted to their young.

The young birds are fed at first on semi-digested food. As the young grow older, the parents begin to feed them small fish and bits of animal matter. They soon become gluttonous feeders. They are guarded and fed by their parents until they can fly. The parents teach them early in life to hide and lie still when danger is near. If the young birds move or start to run before danger is past, the parents have been observed to repeatedly peck them until they are happy to run into the grass and hide. The same is true when it comes to flying. The parents won't allow this hazardous feat until the proper time comes, even to a point that if a young bird attempts to fly before he is strong enough, the parent bird literally batters him to the ground.

Originally, the gull's principal supply of food came from the sea and the mud flats of bays at low tide. Then civilization gave the Western gull an easy way of earning a living as a scavenger. It learned to frequent harbors and populated grounds where it could gorge itself on the refuse of garbage dumps and whatever foodstuff was scattered along the beaches.

Gulls are indiscriminate feeders except on the breeding grounds, where they live primarily on eggs. They do not bother the eggs of other gulls but subsist almost entirely on the eggs and young of the murres, cormorants, and pelicans. This may be why they choose to nest where there is an abundance of the other, more peaceful nesting birds.

The behavior of Western gulls to their non-gull neighbors on the breeding ground is outrageous. They are ever on the alert and never miss a chance to steal and devour the eggs or young from any unguarded nest they can find. Cormorants and pelicans have to sit on their eggs constantly from the day they are laid. Even the young have to be constantly brooded, for the gulls will grab and swallow the smallest young whole, and mutilate and beat to death the larger ones. Cormorants are timid, and if a human walks into a colony of

---

Where to see gulls

AÑO NUEVO STATE RESERVE, IN SAN MATEO COUNTY

AUDUBON CANYON RANCH, IN MARIN COUNTY

CARMEL RIVER STATE BEACH, IN MONTEREY COUNTY

CHANNEL ISLANDS, OFFSHORE OF VENTURA COUNTY
NOTE: Excursions to the waters around the islands are available out of Channel Island and Port Hueneme Harbors.

CLEAR LAKE STATE PARK, IN LAKE COUNTY

FARALLON NATIONAL WILDLIFE REFUGE, OFFSHORE FROM SAN FRANCISCO COUNTY
NOTE: The refuge is about 30 miles offshore of San Francisco and is closed to the public; however, it is possible to view a large variety of wildlife on and near the islands via educational boat tours conducted from June through November by the Oceanic Society.

FISHERMAN'S WHARF, IN MONTEREY COUNTY

GOLDEN GATE NATIONAL RECREATION AREA, IN MARIN COUNTY

LOWER KLAMATH NATIONAL WILDLIFE REFUGE, IN SISKIYOU COUNTY

MCGRATH STATE BEACH, IN VENTURA COUNTY

MONO LAKE, INYO NATIONAL FOREST, IN MONO COUNTY

SANTA ROSA PLATEAU ECOLOGICAL RESERVE, IN RIVERSIDE COUNTY

SONOMA STATE BEACHES/BODEGA BAY, IN SONOMA COUNTY

SUCCESS LAKE, IN TULARE COUNTY

TULE LAKE NATIONAL WILDLIFE REFUGE, IN SISKIYOU COUNTY

---

nesting birds, the cormorants leave. Almost immediately the screaming gulls descend in swarms to break the eggs and eat the young. They have been known to wipe out a whole colony of nesting cormorants.

After the breeding season is over and the young have become strong of wing, they scatter and spread out all along the coast. They follow the fishing boats, chase schools of fish, haunt the mud flats, and roost and associate freely with other species of gulls and other sea birds. Despite some of the gull's less desirable characteristics, people generally welcome it as a peaceful scavenger and admires it as an eye-catching feature in the seashore scenery.

Hawks
Red-Tailed Hawk
American Kestrel

Because a hawk's main mission in life is hunting mice and making little hawks, watching them is always captivating, at times astonishing.

They are fierce raptors, with the size, speed, vision, and talons to make a living nailing mice in fields. Red-tailed hawk and sparrow hawk, also called the American kestrel, are abundant in rural areas wherever there are mice.

That is why many people see their first hawk while driving up and down Interstate 5 in California, between the Grapevine in the Tehachapis on north past Redding all the way to the Oregon border. The birds often sit on fence posts, right along the highway next to fields. Whenever the weather is bad and I can't fly my small plane, I end up cruising I-5, and looking for hawks is a side show with random but often fortuitous results.

A hovering, circling hawk indicates it has spotted a prospect and is zeroing in for a closer look. They have a remarkable ability to hover, circle, and dive, even in wind. If you see a hawk circling, watch closely because you will likely have a chance to see one of nature's most skilled predators in action. Hawks are built something like a fighter jet and have the ability to fold and lock their wings for tremendous power dives. The little mice in the field rarely know what hit them.

When the hawks are sitting on the fence posts, they might be surveying future prospects, digesting a recent meal, or, in some cases, preparing one for consumption. While watching with binoculars, I have seen hawks eat mice whole, head first (down the hatch, so to speak) with that tiny mouse tail disappearing with a quick suck and a slurp. If you find a hawk nest and

Hawks have a remarkable ability to hover, circle, and dive. They are built like fighter jets and can fold and lock their wings for tremendous power dives.

search the waste matter at the base of the tree, you can often pick apart the waste matter with a small stick and find mice skulls intact.

Just watching how a red-tailed hawk sits on its perch, even if it's just a fence post, presents an image of regal grace and noble power. They just seem to know that they are born with the right stuff.

Yet one of the tragic periods of idiocy in California was in the 1940s and 1950s, when many species, including mice, were subject to a large-scale poisoning. Remove the mice, and you remove the food for the hawks. In turn, it won't be long before the hawks are gone, as well as other species that depend on them as a food source, such as owls, coyotes, badgers, and other flesh-eaters. There is also the chance that a hawk could eat poisoned mice and get poisoned itself, though most hawks prefer catching live mice, not scavenging dead ones.

red-tailed hawk

One of the most dramatic scenes imaginable came one day when I was watching these two doves, perched about a foot apart on a deck railing, with the male dove cooing and making eyes, while the female dove was ignoring him. Sound familiar? No matter what that male dove did, a little hop, a twist of the head, and the most romantic "coo-coo" you ever heard, she just sat there, unmoved.

Right then, out of nowhere, this red-tailed hawk shot out of the sky and picked off that male dove with its talons, and, just as fast, was gone with him. The entire incident was over in just a second or two.

The female dove, still sitting there, didn't even notice her suitor had disappeared. After a few seconds, she did turn, look over, and then looked back. Another 20 seconds later, she took off, as if nothing had happened.

I swear there's a lesson there.

Biologists' Notes

RED-TAILED HAWK *(Buteo jamaicensis)*

Hawks belong to the order of birds known as raptors, or birds of prey, and are carnivores, or meat eaters. They have strong hooked beaks, their feet have three toes pointed forward and one turned back, and their claws, or talons, are long, curved, and very sharp. The prey is killed with the long talons, and if the prey is too large to swallow whole, it is torn to bite-sized bits with the hawk's beak.

ANIMAL	Hawk, Red-Tailed
SPECIES	*Buteo jamaicensis*
TYPE	bird
STATUS	OK
SEE ALSO	Eagles, Falcon, Osprey

Hawks can be divided into three different groups: the accipiters, the falcons, and the buteos.

Accipiters include the sharp-shinned hawk, Cooper's hawk, and goshawk. These have long tails and short rounded wings that enable the hawks to dart through and around trees in pursuit of birds, their principal prey food. Typically, they fly low with a series of rapid wingbeats followed by a brief period of sailing, then more series of wingbeats. Accipiters are associated with brush and timbered areas.

The falcons prefer open country. They are the prairie falcon; peregrine falcon, or duck hawk; merlin, or pigeon hawk; and the little American kestrel, or sparrow hawk.

Because of its abundance and wild distribution, the red-tailed hawk is most commonly seen in California. Its shrill, rasping cry attracts attention as it circles high overhead or perches on a dead limb in a tree near the road.

The adult is the more easily identified, for when it leaves its perch on slow, measured wingbeats, or turns when soaring overhead, the broad, rounded tail shows a rich, russet red, hence the name. The red-tailed is our largest hawk. As with most raptors, the female is nearly one-third larger than the male and may have a wingspan up to 56 inches.

Adult red-tails may be found in California throughout the year. Although not truly migratory, they do adjust seasonally by flying to areas with abundant prey. There is conclusive evidence now that 85-90% of their diet is made up of small rodents. They take an occasional bird and infrequently snakes and other small reptiles, but for the most part they live on rabbits, ground squirrels, gophers, and other small rodents.

Mating and nest building begin in early spring, usually in March. This is accompanied by spectacular aerial displays by both male and female hawks. Circling and soaring to great heights, they fold their wings and plummet to tree top level, repeating this display as mamy as five or six times.

The nest sites are from 35 to 75 feet up in the forks of large trees. The nest is large, flat, and shallow and made of sticks and twigs one half inch in diameter. Both birds assist in nest construction. Nest sites may be used from year to year, since there is strong evidence that the hawks mate for life. If the old nest is wind damaged, layers of new nesting material are added each year.

The female usually lays two dull white to bluish-white eggs marked with a variety of irregular reddish spots and splotches. Incubation takes 28 days and is done almost entirely by the female. During this period the male hunts for both of them, bringing her food to the nest. The young when hatched are covered with white down. They grow slowly and require much food, so both parents are kept busy bringing it to them. They remain in the nest for 48 days. During the last 10 days or so the young, appearing nearly as large as the parent birds, will practice flapping their wings and balancing in the wind on the edge of the nest, readying themselves for the days when they will launch themselves into the air.

AMERICAN KESTREL *(Falco sparverius)*

The kestrel is also known as the sparrow hawk. It is the smallest of all North American birds of prey. It is nearly the same size as the pigeon hawk (also known as a merlin), but a glance at the ruddy back and tail of the American kestrel quickly distinguishes the two.

The sparrow hawk is only 11 inches long and has narrow pointed wings. The unusual head markings and bright chestnut upper parts are in sharp contrast with the blue-gray

ANIMAL	Hawk, Kestrel
SPECIES	*Falco sparverius*
TYPE	bird
STATUS	OK
SEE ALSO	Eagles, Falcon, Osprey

American kestrel

wing coverts and mark the sparrow hawk. The small size and bright colors make it easily recognizable.

The American kestrel, or sparrow hawk, is the smallest of all North American birds of prey.

The sparrow hawk, unlike other birds of prey, has thrived with the development of the land. It is a friendly, sociable bird and is fond of perching along roads and near dwellings. When flying, it sometimes soars, but its narrow pointed wings are more suited to rapid flight. When a mouse or grasshopper is sighted, it often hovers on quick-beating wings before it drops on its prey.

The sparrow hawk is the only North American bird of prey that does not build or use an open nest. It wants a cover overhead and prefers holes in trees. In treeless areas along the coast it uses natural burrows or cavities in the cliffs. It is the only one of our hawks that will use a birdhouse as a nesting site. Just before nesting, the male and female spend a great deal of time together near the nesting site. During courtship the male puts on a noisy and spectacular aerial display, returning each time to his mate, and sometimes he presents her with a morsel of food.

Where to see hawks and kestrels

ARASTRADERO PRESERVE, IN SANTA CLARA COUNTY

CHAW'SE INDIAN GRINDING ROCK STATE HISTORIC PARK, IN AMADOR COUNTY

DEVIL'S PUNCHBOWL NATURAL AREA, IN LOS ANGELES COUNTY

GOLDEN GATE NATIONAL RECREATION AREA (HAWK HILL), IN MARIN COUNTY

GRAY LODGE WILDLIFE AREA, IN BUTTE COUNTY

KERN NATIONAL WILDLIFE REFUGE, IN KERN COUNTY

LAKE SOLANO COUNTY PARK, IN SOLANO COUNTY

POINT PINOLE REGIONAL SHORELINE, IN CONTRA COSTA COUNTY

SWEETWATER MARSH NATIONAL WILDLIFE REFUGE, IN SAN DIEGO COUNTY

VENTANA WILDERNESS, IN MONTEREY COUNTY

Other places to see hawks and kestrels

NOTE: The I-5 corridor through the Central Valley offers many fleeting views of hawks perched on telephone poles and highway signs.

ABALONE COVE ECOLOGICAL RESERVE, IN LOS ANGELES COUNTY

ANCIENT BRISTLECONE PINE FOREST, IN INYO COUNTY

CHICO GENETIC RESOURCE CENTER, IN BUTTE COUNTY

COACHELLA VALLEY PRESERVE, IN RIVERSIDE COUNTY

COSUMNES RIVER PRESERVE, IN SACRAMENTO COUNTY

DEL VALLE RESERVOIR AND REGIONAL PARK, IN ALAMEDA COUNTY

EASTMAN LAKE, IN MADERA COUNTY

EATON CANYON NATURAL AREA, IN LOS ANGELES COUNTY

JOSEPH D. GRANT COUNTY PARK, IN SANTA CLARA COUNTY

LAKE BERRYESSA, IN NAPA COUNTY

MOUNT DIABLO STATE PARK, IN CONTRA COSTA COUNTY

SHASTA VALLEY STATE WILDLIFE AREA, IN SISKIYOU COUNTY

STANISLAUS RIVER PARKS, IN STANISLAUS COUNTY

SUCCESS LAKE, IN TULARE COUNTY

The female lays from four to six eggs. They may be nearly all creamy white or so speckled with brown to red spots that the background color is nearly covered. She starts to sit as soon as one egg is laid, and the young may hatch several days apart. It takes from 28 to 30 days for all the eggs to hatch.

It is nearly three or four weeks before the young leave the nest to perch nearby and to start their flying lessons. Both parents feed the young for another week, and then the first lesson in hunting is given. The parent bird brings some food, but, instead of feeding the baby as before, she drops the food in midair, giving a quick cry of killy! killy! killy! The young bird, thus encouraged, leaps from the perch and pursues the morsel to the ground. As soon as the food is clutched in its talons, the parent, with a harsh call, forces the young bird to fly to a nearby perch to finish his meal. The parent bird spends some time teaching the young how to hunt before the family breaks up and the young finally go out on their own.

Heron, Great Blue

Timing can be everything in love, and so it is for great blue herons.

Look for them in mid-summer, fall, or winter, and well, you might get to see them fly around a bit, maybe even fish a little or poke around the mud flats in their daily routines. But in late winter, spring, and early summer? Well, let me tell you about the birds and the bees. Especially the birds. Especially great blue herons, and their neighborly pals, great egrets and snowy egrets.

The feature show is romance for these huge, beautiful birds, from the first shy calls to kicking junior out of the nest. In the middle comes courtship, building a

ANIMAL	Heron, Great Blue
SPECIES	*Ardea herodias*
TYPE	bird
STATUS	OK

home, making some babies, hatching them, then sending them off for future education.

You see, blue herons don't nest in the marshes they frequent so much of the year looking for food. Blue herons typically nest high up in large trees, and the entire process is a wondrous series of events to observe. Spotting scopes or binoculars will provide a glimpse of this inner world.

Blue herons look like something right out of *Jurassic Park*, like pterodactyls lifting off with their huge, labored wingbeats, their wingspans ranging to seven feet. Herons often nest within close range of the great egret, snow white and thin, and about four feet tall. Its cousin, the snowy

great blue heron

Looking like pterodactyls from *Jurassic Park*, blue herons lift off with labored beats on seven-foot-wingspan.

egret, is also pure white, but about half the size.

The birds' courtship starts with nervous glances from afar and then advances to a few tentative squawks. If you watch this closely, you'll see there are times they just seem to look at each other for a spell, as if they are trying to figure out if this is the real deal.

Eventually, somebody has to make a move, or nothing happens, right? End of movie. What often occurs here is that these birds will make a cautious overture, with egrets, for instance, often offering a single twig to its potential mate, as if asking, "Do you wanna?" If there is no response, well, no deal. But if the female gets a twig of her own and offers it in return, the silent answer is, "Yes, I wanna," and off they go to make a nest, often starting with those first two twigs.

As spring arrives, there are plenty of "I wannas."

When the herons' young hatchlings are in the nests, ma and pa heron often will make trips to nearby lagoons or wetlands for food. Upon return of a parent, Junior will grab its beak, which triggers a motor response, where the undigested goodies are regurgitated all over the nest. What could be more fun for Junior and his brothers and sisters than to pounce on the treats and gobble them up as if it's their first meal. Well, in some cases, it IS their first meal.

By the way, what's for lunch?

As spring progresses, and the young birds gain size, strength, and feathers, the viewing evolves to another tradition that might be called "Bon Voyage" or "Goodbye Mabeline."

Starting in mid-June, you can start to see the young birds standing in the nests, practicing stroking their wings, as if simulating the flying experience. They are already big, and it is kind of like watching Mark McGwire take practice swings in the on-deck circle. If you're lucky, you may even see them stray out on a limb.

But then they look down. They see the ground down there about 100 feet, and figure, "Nah, back into the nest. Say, Mom, when's dinner?"

At first, mom puts up with it. Then she gets a little irritated. Then she gets angry, and it's time for the heave-ho.

In late June, the adult herons often just kick the kids right out of the nest with a push. What the youngsters quickly discover is that gravity really is a law. They have about 10 seconds to figure out how to fly before the ground suddenly arrives. Since bird skeletons are extremely rare on the ground, that must be enough time to figure out the correct response.

Wish my kids could learn that fast.

Biologists' Notes

The heron family is worldwide in distribution and consists of many different subspecies of herons, egrets, and night herons. They probably originated in the warmer climates where most of them occur and where they are found in the greatest numbers. They do not exist in the far north or in Antarctica.

The great blue heron, *Ardea herodias,* sometimes called the blue crane, is the largest in size and is the most widely distributed of the herons of North America.

The principal diet of the great blue heron is fish of various kinds, as well as frogs and some aquatic insects. It fishes both day and night using two different methods: still hunting, in which it silently waits for a fish to swim near, or by stalking with slow measured steps until it sees its quarry. A swift stroke of its well-trained bill either impales or seizes the fish. If the fish is small it is tossed in the air to be caught and swallowed head first. If it is

Where to see great blue heron

AUDUBON CANYON RANCH, IN MARIN COUNTY

BOLSA CHICA STATE BEACH TO NEWPORT BAY, IN ORANGE COUNTY

GRASSLAND RESOURCE CONSERVATION DISTRICT, IN MERCED COUNTY

HUMBOLDT BAY NATIONAL WILDLIFE REFUGE, IN HUMBOLDT COUNTY

LAKE HENSHAW, IN SAN DIEGO COUNTY

MERCED NATIONAL WILDLIFE REFUGE, IN MERCED COUNTY

SACRAMENTO NATIONAL WILDLIFE REFUGES COMPLEX, IN BUTTE, COLUSA, GLENN, SUTTER, AND TEHAMA COUNTIES

SHASTA LAKE NATIONAL RECREATION AREA, IN SHASTA COUNTY

WADDELL CREEK, IN SANTA CRUZ COUNTY

too large it may be carried to shore, or beaten on the water and then carried to shore, where it is torn into bite-sized pieces.

When hunting on land, the heron's diet may include lizards, snakes, some birds, and small mammals such as shrews, mice, and gophers, which it secures by stalking. Slowly and carefully, with almost a stately tread, it will move across a field and from a crouch it will strike quickly to either seize or stab its victim. If feeding on grasshoppers, it will stand in one place for as long as two hours and let the grasshoppers come to within striking range.

The heron is exceedingly shy, wary, and difficult to approach. When forced to fly, as when frightened, there is a moment of awkwardness as it scrambles into the air, a tangle of long neck, legs, and vigorously beating wings, accompanied by discordant croaking. When undisturbed it starts more gracefully. By leaning forward with neck extended, it takes a few steps and with a few powerful wing strokes it is airborne. When underway, its flight is strong and sustained by the long, slow strokes of its great black-tipped wings. With its neck folded between its shoulders the long legs are extended to the rear to act as rudders.

Throughout the northern portions of its range, great blue herons are migratory. They move south to escape the winter's snow and ice. In the Sacramento and San Joaquin Valleys and along the coast they may be observed, usually alone, along California's many waterways, in pastures, rice fields, and fenced areas throughout central and southern California.

In the spring, prior to nesting time, males and females will congregate in some remote area and go through an elaborate ritual of choosing mates (see above).

Herons choose a variety of nesting sites in different portions of their wide breeding range, but most herons are gregarious and prefer nesting in closely congested areas. These areas, known as rookeries, may have just a few pairs or hundreds. The rookery may be in a swampy area, along one of California's many waterways, or in the huge oaks out in the middle of the great Central Valley. After a nesting site is chosen, other herons converge on the area and begin to build their nests in or near the tops of the trees. A rookery may be used for many years.

The female normally lays a clutch of four large pale green eggs. The eggs are hatched in 28 days. At first the juvenile heron are feeble and helpless; later they become ungainly and awkward. As soon as a parent bird is seen or heard returning, there is a great excitement and they stand up to clamor and wrestle for their food.

Plumage hunters nearly eradicated herons and egrets in the late 1800s. These magnificent birds are now entirely protected and have been restored to abundant population levels.

Horned Lizards

Horned lizards are such strange looking little guys that they have captured the affection of many in Southern California. In fact, these fellows are one of the best examples of how a creature can be literally loved to death.

Everybody is enamored with the "horned toad," as so many like to call it. They are actually lizards, but the squat body and those prominent little horns make them look like a toad with horns. They also have this peculiar look in their eyes that creates an aura that captivates a lot of people. Their appearance is so peculiar that many people become fascinated with them.

ANIMAL	Horned Lizards
SPECIES	*Phrynosoma* spp.
TYPE	Reptile
STATUS	OK

And that's when the problems start. Many people want them as pets, keeping them in terrariums at home. This is illegal, but that has not stopped prolific black market trade at some pet stores in the L.A. Basin. To keep a horned lizard as a pet is a misdemeanor punishable by a maximum of one year in jail and a $1,000 fine, and it is a felony to collect and sell them. If you know of anybody breaking this game law, or any other, call the Department of Fish and Game's toll-free poacher tip line at 1-888-DFG CALTIP (888-334-2258).

Knowing that, I'll tell you how to find them—just to look! They are most abundant in the state and national parks set in the desert, where it is illegal to disturb, pick up, or remove anything, even a rock. In addition, if you take a horned lizard from a national park, you not only can get the Department of Fish and Game on your case for taking it home, but it's a federal offense to take it out of the park. That's two crimes for the price of one.

What the horned lizards sometimes do on cool nights is emerge from their hiding places and hang out on the edge of asphalt roads, which will retain the heat of the day. It is quite fun to explore the parks at night with a flashlight, trying to find them on the roads, like a treasure hunt. Just don't touch. Don't try to pick them up. And don't take them home. If you were to break any of these laws of nature, the horrible karma you would be inflicting upon yourself would likely ensure you of an eternity in a rattlesnake pit.

During the day, horned lizards are very difficult to find. The coloration is such that they blend readily into their surroundings, making them invisible to most untrained eyes.

After feeding, and when the ground temperature becomes too hot, they seek the shade of a shrub and partially conceal themselves. There they will spend the remainder of the day. In the evening while it is still warm, they often "dig in" for the night. This is a curious process. They stick their nose in the sand like the blade of a plow and wriggle forward to create a short furrow. After flattening the body, they use the spiny border of their sides in a shovel-like fashion to scoop and dig their way into the sand. Sometimes they bury themselves three or four inches, and other times they just leave the top of the head and eyes exposed.

To the uninitiated, their dragon-like appearance is quite fierce. After a while, you realize they're not so fierce after all, and actually cute little gents. In time, you can become quite enamored with them. Just look, don't touch. They are wild creatures, not pets.

Biologists' Notes

Of all the North American lizards, the horned lizards are most distinct. They have very wide, flattened toad-shaped bodies. The tail is broad at the base and short. In most species, the back of the head and temples are crowned with a prominent row of sharp pointed horns. The tail and sides are fringed with sharp spines. On some species the sides are adorned with a double fringe of spines. On the back there are rows of short conical spines.

The back and head are soft and desert gray. The markings are in pastel shades of tan, brown, reddish, or yellow. The underparts are pale yellowish gray. The overall colors are generally close to the predominant color of the soil. Color changes from light to dark (or reverse) can occur in a few minutes.

Horned lizards bury themselves in the sand in the fall and emerge in the spring when the sun warms the sand to a certain temperature.

The horned lizards are found only in the western portions of the United States and in Mexico. There are 14 recognized species.

horned lizard

They range from Arkansas to the Pacific Coast, and from British Columbia south to Guatemala. Four species, all in the genus *Phrynosoma,* occur in California: coast, desert, short-horned, and flat-tailed horned lizards.

These lizards are creatures of hot, dry, sandy habitats. Some of the species inhabit the desert proper where the sun, beating on the arid landscape, produces ground heat that is almost unendurable to humans. Others enter mountainous areas and are found as high as 10,000 feet in elevation.

Regardless of where they occur, there is a similarity in their habits. In the fall, they hibernate by burying themselves in the sand. They emerge in the spring when the sun's rays have reached a certain temperature. The first few hours of the day are spent basking, usually flattened against a rock or on a slanting soil so its back is exposed to the sun. At times while warming up, they may flatten and tilt their bodies toward the sun to obtain maximum radiation.

As soon as their body temperature rises to a certain degree, they commence to forage for food. As the heat of the day progresses, they become more active. They feed on slow-moving, ground-dwelling insects: spiders, ants, sow bugs, an occasional tick, and even items as large as butterfly and sphinx moth larvae. Ants seem to be their major food item. A horned lizard does not pursue its victim hastily, like some lizards, but poises over it and methodically takes it in, in toad-like fashion, with a flick of its long, sticky tongue. The slow motion ceases if disturbed, for the horned lizard will flee as rapidly as a startled mouse. The coast horned lizard's has some well-known defense tricks include inflating itself, biting, and spraying blood out its eyes. Now *that's* the magic of nature.

Mating occurs in late April, peaks in June, and stops abruptly in July. Egg laying starts a few weeks later, usually in late July and early August. The farther north the later the eggs are laid. In some species the eggs are retained within the body, so the young are hatched just before, during, or shortly after laying. Others bury the eggs in the sand, where they require several weeks for further development before they hatch. The eggshells are white and flexible and average about one half inch in diameter. The number of eggs varies with the species. Some have from 10 to 30 eggs with an average of about 15.

The young are called hatchlings. They average seven-eighths of an inch to one and one-eighth inches long, snout to vent. The young have been observed to bury themselves in the sand immediately upon hatching. Hatchlings receive no parental care, so when they emerge, they start to hunt for food. For reptiles, they are cute; the horns on their head are appar-

Where to see horned lizards

AFTON CANYON, IN SAN BERNARDINO COUNTY

COACHELLA VALLEY PRESERVE, IN RIVERSIDE COUNTY

DEVIL'S PUNCHBOWL NATURAL AREA, IN LOS ANGELES COUNTY

PINNACLES NATIONAL MONUMENT, IN SAN BENITO COUNTY

PROVIDENCE MOUNTAINS STATE RECREATION AREA, IN SAN BERNARDINO COUNTY

Other places to see horned lizards

DESERT TORTOISE NATURAL AREA, IN KERN COUNTY

JOSHUA TREE NATIONAL PARK, IN RIVERSIDE AND SAN BERNARDINO COUNTIES

LIVING DESERT, IN RIVERSIDE COUNTY

PALM TO PINES SCENIC BYWAY TOUR, IN RIVERSIDE COUNTY

SANTA ROSA PLATEAU ECOLOGICAL RESERVE, IN RIVERSIDE COUNTY

ent, although the rest of their skin, while well marked, is relatively smooth. They grow most rapidly in late summer and early spring when there is an abundance of food. There is no evidence that they reproduce the first year, but they are classed young adults by the end of the second summer and probably reach full growth in three years. Some species reach a snout-to-vent length of six inches. Most species are less than five inches in length.

Jays

Jays used to bug the heck out of me, but after being adopted by this one baby Steller's jay I named Joey, I decided that they aren't such bad fellows after all.

Jays are a prominent member of California's wildlife family, of course. They can be found at nearly all places where there are people, especially in parks with picnic sites, campgrounds, and natural rest spots on trail. And that's the trouble.

In one succession of trips to several state parks to research my hiking book, all I would have to do is stop, sit on a rock, pull out my trail lunch, and here they would come— always begging, loud, persistent, and no matter what you'd do, they would not go away. In this situation, they are cute for about 10 seconds. If you make a mistake and give one a peanut or something, then

ANIMAL	Jays
SPECIES	Steller's - *Cyanocitta stelleri* Scrub - *Aphelocoma californica*
TYPE	bird
STATUS	OK
SEE ALSO	Magpie, Raven

you will shortly be in for the full onslaught, where a few squawks will bring every jay from miles around to seek a handout. Finally, they drive you out.

Sound familiar? You ain't lyin' that sounds familiar.

Then one day, I was having some firewood stacked at my mountain cabin, and there was a knock on the door. The two boys stacking the firewood looked up at me, cradling a baby bird in their hands.

"We found it on the ground," one said.

"We didn't know what to do, so we thought we'd bring it to you for you to raise," added the other.

Well, this is not the best solution, I explained. And we walked to the edge of forest where the baby bird had been found, then placed it back on the ground.

"Now, watch what happens," I explained, and then led the boys away to a hiding spot.

A moment later, the momma jay came out of nowhere, hopping about, and then on the ground, led its baby to safety in the brush. Apparently it had been kicked out of the nest but wasn't ready to fly.

Well, the next week I looked out to my homemade bird feeder, and to my surprise, saw what appeared to be these same two birds, the mother with junior, pecking away. For the next two months, every morning just after dawn, I'd look out at the bird feeder and see them. Week by week, I watched that little jay get its color, develop a crest, and double in size into a more mature bird.

Then one morning, after having returned from a hike from Yosemite to Tahoe, I was awakened by this pecking at the sliding glass door that led to an upstairs deck outside my bedroom. First I tried to ignore it. But the pecking not only kept on but was supplemented by squawking. Well, like anybody, I know a jay squawk when I hear one. I finally pulled myself out of bed, opened the blinds, and there, pecking away at the window, was Joey, while momma jay was perched on the railing, squawking.

My first response is that the situation was not only wrong, but my own fault for feeding a wild creature and promoting its semi-dependence on me for food. But then I remembered those two boys, how they first held that baby jay in their hands, and, yep, how I wanted it to survive—and how thrilling it was when it appeared at my feeder, and the satisfaction I had taken in watching it grow up.

Jays are part of the crow family, and, like crows, they are a noisy bunch. When nesting, however, they are silent and flit like shadows through the trees. They lay from three to six beautifully marked eggs, the color variations of which may exceed that of any other bird in America.

It is episodes like these that make bird feeding the number one wildlife activity in North America.

scrub jay

Biologists' Notes

The jays are one branch of the crow family, but unlike crows, which are black, jays are brightly colored in various shades of blue. Although there are several species and subspecies of jays in California, the two that are most familiar and most easily recognized are the Steller's jay *(Cyanocitta stelleri)* and the Western scrub jay *(Aphelocoma californica)*.

Different races of those bold and impudent fellows are abundant throughout California except in the higher mountains and desert regions. Nature students can tell them apart by size, color, and habitat, but to the casual observer they are all blue jays. Technically, though, "blue jay" is the name for jays east of the Rockies.

The Steller's jay inhabits the higher forests of the Sierra and Cascade Mountains and the northwest Pacific regions. Although more shy and retiring than the scrub jay, it is easily identified by the large saucy crest and the dark blue to sooty black of its head and neck and the upper portions of its back.

Where to see jays

CACHUMA LAKE RECREATION AREA, IN SANTA BARBARA COUNTY

CUYAMACA RANCHO STATE PARK, IN SAN DIEGO COUNTY

EATON CANYON NATURAL AREA, IN LOS ANGELES COUNTY

MOUNT SAN JACINTO STATE PARK AND STATE WILDERNESS, IN RIVERSIDE COUNTY

MOUNT TAMALPAIS STATE PARK, IN MARIN COUNTY

Other places to see jays

BIG MORONGO CANYON PRESERVE, IN SAN BERNARDINO COUNTY

JOSEPH D. GRANT COUNTY PARK, IN SANTA CLARA COUNTY

PALM TO PINES SCENIC BYWAY TOUR, IN RIVERSIDE COUNTY

SHASTA LAKE NATIONAL RECREATION AREA, IN SHASTA COUNTY

SILVERWOOD LAKE STATE RECREATION AREA, IN SAN BERNARDINO

SMITH RIVER NATIONAL RECREATION AREA, SIX RIVERS NATIONAL FOREST, IN DEL NORTE COUNTY

TOPANGA STATE PARK, IN LOS ANGELES COUNTY

YOSEMITE NATIONAL PARK, IN MARIPOSA COUNTY

The jays as a group are a noisy bunch. They have raucous squawks. Their flight from tree to tree is at a relaxed speed, and they are easily observed.

In the spring after they have paired and are nesting, they are silent and seldom raise their voices above a whisper as they flit like shadows through the trees. The jays on the whole are notorious thieves, and like thieves, when they are searching for a nest to rob or stealing almonds or cherries, they slip quickly and quietly through the low shrubs.

The jay's nest is rather bulky. The construction is of small twigs, but the cup of the nest is well defined and nearly always is lined partly with the hair of some small animal. The nest of a Steller's jay may be from 10 to 50 feet up on a limb of a fir tree. The scrub jay's nest is well hidden, usually in brush or shrubbery within six feet of the ground.

They lay from three to six beautifully marked eggs, the color variations of which may exceed that of any other bird in America. The male assists in the nest building, but it is not known for certain if he helps in sitting on the eggs. The young birds are hatched in 14 to 16 days and within another week are able to leave the nest. They follow the parent birds for some time, probably to learn the habits of other birds, when the cherries are ripe, which nests to rob, and all the other nefarious little tricks that jays seem to know.

Killdeer

The killdeer's shrill call, its ability to fly at high speeds, including at night, and its great range make encounters with them an interesting, friendly, and common experience.

They can be seen in the coastal foothills, in farmer's fields, in deep canyons along rivers, and the edge of desert, from the Oregon border to Mexico. When you least expect it, killdeer will be there, as if they are showing off for you, darting about and calling. Each sighting offers something special.

At one meadow in the coastal foothills, I used to see killdeer nearly every night of summer. By day, they would be nowhere to

ANIMAL	Killdeer
SPECIES	*Charadrius vociferus*
TYPE	bird
STATUS	OK

killdeer

Killdeer can run five miles per hour, one of the few birds has developed ground speed as well as flying skills. Killdeer parents are noted for using the old "broken-wing trick" to lure intruders away from the nest.

be seen. By night, with the fog encroaching, I would take my dog for a walk, and the killdeer would start flying. They are like miniature fighter jets, capable of flying 35 mph, typically in a scattered group, not in formation like the Blue Angels but loosely organized. They seemed to enjoy taunting me, flying about in a swirl, with that piercing call shooting through the night.

Among birds, this is very unusual. Many birds do not fly at night. But there is nothing typical about the killdeer, except in their abundant numbers that make sightings of them common for many wildlife observers.

Another anomaly about the killdeer is that they can run five miles per hour, one of the few birds with flying skills that have developed ground speed as well. The reason, I believe, is because they often nest in fields, on the ground, not in trees. When facing a potential problem, such as an invasive cow, they start by running and hiding. If the cow keeps coming, the killdeer will then rise up and fly into the face of the startled intruder. I've seen this, and it is quite a show, watching this relatively small bird scare off a giant cow.

Once the young hatch, another protective maneuver for which killdeer parents are noted is the "old broken-wing trick." When a threatening creature comes too close to the nest, the adult killdeer will depart, calling repeatedly, loud and shrill, attracting attention to itself, and then drag a wing on the ground as if it is broken and the bird is in great distress. In turn, the intruder will be decoyed away from the nest, typically without even knowing how close it was to an easy lunch. Get this: Once the predator has been led away, a sudden, miraculous recovery occurs, and the killdeer takes to air, sometimes even divebombing the invader for spite. If it could talk, it would then shout, "Gotcha!"

Many people who enjoy the outdoors like watching killdeer. My favorite place to see them in action is in river canyons. On multi-day rafting or canoe trips, when we pull up for camp at a sandbar on the far side of a bend in the river, there have been many pleasurable evenings watching killdeer.

One of the most satisfying ways to end a day on the river is to finish dinner, get the camp clean-up finished and gear stowed, and then at dusk, sit against a rock and just watch the river run past while the killdeer are flying and calling. At the bottom of steep canyons, the calls can echo across the water and against the rock walls. Even now, as I write this, I can hear that sound.

Biologists' Notes

The killdeer is a member of the plover family and as such is classified as a shorebird.

The earliest mention of plovers is in the writings of Aristotle, who referred to them as "Charadrios; an inconspicuous waterbird." But the killdeer is not quite that retiring. At the first hint of danger, it will run ahead of or fly around an intruder—one or two birds ever circling and warning one and all with loud piping, "Killdeer! Killdeer! Killdeer!" This call and a long trilling note made when displaying or fighting have earned the killdeer the scientific name, *Charadrius vociferus*.

It is also called field plover, noisy plover, and chattering plover.

It is the size of a robin and its body plumage is gray-brown above, shading to bright orange on the lower back, rump, and tail coverts. It has a white belly, chest, and neck with two black stripes across the chest, while its tail has a black band tipped with white. All this, a slender black bill,

Where to see killdeer

Anderson Marsh State Historic Park, in Lake County

Big Basin Redwoods State Park, in Santa Cruz County

Bolinas Lagoon, in Marin County

Grassland Resource Conservation District, in Merced County

Harper Lake, in San Bernardino County

Humboldt Bay National Wildlife Refuge, in Humboldt County

Las Gallinas Wildlife Ponds, in Marin County

Lower Klamath National Wildlife Refuge, in Siskiyou County

Mattole Recreation Site, in Humboldt County

Mono Lake, Inyo National Forest, in Mono County

Morro Bay State Park, in San Luis Obispo County

Point Lobos State Reserve, in Monterey County

Torrey Pines State Reserve/Los Penaquitos Marsh, in San Diego County

and straw-colored legs and feet make it a handsome bird. The sexes are alike in appearance.

Found in the United States from Maine to the Pacific Ocean, the killdeer lives in open meadows, on agricultural lands, in rolling foothills, or in flat, semi-arid areas, even many miles from water.

Although most plovers are migratory, here again the killdeer asserts its independence. When it does migrate, it usually does so in small, irregular bunches or flocks, almost never in any formation as seen in other shore-birds. Its winter migration can be from Canada south through the Pacific Coast of North America, the Midwest, and the western fringe of the Atlantic states to Bermuda, the Greater Antilles, upper ranges of Venezuela, and the northwest section of Peru.

Breeding can take place from upper British Columbia, Ontario, and southern Quebec all the way to Florida, the Bahamas, and across central Mexico to the tip of Baja California.

The nest is usually built in a slight depression on bare ground, lined with grass, small twigs, and pebbles. Four, rarely five, buff-colored eggs spotted with black and brown are laid. The eggs are usually arranged with the smaller ends together in the center of the nest. If disturbed, the eggs are quickly rearranged to their original positions.

The incubation period is 24 days with both parents sharing the brooding. Their plumage readily identifies the chicks as killdeers, except the chicks have only one black chest band, the second appearing after subsequent molts. As soon as their down feathers are dry, the young are able to pick up their own food from the ground. The chicks stay with the parents until they learn to fly, in about two and a half weeks. In some areas, and under favorable circumstances, two broods in one season are not uncommon.

Killdeer are often seen following a farmer's plow to feed on uncovered invertebrates and insects. Almost any small thing that moves is eaten, including earthworms, grubs, beetles, crayfish, grasshoppers, caterpillars, ants, snails, scorpions, dragonflies, caddis flies, centipedes, spiders, mosquitoes, and small crabs. When feeding, the family group will run a short distance, stop and seem to look and listen intently, then stab at food on the ground with their bills.

Kingfisher, Belted

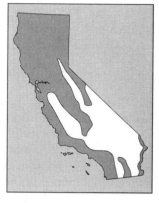

The first time I saw a kingfisher, I knew it had to be a fisherman, just by the way it acted toward me.

When I paddled my canoe near its apparent fishing spot, it made its displeasure known like any fisherman who feels another angler is horning in, letting out this raucous, rattling cry. In kingfisher language, it meant, "This is my spot. Get the heck out of here." Such was my introduction. Over the years, as I watched the behavior of different kingfishers, I realized that each kingfisher patrols a well-defined fishing territory and they don't take kindly to rude behavior like an outsider moving in on the action.

ANIMAL	Kingfisher, Belted
SPECIES	*Ceryle alcyon*
TYPE	bird
STATUS	OK

The kingfisher has a striking appearance, usually recognized by most with even a remote interest in wildlife. Its body shape is roughly like a large jay, about 10 inches to a foot tall, with a blue-gray head, wings, back, and tail feathers. Its head is crested, and its chest and neck are white, as if a white belt has been painted is around its neck, hence the name. But what is

belted kingfisher

The kingfisher's beak is long and pointed, like needle-nose pliers, well adapted to picking up small fish. Kingfisher parents dig a deep burrow that extends inward and slightly upward some three to eight feet. The tunnel ends in a chamber in which a sparse nest is built.

most striking is not that white belt but the beak. It's a real honker for such a small bird.

That beak is long enough to take in small fish, yet pointy enough, like needle-nose pliers, to pick up small tidbits. For this fisherman, it's the perfect combination.

That is because kingfisher have a diet made up primarily of small fish. The heavy beak and the form of its head is ideal for use in its deep plunges. The stocky build allows the kingfisher to withstand the shock of frequent dives for food.

What kingfisher like to do is land or perch on a dead tree or leafless limb that offers an unobstructed view of the water. If you see this, get out the binoculars and watch closely. The kingfisher is the only bird that will dive for fish from a perch; other birds, such as osprey and pelican, for instance, conduct their searches while flying, typically hovering and circling. So with binoculars to eyes and a little persistence, you'll be able to see the kingfisher drop from its perch and head straight into the water, typically hunting for two- to four-inch fish.

Keep watching. It then heads right back to its perch, and then will thump its prey on the perch a few times, then toss it into the air to deftly catch and swallow it head first.

No foolin'. No wonder the kingfisher squawks whenever I paddle into its territory.

Biologists' Notes

The belted kingfisher *(Ceryle alcyon)* occurs in nearly all of North America, breeding from northern Alaska and Labrador southward to the southern border of the United States.

The kingfisher is essentially a fish-eating bird, so its haunts are naturally near bodies of water that contain an abundant supply of small fish. It is rather common along the seacoast and nearby estuaries, where it may be seen perched on a piling or pier watching for its prey.

They are solitary birds and like to fish alone, except during nesting season. The nest of the kingfisher is almost always in a deep burrow, a sandy clay, or a gravelly bank. Both the male and female dig the nest. They use their strong beaks to loosen the soil, and their little shovel-like feet to kick out the dirt. They seem to prefer a sheer bank or cliff near a favorite fishing ground, but sometimes they must go a long distance from water to find a suitable nesting site. The burrows are quite deep, extending inward and slightly upward for three to six or even eight feet. The tunnel ends in a chamber in which a sparse nest is built. Depending on the consistency of the soil, the pair might take from three days to three weeks to complete a suitable home. If undisturbed, they may use the same burrow each succeeding year, as it would only require a little housecleaning to prepare it for the new brood.

The female lays from six to 10 pure white eggs, the most common number being six or seven. The incubation period is from 23 to 24 days.

The overall form of the young looks terribly out of proportion, with the large, wobbly beak and head atop the skinny, unfeathered gangly bodies. They do not open their eyes for two weeks. They cling to each other, possibly for warmth, for the mother's legs are so short she can't stand over them to keep them warm. However, the nest cavity, deep in the earth, offers good protection from the weather.

Both parents are attentive to the hatchlings' needs in both feeding and keeping the nest clean. The food brought to the young for the first week is partly digested and regurgitated directly into the babies' mouths. After a week, the diet is graduated to tiny fish one or two inches in length. After a month, now fully feathered, the young will leave the nest and start practicing short, erratic flights between feedings.

At this time the parents begin to teach the babies to dive for their own fish. This is accomplished by bringing a small fish back to the nest, and, instead of giving it directly to one of the young birds, dropping it into the water. Eventually, one will make a dive for it, and thus the instruction begins. It takes only a few days until the lesson is complete, and within a week, the parents will abandon the babies. Within another week, the young birds will disperse and leave the area to find fishing territories of their own.

Lobster

You can't believe how hard it can be to catch a lobster. Or how easy it is to become a felon when making the attempt.

You might think that a five-pound lobster would be pretty easy to catch, especially if you were a skilled swimmer with scuba diving gear, that you could just swim right up and nab it. Nope. Not in the real world.

Let me tell you what does happen. Equipped with full scuba gear, you spot "the bug," as they are called by divers, and then start sneaking up on it. As you swim, it seems as if the lobster has no idea that you are in the same universe. About 15 feet away, your heart starts to pound. After all, there it is, right in front of you, yours for

ANIMAL	Lobster
SPECIES	*Panulirus interruptus*
TYPE	crustacean
STATUS	OK
SEE ALSO	Crayfish

the taking. As you reach out with your hand to finish the deed, the most amazing scene unfolds.

Just as you are about to grab it, that lobster will explode forward 25 to 50 feet, propelling itself with that giant tail, shooting away like a drag car at the starting line. For a second there, with such high hopes and zero results, you might feel like a groom left at the altar.

But then again, you can still see the lobster, and off you go in the chase. It again rockets off, this time with maybe two or three tail blasts, into cover, and it's goodbye. Never really loved her anyway, right? Yeah, suuure.

What makes lobster so desirable is the giant tail, of course, considered one of the most loved delicacies at a seafood restaurant, with the price to prove it. And lobsters didn't get a tail that big by letting scuba divers nab them. The lobster may have lousy vision but over the eons has evolved a remarkable ability to detect motion, then to blast off into oblivion to avoid getting caught.

So there is nothing easy about catching a lobster. In fact, there is an art to it among the few who successfully answer the challenge. Unfortunately, the difficulty of the feat also means that many will cheat and take short cuts. People who fish with hoop nets from piers, as well as sport divers and commercial fishers with traps, break the law in order to capture the prize shellfish.

California rock lobster

The spiny antennae and armored shell protect the lobster from smaller enemies, but as many as 10 lobsters have been found in the stomachs of larger fish such as the octopus or giant black sea bass. The lobster's eyes are set on the end of stalks and are compound, like those of an insect.

The small ones are a lot easier to catch, and the big ones are highly desirable, and so the problems start. Although limits for size and take are clearly written, many undersize lobsters are illegally kept, undersize meaning any lobster measuring less than 3.25 inches from the eye stalk sockets to the rear edge of the body shell, or carapace. In addition, many poachers will illegally tear the tail off and hide it, then dispose of the rest of the creature; this is called "tailing." At the Ocean Beach Pier in San Diego, Warden Mark Crossland of the Department of Fish and Game told me that he has found poachers hiding tails inside car seats, in backpacks, and in trash cans, under a plastic liner. "Lobsters bring out the larceny in people," he said.

The take of undersize lobsters, or "shorts" (tailed lobsters), has caused a significant decline in the population of the species. Lobsters are being taken before they have had a chance to spawn. At the same time, taking the rare giant ones, the 10-pounders and up, removes prolific spawners from the system.

The logic of game laws is that a resource is managed like a lucrative bank account; the public is allowed to take the annual interest but never cut into the principal. But poaching has cut deeply into that bank account, and, in the case of such a desirable species as lobster, there have been loans taken out on the future.

So maybe it's justice that nature has endowed this creature with such a remarkable ability to jettison itself away from its predators.

Biologists' Notes

Many species of lobsters live in the oceans of the world. Four species inhabit the waters along the west coast of the Americas, but only the California rock lobster *(Panulirus interruptus)* is found along our shores. Its range extends from San Luis Obispo County south, nearly to the tip of Baja California.

The rock lobster, a.k.a. spiny lobster, is easily distinguished from its cousin, the American lobster that inhabits the north Atlantic Ocean, by the absence of large claws and, as its name implies, by numerous forward-pointing spines on the carapace, the shell-like covering on the back.

The spiny lobster sports a pair of heavy spiny antennae that are long and sweeping, normally longer than the body. A second pair of short double-ended antennae extends from the area between the longer pair. The lobster's antennae and 10 legs are easily broken but in time regenerate themselves. This process enables the lobster to more easily escape from its enemies.

Two spots or false eyes are located just above the base of the short antenna of the spiny lobster. The real eyes are like tiny black beads set on the end of stalks. Each eye stalk is set beneath a long sharp spine that extends forward. The eyes are compound, like those of an insect, and are designed to detect the slightest movement. Creatures with this kind of eye are wary and quick to flee from their enemies.

The body color ranges from brick red to brown with greenish overtones; in nature it does not develop the bright orange coloration of the cooked lobsters seen in the market. The male attains the greatest size of any of the world's spiny lobsters. There are authentic records of bulls weighing over 26 pounds and reaches lengths of over two feet, excluding the antennae. However, lobsters over 10 pounds are now rare.

The tail has a segmented covering of shell-like material that ends with a fan of rounded fins. Folding across the abdomen are two rows of small leaf-like fins called swimmerettes. At the lower edge of each tail segment is a sharp spine that is capable of inflicting a nasty wound when the tail is

Where to see lobster

Cabrillo National Monument (tidepools), in San Diego County

Catalina Island, offshore from Los Angeles

Channel Islands, offshore from Ventura County

San Clemente Island, offshore from San Diego County

flexed, so care must be used when handling live lobsters. The best method is to grasp them firmly by the back, behind the spines that stick out over the eyes. Although they can be held barehanded, gloves are advisable.

Lobsters prefer to live in and near the kelp beds along the rocky shores and bottoms of the mainland and around the Channel Islands to depths of over 100 feet. The holes and crevices formed by the rocky bottoms and the kelp offer protection in which lobsters can move while feeding.

In shallow waters the lobsters move around more during the night. They climb slowly over and around the rocks in search of food. They can walk forward, backward, and sideways with equal skill. Lobsters feed on a wide range of both plant and animal material and readily dine on decaying foodstuffs.

The spiny antennae and an rmored shell protect the lobster from many of its smaller enemies, but it falls easy prey to the octopus and the giant black sea bass. It is recorded that 10 lobsters were once found in the stomach of one of these large fish.

The female is distinguished by a small pincer on her last leg and by swimmerettes that are much larger and more fleshy than those of the male. The eggs are carried under the swimmerettes of the female.

Spawning occurs from March through August, with the greatest number of egg-bearing females evident in June. The eggs are coral red in color and may number from 50,000 to 800,000. They are fertilized by a gray putty-like substance, which the male deposits on the stomach of the female before she lays her eggs. Upon hatching, the tiny, strangely shaped larvae are free swimming and are at the mercy of the ocean currents. The larvae have been collected in water 75 fathoms deep and as far as 150 miles offshore. They drift around for seven or eight months and go through 12 developmental stages before settling to the bottom as baby lobsters.

Spiny lobsters grow by repeatedly shedding their entire shells, which is known as molting. They increase in size immediately after each molt and before the "new" shell hardens. In the soft-shell stage they are particularly vulnerable to predation. The shedding of their shells occurs annually right after the period of reproduction.

Like all animals subject to both sport and commercial exploitation, the spiny lobster population appears in danger of becoming seriously depleted.

Marlin

A hook-up with a big marlin is likely the single most exhilarating moment in all of fishing. After connecting, once you have the first sense of its immense weight, the fish often then vaults out of the water, hurtling and shaking, its phosphorescent blue sheen sparkling in bright sun.

It's all right in front of your eyes, a giant fish, typically 10 feet long, leading with his spear, tail-walking across the surface, just showing off before launching a sizzling 150-yard run.

In the fishing world, this is called getting your pancake flipped, getting your chain pulled, dinging your dong, or floating your boat. For many it is simply the best of the best.

ANIMAL	Marlin
SPECIES	Striped - *Tetrapturus audax*
TYPE	fish
STATUS	OK
SEE ALSO	Swordfish

There are three marlin found in Pacific waters, the striped, the blue and the black. The striped marlin is the most beautiful and prized member of the billfish family, sought by big game fishermen along California's southern California coast. It is also the most abundant, and it occurs throughout the tropical range and typically migrates as far north as Catalina Island in the fall.

Marlins' arrival in Southern California waters always sets off incredible excitement for those who heed the call. It starts in San Diego, with anglers tracking water temperatures, Pacific currents, and baitfish migrations. The chase heightens in summer then crests in September during peak water temperatures. Catalina Island is the capital of offshore fishing in California, primarily because it is located 20 miles out, a giant head start for boats heading out to search the offshore currents, the warm, clear, and azure blue waters that attract marlin, albacore, and tuna.

marlin

The spear of the marlin is used to slash and stun prey, rather than spear it. The food of the marlin is predominantly fish, although some invertebrates such as octopus, squid, and red crabs are found in their stomachs.

In El Niño years, marlin have been documented as far north as Santa Cruz and the Farallon Islands off of San Francisco, and in 1983, a wayward striped marlin somehow found its way all the way to Oregon, but these are anomalies.

The average fish is 100 to 125 pounds, but they get much bigger. The state records in California are 339 pounds for striped marlin and 692 pounds for blue marlin. The world records are 494 pounds for striped marlin and 1,376 pounds for blue. There are 2,000-pound black marlin off of Australia and Hawaii.

Marlin fishing is much like flying a small airplane: Long periods of boredom interspersed by moments of sheer terror, just like *The Old Man And The Sea*. To find the fish, you have to practically troll your little petunia off while a spotter high on the boat searches across the surface for the high crescent-shaped tail that marks a marlin finning on the surface. It can be many hours between action. Marlins are moody fish, but when feeding they will strike live bait as well as a variety of feathered lures.

One of the crowning achievements in the flyfishing world is to entice a marlin to strike with the boat dead in the water, then land a big fish inside of an hour. Ed Rice, one of the world's renowned flyfishers, has caught over 150 species of fish on his life list, and he has caught and released striped marlin over 200 pounds on the fly rod. "Each fish is different," Rice said. "They have a personality, and you never know what you're in for until the moment of hookup. I've had 80-pounders beat the heck out of me, and I put down a 200-pounder in 45 minutes."

Many one-timers will make a charter trip, then kill a 100-pounder in order to later brag about their great deed. The truth is that a 100-pound marlin is only three or four years old, and to kill it is to threaten the future of this fishery. Hence, there is growing pressure in the fishing community to support catch-and-release fishing, just as Rice urges, so marlin will not only have the chance to grow much bigger but will be able to fight again— and who knows how big when the chance comes.

I once fought a big marlin on light tackle, a battle with a dozen jumps and a half dozen 100-yard runs, one of the most exhilarating fights imaginable. But you know what I remember best? It was after finally persuading that fish alongside the boat, when I reached down, unhooked it, and watched its giant form swim off free. It was a moment of quiet satisfaction after an electrifying battle, like a soothing summer rain on a dusty prairie.

Biologists' Notes

The striped marlin, *Tetrapturas audax,* is the most prized member of the billfish family. There are three marlin found in Pacific waters, the striped, the blue, and the black. The striped marlin is the most abundant, and it occurs throughout the tropical Pacific.

Members of the billfish family all have the same general configuration: long slender bodies, high dorsal fins, and crescent-shaped tails. The nose of each is adorned with a long, sharp spear, or bill. However, the striped marlin is easily recognized, for the sides of its body are marked with distinctive light-colored vertical stripes.

The spear of the marlin is used when feeding, which it does by slashing and stunning its prey rather than by spearing it. The marlin then turns and picks up the stunned fish.

There are two distinct populations of striped marlin. One group inhabits the Western Pacific from Japan down to and around the Hawaiian Isles. The other group occurs in the Eastern Pacific from Peru north to Point Conception on California's southern shore.

Studies of the Eastern Pacific marlin indicate that spawning occurs off Central America in the general area of the Galápagos Islands and as far north as the Revilla Gigedo Islands. They prefer water temperatures of 75°F in which to spawn. After spawning they make their way north, following the warm ocean currents as far north as Point Conception, near Santa Barbara. The northward migration peaks in September, when marlin are found in the greatest numbers off Catalina Island.

Many of the marlin taken from California's waters are immature fish weighing from 100 to 150 pounds. It has been determined that at that weight they are from three to five years old. Mature adults have been taken in February and March around the Hawaiian Islands.

The food of the marlin is predominantly fish, although some invertebrates such as octopus, squid, and red crabs are found in their stomachs. In California waters, anchovies, saury, and flying fish are the most common food sources.

In 1937, legislation designated the striped marlin a recreational resource, and the buying and selling of marlin became prohibited in California. Although some marlin inhabit California waters year-round, August and September show the greatest number of fish caught. Californians seek marlin through the summer and fall months in the area from San Diego to Point Conception.

A tag-and-release program is carried on by state and federal agencies in the United States and Mexico. Many of the marlin clubs as well as private citizens are now tagging and releasing their catches as an aid to the study. Recovered tags have revealed valuable data. Marlin tagged off Catalina Island have been recovered from the Baja California fishing grounds, and one fish tagged at Catalina was caught off the Marquesas Islands. The longest movement of the fish recorded from California waters was to the west of the Hawaiian Isles.

Where to see marlin

CATALINA ISLAND, OFFSHORE FROM LOS ANGELES

CHANNEL ISLANDS, OFFSHORE FROM VENTURA COUNTY

LOS ANGELES DEEP SEA, OFFSHORE FROM LOS ANGELES COUNTY

OCEANSIDE DEEP SEA, OFFSHORE FROM SAN DIEGO COUNTY

SAN DIEGO DEEP SEA, OFFSHORE FROM SAN DIEGO COUNTY

SANTA BARBARA DEEP SEA, OFFSHORE FROM SANTA BARBARA COUNTY

SANTA MONICA/REDONDO DEEP SEA, OFFSHORE FROM LOS ANGELES COUNTY

VENTURA DEEP SEA, OFFSHORE FROM VENTURA COUNTY

Marmot

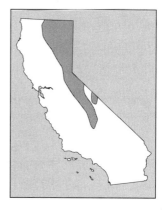

Marmots are the most lovable little fluffballs in all the high country of California, but you've got to keep track of the little buggers.

From Mount Whitney north about 50 miles on the Pacific Crest Trail (PCT), it seems every natural rest stop you come upon—you know, great view, perfect rock to lean against—will have a marmot on Corn Nut Patrol. You'll be enjoying the view, perhaps scanning across a canyon into a perfect example of a glacial cirque, maybe break out a snack of Corn Nuts, and then you'll turn to see, about 20 feet away, sitting up on a boulder, staring at you, this little brown marmot hoping to get a nut.

After a while, they seem to become the official mascot of the PCT. As you hike far-

ANIMAL	Marmot
SPECIES	*Marmota flaviventris*
TYPE	mammal
STATUS	OK
SEE ALSO	Chipmunks, Squirrels

ther north, particularly in the Sierra Wilderness from roughly Tahoe on, the marmots are not only fewer but seem far more wary of humans.

They have the personality of an advanced form of guinea pig, coupled with the fur of a mountain dweller and the begging ability of a well-trained chipmunk. After departing one lunch site north of Glen Pass, instead of hiking onward, I instead hid about 40 yards above the site; within minutes, several marmots appeared and combed over the area for leftovers like homicide detectives with a metal detector looking for a gun. They are vegetarians and like to find their bonus nut for the day.

The problem is, you see, is that sometimes they want more.

yellow-bellied marmot

The body temperature of a marmot in hibernation drops from 97°F to 40°F. The heartbeat drops from 100 beats per minute to four and a breath is taken once in about six minutes. All growth stops, and fat is absorbed to keep the animal alive. When the marmot emerges from its den, it is lean, hungry, and somewhat groggy.

At one time or another, at the wilderness trailheads for Inyo National Forest and Kings Canyon National Park, marmots have been known to crawl inside engine compartments of vehicles and gnaw on the water hoses of vehicles to get to the sweet-tasting antifreeze. (Unfortunately, antifreeze is toxic to all mammals.) The worst spot seems to be the trailhead for the hike up to Kearsage Pass. Some hikers will actually bring back-up hoses for their engines, in case a marmot decides to start chewing.

Marmots will also get into your food bags, if you leave them unattended. Of course, bear-proof food canisters are now required in much of the same wilderness areas that provide habitat for marmots, and these canisters are also marmot-proof.

For the most part, marmots are harmless and also provide a food source for larger carnivores. Their main aim in life seems to be to avoid being eaten, make little marmots, and stake out lunch sites for backpackers.

The wilderness hikers and sportsmen who venture into the higher elevations of our western mountains and deserts find the presence and shrill whistle of the marmot a pleasing touch.

Biologists' Notes

Marmots are common to Europe, Asia, and North America. The group contains many species and geographic races, which vary in size and color. North America contains several species of marmots. The one found in eastern Canada and the midwestern and eastern United States is commonly known as the woodchuck or groundhog. It occurs from sea level to near the tops of the highest mountains.

The most common western marmot occurs in the mountains and cold deserts of North America and is called the yellow-bellied marmot, whistler, or rockchuck.

The marmot found in California is the yellow-bellied marmot, *Marmota flaviventris*. Its underparts and feet are usually light yellowish brown, or tawny yellow. The fur is much thicker and of a better quality than the Eastern woodchuck's. Its body is grizzled brown, shoulders are buff-washed, and the muzzle has a light-colored band around the mouth. Because of variation in climatic conditions and isolation in different parts of its range, several geographic races have developed. It is most commonly found from about 4,000 feet elevation in the north to above timberline, which in the southernmost part of its range in California and New Mexico could be well above 10,000 feet.

High in the mountains, the marmot usually inhabits rock slides or rocky points on the edges of small glacial valleys. It lives in dens or burrows, which it digs for itself. Ordinarily the dens are hidden in rock slides and broken ledges, or they are dug under the shelter of large boulders. Occasionally a den might be found out in open ground. The dens are a complex of tunnels from six to 12 feet long with one ending in a small round room lined with grasses, in which the marmot spends the long winters.

The marmot is a true hibernator. Unlike bears, skunks, and chipmunks, which spend much of the winter in only a torpid state, the marmot, fat from a summer's feeding, goes into its winter burrow, curls into a ball, and gradually goes into a deep sleep. The body temperature drops from 97°F to 40°F. The heartbeat drops from a rate of more than 100 beats per minute to four; circulation slows and a breath is taken only once in about six minutes. All growth stops, and fat is absorbed to keep the animal alive.

When the marmot emerges from its den in February and March, later in the northern regions, it is lean, hungry, and somewhat groggy. It may be seen running around, searching for the first green grasses to come up between the remaining patches of snow. The females dig new burrows, and the males wander from burrow to burrow searching for a mate. Although a male may be driven out time and again, he is finally allowed to stay and they settle down to make a family. Four is the average number in a litter. The gestation period is about 30 days, so most marmot babies are born in April and early May. Just before the young are born, the male either leaves or is evicted and wanders away to dig its own burrow.

The young are totally dependent on the mother for about six weeks. By the time they emerge from the den, it is warm and there is plenty of vegetation for them to eat. They remain in the immediate vicinity of the mother's den for some time. They have been observed wrestling and playing "king of the mountain" on the mound at the entrance to the den.

By mid-June, the young marmots weigh more than one pound and are commencing to overcrowd the burrow. At this time, the mother takes them one at a time to their own burrows, which she has prepared in advance. From this time on, the young are on their own. Although they are subject to some predation by coyotes, bobcats, bears, and eagles, if they have paid attention to their mother's teachings, they know what to eat and how to remain alert to danger.

Where to see marmot

HOPE VALLEY WILDLIFE AREA, IN ALPINE COUNTY

LASSEN VOLCANIC NATIONAL PARK, IN LASSEN COUNTY

SEQUOIA AND KINGS CANYON NATIONAL PARKS, TULARE AND FRESNO COUNTIES

SHASTA VALLEY STATE WILDLIFE AREA, IN SISKIYOU COUNTY

Disregarding the squeaks and grunts typical of all large rodents, the only sound the marmot makes that is generally heard is a short, shrill whistle. The whistle is common to all marmots but clearer and louder among the yellow-bellied marmots. The sound is very close to that of a man whistling with two fingers between his teeth. The whistle's primary function is to warn other marmots that an intruder is approaching.

If an observer approaches a mountain meadow cautiously, even though the vegetation is tall enough to conceal a feeding marmot, a sharp whistle may cause it to sit up where it can be seen. Marmots are vegetarians and feed heavily on grasses, broad-leafed plants, and a large assortment of wild fruits and berries. After feeding, the marmot may be seen sunning itself, stretched out on a large boulder or a log in full sun, but ever alert to danger.

Marten, Pine

You aren't going to see many pine marten in a lifetime. Those with a passion for tracking wildlife, however, are likely to see their tracks. By following and reading their tracks, you can re-create many scenes that once transpired in the wild.

Rich Fletcher, an expert tracker and executive director of the Mule Deer Foundation, taught me this. On the cold morning of an early spring day in the alpine zone of California's mountain country, I was able track such a scene. It turned out to be one of the most memorable wildlife adventures I've ever had.

The tracks started in the snow off a Forest Service road. The snow was just an inch deep and the tracks were outlined perfectly, as if a cookie-cutter was punching patterns in soft dough.

ANIMAL	Marten, Pine
SPECIES	*Martes americana*
TYPE	mammal
STATUS	OK
SEE ALSO	Badger, Fisher, Mink, Otters, Raccoon, Skunks

A pine marten was following a squirrel, no doubt about that, with the little squirrel tracks, with the typical drag mark from its little paws, followed by the distinct marten tracks, with the distance between the prints indicating an animal about a foot long, the size of an adult marten.

pine marten

After following the tracks for a short way, about 25 yards, through a meadow edged by thick forest, the squirrel apparently became aware that it was being followed. Because here the squirrel tracks suddenly lengthened, twice the stride, indicating it was running, not walking. I followed those squirrel tracks to the base of a Douglas fir, where they stopped. At the same time, the marten's tracks had also lengthened, now apparently in all-out chase, and had followed the squirrel to the same tree.

I then searched the perimeter of the tree, trying to determine if the chase continued back on the ground, if the marten had in fact caught the squirrel in the tree, leaving evidence of the kill, or this saga ended here and now, with the squirrel getting away, hopping from tree to tree in the thick forest.

What I found instead provided a chilling insight into the real world of nature.

Instead of finding more squirrel tracks or remnants of a kill, I saw another set of tracks, that of a third animal. They looked similar to dog prints, yet without the claws. That could mean only one thing: mountain lion.

For nearly an hour, I searched the perimeter. Finally, I found it: A piece of fur from the pine marten.

Yes, the chaser had become the chased, the hunter had become the hunted. While trying to nab that squirrel in the tree, the pine marten had apparently aroused a mountain lion—and while the squirrel escaped the marten, the marten did not escape the lion. The lion had apparently caught the marten in the tree.

As I made this find, a squirrel in a giant Douglas fir above was chattering like a nattering nabob. I wondered if this was perhaps the same squirrel that had taken part in the incident and perhaps had witnessed the entire affair.

Such is the magic of tracking. Pine marten are easier to track than see because while they are secretive fellows, they can cover up to 10 miles in a day of hunting for prey and thus leave lots of tracks. It's my experience that Sierra pine marten are similar to mink, but their range generally extends to higher elevations than mink, with a small overlap at the bottom edge of the snowline. They also have a preference for wilderness, heavily treed in winter, but will eagerly go above treeline to find chipmunks and the like in summer.

Like most in the weasel family, the marten is a keen predator, and where there are ample mice, squirrel, or chipmunks, the pine marten can have a field day every time it goes out to hunt.

Unless, that is, it too is being hunted.

Biologists' Notes

The pine marten *(Martes americana)* looks about like a slender, medium-sized house cat. It has beautiful fur. Its color ranges from a honey-brown to a dark sable brown, but it is always paler around the head and neck. It has a characteristic throat patch, which ranges in color from yellowish orange to cream. The patch varies in size from a triangular spot to a stripe that extends the full length of the belly. Its long, silky underfur is overlaid with dark shiny guard hairs that give the fur a dusky brown luster.

The pine marten lives on mice, birds, bird eggs, rabbits, and pine squirrels, which it catches by running them down in the trees. Martens breed in July and August, but due to a phenomenon called delayed implantation, the ovum is not implanted until January of the following year.

Its legs are rather long and its feet are dark in color and fully furred. It has nearly white semi-retractable claws. Its tail is dark brown and tapers to a tip that is nearly black.

The marten is most agile, running through trees in the manner of a gray squirrel. It is more powerful than a squirrel and is able to span greater distances when jumping from tree to tree. It spends some of its time in trees, but observations in winter show that it spends a great deal of time on the ground. Tracks in the snow may cover as many as 10 miles in its never-ending search for food.

The Sierra pine marten prefers to live in the seclusion of dense uncut fir forests from 4,000 to 7,000 feet elevation in the Sierra. In summer, it ranges from 7,000 to 13,000 feet, the latter well above timberline. Rock slides support many small rodents on which the marten preys. It is found from Tulare County north to Mount Shasta and then west into Siskiyou and Trinity Counties. The most common sightings have been reported in the Mount Lassen area and in Trinity County.

The Humboldt pine marten, a geographical variation, was originally found from Sonoma County up through the redwood belt to Del Norte County. It ranged at lower elevations and, because of the lack of snow, was trapped nearly to extinction. Trapping for marten was prohibited in 1952. Sightings have been recorded in recent years in Mendocino, Humboldt and Del Norte Counties.

The pine marten, like other members of the weasel family, is a tireless hunter. It lives on mice, birds, bird eggs, rabbits, and squirrels. It catches the latter by running them down in the trees.

The marten builds its home in hollow trees and rocky ledges The breeding season occurs in July and August. The most births occur in April of the

Where to see pine marten

EMERALD BAY STATE PARK/D.L. BLISS STATE PARK, IN EL DORADO COUNTY

LASSEN VOLCANIC NATIONAL PARK, IN LASSEN COUNTY

TRINITY LAKE, SHASTA-TRINITY NATIONAL FOREST, IN TRINITY COUNTY

following year. The seemingly long gestation period is actually caused by an unexplained phenomenon called delayed implantation. The ovum lays inactive in the uterine horn at least from October until January. Near the latter month, they become implanted in the walls of the uterus and develop to full term by April.

The female does not breed until she is two years old, so the first young are not born until she is three years old. The average number of young is only three per litter, and only one litter is born per year. The young grow rapidly and by fall are nearly as large as the parents. The males are about one-quarter larger than the females.

Mink

Many fur-coat lovers might find it difficult to believe how closely related the beloved mink is to the skunk. They are just a beat apart, both in the weasel family and both capable of producing a smell that can make your eyeballs spin.

The difference is that the mink does it to attract mates, and the skunk, well, you know all about the skunk.

All members of the weasel family have scent glands near the base of the tail. The mink's scent glands are highly developed, and though few people get the full dose, in the field the odor is more repugnant than that of a skunk. Mink use the scent not as a defense, but rather as a means of communicating with other mink. The mink, like many

ANIMAL	Mink
SPECIES	*Mustela vison*
TYPE	mammal
STATUS	OK
SEE ALSO	Badger, Fisher, Marten, Otters, Raccoon, Skunks

other animals, has a defined territory in which it lives and hunts, and the territory is marked by deposits of this scent. In the frontier days, trappers used the scent to attract the mink to their sets.

Fur coats are on the way out, an anachronism in the 21st century, definitely to the benefit of mink and other wildlife. But in New York, Chicago, Baltimore, and other northeastern cities, as well as on many fashion runways, a mink coat is still thought of as the ultimate luxury for some high-dollar men and women. You wonder how many of them realize that mink are actually smelly skunk-like little animals that live near bogs.

But in the wild, mink are captivating to many, starting with that beautiful coat of fur. However, they prefer to keep it on their own backs.

In the early winter months when nights grow cold, a mink's soft underfur grows dense for warmth, and the outer hairs, called guard hairs, grow to their fullest length and literally gleam with iridescence. The coat gains and retains its greatest beauty from early December through January. It then becomes a little shopworn with broken guard hairs and rubbed spots beginning to show. The hunting technique of the mink, squeezing in and out of the nooks and crannies where its prey lives, can give the fur its worn appearance.

Mink kits are born in litters of six to eight in midsummer. The fur is so short and fine that they appear naked, but soon they grow a very short silky coat of pale blue fur, which against the pink skin appears lavender. The mink's scent glands are highly developed, and the odor is considered by many to be more repugnant than that of a skunk.

And hunt they do. Like its smaller cousins in the weasel family, the mink kills wantonly when prey food is found in numbers, such as a nest of mice, rabbits, or broods of chicks or birds, without regard to its needs. It has a varied diet; it eats birds, small rodents, fish, crayfish and other aquatic animals, and insects. Muskrats don't stand a chance.

They also have their own enemies, of course. On one hike, I found the partial hide of a mink, immediately identified by its amazing coat. But it was just a small piece. Couldn't

mink

even make a fig leaf with it. Something had gotten the rest, perhaps a golden eagle, maybe a badger, possibly a bobcat or mountain lion, or a pack of coyotes. Despite a lengthy search, I found no tracks or signs of the skirmish to try to re-create the scene.

Few people see mink because the mink lives in seclusion by day, often in burrows or complex thatches along rivers, and hunts at night. They have a remarkable stealth ability, and if you are exploring along a valley creek, for instance, you can often walk right past a burrowed mink without the slightest hint of recognition. Though I have seen a few mink, always by accident, I bet there have been hundreds of times when I have been within 25 feet of one with nary a clue.

And when dealing with people who like fur coats, that is exactly how mink like it.

Biologists' Notes

The mink, *Mustela vison*, is a member of the weasel family. The body is long and slender. The legs are short, and for such a small animal, very muscular. The head is small and round. The little half-round ears barely show above the short dense fur. The round tail is densely furred and is six to eight inches in length.

The color is uniform except for a dark tip on the end of the tail, a white spot on the chin, and occasionally a white spot on the throat or chest. The fur of the wild mink ranges from a dark honey color to a rich dark brown to nearly black. The male is larger than the female, sometimes a little over 24 inches in length.

The mink is at home on land or in the water. It prefers to live along the waterways of ditches and streams that have a thick jungle-like growth of brush, vines, and tules.

The den may be in an abandoned muskrat or beaver burrow, an old log jam, or under the tree roots that overhang the water's edge. For such a small animal, the mink claims a rather large territory and may travel as many as six or eight miles in a night of hunting. The mink is a tireless hunter and will leave the larger rivers to hunt along small tributary streams and ditches. Close observation reveals that the males travel over their territory with a certain degree of regularity. They usually return to the home denning area by daylight the following morning. The female mink's hunting grounds are smaller than the male's. Her territory is usually a confined area near her den.

The kits are born in mid-summer. There may be up to six or eight in a litter, although the average is four. They are quite helpless while young and do not open their eyes for nearly six weeks. The fur is so short and fine that they appear naked at first, but they soon grow a very short silky coat of pale blue fur, which against the pink skin, almost appears lavender. Baby minks are not very cute. The body seems disproportionately long, for the little head is blunt, the muzzle short and almost square, and both the tail and legs are short and stubby. At three weeks they are only about as big as a mouse but can squirm out of cupped hands.

In two and a half months, the mother begins to take them with her on short hunts to teach them how to find and catch their own food. They learn rapidly and in the fall the litter breaks up and the young mink go out on their own.

The mink, although semi-aquatic in habits, is not bound to water. However, it is found along most of the waterways from San Francisco Bay north. Its tracks may be seen on the sands of many beaches. It is interesting that there is no record of mink occurring along the coast south of San Francisco Bay. It is found in the Sierra, on the east side from Inyo County north and on the west side from the San Joaquin River watershed north. Although the greatest abundance of mink appears to be in the Delta region at the confluence of the Sacramento and San Joaquin Rivers, the sleekest mink are found in Humboldt and Trinity Counties, where their fur is the darkest and most silky in texture.

Where to see mink

ANDERSON MARSH STATE HISTORIC PARK, IN LAKE COUNTY

BRANNAN ISLAND STATE RECREATION AREA, IN SACRAMENTO COUNTY

COSUMNES RIVER PRESERVE, IN SACRAMENTO COUNTY

EAST WALKER WILDLIFE AREA, IN MONO COUNTY

LAKE SOLANO COUNTY PARK, IN SOLANO COUNTY

NAPA RIVER ECOLOGICAL RESERVE, IN NAPA COUNTY

Other places to see mink

GRIZZLY ISLAND WILDLIFE AREA, IN SOLANO COUNTY

McCLOUD RIVER PRESERVE, IN SISKIYOU COUNTY

PAYNES CREEK WETLANDS, IN TEHAMA COUNTY

Mountain Lion

The first time I saw a mountain lion, the most feared animal in California, I thought it was a big dog.

It was at a small lake in the foothills of the San Francisco Peninsula, about sunset, when what looked like a short-haired golden retriever emerged from the brush and started walking along the shoreline.

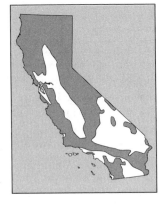

"What's a dog doing out here all by itself?" I remember wondering. Then I looked closer and discovered that it was no dog.

Its shoulder muscles were sculpted, flexing and rolling with each step, and it had a rhythm to its walk as if gliding, so smooth that seemed the grass wasn't even bending.

ANIMAL	Mountain Lion
SPECIES	*Felis concolor*
TYPE	mammal
STATUS	OK
SEE ALSO	Bobcat

Its hair was short and smooth, like it was oiled down, and its tail was long and thick. About 125 pounds, I figured, healthy, lean, and powerful.

"That's no dog! That's a mountain lion!" I remember mumbling to myself, and a tingle shot through my body. A moment later, the cougar disappeared back into the brush, then was gone. For days, I was astonished.

Most encounters people have with mountain lions are exactly like this, chance meetings, always brief and surprising. In 20,000 miles of hiking, I have seen only three. My three best hiking pals, all with 5,000 to 10,000 trail miles in their boots, have seen only two mountain lions between them, and both were fleeting chance meetings.

Despite this reality, there is shock lingering in California from the potential danger of a mountain lion attack. It shadows the thoughts of many people who love the outdoors, even though you actually have a far greater chance of dying from a bee sting, lightning bolt, or a Great White shark. The idea that there is even a remote chance of attack renders California hikers nervous and vulnerable. At trailheads throughout the state park system, for instance, there are now warning signs that you are entering mountain lion habitat. In addition, the Department of Fish and Game has issued a special mountain lion pamphlet, which was widely promoted.

From 1992 to 1995 there was at least one mountain lion attack on a person in California, most notably in the Sacramento foothills near Auburn, and also near San Diego. In the four years that followed, however, there were no documented attacks. In many areas, especially in Los Angeles and the Bay Area, the issue of safety has virtually evaporated from public consciousness. In the Bay Area, for instance, there has only been one attack in history, in Gilroy in 1911, with a rabid lion—an aberration.

But the Department of Fish and Game receives 350 to 400 incident reports on mountain lions per year, that is, where people are concerned enough about a situation to report it. Most of the encounters occur in the foothills of the Sierra Nevada, roughly from Mariposa north past Placerville on up to Auburn and beyond to Cottonwood. In Placerville, one woman and her children stayed locked in her car at her home for hours, kept at bay by a 200-pound lion waiting alongside, just looking at them.

The onset of winter is a particularly critical time in the Central Valley foothills because as snow arrives to the Sierra Nevada, deer migrate down to their winter range in the foothill country. Mountain lion, which eat an average of one deer per week, follow them right down and find themselves encountering people on the outskirts of Sierra foothill towns. But any region that has both deer and mountain lions, such as the Bay Area foothills, or the foothills of Humboldt Country, Monterey, Santa Barbara, and San Diego, can provide the scene for an encounter.

An adult mountain lion requires about 70 square miles of range, so as young lions mature, the adults push them out into new areas. As the lion population grows, these new areas include where people are apt to be. The mountain lion is the only animal in California to be designated a "Specially Protected Mammal" by public referendum.

mountain lion

Mountain Lion Truths

Mountain lion expert Steve Torres of the Department of Fish and Game provided the following list of 10 truths regarding mountain lions:

1. Mountain lions are very shy and wary of humans. Attacks on people are extremely rare. That is why any threatening encounter can make news, because it is an anomaly.

2. Mountain lions are rarely seen. They are masters of stealth. That is why repeat sightings are alarming and should be reported to Torres at the Department of Fish and Game headquarters in Sacramento.

3. Mountain lions are known for their silence and are rarely vocal. If you hear the cry or roar of a lion, very rarely heard during an attack on a deer, your experience is likely a once-in-a-lifetime event.

4. In the past 100 years, there have been only 15 documented fatal mountain lion attacks in North America, but 75% of the attacks (66) on record have occurred since 1970. In the 1990s between 1 and 10 attacks have occurred each year in the U.S. and Canada, with about 50 since 1970, but before 1970, there were less than 20. In California, there were attacks in four straight years from 1992-1995, but no documented attacks in the four years that followed.

5. The home range of male mountain lions does not overlap those of other males. That is why if a problem mountain lion is transported to a new habitat, it will get driven out by the resident male lion already present, and forced to go elsewhere; that is why moving problem lions does not work. Female mountain lions are a bit more tolerant, at times their range may overlap, but they avoid each other. As a result, an expanding mountain lion population will force young lions to try to find new range. That is why they can end up on the outskirts of expanding towns in the Sierra foothills. Both the mountain lions and the towns are expanding to the point where their range can overlap.

One reason is because there are just more mountain lions out there, no doubt about it. An adult mountain lion requires a lot of territory, about 70 square miles in Coastal Ranges, and as young lions mature, they get pushed out by the adults into new areas. In the past 10 years, as the lion population has grown, those new areas include places where people are apt to be.

How dangerous is the situation? Even when encountering wildlife with the most menacing reputations, such as mountain lions, bears, and wild boar, the confrontations almost always turn out to be less perilous than the average commute to work. The most dangerous part of a hike is

6. Mountain lions are solitary. After breeding, the males depart quickly, and take no role in rearing the young.

7. Mountain lions generally feed only on animals that they have killed. However, sometimes they can feed on the kill for weeks.

8. Regulated hunting has little or no effect on mountain lion populations. Several western states that permit mountain lion hunting have lion populations that are increasing. In addition, allowing hunting has no apparent effect on the number of mountain lion attacks, such as in British Columbia, where hunting is permitted, yet attacks have still occurred.

9. Mountain lions are not threatened or endangered in any way. Populations are stable to increasing. The biggest threat to mountain lions is loss of habitat to development.

10. Mountain lions are not afraid of dogs. While packs of trained hounds are capable of putting a lion in a tree, solitary pets of all kinds, including dogs, are fair game for mountain lions. In areas with documented mountain lion habitat, dogs should be kept inside at night.

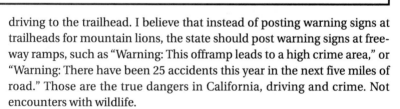

driving to the trailhead. I believe that instead of posting warning signs at trailheads for mountain lions, the state should post warning signs at freeway ramps, such as "Warning: This offramp leads to a high crime area," or "Warning: There have been 25 accidents this year in the next five miles of road." Those are the true dangers in California, driving and crime. Not encounters with wildlife.

The mountain lion represents the ultimate paradox, because it is loved enough to win designation by ballot as the state's only "Specially Protected Mammal," yet the population is growing and causing problems in many rural areas.

Wildlife experts say the real issue is not safety, but the devastating impact that lions have on deer and other wildlife. In one test area, Round Valley near Bishop, the deer herd fell from 5,500 to fewer than 1,000 adults in eight years, with 51% of the deaths from mountain lion kills, 22% from coyote kills, 14% from road kill, 7% from hunting, and 6% from other factors. At the same time, the Sierra bighorn was listed as an endangered species in California, and 106 of them were fitted with radio collars so their migration routes could be tracked. Biologists discovered instead that within a year, 24 were killed by protected mountain lions, which are not a threatened or endangered species.

My most recent mountain lion confrontation was at Point Reyes National Seashore, hiking out toward Tomales Point. Suddenly, 40 yards in front of me on the side of the trail, this mountain lion sat straight up, perched on his haunches, staring straight at me. Those cold eyes felt like laser beams. For

---

Where to see mountain lion

ASH CREEK WILDLIFE AREA, IN MODOC AND LASSEN COUNTIES

AUBURN STATE RECREATION AREA, IN EL DORADO AND PLACER COUNTIES

CALAVERAS BIG TREES STATE PARK, IN CALAVERAS COUNTY

CUYAMACA RANCHO STATE PARK, IN SAN DIEGO COUNTY

MOUNT TAMALPAIS STATE PARK, IN MARIN COUNTY

POINT MUGU STATE PARK, IN LOS ANGELES COUNTY

SINKYONE WILDERNESS STATE PARK, IN HUMBOLDT COUNTY

Other places to see mountain lion

ANZA-BORREGO DESERT STATE PARK, IN SAN DIEGO COUNTY

CHINA FLAT/SILVER FORKS CAMPGROUNDS, EL DORADO NATIONAL FOREST, IN EL DORADO COUNTY

FOOTHILLS FROM AUBURN TO PLACERVILLE, IN EL DORADO AND PLACER COUNTIES

HENRY W. COE STATE PARK, IN SANTA CLARA COUNTY

MONTANA DE ORO STATE PARK, IN SAN LUIS OBISPO COUNTY

MOUNT DIABLO STATE PARK, IN CONTRA COSTA COUNTY

MOUNT SAN JACINTO STATE PARK AND STATE WILDERNESS, IN RIVERSIDE COUNTY

PALOMAR MOUNTAIN STATE PARK, IN SAN DIEGO COUNTY

POINT REYES NATIONAL SEASHORE, IN MARIN COUNTY

40 seconds, it was a standoff, then suddenly, the cougar dropped back down to all fours, then slinked off down into a gully.

I tried to follow it, but in seconds there was no trace, even though the habitat here is coastal grasslands with no apparent place to hide.

Almost the same thing occurred in another encounter with a mountain lion, in the coastal foothills of San Mateo County, near the San Francisco Fish and Game Refuge.

I wish a lot of highway drivers could take such a non-combative approach.

Biologists' Notes

The mountain lion *(Felis concolor),* also called cougar and puma, is California's largest cat. Healthy adult males can reach 200 pounds, though they are often smaller, and females can reach 150 pounds.

They are instantly recognized by almost everyone. They are colored golden, actually more of a brownish-yellow, with a white underside. Mountain lions have lean and powerful bodies, the classic cougar head with small ears, large paws, and a long tail.

Unlike many species, mountain lions can breed in any month during the year. At age two, the female often has her first litter, two to four kittens, and will care for and supervise them for more than a year. When the juveniles depart, they must establish their own range. Males will not tolerate an intruding male mountain lion in their established range, thus mountain lions are being found in new areas, often near rural towns, and also in rural areas where development is taking place for the first time.

Mountain lions live about 10 years in the wild, though in captivity they have been known to reach as old as 20. Their diet is typically deer, but they will eat other animals if the opportunity presents itself, including bighorn sheep, wild pig, rabbit, marmot, and squirrels. They will also kill domestic animals such as dogs, cats, sheep, pigs, and llamas.

Opossum

Most people don't think of an opossum as cute. In fact, upon first appearance, many think they seem about as cute as a tarantula. But the evening I saw a momma possum with a passel of babies, well, that perception changed forever for me.

It was just after nightfall, on the coastal foothills about a mile from the ocean. I was out with my flashlight, exploring where a thicket of wild berries gave way to grasslands, with a forest of cypress trees and a creek nearby. It is changes of habitat such as these, interfaces between forest, meadow, and cover, with nearby water, where you are most likely to see wildlife. I heard a rustling, and my dog tugged at his leash. I pointed the light beam ahead, and there, waddling just 10 feet away, was a momma possum with all these babies hanging from her.

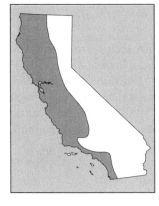

ANIMAL	Opossum
SPECIES	*Didelphis virginiana*
TYPE	mammal
STATUS	Introduced

The baby possum were all about three inches long, and a line of them, about six in a row, were hanging along the side of the mother, grabbing on to her fur with their little claws, like a row of small bells swinging back and forth as she waddled along. A seventh baby was hanging on to the base of her tail. Though it was impossible to see, it is likely that another half dozen were tucked away in her pouch, which momma possums use as a nursery. It was an extraordinary sight, especially for an animal that can seem to many observers to be more like a large rat than anything else. The official name for possum is "opossum," of course, but everybody I know calls them possum.

opossum

They are active only at night and seek cover in any protected spot during daylight, sleeping until dark. In two chance encounters, for instance, one was found in the manger of a barn, and another was found curled up in an open crow's nest.

So many people never see a possum, that is, unless it is on a road, having been hit by a car, or in the mouth of an aggressive dog. Those are their two biggest enemies: car strikes at night, and dogs allowed to run free in rural areas, which play havoc with wildlife. The opossum, upon an encounter with a dog, doesn't have a chance. One bite and it's over.

It's wrong to say an adult possum is like a giant rat. A rat is much cuter, heh heh. When viewed close up, you discovered that the hair of a possum is coarse and gray, with the head and eyes of a rat, but with a long curved snout that hides a menacing row of chompers. Their bodies are typically fat with no muscle definition, leading to a tail that is long and often curling.

But everything has its place in nature, and so it is with opossum. Their ability to reproduce in large numbers, their nocturnal activity, and poor ability to defend themselves make them an excellent food supply for many predators, including owls, foxes, coyotes, and many wolverine-like predators.

Their most endearing trait is their fantastic ability to defend themselves by faking death, that is, "playing possum." Frequently, when attacked or severely shaken, an opossum will literally "faint," that is, fall over, limp and inert. Only its warmth and heart beat will betray that it is very much alive. If left alone it will "come to" and quietly slip away to go about its business.

I was out with my flashlight, exploring where a thicket of wild berries gave way to grasslands, with a forest of cypress trees and a creek nearby. It is changes of habitat such as these, interfaces between forest, meadow, and cover, with nearby water, where you are most likely to see wildlife. I pointed the light beam ahead, and there, waddling just 10 feet away, was a momma possum with all these babies hanging from her.

The first time I witnessed this, I suddenly understood an episode from my childhood: When I was 10 I faked being sick in bed, the covers pulled up, in order to miss school and later watch a World Series baseball game. However, upon inspection by my worried, loving mother, she took one long look and announced, "Mr. Tom Stienstra, you are playing possum."

Biologists' Notes

There are many species of opossum worldwide, but only one *(Didelphis virginiana)* occurs in the United States.

Although native to North America east of the Rockies, records show that it was introduced into California in the 1900s near San Jose. Apparently it adapted readily to its newfound home, for it increased in numbers rapidly and, with the help of man, it now occupies most of the habitat that is suitable. It is now found throughout the Sacramento and San Joaquin Valleys; in the foothills of the western slopes of the Sierra, up to 3,000 feet elevation; and in the Coastal Ranges west of the Mojave Desert, from Mendocino County south to the Mexican border. Since the opossum does not hibernate it is doubtful if it could exist where snow lies deep for long periods of time.

The opossum is a true marsupial, that is, it is the only mammal in North America that has a pouch on its stomach in which it rears its young.

The opossum is about the size of a large house cat. Except for its color, it resembles somewhat a large, slow-moving rat. Its long round tail is nearly hairless. Its papery thin ears are small and round. The resemblance to a rat ends at the mouth, for in an opossum's primitive widespread jaws are 50 teeth, more than any other native mammal in North America. The long, narrow face is white, which accents the black beady eyes. Its lower legs and feet are black. The feet look like little hands. The hind feet have clawless thumbs and can be used for clasping. The rough-skinned tail is prehensile and is used as an aid in clinging to things.

The opossum is accused of being slow, stupid, and weak—characteristics which have, over the years, rendered many animals extinct—yet it has survived in its present form from the time prehistoric animals roamed the land. In fact it has been called a "living fossil." Zoologists have pondered this, and many believe the most logical reasons for its survival are that it isn't an aggressive fighter; it can eat anything, vegetable or animal, dead or alive; and it produces lots and lots of little possums.

The opossum is a solitary animal except during the breeding season. Females may start to breed when only six months old. From the time the female is bred, the young are born in 13 days. There can be from 15 to 18 born at a time. The young are tiny things, no larger than a honeybee. When born they are still in a partially embryonic stage—hairless, earless, and blind. The front legs are the most highly developed of any part. In preparation for the birth, the mother prepares a pathway of saliva to the pouch. Using their strong forelegs, the babies make their way up this path to the pouch, where they attach themselves to an active nipple. The tiny mouth is encircled by a tight ring of muscle. The nipple becomes engorged inside the baby's mouth. The baby remains fastened there for 65 days for the final stages of development. Female opossums have from

Where to see opossum

ANDERSON MARSH STATE HISTORIC PARK, IN LAKE COUNTY

BIDWELL PARK, IN BUTTE COUNTY

CASWELL MEMORIAL STATE PARK, IN SAN JOAQUIN COUNTY

CHINA FLAT/SILVER FORKS CAMPGROUNDS, IN EL DORADO NATIONAL FOREST

COACHELLA VALLEY PRESERVE, IN RIVERSIDE COUNTY

CUYAMACA RANCHO STATE PARK, IN SAN DIEGO COUNTY

NAPA RIVER ECOLOGICAL RESERVE, IN NAPA COUNTY

OROVILLE WILDLIFE AREA, IN BUTTE COUNTY

eight to 13 active nipples. Any young that do not find a "place at the table" soon die of starvation. It is not unusual to find from six to 10 young in the pouch. When fully developed they emerge from the pouch well formed and with their round, black, beady eyes wide open. Baby possums, like all wild babies, are cute. While small they sometimes hitch a ride by clinging to the mother's fur, then return to the pouch to hide and suckle. A female opossum is a good mother and she cares for the young until they are about four months old. Then they go their solitary way.

Osprey

My favorite time, in the natural world, is the last two hours of every summer day. This is when the mountain landscape is transformed to a place where anything seems possible in nature. The changes occur minute by minute, and those who are aware enough to watch this—the world of nature coming to life—are often blessed by an array of sights and share in a world that relatively few enjoy.

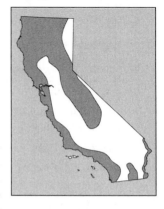

ANIMAL	Osprey
SPECIES	*Pandion haliaetus*
TYPE	bird
STATUS	OK
SEE ALSO	Eagles, Falcon, Hawks

When the sun hits the mountain and the first shade is cast on a lake or stream, it triggers a round of insect hatches, a variety spanning from tiny midges to large mayflies. In turn, the emerging arthropods attract trout to the surface, as well as small flocks of swallows, both feasting on the insects. In addition, this is when deer often come to lake's edge to drink, when an otter may hide behind a log and ambush a trout, and even a bear will start its evening rounds.

And at hundreds of lakes across California, this is also when the osprey, the greatest fisherman of them all, comes out for its dinner.

The osprey's silhouette against an evening sky is a classic sight, smaller than an eagle and in monochrome, but nearly as skilled a flyer. They will fly over the lake, just cruising, looking for trout swimming to the surface to feed on the emerging insect hatch. Suddenly, the osprey will turn, and, at the point of recognition, without hesitation, fold and lock its wings and then plummet in warp drive, crashing into the lake. Just as quickly, the osprey will emerge with the trout in its talons and off it goes to a quiet perch to enjoy the meal. The entire attack, from recognition to kill, can occur in seconds.

Of all the fish-eating birds, I believe osprey to be the most highly skilled hunters. Once they start their dive, they almost never miss their fish. Nearly every mountain lake with fish has an osprey or two that will pop a trout about every evening. They come and go so quickly, fishing with such supreme natural abilities, that many less-than-alert observers can miss the show.

Ospreys also have many curious flying habits. When they cruise at lake level, for instance, many people believe they are looking for fish. Nope. If you watch closely, they often fly just above the lake surface, dipping their talons for moment in the water. You know why? Because this is how they clean their talons. No foolin'.

When fishing, they always fly well above the lake, scanning for fish, sometimes circling when they see one, occasionally hovering for a moment to make sure, before starting the power dive. They are also fast birds, capable of tremendous bursts of speed when needed. Their vision is razor-sharp, a physical gift perfected by thousands of years of necessity.

They are such skilled fishermen that I've seen bald eagles wait for an osprey to catch a fish, then team up, attack the osprey, force it to drop the fish.

Occasionally youngsters and adults alike ask themselves, "If you could be any animal, bird, fish, or reptile,

When osprey cruise at lake level, many people believe they are looking for fish. They are actually dipping into the water to clean their talons. An osprey looking for fish does so from a high vantage point and typically dive from heights of over 100 feet. They dive head first at great speed with wings folded, and just before hitting the water, they pull back and enter feet first to clutch their prey.

osprey

what would it be?" For me, it would have to be Bigfoot. Heh, heh. No, seriously, it would be osprey, the predator bird with remarkable natural skills, capable of precision flying, blessed with telescope vision, a skilled fish hunter, big enough to protect itself, always prospering in some of the most beautiful places on earth.

All this can be seen in the last two hours of day at many mountain lakes, the transition from day to dusk to dark, when nature comes to life and the wildlands of California are transformed—and osprey emerges from its roost.

Biologists' Notes

The osprey *(Pandion haliaetus)* is a bird of prey. Its unique facility as a catcher of fish differentiates it from eagles, hawks, and falcons. Its species name, *haliaetus,* means "sea eagle," and osprey are also commonly called sea hawks.

The osprey is uniquely adapted to fishing success, having oily feathers that protect against water saturation, crooked wings that soften collisions with the water, and long legs with short stiff feathers, allowing the talons to penetrate the water with little resistance. The curved, razor-sharp talons and spiny bumps on the feet assist in gripping slippery prey. It can make dives from heights of over 100 feet, with wings folded. They dive head first at great speed, then just before hitting the water, they pull back, entering feet first to clutch their prey.

The osprey is about two feet long, dark brown above and white below, with a white cap on its head and a wingspan of nearly six feet. The feet of the osprey are a light grayish-blue with a brown tinge. Males lack the brown chest spots of the female and have a more upright stance.

Osprey live near fresh and salt water all over the world, on every continent but Antarctica. North American osprey cluster on the Atlantic seaboard, in states bordering the Great Lakes, and on the west coast from the northern Rocky Mountains to the California coast, migrating from temperate to subtropical areas in the West Indies and Central and South America for the winter and returning in early spring. Like most raptors, osprey ride thermal updrafts, soaring in circular motions and conserving energy on long migration flights.

Osprey thrive in shallow water systems, where there is an abundance of fish and dead trees to nest in. Osprey are buoyant and can only penetrate about one meter below the surface, limiting the catch to surface fish or

Where to see osprey

AHJUMAWI LAVA SPRINGS STATE PARK, IN SHASTA COUNTY

ANTELOPE LAKE/INDIAN CREEK, IN PLUMAS COUNTY

CRYSTAL COVE STATE PARK, IN ORANGE COUNTY

HUNTINGTON LAKE, SIERRA NATIONAL FOREST, IN FRESNO COUNTY

JUNE LAKE, INYO NATIONAL FOREST, IN MONO COUNTY

LAKE ALPINE, STANISLAUS NATIONAL FOREST, IN ALPINE COUNTY

STAMPEDE RESERVOIR, TAHOE NATIONAL FOREST, IN SIERRA COUNTY

Other places to see osprey

ARCATA MARSH AND WILDLIFE SANCTUARY, IN HUMBOLDT COUNTY

AUDUBON CANYON RANCH, IN MARIN COUNTY

BOLSA CHICA ECOLOGICAL RESERVE, IN ORANGE COUNTY

HIGH SIERRA RECREATION AREA, IN FRESNO COUNTY

JENKINSON LAKE/SLY PARK RECREATION AREA, IN EL DORADO COUNTY

LAKE TAHOE VISITOR CENTER AT TAYLOR CREEK, IN EL DORADO COUNTY

POINT REYES NATIONAL SEASHORE, IN MARIN COUNTY

RUTH LAKE, IN TRINITY COUNTY

SHASTA LAKE NATIONAL RECREATION AREA, IN SHASTA COUNTY

SHASTA LAKE, SHASTA-TRINITY NATIONAL FOREST, IN SHASTA COUNTY

SILVERWOOD LAKE STATE RECREATION AREA, IN SAN BERNARDINO COUNTY

SONOMA STATE BEACHES/BODEGA BAY, IN SONOMA COUNTY

those found in shallow water and near shore. Many reservoirs meet these conditions and have become prime osprey habitat.

The osprey builds the largest nests of any North American bird, some measuring up to six feet high. Nests are built in trees (preferably cedar trees), jagged rocks, power poles, low bushes, and on the ground, of materials such as seaweed, bones, sticks, driftwood, and just about any suitable debris. Because osprey pairs can return to the same nest each year for a decade or more, each year's added material can result in a nest approximating a total weight of half a ton or more. Such nests are vulnerable to strong winds.

In the spring, osprey pairs generally produce, over a period of three to seven days, from two to four eggs, pinkish and heavily marked with brown. Both parents take turns incubating the eggs for a period of 30 to 37 days. The male osprey feeds the female during the courting period and delivers about six pounds of fish per day to the nest after the young hatch. The female feeds the shredded fish to her young, who grow to 80% of their adult weight in one month and are typically ready to leave the nest in eight weeks, generally in August.

Osprey tend to hunt alone, in the early to mid-morning hours and in the early evening, with much of the foraging activity taking place from a perch.

Nest predation is a threat to the osprey, sometimes from climbers like the raccoon or egg-collecting humans, but primarily from crows, ravens, and owls. In the 1950s, however, the use of the insecticide DDT caused a major disturbance problems in nesting success. Fish accumulated large amounts of the pesticide in their bodies and were later consumed by osprey and other fish-eating birds. The osprey was especially vulnerable, as fish makes up nearly 99% of its diet. The accumulation of DDT in the osprey caused the bird to lay thin-shelled eggs, which either failed to develop or were broken during incubation.

Multiple efforts have since been made to conserve osprey habitat and that of the fish critical to their survival. In fact, the osprey's sensitivity to the environment has led to its being considered an "indicator species," that is, success of nesting pairs is tracked as a measure of environmental rehabilitation efforts.

Concern for the continued welfare of osprey populations can be witnessed throughout California in public forests and parks, where every effort is made to limit disruption of nesting pairs by banning tree and snag cutting and restricting public access during critical periods.

Otter, River

River otters rate a 10 on the cute scale, but you haven't seen anything until you spot them in action, in a river, where you can witness their extraordinary swimming skills.

Especially for youngsters, river otters seem adorable. They pop those little heads up from the water like periscopes from a miniature submarine and often look right at you—always a thrill. But it can get better. On the McCloud River on the section of property managed by the Nature Conservancy, in early April when no one else is around, I have seen otters body surfing the rapids as if riding boogie boards.

ANIMAL	Otter, River
SPECIES	*Lutra canadensis*
TYPE	mammal
STATUS	OK
SEE ALSO	Badger, Fisher, Marten, Mink, Otter (Sea), Raccoon, Skunks

One time, when I was sitting on a rock munching a trail lunch, just watching the water go by, these two otters came surfing down the river. Instead of just ripping past when they spotted me, they dove down, then popped their heads up directly adjacent to me, swirled around on the surface in an eddy, showing off, playing, then swept back out into the fast water, caught a small wave from a rapid, and went hurtling again downstream.

Another time, in the same area, I saw a river otter flashing downstream that managed to breach like a whale, then lift up its head and stare at me nearly eye-to-eye, then duck back down into the river, all while traveling at nearly 15 or 20 mph downstream.

I have also seen river otter at wilderness lakes where the feeder streams were nothing but a trickle of a creek. In the Ukonom Basin of the Marble Mountain Wilderness, where there are more bears per square mile than anywhere, I got the surprise of the evening, when, instead of a bear, a pair of river otters showed up near our lakeside campsite.

river otter

River otters are not instinctive swimmers; their mother has to coax her pups into the water to teach them to swim. Although there wasn't a river to go with the river otter, a pair of them were still having a field day, playing in the shallows, as if in a game of hide-and-seek, popping their heads up, then ducking down, swirling about.

Now just a minute—a river otter in a lake? Well, your best chance of seeing a river otter isn't always in a river at all. It can be in a lake, and I'll tell you why.

After weeks of hot weather, water temperatures in lakes can rise to high levels, even 75-80°F on the surface at reservoirs in the foothills of the mountain country. Fish that want cool water must do one of two things: Head down to the thermocline, a cool, oxygenated layer of water that typically establishes itself 35 to 60 feet deep in summer, or migrate to the head of the lake, then catch the cool inflows from the primary river that is feeding the lake. (In winter and spring, when the temperatures in a lake are the same as in a river, and also when there is no midwater thermocline, this strategy does not apply, of course.)

But in summer, this is why there are typically more river otters at the heads of lakes than anywhere else. Come the last two hours of a summer day, when shade is cast on a lake and the trout begin to feed, that is when the otters will also make their appearance. After all, it is a lot easier to catch trout when you go where they are, just as human fishermen know.

Some fishermen groan at the sight of the fish-eating otters, since they think it means the end of that day's fishing, and, worse, that otters cause declines in fish. The truth is that I fish a ton, and otters have never bothered my catches. If anything, they will tell you where the fish are, and in addition, the otter, in order to get dinner, has no desire to scare fish into hiding. Otter and fish have co-existed since practically the beginning of time, with their populations cycling up and down without regard to each other. They are not, as biologists term it, a limiting factor.

What they can do is put on a swimming show that is unrivaled at a lake or stream. And be finalists in the cute contest of California wildlife.

Biologists' Notes

When first seen, the long, slender, short-legged body of the Northern river otter (Lutra canadensis) can remind the observer of a small pet. The otter is a dark, rich brown, and the muzzle and underparts are tawny, tinged with gray. The luxurious fur is short and dense and evenly interspersed with

Where to see river otter

ARCATA MARSH AND WILDLIFE SANCTUARY, IN HUMBOLDT COUNTY

ASH CREEK WILDLIFE AREA, IN MODOC AND LASSEN COUNTIES

COSUMNES RIVER PRESERVE, IN SACRAMENTO COUNTY

EAST WALKER WILDLIFE AREA, MONO COUNTY

GRIZZLY ISLAND WILDLIFE AREA, IN SOLANO COUNTY

LAKE EARL WILDLIFE AREA, IN DEL NORTE COUNTY

OROVILLE WILDLIFE AREA, IN BUTTE COUNTY

PAYNES CREEK WETLANDS, IN TEHAMA COUNTY

SACRAMENTO NATIONAL WILDLIFE REFUGES COMPLEX, IN BUTTE, COLUSA, GLENN, SUTTER, AND TEHAMA COUNTIES

YOLO BYPASS WILDLIFE AREA, IN YOLO COUNTY

Other places to see river otter

CACHE CREEK MANAGEMENT AREA, IN LAKE COUNTY

LEWISTON LAKE, IN TRINITY COUNTY

MCCLOUD RIVER PRESERVE, IN SISKIYOU COUNTY

REDWOOD NATIONAL AND STATE PARKS, IN DEL NORTE COUNTY

RUTH LAKE, IN TRINITY COUNTY

SHASTA LAKE, SHASTA-TRINITY NATIONAL FOREST, IN SHASTA COUNTY

short, wiry guard hairs. It is considered one of the most beautiful and durable of all furs. The otter's head is small, round, and short-eared. The tail is long and thick, tapering with little definition from the body to the tip. The legs are short and powerful, and all four feet are webbed.

Its lithe, muscular body and webbed feet make it well suited to an aquatic life. When seen in the depths of clear water, its fluid swimming motions leave the impression of a bodiless shadow. When it surfaces, the round, slightly flattened head and drooping whiskers give it a quizzical expression.

The river otter prefers to live on the larger rivers, lakes, and sloughs. Its home is in carefully concealed dens along the water's edge. In the delta regions of the Sacramento and San Joaquin Rivers, it sometimes dens in the thick tules.

The otter in the same form is found on all the major land masses on earth, including North and South America, Europe, Asia, and Africa. In California it ranges through northern and central California from the floor of the great valleys up to 5,000 feet, and in summer, has been documented to expand its range high into the alpine zone of the mountains of Northern California as well as the Sierra Nevada. It inhabits the coastal streams from the Russian River north to the Oregon border and throughout the watersheds of the Klamath, the Sacramento, and the San Joaquin Rivers. There is no record of river otters in the coastal streams south of San Francisco.

Mating occurs in summer, with the young being born blind and helpless the following April and May. There are from two to four in a litter. The young develop slowly and live with their mother for one year. They are not instinctive swimmers; mother has to coax them into the water to teach them to swim.

The otter's food is chiefly aquatic, consisting of fish, crayfish, frogs, and aquatic insects, although it occasionally eats small mammals, birds, and bird eggs. Along coastal streams an otter is occasionally seen with steelhead trout or salmon, but, when available, the otter subsists on the slower-moving rough fish such as carp, suckers, and squawfish. There is no evidence that otters have any effect on wild fish populations.

Otter, Sea

With many kinds of wildlife, that magical first sighting is elusive, often an accident. Not so with sea otter. This is not only one of the most lovable species to watch in California, but you can make it a mission to watch them and have a near guarantee of success.

So it was the first time I headed out to find them, filled with more anticipation than certainty. I was exploring the Big Sur coast in Monterey County, and at Andrew Molera State Park, decided to hike out on a trail to the beach, then explore a bit. At this one spot, there was this huge washed-up log, perfect for a backrest, so I took a seat, just sitting in the sand and watching the water lap at the beach. It was a fall afternoon, when the Monterey coast gets its best weather of the year, and it was a clear and almost balmy day.

ANIMAL	Otter, Sea
SPECIES	*Enhydra lutris*
TYPE	mammal
STATUS	OK/Threatened
SEE ALSO	Badger, Fisher, Marten, Mink, Otter (River), Raccoon, Skunks

Just offshore were a few shallow kelp beds. Out of the corner of an eye, I detected movement, and instinctively, turned and focused in on the edge of a kelp bed. Just like that, this little brown head popped up, looking at me. A moment later, there was another. For the next hour I watched these little guys play hide-and-seek, as amused at putting on a show for me as I was to be watching it.

With that sighting, I immediately understood the fascination with sea otters. They are cute beyond belief, fuzzy and furry, with dark eyes and little paws, and when not playing "now-you-see-me, now-you-don't" on the kelp beds, they like rolling on their backs, then floating about on the surface, their hind flippers aimed to the sky.

Anybody who has watched sea otters knows exactly what I'm talking about.

At Big Sur and Andrew Molera State Park, the rangers will often provide a sheet listing the best places to watch sea otters.

They are most abundant in California along the Monterey County coast, specifically from Big Sur south to San Simeon. Their ideal habitat is available here, expansive inshore kelp beds. They typically hang out in compact

sea otter

Lacking a protective layer of blubber, which keeps other marine mammals warm, the sea otter uses digestion to stay warm and cannot go without food for long. A minimum of six to eight pounds of food per day is required, and an adult may consume as much as 15 pounds or nearly one quarter of its weight per day.

groups and have a ravenous appetite for abalone. Because of the overharvest of abalone by commercial divers, the food supply for sea otters is a limiting factor to population expansion.

However, sea otters have also been discovered at Elkhorn Slough near Moss Landing in Monterey Bay, with most of the otters at Seal Bend feeding primarily on clams. While some cheered the arrival of sea otters here, many believe they will simply wipe out a large portion of the clam population, then head back out, looking for more traditional food sources. In a five-year study, populations of sea otter in Elkhorn Slough fluctuated dramatically, from as few as four to as many as 75.

The reason the latter is of great note is because sea kayak rentals are available in Elkhorn Slough, with special package deals for families with children. With the otters taking up home, that makes for an extremely enticing adventure. Can you imagine a better introduction to nature than for a youngster to be paddling a kayak with mom or dad, and then have a few sea otters poke their heads up, or play a bit, within a boat's length? You would have an outdoors convert for life.

After all, look what happened to me after just an hour on the beach, watching them play.

Biologists' Notes

At one time sea otters *(Enhydra lutris)* numbered in countless thousands, in an arc-like range nearly 6,000 miles long from Japan to Baja California.

One of the most notable things about the sea otter is its fur, which is unusually fine, soft, and dense. It was the fur's great value that almost led to the sea otter's extinction. The silken beauty of its fur was prized by the mandarins of Asia as early as 1700, and later in the mid-1700s it added much to the elegance of the courts of Russia. Because of the great demand, the animal was hunted without mercy.

Incomplete records between 1741 and 1911 show that over one million skins were taken, about 200,000 of which were from California and Baja California waters. As early as 1867, when the United States purchased Alaska from Russia, floods of letters and petitions urged the protection of the sea otter and fur seal, but the ruthless killing continued until the early 1890s.

The sea otter was nearly extinct, with only a few otters left along central California and some of the island waters of Alaska.

In 1911 the Fur Seal Treaty was signed by the U.S., Russia, Japan, and Great Britain, affording protection to the sea otter in Pacific waters. State law in 1913 supplemented the treaty and gave rigid protection to the remaining few otters along the California coast from all but the occasional poacher. As added protection from shooting, in 1941 a sea otter refuge was established, and in 1959 the refuge was expanded. This refuge included the land west of Highway 1 from the mouth of the Carmel River south to Cambria.

Under complete protection, the sea otter has made a strong recovery, though it is still a protected as a federally threatened species. They have increased in numbers and expanded their range north to Santa Cruz and south to Point Buchon in San Luis Obispo County.

The sea otter is a member of the weasel family, most closely related to the river otter. A large animal, the male is about four and a half feet long, including its 10- to 12-inch tail. Males can weigh as much as 86 pounds in California, while the female is smaller.

Although the forepaws are rounded and stubby, the sea otter is able to make use of them for holding food and other objects. The hind feet are large and webbed and the tail is slightly flattened horizontally. The most common position for swimming or resting is on its back, but when in a hurry it swims on its belly at speeds of up to five miles an hour.

Where to see sea otter

ANDREW MOLERA STATE PARK, IN MONTEREY COUNTY

AÑO NUEVO STATE RESERVE, IN SAN MATEO COUNTY

CARMEL RIVER STATE BEACH, IN MONTEREY COUNTY

MORRO BAY STATE PARK, SAN LUIS OBISPO COUNTY

PISMO STATE BEACH, IN SAN LUIS OBISPO COUNTY

VENTANA WILDERNESS, IN MONTEREY COUNTY

Sea otter pups may be born at any time of the year; however, the peak of the pupping season in California is from November to March, and the gestation period is between eight and nine months. The young are born with their eyes open and some teeth already present. The pup's coat is woolly for five or six months. The baby first learns to swim on its belly but floats on its back when left alone. After some weeks it learns to swim on its back.

The mother is devoted to the pup. When she is on the surface of the water, the baby spends most of its time resting on her, nursing and hitching rides when she moves to a new feeding ground. Although the baby nurses for nearly one year, it starts eating solid food after a few weeks and is fully grown in four years.

Unlike the northern sea otters in Alaska, which in some areas frequently come to shore, the California sea otter spends almost all its life in the water. The sea otter's food consists almost entirely of animal life from the ocean floor and kelp beds. This limits the otters to fairly shallow water.

Food habit studies have shown that in the kelp-rocky reef areas within its present range, sea otters' preferred foods are abalone, sea urchins, and rock crabs. In the sandy beach areas it turns to clams and a variety of other shellfish. The sea otter is one of the few animals to use a "tool" in its quest for food, using a rock to dislodge organisms from the ocean's bottom and to crack shells at the surface.

Lacking the protective layer of blubber, which keeps other marine mammals warm, the sea otter cannot go without food very long. The sea otter requires a minimum of six to eight pounds of food per day, and an adult may consume as much as 15 pounds or nearly one quarter of its body weight per day. Thus, a herd of sea otters is capable of a profound effect on the near-shore marine environment.

Owls
Great Horned Owl
Barn Owl

The forest night was quiet and black, and at midnight at my camp, I awoke to the soft but haunting call of an owl: "Hoo," it started, a deep, booming hoot, then "Hoo, hoooo." That last "hoooo" was softer and had a ripple on the end as if for special effect, like a yearning call for a lost love off in the distance.

At dusk the next evening, I set out into the forest with my boys, Jeremy and Kris. We listened closely. Nothing. Then suddenly, amid a maelstrom of feathers, it sounded like a small helicopter was buzzing us. We instantly looked up and a two-foot great horned owl ripped overhead, its wingspan as wide as that of a hawk, but with its chunky body silhouetted against the sky, then popped up to the top of a Douglas fir.

By itself, the roar of the wings was remarkable because owls are best known for silent flight, a product of the serrated edges of their outer wing feathers, which allows them to hunt mice, gophers, voles, and rabbits (and cats, near towns) without being heard.

The big owl sat there, perched, its ear tufts propped up, staring at us with its yellow eyes, dark centers.

barn owl

"It's kind of creepy," I said to Kris, 8.

"Yeah, it is kind of creepy," he answered.

"Like Darth Vader," answered Jeremy, 11.

Then we saw it. Sitting on the forest floor, next to a small downed log just 25 feet away to our left, was another owl, about a foot tall. It was maybe four weeks old, a baby, suggested by the down-like fluff on its breast feathers.

This was the start of a tale of two owls, a wildlife rescue, and rarely seen glimpses of the realities of nature, and as an Indian friend told me, perhaps a story with a moral of the wild outdoors.

The first thing we did was get to a telephone and call the Department of Fish and Game's regional office; each regional office keeps a list of wildlife rescue specialists. Only a trained wildlife professional should conduct a wildlife rescue, of course. The next morning, Rich Callas, a Department of Fish and Game biologist and bird expert, called back, and shortly later, he arrived—and out we went into the forest. It wasn't long before we found the young owl, still sitting there.

An owl's eyesight is about 100 times as sensitive to light as that of a human. Its hearing is also acute and, because its right ear opening is higher than the left opening, the bird can pinpoint the source of sounds. Prey is torn apart and swallowed—bones, skull, and all. Indigestible parts are formed into pellets and disgorged at the roosting area. Two hundred pellets examined by scientists were found to contain the skulls of 406 mice, 20 rats, 20 shrews, one mole, and one sparrow.

"It's eyes are closed tight," Callas said, "that's not right."

Callas then walked up and examined it further. The other owl was nowhere to be seen. "His craw smells. The waste matter here doesn't look right. He hasn't moved in some time."

A minute later, Callas concluded, "This owl is dehydrated and starving to death."

We then checked the base of a giant nearby Douglas fir. Callas quickly found a variety of waste matter, including one pellet chunk which included the skull pieces of a mouse or gopher. Then he looked up and burst out, "There it is!"

About 80 feet high in that fir was a huge owl nest, maybe three feet across. Just 40 feet away, we found a rabbit that had been caught, killed, and beheaded, apparently by a hungry adult owl.

"Either the baby owl fell out of the nest or was pushed out," Callas said. "I have another owl, a little bit younger, at home that was found the same way. What I'd like to do is rehabilitate this owl for four or five days, get it strong enough to compete with any others up there, then climb up the tree and put it right back in the nest."

The next night, at Callas' wildlife rescue center at his home, Jeremy and Kris were mesmerized by the two owls in rehabilitation. In just 24 hours the one we had found had gained considerable strength; Callas had forced water into it with a catheter, then fed it small chunks of deer meat.

At one point, the boys took turns feeding it. Callas showed them how to barely touch the owl's down-like feathers below its beak, which triggers a sensory response, where the young owl intuitively grabbed the meat, tilted its head back, and took it down whole in a quick gulp.

But something was still not right. The owl's eyes were still tightly shut. When Callas examined them, there was a gray film across them, and they seemed dry. He had applied ointment to the eyes, but it seemed to do little good. Apparently, the owl was blind.

The other young owl being rescued, meanwhile, appeared alert, sharp and hungry. Its eyes were clear, yellow with the dark center, staring at us as if with X-ray vision. A week after its original rescue, the healthy owl was ready to "start training," as Callas called it.

"In a secure area, we'll let it chase live mice so it can learn to hunt for itself," Callas said. "When it can fly, understand hunting, and get food and water for itself, it will be ready to be released back into the wild, the same place where it was found."

The other owl, the one we had found, was not doing as well. Its eyes were still closed and its general health was fair at best. At one point, Callas had to administer antibiotics.

"This owl may never be able to compete in the wild," he said. "If it can't see, then it can't hunt. If it can't hunt, it won't eat. If it can't eat, it won't live. The best we may be able to do for it is to place it in a children's museum or small zoo, and even then, it will take a lot of care to keep it going."

An Indian friend of mine, Cloud Dancer, was told of the incident, and he asked if I had been hearing or seeing other owls recently. Yes, I answered, in fact, several on my last two camping trips this month.

"Seeing a certain bird or animal over and over again is never an accident," said Cloud Dancer. "They are messengers. Owls are particularly potent. They represent wisdom because they are able to see the truth through all deception. For you to see owls and rescue one is a message that you are being given a message of truth."

If so, then of what? Perhaps the one truth I have learned by spending so much time in the field is the brutal reality of nature. It is an unforgiving reality, with no sentiment between animals, even between a mother owl and its blind son, kicked out of the nest. For wildlife, there is none of the harmony that so many people find in wild places. Birds, animals, fish, and reptiles spend most of their time looking for something to eat and trying to keep from being eaten. The weak are killed quickly by other animals.

But what I keep remembering is that baby owl we found, how it felt in my hands, and our hopes for it amid the uncertainties of the natural world. Maybe the young owl will live. Maybe it will not.

Out in the wildlands, the battle for survival is fought each day, and the saga will never end.

Biologists' Notes

GREAT HORNED OWL *(Bubo virginianus)*
The great horned owl lives up to its reputation of being a "winged tiger." Its silent flight is like a big cat's soundless stalking. It has a greedy appetite, consumes almost anything, and attacks prey with frightening effectiveness. "Hoot owl" and "cat owl" are also common names for this large "eared" owl.

California has four subspecies of this New World owl. When owls are mentioned, this species most commonly comes to mind. It gives a "hooting " call, one of the most

ANIMAL	Owl, Great Horned
SPECIES	*Bubo virginianus*
TYPE	bird
STATUS	OK

famous of bird sounds. Birders learn the call of this and other owls to locate them at night.

Through natural selection, owls have developed special powers of sight and hearing. An owl's eyesight is approximately 100 times as sensitive to light as that of a human. Its hearing is also acute and, because its right ear opening is higher than the left opening, the bird can use this assymetry in sound reception to pinpoint the origin of sounds.

This large owl—20 inches long with a wingspread of 55 inches—has a general dark brown coloration, large head, and short neck. Its flight is direct and deceptively quick. It is twice the size of the crows that often harass it during the day. Weighing up to five pounds, the great horned owl is even larger than the common red-tailed hawk. This species is the largest owl with ear tufts or horns. The long-eared owl is the only other owl it may be confused with in the field. As its name implies, long-eared owl also has ear tufts but it is much smaller, about the same size as a crow.

Generally, great horned owls are gray-brown, mottled with darker brown on the back and wings. On the underparts it is lighter in coloration, finely barred with dark brown or black. A distinctive white bib can be seen upon close observation. A brownish facial disc surrounds bright, piercing yellow eyes.

Owls are nocturnal birds of prey, hunting primarily at night or in the early evening when light conditions are poor. The facial disc may act like a radar disc, funneling light to the eyes and sound to the ears. The horn tufts have nothing to do with hearing; they just add to the fierce appearance.

An owl is unable to move its eyes as humans can, so it is constantly turning its head to see what is going on around it. With the ear openings on each side of its face, it also hears sounds emanating from the same direction it is looking, an unusual workable adaptation for nocturnal birds of prey. Owls can turn their heads so quickly that, in poor light, it appears they are twisting their heads off.

Great horned owls are widespread in California. They are resident birds from the timberline in the Sierra Nevada to the grasslands and canyons of the coast. They can even be seen below sea level in the Mojave Desert. Suitable habitat can be almost any locality with protected daytime roosts and nesting sites. Look along wooded river bottoms in the valleys, in wooded foothill ravines, or in forests of mountainous areas.

Watch for this dark bird to fly silently, deeper into its territory to another hidden perch. Often, great horned owls are located by a noisy mob of crows, jays, or other birds, which attack them during the day. Although great horned owls may raid these other birds' nests, the conflict among them is more like a "dog and cat" relationship. They just seem to be natural enemies. These owls are non-migratory and will be found in established breeding territories all year long if an adequate food supply is available. A minimum of one square mile of habitat is needed to raise a family of two to three young per year.

Dinner for the great horned owl is usually whatever is most abundant, although a rabbit may be favored. When hunting, this owl most frequently waits on a perch to locate its prey, then drops silently on it. It is so powerful and aggressive it takes down surprisingly large birds and mammals.

Great horned owls regularly use a feeding perch or station. When you are in the field, watch the ground for bird feathers, discarded animal parts, and regurgitated pellets made up of undigested materials. These are found under the perch.

While this owl remains hidden during the day, it will hunt at any time when necessary. The sense of smell is not well developed. Often it will take skunks as prey with no apparent ill effects. It dislikes spoiled meat but will always taste it before discarding it. The male furnishes all the food for the female and young when they are in the nest. Females are in constant attendance of a nest with eggs or young, defending it against any intruders, especially birds of the same species.

The great horned owl is the earliest breeder, often as early as mid-January in the lower latitudes. Females have been seen with snow on their backs while incubating a clutch. They do not build their own nest. Instead, they renovate an abandoned nest from the previous year that was built by a hawk, eagle, heron, or other large bird. These sites may be in trees or cliff ledges.

Look closely at any large stick nest in the late winter or early spring, you may see a pair of ear-tufts and yellow eyes peering over the nest edge. Owls are very alert and the chance of your surprising one is unlikely.

Horned owls are disliked by many bird species, but none are a real threat. The only real enemies are humans and, occasionally, one of its own kind. Adults usually show extreme anger and recklessly dive again and again at an intruder when their eggs or young are threatened. They frequently keep up a constant crackling or snapping of their bill.

Great horned owls have earned a place on the list of "beneficial" birds. They take far more obnoxious species as prey than they do game animals or poultry. It is an important species to the farmer and rancher because of its diet of rodents and other mammals that cause great economic losses each year.

Barn Owl *(Tyto alba)*
The barn owl is a worldwide species, but only one form is found in North America. It is widely distributed in the United States. The breeding range in California is generally south of Redding. Barn owls have been seen as far north as the southern border of British Columbia, but they increase in abundance southward and occur in greater numbers in Southern California.

The barn owl can readily be distinguished from other owls by its unique shape and

ANIMAL	Owl, Barn
SPECIES	*Tyto alba*
TYPE	bird
STATUS	OK

color. The color varies somewhat but is prevailingly white with buff, yellow, and tawny shadings. It is delicately freckled with dark specks and the blending of colors in daylight has led some to call it, appropriately, the "golden owl". Other common names are white owl and monkey-faced owl.

The barn owl's face is arresting. There are no ear tufts. The eyes and beak are completely encircled by a heart-shaped facial ruff of white, rimmed with buff. The ruff is composed of narrow, stiff, slightly curved feathers that radiate out from the small dark eyes. They see well at night and, like great horned owls, also must move their heads to see to the side or back. Their hearing is extremely acute, for it is known that a barn owl can strike a mouse in the dark.

Sitting, the barn owl looks and acts awkward, but in flight it is airy and graceful. The long, broad wings support the slight body with ease and enable it to dash swiftly and silently on its prey.

Barn owls are distinctly birds of open country rather than woodland areas. They find the food they prefer in open fields, orchards, and gardens and seem to favor humans' old and seldom used buildings. They are more nocturnal than other owls. They wait until dark before starting out to hunt, except when the demands of their young may start them hunting at twilight. Normally, before daylight, they retire to some shadowed or enclosed area in an old building, a hollow tree, or a hole in a rocky cliff and remain there, drowsily inactive, all day.

Their silent coming and going is seldom observed, and it is interesting to see how long they can remain unnoticed even in a thickly settled community.

When hunting at night, it sweeps the fields on silent wings, catching its prey with its long, slender claws. It prefers small mammals but occasionally, in winter, when mice and gophers are scarce, will take small birds. Studies indicate that in California the pocket gopher, which is quite destructive in orchards and gardens, seems to be preferred.

The prey is torn apart and swallowed—bones, skull, and all. Indigestible parts are formed into pellets and disgorged at the roosting area or about the nest. Scientists examined 200 pellets from the nest of one pair of barn owls. In this study, they found 406 skulls and three different kinds of mice, the skulls of 20 rats, 20 shrews, one mole, and one sparrow.

Barn owls choose nesting sites almost anywhere, in old buildings, hollow trees, and on and in the ground. No effort is made to build or line the nest. The female lays from five to seven white, spotless eggs at intervals of two to three days. Incubation starts after the first egg is laid. It takes from 32 to

Where to see the great horned owl and/or barn owl

GRAY LODGE STATE WILDLIFE AREA, IN BUTTE COUNTY

KERN NATIONAL WILDLIFE REFUGE, IN KERN COUNTY

LAVA BEDS NATIONAL MONUMENT, IN SISKIYOU COUNTY

LOS BANOS STATE WILDLIFE AREA, IN FRESNO COUNTY

MENDOTA STATE WILDLIFE AREA, IN FRESNO COUNTY

MODOC NATIONAL WILDLIFE REFUGE, IN MODOC COUNTY

SWEETWATER MARSH NATIONAL WILDLIFE REFUGE, IN SAN DIEGO COUNTY

TEHAMA STATE WILDLIFE AREA, IN TEHAMA COUNTY

34 days for the first egg to hatch, so a nest may contain four or five young of different sizes and ages.

The young are called owlets. They are covered with snow white down for six days. This is gradually replaced by a buff-colored down that develops into a thick, woolly covering that is in evidence for about 50 days.

The little owlets are hungry all the time. Both parents are busy night after night ransacking the adjoining fields to catch an unbelievable number of small ground creatures to feed their ravenous babies.

Adult plumage is acquired in about seven and a half weeks, at which time, after much practicing about the nest, the young venture out for their first lessons in hunting.

Pelican, Brown

When it comes to fishing, birds never lie. And when it comes to birds, the greatest lie detector of them all is the pelican.

Let me explain. A fisherman can generally be defined as a liar standing next to water. Hence they tend not to trust, especially in each other. So on the ocean, anglers turn to birds for advice, because there is no one better at fishing than marine birds. And on the California coast, there is none better at telling the truth than the pelican.

ANIMAL	Pelican, Brown
SPECIES	*Pelecanus occidentalis*
TYPE	bird
STATUS	Endangered

A hovering pelican means it is searching for food. A diving pelican means he has found it. A pelican flying low and fast means it is traveling to a specific destination. A V-squadron of pelicans cruising the coast typically means they are migrating. And a pelican sitting on a dock or buoy means it is fat and happy, likely content to rest after a recent gorge session.

The reason this pelican code is critical is the marine food chain. Pelicans like nothing better than divebombing a horde of anchovies near the surface. And those anchovies have been driven to the surface likely because beneath them is a school of game fish. Fishermen know that following pelicans will get you to the fish every time, earning them a special place in the minds of anglers.

In recent years, however, as the pelican population recovers from its catastrophic collapse to endangered species status in the early 1970s, they have gained a place in the hearts in much of the general public as well.

brown pelican

When they first lift off, their large, awkward wingbeats make them look like clunky flyers. Wrong! With a slight wind to provide lift under those big wings, pelicans have the ability to fly the inshore coast like F-15 jet fighters in V formation, just a few feet above the ocean surface as if avoiding radar, cruising up and down the swells in sync with the rhythms of the ocean.

Watching them in a divebomb feeding frenzy is a thrill to anglers—because it means fish—and a spectacle for everybody else. Pelicans hover almost like a helicopter, then collapse their wings and freefall straight down like a dropped bowling ball, crashing into the water with a gigantic splash, with the monstrous scoop of a mouth making a slashing dip for food as if it were a huge ladle.

A hovering pelican is looking for food; a diving pelican has found it. When flying low and fast, a pelican is heading to a specific destination. A V-squadron cruising the coast generally means migration. A pelican sitting on a dock or buoy is fat and happy, resting after a gorge session. The pelican's method of fishing is unique. After entering the water, it turns completely around, rises to the surface to drain about a gallon or more of water from its pouch, then points its bill upward to swallow its fish.

As with so many fish-eating birds, the population of brown pelicans collapsed in the 1970s due to the pesticide DDT. In 1970 only one baby pelican was produced in 552 nesting attempts at Anacapa Island, at the time the last breeding population in the state. Since the ban, pelicans have come back strong and can be seen all along the California coast at different times of the year.

Pelicans can usually be spotted year-round along the Southern California coast, especially along San Diego, San Clemente, and out to the Channel Islands and Catalina. If you watch them closely, you will discover that they provide an excellent weather forecast: Pelicans flying offshore at sea means good weather ahead. When a storm is about to arrive, they typically will fly to land for shelter, 12 to 24 hours in advance of the front.

As the migration of anchovies arrive to the Bay Area coast in July, the pelicans begin flying north in large numbers. By the end of July, it is common to see pelicans all along the California coast from San Diego to Crescent City, typically hanging around together near docks and marinas, picking up handouts and leftovers before heading out and looking for a main course.

When they do, it is always a production. They take their eating seriously. In the process, a lot of people pay attention. After all, pelicans are the world's most honest fishermen.

Biologists' Notes

The brown pelican *(Pelecanus occidentalis)* is a large grayish-brown coastal bird with a long, pouched bill. Adults have white heads and necks, but immature birds are dark-headed. It flies with its neck and head folded back on its shoulders, alternately flapping its wings and sailing.

The California brown pelican differs from its eastern relatives chiefly in its much larger size. The color of the back of its neck is much darker, nearly black, and the color of its pouch is reddish at certain seasons. This subspecies nests on California's Channel Islands, on the coastal islands off Lower California, and in the Gulf of California.

The California brown pelican is not truly a migratory bird. However, after the breeding season they do extend their range northward along the California coastline with an occasional sighting as far north as British Columbia.

The pelican's diet consists almost entirely of fish, which it catches in its large pouch. The method of fishing is unique. It enters the water with a splash and does a complete turnover under water. The bird's body buoyancy brings it quickly to the surface. Upon emerging, after it shakes the water from its plumage, it first points its bill downward to drain the water—which may be a gallon or more—from its pouch, then upward to swallow the fish.

California brown pelicans' main nesting area is on remote islands off the coast of Mexico. Here they prefer the steep, rocky slopes and build large, bulky nests of sticks, grasses, and other convenient material. The female usually lays three and occasionally four large white eggs that appear dirty and sometimes stained. It takes four weeks of incubation before the eggs hatch. There is no difference in the appearance of the male or female, so it is difficult to determine which is sitting on the nest.

When first hatched, the young are far from attractive. They are unable to hold up their heads and really look more like a shapeless mass of half-dried flesh than a bird. However, within a few days, their eyes open and the dark red skin turns to a dull black. Within one week they can sit up and take notice of things. At two weeks they become covered with white down.

The youngest birds are fed by their parents on regurgitated, partly digested fish that flows from the tip of the adult bill, where it can be easily reached by the nearly helpless young. As the young increase in size, they learn to stick their heads down into the pouch, where they find a hearty meal of whole and partly digested fish.

Unlike the adult birds, which seldom make any sounds, the youngsters are quite noisy, continuously clucking to themselves, and as they grow older they utter a shrill scream when the mother approaches with another pouch full of fish. Later, when they have learned how to fly, they are taken in small flocks and taught how to catch their own food.

They go out in groups of five to 20. Their first efforts to take flight are quite laborious, with much wing flapping and running a few steps on the water. Once airborne, the flight of the pelican is strong, graceful, and well sustained on their long powerful wings. They relieve their slow, sweeping wing strokes with frequent periods of scaling or soaring. At times they congregate and may be seen soaring high in the air for sport or exercise, but they are by no means equal to the white pelican, which stays aloft for long periods of time.

When the feeding grounds are reached, they fly in a straight line near the surface until fish are found. If a school of fish is near the surface, there is a great flurry of diving and circling until the fish disappear. Once more in the air, the search continues until all are fed.

Where to see brown pelican

CABRILLO NATIONAL MONUMENT, IN SAN DIEGO COUNTY

CHANNEL ISLANDS, OFFSHORE FROM VENTURA COUNTY

FORT FUNSTON SUNSET TRAIL, IN SAN FRANCISCO COUNTY

GOLETA BEACH COUNTY PARK, IN SANTA BARBARA COUNTY

HUMBOLDT BAY NATIONAL WILDLIFE REFUGE, IN HUMBOLDT COUNTY

MONTEREY BAY, FROM MOSS LANDING TO FORT ORD, IN MONTEREY COUNTY

SUNBEAM LAKE / FIG LAGOON, IN IMPERIAL COUNTY

Other places to see brown pelican

FISHERMAN'S WHARF, IN MONTEREY COUNTY

FISHERMAN'S WHARF, IN SAN FRANCISCO COUNTY

LOPEZ LAKE, IN SAN LUIS OBISPO COUNTY

PATRICK'S POINT STATE PARK, IN HUMBOLDT COUNTY

SWEETWATER MARSH NATIONAL WILDLIFE REFUGE, IN SAN DIEGO COUNTY

TIJUANA SLOUGH NATIONAL WILDLIFE REFUGE, IN SAN DIEGO COUNTY

Pheasant, Ring-Necked

Pheasants are not wild because they're hunted, Bob Simms told me, they're hunted because they are wild.

Simms, who hosts one of the West's most popular radio shows on the outdoors, is an avid outdoorsman who has a natural passion for wildlife, wild places, and California history. I have spent many days with him, from searching for Indian artifacts in the Ishi Wilderness to fishing for bass at his secret home water, amid other adventures, including just driving around the woods. But it is pheasant that provides a particular fascination for him, as well as inspiring many adventures from his home base in the Central Valley.

ANIMAL	Pheasant, Ring-Necked
SPECIES	*Phasianus colchicus*
TYPE	bird
STATUS	Introduced
SEE ALSO	Quails

On one such escapade, Simms ventured out to explore a long swath of riparian habitat set along a river bank near farmland, looking for pheasant. "Riparian" means wild habitat along a watershed, and in the Central Valley, there are riparian zones between rivers and farmland. This, Simms explained, is where you can find pheasant, along with so much other wildlife.

As the hike started, from time to time you could hear the distant cackling of pheasant. "You know they're in here," Simms said. "You can hear them."

In the next few hours, Simms combed that riparian zone. Guess what? Nothing. The search thus became more systematic, dividing the habitat into zones, then methodically probing in 10-foot swaths, back and forth. Nothing could elude such a careful search, right? Guess what? Nothing. Finally, it had been some time, and even the call of pheasants had ceased. Nothing.

Simms then sat down on a rock, a bit piqued,

ring-necked pheasant

In 1889, several varieties of pheasant were introduced in California; only the Chinese ring-necked pheasant, native to eastern Asia, was successful in establishing breeding populations.

and talked some about how the Department of Fish and Game was reacting to the illegal introduction of the predator fish pike into California waters, then said, "Well, I guess the pheasant all took off. We looked everywhere."

At that exact moment, you could hear a pheasant cackle about 50 yards off, an area that had been thoroughly explored. He raised his eyebrows, then turned to the sound, and right then, another pheasant emerged from the brush and went flying down along the rivercourse.

"The way we looked, you would think that it would not be possible for a pheasant to be in there," he said with a grin. "But there they are. The difficulty of finding wild pheasant is a key to the attraction for me."

And that's why they are hunted. Because they are wild.

There have been many times, when looking for quail, when I have almost stepped on a pheasant in high grass. They typically stay quiet and motionless to the last second, then suddenly burst into the air amid a wild flurry of pounding wings and feathers. When you surprise one like this, the commotion they create is so great that you can just about have a heart attack. They can just plain stun the heck out of you in surprise flight.

They are beautiful, big birds, one of the great prizes of upland game, of course. Artists have painted their likeness in every form imaginable, on glasses, dishes, towels, seat cushions, wrapping paper.

If they were easy to find, such as at the game bird farms where domestic-raised pheasants are planted, there would be no such mass appeal. After all, few things worth remembering come easy.

Biologists' Notes

The pheasant is the most spectacular upland game bird in California. It is native to China and other parts of eastern Asia, but in 1889 the Department of Fish and Game (then the State Board of Fish and Game Commissioners) introduced several varieties of pheasant into California. The Chinese ring-necked pheasant (*Phasianus colchicus*) is the only species that was successful in establishing breeding populations.

The Chinese ring-necked pheasant is a gaudily colored bird with distinctive brilliant plumage, a white ring around his neck, and, when fully matured, a black-banded tail that may be as much as 21 inches in length.

The female is smaller and also has a pointed tail. She is quite drab by contrast. Her coloring could be described as a mottled blend of grays and browns with some buff and dusky markings.

During the winter, pheasants tend to separate into bands of hens and bands of cocks. In February and March the cocks spread out to look for a territory of their own. These home areas are defined by crowing and display and defended by much bluffing and even fighting. The size of the home areas varies from three to 13 acres according to the density of the cover and the availability of food and water.

In late March and early April the hens gradually disperse and join the roosters in the crowing grounds for harem formation, which is usually three to five hens per rooster.

The hen builds her nest in grassy or weedy places. She lays from 10 to 12 pale olive-colored eggs, which are hatched in 23 to 25 days. The young are ready to leave the nest when they are dry. Both the father and mother are good parents. The father guards the young of all the hens in his harem, and although he is not with any one of his families, he responds immediately at the first note of alarm.

The baby pheasants' food the first week is made up almost entirely of insects, but by the time they are 12 weeks old they eat the same diet as their parents, which is made up of cereal grains, wild weed seeds, the green leaves of plants, and some insects.

Young pheasant broods are reclusive and are difficult to flush. Although they can fly when three weeks old, they prefer to run when danger threatens, even after they are grown. In August the young show some independence, and by late September the fully feathered birds from different territories join each other in areas that have the most suitable protective cover.

The flight of an adult pheasant is strong. When cornered at the edge of cover it bursts from the ground, sometimes with a raucous cackling cry. The wing action is rapid and the speed of flight may reach 35 miles per hour. The flights are usually low, 10 or 15 feet from the ground, and pheasants may coast on set wings for 200 yards or more.

Ring-necked pheasants have been introduced into every county in California, but satisfactory breeding populations became best established in the fertile valley areas of diversified agriculture, where there is a plentiful year-round supply of water and some grain forming.

The largest populations are found in the rice-growing areas in the Sacramento and upper San Joaquin Valleys, and in the Tule Lake area of extreme North California. The most important of these is the rice-growing area of

Where to see ring-necked pheasant

COLUSA NATIONAL WILDLIFE REFUGE, IN COLUSA COUNTY

GRASSLAND RESOURCE CONSERVATION DISTRICT, IN MERCED COUNTY

GRAY LODGE STATE WILDLIFE AREA, IN BUTTE COUNTY

MERCED NATIONAL WILDLIFE REFUGE, IN MERCED COUNTY

SAN JACINTO WILDLIFE AREA, IN RIVERSIDE COUNTY

SAN PABLO BAY NATIONAL WILDLIFE REFUGE, IN CONTRA COSTA COUNTY

the Sacramento Valley. The abundant water needs for rice culture promotes heavy growths of cover along the many canals, ditches, sloughs, and low spots suitable for high pheasant populations.

Pig, Wild

Most people like to think that wild boars roam the woods something akin to a Hells Angel running his Harley-Davidson over a highway. You'd best get out of the way, right?

The vision of a charging boar, nostrils flaring, tusks ripping everything in range is, well, largely an illusion. That just isn't how it works out in reality. Once, in the Ishi Wilderness, I was hunting in caves for Indian artifacts, and after discovering several acorn grinding bowls in rocks, I turned and found myself looking nearly face-to-face with not one boar, but two, dead-on. I figured, "I must be dead," and they came charging out. Reacting on instinct, I stepped aside, and those pigs roared right on past, close enough for me to swat one on the butt.

ANIMAL	Pig, Wild
SPECIES	*Sus scrofa*
TYPE	mammal
STATUS	Introduced

So I did! A nice, clean, hard swat. The pig let out a grunt and kept on going.

So the reality is wild pigs are not violent animals towards people. When you spot, stalk, and track wild pigs, what you discover is that their violence is directed towards the habitat of other wildlife. They plow up native grasslands and oak woodlands like rototillers, plowing and eating acorns, roots, saplings and bugs. After a herd of wild pigs goes through an area, there is often little left behind for other wildlife on which to feed. But dangerous for people? You've got to be kidding.

Today's wild pigs are a mix of true black Russian boar and wild feral pigs. In good conditions, they have two litters per year, with an average of five piglets per litter, and hence, there are several areas where their population is expanding to the point that they are eating other wildlife out of house and home.

California wild pigs are a mix of feral domestic swine and true black Russian boar, introduced in the 1920s. They now rank second only to deer among big game in population size. Wild pigs have poor eyesight but a keen sense of hearing and of smell.

But let me tell you, stalking wild pigs is great sport. You have to be a combination of athlete and detective: an athlete to stand up to hiking through wild and rugged country, and a detective to find the smart and wary animal without uncovering your own presence.

To do it right, you must be out at dawn or dusk, the periods when wild pigs are either emerging from or returning to dense cover in canyons. Most of their foraging is done at night. You start by searching for any sign. It might be nothing more than an uprooted boulder or log, a sign that a pig has been rooting for food, or a few tracks found in the mud. If the signs appear fresh, you will know right off that you are close.

In morning and evening, when wild pigs are often feeding and on the move, my preference is to head out to valley overlooks and ridges, and then scan the broad areas below with binoculars. During midday, when the pigs often bed down, I take the opposite approach, hiking up the center of canyons that have plenty of protective cover.

Once you spot a group of pigs, the excitement starts. Wild pigs have very poor vision, which means that the careful stalker, with patience and intuition, can

wild pig

get remarkably close to them. I've snuck within 30 and 40 yards many times. Of course, keep any breeze in your face, so they don't pick up your scent, and stay out of sight by creeping in gullies and behind boulders and trees.

Without experience in stalking, you can spend a whole weekend and not see a single wild pig. It will drive you crazy, because you will likely see all the rooting damage from previous nights of work by their packs and know they are there.

In the end, wild pigs can be hard to find, particularly on public land. In addition, the danger factor is completely overblown. But what is not is the thrill of searching out and finding wild pigs on their own terms. In a world spinning like a 78-rpm record, this kind of adventure has a way of reaffirming a general sense of reality in the world that many never discover.

Biologists' Notes

Wild pig *(Sus scrofa)* populations in California are descendants of feral domestic swine and imported European wild boar. Since the two subspecies readily hybridize, few pure strains of European wild boar remain in California.

Domestic swine were released into the wild in California prior to 1800. They soon developed small feral populations in the coastal foothills. In the early 1920s European wild boar were introduced into Monterey County and subsequently dispersed south to San Luis Obispo County. They readily interbred with the already present feral pigs. Wild pigs are now found in approximately one half of the counties in the state, with most found on private lands. Substantial populations also exist offshore at Catalina and Santa Cruz Islands, despite programs designed to deplete them.

The wild pig in California ranks second only to deer among big game in estimated population size.

Wild pigs appear long-legged compared to domestic swine. They reach a length of about five feet and adults measure two or three feet high at the shoulders. Their hips tend to be angular, with both boars and sows looking generally alike. Although adult boars are reported to weigh up to 600 pounds, live weights above 300 pounds are unusual in California. Sows typically weigh less than 200 pounds, and 100- to 125-pounders are average.

Wild pigs range in color from pure white to pure black and include many color patterns resembling common breeds of domestic swine. Although both sexes have canine tusks, they are more obvious in adult boars, sometimes exceeding three inches in length. Pigs use these razor sharp teeth for feeding and fighting.

Wild pigs have poor eyesight, but keen senses of hearing and smell. Ordinarily wary, wild pigs will fight fearlessly and are considered among the most dangerous wild animals when wounded, cornered, or threatened when with their young. Although wild pigs may breed throughout the year, most breeding occurs in fall and winter. The gestation period is approximately four months. Litter sizes generally range from two to nine piglets, with most born during spring. Wild pigs reach sexual maturity at about six months of age. Although males appear to travel more than females, wild pigs are generally considered nomadic. Adult boars commonly lead a solitary life except during the breeding season. Several sows and their young often form groups.

Wild pigs inhabit a wide variety of habitats in California, but oak grasslands consistently support the largest pig populations. Once they locate food and water, pigs usually stay until the supply is gone or they are disturbed. Wild pigs are most active during morning and evening hours, but they may become essentially nocturnal.

Wild pigs are omnivorous and shift their diets seasonally to take advantage of nutritious sources of food. They rely on acorns, grasses, forbs, bulbs,

---

Where to see wild pig

HENRY W. COE STATE PARK, IN SANTA CLARA COUNTY

ISHI WILDERNESS, IN TEHAMA COUNTY

LAKE SOLANO COUNTY PARK, IN SOLANO COUNTY

LAKE SONOMA, IN SONOMA COUNTY

PINNACLES NATIONAL MONUMENT, IN SAN BENITO COUNTY

TEHAMA STATE WILDLIFE AREA, IN TEHAMA COUNTY

Other places to see wild pig

ANNADEL STATE PARK, IN SONOMA COUNTY

BIDWELL PARK, IN BUTTE COUNTY

DYE CREEK PRESERVE, IN TEHAMA COUNTY

JOSEPH D. GRANT COUNTY PARK, IN SANTA CLARA COUNTY

LAKE SONOMA RECREATION AREA, IN SONOMA COUNTY

roots, and insects. Feeding on carrion is common where pigs encounter carcasses of livestock or other wildlife. Reproductive success of pig populations has been directly linked to acorn availability during the fall. Riparian and marsh vegetation are important sources of succulent forage, preferred by pigs during summer.

Pigeon, Band-Tailed

The erratic, swooping, high-speed flight of band-tailed pigeons, also known simply as "bandtails," makes them like no other creature in the air.

I've spent hours at a time watching them fly. They arrive in flocks of all sizes—singly, in pairs, or in groups of tens and twenties— and not a one simply cruises on past. They rise up, then drop down, sometimes locking their wings in power dives, then bank to one side, rise up, then drop again in a dipsy-doo. To watch a half dozen in this dance across the low sky is a little piece of nature's magic.

Don't confuse a bandtail with the domestic pigeon found in cities. They don't look or act the same, and, in fact, are separate species.

ANIMAL	Pigeon, Band-Tailed
SPECIES	*Columba fasciata*
TYPE	bird
STATUS	OK
SEE ALSO	Doves

Band-tailed pigeons are migratory nomads, roaming from Canada to California on the annual fall migration south, and then back again in the summer.

If you do a little homework you will have plenty of opportunities to find bandtails. Most of their habitat is on public land, where access is free. To find a prime spot, first pick one of the areas on the list at the end of this section. Then find the locale that provides the appropriate combination of food and water these birds must have. They never go a day without watering, so you should stay close to a river or freshwater or mineral spring. Then search for a habitat where you might find acorns, pine nuts, madrone or toyon berries, or dogwood or oak buds.

Finding a stream with a few of these shrubs and trees along with a nearby mineral spring nearly guarantees that you will see plenty of bandtails perform their ballet across the sky.

Typically, bandtails will feed before dawn breaks, then fly to water, so the best way to find them is to position yourself near a mineral spring or river from dawn to about 9 a.m. By mid-morning, having fed and watered, they often take roost in trees, preferring dead tree skeletons to live tree branches. They then take flight sporadically through the rest of the day.

John Reginato, an old-timer who is an outdoors legend among many outdoor writers across the West, has a singular passion for bandtails. Some 20 years ago, he took me under his wing to share his experience with band-tail pigeons, taking me to his favorite stand above a mineral spring, adjacent to a creek, and near a hillside loaded with oaks, dogwood, pine, and madrone. The spot had everything: water, food, and cover.

From dawn to 8 a.m., we'd watch hundreds and hundreds of bandtails fly into that mineral spring like fighter jets approaching a landing strip, often locking their wings and dive-bombing into the river canyon, or veering off, fluttering like butterflies. It seemed as if they exulted in flying, and for hours, they'd just keep on coming. After a while, their light-spirited flight would start to rub off on you, and you'd notice that suddenly, you felt pretty good yourself.

band-tailed pigeon

Biologists' Notes

The band-tailed pigeon *(Columba fasciata)* gets its name from the wide blackish band that crosses the midtail. It resembles the domestic pigeon in size and shape and is easily distinguished from the dove by its broad rounded tail and dark overall bluish color. Unlike the domestic pigeon, its bill and legs are yellow and the eyelids are naked and bright red. Adults have a narrow white crescent that forms a collar at the base of the neck.

The bandtail is migratory. These pigeons live primarily in natural forests and in summer prefer high elevations, though there are some reports of them living in city environments in the northwest United States. Their breeding range is mostly in the north Coastal Ranges and at higher elevations on the western slopes of the Sierra Cascade Mountains. They start their northern migration as early as January and are found nesting in northern California through western Oregon, Washington, and into British Columbia, arriving there by mid-May.

Their courtship is typical of the pigeon family. Males perform a display of short flights followed by much cooing. After the female chooses a mate, the pair selects a nest site. Nesting is usually done singly in widely scattered spots, although sometimes food conditions will draw a number of birds into a loose colony.

The female builds a flimsy nest. In California it may be in a small shrub or in a huge Douglas fir tree. She may take a week or so to complete the nest; when finished, observers wonder how it can hold an egg or a baby pigeon.

The female lays one pure white egg, rarely two. Both parents help with the incubation. In 18 to 20 days the young are hatched, clothed in a thin coat of yellowish down. Both the mother and father feed the squab by regurgitating thick whitish "pigeon milk" that is manufactured in glands on the walls of the pigeon's crop. After a diet of pigeon milk for one week, fruit and insects are added, and soon the baby is nearly as large as its parents. By the 30th day it is fully feathered and ready to fly. In California, marked pairs of pigeons have been observed rearing two broods, using the same nest. Sometimes the pigeons produce only one egg each year.

In the fall they start their southern migration. Most of the migrating flocks range in size from 10 to 40 individuals, although some years see them in bands of hundreds to thousands. Their migratory habits are so erratic that it is hard to predict when or where they will appear next. If food is plentiful they dally along the way. When food is scarce they travel hundreds of miles and appear suddenly in a good food area in flocks of thousands. Normally it takes about three months for them to reach southern California in the fall flight.

When not actually migrating, they generally roost at high elevations. At daybreak the large roosting flock breaks up into smaller groups that swoop down to lower elevations to feed. The morning flight may take them to a hillside of madrone berries, or to a farmer's harvested grain field. Usually by 9 or 10 a.m. the feeding period is over, and they will spiral upwards to return to roost in the tall trees at higher elevations. They sit quietly through the day and repeat the feeding activity from late afternoon till dark.

Band-tailed pigeons are seed and fruit eaters. Acorns make up the bulk of their diet. They prefer the acorns of the blue oak and also the California live oak. They eat the fruits of dogwood and madrone trees. It is interesting to watch the pigeons feed on manzanita blossoms in the spring; the slender twigs bend with the weight of the bird, which executes all sorts of acrobatics while holding on and trying to eat at the same time.

Where to see band-tailed pigeon

CASTLE ROCK STATE PARK, IN SANTA CLARA COUNTY

CHEWS RIDGE, LOS PADRES NATIONAL FOREST, IN MONTEREY COUNTY

CLEAR LAKE NATIONAL WILDLIFE REFUGE, IN SISKIYOU COUNTY

HOBO GULCH TRAIL, SHASTA-TRINITY NATIONAL FOREST, IN TRINITY COUNTY

LAKE MORENA, CLEVELAND NATIONAL FOREST, IN SAN DIEGO COUNTY

Other places to see band-tailed pigeon

GROVER HOT SPRINGS STATE PARK, IN ALPINE COUNTY

LAKE SOLANO PARK, IN SOLANO COUNTY

MOUNT PINOS OBSERVATION POINT, IN VENTURA COUNTY

PINECREST LAKE, IN TUOLUMNE COUNTY

SANTA ROSA PLATEAU ECOLOGICAL RESERVE, IN RIVERSIDE COUNTY

STANISLAUS RIVER PARKS, IN STANISLAUS COUNTY

YOSEMITE NATIONAL PARK, IN MARIPOSA COUNTY

Porcupine

When people see their first porcupine, nearly everybody immediately asks the same question: Can they shoot their quills like darts?

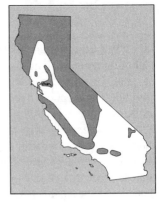

The answer is no, but I knew this dog named Sam, belonged to my old buddy Foonsky. If you could speak dog, ol' Sam would swear to you that porcupines could shoot their quills.

How else could he explain the quills in his nose and mouth, and the pain he was experiencing? "I'd never be so stupid to try and sniff a porcupine," Sam seemed to say as he leaned forward for a little commiseration. "And, of course, I'd never try to take a bite out of one. No, that porcupine shot his quills at me, and got me good."

ANIMAL	Porcupine
SPECIES	*Erethizon dorsatum*
TYPE	mammal
STATUS	OK

Well, the vet removed the quills and explained that despite Sam's story, porcupines just plain don't shoot their quills.

What they do, you see, is whip that tail around and nail the intruder like a hammer on an anvil. In a split second, the offender can have a mouthful of quills, or in the case of a dog, a noseful as well, resembling something like a pin cushion. In some cases, the force of the tail whipping around can cause the quills to carry perhaps a foot, but they never shoot like darts.

When you first see a porcupine, it can be amazing how clunky they appear. They kind of waddle like a fat, drunk raccoon covered with spikes. Then you realize that through the laws of natural selection, with their built-in natural defense, they have never had a need to be in much of a hurry, or for that matter, worry about being slim enough to move quickly.

And so they don't run. These roly-poly fellows are content to stumble about, afraid of nothing, looking for food, with a diet similar to that of a beaver. They not only gnaw on the base of trees but are one of the few animals to feed on the needles and branches of conifers. If inspired, they'll even chew on boots on a campout.

I used to always wonder: How could a porcupine be born? After all, it sounds like a painful experience for mom, right? Department of Fish and Game biologists provided the information: When a porcupine is born the juvenile comes equipped with hundreds of inch-long quills, but they do not become sharp until they dry and harden, a matter of hours.

At a children's zoo, I saw a porcupine that seemed as gentle as a guinea pig. But how do you pet a porcupine? Actually, when born in captivity and handled repeatedly, they display a pleasing amount of affection. Everything but purr like a kitten.

But if alarmed . . . then they go on alert and out come the quills.

One of the most memorable scenes in all of nature is when a bear decides it wants to eat a porcupine, but must somehow get to its soft underbelly to

porcupine

get a bite. The bear will track and circle a typically plumped-out fellow, which simply ignores the bear, his quills at attention. The bear knows to keep its distance of that tail, which can whip around like a boomerang and smite him like the sword of Lancelot, but remains fascinated with the hope of an easy meal of such a fat, slow-moving customer.

Porcupines are born with hundreds of inch-long quills which do not become sharp until they dry, several hours after birth. The tips of the quills are barbed.

This is an example where sheer perseverance of will means nothing. It's like a horse race; you can train a donkey from sun-up to sun-down but it ain't gonna win the Kentucky Derby. No matter how hard that bear tries, no matter what tricks it pulls, the bear is not going to win this race; that porcupine has about the most perfect defense in the world.

Even though it can't throw its quills like darts, no matter what Sam says.

Biologists' Notes

Although most of the world's porcupines make South America their home, two species are found in North America. And one of these, the common or yellow-haired porcupine, *Erethizon dorsatum,* is the only species found in California. The other is the Canadian porcupine.

Like the skunk, the porcupine is one of the few California animals born with a ready-made defense against enemies. Except for its throat and underparts, the porcupine has a long yellowish coat of rough fur partially concealing literally thousands of sharp, barbed quills.

The porcupine has short ears, a short blunt tail, and bright shoebutton eyes nearly buried in hair. As the animal waddles slowly along the ground on its squat bowed legs, it looks like easy prey for any meat-eater that finds it. When at ease, it appears deceptively inoffensive, for the quills lie flat and are nearly concealed by the thick dark fur and the long yellow-tipped guard hairs.

However, the quills are attached to a layer of muscle beneath the skin that allows the porcupine, if startled by an enemy, to raise the quills rigidly, presenting a fearsome defense.

The tip of the quills are barbed and can only be removed from a creature that has lost the battle against the porcupine by a strong pull with pliers. If the quills are not removed, some may work their way into the flesh, and others may be harmlessly absorbed. But if embedded quills reach a vital spot such as the heart or lungs, or become infected, the animal may die.

The loosely embedded quills in the tail may fly several feet from the violence of the switching action during an attack. Several hundred quills may be lost during an encounter, but these are being constantly replaced by new ones coming through the skin. Those who seem to be able to prey on the porcupine with the most success are the mountain lion, fisher, and wolverine.

In California the porcupine ranges from valley floors all the way to timberline. They seem to prefer the ridges where food trees are most abundant, and yellow pine in the west seems to be the favorite. They show a preference for the sweet cambium layer under the outer bark, but they also eat pine needles and other coniferous foliage. Mistletoe is a favorite food during the colder months. Although they are not meat eaters, they do gnaw on and consume bones and the shed antlers of deer.

Porcupines make their dens in the crevices of rocky ledges and in hollow trees and logs. Dens are frequently marked by piles of smooth greenish-brown pellets, and the animals travel to and from the den to the feeding areas. Although they do not seem to mind the cold, in winter they will sometimes stay in the same food tree for weeks at a time rather than trudge back and forth through the snow.

Mating takes place in September and October, and the act is performed in a manner similar to that of other animals. The young are born in April and May, and each mother gives birth to only one baby; twins are very rare.

Because of the long gestation period, the baby porcupine is born highly developed. It is nearly 12 inches long and weighs about one pound. Its eyes are open, teeth are formed, and it is completely covered with dense black hair that later turns yellowish; hence the name yellow-haired porcupine. In its fur already are hundreds of inch-long quills that become hard and sharp as soon as the baby is dry. Although unsteady on its feet, if startled, the young porcupine will display its quills in defense and swing its tail sharply.

Within two days it can climb and is soon following its mother on feeding trips. It eats green herbage with increasing enjoyment and after 10 days is completely weaned. The youngster stays with its mother for five or six months and then takes off on its own to live a rather solitary existence, for except during the mating season and when denning in the winter, porcupines are seldom seen together.

Although seemingly slow, clumsy, and rather dull, porcupines like to play. They frisk individually with pine cones and sticks, and when together the young wrestle with lots of grumbling and whining. Even the oldsters have been observed doing a sort of dance, standing erect and rocking from one hind foot to the other.

Where to *see* porcupine

BIZZ-JOHNSON TRAIL/SUSAN RIVER, IN LASSEN COUNTY

HOPE VALLEY WILDLIFE AREA, IN ALPINE COUNTY

PAYNES CREEK WETLANDS, IN TEHAMA COUNTY

SINKYONE WILDERNESS STATE PARK, IN HUMBOLDT COUNTY

Foresters are often worried about the damage porcupines do in girdling the trees, and in yellow pine this damage can be considerable. However, surveys have shown that in mixed conifer and hardwood forests where the porcupine population may be 25 per square mile, the damage only amounts to a few cents an acre.

Pronghorn Antelope

Of all the large animals in California and across the West, the pronghorn antelope can be one of the easiest to find and see—especially when compared to bears and mountain lions. At the same time, antelope can be difficult to sneak up on for a close-up photograph, even when you are equipped with professional equipment and a telephoto lens.

The only difficult part about finding antelope is the long drive most people in California have to make to reach antelope habitat. If you had lived a hundred years ago, you wouldn't have had to travel far at all—pronghorn ranged all over the state in great herds. But now, their primary range is in the high semi-desert flats of Lassen

ANIMAL	Pronghorn Antelope
SPECIES	*Antilocapra americana*
TYPE	mammal
STATUS	OK
SEE ALSO	Bighorn, Deer, Elk

and Modoc Counties in the northeastern corner of the state, a region so remote and unpopulated that it can be difficult to believe it is part of California. The habitat is a mix of chaparral and juniper with occasional pine, across flatlands set on the edge of the West's Great Basin.

What I do is cruise along Highway 395 between Susanville and Alturas, where the Likely Flats is one of the best regions for pronghorn. Here there are a number of dirt roads that split off the highway, including a personal favorite that is routed out to the South Warner Wilderness. Another good road to find antelope is in the vicinity of Eagle Lake on County Road A1, as well as nearby Antelope Mountain. Much of this region provides sweeping, long-distance views across a landscape that seems to have stood still since the beginning of time.

Pronghorn antelope have been clocked at 60 miles per hour, the swiftest mammal in the Western Hemisphere.

What usually occurs when you are cruising around out here, on vacation in the middle of nowhere, is that somebody in your car spots something moving far off in the distance and then discerns a clear animal shape. You stop the car, look closer, and perhaps the outline of a deer-like animal comes into view. At that point, when you bring your binoculars up to your eyes and focus, there is suddenly not one pronghorn antelope amid the sagebrush, but usually several.

That's when the real fun starts. Your mission, should you decide to accept it, is to try to sneak close enough for a photograph. First, of course, make certain you are not trespassing on private property, as the good ol' boy ranchers up here take intense exception to trespassers. Pay attention to posted private property signs, and in addition, check out U.S. Forest Service maps of Lassen and Modoc National Forests that show what land is public and what is private.

pronghorn antelope

After parking and starting your sneak, you will quickly discover that the antelope are farther away than you likely believed when first spotting them from your car. Then you will also discover that there are very few trees to hide behind, or anything else to cloak your presence during your sneak. Antelope are quick to discern any movement across the plains, and your approach is thus quite easy for them to detect. They just tend to move off, staying out of range.

Most people like myself don't give up. But I've learned that the only way to get a good sneak on antelope is to commit to a long, slow crawl in the sagebrush. As in most stalks, keeping the sun at your back and the breeze in your face can provide a critical advantage. That is because if an antelope looks for you, it will be somewhat blinded by looking into the sun, and if it sniffs for your scent, the wind will carry it away in the opposite direction.

On one sneak where everything seemed perfect, I spent two hours creeping up on a small band about 500 yards away. I would crawl about 20 feet at a time, then rest, and then move again, trying to keep low and out of sight. It seemed endless, yet it was exciting, because the game was afoot. It requires the attention to detail of a detective, the sneaking ability of a burglar, and the ability to sustain the physical effort of an athlete.

As I neared for the perfect photograph, I felt like a burglar sneaking through an unlocked window. When I rose and cleared the sagebrush for the picture, the antelope were again 500 yards off.

Turns out they knew I was there the whole time. They just kept moving along, nibbling as they went, leading me out across the sagebrush, luring me into an adventure with no end.

And so it is with antelope, as with so many wild creatures. The chase never ends.

Biologists' Notes

They are commonly called antelope, but their true name is pronghorn or pronghorn antelope, *Antilocapra americana*. They are not actually a true antelope but are classified in a family all by themselves (Antilocapridae), mainly because of their unique horns. This species is the only antelope-like form that has branched horns. It is strictly a North American mammal and does not occur naturally on any other continent in the world.

The horns are true horns that grow over a bony core, like the horns of cattle, sheep, goats, and true antelopes. Unlike that group, which keeps the same horns through life, the pronghorn sheds the outside shell each year, more like antlers. (Strictly speaking, antlers are bony growths that are shed in their entirety on a regular basis and regrown; horns are permanent growths that are never shed.) The horns of the female are much smaller than the male's. The buck's horns have been recorded at over 20 inches in length.

Pronghorns are about the size of a black-tailed deer, around three feet high at the shoulder. Does average about 90 pounds while the bucks average 110 pounds. Unlike deer, they don't attempt to hide in heavy brush or timber but prefer to live in open, grassy plains where they can see long distances. They depend on their exceptionally keen eyesight and speed to escape from their enemies. Their eyes protrude like a rabbit's and are placed so they can see in all directions. They appear awkward when walking but are most graceful when running at top speed. They seem to enjoy running and will race beside a car, suddenly spurt ahead, and cross over in front of a speeding car as though to prove their swiftness. They have been clocked running at 60 miles per hour, the swiftest mammal in the western hemisphere.

To provide added protection, nature gave pronghorns a bright coat of reddish tan, marked with white and black. Up close the coat appears colorful; however, when viewed from a distance, the peculiar markings tend to break up the outline of the body so that it is difficult to recognize while the animal is lying down or standing still. The long white hairs on the rump can be raised at will. When alarmed, a band of pronghorns will face an intruder and rapidly raise or spread these hairs, possibly as a warning signal to other distant bands of their own kind.

In summer they eat grasses and many leafy plants; in winter sagebrush is their main source of food. They move in bands from summer range to winter range where the snow is not as deep.

The breeding season is in September and October. The mother carries the young eight months before giving birth in late spring or early summer. A young doe usually has only one kid, but twins are common in subsequent births. The kids are not spotted like fawn deer, but are grayish brown so they can hide in the grass and sagebrush. By the time they are three weeks old they can run tirelessly with the band. They grow rapidly and by fall they can take care of themselves; it is then hard to tell them from adults.

In the early days of California the pronghorn antelope was found in great numbers all through the state's central and southern open spaces. The rapid development of the state and unrestricted killing by the early settlers soon reduced their numbers to the northeastern part of the state and to a

Where to see pronghorn antelope

EAGLE AND HONEY LAKES, IN LASSEN COUNTY
NOTE: Near Eagle Lake, look for antelope along County Road A1 and
Highway 139. Near Honey Lake, look for antelope along Highway 395 near
Honey Lake.

GOOSE LAKE, NEAR DAVIS CREEK, IN MODOC COUNTY

INYO NATIONAL FOREST, HIGHWAY 270, IN MONO COUNTY
NOTE: Look for antelope along Highway 270 and on the dirt road that leads
to Bodie State Historic Park.

LOWER KLAMATH NATIONAL WILDLIFE REFUGE, IN SISKIYOU COUNTY
NOTE: The best viewing months are May through August, along Highway 161
between Highway 97 and Hill Road on the way to the visitor center.

MADELINE PLAINS, SOUTH OF LIKELY, IN MODOC AND LASSEN COUNTIES

MODOC NATIONAL WILDLIFE REFUGE, IN MODOC COUNTY
NOTE: Look for antelope south of the refuge along the route from Alturas to
Likely on County Road 60/Westside Road, particularly in the area from two
miles to 10 miles south of Alturas. South from Alturas on Highway 395, turn
west on Carlos Street and drive to the first stop sign. Turn south on County
Road 54 and drive about one mile to a "Y" intersection. Turn left (south) on
County Road 60/Westside Road and drive south to Likely.

small band in Mono County. The use of sheep-tight fencing has also
restricted the pronghorn's range. Although pronghorn can jump 20 feet in
one bound, a sheep-tight fence will stop them if they can't go through it
or under it. Unlike deer, they do not jump over fences. Reintroduction of the
antelope to its historic range has been ongoing, however, and they can now
be found not only in Mono and the northeastern counties (Modoc, Siskiyou
and Lassen), but in Colusa, San Luis Obispo, Kern, Los Angeles, Santa Clara,
San Benito, and Monterey Counties.

The areas in which they prefer to live have also been used heavily for
years by native deer and introduced grazers such as cattle, sheep, and wild
horses. The competition limited the number of pronghorn that could live
there. When the sheep industry collapsed in the 1960s in northeastern California, it was the best thing possible for antelope, as it resulted in a drastic
reduction of the number of sheep grazing on winter ranges that historically had been used by the antelope. Since then, grazing permits on public
land have also been gradually reduced for other livestock. This, plus a wet

cycle in weather, has increased the pronghorn's range to a point that population actually began to increase. Numbers in California have fluctuated between 5,000 and 8,000, in response to weather conditions. Antelope are easily observed from the air, making it possible for game managers to keep a close check on their numbers.

Quails
California Quail
Mountain Quail

We knew the quail were in there, in that bush, but we just wanted to see if we could get them to come out.

You could hear them. That little whistle-like call of quail, along with the scratching of their feet as they hopped around the underbrush in the thicket. You know the phrase, "A bird in the hand is worth two in the bush," well, it was invented to describe quail.

It was midsummer in the central Sierra, and I was visiting my wildlife mentor, Ed Dunckel, at his wilderness property. The day had started with a hike out to investigate some beehives that had been set in a small apple orchard. To our surprise, we found that the beehives had been completely destroyed, plundered, and splintered into little wood pieces, apparently by a sweet-toothed bear looking for honey. In some of the wood pieces, you could see the tooth and claw marks.

While surveying the damage, suddenly in the background we heard this noise, a cross between a squeak and a whistle.

mountain quail   male California quail   female California quail

California quail – male, female

We both perked up. Dunckel had taught me that searching and finding wildlife—for no other reason than the discovery—is one of the great adventures in all of nature.

"You know those little guys are in there," he said. "Let's see if we can get them to come out."

We hid ourselves along a brush line and stayed quiet for 20 minutes. Then we started making our own little noises, trying to sound like quail, a light, short whistle, hoping they would come out of that bush to investigate.

This is not how you usually see quail. Usually you drive along a country road, and they suddenly shoot out of the bush alongside the road, and fly in a short burst right in front of your car, then back into the brush. I've had this happen so many times, hundreds and hundreds of times, that I'm starting to think a quail's DNA coding contains a genetic aberration that causes them to wait until the last minute . . . "I'm gonna do it, I'm gonna do it, I'm gonna do it" . . . then go shooting across the road, right in front of you. It is almost as if they say to themselves, "I know it doesn't make any sense, but darn it, there are just some things a quail has gotta do."

Mountain quail live primarily in the alpine zone of mountain ranges, typically in areas that are high enough in elevation to get snow, have four full seasons, and avoid exposure to extended droughts, but not so high that they must survive six-month winters. These birds get around, not so much by flying, but by walking and running, with the ability to fly in short bursts, perhaps just in front of your car.

Even after a fresh quail hatch, I've seen a mother with eight one-inch chicks go propelling across the road, right in front of me. With the chicks, I always stop and watch them scurry into the bush after momma. At one such opportunity, I saw exactly where they had lit down. But when I tried to find the covey, it was as if they had been beamed off the planet. You might as well try to find a polar bear in the desert.

I whispered this story to Dunckel, and he answered, "I know, I can never get them to come out either. But let's keep trying."

He whistled again, a short whistle in a one-two cadence, three times.

Suddenly, we heard an answer. It was muted, more like a tweak, but several of the quail in that bush were cackling among themselves.

We whistled back. Then there was a rustling in the brush. A moment later, a quail popped its head out of the bush, then hopped a few steps. A moment later, two others joined. It was the only time in my life I have successfully called quail out of the bush.

Now with confidence, we whistled our best quail call, loud with urgency. You know what happened?

Those quail heard that, figured it for a fake, then turned around and went right back in the bush, never to return.

Well, we gave up, got in my four-wheel-drive, and headed out of the woods, driving on the dirt Forest Service roads for town. Guess what happened? We had three different full coveys shoot out right in front of us while we were driving, and twice I had to stop to keep from running over them.

They just gotta do it, I tell ya.

Biologists' Notes

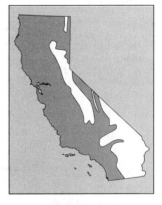

CALIFORNIA QUAIL *(Callipepla californica)*
The California quail is our official state bird, adopted by the legislature in 1931. They are well loved because of their large coveys, the common sightings along roads, and clear distinct notes of their call.

The California quail is found almost everywhere in California except in the high mountains and desert areas in southeastern California. The Gambel's or desert quail *(Callipepla gambelii)* is found in the deserts of southeastern California and along the Colorado River.

If there is such a thing as a conversationalist among birds, it would be the California quail. When birds are busy feeding, a number of different calls may be heard at close

ANIMAL	Quail, California
SPECIES	*Callipepla californica*
TYPE	bird
STATUS	OK
SEE ALSO	Pheasant

range. A scolding call is often given as birds scurry from danger. The year-round assembly call is most commonly heard and is a loud, clear "cuc-ca-coo." It has been interpreted as "chi-ca-go," "come-right-home," "get-right-up," and many other expressions. During the breeding season from April to July, the male, perched on a post, repeats at intervals a single resonant note. The large flocks post sentinels to warn of danger. Birds seem to be constantly conversing.

Quail belong to the gallinaceous, or chickenlike, bird family. They spend most of their time on the ground scratching for food, and at night they perch in bushes or trees where they are safe from their enemies. During the fall and winter months they live in coveys of from six to 60 or more.

In early spring the coveys break up, and after considerable fussing the quail begin to pair off and commence nesting. Quail use a great variety of sites, but generally their nests are built on the ground. Although rather poorly constructed, they are well hidden from view.

The California quail, a member of the gallinaceous family of chicken-like birds, is California's official state bird. To ensure a supply of drinking water for quail and other wildlife in semiarid areas, Department of Fish and Game has installed 3,000 rain collectors called "gallinaceous guzzlers."

The female lays from 10 to 15 creamy white eggs lightly splotched with golden brown. The eggs must be kept warm for 22 days, so the female and sometimes the male sit on them day and night. The eggs hatch within a few hours, and as soon as the chicks are dry they are ready to leave the nest.

The mother is quite attentive to her young, holding them in a close-knit group with soft warnings as they make their way through the grass and weeds in search of their first food. Their feathers grow rapidly and after 10 days they are ready to fly short distances.

The diet of the California quail consists mainly of weed seeds during the drier seasons and greens in the winter and spring. The chicks' diet is composed of insects, greens, and seeds until they are several weeks old, at which

California quail

time their diet becomes similar to that of the adults. Important weed seeds found in their diet in many areas of the state are filaree, turkey mullein, fiddleneck and acorn fragments, and especially important are members of the pea family such as the clovers, lupines and trefoils. A number of other seeds are taken on occasion.

In the early days of California, quail were more numerous than they are today. It was a common bird on the market. Quail on toast could be ordered at almost any restaurant or hotel in California. In the early 1880s, 32,000 dozen were shipped into San Francisco from Los Angeles and San Bernardino Counties. By the late 1880s, quail were becoming so scarce that market hunting was no longer profitable. Changes in agricultural practices, including overgrazing, have destroyed the homes where quail once lived, reducing the quail population in many areas. However, quail are easily managed. They need three things: food, water, and cover in which to escape from their enemies.

With the high breeding potential they have, quail respond quickly in numbers in areas where desirable habitat and water improvements are made. Water is often the governing factor with respect to quail numbers in some semiarid areas. Where this is a factor, the Department of Fish and Game has developed and installed underground storage devices designed to collect water during the rainy season for use by quail and other wildlife during the dry season. Some 3,000 of these devices, called "gallinaceous guzzlers," have been installed in California.

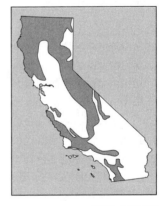

Mountain Quail *(Oreortyx pictus)*

The mountain quail is the largest native quail in North America. It is widely distributed over approximately 45% of California from the Mexican to the Oregon borders in both the Coast and Sierra Nevada Ranges. It is also found in the high desert ranges of southern California.

Unlike other quail species, the sexes look generally alike. The male and female have a long, slender, erect black plume of two feathers. The throat is chestnut bordered

ANIMAL	Quail, Mountain
SPECIES	*Oreortyx pictus*
TYPE	bird
STATUS	OK
SEE ALSO	Pheasant

with white. The breast, upper back, and head are bluish-gray, and the flanks are chestnut with broad white stripes.

Sexes may be determined under close scrutiny, however. The plume is slightly shorter on the female and the color shading on the back of the neck is a clear gray in the male and a dull gray in the female. Birds are typically eight to 11 inches long, and their average weight is eight to nine ounces.

Mountain quail migrate to higher elevations in the spring and down to winter range in the fall, making a journey of more than 50 miles almost entirely on foot.

Mountain quail in California consist of both resident and migratory populations. In the desert and lower elevations they are resident; any movements of local populations are due to the search for food and water, or in response to the weather.

One of the main ways in which mountain quail differ from other quail species is in their mobility. In the Sierra Nevada and high mountain areas of the Coastal Ranges the species will migrate to higher elevations to nest during the spring and early summer. This way quail can take advantage of soil moisture available from snowmelt and spring rains. In the winter, the quail will migrate down to lower elevations and spend the winter months below the snowline in the valley foothills.

Where to see quails

ANZA-BORREGO DESERT STATE PARK, IN SAN DIEGO COUNTY

BIG MORONGO CANYON PRESERVE, IN SAN BERNARDINO COUNTY

CHAW'SE INDIAN GRINDING ROCK STATE HISTORIC PARK, IN AMADOR COUNTY

CHILAO VISITOR CENTER, ANGELES NATIONAL FOREST, IN LOS ANGELES COUNTY

COACHELLA VALLEY PRESERVE, IN RIVERSIDE COUNTY

HENRY W. COE STATE PARK, IN SANTA CLARA COUNTY

JOE DOMECQ WILDLIFE AREA, IN STANISLAUS COUNTY

JOSHUA TREE NATIONAL PARK, IN RIVERSIDE AND SAN BERNARDINO COUNTIES

MOUNT PINOS OBSERVATION POINT, IN VENTURA COUNTY

PICACHO STATE RECREATION AREA, IN IMPERIAL COUNTY

SALTON SEA NATIONAL WILDLIFE REFUGE, IN IMPERIAL COUNTY

SHASTA LAKE, SHASTA-TRINITY NATIONAL FOREST, IN SHASTA COUNTY

SUNBEAM LAKE/FIG LAGOON, IN IMPERIAL COUNTY

WADDELL CREEK, IN SANTA CRUZ COUNTY

This migration is made almost entirely on foot. During the upward migration most birds are found in pairs, while the downward migration consists of one or more family groups. Distances from summer to winter ranges are reported in some remote areas to be as much as 50 miles.

Birds stay together in family groups during the summer and fall. They do not appear to have strong tendencies to form giant coveys as do California quail. An average winter covey of mountain quail is six to 12 birds, with up to 20 in high population areas.

Both sexes care for the eggs and young. The nest is a shallow depression on the ground, lined with leaves, pine needles and grass. It is built under the protection of a bush, log, rock, clump of grass or other suitable site. Average clutch size is nine to 11 plain, reddish-buff eggs. Incubation period is 24 days. During the laying period the cocks reach the height of their territorial activity. Much crowing occurs, although not in the vicinity of the nest. Crowing decreases during the incubation period and after the chicks hatch it is seldom heard.

Great fluctuations are the rule in mountain quail populations. A sudden drop in a population is almost entirely caused either by drought, which results in hatching failure, or by severe winter weather, which results in birds dying off during the winter. Water installations in desert areas offset the effects of drought by preserving a larger nucleus population. Mountain quail require water in summer only, unless drought conditions prevail, when they may drink in winter. Chicks require water soon after hatching.

Many species of shrubs are used as cover, as well as trees, rocks and large annuals. Shrub cover that is too dense can be the greatest single adverse factor to mountain quail populations. Cover should not be clumped and should extend over 20-50% of the ground area. Ideal mountain quail cover is a homogenous arrangement of small and large plants. In such cover it is possible for birds to hide, loaf, roost, forage, or nest practically any place within the covey range.

Rabbits and Hares
Cottontails
Jackrabbits

Rabbits inspire a lot of smiling faces as they romp and play. Little cottontails seem to love kicking up their tails, playing in the dust of a little-used ranch road, or nibbling on the clover of a meadow. Jackrabbits seem to live for darting about in front of cars on ranch roads, hopping at 20 and 30 mph, zig-zagging every which way as if juiced by 110 volts.

But a rabbit's life is hardly the carefree existence so many believe it to be.

There is a reason that rabbits breed in such prolific numbers. In temperate zones of California, they can breed three or four times a year, with two to eight babies per litter. That means a single female rabbit can create 15 to 25 baby rabbits in a year. So you might think they would be every place you turned, with people pulling rabbits out of their hats, as it were.

Well, that would be the case except that just about everything out there likes to eat the little fellers.

From the air, eagles, hawks, falcons, and owls love swooping down and nabbing rabbits. From the ground, they practically line up: Mountain lion, bobcat, coyote, badger, fisher, mink, rattlesnake, and gopher snake. There are other predators, of course. Rabbit, they say, "tastes like chicken." I've even seen house cats stalk and pounce on cottontails.

At first, cottontails provide a lot of aesthetic enjoyment as they romp and play. The easiest way to find cottontails is to hike during the last two hours of the day on into dusk and sunset at meadows, big grassy areas next to forest, and along the edge of farmers' fields. The last is true throughout the coastal foothills of California and in the Central Valley, where cottontail will eat the outside edge of crops. It drives the farmers crazy, and many field hands are given permission to hunt them; they love eating the *conejos*. Tastes like chicken, you know.

Upon first being sighted, cottontails always freeze, as if not moving will make them invisible. Big mistake. All that does is give a predator a good head start to nab it.

In hiking the edge of farmers' fields, I can always count on seeing cottontails wherever there is a half-inch or so of dust, typically on corners of the dirt roads. About an hour before sunset, the little cottontails love playing in the dust at such spots. I walk up; they immediately freeze. If I were a golden eagle, I could pop a rabbit for dinner every evening. Some do just that.

All rabbits need is food, cover, and water. With so many ranches edged with brush and with nearby ponds for irrigation, there is no shortage of habitat. And thus the entire wildlife food chain is created. Lots of rabbits will make for lots of all other creatures; they are the most attractive food source for so many predators high on the food chain.

Jackrabbits are more difficult to catch, but under a full moon I've seen a great horned owl nail an unsuspecting jackrabbit.

Sometimes jackrabbits appear to have a screw loose. Hundreds of times, while driving ranch roads or gravel county roads in the foothills, I've had jackrabbits pop out in front of my truck, then sprint as if in the Rabbit Olympics. Of course, they could just hop into the brush, but nature has not endowed them with much brainpower.

On one trip with my boys, Jeremy and Kris, we had a jackrabbit zig-zag in front of the truck at 25 mph for two minutes. We had been fishing at private farm ponds, catching bass and bluegill, but seeing that jackrabbit was just about as exciting as anything that happened that evening.

On an individual basis, rabbits are gentle creatures that must live in fear of constant predation. Collectively, they can do damage to farmers' crops. Most people don't worry about the ecological impact but just want to see the rabbits playing and hopping around adorably. Even if they do "taste just like chicken."

Biologists' Notes

CottONTAILS (*Sylvilagus* spp.)

The cottontail rabbit is perhaps the best known and most widely hunted small game animal in the United States. Subspecies and geographical variations can be found coast to coast and in California from sea level to high mountain elevations.

In California there are four cottontails: the desert or Audubon's cottontail *(Sylvilagus audubonii)*, mountain or Nuttall's cottontail *(S. nuttallii)*, brush rabbit *(S. bachmani)*, and pygmy rabbit *(S. idahoensis)*. The pygmy rabbit is scarce and lives at high elevations in remote areas in eastern and northeastern California. The riparian subspecies

ANIMAL	Cottontails
SPECIES	*Sylvilagus* spp.
TYPE	mammal
STATUS	OK/Endangered

of the brush rabbit *(S. bachmani riparius)* is a state-listed endangered species.

pygmy rabbit

Nuttall's cottontail lives in the brushy, rocky places in the sagebrush country, generally on the east side of the Sierra-Cascade crest. Audubon's cottontail is the most common and is found in the lowlands of California ranging up into the low foothills on either side of the Sacramento and San Joaquin Valleys. The little brush rabbit inhabits the dense brushlands of the hills and mountainous areas in the western half of California from Oregon clear to the Mexican border.

The cottontails are true rabbits. They all have one thing in common, which makes them different from jackrabbits or hares. The cottontails build a nest, and their babies are born naked with their eyes closed, whereas the true hares do not build a nest, and their babies are born with fur, eyes open. The gestation period is from 26 to 30 days. There may be as many as three litters of two to six babies born each year. The cottontail digs a shallow hole and lines it with the soft downy fur, which she plucks from her own chest. She crouches over the nest while the babies nurse. When she leaves the nest to feed, she carefully covers the babies completely with fur. About a week after birth the young open their eyes and commence to nibble on grass. Soon the babies are eating the same things as their mother, usually grass, leaves of various plants, fallen fruits, and sometimes acorns. They rarely eat the bark of trees or shrubs.

The Audubon cottontail, because of its abundance and wide distribution, lives both in conflict and harmony with man. In the agricultural areas of the San Joaquin Valley and Southern California, cottontails are sometimes considered a pest. They can cause a great deal of damage to alfalfa and other crops.

JACKRABBITS (*Lepus* spp.)

Jackrabbits are true hares. The hares, unlike the cottontail rabbits, do not build a nest. The mother just chooses a place to her liking and the young are born, fully furred, with their eyes wide open. They are able to hop around soon after they are born.

There are three members of the hare family native to California: the black-tailed (*L. californicus*), the white-tailed (*L. townsendii*), and the snowshoe or varying hare (*L. americanus*). The black-tailed and white-tailed hares are commonly called jackrabbits. The snowshoe or varying hare is known as the snowshoe rabbit.

The white-tailed jack is the largest of California's hare family. It weighs from six to eight

ANIMAL	Jackrabbits
SPECIES	*Lepus* spp.
TYPE	mammal
STATUS	OK

pounds. In winter, it is sometimes mistaken for the snowshoe rabbit, for in the colder parts of its range, individuals turn completely white. The range of the white-tailed jack in California is restricted to the east side of the Sierra Nevada and Cascade ranges from Tulare County north to the Oregon border. Unlike the black-tailed jack, which prefers to live in the flat open country and in the valley, the white-tailed jack lives in the hills and mountains. In areas where the ranges of these two jackrabbits overlap, when the hares have their summer coats, there may be some confusion as to identity. However the two may be distinguished by the color of the underside of their tails. The tail of the black-tailed jack is brownish underneath; the tail of the white-tailed jack is white.

Where to see rabbits and/or hares

CHAW'SE INDIAN GRINDING ROCK STATE HISTORIC PARK, IN AMADOR COUNTY

DEATH VALLEY NATIONAL PARK, IN INYO COUNTY

EATON CANYON NATURAL AREA, IN LOS ANGELES COUNTY

HENRY W. COE STATE PARK, IN SANTA CLARA COUNTY

JOSHUA TREE NATIONAL PARK, IN RIVERSIDE AND SAN BERNARDINO COUNTIES

MODOC NATIONAL WILDLIFE REFUGE, IN MODOC COUNTY

MONO LAKE, INYO NATIONAL FOREST, IN MONO COUNTY

PESCADERO MARSH NATURAL PRESERVE, IN SAN MATEO COUNTY

POINT REYES NATIONAL SEASHORE, IN MARIN COUNTY

SUCCESS LAKE, IN TULARE COUNTY

TIJUANA SLOUGH NATIONAL WILDLIFE REFUGE, IN SAN DIEGO COUNTY

WHITTIER NARROWS NATURE CENTER, IN LOS ANGELES COUNTY

Other places to see rabbits and/or hares

ANCIENT BRISTLECONE PINE FOREST, IN INYO COUNTY

CACHUMA LAKE RECREATION AREA, IN SANTA BARBARA COUNTY

COACHELLA VALLEY PRESERVE, IN RIVERSIDE COUNTY

COTTONWOOD CREEK, IN INYO COUNTY

LOPEZ LAKE, IN SAN LUIS OBISPO COUNTY

MOUNT DIABLO STATE PARK, IN CONTRA COSTA COUNTY

NEW HOGAN LAKE, IN CALAVERAS COUNTY

PISMO STATE BEACH, IN SAN LUIS OBISPO COUNTY

SAN JACINTO WILDLIFE AREA, IN RIVERSIDE COUNTY

The snowshoe or varying hare is more easily identified. It is the smallest hare. It looks more like a cottontail rabbit. Its ears are shorter than its head, but the underside of its tail is brown, not white like the cottontail. The snowshoe rabbit, like the white-tailed jack, also goes through two annual molts. In early winter it turns snow white, except for the tips of its ears, which remain black. Its feet become covered with a mat of long hair, to help it run over the soft snow, hence the name "snowshoe." In late spring it molts again to a summer coat of grayish brown.

The snowshoe rabbit's range is a long narrow strip from the Oregon border down through the higher elevations of the Klamath, Cascade, and Sierra Nevada ranges as far south as Tuolumne County. There are a few snowshoe rabbits in the Warner Mountains in Modoc County. The snowshoe is seldom seen, for it prefers to live in dense fir thickets and in winter is isolated by deep snow.

The snowshoe rabbit and the white-tailed jack may have more than one litter a year. There can be as many as seven or eight babies in a litter, although the average litter is from two to four.

jackrabbit

The black-tailed jack is by far the most common and is found all over California except in the mountainous areas at elevations above 12,000 feet. They adapt themselves readily to humans' use of the land and thrive even in highly developed areas.

In the more temperate areas of the black-tailed jack's range, breeding may continue the year around. Usually several litters are born each year. Here again there may be as many as eight, but the average litter is from two to four. The mother hides her young when she goes out to feed, and, upon returning, mother and young call to locate each other.

The hares are mostly active at night. During the day they lie crouched in a form, a slight depression in vegetation which they have made by using the same spot in clumps of grass or weeds. With their long ears flattened against their backs, they are difficult to see. Frequently on hot summer days they can be seen resting in the shade of a small bush or even a fencepost. When frightened they run with such speed that few dogs can catch them. At the start of the chase their speed is broken by high long leaps.

True hares, or jackrabbits, do not have hairless babies like the cottontail rabbit. Jackrabbit babies are born fully furred and with their eyes open.

Hares are strict vegetarians, eating a great variety of herbs and shrubs. In agricultural areas the black-tailed jack may become a serious pest in young orchards and other agricultural crops.

Raccoon

It was close to midnight when I suddenly awoke in my tent. There was noise out at camp. "A bear," I figured, "trying to get our food."

I usually sleep right through bear raids, that is, when a bear slinks in as silently as possible through camp, hoping for an easy munch. But this time it was louder than normal.

I poked my head out the tent and all was blackness. I retrieved my pocket flashlight and shined its narrow beam up toward our food hang, where our camp food had been secured in plastic garbage bags, held in place by a rope, well out of reach of any bear with Tang on his mind. Nothing. Then I scanned around beneath the hang. Nothing.

Suddenly, there was that noise again. It was coming from where I had rested my backpack against a tree, and I swung the flashlight, and there exposed in the light beam was not one raccoon but two, working in tandem to get into my backpack. They looked like bandits, complete with black mask, and had this cute but guilty look on their faces, those long claw-like hands of theirs on the goods.

"Hello little fellers," I said, then walked toward them. As most animals do when confronted, after a momentary freeze,

ANIMAL	Raccoon
SPECIES	*Procyon lator*
TYPE	mammal
STATUS	OK
SEE ALSO	Badger, Fisher, Marten, Mink, Otters, Skunks

raccoon

they scurried off, that long coon tail dragging behind. One of these raccoons was quite big, maybe 15 pounds, and it waddled more than ran.

This is typically how you see raccoons. After Mr. Bear, raccoons are the best around in the food-raiding business. They'll eat just about anything, from leftovers from camp dinner in the mountains to left-out food in the backyard of a San Francisco Victorian. They have an amazing ability to adapt, even in urban areas, providing they have food to sneak. That makes their habitat extremely widespread, and they are found just about everywhere but the high mountains, extreme desert, and downtown Los Angeles.

They have this nasty habit of beating the tar out of house cats in fights, and in rural areas, will sneak in and kill chickens. They can be a major nuisance at campgrounds and are so prevalent at many state parks that it's a must to keep your food in the secure lockers that are provided at each campsite.

But regardless of these habits, it is difficult to stay mad at raccoons for long. You know why? Because they are not only cute, but they look like real-life cartoon characters.

One evening I was exploring this small coastal stream, really more of a creek set in a wooded canyon, dark, moist, and looked up, and there were a whole passel of them. There was one big one, a momma raccoon, and a whole string of babies, all these little miniature bandits, lined up single file, following momma as she made her rounds.

The feet of a raccoon are bare on the bottom, and the long, slender "fingers" on the front feet are so dexterous they can be used like hands. The raccoon is in the carnivore family, but it has one of the most varied diets of all mammals —it will eat darn near anything.

As for that night at camp, I was following them with the flashlight beam as they disappeared into the woods and smiled at my good fortune of experiencing another chance encounter with wildlife. I then checked my pack for food; after all, anything edible or with a scent should be up in the food hang. Sure enough: I found an empty wrapper for meat sticks. It was just a piece of trash, but for all those raccoons knew, they were one discovery away from a feast.

Satisfied, I headed back to the tent. Suddenly, I heard another noise. I pointed that flashlight beam, and there, looking like a burglar sneaking through an unlocked window, was a raccoon scurrying through a hole it had chewed right out of the back of my tent.

Just like organized crime, I thought. Maybe the whole thing had been a set-up. Draw the victim out, decoy him, and then when he's not looking, send in the stealth team to get the goods. Well, I checked, and the bandit didn't get anything.

'Course, what's a raccoon going to do with size 13 hiking boots?

Biologists' Notes

Of all the furbearers in California, the raccoon, or "coon" as it is commonly called, is probably the best known. The black-masked face and ringed tail have been popularized in children's books and animated cartoons until even the youngest recognize it.

A huskily built animal, the average raccoon *(Procyon lator)* weighs from 10 to 16 pounds. The color of its coarse, shaggy fur is generally gray with a light shading of brown on the flanks. The black guard hairs give it a blackish appearance on its back and the back of its head. Its tail is round and heavily furred, and it is pale brown with black rings.

Its feet are bare on their bottoms and the long, slender "fingers" on its front feet are used with great dexterity in searching for, and grasping, small objects. Its hind feet have a large surface that allows the coon to balance easily on its hind feet while using both "hands" for feeling, or catching or holding food. A peculiar characteristic is the coon's habit of washing its food, if water is available.

It is nocturnal, that is, seldom moving around in daylight. Tracks in the mud and in the dust of dry trails reveal that it is quite common even in areas where it is seldom seen. The raccoon is normally associated with water sources, but in late summer and fall it may wander far in search of seasonal foods. It is a meat eater yet has the most varied diet of any of the furbearers.

In the spring, both ground and tree nests of birds are eaten; in the summer, ripening fruits and vegetables; and in the fall, ripe fruit, nuts, melons, and seeds of both trees and plants are used. All year long the waterways offer a great variety of food. The raccoon eats fish, shellfish, reptiles, and insects and is constantly foraging on small birds and mammals. Crippled ducks around shooting areas, and Farmer Brown's chickens are easy prey for the coon. The density of the coon population is probably governed by the availability of seasonal foods.

It does not dig its own den but prefers holes in hollow trees and natural holes in rocky ledges. Along rivers, it sometimes dens in dense tule growth.

The male raccoon, unlike some furbearers, mates with more than one female. The gestation period is 65 days, with most young being born in April and May. The litters vary from two to eight, with four as an average. Only one litter is born a year.

The newborn young are hairless and still have their eyes shut. The square, muzzled head gives them an odd homely appearance, but the mother loves

Where to see raccoon

Bidwell Park, in Butte County

Big Basin Redwoods State Park, in Santa Cruz County

Big Morongo Canyon Preserve, in San Bernardino County

Caswell Memorial State Park, in San Joaquin County

Mount San Jacinto State Park and State Wilderness, in Riverside County

Mount Tamalpais State Park, in Marin County

Oroville Wildlife Area, in Butte County

Whittier Narrows Nature Center, in Los Angeles County

Yolo Bypass Wildlife Area, in Yolo County

Other places to see raccoon

Andrew Molera State Park, in Monterey County

Bizz-Johnson Trail/Susan River, in Lassen County

Cuyamaca Rancho State Park, in San Diego County

Effie Yeaw Nature Center, in Sacramento County

Lake Solano County Park, in Solano County

Lewiston Lake, in Trinity County

Malibu Creek State Park, in Los Angeles County

Martis Creek Lake, in Nevada County

Montana de Oro State Park, in San Luis Obispo County

Mount Diablo State Park, in Contra Costa County

Morro Bay State Park, in San Luis Obispo County

Napa River Ecological Preserve, in Napa County

Patrick's Point State Park, in Humboldt County

Paynes Creek Wetlands, in Tehama County

Piru Creek, in Los Angeles and Ventura Counties

Point Reyes National Seashore, in Marin County

Shasta Lake, Shasta-Trinity National Forest, in Shasta County

Shasta Lake National Recreation Area, in Shasta County

Yosemite National Park, in Mariposa County

them and rears them with such care that by late summer the young are able to support themselves.

Raccoons are found in most parts of California except above elevations of 6,000 feet, in a narrow strip south of Mono County, east of the Sierra, and in the true deserts west of the Colorado River.

Rattlesnakes

Rattlesnakes aren't really such bad fellows; it's just that people keep stepping on them. And then out come the fangs, in goes the poison, and then you're in a heck of a mess, and in for a trip to the hospital.

Typically a bite means some pain and remarkable numbness, an anti-venom shot in the emergency room, and then, in the coming week, the affected area will turn black-and-blue. In time, you'll shed a layer of skin just like the rattlesnake. In a few months you may be as good as new, but you will discover this newfound ability to watch every step you take for the rest of your life.

ANIMAL	Rattlesnakes
SPECIES	*Crotalis* spp.
TYPE	reptile
STATUS	OK
SEE ALSO	Snakes, Garter and Gopher

Over the years, I've run into quite a few rattlers. So have many of my friends who spend so much time in the outdoors. Some have been bitten once. Nobody twice. Most others never. All carry the episodes around in their brain, forever branded by the instant shock of the sound of a shaking rattler.

John Higley, who was taking pictures of his pet quail for a magazine cover, reached down for his camera bag while looking at his quail, and suddenly found himself shaking hands with a rattlesnake. Before he knew what happened, it bit him in the finger, a sharp sting followed by a para-lyzing numbness. As he drove himself to the hospital, the numbness spread into his hand and arm. After the anti-venom shot, in the days that followed, his skin turned black and blue from his hand all the way up to his shoulder, and he told me he was quite sore for weeks. Now when he takes his quail out, he keeps it on a leash made out of fishing line so he can keep a lookout for a surprise rattlesnake.

Another pal and outdoors writer, Phil Ford, was out on a hike, fishing a mountain stream in Sierra County about five miles in from the trailhead when he got the surprise of his life. This is how he recounted it:

"I was hiking along on the edge of the stream, in about ankle deep water, and I had just planted my left foot. As I stepped forward, it suddenly felt like I had pushed a tree limb forward and it had snapped back and hit me in the ankle. I looked down where I felt that sting, here is this rattlesnake lying in the water, about three feet long, a timber rattler.

"You know they tell you, 'Don't get excited'—what a joke! My heart was beating like a jackhammer. First I rocked that snake to sleep, so that was the end of the snake. Then I cut a single slit across the bite, then squeezed it like a pimple, trying to get the poison out. Because I was so far from the trailhead, I didn't try to hike out. I stuck my leg in the cold water of the stream and stayed there all night. The next day I did hike out."

The rattlesnake is the only poisonous snake native to California. Rattlesnake eggs are retained in the mother's body until hatched and the young are born alive. Sometimes the female rattler is killed with the young in her body, and they can still be born alive afterward. This phenomenon may have given rise to the folk tale that female rattlesnakes swallow their babies temporarily to protect them from danger.

rattlesnake

After treatment, Ford's leg was swollen from foot to hip, black-and-blue. It was a few days before he could get around, more than a week for his skin to undergo several color changes; in the end, he shed a layer of skin.

Most rattlesnakes are three to four feet long. Though their coloration varies from being tinted green, brown, and even blackish from area to area, there is a universal response when you hear that unmistakable rattle noise. First you freeze, then you look for the snake, then you get the heck out of there, followed by a prayer of thanks that you were not bitten.

If you do get popped, most doctors advise simply getting yourself driven to the hospital immediately, then letting them deal with it. A smaller number suggest a single incision across each fang mark, then trying to squeeze the poison out with your thumb and forefinger. The old methods of cutting an "X" across the wound, or sucking the wound, are ineffective.

Upon an encounter, also remember that rattlesnakes will not chase you down and hunt you. They have the ability to strike just a foot or two, and often only strike within six to eight inches. If you can keep from rustling them, you typically won't get bitten, even at close range.

But let me tell you, once you have heard that distinctive rattle buzz, you never forget it. My old compadre John Korb told me that while driving, he once hit and killed a big rattlesnake with his pick-up truck by accident, so he went back and cut the rattler off, and put it on his dashboard. "About a week later, I was driving along and I turned the air conditioning on and suddenly, I heard the sound of a rattlesnake getting ready to strike," Korb remembered. "I completely froze, in shock, and then I jammed on the brakes and jumped out." It was all-out shock and panic.

It turned out that rattle had fallen off the dashboard and into the air conditioning unit, and when he turned on the fan, it rattled as if it was a live snake. He said, "It was completely unsettling to hear that noise. Drove me crazy, so I took the whole dashboard off to get it out of there."

My own near miss came when I was leading a hike to a mountain peak, amid manzanita and other brush near the summit. I was in mid-step when I heard that one-of-a-kind rattling, instantly froze, looked down, and saw that I was four inches from planting my left boot on top of a coiled rattlesnake. In shock, I put the movie in slow rewind, backed up in the opposite direction, and managed to avoid an attack.

Later, I was explaining about rattlesnakes, how you deal with them, and of course, how important it is to always remain calm.

At that exact moment, a four-inch lizard scurried across the trail at my feet, and I just about levitated, letting out a yowling cry of shock.

"Like I said, always remain calm."

Biologists' Notes

Throughout the world there are many snakes whose poisonous bite can be fatal to man. But in the United States there are only four different types: the coral snake, the copperhead snake, the cottonmouth water moccasin, and the rattlesnake. The last is the only poisonous snake native to California.

Rattlesnakes (genus *Crotalus)* come in 16 distinct varieties. There are numerous subspecies and color variations, but they are all positively identified by the jointed rattles on the tail. While most of the rattlers are concentrated in the southwestern United States, they extend north, east, and south in lessening numbers and kinds so that every contiguous state has one or more varieties.

Along the coast north of southern California, the Pacific rattlesnake has the territory all to itself. It is found over a variety of places in the state from coast level, the inland prairies, and desert areas to the mountains at elevations of more than 10,000 feet.

In southern California, the Pacific rattler overlaps the ranges of several other species and subspecies, except that of the large Western diamondback rattler along the Colorado River and the southeastern California deserts.

From Lake Tahoe north, on the east side of the Sierra, you might see the Great Basin rattler; from Tahoe south through Death Valley, the sidewinder and Panamint rattlers; along the Colorado River, the Western diamondback; in the southwestern area, the red diamondback and speckled rattlers; and in the Mojave Desert, both the Mojave rattler and the sidewinder.

In favorable areas where there is a constant and abundant supply of small rodents, the Pacific rattler sometimes attains a length of five feet, but the average adult size is between three and four feet. It is more slender than the heavy-bodied diamondbacks of the south and eastern United States. The color of the Pacific and pattern of its markings are varied, ranging from brown to grayish or greenish tones with large blotches of lighter hues along its back.

In the northern areas of their range and at higher elevations, snakes congregate in the fall at crevices in rocky ledges to hibernate for the winter, returning to these places annually. These spots are known as snake dens.

When outside temperatures begin to warm, the snakes come out of hibernation. They remain around the den entrance for a few days, sunning themselves, and then make their way to where they will spend the summer. They hardly ever go more than one mile from their dens. Most snakes

Where to see rattlesnakes

AFTON CANYON, IN SAN BERNARDINO COUNTY

ANDERSON MARSH STATE HISTORIC PARK, IN LAKE COUNTY

ANDREW MOLERA STATE PARK, IN MONTEREY COUNTY

BUTTE VALLEY NATIONAL GRASSLANDS, IN SISKIYOU COUNTY

DESERT TORTOISE NATURAL AREA, IN KERN COUNTY
NOTE: Be alert to the presence of the Mojave green rattlesnake, which is resident here.

DEVIL'S PUNCHBOWL NATURAL AREA, IN LOS ANGELES COUNTY

GRASSLAND RESOURCE CONSERVATION DISTRICT, IN MERCED COUNTY

HENRY W. COE STATE PARK, IN SANTA CLARA COUNTY

HIGH SIERRA RECREATION AREA, IN FRESNO COUNTY

JOSHUA TREE NATIONAL PARK, IN RIVERSIDE AND SAN BERNARDINO COUNTIES

LIVING DESERT, IN RIVERSIDE COUNTY

SANTA ROSA PLATEAU ECOLOGICAL RESERVE, IN RIVERSIDE COUNTY

SEQUOIA AND KINGS CANYON NATIONAL PARKS, TULARE AND FRESNO COUNTIES

SILVERWOOD LAKE STATE RECREATION AREA, IN SAN BERNARDINO COUNTY

are secretive in their summer activities, hunting at night and remaining inactive and out of sight for days at a time during the digestive period after eating a squirrel or small rabbit. Consequently, more snakes are seen in the spring and fall migrations to and from their winter homes.

The eggs are retained in the mother's body until hatched and the young are born alive. Sometimes the female rattler is killed with the young still in her body, and they can still be born alive. The female Pacific rattler may contain from four to 25 eggs, from which an average of nine or 10 healthy young are born live.

Except in the extreme northern part of California, mating takes place in the spring and the young are born between August and October. The newborn Pacific rattlesnake is about 10 inches long and has a small horny button on the tip of its tail. Rattler babies have venom and short fangs and are dangerous at birth. In fact, they are more pugnacious than the adults. Although unable to make a rattling sound, the youngsters throw themselves into a fine defensive pose and strike repeatedly when disturbed.

Young rattlers are completely independent of the mother. They remain in the area of their birth from seven to 10 days, when they shed their first baby skin and add their first rattle. The litter then begins to break up and start the search for food. Many of the babies do not survive the first year, either dying of hunger or being eaten by birds and animals. Even if they make it through the first summer, they may perish during the first winter if they can't find a suitable warm crevice in which to hibernate.

If all goes well, the youngsters grow rapidly. As they grow, and each time they come out of hibernation, they shed their skin, and with each skin shedding a new rattle is added. During the rapid growth of the first few years they may shed their skin three times a year. Thus, the number of rattles is not a true indicator of age. Rattles also wear out or break off, so it is unusual to find an adult snake with more than eight to 10 rattles.

Rattlesnakes eat lizards and small rodents such as ground squirrels, small rabbits, rats, and mice, striking rather than attempting to hold their prey. When the hollow fangs of the rattler penetrate the flesh of its victim, venom is injected as though from twin hypodermic needles. The small prey is usually stunned. If a larger animal runs some distance before it dies, it is trailed by the snake and swallowed whole.

Many persons spend a lifetime enjoying the outdoors and never see a rattlesnake. Very few people are bitten. Yet, because the bite is extremely painful, you should always keep alert and watch where you step or put your hands when you are in the field. Be careful after dark, for on warm nights the rattlesnakes move around searching for food.

One rule of thumb for rattlesnakes is that they will not share habitat with king snakes. If you see a king snake—and note that the mountain king snake is the most beautiful of all California snakes (and harmless, too)—it is unlikely you will see any rattlesnakes. When they can find them, adult king snakes will eat baby rattlers.

Most rattlesnakes, when disturbed, normally try to withdraw. But if they think they are cornered, the explosive sizzling buzz of their rattles is an unmistakable warning and a sound that will long be remembered.

Raven

When this book was first created, we were constantly challenged by what to leave in and what to leave out. Scientist Michael Furniss, my lifetime friend of so many adventures across the land, was reviewing the original cast of characters and exclaimed, "Raven! You've got to have raven!"

Furniss is an extremely rare individual who is able to blend the remarkable intellect of a scientist with deep, spiritual passions. We have seen raven on many of our adventures, and over the years, he has become fascinated with them.

In the ancient world, the raven symbolized the carrier of magic energy and was

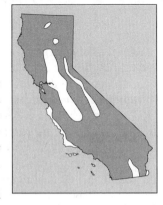

ANIMAL	Raven
SPECIES	*Corvus corax*
TYPE	bird
STATUS	OK
SEE ALSO	Jays, Magpies

revered as big medicine by many Native Americans. Today, while relatively few are aware of the esteemed place of raven in ancient cultures, those few do not take a frequent appearance of the bird as an accident. If raven keep appearing amid an adventure, then they believe it is a symbol of magic energy, that a special event is at hand. When we come across them, we always note this, then see what will happen next. It is nothing you can control.

The last such episode was when we climbed to the rim of the Mt. St. Helens volcano in Washington state, the trip inspired by the hope of literally staring into the steaming bowels of the earth. Instead, we found much of the "steam" from the volcano is actually dust from perpetual landslides. What was most electrifying was not the volcano, but the view—into the caldera and across the blast zone to Spirit Lake, and also of the distant landscape and mountain peaks, 14,411-foot Mt. Rainier to the north, 12,276-foot Mt. Adams to the east, and 11,235-foot Mt. Hood to the south. Yet just as we were enjoying the spectacular scenery, several ravens suddenly appeared, gliding on the thermals on the mountain rim. Furniss took note of their appearance, then looked at me like I had antlers growing out of my head, like "What's going to happen next?"

Ravens are spectacular to watch, fantastic flyers, capable of all kinds of aerobatics, but my favorite raven show is how they can catch thermals along a mountain wall, then ride them with hardly a wingbeat. They are also fast and elusive, and I have seen them buzz hawks, and, a few times, actually drive a hawk off.

Many confuse the raven with the common crow. They look largely similar, but the raven is lesser known because it occurs in smaller numbers and inhabits the more remote areas along the coast and the higher, sparsely settled inland areas. The Western crow, on the other hand, is partial to areas devoted to agriculture and to a large extent is now dependent on them. If you are unfamiliar with the difference, note that if you are seeing a flock of large black birds in the Central Valley or other farming area, it is crow.

Another difference is that ravens are bigger, up to 27 inches long, and much heavier. They also have a remarkable black sheen. And unlike crows, ravens typically travel in singles and doubles, occasionally in small groups, but never in massive flocks.

Now I know what you're probably wondering. After seeing that raven, what magical experience proceed-

Many confuse the raven with the crow. They look similar, but the raven occurs in smaller numbers and inhabits the more remote areas along the coast and higher, inland areas. The crow, on the other hand, is partial to agricultural areas and is to a large extent dependent on them. If you see a flock of large black birds in the Central Valley or another farming area, for instance, they are crows.

raven

ed, right? Well, it wasn't long after that the idea for this book came to me, just kind of popped into my head as I was walking down off Mt. St. Helens.

"Got to have raven in the book," Furniss said.

"Of course," I answered. "After all, remember Mt. St. Helens?"

Biologists' Notes

The raven *(Corvus corax)* belongs to the Corvidae, or crow family, along with the crow, jay, rook, magpie, and jackdaw. Both crows and ravens are intelligent, large, and black, but the raven is larger, from 22 to 27 inches long compared to the crow's average length of 17 to 21 inches. The raven also differs in having a thicker, less pointed bill and shaggy throat feathers. There is a characteristic luster to the raven's intense black feathers, a purple-blue cast, except for the blue-green on the head, wings, and underparts.

The common raven prefers wilder places than the crow and is found in remote forests, deserts, sea cliffs, and mountains throughout North America, ranging in the west from the Arctic south to Nicaragua. In California, ravens are found everywhere but in the Central Valley, where crows predominate. Preferred habitat includes open terrain for foraging and the face of cliffs, bluffs, or seawalls, which provide nesting opportunities. Active raven nests have been noted from below sea level in Death Valley up to 7,500 feet in the Inyo Mountains and in parts of the Mojave Desert, as well as along the coast of the northern counties. Ravens feed on carrion, insects, worms, eggs, young birds, small mammals, fruits, and grains. Intelligent and opportunistic, the raven is drawn to the food scraps found in campgrounds and picnic areas, and when their numbers increase to what are considered unmanageable levels, they can become subject to eradication efforts.

In late winter, nests are built in trees or on cliffs, of sticks, grass, and lumps of earth and are lined with wool, hair, and plant fibers. Three to six spotted eggs are produced in one season. The female alone incubates the eggs for about 18 days, but both parents feed the young, first removing any hair, feathers or bones in the offering. The parents continue to care for the young ravens for almost half a year after they begin to fly at about six weeks.

Ravens have a distinctive deep, rumbling croak which can vary considerably in tone and range, leading to the speculation that these birds communicate in a sophisticated manner among themselves and probably also to their mention in early mythology. The Norse god Odin kept sacred ravens that flew around the world, returning at each day's end to report all they had seen.

Where to see raven

AFTON CANYON, IN SAN BERNARDINO COUNTY

ANCIENT BRISTLECONE PINE FOREST, IN INYO COUNTY

BUTTE VALLEY NATIONAL GRASSLANDS, IN SISKIYOU COUNTY

CABRILLO NATIONAL MONUMENT, IN SAN DIEGO COUNTY

CACHE CREEK MANAGEMENT AREA, IN LAKE COUNTY

DEATH VALLEY NATIONAL PARK, IN INYO COUNTY

DESERT TORTOISE NATURAL AREA, IN KERN COUNTY

DOS PALMAS PRESERVE, IN RIVERSIDE COUNTY

Other places to see raven

ANZA-BORREGO DESERT STATE PARK, IN SAN DIEGO COUNTY

BISCAR WILDLIFE AREA, IN LASSEN COUNTY

EMERALD BAY/D.L. BLISS STATE PARK, IN EL DORADO COUNTY

HAIWEE DEER WINTER RANGE, IN INYO COUNTY

KING RANGE NATIONAL CONSERVATION AREA, IN HUMBOLDT COUNTY

LASSEN VOLCANIC NATIONAL PARK, IN LASSEN COUNTY

LAVA BEDS NATIONAL MONUMENT, IN SISKIYOU COUNTY

MCARTHUR-BURNEY FALLS STATE PARK, IN SHASTA COUNTY

MOJAVE NATIONAL PRESERVE, IN SAN BERNARDINO COUNTY

MOUNT TAMALPAIS STATE PARK, IN MARIN COUNTY

PINNACLES NATIONAL MONUMENT, IN SAN BENITO COUNTY

REDWOOD NATIONAL AND STATE PARKS, IN DEL NORTE COUNTY

Roadrunner

You know where most people see their first roadrunner?

In the Southern California desert? Nope. In the Central Valley? Nope. I'll tell you where: Just like my boys, Jeremy and Kris, most people make their first sighting on TV, Looney Tunes cartoon style. You know, Roadrunner— that crazy bird that goes "Beep-beep" and then zooms away at 100 mph, while making nemesis Wile E. Coyote out to be a fool.

In real life, roadrunners don't beep and they don't run at 100 mph, but they do have enough idiosyncrasies that make them seem something like a cartoon character.

ANIMAL	Roadrunner
SPECIES	*Geococcyx californianus*
TYPE	bird
STATUS	OK

The fact is that they run at a documented rate of about 15 mph, but when you see one darting about the desert, it seems much faster than that. The reason is that a roadrunner's facility for split-second dodging heightens the illusion of phenomenal speed.

What they typically do is to sprint as if they are going run headlong into a bush, then, at the last second, suddenly stop. This is how they hunt. From behind the bush, they go into stealth mode and sneak a look on the other side, hoping to spot a meal, perhaps a lizard, small snake, or insects. If that hope is realized, they will use that extraordinary ability to zig and zag in order to catch their prey. If there's no meal in sight, then it's on to the next bush, where the hunting procedure is repeated.

The roadrunner is a member of the cuckoo family. The unusual feet, with two toes forward and two toes in back, leave a distinctive "X" track in the dust.

One of my favorite cowboy campfire tales involves the roadrunner and the rattlesnake. I have heard it told in various forms, and some old-timers swear it is true: The roadrunner builds a fence of cactus spines around the sleeping rattler; then after the snake perishes in its struggle to escape, the roadrunner returns to eat the snake. Of course, it makes no sense, since rattlesnakes can live and crawl through tangled masses of cholla, the spiniest of cacti, with no apparent harm. Don't worry about that, warn the cowboys, never let the facts get in the way of a good story.

Over the years roadrunner has always been a vital part of the desert world, adding an eccentric personality to an often still landscape.

Unlike on the cartoon show, the real roadrunner has big problems with coyotes. Coyotes can outrun a roadrunner, and once a pack has trapped a roadrunner without a bush to hide in, only rarely is there occasion where roadrunner's fantastic zig-zagging allows it to elude the faster wild dog of the desert.

The other problem is uninformed humans. Because roadrunners have been seen eating quail eggs, a desirable bird for hunters, roadrunners have at times been shot for this lone reason. This persecution is groundless and certainly not justified, for according to biologists, less than one roadrunner meal in thousands will consist of quail eggs or young quail. State and federal laws protect the roadrunner, but some people pay no attention to laws or to science. Maybe they've watched too many cartoons.

Biologists' Notes

The roadrunner *(Geococcyx californianus)* is a member of the cuckoo family. In California it occurs in most abundance in the desert areas, but it ranges north along the coast to the Navarro River in Mendocino County and occasionally is found in Humboldt County. The roadrunner also ranges in the Central Valley north to Redding, where it occasionally is seen in open fields and chaparral-covered foothills.

Sometimes called the chaparral cock, the roadrunner is distinguished by his long tail, long strong legs, and slender overall length of nearly two feet. His plumage is soft tan in color, coarsely streaked with greenish bronze and black. When preoccupied in its search for food, the feathers on its head rise and fall in a noticeable crest. The unusual feet, with two toes forward and two toes in back, leave a distinctive "X" track in the dust.

Roadrunners have a voracious appetite, which keeps them busily engaged in a search for food, save for the extreme heat of summer days. They are omnivorous and will eat almost anything that walks or crawls and is small enough to swallow. Their diet also includes some seeds and fruits and even small birds.

roadrunner

Where to see roadrunner

Afton Canyon, in San Bernardino County

Little Panoche Wildlife Area, in Fresno County

Providence Mountains State Recreation Area, in San Bernardino County

Salton Sea National Wildlife Refuge, in Imperial County

San Jacinto Wildlife Area, in Riverside County

Other places to see roadrunner

Big Morongo Canyon Preserve, in San Bernardino County

Coachella Valley Preserve, in Riverside County

Death Valley National Park, in Inyo County

Desert Tortoise Natural Area, in Kern County

Santa Rosa Plateau Ecological Reserve, in Riverside County

Sunbeam Lake/Fig Lagoon, in Imperial County

When a meal is found, whether it be a snake, lizard, scorpion, tarantula, centipede, horned toad, or large insect, a lightning-like blow is struck with the strong beak, then the victim is grabbed and battered and thumped upon the ground. Then, if it is small enough, the tenderized mass is swallowed whole. Small snakes, including rattlesnakes, are swallowed head first. If the snake's length has been misjudged, several inches of the snake's tail may be left dangling form the side of the roadrunner's strong bill.

They seem to prefer to run but can fly if necessary. Their short, rounded wings carry them to treetop heights as they sail long distances to safety.

When irritated, the roadrunner makes a clacking sound with his strong bill, but in early spring it gives vent to a song consisting of soft dove-like coos.

Upon attracting a mate, the male puts on a mating display of drooping wings and fanned tail. The crest on the head is erect and the male jumps up and down in excitement. If the female accepts his attention, choosing a home site comes next. Nests are rarely built on the ground; rather, they are from three to 15 feet up, out of sight in a thick, thorny retreat. The easiest way to find their nest is by closely observing the parent bird's activities and visually trailing it back to the nest. Normally, three to seven cream-colored eggs make up a clutch. In the cuckoo tribe, two females may use the same nest. Incubation takes 18 days, and since the female starts to set as soon as the first egg is laid, there can be newly hatched birds and some half grown occupying the same nest.

The newly hatched young are featherless, greasy black, and strangely reptilian in appearance. Because of the differences in size, a nest full of young present a tangle of huge beaks, scrawny necks, and long weak legs. Because of their extreme hunger, it is a full-time job for the parent to feed them.

Salmon

It was a cool November day when fisherman Lindy Lindberg hooked something that acted like a living telephone pole in the Sacramento River near Anderson.

For two hours, this fish hugged the bottom in a deep river hole, wearing out Lindberg and his gear. Finally, the fish rose to the surface and showed itself for the first time, and Lindberg almost fell out of his boat: It was five feet long and looked like a whale, but it was a salmon.

Like a submarine, the enormous salmon went back down for two more hours. It wasn't until Lindberg drifted his boat to shallow water that he was finally able to gain the upper hand, four hours after hook-up, even-

ANIMAL	Salmon
SPECIES	*Oncorhynchus* spp.
TYPE	fish
STATUS	OK/Endangered
SEE ALSO	Steelhead, Trout (Golden)

tually leading the fish to his grasp. As in *The Old Man and The Sea,* the fish was too big to bring in, so Lindberg lashed the salmon to the side of his small boat and headed for home. Hemingway should have been there.

At the dock, everybody in sight was amazed. The fish weighed 88 pounds, the largest salmon ever caught in California.

Do you hear those cannons going off in the distance? It is more likely the pounding hearts of fishermen about to head out salmon fishing, imagining what the day's catch might bring.

Salmon are among the earth's most remarkable creatures. As an anadromous fish, they live most of their lives in salt water, but spawn in fresh

silver salmon

pink salmon

water, using their olfactory systems to return to the water of their birth. As smolts, they swim with the river current downstream and out to sea, and then in the next few years, are capable of roaming as far as 1,800 miles from their place of birth. When feeding conditions are optimal, they can grow an inch per month, and, in their typical three-year life cycle, reach 15 to 25 pounds. Those that swim the ocean for four years can reach 30 to 40 pounds, and the rare five- to seven-year-old fish can go 50 pounds and up.

Tag studies show that they travel as far south as off Ensenada in Baja, and in warm water years, salmon from the Golden Gate have been caught off the coast of Canada. As a migratory fish, they roam in schools to wherever conditions are ideal and food is abundant. That is why many salmon choose to stay in the vicinity of the Gulf of the Farallones off the Bay Area coast year-round, where ocean temperatures are generally 50-60°F and populations of anchovies, herring, sardines, squid, and shrimp provide an abundant food supply. In turn, the Golden Gate fleet has the highest catch rate per hour of salmon of any place in the world, including Alaska.

Tag studies document that salmon spawned from the Sacramento River near Redding can be found as far south as Ensenada in Baja, and in warm water years, as far north as Canada. The largest king salmon ever documented weighed 127 pounds and was caught by a commercial fisherman in Alaska.

Salmon are so fascinating that I could write a whole book about them; in fact, I did! (My first, now out of print.) But of all the fish stories, research, and data that have been compiled about salmon, what I remember best is a day on the briny green with underwater film wizard Dick Pool. He invented a way to suspend an underwater camera in the water behind the boat, so we could watch the salmon on a TV screen as they attacked our trolled baits and lures. We figured it would be like looking into a crystal ball to tell the future.

But instead, we got the surprise of our lives. Instead of viewing one savage attack after another, we watched salmon of all sizes race up to our baits, follow them for a while, then veer off at the last instant without striking. At first it drove us crazy. One fish followed the bait for nearly a half hour and made 17 passes before finally being hooked. In the years that followed, we learned how four factors affect salmon: bait action, fishing depth, color section, and proper use of attractants, such as dodgers. Put it all together and you can't miss.

For those who love salmon, it's a shame that the same government that set aside Yosemite as a national park in 1890 later funded water and development projects that have led to major decreases in salmon populations, in some cases nearly destroying an entire fishery. First federal dams blocked rivers and destroyed 90% of the salmon spawning habitat in California. Then, as some runs became depleted, the Delta pumps continued to take 70,000 gallons of water per second, killing fish, and helping to turn the winter- and spring-run chinook into endangered species. ("Winter run" and "spring run" are descriptions of salmon groups that spawn in winter and those that spawn in spring; these groups are effectively different subspecies since the timing of their life cycles means that a winter-run salmon can never spawn with a spring-run salmon.) More recently, the National Marine Fisheries Service has been cutting back on hatchery funding, even though hatcheries were originally built as mitigation to replace fish lost because of federal water projects.

The truth is, however, most anglers do not worry about these things. Less than 1% belong to conservation organizations.

What they spend their time thinking about, rather, is the next trip out. Maybe even a five-foot salmon.

chum salmon

Most state record fish have been mounted. But as for the 88-pound state record salmon, it will never be seen again. It never made it to a taxidermist.

Instead, to everyone's disbelief, Lindberg cut the fish into several sections. Then, over the course of winter, he ate it.

sockeye salmon

Biologists' Notes

There are five species of salmon (*Oncorhynchus* spp.) native to North America. They are, in order from least to most abundant, the pink salmon (*Oncorhynchus gorbuscha*) sockeye or

king salmon

red salmon *(O. nerka)*, chum *(O. keta)*, coho or silver salmon *(O. kisutch)*, and chinook or king salmon *(O. tshawytscha)*.

In California waters, the kings and silvers occur in the greatest numbers along the coast. The pink salmon is erratic and uncommon in its occurrence. The chum salmon is rare and the sockeye in the sea-run form is exceedingly rare. However, a landlocked form of the sockeye salmon, called kokanee, has been introduced into numerous cold water lakes and reservoirs in California and is reproducing satisfactorily in some of them.

The king salmon at sea is a beautiful fish: bluish to gray on the back and silvery on the sides and belly. There are numerous black spots on the back, dorsal fin, and on both sides of the tail. A king salmon and silver salmon of the same size are similar in color and shape. However, a quick examination of the inside of the mouth is a ready identification. The silver salmon has white gums around the teeth, while the gums of the king salmon's mouth are all dark.

When salmon enter fresh water to spawn, they gradually lose their silvery color and turn darker. Females turn blackish. Males, especially the larger ones, often have blotchy dull red sides. The smaller males tend towards dull yellow rather than red.

The average weight of the king salmon at spawning time is about 20 pounds; some exceed 50 pounds. The largest ever documented weighed 127 pounds and was caught by a commercial fisherman in Alaska.

Spawning king salmon are most abundant in the Sacramento-San Joaquin river system. Other important spawning areas along the northern coast of California are the Klamath, Mad, and Eel Rivers and Redwood Creek. Silver salmon, on the other hand, prefer small coastal streams.

King salmon spawns in cool or cold streams that have gravel bottoms. The preferred spawning areas are at the lower end of pools where the water picks up enough speed to move the loose rocks and gravel. The female selects the spot and digs the nest. She does this by rolling on her side on the bottom, and, with a pumping motion, stirring up the sand and gravel, which is carried downstream by the current. This leaves a pit in which she deposits some eggs. The eggs are immediately fertilized by a waiting male. The female then moves upstream a short distance and repeats the process, digging up more gravel to cover her previously deposited eggs and extending the nest upstream. More eggs are deposited and the process repeated until she is spawned out. After spawning, all adult king salmon die, both males and females.

The eggs, which are safely buried in the cracks and crevices of the coarse rocks and gravel, hatch in 50 to 60 days. When newly hatched, the young have a large pinkish yolk sac, which gives them a tadpole-like shape. They remain safely in the gravel, living on the yolk sac for several weeks until it is absorbed. They then wriggle up through the gravel as miniature young salmon and begin feeding on minute forms of life in the stream. In California, most young king salmon migrate to the ocean in their first few months of life. A small percentage remain in the stream until they are over one year old.

After returning to the ocean, many king salmon remain in the vicinity of the mouth of the river in which they were spawned. Others will migrate long distances. When a king salmon is approaching maturity, it returns to the stream from which it migrated to the ocean. Very few salmon will enter any other river. Straying into the wrong tributary is more common. In exceptionally wet years, kings sometimes enter the flood water of small tributaries that do not remain large enough to accommodate them, which leaves them stranded in some strange places.

Sea Lions

Some creatures are born to be wild, like the badger, golden eagle, and white shark. Some seem born to conceal themselves from humans, like Bigfoot, mink, and fisher. Others are born performers, like dolphins, chipmunks, and osprey.

The sea lion, on the hand, seems born to beg, mooch, and steal.

They are incredible hams, begging handouts at the coastal wharves wherever there are tourists, most notably at Monterey's Fisherman's Wharf and at San Francisco's Pier 39. And they usually succeed. Like a doggy who knows exactly how to use its big brown eyes to get its owner to do anything, the sea lions have developed a melange of wiles and contrivances in their apparent sole mission to keep from having to work for a living.

ANIMAL	Sea Lions
SPECIES	Steller's - *Eumetopias jubatus* California - *Zalophus californianus*
TYPE	mammal
STATUS	OK/Threatened

A sea lion barks like a dog, lays around like a bum, begs like a zoo bear for a handout, and has the smarts of a safe-cracker. The entire time, they know exactly what they are doing. Once they get a taste of the easy life, why worry about a profession? After all, they already have one: Professional beggar and thief.

The droves of sea lions mooching handouts has turned into a major tourist attraction. Though signs are posted warning the public not to feed the sea lions, it is similar to what happens in Yosemite National Park when tourists see their first bear. Something takes over—they *must* feed it. This occurs day after day, with new and willing tourists arriving all summer long, and, in time, you get a breed of sea lions that panhandles for a living.

But not all of them are completely lazy. Some like to steal. Sea lions love following fishing boats out to sea, waiting until fish are hooked up, and then stealing the fish right off the hook. Hey, it's a lot easier than having to catch it yourself, right?

Another way they burglarize is for several to swim beneath the submerged net pens where commercial fishers keep live anchovies to be sold for live bait. Once under the pens, the sea lions will blow air bubbles through the bait, killing large quantities. When those dead anchovies are then skimmed off the surface and thrown to sea, the sea lions have a field day—free eats again.

Here's a little crazy fact about them, one that shows not even sea lions have it perfect. When sea lions are lying around in the sun, it's not just because they might be tired from eating. One of their curses is that their circulatory system does not extend to their flippers, nor are their flippers covered by a neoprene-like layer of skin. So after long periods in the water, their flippers get cold. The only way to warm them up is to lie there.

And all is not easy, not even for sea lions living the good life. Since the Marine Mammal Protection Act of 1974, the sea lion population has grown steadily. The white shark population has grown on a parallel course. You see the connection? More sea lions means more food for white sharks.

While fishing in the vicinity of white shark habitat, I have seen sea lions suddenly start jumping and sprinting for the nearest land, like a hurdler racing to the finish line. You know what that means? Sure—Whitey is looking for lunch. Often, they get it. I have seen white sharks completely massacre a sea lion in a few minutes. Some biologists believe that the sharks will bite its victim, then back off, avoiding the struggle and waiting for its prey to bleed to death. Not always. In one

When sea lions are lazing around in the sun, they are actually warming their flippers. Their circulatory system does not extend to their flippers, so after long periods in the water, their flippers are cold. Sea lions consume from 15 to 20 pounds of fish a day.

California sea lion

episode, I saw a white shark consume a 650-pound sea lion in two minutes. Several of my field scouts who have fished in the vicinity of white sharks say they have seen the same thing.

So you see, even a sea lion that has perfected the art of begging, mooching and stealing doesn't have life too easy—they always have to keep an eye out for a large, black shadow in their midst.

Biologists' Notes

Sea lions, perhaps the best known of all our marine mammals, are the sleek, seal-like animals commonly seen swimming near shore or hauled out on the rocks of California's coastline. They belong to one of the three families that make up the order Pinnipedia (feather- or fin-footed), a group of specialized animals well adapted to live in the sea.

All pinnipeds have thick hides covering heavy layers of fat for thermal insulation, and some species have fur for additional protection from the

---

Where to see sea lions

CHANNEL ISLANDS, OFFSHORE OF VENTURA COUNTY

CRESCENT CITY HARBOR, IN DEL NORTE COUNTY

CRYSTAL COVE STATE PARK, IN ORANGE COUNTY

FARALLON NATIONAL WILDLIFE REFUGE, OFFSHORE FROM SAN FRANCISCO

FISHERMAN'S WHARF, IN SAN FRANCISCO

MORRO BAY STATE PARK, SAN LUIS OBISPO COUNTY

POINT MUGU STATE PARK, IN LOS ANGELES COUNTY

Other places to see sea lions

FISHERMAN'S WHARF, IN MONTEREY COUNTY

GOLDEN GATE NATIONAL RECREATION AREA, IN MARIN COUNTY

MATTOLE RECREATION SITE, IN HUMBOLDT COUNTY

MONTANA DE ORO STATE PARK, IN SAN LUIS OBISPO COUNTY

POINT REYES NATIONAL SEASHORE, IN MARIN COUNTY

SONOMA COAST STATE BEACH, IN SONOMA COUNTY

VENTANA WILDERNESS, IN MONTEREY COUNTY

---

cold. Their forefeet and hind limbs are modified to form flippers, as their name suggests, and the tail is short or rudimentary. They are excellent swimmers and often spend long periods at sea.

Sea lions and fur seals belong to the eared seal (Otariidae) family and are joined in the pinniped order by the earless seal (Phonidae) family, such as the harbor seal, and the walrus (Odobenidae) family. While the earless seals move on land with a sort of squirming forward motion, the sea lion and fur seal have flippers that turn forward, enabling them to travel at an awkward but fairly rapid gallop.

Sea lions choose offshore islands, rocky points, isolated beaches, or sometimes bell buoys—areas known as haul-outs to sleep or rest. Seal Rock near the old Cliff House in San Francisco is famed as an observation point for both Steller's and California sea lions, the two kinds found along the California coast.

Of the two sea lions, the California sea lion *(Zalophus californianus)* is by far the better known. Did you ever see trained seals? They are the gentle, intelligent, easily trained California sea lion, found from the Trés Marias Islands in Mexico north to British Columbia. Male sea lions are mostly used because trainers find females in estrous hard to work with. The male reaches a length of seven or eight feet and weighs 500-900 pounds; females are considerably smaller. They rarely reach a length of six feet and weigh 200-500 pounds.

A much larger animal is the Steller's or Northern sea lion *(Eumetopias jubatus)*, which may attain a length of 13 feet and a weight of 1,500 or 2,000 pounds. It is found from the Bering Straits in Alaska to southern California. The Steller's sea lion has been a federally threatened species since 1990.

In contrast to the rich, dark brown coat of the California sea lion, the Steller's has a tawny, yellowish brown coat. The coats of both are coarse and have no value as fur. Another distinguishing characteristic is the almost incessant barking of the California sea lion on the hauling and breeding grounds. The Steller's remain fairly quiet while hauled out, except when disturbed, but roar almost constantly on the breeding grounds.

Sea lions have preferred breeding grounds or rookeries to which they return year after year. California sea lions breed mostly on offshore islands from the Channel Islands south into Mexico. The breeding grounds of the Steller extend throughout most of its range; however, little or no breeding occurs south of central California.

Males of breeding age arrive first at the rookeries and battle other males until there are relatively few left, each in possession of his own territory.

Vanquished males are forced out of the breeding grounds for the rest of that year. When the females arrive to give birth, there is the din of literally thousands of elephant seals and sea lions crowded side by side along the shoreline, the roar of battling seals, the plaintive bleat of newborn pups, and the bedlam of victorious males each trying to hold a harem of 10 to 20 females.

Sea lions breed in June and July within a few days after the single pup is born. Mortality among the newly born may be as much as 50%, as many are crushed in these overcrowded conditions. Males remain on the breeding grounds for as long as two weeks without food, zealously guarding their harems.

Females go to sea for food, returning every two or three days to nurse their young. It is amazing that a female can make her way through the bedlam directly to her own pup. Newly born pups are quite trusting. They are covered with a rich, soft, purplish-brown fur and have large limpid eyes that make them most appealing. They remain on land for several weeks until the mothers can coax them into the water to learn the ways of the sea.

The food of the sea lion consists largely of squid, octopus, and a variety of fishes It is not known how much a sea lion eats in the wild, but one in captivity consumed from 15 to 20 pounds of fish a day.

Sharks

In the depths of sleep, I was dreaming that I had fallen in the ocean and giant white sharks were attacking me. I was punching them, trying to fight them off. Then I awoke in a sudden fury, sweating, my arms and legs twitching. It was 2 a.m. An hour later, still wide awake, I got up and headed for the boat. You see, we were going fishing. For white sharks. As I cruised down the empty highway, I couldn't get that dream out of my mind.

At the dock, Ski Ratto and his brother, Robert, had already arrived, also an hour early. "I slept about an hour," Ski Ratto said.

ANIMAL	Shark
SPECIES	*Carcharodon carcharias*
TYPE	fish
STATUS	OK

great white shark

"This is getting to me. I keep thinking about how big they are."

A few minutes later, up drives Abe Cuanang, also ready for the trip. "Couldn't sleep," he said. White sharks have a way of doing that to you. Every one of us, faced with the prospect of tangling with a man-eater, not only could not sleep, but found ourselves at the dock in the middle of the night, consumed by the passion of the adventure.

It wasn't long before our two skiffs, 17-foot Boston Whalers, were whipping across San Francisco Bay, heading out to sea. After passing the orange glow of the Golden Gate Bridge, the Pacific Ocean was as dark as the sockets of a skull.

In 1994, the California State Fish and Game Commission passed a law that prohibits sportfishing for white sharks. But before that happened, I spent years fishing for white sharks with several different expert anglers, including the brothers Cuanang, Abe and Angelo, two of the finest saltwater anglers and boatmen in the country. We never planned on trying to kill a fish like that, but to go one-on-one with it, then cut it free. Man versus man-eater.

The key to the expanding population of white sharks on the Pacific Coast is the Marine Mammal Protection Act of 1974. Since sea lions and elephant seals have been protected, they have provided a much larger food source for Whites. In turn, baby white sharks started having much higher survival rates in the early 1980s and '90s. There are so many whiteys that someone gets bitten nearly every year, usually a surfer dressed up to look just like shark food.

At the same time, the abundance of white sharks off the California coast has become critical to keeping the marine ecosystem in balance. Because sharks eat sea lions, and sea lions eat fish, more sharks mean fewer sea lions and more fish. Marine mammals, such as sea lions, eat five times as many fish as are taken by sport and commercial fishermen put together.

Thus, if you remove the sharks, the sea lions have no enemies, and ultimately, fisheries can be damaged by increased sea lion predation. That is why it is illegal to kill sharks. Their survival is vital for other fish. But you won't find me dangling my legs from a surfboard.

That is because there have been more shark attacks off the Bay Area coast than anywhere else in the world. John McCosker, one of the world's leading shark scientists, tries to keep track of each one. Scientists call the area bordered by Año Nuevo to the south, the Farallon Islands to the west, and Bodega Bay to the north the "Red Triangle" or the "Farallon Triangle." Whites live here year-round, feeding on abundant populations of sea lions and elephant seals.

For many years sharks were thought to be cold-blooded, taking up pretty much the temperature of their environment. Recent detailed anatomical examinations and experimental work show that great whites are able to maintain a body temperature slightly above that of their environment.

Out at sea, just as Ratto was bringing a small rockfish aboard, he looked down and saw it. A white shark four feet across at the head was looking right at him, just two feet from the boat, about a foot below the surface.

"He had a giant eye that looked right at me," Ratto said. "A strange feeling went through me like nothing I have ever felt. I panicked and gave the boat full throttle and got the hell out of there."

It was the seventh white shark episode experienced among Ratto, Abe Cuanang, and me in a 10-day span, including twice watching 600-pound sea lions get annihilated in less than two minutes. So we were back, this time prepared.

We moved the boats to the prime area, then hooked a live lingcod through the back with a hook about 10 inches long and four and a half inches wide. Clamped to the hook was three feet of chain, then 12 feet of four separate 1,000-pound test strand wire for leader. We had heavy big-game tuna rods with roller guides, and for reels, Penn Internationals with 500 yards of 130-pound test line.

We set two lines out at 70 feet deep, the chain providing all the weight necessary to get it there, and let the live lingcod swim about. We set two other lines about 40 yards off the boat, about 30 feet deep, with large red balloons tied on as "bobbers." Kind of like fishing at a pond for bluegills,

Shark Facts

- A typical white shark off California is a 12-footer that weighs about 1,500 to 1,700 pounds. There are a number of 14- to 15-footers in the 2,500- to 3,000-pound class, and there is the remote possibility of a 19- or 20-footer weighing perhaps 5,000 pounds.

- The biggest white shark documented on the Pacific Coast washed up at Año Nuevo State Park on the San Mateo County coastline. The shark was 18 feet long, weighed an estimated 4,500 pounds, and had a mouth big enough to eat a man in one bite and two gulps. It may have been the same white shark that was responsible for two deadly attacks in the same area. At nearby Pigeon Point, an abalone diver was nearly bitten in half and killed by a shark, and in Monterey Bay, a surfer was ripped right off his board and killed.

- Considerable dispute rages over the size of the largest white shark in history. A 36-footer in England and a 29-footer in the Azores are the largest documented. The largest white shark ever weighed was 7,300 pounds and measured 21 feet, three inches long. It was snarled in a net off Cuba in the 1930s. However, there are tales of 40- and 50-footers. Based on projections of the size of shark teeth from prehistoric times, white sharks once perhaps ranged up to 70 feet long.

- Sharks do not bite everything in sight, as is their reputation. They often go months without feeding. Even when chummed and baited, they appear to be the most finicky of eaters.

- When a shark takes a bite out of a person along the California coast, it rarely finishes the job but often spits the person out, perhaps disappointed at the taste and that it was not a sea lion.

right? Well, not quite. One "bait" we used was a 60-pound bat ray Abe Cuanang had caught in San Francisco Bay and saved for the Big Day.

There were no other boats in view for miles. The ocean had just the slightest roll to it and our only companions were passing gulls, murres, and shearwaters. Occasionally a few sea lions would cruise by and start hopping across the sea like trained porpoises, then jump like penguins out of the water and onto an island. We all saw this and immediately knew why.

"The big guy is down there," said Cuanang. "There's no other reason for them to hop like that." You see, when a white shark is cruising around, even sea lions are smart enough to get the heck out of the water.

There was a violent jerk on one of the rods, the one hooked with a three-and-a-half-foot lingcod swimming 60 feet deep. For the flash of an instant, we all froze. Then Cuanang, who was closest, grabbed it. His eyes looked as if they were going to pop out of his head. Later, Ratto said I had the same look.

"I can feel his head jerking side to side with the bait," Cuanang shouted. "He's eating it!"

He put the reel on free-spool and the shark started to swim off, straight ahead of the boat. The line peeled off the revolving spool. I was just about to shout "Strike!" when Cuanang put the reel in gear to do exactly that. But nothing happened.

"Something weird's happening," Cuanang said. Then it hit him. "He's swimming for the boat! He's swimming for the boat!"

Cuanang reeled with ferocity to pick up the slack. But when the line tightened, the shark was gone, and so was the bait.

We all looked at the bare hook. The only sound was a seal barking in the distance.

"He robbed our bait," Ratto said.

Well, somewhere out there in the briny deep was a white shark with a lingcod in its belly.

Shark Tales

- At the mouth of Tomales Bay, a giant white shark came up behind the boat and breached like a whale, then with its head out of the water, began barking like a dog, perhaps gulping air.

- Ski Ratto, Abe and Angelo Cuanang, and I had been fishing for rockfish and lingcod, and when Ratto turned on the depth finder, the bottom registered 120 feet deep. But later, suddenly, on the screen, the bottom of the ocean appeared to be rising to 80 feet, then 50 feet, then 40 feet. But the boat had not moved. Impossible? A malfunction? No: It was a shark under the boat, a fish so gigantic that the electronic sonar impulses sent by the depth finder were bouncing off the shark and reading it as the ocean bottom.

- A white shark tagging program was directed at the Farallon Islands by Peter Klimley of Scripps Institute. He tagged several sharks, including two 17-footers, in a 45-minute span. As many as 13 or 14 of this size have been documented at one time. One night, Klimley's Zodiac rubber boat was bitten and sunk by a white shark. At the time of the attack, nobody was in the boat, which had been used to shuttle scientists from the island to research vessels. "I'm thankful for that," he told me.

Biologists' Notes

The white shark, called *Carcharodon carcharias* by scientists, is in the mackerel shark family. These are large, stout-bodied sharks of which the white is most notorious. All members of this group are found in the upper layer of the open tropical temperate seas.

To the experienced eye, its identity is unmistakable. Its body ranges in shade from gray to black above and is usually white below. A blackish dorsal fin slices the water's surface as it speeds along the way. White sharks have well-developed jaws with bony, replaceable teeth. The skeleton is cartilaginous and may be so hardened with deposits that it resembles bone. Their scales are abrasive and toothlike when viewed under a microscope.

The white shark differs from bony fishes in that it lacks an air bladder and must be constantly on the move to maintain its buoyancy and water flow over the gills.

The white is a live bearer, as are most other sharks found in the open sea. While most fishes complete the spawning process by externally fertilizing the deposited eggs, the great white shark breeds much as do mammals. Males have a pair of copulatory organs, or claspers, near the pelvic fins, which are used for depositing sperm in the female during mating.

Fertilization is internal and the young develop within the mother's body. The young are born as miniature versions of adults, perhaps three to four feet in length, and must fend for themselves. At this size they can't pursue the large seals and sea lions preferred by their parents but must search out areas with prey more their size, such as lingcod, rockfish, flatfish, bottom-dwelling invertebrates, and other small sharks.

For many years sharks were thought to be cold-blooded, taking up pretty much the temperature of their environment. Recent detailed anatomical examinations and experimental work show that great whites are able to maintain a body temperature slightly above that of their environment. This is significant to the predatory performance of the great white shark since muscles function better as the temperature of the muscle is increased. This ability to control body temperature allows great whites to tolerate a wider range of water temperatures.

They have a keen sense of smell, allowing them to detect blood as dilute as one part per billion. In addition, white sharks, like other sharks, have special nerve sensors or pores on their snouts. These nerve sensors are able to detect the very weak electric fields that surround all aquatic animals. Once the general location of possible prey has been determined through

Where to see sharks

AÑO NUEVO STATE RESERVE, IN SAN MATEO COUNTY

CATALINA ISLAND, OFFSHORE FROM LOS ANGELES

CHANNEL ISLANDS, OFFSHORE FROM VENTURA COUNTY

DANA POINT HARBOR, IN ORANGE COUNTY

FARALLON NATIONAL WILDLIFE REFUGE, OFFSHORE FROM SAN FRANCISCO

POINT CONCEPTION, IN SANTA BARBARA COUNTY
NOTE: Great white sharks are sighted off of the point, but land access is private.

POINT MUGU STATE PARK, IN LOS ANGELES COUNTY

TOMALES BAY STATE PARK, IN MARIN COUNTY

chemical sensing and sound wave detection, the shark can more accurately locate the prey through reception of electrical discharges by the ampullae. The great white's highly developed eyesight comes into play about 50 feet from the prey and is critical to get the shark to within range of the electrical discharges.

Sharks have a unique role to play in the ecological balance of nature as it exists in the ocean. Sharks prey upon the smallest and the largest creatures in the sea using some of the most intricate biological detection equipment ever evolved. Their long evolutionary history dates back to the Silurian period, 420 million years ago.

Skunks

Skunks are actually cute little fellows, especially the babies. They just have this problem now and then, and let me tell you, if they get in position—head down, tail up—get yourself and your animals clear, and fast, then brace yourself.

Never experienced a skunk blast? Imagine this heavy, gaseous but invisible cloud

ANIMAL	Skunks
SPECIES	Striped - *Mephitis mephitis* Spotted - *Spilogale gracilis*
TYPE	mammal
STATUS	OK
SEE ALSO	Badger, Fisher, Marten, Mink, Otters, Raccoon

that seemingly drips with an acrid stench. It hovers over the land like a nebula in space. It's like nothing else in the world. And for some reason, dogs that have never experienced the sensation are often attracted to the little weasel, and, boom, they get blasted head-on.

But cute? A passel of baby skunks is cuter than a truckload of baby ducks. They seem so innocent. So nice. So charming. I'm serious. Say the word "skunk" and most people act like they've bit into a lemon. But when you actually see a skunk family, they don't seem so bad at all—in fact, just the opposite. They're so delightful that you might invite them for dinner under your house.

Well, maybe not. Skunks inevitably wear out their welcome. The first thing they usually do wrong isn't letting off an A-bomb level blast. It's getting into stuff, like for folks living in rural areas, into chicken coops. They have a way of getting under a porch, into left-out dog food, and into anything else that seems interesting to them. In turn, your dog or cat, who thinks it is chief of security, decides to check out the intruder.

A threatened skunk stamps its front feet in warning and, when that is not a sufficient deterrent, can eject a powerful oily spray about 10 feet.

And they get nailed, like, fast, so the story does not have a happy ending. My old dog Rebel, when just two years old, had never seen a skunk, and on a hike across coastal farmland, he trotted right up to one, curious, and was sniffing its tail—no foolin'—and got hit right between the eyes. His girlfriend dog, Kaya, came up to investigate and got hit, too, mainly on the side.

You see, the skunk actually shoots an oil at close range, like scented pepper spray in an animal's eyes, and once it gets on fur, it's mighty tough to get off. Soap doesn't work. Tomato juice can do the job, but if you wash the dog at home, it can stain the tub. Some pet shops sell a skunk oil antidote that works fairly well. Imagine if you were a coyote and got skunk-sprayed? All you could do was endure the odor for weeks.

Striped skunk

In Native American lore, skunks are revered, not shunned, though I suspect even Chief Sitting Bull would advise keeping some distance. Skunks' unique abilities give them great presence and respect from Native Americans. When I drew the skunk card in my totem, my friend Cloud Dancer told me that it is actually the animal of self-empowerment, and that when you walk around, some people can feel uncomfortable by the natural projection of power. I always wondered why everybody flees for the horizon when I show up.

Biologists' Notes

There are two kinds of skunks in California, the striped skunk *(Mephitis mephitis)* and the Western spotted skunk *(Spilogale gracilis)*. They are similar in many ways; both have glossy coats of black marked with white in stripes or spots, which give them their respective names.

The striped skunk is about the size of a plump house cat. The Western spotted skunk is smaller; about as big as a half-grown cat. Both of these skunks belong to the weasel family.

Skunks are not very good fighters or runners but they possess a potent secret weapon, and you know what that is: a strong smelling scent gland at the base of their tail. When cornered or molested they stamp their front feet in warning and turn so the gland opening is aimed at the intruder. The little spotted skunk may become so excited that it will whirl around and stand up on its front feet. This may look cute, but duck—he's just taking better aim. If

spotted skunk

Where to see skunks

ARCATA MARSH AND WILDLIFE SANCTUARY, IN HUMBOLDT COUNTY

CASWELL MEMORIAL STATE PARK, IN SAN JOAQUIN COUNTY

EFFIE YEAW NATURE CENTER, IN SACRAMENTO COUNTY

LAKE EARL WILDLIFE AREA, IN DEL NORTE COUNTY

LAKE SOLANO COUNTY PARK, IN SOLANO COUNTY

MODOC NATIONAL WILDLIFE REFUGE, IN MODOC COUNTY

NAPA RIVER ECOLOGICAL RESERVE, IN NAPA COUNTY

POINT MUGU STATE PARK, IN LOS ANGELES COUNTY

POINT REYES NATIONAL SEASHORE, IN MARIN COUNTY

skunks are attacked the powerful oily scent can be ejected in a spray for about 10 feet. If left alone they will turn and scamper away.

Skunks eat a variety of food. In spring and summer they eat fruits, berries, eggs, and all kinds of insects, small rodents, and reptiles. In winter they dig insects and small rodents out of the ground. Their digging leaves little cone-shaped holes.

They usually live in underground burrows, which they may dig if the ground is soft. Otherwise they use hollow logs, rockpiles, or the vacant homes of other small animals. They also like to live in haystacks and in the space under old buildings. Both skunks are nocturnal and are seldom seen in daylight hours.

The skunks do not hibernate, although they do sometimes group together in one den and sleep through short periods of the coldest weather.

The mating season is in February and March, and the young are born in 63 days. The striped skunk has from four to 10 babies in a litter. The spotted skunk rarely has more than six. Although skunks are born blind and helpless, like kittens, they develop rapidly and are out hunting with their mother in six weeks.

Skunks are distributed widely in California. They adapt themselves to a variety of surroundings. The striped skunk thrives in low mountains, valley farmlands, and even among suburban dwellers. It never strays far from water and seems to favor old ditches and stream banks where the brush is dense. The spotted skunk does not confine itself so closely to water and prefers the rocky, brushy hillsides over the open floor of the valley.

Because of their nocturnal habits and shy nature, skunks are very little bother to people. For the most part, skunks are good animals to have around because they eat so many destructive insects and rodents.

Snakes, Garter

It seems that every person has one of two severe reactions upon seeing a garter snake, and they are as far apart as the North and South Poles.

The best example occurred when I was just about to sell a house, having already moved out to a ranch. The moment of truth came as we walked out the front door, when the buyer and her two sons and I were about to shake hands on the deal, but this little garter snake suddenly appeared out of nowhere, slithering through the grass in the front yard, right at the woman's feet.

She about jumped on the roof of the house, and let out a Richter Scale-level "Eeeeek!"

Meanwhile, her sons were enamored with the little guy, chasing it down, following it, wanting to pick it up and stroke it as if it was a pet guinea pig.

ANIMAL	Snakes, Garter
SPECIES	*Thamnophis* spp.
TYPE	reptile
STATUS	OK/Endangered
SEE ALSO	Rattlesnake, Snake (Gopher)

Well, the deal fell through, but it was a good wildlife lesson for me. Because the reality of garter snakes is that you should treat them somewhere in the middle of those two reactions: They aren't dangerous enough to inspire leaping tall buildings in a single bound, nor are they so tame that you should pick them up, pet them, and let them wind around your body, perhaps even inside your shirt and out the neck hole.

Garter snakes aren't poisonous, of course. In terms of the wild kingdom, they are fairly docile, living near water, then spending most of their time hunting crawdads, minnows, and insects, occasionally also feeding on frogs, toads, and earthworms.

But they aren't so docile that you can treat them like a pet bunny.

In fact, garter snakes will bite, actually more of a nip. While their bite is not poisonous, if the skin is broken, some form of disinfectant should be used. (Of course, this applies to the bite of any animal.) In addition, when disturbed, and especially if handled, these snakes can secrete an exceedingly vile-smelling fluid from the scent glands near the base of the tail.

Since the earliest times, people have been fascinated with snakes, and some of the craziest yarns ever told have been about snakes—some of them true, most of them not.

All garter snakes are viviparous, that is, they bear their young alive.

My favorite such tale applies particularly to the garter snake. There's a campfire story that goes when a mother snake is threatened with danger, she will give a warning hiss, then allow her baby snakes to crawl into her open mouth to safety. When the danger passes or the mother is killed or injured, the baby snakes then miraculously climb out of her mouth unharmed.

This is, of course, ridiculous. The origin of the tale is probably the fact that garter snakes give birth to live young, rather than laying eggs. Perhaps once an expectant mother was killed, and the soon-to-be-born young managed to escape her body. Perhaps somebody witnessed such an event, and thus, the legend was born.

garter snake

But when it comes to the outdoors, and especially campfire tales, what I've learned is that a lot of people don't like the facts to get in the way of a good story. I admit that at times I have been among the guilty.

Serpentine Folklore

The fear some people experience when encountering a snake may stem from old wives' tales that are kept alive by persons with little knowledge of reptiles. Most of these stories are somewhat threatening, so imagination also increases that fear. The following are some examples of such folklore:

- *Snakes can charm people or other animals.* This is not true. A small mammal or bird may watch a snake closely, but the animal is not held spellbound.

- *The fabled "hoop snake" is said to grasp its tail in its mouth and roll downhill like a bicycle tire, then release its grip, straighten out and strike with a horn-like stinger on the tip of its tail.* The "hoop snake" does not exist.

- *Milk snakes can milk cows.* The milk snake does enter barns and cow pastures to forage for rodents, but it is doubtful it could effectively milk a cow, even if the cow could tolerate the snake's teeth.

- *Many people still believe that the glass snake—whose tail breaks off in pieces when seized—will come back before sundown to reattach itself to the tail.* The "glass snake" is actually a lizard and the tail will regenerate slowly after being broken.

- *The coachwhip snake hangs from tree limbs to whip a passerby.* Even though the pattern of scales on its tail does resemble a braided leather whip, the coachwhip is actually one of California's harmless racers.

- *A horsehair rope around one's sleeping bag is protection against snakes.* Experiments have shown that snakes crawl over horsehair ropes with impunity.

Biologists' Notes

Garter snakes, genus *Thamnophis,* are among the most common and widely known of American snakes.

There are 13 species in North America, five of which occur in California. Garter snakes are sometimes called striped snakes, ribbon snakes, and water snakes, the latter name being officially associated with the genus *Nerodia,* to which garter snakes are closely related.

Garter snakes are generally marked with bright colors and most of them have dorsal and lateral stripes. Color intensity and pattern vary greatly among species.

Of all the garter snakes in California, the most spectacularly marked is the San Francisco garter snake, *Thamnophis sirtalis tetrataenia,* an endangered species found only in parts of San Mateo County. This beautiful animal has rich red stripes bordered by black and lighter stripes on each side, with a lovely red head.

Garter snakes are one of the most adaptable of all the American snakes. They can be found in reclaimed land and in farming areas where other snakes could not adjust to humans and their ways. They are also found in the suburban parts of many large cities.

In the northern regions, the habitat of the garter snake is mostly terrestrial. However, they prefer damp areas near water. These northern snakes appear far more tolerant of cold than their various cousins. In the warmer southern country, the genus tends to become more aquatic in its lifestyle.

Where to see garter snakes

AFTON CANYON, IN SAN BERNARDINO COUNTY

ANDREW MOLERA STATE PARK, IN MONTEREY COUNTY

BUTTE VALLEY WILDLIFE AREA, IN SISKIYOU COUNTY

DEVIL'S PUNCHBOWL NATURAL AREA, IN LOS ANGELES COUNTY

EATON CANYON NATURAL AREA, IN LOS ANGELES COUNTY

HIGH SIERRA RECREATION AREA, IN FRESNO COUNTY

KING RANGE NATIONAL CONSERVATION AREA, IN HUMBOLDT COUNTY

PESCADERO MARSH, IN SAN MATEO COUNTY

SEQUOIA AND KINGS CANYON NATIONAL PARKS, TULARE AND FRESNO COUNTIES

STONE LAKES NATIONAL WILDLIFE REFUGE, IN SACRAMENTO COUNTY

There they live along streams and ponds, into which they dive immediately when surprised or disturbed.

All garter snakes are viviparous, that is, they bear their young alive. Mating occurs in the spring and the young are born in late summer. The number of young varies considerably in the different species, but 20 in a litter would be a good average. The young are usually about six inches long and are always a replica of the parents in markings and characteristic shape. The female garter snake is slightly larger than the male. Adult garter snakes rarely exceed three feet in length. However, the rare giant garter snake, *Thamnophis couchi gigas,* of California's Central Valley may exceed 50 inches in length and is listed as a state and federal threatened species.

Snakes do not stay together as families, nor is there any confirmed instance of a mother watching or otherwise caring for the litter.

Snake, Gopher

The gopher snake is the biggest snake in California and the most geographically widespread. They are often colored somewhat like a rattlesnake, with distinct black and brown splotches along its back.

Too bad for that.

Because the gopher snake's size, plentiful numbers, and coloring puts it in peril. Upon an encounter with a gopher snake, many people mistake them for rattlers and react with chilling fear, and often will even try to kill them in any manner possible in the moment.

What a waste. Gopher snakes are dangerous to no one, except perhaps causing a few heart attacks when people occasionally step on one. In fact, a gopher snake's primary job in life is to eat mice, rats, and gophers, a

ANIMAL	Snake, Gopher
SPECIES	*Pituophis melanoleucus*
TYPE	other
STATUS	OK
SEE ALSO	Rattlesnake, Snakes (Garter)

charge beneficial to most landowners. They are mild-mannered and try to stay out of the way, but, like I said, they are not only the biggest snake in California, but they are prolific, so sooner or later, you are bound to see one. One thing I have noticed is that in areas where there are lots of gopher snakes, you rarely see rattlesnakes, even though the habitat is often ideal for them. There are typically five to 10 gopher snakes for every rattlesnake.

So if you come across one, hey, lighten up and enjoy the moment. Upon meeting a typical four- to five-footer, if you don't immediately identify it, just look down at the tail. Do you see rattles? No? Then you have yourself a gopher snake. They tend not to move quickly when encountering humans. Often they will lay in the sun after cool nights to warm up. Other times they will search out hiding places for mice or even try to enter a gopher den. If you see this activity in the wild, consider yourself lucky to get an insider's look at wildlife.

The gopher snake is the largest snake in California, reaching a length of eight feet. It kills its prey by constriction, then swallows it whole. They have been known to do this with prey as large as a ground squirrel.

Remember this: There is only one snake in California capable of inflicting painful injury, rarely death, and you know what that is, right? Of course—duh—the rattlesnake. So don't sweat the other guys. Which is not to say that the gopher snake will *never* strike—if threatened and cornered, any animal can be forced into doing something that is contrary to its nature. The bite is like a little jolt, in which you get some redness, but that's it. It's best to treat the gopher snake with the same amount of respect that it has for you.

gopher snake

What fascinates me most about the big gopher snakes, the six-footers and up, is when they shed their skin. Often it comes off in pieces, like little plastic crinkles, but occasionally you might find the whole thing nearly intact, an extraordinary find, especially for youngsters.

Two of the most outrageous tales I've heard regarding snakes have added a lot of fear toward the mild-mannered gopher snake.

One is that gopher snakes are capable of interbreeding with rattlesnakes to produce a dangerous hybrid called the "bull rattler," which looks like a rattlesnake but without rattles. In other words, according to the myth, it looks like a harmless snake but can kill with a single bite. The reality is that there is no such critter. It is biologically impossible for gopher snakes to breed with rattlesnakes; the species are too different. In addition, rattlesnakes bear live young, while gopher snakes lay eggs.

The other story is that though gopher snakes may not have rattles, their flicking red tongue is a stinger, and though it cannot inflict death, it is still perilously dangerous. I've heard this one several times, and still wonder how folks come up with stories like these. A snake's tongue is simply a tongue, a sensory organ used to find prey.

In a typical year of roaming California, hiking everywhere imaginable, I'll see about three to six gopher snakes a year. In their habitat, especially grasslands where there are plenty of mice, I'm always on the lookout for them. But I'm looking for them not out of fear but out of wonder. They have managed to not only survive, but flourish in an era where uncounted thousands of uninformed humans try to kill them, simply because they are a snake.

Biologists' Notes

California's varied climate and topography provide living conditions for a wide variety of reptiles, including 33 species of snakes. As the weather warms in the spring, snakes come out from their winter hiding place and are most apt to be seen.

The largest snake in California is the gopher snake *(Pituophis melanoleucus)*. It is probably the most commonly seen snake, not because it is most numerous, but because of its wide distribution and its habit of hunting by day and night. The gopher snake ranges throughout California, except in the mountains above 9,000 feet.

The gopher snake reaches a length of three to six feet, with some individuals attaining a length of eight feet. It is a slender-bodied snake with a slim, pointed tail. It is distinctively marked. The general ground color is

Where to see gopher snake

DEVIL'S PUNCHBOWL NATURAL AREA, IN LOS ANGELES COUNTY

HARPER LAKE, IN SAN BERNARDINO COUNTY

HENRY W. COE STATE PARK, IN SANTA CLARA COUNTY

KELLY RESERVOIR, IN MODOC COUNTY

PLACERITA CANYON PARK, IN LOS ANGELES COUNTY

SAN LUIS DAM AND RESERVOIR, IN MERCED COUNTY

yellow to cream, with black, brown, or reddish-brown blotches along the back clear to the tip of the tail. There are corresponding rows of smaller markings along each side. The belly is white to yellowish and sometimes flecked with black. In desert regions, the markings are more distinct. Occasionally, striped individuals are found in Sonoma, Napa, and Yolo Counties.

In general, this snake is active in the daytime but in the inland valleys and deserts, especially in summer, most activity occurs at dusk and at night. In the daytime, the gopher snake hides in rodent burrows, under old boards and logs, and in other places of refuge. It is capable of digging in loose soil and is a good climber. It has been found high in trees, searching for the eggs and young of birds.

The gopher snake preys on mice, gophers, rats, and occasionally ground squirrels, rabbits, bird eggs, and nesting birds. It kills its prey by constriction, then swallows it whole.

Gopher snakes do not give birth to live young. They lay from three to 12 elongated, soft, leathery-shelled eggs. The eggs are nearly white. Loosely concealed in dirt, the eggs hatch in about 65 to 70 days. The young receive no parental care and, while small, are subjected to considerable predation by hawks, small mammals, and other snakes.

All snakes have scales and dry skin. As growth and wear take place, the skin is periodically shed. The old skin loosens at the mouth and, as the snake squeezes through sticks and rocks, the skin is rolled back, inside out, and is gradually shed. The snake literally crawls out of its skin. Even the glass-like covering over the eyes is shed. Sometimes the skin is torn off in pieces, although sometimes it comes off intact.

Although a snake may feel cool to the touch, its body temperature is controlled chiefly by its surroundings. It can partially control its temperature by moving from sunlight to shade. Snakes are most active when the temperature stands between 70 and 85°F.

Snipe

I was just a lad on a campout when I fell for the old snipe-hunt trick.

It was just after nightfall, the glow of the campfire starting to poke a hole through the darkness, set deep in remote forest wildlands near the Tuolumne River, high on the west slopes of the Sierra, when I was asked innocently, "Want to go on a snipe hunt?"

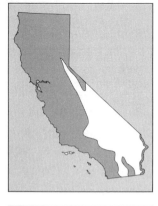

"Yeah!" I answered with enthusiasm. But, actually, I was not sure what a snipe hunt was, just that I was the youngest person there, about 90 pounds at that time, and did not want to give the impression that I was lacking experience in any way. "Let's go!"

ANIMAL	Snipe, Common
SPECIES	*Gallinago gallinago*
TYPE	bird
STATUS	OK

My dad, Bob Sr., fetched a bag. My brother, Bob Jr., six years my senior, appeared to analyze a map. My Little League baseball coach, Mr. Ed Dunckel, sat there looking wise.

With flashlights beaming the way, the three led me out in the woods. We walked for about 10 minutes.

"There's a real good spot I know about," explained Mr. Dunckel.

"Looks like a good spot," answered my brother.

"An excellent spot," echoed my dad.

Then they got deadly serious as we stopped, and I was given the bag.

snipe

"Stay perfectly still and quiet," Dunckel explained. "You don't want to scare the snipe. The rest of us will go back to camp and let the woods settle down. Then when the snipe are least expecting it, we'll form a line and charge through the forest with sticks, beating bushes and trees, and we'll flush the snipe out right to you. Be ready with the bag. When we flush the snipe out, bag it. But until we start our charge, make sure you don't move or make a sound or you will spook the snipe and ruin everything."

I sat out there in the woods with my bag for hours, waiting for the charge. I waited, waited, and waited. Nothing happened. No charge, no snipe. About midnight, my brother finally came out and dragged me in, despite my protest. When I finally returned to camp, everybody was sleeping.

For the rest of summer, I wondered why they didn't charge through the forest, like we'd planned. "No snipe," my brother finally confided. It took me a year or two to figure out that the "old snipe hunt" was actually a practical joke. It was years after that when I discovered that a snipe is a bird after all, a friendly little fellow, and they have nothing to do with campouts.

Snipe don't look anything like I figured they would. They are about eight to 10 inches long, but what surprised me was their long, derrick-like bill that is used to feed in mud, lagoons, and wetland areas. They're not in the woods at all, like I'd been led to believe as a boy, but a shorebird. It's a pretty bird, though often well camouflaged amid its wetland and inshore habitat. Snipe hop and walk about, probing with that derrick, typically feeding when low tides unveil miles of flats filled with tiny marine life. The best spots to see them are lagoons and preserves along the coast, and wildlife refuges and rice farms in the Central Valley.

Real snipe, as opposed to the joke snipe, migrate long distances over the course of the year. The best time to see them in California is from late fall through early spring, and though there are resident birds that stay year-round, particularly in northern California, by the start of May most head for the northern climates.

Those who have fallen for the old snipe hunt owe it to themselves at some point to see the real thing.

The aerial courtship dance of the snipe is conducted hundreds of feet above the ground in a series of undulating swoops ending in a sudden dash to the ground from about 50 feet.

Biologists' Notes

Snipes are worldwide in distribution. The species found in America is the common snipe *(Gallinago gallinago)*, although in the west it is usually referred to as the Wilson or jacksnipe.

It is a shorebird that is typically solitary and quiet in its habits, in migration it travels at night and on dull sunless days. Most of its feeding occurs in early morning and late afternoon, so finding this bird is not always easy.

The snipe is nearly 11 inches long. Its size should make it easy to see, but the beautiful blending of blackish brown feathers margined with white, along with the horizontal stripes on its head and back, produce a pattern of light and dark that render it nearly invisible as it moves along the grass and weeds. While feeding, it probes and prods the mud in search of its favorite foods, and when approached it crouches motionless close to the ground. It is rarely seen until it springs into the air from almost directly underfoot.

The rasping cry of the snipe and the crazy erratic manner in which it dashes away is usually a surprise to even the most experienced wildlife watcher.

Breeding grounds of the snipe are transcontinental. When the ground in the marshes and boggy lands of its summer range commence to freeze, the birds start their southern migration. The bulk of the population arrives in central California in two peak periods, the first about the last week of October and the second and highest numbers during the first week in December. Some birds stay in central California, but biweekly counts have indicated that the majority of migrating birds continue on to more southerly wintering areas. They prefer wetlands such as irrigated pastures and ponds with surrounding marshy areas. In central California the harvested rice fields offer an ideal place to hide and feed.

Shorebirds seem to sense when the frozen ground in the north starts to thaw, for in the spring they start their northerly migration. By the end of April most of them have disappeared from central California, but some linger to nest on the marshes in the northern part of the state.

The courtship performance of the snipe is a charming thing to watch in May and June. It may occur at any time of day, but most often it takes place at dawn and dusk. Some of the display occurs on the ground near the nest. The male struts proudly around with spreading tail and dropping wings and occasionally rises into the air in short, graceful spirals.

Most exciting and more easily seen is the aerial courtship dance carried out several hundred feet above the ground. Here the snipe flies in wide, irregular circles and makes a series of undulating swoops. The descent of each swoop is accompanied by a peculiar song or roll of syllables, which intermingles with the sound of rapidly beating wings as the bird ascends to the original height of the flight.

This has been called the winnowing of the snipe. Once heard, it leaves an unforgettable memory of the bird's delightful behavior. The aerial display ends with a dash toward the ground. Usually, about 50 feet from the ground, it seems to collapse and fall a few feet, recovering and falling, recovering and falling. It completes the descent to alight suddenly, usually in the immediate area of the nest.

Nesting begins in the latter part of May. Wet, marshy ground seems preferred, especially if there is low brush and small grass or weed-covered humps of ground. The female hollows out a spot on one of these humps and builds a nest of grasses and leaves. There are four, occasionally five, tan eggs marked boldly with splotches of brown and black. Both parents help in sitting on the eggs. It takes from 18 to 20 days for the young to hatch.

Babies leave the nest as soon as they are dry and then commence to creep around in the nearby grass. They are most handsome in their rich down coats of dark brown and black. Each wears a distinctive white spot on the crown of its head, and the backs are covered with little white dots that are on the tips of the filaments of down. The downy coat is worn for about 15 days before the first feathers begin to show.

Both parents care for the young and make quite a show of distress when approached. They fan their tails and, with widely spread, quivering wings, they limp and flutter pitifully, always just out of reach, to lead their pursuers away from their carefully hidden young. By fall, after molting, the young and the adults look alike, and in their bright new feathers they begin their migration to the southerly wintering grounds.

Songbirds and Other Favorites

Cedar Waxwing
Dipper
Finches
Magpie
Mockingbird
Red-Winged Blackbird
Robin
Western Meadowlark

Let me tell you a little secret.

When it's the dead of winter, the weather has been dreary for days, and I'm getting a terrible dose of cabin fever, I've found a secret way to bring the magic energy of nature back into my life.

This is how: I pull out my mini tape recorder and the microcassettes I used when recording notes for hiking the Pacific Crest Trail, from Mount Whitney to Lake Tahoe, and insert the tape for the Mokelumne Wilderness. Because, you see, while I was recording my description of the area and its unique mix of volcanic and glacial-based geology, in the background are the repeated calls and answers of meadowlarks as they play hide-and-seek in the volcanic-based tablelands.

While I play the tape, I block out my voice and just listen to the songs of those meadowlarks. It is beautiful, lyrical, and sweet, and I listen to it over and over again. And for a moment, I am transported to a day when everything was simple and good, and the meadowlarks were happy. It feels like taking a shower and washing off the grime after having been coated with dust.

For those who pay attention, birds always have this positive effect.

Most people don't start out with the specific intent to become bird-watchers, yet in the end, they discover this activity is one of the best ways possible to share in a world where all seems gentle and joyous. Most people get involved just as I have, as a by-product of another adventure, whether walking, boating, fishing, or camping. You see the birds, watch them, and soon start wondering what they are. If you take the next step and find out, well, guess what? You have become a birdwatcher.

My favorite song is that of the meadowlark. My favorite bird to watch is a single water ouzel. My favorite flock is a horde of blackbirds. My favorite first bird of spring is the robin. My favorite city bird is the finch. And the magpie, mockingbird, and cedar waxwing fit right in there as well, a mix of all the best qualities. You may have other favorites yourself out of the hundreds of species of birds.

The water ouzel may not be well known among the general public, but the little guy is truly one of the most loved of all birds in California wildlands. The ouzel is also called the "dipper." By any name, there's no other creature like it on the planet.

Dippers can fly, swim underwater, and actually walk on the bottom of a stream as if on land, looking for food such as stonefly nymphs, and can also fly like a fighter jet, darting up and down canyons, swooping, plunging, occasionally picking insects off the water surface as they go. Ouzels are typically found in canyons with streams and waterfalls; they usually make their nest right behind the waterfall in crevices, fissures, and cracks, literally within inches of the rushing fall of water. In the spring, you can watch the ouzels making their nests, darting in and out of the nest site, often flying right through the waterfall to reach the nest.

Dippers also seem to have more personality than any non–flesh-eating species of bird. That's because when they stand on a rock, they don't just stand there but perform these little knee bends as if on an aerobics program. The little guys are mesmerizing, hopping around, knee-bends and all, then maybe swimming underwater or even walking on the bottom of a stream, then emerging and rocketing down the canyon, perhaps right through a waterfall to a nest.

I first discovered dippers while flyfishing for trout and found them more entertaining than the fish. Just love the little guys.

If you live in an area where there are four distinct seasons, then seeing the first robin of spring is always a magical day. There is no better validation that winter is over and that the annual rebirth of nature is at hand. You can almost always attract robins in the summer simply by watering your lawn extremely heavily. The water will bring worms and nightcrawlers to the surface, and at sunset and dawn, the robins will be there, jumping around, finding the worms.

Sometimes the sheer numbers of birds can be a staggering display. So it is with blackbird, best seen in the flocks of thousands as a marsh comes to life at dawn at wetlands in the Central Valley. This occurs at nearly all the state and federal wildlife refuges in the Sacramento and San Joaquin Valleys. I have seen so many blackbirds at sunrise that they looked like a black cloud, and as that cloud neared, it seemed as if there was a symmetry to their flying patterns, as if they were somehow connected by mind and body, not individual birds simply choosing to be together. Of the blackbirds, the redwing is most beautiful, and every time I see one, I always stop and say to myself, "red-winged blackbird," reminding myself that even though they are plentiful, never take them for granted.

In the city, finches are common but seem especially friendly. One winter, I actually kept two finches in a cage, the only time I've ever kept birds as pets. One morning right at daybreak I heard some pecking on a nearby window, and in the cage, my finches were calling out with their little cheep-cheeps. This continued for several days, waking me every morning. Finally, I got out of bed and found three finches pecking on the window, and my caged finches calling them back. The next day, when it was repeated again, I took the cage outside, and for an hour, watched the finches interact. I realize that not all birds speak the same language, often having different dialects even within a species for different areas, but these finches acted as if they were long-lost friends. Who knows, maybe they were.

You know what I did? I opened the door on the cage and let them go. And out they went, joining their new friends.

For years after that, I put seed for the finches outside that window, and nearly every morning, I could go out and watch them feed, and enjoy my old friends as they rejoiced in their freedom.

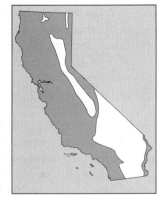

Biologists' Notes

CEDAR WAXWING *(Bombycilla cedrorum)*
Commonly seen in central California is the cedar waxwing, which ranges from central California to western Panama and breeds from northwestern California to western British Columbia. Within this area the cedar waxwing is irregular in occurrence, sometimes present one year and absent in other years.

Cedar waxwings nest peaceably in loose colonies. As many as 12 or 15 nests have been found within a radius of 150 feet, with the average nest rather high from the ground.

ANIMAL	Cedar Waxwing
SPECIES	*Bombycilla cedrorum*
TYPE	bird
STATUS	OK

cedar waxwings

There is little noticeable difference between the male and female. However, since two birds work together, it is assumed that the male helps in nest building, brooding, and rearing the young. Nests may be large and loosely built or small and compact, but the inner portion is a well-formed cup lined with soft materials.

The female lays from three to five dull-grayish eggs, lightly marked with small spots of gray-brown and black. It takes from 10 to 16 days for the eggs to hatch. Unlike some birds whose newly hatched young are ready to leave the nest as soon as their downy well-marked coats are dry, the waxwings are hatched perfectly naked. It is nearly a week before the first feathers break through and 10 days before the eyes are completely open. Until the first feathers appear, the female broods them closely, seldom leaving the nest. Her mate brings food, which during spring is usually berries or cherries that he carries in his gullet. These are carefully regurgitated and offered one at a time. As many as five undamaged cherries have been seen delivered in this manner.

California has a great variety of ornamental trees and shrubs that ripen at different times and offer an abundance of foods. Following a ripening food supply may account for the erratic movements of the small flocks of waxwings seen in mountainous areas and around valleys and cities. They like berries from trees and shrubs such as toyon, manzanita, pyracantha, madrone, camphor, pepper, mountain ash, and rose hips and blossoms of spruce, apple, and pear trees.

DIPPER *(Cinclus mexicanus)*

The dipper (also known as a water ouzel) is found along rushing mountain streams. This small dark bird has the ability to dart down the canyon, swim, and actually walk on the bottom of streams looking for food, the only bird that can do all three. Both the male and female are short-tailed and slate gray. Their flying ability is a spectacle; they rocket up and down river canyons with their rapid wingbeats, skimming the water for bugs. They are also famous for their bobbing motions, as if doing knee-bends.

> The water ouzel, or American dipper, can fly down a canyon, swim, and walk along the bottom streams looking for food; it is the only bird that can do all three.

ANIMAL	Dipper
SPECIES	*Cinclus mexicanus*
TYPE	bird
STATUS	OK
SEE ALSO	Ducks, Wood Duck

Dippers nest in the crevices of rocks along streams, often just beyond the free-fall of a waterfall. Here they lay three to five plain white eggs.

FINCHES *(Carpodacus* spp.)

The finch comes in several species, including the house finch *(Carpodacus mexicanus),* a very common non-native species. They are small, friendly birds, roughly four to five inches long, with their well known "cheep-cheep" call to other birds. They are extremely common sights feeding in urban areas at bird feeders. They have short stubby bills, ideal for eating seeds. Many finch have a colored head, best known by the reddish head and upper back of

dipper

the Cassin's Finch *(C. cassinii)*, common in the mountains, and the house finch, which lives throughout California. They have a unique flight pattern, noted by quick wing-beats alternated with short glides.

house finch

ANIMAL	Finches
SPECIES	*Carpodacus* spp.
TYPE	bird
STATUS	OK

MAGPIES *(Pica nuttalli and P. pica)*

Two magpies, the yellow-billed and black-billed, are the only large black and white land birds in North America. A simple way to classify them at a distance is that if you are east of the Sierra, it is probably a black-billed magpie *(Pica nuttalli)*, for the yellow-billed magpie *(P. pica)* has a limited range west of the Sierra and is found nowhere else in the world. The center of its population is in the Central Valley, and although the distance between the two narrows in places to less than 50 miles, the ranges of the two magpies do not overlap.

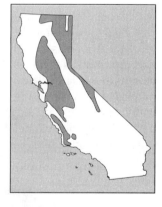

The range occupied by the yellow-billed magpie is entirely within the borders of California. It is about 500 miles long extending from Shasta County in the north to Kern County in the south. The area is less than 150 miles wide and includes some of the coastal valley south of San Francisco.

ANIMAL	Magpies
SPECIES	*Pica* spp.
TYPE	bird
STATUS	OK
SEE ALSO	Jay, Raven

The yellow-billed magpie thrives on land that has been occupied and cultivated by man. It likes the open ground—grassy pastures, freshly plowed fields, and the bare ground of well-kept orchards in which to forage. Much of their search for food is on the ground. In the fall they eat some acorns and certain nuts before the shells harden, but stomach examinations show about 70% of their diet is animal matter: grasshoppers, beetles, ants, flies, and other bugs. It is not unusual, in winter months, to see them picking at the remains of a road-killed animal.

The magpie nest is a large, bulky affair resembling a clump of mistletoe; some are even built in mistletoe clumps.

They are found in most abundance where there are long lines of tall trees bordering streams—great valley oaks and groves of tall eucalyptus trees in which to nest and roost. Farmlands provide year-round availability of food and water for drinking and nest-building.

The mild climate of the Sacramento and San Joaquin valleys seem to encourage an early start in nest-building. Magpies have been observed in January carrying large twigs and puttering around, either repairing old nests or starting new ones. Storms stop or delay this activity, but as the season progresses and the days begin to warm, the nesting activity increases. This is to make sure the nest is completed by egg-laying time in March.

The yellow-billed magpie, unlike the black-billed, makes its nest in tall trees, usually 40 to 60 feet above the ground. Cottonwoods, sycamores, and valley oaks are commonly used, particularly if the tree is infested with mistletoe. The nests are built far out on the smaller limbs. They are rather large, bulky affairs and resemble clumps of mistletoe; some are even built in clumps of mistletoe. The nest has two entrances and is domed over for protection from the weather. The cup of the nest is made of mud and lined with fine grasses. Both the male and female assist in nest-building and both defend the nest site, driving away other birds who attempt to use it.

yellow-billed magpie

mockingbird

MOCKINGBIRD *(Mimus polyglottos)*

The mockingbird shows a decided preference for the society of man. It often makes itself at home in front yards, sits and sings on the chimney top, teases the family cat, and has even been found entering the house through an open door or window. The bird is slim, neat, graceful, imitative, and amusing with such a rich tender song that only a thrush could hope to rival. The mocker is everyone's favorite, including the folks who testily protest its moonlight serenades.

The mockingbird is easily recognized. It is about the size of a robin, 9-10 inches long, but more slender. The male and female are the same in appearance, gray above, with the wings and wedge-shaped tail having a brownish cast. The upper wing feathers and outer edge of the tail feathers are white and

ANIMAL	Mockingbird
SPECIES	*Mimus polyglottos*
TYPE	bird
STATUS	OK

quite conspicuous in flight. The underparts are light gray and shading to white.

Except at nesting time, there is nothing secretive about either the male or female and they are readily observed if you are fortunate enough to have a pair or more become attached to your home or yard.

There seems to be no sound of bird or beast that a mockingbird cannot imitate clearly. It could be the cackle of a hen, the bark or whine of a puppy, the squeak of a rusty hinge, or even the note of some musical instruments.

The mockingbird belongs to the family Mimidae. *Mimus polyglottos* means "mimic in many tongues." There seems to be no sound of bird or beast that it cannot imitate so well as to deceive everyone but himself. The mocker seems to improve on most of the notes it reproduces. It could be the cackle of a hen, the bark or whine of a puppy, the squeak of a rusty hinge, or even the note of some musical instruments.

In the spring just prior to and during the mating season it launches itself into the air from some tall vantage point and literally puts body and soul into an improvised song. Exhausting itself, the mockingbird will float on quivering wings until it sings, sometimes, clear to the ground. On moonlit nights the performance is repeated. The night air is filled with the exquisite swells and trills, liquid and sweet, of its unparalleled melody.

The mocker usually builds its nest near a house, in the most dense tangle of shrubbery in the yard. The nest is almost always near the ground and without exception a loosely, poorly constructed affair of coarse twigs, leaves, and grass, and sometimes scraps of rags.

For many years the mockingbird in California was considered a southern bird. As the state's population grew, it has gradually made its way north, first to central California, then up the coast as far north as Eureka, up the great Central Valley to Redding, and has even been seen up the easternside of the Sierra as far north as Honey Lake in Lassen County. It is seldom seen in mountainous or forested areas.

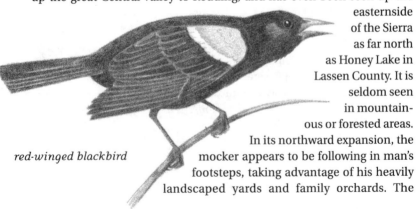

red-winged blackbird

In its northward expansion, the mocker appears to be following in man's footsteps, taking advantage of his heavily landscaped yards and family orchards. The pyracantha and other flowering and fruiting shrubs offer both food and nesting cover.

Red-Winged Blackbird
(Agelaius phoeniceus)

The male is sleek and blue-black with a red and yellow shoulder patch; the female is brown with stripes. They are almost always seen near water. It commonly nests in tules and reeds two or three feet above the water, producing eggs that are pale blue, lined heavily. For many, seeing the bright cardinal red patch on the upper edge of their wing is a thrill, with the immediate response, "Look! A red-winged blackbird!"

ANIMAL	Red-Winged Blackbird
SPECIES	*Agelaius phoeniceus*
TYPE	bird
STATUS	OK

Robin *(Turdus migratorius)*

The robin is the largest member of the thrush family. It is well known to millions of people, for it is widely distributed throughout the United States and Canada. It is so common that it is probably the first bird we learn to call by name. Its cheery morning and evening song is loved by all.

The American robin is easily recognized by its dark gray back, brick-red breast, broken white eye ring, and yellow bill. Young robins have speckled breasts, but the gray back and rusty underparts identify them.

At any time in late fall and early winter large flocks of robins may be seen moving from one locality to another in search of suitable feeding grounds. In the spring large flocks can be seen flying north and up into the mountains. However, many pairs of birds remain to nest in the developed lowlands of California.

ANIMAL	Robin
SPECIES	*Turdus migratorius*
TYPE	bird
STATUS	OK

Most nests are rather large and sturdily built in the crotches of trees and shrubs less than 10 or 12 feet above the ground. Both male and female assist in nest-building. They bring twigs, grass, and mud. The female shapes the nest, turning her body in the mud-lined nest to form a deep cup.

When the nest is completed, she lays from three to six eggs. Three seems the most common number. Their color is such that it gives rise to the figure of speech "as blue as a robin's egg." The female, with a little help from the male, broods the eggs for 14 days, during which time she leaves the nest for only brief periods. The male, when not feeding, spends much of his time on his song perch and may be heard singing at any time of day.

When the young birds hatch, both male and female are kept busy feeding the hungry fledglings. They are fed by regurgitation the first few days and then are given whole worms and larger insects. Because the nests are large and usually in plain sight, baby robins are subject to being hunted by cats, hawks, and jays. The jay is the worst offender as it craftily and persistently robs the nest of eggs and young. The parent birds defend the nest vigorously and keep it scrupulously clean, for soon after the fledglings leave the nest the female begins laying more eggs for a second and sometimes a third brood.

> Robin parents keep the nest scrupulously clean, for soon after the first fledglings leave the nest, the female begins laying more eggs for a second and sometimes a third brood.

When the young leave the nest they flutter weakly to the ground where they squat in the grass waiting to be fed. The male then takes over the rearing of the young. The babies at first show little fear and chirp loudly for attention. The male parent is kept busy bringing plump worms, which he shakes briskly before stuffing them into the hungry mouths. At this point in their growth the young are vulnerable to being caught by an alert house cat or a bird of prey. They soon become wary and able to run swiftly and fly up out of danger. In a few more days they acquire the manners of adult birds and in two weeks, although not always willingly, are able to find their own food. This frees the male to aid in rearing the nest brood, which is then nearly ready to hatch.

robin

WESTERN MEADOWLARK
(Sturnella neglecta)

The meadowlark is a common species in our gardens and fields, and its cheerful song makes the bird's appearance in the spring welcomed by all.

Two species of meadowlarks are found in North America from southern Canada to northern Mexico. The Western meadowlark, with the exception of its more melodious song, is similar in size and appearance to the Eastern meadowlark. However, the Western meadowlark occurs only from the prairies and great plains to the Pacific Ocean. There is little overlapping of their ranges.

The meadowlark is nearly the same size and shape as a quail and, like the quail, walks instead of hopping when on the

ANIMAL	Western Meadowlark
SPECIES	*Sturnella neglecta*
TYPE	bird
STATUS	OK

ground. Although flight characteristics of the two birds are similar, the meadowlark is readily distinguished by three well-known features—the white lateral tail feathers, yellow breast, and black crescent.

The fall migration seems almost casual, the bird moving only a few miles at a time and stopping to feed and stay awhile. It is a gradual drift towards the warmer climate away from areas where winter snows cover the feeding grounds. The birds move leisurely in small groups of a few to flocks of 100 or more to their wintering areas.

They return to the breeding grounds in early spring in much the same fashion. The male's arrival is announced by a glorious burst of song, proclaiming to the bird world that this is where he and his mate intend to nest. The meadowlark claims a territory that may vary from five to 10 acres and defends it fiercely from others of the species. If another male even flies across it, he will pursue and attack until the interloper is chased from the territory.

His joyous song throughout the early spring soon attracts a mate, and after a modest courtship display the serious business of nest-building begins, which may be as early as April along the coastal states. In California they prefer to nest in open pasture and grasslands. The nest is always constructed on the ground, hidden in a clump of grass, and is domed

Western meadowlark

The meadowlark claims a territory of from five to 10 acres and defends it fiercely from others of the species. If another male flies across it, it will pursue and attack until the interloper is chased from its territory.

completely with a canopy of grass and weed fibers. There is a small opening on the side and a carefully concealed runway from two to four feet long leading into the nest. The nest, if lifted from the ground, would appear almost globular. Because they prefer to live in open areas, the birds are constantly alert for predators from the air and on the ground, so the nest must be carefully concealed.

The nest is lined with fine grasses in which the female lays from three to seven eggs, with five being an average set. The eggs are white, rather evenly splotched with brown, and sometimes are faintly tinted with green. Both the male and female help in nest-building and incubation of the eggs. The eggs are laid on consecutive days until the set is complete.

Incubation takes about 17 days. The young leave the nest before they are ready to fly, roaming the area with their parents and learning the things young meadowlarks need to know, such as how to catch bugs, which seeds to eat, and especially how to hide from danger. The babies' coloring is a yellowish light brown, streaked with black. As long as the young meadowlarks are still, the color pattern will protect them from harm. Within several weeks, as soon as the young have learned to fly, perch in low shrubbery, and fend for themselves, they are no longer dependent on the adults and are on their own.

Where to see songbirds and other favorites

ANDERSON MARSH STATE HISTORIC PARK, IN LAKE COUNTY (WESTERN MEADOWLARK)

AUDUBON CANYON RANCH, IN MARIN COUNTY (CEDAR WAXWING, FINCHES, RED-WINGED BLACKBIRD, MAGPIE, MOCKINGBIRD, ROBIN)

BEAVER CREEK, NEAR MCARTHUR, IN SHASTA COUNTY (CEDAR WAXWING, FINCHES, RED-WINGED BLACKBIRD, MAGPIE, MOCKINGBIRD, ROBIN)

CRYSTAL COVE STATE PARK, IN ORANGE COUNTY (CEDAR WAXWING, FINCHES, RED-WINGED BLACKBIRD, MAGPIE, MOCKINGBIRD, ROBIN)

GRAY LODGE STATE WILDLIFE AREA, IN BUTTE COUNTY (CEDAR WAXWING, FINCHES, RED-WINGED BLACKBIRD, MAGPIE, MOCKINGBIRD, ROBIN)

JACKSON MEADOWS RESERVOIR, IN NEVADA COUNTY (DIPPER)

LAKE SAN ANTONIO, LOS PADRES NATIONAL FOREST, IN MONTEREY COUNTY (CEDAR WAXWING, FINCHES, RED-WINGED BLACKBIRD, MAGPIE, MOCKINGBIRD, ROBIN)

LASSEN VOLCANIC NATIONAL PARK, IN LASSEN COUNTY (DIPPER)

LEWISTON LAKE/TRINITY RIVER HATCHERY, IN TRINITY COUNTY (DIPPER)

LITTLE PANOCHE WILDLIFE AREA, SOUTH OF LOS BANOS, IN FRESNO COUNTY (WESTERN MEADOWLARK)

MARTINEZ REGIONAL SHORELINE, IN CONTRA COSTA COUNTY (WESTERN MEADOWLARK)

NEW HOGAN LAKE, IN CALAVERAS COUNTY (WESTERN MEADOWLARK)

PALM TO PINES SCENIC BYWAY TOUR, IN RIVERSIDE COUNTY (CEDAR WAXWING, FINCHES, RED-WINGED BLACKBIRD, MAGPIE, MOCKINGBIRD, ROBIN)

PINECREST LAKE, IN TUOLUMNE COUNTY (CEDAR WAXWING, FINCHES, RED-WINGED BLACKBIRD, MAGPIE, MOCKINGBIRD, ROBIN)

POINT MUGU STATE PARK, IN LOS ANGELES COUNTY (CEDAR WAXWING, FINCHES, RED-WINGED BLACKBIRD, MAGPIE, MOCKINGBIRD, ROBIN)

PRAIRIE CREEK REDWOODS STATE PARK, IN HUMBOLDT COUNTY (CEDAR WAXWING, FINCHES, RED-WINGED BLACKBIRD, MAGPIE, MOCKINGBIRD, ROBIN)

SKYLINE RIDGE OPEN SPACE PRESERVE, IN SANTA CLARA COUNTY (CEDAR WAXWING, FINCHES, RED-WINGED BLACKBIRD, MAGPIE, MOCKINGBIRD, ROBIN)

SWEETWATER MARSH NATIONAL WILDLIFE REFUGE, IN SAN DIEGO COUNTY (WESTERN MEADOWLARK)

Other places to see songbirds and other favorites

BIDWELL PARK, IN BUTTE COUNTY (CEDAR WAXWING, DIPPER, FINCHES, RED-WINGED BLACKBIRD, MAGPIE, MOCKINGBIRD, ROBIN)

BIG BASIN REDWOODS STATE PARK, IN SANTA CRUZ COUNTY (CEDAR WAXWING, FINCHES, RED-WINGED BLACKBIRD, MAGPIE, MOCKINGBIRD, ROBIN)

GROVER HOT SPRINGS STATE PARK, IN ALPINE COUNTY (DIPPER)

HENRY W. COE STATE PARK, IN SANTA CLARA COUNTY (CEDAR WAXWING, FINCHES, RED-WINGED BLACKBIRD, MAGPIE, MOCKINGBIRD, ROBIN, WESTERN MEADOWLARK)

MCCLOUD RIVER LOOP, IN SISKIYOU COUNTY (CEDAR WAXWING, DIPPER, FINCHES, RED-WINGED BLACKBIRD, MAGPIE, MOCKINGBIRD, ROBIN)

NEW HOGAN LAKE, IN CALAVERAS COUNTY (CEDAR WAXWING, FINCHES, RED-WINGED BLACKBIRD, MAGPIE, MOCKINGBIRD, ROBIN)

OROVILLE WILDLIFE AREA, IN BUTTE COUNTY (CEDAR WAXWING, FINCHES, RED-WINGED BLACKBIRD, MAGPIE, MOCKINGBIRD, ROBIN, WESTERN MEADOWLARK)

SAN PABLO BAY NATIONAL WILDLIFE REFUGE, IN CONTRA COSTA COUNTY (CEDAR WAXWING, FINCHES, RED-WINGED BLACKBIRD, MAGPIE, MOCKINGBIRD, ROBIN, WESTERN MEADOWLARK)

SEQUOIA AND KINGS CANYON NATIONAL PARKS, IN TULARE AND FRESNO COUNTIES (CEDAR WAXWING, DIPPER, FINCHES, RED-WINGED BLACKBIRD, MAGPIE, MOCKINGBIRD, ROBIN)

SUCCESS LAKE, IN TULARE COUNTY (CEDAR WAXWING, FINCHES, RED-WINGED BLACKBIRD, MAGPIE, MOCKINGBIRD, ROBIN, WESTERN MEADOWLARK)

The parent birds may then nest again, bringing forth a second brood by the middle of June. Because there are many natural enemies (skunks, weasels, mink, raccoon, coyotes, foxes, snakes, hawks, and owls), having two large broods is nature's way of ensuring that there will be enough meadowlarks to withstand natural mortality.

As a destroyer of cutworms, caterpillars, and grasshoppers, three of the worst insect pests in California, the Western meadowlark is probably unequaled by any other bird species in its benefits to mankind.

Squirrels

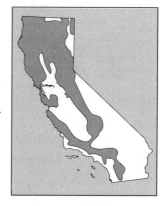

For years I kept a homemade bird feeder available for wildlife, along with a sunken, shallow tub of water amid a small grove of cedar, pine, and fir, surrounded by a small meadow, which, in turn, was edged by forest. It created a small habitat with food, water, and cover for a variety of birds and animals. It was just outside my mountain cabin, and from the upstairs room I kept as an office for writing, I could watch the activity every morning, where the squirrels were often more fascinating than the birds.

Note that to prevent a dependence on the feeding site, I would never keep the feeder full of seed. Instead, at dusk, I would place half a cup of sunflower seed and wildflower seed on the flat surface, mounted on a four-foot high stump of a four-inch diameter fir, as well as sprinkle an additional half cup in the general vicinity. That accomplished two things: 1. By sprinkling the seed in a large area, instead of a single feeding site, it avoided potential competition and conflict

ANIMAL	Squirrels
SPECIES	Squirrel - *Sciureus* spp. Douglas' - *Tamasciurus douglasii* Northern Flying - *Glaucomys sabrinus*
TYPE	mammal
STATUS	OK/Endangered/ Introduced
SEE ALSO	Chipmunks, Marmot

between birds, squirrels, chipmunks, and occasional deer and bears that might come by for a snack. 2. By putting the seed out at night, the wildlife would thus arrive at dawn, with enough seed for maybe an hour or so of feeding—that's all—and then they were off to their other haunts.

It was the squirrels that seemed most like circus animals. They would scurry about, often amid juncos, jays, and flickers, and collect the seed in their cheeks. Sometimes they would jump from tree to tree, scurrying about, flying from the cabin roof to a branch of a Douglas fir, and then jump across to a cedar, then down the trunk, circling it, into a hole at the base, then out, with several often playing tag. Nearby sat an old snag of a Douglas fir that had been snapped in half by a windstorm. Much of it was dead, but it was filled with holes from the nesting squirrels; dead trees should always be left standing, not cut down for firewood, for they provide outstanding wildlife habitat.

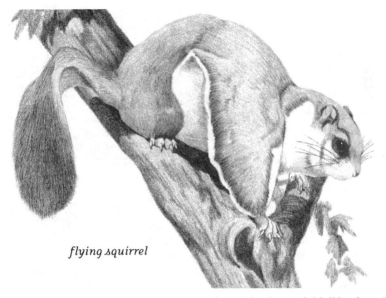

flying squirrel

There was one gray squirrel in particular, with a beautiful full bushy tail about 10 inches long, that would try to pack so much seed in its mouth that it appeared it might be the first squirrel in history with an exploding head. I always wondered if that squirrel would cough or hiccup, if that seed would be jettisoned like a rocket blast, but it never happened.

Studies show that over half of the diet of gray squirrels in northern California is made up of truffles, a type of subterranean mushroom, which they dig up from just below the ground surface.

Of course, squirrels are best known for gathering food for winter. It's half blessing, half curse. A blessing because it gives them the ability to make it through long winters when no food is available. A curse, though, because they seem to live in fear, hoarding everything they can get, believing they never have enough. Many people who maintain bird feeders can't stand them, and instead use squirrel-proof feeders; I've learned by sprinkling the seed around, rather than using a single site, you can largely avoid the problem.

Squirrels have such personality that it can be easy for many people to forget they are wild animals, and that one of their chief purposes in the scheme of nature is to provide food for flesh-eating predators. That is why squirrels are so "squirrelly," often high-strung and chattering in fear, because a lot of them disappear each day, caught by eagles, hawks, owls, minks, fishers, martens, skunks, mountain lions, bobcats, and foxes. Along with chipmunks, mice, pocket gophers, and other rodents, squirrels are members of the club that can have a heck of a summer trying to keep from ending up as someone's dinner.

But just about everybody seems to love the little guys, out looking for their nut for the day.

Biologists' Notes

There are three different species of tree dwelling squirrels within the forests of California's mountains, and in the oak woodland areas of the foothills and valleys. They are the Western gray squirrel, the little Douglas' squirrel or chickaree, and the nocturnal flying squirrel. They are the only tree squirrels in California except the Eastern red squirrel (also called Eastern fox squirrel, *Sciurus niger),* and the Eastern tree squirrel *(S. carolinensis)* that were intro-

duced into some of the city parks and has since spread into some of the central coast counties.

Douglas' squirrel, or chickaree

The Western gray squirrel *(S. griseus)* is the largest, being nearly two feet from the tip of its nose to the end of its long bushy tail. Its coat and tail are clear gray with white on the underparts of the body. It lives both in the forests of the mountains and in the oak woodland areas in the valleys and foothills.

On the ground, gray squirrels appear leisurely and graceful, but if danger is present they climb and run through the treetops with ease. They make their homes in hollows in the trees and sometimes make a shallow nest of twigs on a limb 30 feet or so above the ground. The breeding season extends from January through July. They have from three to five babies in a litter and sometimes two litters a year. The babies are born blind and helpless and are nearly six weeks old before they are ready to leave the nest. They spend considerable time on the ground foraging for food. They eat mushrooms, acorns, pine nuts, and grain if it is available. They store a large amount of their food. Studies show that over half of the diet of gray squirrels in northern California is made up of truffles, a type of subterranean mushroom, which they dig up from just below the ground surface.

The little Douglas' squirrel, or chickaree *(Tamiasciurus douglasii)*, is much more active than its larger cousin the gray squirrel. It lives at higher elevations in the pine forests. These animals are curious, noisy, and active. Their chattering call, accompanied by a series of explosive little grunts, growls, and clucks, attracts quick attention. The Douglas' squirrel's day begins early. At sunrise they will be 200 feet high in a tree cutting pine cones, which they store in great quantities. Pine nuts are their favorite food. The husked cones are found in neat piles near the base of a tree or rock. They also eat animal food such as nestlings, bird eggs, and some insects. They live in old woodpecker holes and hollow limbs in trees high above the ground. In California the Douglas' squirrel is seldom hunted as a game animal, even though there is an open season.

The smallest of the California tree squirrels is the flying squirrel *(Glaucomys sabrinus)*. Its coat is a soft gray with cream-colored underparts. Its tail is flattened and is the same color as the back. Like other strictly nocturnal animals, its eyes are large and its whiskers are long. The most interesting difference about the flying squirrel is the soft furry membrane that connects its front and hind feet. When they spread their legs and tails they are about five or six inches square and quite flat. This enables them to glide long distances.

Because flying squirrels are seldom seen, few people realize that they are quite common in California's forests. However, if you were to sit quietly around a camp in the woods after sundown, you could hear them scrambling around in the tall trees. These little squirrels are extremely fast climbers. They leave one tree by gliding as far as 100 feet to reach a spot at a lower elevation. They land with an audible thump and then climb to a higher elevation to glide again, veering upwards to alight. Vocal sounds are small and birdlike, and when they are in distress, they emit a shrill squeal.

Where to see squirrels

CALAVERAS BIG TREES STATE PARK, IN CALAVERAS COUNTY

CHINA FLAT/SILVER FORKS CAMPGROUNDS, EL DORADO NATIONAL FOREST, IN EL DORADO COUNTY

GROVER HOT SPRINGS STATE PARK, IN ALPINE COUNTY

PALOMAR MOUNTAIN STATE PARK, IN SAN DIEGO COUNTY

SILVERWOOD LAKE STATE RECREATION AREA, IN SAN BERNARDINO COUNTY

WADDELL CREEK, IN SANTA CRUZ COUNTY

Other places to see squirrels

NOTE: Squirrels are widespread—you can see them in all of California's 19 national forests, in more than 100 of California's state parks, and nearly all the national parks.

LAKE SONOMA RECREATION AREA, IN SONOMA COUNTY

LASSEN VOLCANIC NATIONAL PARK, IN LASSEN COUNTY

MARBLE MOUNTAIN WILDERNESS, IN SISKIYOU COUNTY

PAYNES CREEK WETLANDS, IN TEHAMA COUNTY

They also spend a good deal of their time foraging on the ground. They eat nuts, berries, insects, and some fungi. They also like meat, and they feed on any carcasses they might find. They live in old woodpecker holes and natural cavities in trees and also make a shallow twig nest on a limb. The breeding season is in late winter. They have from two to six pink hairless babies in a litter, and sometimes there are two litters per year. At birth the eyes of the babies are closed and the gliding membranes are transparent. Their eyes open in 28 days and they are weaned at five weeks. If the nest is endangered the mother will move the babies by holding them firmly in her teeth and gliding to safety. The young can make short glides in eight weeks.

For information on the golden-mantled ground squirrel *(Spermophilus lateralis),* see the discussion on chipmunks.

Steelhead

The "One Percent Club" is a special group, recognized among most steelhead fishermen. You can't buy your way in, and, for the most part, you can't will your way in. What it takes is time, skill, persistence with spirit, and days when you have to be both lucky and good.

According to a survey conducted by the Department of Fish and Game, 97%of California's anglers have never caught a steelhead. Of the 3% that have, perhaps just one-third have caught a 15-pounder. Thus comes Club Membership. There's a reason so few are in the Club—in fact, many reasons.

ANIMAL	Steelhead
SPECIES	*Oncorhynchus mykiss*
TYPE	fish
STATUS	OK/Endangered
SEE ALSO	Salmon, Trout (Golden)

It starts with the fish. There's nothing else like steelhead, especially the big, fresh-run steelhead that arrive to coastal rivers strong from years of hunting down food and roaming free in the ocean. A big steelhead is the fastest freshwater fish in California, capable of a speed burst of 27 feet per second.

The first one I ever hooked jumped 100 feet to my left, landed with a gigantic splash, and then a few seconds later, jumped 100 feet to my right. By the time I figured out it was the same fish, it was another 100 feet down stream, and a moment later, now with a full head of steam, into the white water and gone forever. They'll drive you crazy, I tell you.

They live primarily in 20 California streams, the significant coastal rivers mainly from the Smith River near the Oregon border south to the Carmel River near Monterey,

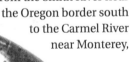

steelhead

with specimens documented as far south as San Luis Obispo County and even the Ventura River. The state record is officially 27 pounds, 4 ounces, from the Smith River, but I have a newspaper clipping from 1906 that documents a 30-pound specimen, complete with photograph, landed on Lagunitas Creek (the same small stream that holds the state record for silver/coho salmon).

The first thing to remember is that a steelhead is basically a trout, that is, a rainbow trout that lives most of its life in the ocean, getting big and strong before returning to rivers during the winter to spawn. What makes the difference between a summer trout stream in the mountains and a winter steelhead stream near the coast is size: Everything is bigger. The water is bigger, the tackle is bigger, and the fish are way bigger.

Why aren't more people in the One Percent Club? Many reasons: It starts with the long, mind-numbing drive required from population centers to reach the best rivers. On top of that comes the cold, rainy weather that often greets anglers in the winter, and with it, the perpetually changing stream conditions. Then, of course, there is the elusive nature of the fish and the super-powered strength and speed of the big ones, even if you should manage to hook one. Collectively, it makes big steelhead the challenge of a lifetime.

A large steelhead is capable of a burst of speed of 27 feet per second, making it the fastest freshwater fish in California. Only 3% of California anglers have ever caught a steelhead, which is spawned in a coastal stream but spends much of its life at sea.

Steelhead use the river as a highway, then spawn in the tributaries, for the most part. They don't like to stop moving, but they will in order to rest a bit, especially after swimming through some rough water. This is when anglers get their chance. I like to fish the pools and long slicks, especially just above white water. After a steelhead charges through that white water, it is bound to hole up for a while to rest before heading on upstream.

During extended rainless periods, it is possible to stand on the canyon rims of rivers and gaze down at the pools with binoculars and see the dark outlines of steelhead in the clear water. One of the best spots for this is on the Smith River, the clearest-running steelhead stream in California, best at the forks of the river in Gasquet, as well as on the South Fork where bridges cross the river.

It is well documented that steelhead populations have suffered declines because of damage to their spawning habitat, especially siltation of spawning gravels because of topsoil damage from past logging and clear-cuts in watersheds. Fishery officials have responded by creating fishing rules so complicated that you need a lawyer standing next to you on a river to explain it all. But meanwhile, these rules have done nothing to bring the fish back, and the habitat degradation remains.

In fact, the National Marine Fisheries Service has a perfect record: More than 500 aquatic species have been listed as endangered species in the United States, and in 25 years, not a single one has been recovered and delisted. For this they have been entrusted and paid highly as guardians of the resource? I'd rather take my chances in Las Vegas than with NMFS.

Regardless, most fishermen are trying to do their part to aid the restoration. On the Smith, where more anglers join the One Percent Club than anywhere else, you can purchase a beautiful silver steelhead hat pin at local shops inscribed with the words "Catch & Release." Of course, you have to get yourself a 15-pounder and let it go so you can wear the thing.

Let me tell you, after a fantastic 30-minute fight with a 16-pounder, a steelhead that jumped three times, ripped line on countless power runs, then bulldogged in a pool for 15 minutes, and just about slipped downstream into the rapids on me—well, watching that bomber swim away after I released it was one of the most satisfying moments in all the outdoors.

Biologists' Notes

The steelhead is a rainbow trout *(Oncorhynchus mykiss)*, a fish known to the majority of anglers in California. The steelhead is special because it is spawned in a coastal freshwater stream and then swims out to sea, where it spends much of its life. The steelhead, unlike salmon, does not die after spawning. On shorter streams where the swim is not long or hazardous, many return to spawn a second or third time.

Steelhead have from nine to 12 rays on the anal fin (salmon have from 13 to 19). Steelhead also have small, round, black spots on their backs (salmon have larger, irregularly shaped spots). Steelhead that have been in fresh water for a time develop a broad red stripe on their sides and look like a large stream rainbow; this is most common on the Klamath River. In the ocean, both salmon and steelhead are steel-blue on the back and silvery on the sides.

California steelhead are divided into three classes, based on the time they first enter fresh water on their spawning migration: fall, winter, or spring. In the Klamath, both half-pounders and adult fish will enter as early as August. As water temperatures drop and flows increase, the fish move

Where to see steelhead

EEL RIVER, IN HUMBOLDT COUNTY

FEATHER RIVER HATCHERY, IN BUTTE COUNTY

KLAMATH RIVER, IN HUMBOLDT AND SISKIYOU COUNTIES

NIMBUS/AMERICAN RIVER HATCHERIES, IN SACRAMENTO COUNTY

REDWOOD CREEK, REDWOOD NATIONAL PARK, IN HUMBOLDT COUNTY

RUSSIAN RIVER, IN SONOMA COUNTY

SMITH RIVER, IN DEL NORTE COUNTY

WADDELL CREEK, IN SANTA CRUZ COUNTY

Other places to see steelhead

GARCIA RIVER, IN MENDOCINO COUNTY

GUALALA RIVER, IN MENDOCINO AND SONOMA COUNTIES

MATTOLE RIVER, IN HUMBOLDT COUNTY

NAVARRO RIVER, IN MENDOCINO COUNTY

VAN DUZEN RIVER, IN HUMBOLDT COUNTY

upstream and spawn in the headwaters and smaller tributaries in January and February. Other adults, called winter-run fish, enter the rivers in December and January and move more quickly to the spawning grounds. Although spawning occurs at different times in different rivers, January, February, and March are the peak months. Since 1997, the geographic populations of steelhead from four river drainages are federally listed as threatened or endangered—Central California Coast, South/Central California Coast, Southern California Coast, and the Central Valley.

In some of the small coastal rivers and streams, sandbars form across the mouth of the river or stream as a result of low summer flows and wave action. This often creates lagoons in the lower river, which juvenile steelhead often use as a nursery area. In winter, high flows will blow out the sandbar, allowing the juvenile fish to head out to sea and allowing older ocean migrants to return to the river of their birth.

The spawning and early life history of steelhead are very similar to that of the salmon. The female steelhead digs the nest and, as she lays some of her eggs, the male simultaneously fertilizes them. The female moves slightly upstream and digs another nest, the gravel from the second nest covering the eggs in the first nest. This process continues until the female has no more eggs. As the eggs hatch, the young fish develop and work their way slowly out of the gravel. Once out of the gravel, they will feed and grow. Young steelhead remain in fresh water from one to four years before moving downstream to the ocean, where they will feed and grow for an additional one to four years before returning to spawn the first time.

Sturgeons

There are fish stories, and then there are stories about sturgeon, which go beyond all other yarns. Mr. Sturgy, the giant fish with prehistoric roots, can inspire war stories in which the line blurs between myth and legend. And the legends are many.

On a magic day in the Bay Area, for example, Joey Pallotta hooked a sturgeon in Carquinez Strait off Benicia, and when the fish rolled near the surface, it looked as big as a whale. Turns out it was: The fish weighed 468 pounds and measured nine feet, six inches, a world record. With a six-foot maximum size limit now enforced in all western

ANIMAL	Sturgeons
SPECIES	*Acipenser* spp.
TYPE	fish
STATUS	OK

states, that is, all sturgeon measuring six feet and longer must be released, this record will never be broken.

Now get this: according to the late Larry Green, some divers who were laying cable on the bottom of Carquinez Strait say they came across a sturgeon that they paced off at something like 12 feet long. Another time, a big ship's propeller cut a sturgeon in two, and, according to witnesses, both pieces washed up on shore and added up to 11 feet.

It seems anything is possible, and so it is. Perception, when talking about the legend of Mr. Sturgy, often becomes reality.

But it all makes sense, you see, because sturgeon are capable of living 70 or 80 years, perhaps even longer, and can therefore grow to fantastic sizes. They live primarily in the ocean and spawn only once every seven or eight years, passing through San Francisco Bay and entering the Sacra-

sturgeon

mento River or San Joaquin Delta. They have also been documented in the Klamath River, and, very rarely, in the lower Smith River. Some individuals have been tagged in San Francisco Bay and then migrated a thousand miles north and caught in the Columbia River.

What draws them in from the ocean are excellent feeding conditions, such as herring, smelt, or disrupted beds of mud shrimp, or ideal spawning conditions—high freshwater outflows from the estuary to the ocean. Hence there can be dramatic fluctuations in population levels in a given body of water from year to year.

The sturgeon is capable of living 100 years and is the largest freshwater fish in the world. Age is determined by counting the microscopic growth rings on the rays of the pectoral fin.

I am a strong supporter of the six-foot maximum size limit, after all, these are the big spawners. In fact, I support releasing all sturgeon, since they can live to such old ages, and have released every sturgeon I have caught in the past 15 years.

Sturgeon have a strange, round mouth that they often use like a tool on a vacuum cleaner, filter feeding the mud on the Bay bottom for shrimp, crabs, and small fish. They also love munching on freshly spawned eggs from herring, and herring themselves, which migrate into San Francisco Bay in the winter months.

The unique feeding pattern is why sturgeon are most active in winter during strong outgoing tides. The infusion of fresh water from winter rains draw sturgeon in to the Bay estuary, and the fresh water on top of outgoing tides stirs up the bottom, uncovering all matter of food for Mr. Sturgy.

You never know when the next giant sturgeon will come along.

Like the November day when Bill Stratton was on his first trip on a new boat with a new rod. He was fishing for striped bass when he hooked a monster sturgeon by accident. After nearly losing all his line, he had to hop aboard another boat, piloted by my longtime pal Barry Canevaro, to continue fighting the fish. After several hours, he landed a 390-pound sturgeon that stands as the world record for 30-pound line.

On one trip on a late winter day with Keith Fraser, the Bay Area's Sturgeon General, and Jerry Goff, a former professional baseball player, we anchored our boat in San Francisco Bay near the Richmond Bridge—and almost immediately my rod tip dipped, I set the hook, and just like that, a huge sturgeon jumped completely out of the water and landed like a Volkswagen.

I fought that fish for over an hour, and while I was doing so, Fraser and Goff caught and released two sturgeon weighing 70 and 90 pounds, respectively. It was nearly dark when the fish came alongside the boat, the lights of a traffic jam on the Richmond Bridge shining overhead. The sturgeon measured seven feet, one inch, and weighed 150 pounds. Now get this: On my first cast the next day, I caught a six-foot, 100-pounder in another tremendous fight, featuring a series of 150- and 100-yard runs.

But that's nothing. I hooked another one that was so big that I fought it all day long without gaining an inch. So I tied the line to the trailer-hitch on my four-wheel drive, figuring I'd pull it out like a boat. Let me tell you, the last I saw of my truck was the hood ornament disappearing in the water.

Biologists' Notes

The sturgeon is the largest freshwater fish in the world. There are twenty or more species or subspecies that occur in Asia, northern Europe, and North America. They do not live in the tropics. Seven of these species live in North America, four of which are anadromous (spawn in fresh water but spend a good part of their life at sea). Only the white and the green sturgeon are found on the Pacific Coast. They range from northern California to northwestern Alaska.

The white sturgeon *(Acipenser transmontanus)* is the largest freshwater fish in North America. It is sometimes called the Columbia River, Sacramento, or Pacific sturgeon. It generally reaches a length of 20 feet and a weight of 1,000 pounds. One specimen weighted 1,900 pounds.

Green sturgeon (*A. medirostris*) reach a length of seven feet and a weight of 350 pounds. In the Sacramento-San Joaquin estuary they are much less common than white sturgeon; however, they are apparently the only sturgeon in the larger rivers of northwestern California. Tagging studies have demonstrated that some green sturgeon travel long distances at sea. Individuals tagged in San Pablo Bay and in the Klamath have been recaptured in Oregon and Washington rivers and bays.

Sturgeon grow slowly and live for many years, some reaching 100 years of age. The age is determined by counting the microscopic growth rings on the rays of the pectoral fin. Sturgeon do not look like other fishes. The eyes are small. The mouth is on the underside of the head. The mouth is small but it can be extended, purse-like, to suck up small pieces of food. There is a row of four rubbery whiskers or feelers in front of the mouth. The diet of sturgeon living in San Pablo Bay is composed mostly of clams, grass shrimp, mud crabs, and herring eggs, in that order. When feeding, sturgeon root in the mud with their snouts, feeling around with their sensitive whiskers. When food is located, the sturgeon protrudes its mouth and sucks the food up from the bottom. There is a vacuum cleaner-like action, for rocks, twigs, and other odd items have also been found in its stomach. It is reported that one white sturgeon from the Snake River in Idaho had eaten a half bushel of onions it found floating in the river.

Sturgeon spawn in freshwater in the late winter and spring. Females are said to spawn for the first time when about 13 or 14 years old, the males a little earlier. At this age they are about three feet long. It appears that an individual fish does not spawn every year, as do most other fish, but can spawn once every six or seven years. Because the fish may choose to live at sea for periods of time, the variance in its presentation in Bay waters can give the appearance of great population fluctuations.

In the Sacramento River most sturgeon spawn between Knights Landing and Colusa. They do not build a nest. The eggs are discharged in large grayish masses that cling to vegetation, stones, or other material on the bottom. After spawning, both the male and female leave the area and return to the feeding grounds. The eggs hatch in three to seven days. The baby sturgeon lives the first few days on the egg yolk. When it is about three-quarters of an inch long, it commences to eat the minute animal life it finds in the water. It grows rapidly and in a month it is four or five inches long and begins to feed on small shrimp and other crustaceans.

In the 1870s white sturgeon six to 12 feet long were caught in such large numbers that California markets were flooded. By 1880 the commercial

Where to see sturgeons

BRANNAN ISLAND STATE RECREATION AREA, IN SACRAMENTO COUNTY

CARQUINEZ STRAIT, CROCKETT PIER, IN CONTRA COSTA COUNTY

SACRAMENTO RIVER, FROM RED BLUFF TO COLUSA, IN COLUSA COUNTY

SAN PABLO BAY, LOCH LOMOND MARINA, IN MARIN COUNTY

SOUTH SAN FRANCISCO BAY, OYSTER POINT MARINA, IN SAN FRANCISCO COUNTY

SUISUN BAY, MARTINEZ PIER, IN CONTRA COSTA COUNTY

Other places to see sturgeons

SAN PABLO RESERVOIR, IN CONTRA COSTA COUNTY

SHASTA LAKE, IN SHASTA COUNTY

catch had reached 700,000 pounds, but the sturgeon soon began to disappear. Overfishing, stream pollution, and dams on the rivers and spawning streams took their toll, and in 1901 the fishing season was closed for eight years. The season was reopened in 1910, but in 1917 a complete closure was put into effect until 1954, when sportfishing for sturgeon again became legal. To protect juvenile sturgeon and large adult spawners, it is illegal to keep sturgeon under 46 inches or over 72 inches.

Sport fishermen now regard the sturgeon as a world-class fishery, with many encouraging catch-and-release fishing to help ensure future successful spawns, many large fish, and a productive future.

Swans

To many, the swan is the most beautiful of all birds. Watching them float about a pond, lake, or marsh, they seem graceful and almost fragile, as if touched by an angel.

The truth is that angels can be pretty tough, and there is nothing fragile about swans. Many people see swans as a bird of peace, an image similar to that of a rare, white dove. But what you will notice, if you watch them in their native habitat, is that they are often the only game in town. That is, you won't typically see an abundance of other waterfowl sharing the same habitat, at least in close proximity. You know why? Because a swan can be something of a bully.

ANIMAL	Swans
SPECIES	*Cygnus* spp.
TYPE	bird
STATUS	OK
SEE ALSO	Goose, Canada

Yep, these snow-white, peaceful-looking creatures usually don't like to share, and they are big enough to drive off most any cousins they don't want around. It often seems that the only other waterfowl that will put up with them, or at least force them to cooperate, is the Canada goose.

However, swans have a special grace that captivates people. This large, often pure-white bird with its classic form is best enjoyed at a small pond. I know two ranchers who have even spent small fortunes building ponds where swans live as unrestrained pets, and where occasional migrants join them. The swans could leave, but they choose not to. After all, they've got it good.

tundra swan

The image of a mated pair of swans floating peacefully about the surface of a lake is the picture that comes first to mind for many. What is actually more memorable, I believe, is seeing a flock of

20 or so outlined against an early-morning sky in Central Valley, in migratory flight, their distinct calls audible for miles.

From a distance, they appear to be moving slowly and gracefully. That is because swans' long wings are flapped with such long strokes and so methodically, the birds often lined up in skeins or Vs as they propel themselves across the sky. They are so big, four to six feet from wingtip to wingtip, that a skein of 50 can seem to stretch across the horizon.

When swans rise from the water, they face the wind and patter along the surface for 15 or 20 feet to gain enough speed to lift into the air. They mate for life and only an accident or death will separate a mated pair. If this happens, the surviving bird will choose another mate.

On a quiet morning, you can hear swans' high-pitched notes from miles away, especially striking from the trumpeter swan, but always memorable. As they near, suddenly you realize that these birds aren't the clunks they might appear from so far away, but are fast, graceful flyers. In fact, they can reach speeds of 50 mph, and when they pass overhead, their speed suddenly becomes evident relative to your position on the ground. They seem like evolutionary perfection, built to fly fast and far.

That is how I think of them. The perfect migratory machine.

Most love watching them float around, a picture of peace. But it is their wild state in which their true character is best beheld.

Biologists' Notes

The whistling or tundra swan *(Cygnus columbianus)* is the common wild swan of North America. Both in the air and on the water, this magnificent snow-white bird is the most striking of all the waterfowl that winter in California. It is by far the largest all-white bird commonly seen; the trumpeter swan *(Cygnus buccinator)* which is slightly larger, is a rare visitor to California.

With the approach of cold weather in the far north, these great birds leave their breeding grounds in small family groups to start their southern migration to spend the winter below the mean freeze line.

The severity of the storms in the north accounts for the variance in the numbers that come to California. They occur in the greatest numbers in the Sacramento-San Joaquin Delta. Here the pastures and flooded fields offer them adequate feeding and resting areas.

Swans are easily recognized in flight by their very large, snow-white form; long necks; triangular, slow-moving wings; and black bills and feet. When landing they alight gracefully into the water with hardly a splash; student pilots would do well to study the perfect landings. When rising from the water they face into the wind and patter along the surface for 15 or 20 feet to gain enough speed to lift into the air.

Unlike the domesticated mute swan, which, while in the water, arches its neck with the bill pointed downward, both the whistling and trumpeter swans sit gracefully on the water with the neck erect and the bill held parallel to the water.

Swans are relatively quiet on the water but when they take wing, and in flight, their voices are so distinctive that they are easily distinguished from other waterfowl. The notes of the swan's call sounds like repeated *whoo-whoos* followed by a lower note, *wow-WOW-ou,* heavily accented on the second syllable. When flying low overhead, especially in the fog, the yelping and hooting has an almost musical quality.

The swan feeds in shallow water by reaching down with its long neck to pull weeds and grasses, from which it eats the tender roots and bulbs. It does not dive in deep water to feed. On the winter range, on land, it eats corn and the tender roots of planted grains. It is a thrilling sight to see large bands of these majestic birds trading back and forth between resting and feeding areas.

Early in the spring they become restless and uneasy. Large flocks spend considerable time preening their feathers and keeping up a constant conversation, almost as though discussing the weather and which routes to take in preparation for a long migration to the frozen tundra, north of the Arctic Circle. By the first of March, they are generally on their way. Late spring storms delay them from time to time, but usually in early May they reach their destination.

Upon arrival, the birds separate in pairs, usually when at least three years old, and almost immediately commence the business of nest-building and rearing their young. Each pair claims a rather large territory so the nests are widely separated. Unmated birds join large molting flocks to spend the summer in coastal estuaries. Swans mate for life and remain in family groups through the spring migration the following year. Only an accident or death will separate the parent birds. If this happens, the surviving bird will choose another mate.

The nest of the tundra swan is made up largely of native vegetation. It is a rather bulky flattened mound about three feet in diameter at the base, tapering up to about 18 inches, and is 12-18 inches in height. The nests are usually located on islets in ponds and lakes or carefully hidden in the tundra.

Where to see swans

Cosumnes River Preserve, in Sacramento County

Grassland Resource Conservation District, in Merced County

Honey Lake Wildlife Area, in Lassen County
Note: November, February and March are peak months for waterfowl.

Shasta Valley State Wildlife Area, in Siskiyou County

Yolo Bypass Wildlife Area, in Yolo County

Other places to see swans

Ahjumawi Lava Springs State Park, in Shasta County

Butte Valley Wildlife Area, in Siskiyou County

Delevan National Wildlife Refuge, in Colusa County

Humboldt Bay National Wildlife Refuge, in Humboldt County

Modoc National Wildlife Refuge, in Modoc County

Swans lay from two to seven creamy dull-white eggs, averaging four or five to the clutch. It takes 35-40 days for the eggs to hatch and both the male and the female assist in nest-building and incubation.

Soon after they are hatched, the young are led by their parents to nearby water. The swans are very attentive to their young; they keep a close watch over them while teaching them how to find the most tender food, even giving them a piggyback ride now and then. Newly hatched cygnets are pure white, but in about five to six weeks their new feathers start to emerge and eventually they are covered with an unassuming brown plumage. Also during this period, the older birds, like other waterfowl, shed their flight feathers. For a time, they, like their young, are flightless. In a few weeks the flight feathers of the adults have regrown, and the young start practicing flying in preparation for the long southward migration. The young swans retain their brownish gray immature plumage and flesh-colored bill and feet for their first year, making them easily recognizable amidst the gleaming white of the mature adults.

Swordfish

Many people get swordfish confused with marlin. After all, aren't they both highly desired billfish that grow to large sizes? Aren't they abundant off the Southern California coast on south all the way to equatorial waters? Yep, they be the ones, but other than those similarities, the twain definitely doth part.

Marlin are the prize sportfish, gifted with a remarkable phosphorescent sheen and pointed spear, known for their ocean-quaking jumps and long power runs.

ANIMAL	Swordfish
SPECIES	*Xiphias gladius*
TYPE	fish
STATUS	OK

Swordfish don't have a magical radiant glow about them, they don't have a spear (but rather a sword) attached to their nose, and while extremely powerful fish capable of great speed, they don't quite merit the zealous pursuit of the world's most talented anglers, as do marlin.

swordfish

Regardless, they are among the most interesting fish in the world and also one of the most coveted on the dinner table. In turn, they are the cause of an ongoing battle between commercial fishermen and conservationists (and we'll get to that).

Swordfish get big, most ranging 75 to 150 pounds, with the California state record weighing 337 pounds. Yet one-third of their length is in the bill, which is shaped like a long, flattened sword. Its scientific name, *Xiphias gladius,* means "sword-like" in Greek and Latin. Swordfish was popular in the ancient days of Aristotle, well known in the Mediterranean, and named "Xiphias" by Aristotle after its sword-like bill.

The skin of a swordfish is also nothing like that of a marlin. It is rough to the touch, like sandpaper, as is a shark, and if you try to handle a larger specimen without gloves, you can scrape up your hands.

One of the unique features of the swordfish is its ability to almost wallow on the surface, resting, seemingly at peace. That is because they are blessed with massive air bladders that allow them to float without constant finning. They also have a large tail or caudal fin that can propel the torpedo-shaped body through the water at amazing speed. Adult swordfish have been observed feeding at a depth of 2,000 feet.

One of the rare wonders of swordfish is their ability to wallow on the surface of the water, resting, seemingly at peace. That is because they are blessed with massive air bladders, which, unlike many big fish, allow them to float without constant finning. Anglers often will bring binoculars and scan the surface for them. In earlier times, they were spotted and stalked by boat, then taken with harpoons.

Most people are familiar with swordfish on the dinner menu of a seafood restaurant, with its rich textured white meat. Mesquite grilled and served with lime and cilantro, I believe it to be the best of steaks, better than a T-bone or New York. Yet I do not eat swordfish anymore, and I will not until the commercial fishers use less harmful forms of take. Many members of the International Game Fish Association (IGFA) are taking part in a worldwide boycott.

The reason is because the No. 1 method commercials use to catch swordfish is a longline, that is, fishing lines that are miles long with 5,000 to 6,000 hooks, sometimes more. The lines are allowed to drift at sea, snaring and killing many kinds of sea creatures; when the lines are brought aboard, the unintentional catch is simply tossed overboard, dead, to waste. A number of commercials also use drift gillnets, with a similar result—an unacceptable by-catch wasted without regard to anything but the fishermen's own greed.

In response, the IGFA passed a resolution calling on the U.S. government to prohibit the use of drift longlining gear. The National Marine Fisheries Service has been pressured for years to stop the damage from longlines, with no response. The biggest offenders are typically the giant Japanese commercial ships, which try to sneak inside U.S. and Mexican waters, having already cleaned out the fishing areas near their own country. However, there are many U.S. commercial longliners and netters who do their share of damage as well.

After all, there is only one world—we share it with all the mammals, birds, reptiles, and fish, including the majestic swordfish. We'd best take care of it.

Biologists' Notes

California is visited during the summer and fall by one of the world's most unusual fish, the broadbill swordfish *(Xiphias gladius)*. It is recognized mainly by the long, flattened bill.

Broadbill swordfish are a well-represented species, found in most of the oceans of the world where surface temperatures are above 60°F. The most important fishing areas are in the more temperate areas of the fish's range, such as the west coast of Mexico, the New England and Newfoundland Banks, the Baltics, the west coast of France, and the east coasts of New Zealand and Australia. The commercial fishery in California is important primarily to in-state markets.

Swordfish are stoutly built with a large tail or caudal fin which can propel the torpedo-shaped body through the water at amazing speed. The adult has a large, sickle-shaped dorsal fin and a smaller dorsal fin, or finlet, near the tail. There are two anal fins on the underside and a pectoral fin for maneuvering.

Projecting from the nose of the fish is a hard, bony blade or bill. The bill is wide and flattened and is used by the fish as it attacks a school of forage fish or squid. It slashes through the school, wounding many of the members, which are then devoured. Embedded in the sandpaper-like skin on each side is a well-developed lateral line system that lets the swordfish detect motion around it.

Spawning may occur during any time of the year in the eastern Pacific, but fish about to spawn are most abundant from March through July in northern latitudes and around January in southern latitudes. The eggs are buoyant in sea water and contain a single oil globule inside the yolk. The young swordfish hatch in about 60 hours, soon begin feeding, and reach a length of one-third inch in 13 days. In one year of life, the young swordfish

Where to see swordfish

CHANNEL ISLANDS, OFFSHORE FROM VENTURA COUNTY

LOS ANGELES DEEP SEA, OFFSHORE FROM LOS ANGELES COUNTY

MONTEREY BAY DEEP SEA, OFFSHORE FROM MONTEREY COUNTY

SAN DIEGO DEEP SEA, OFFSHORE FROM SAN DIEGO COUNTY

SAN LUIS OBISPO BAY DEEP SEA, OFFSHORE FROM SAN LUIS OBISPO COUNTY

will be 18-22 inches, 33-37 inches by the second year, and 39-49 inches by the third year. A total length of about 15 feet is possible. A fish this size would weigh over 1,100 pounds. The largest fish on record was taken by rod and reel off Chile and weighed 1,182 pounds.

Swordfish are considered to be highly migratory, probably moving great distances over the edges of continental shelves during summer migrations.

Swordfish are quite hardy and have the ability to adapt to wide changes in their environment. They are opportunistic feeders and will forage for food from the bottom of the sea to the surface, over great depths and distances. Adult swordfish have been observed feeding at a depth of 2,000 feet. Over deep water their diet consists mainly of pelagic fish and squids, while in shallow water near shore, they will feed near the bottom on species such as hake, rockfish, and cod.

Swordfish usually appear off the coast of California in early summer, then become more available in late summer and fall.

Tarantulas

We were breaking camp in the high desert country near Joshua Tree, a cool morning in late winter, and I was sitting on a rock, just about to put my boots on for the day.

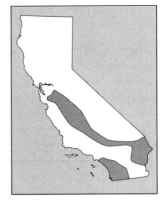

I grabbed ahold of my size 13s and started to point my right toe into the opening when, in the back of mind, this echo from the past resonated: "Always shake out your boots." It was advice my dad, Bob Stienstra, Sr., had given me on a campout when I was just a lad.

ANIMAL	Tarantulas
SPECIES	*Aphonopelma* spp.
TYPE	insect
STATUS	OK

Well, most of the time you obey those little voices in the back of your head, so in one motion, I grabbed that boot by the heel, turned it upside down, and gave it a shake. With a clunk, a tarantula fell out and I just about levitated into orbit around the moon.

Tarantulas are so fearsome in appearance that the first response upon an encounter is a desire to evaporate into thin air. That being impossible,

tarantula with parasitic wasp

some people jump, others run, and almost nobody sticks around for the show. They look like giant spiders with fur, with even their long brown legs covered with the hair. This scary appearance belies their true nature, but most people don't know this.

There was even a 1950s low-grade horror film called *Tarantula* where a scientist's nutrient experiment turned a tarantula into the size of a large building. When the creature is released it menaces the residents of Arizona, crushing everything in its path.

Like most films, the producers didn't want to let the facts get in the way of a story. For the most part, tarantulas are harmless creatures in California.

Even if through carelessness a bite should occur, the venom in the bite causes only slight swelling, with some numbness and itching, which disappears in a short time. The chances of being bitten are so small that one has little need to worry. Tarantulas also don't jump over bridges to crush cities, except in the movies. In fact, they can only jump forward a few inches, and it's usually to catch something to eat or get away from a considerable list of enemies in natural settings.

> Tarantulas can live 25 years and don't reach sexual maturity until about age 10. Horror stories to the contrary, tarantula venom causes only slight swelling, with some numbness and itching, which disappears in a short time.

Some people are so scared by tarantulas that, upon a chance meeting, will do whatever is necessary to kill it. This is one of the best examples in all of nature where ignorance and fear can usurp intelligence and logic.

Killing a tarantula is about as idiotic as taking a starfish home from a coastal tidepool; both can live 20 to 25 years and don't reach sexual maturity until about age 10. In each case, you impact a natural setting, because of the length of time it takes for the species to reach maturity.

What's a tarantula's intention? Might get some bugs. What's the danger? Virtually none. Why the reaction? Because of the way they look.

In California, many junior museums have specimens in terrariums, with interpretive specialists available to explain that tarantulas are not dangerous. Many kids, who apparently learn from their parents and dreadful movies like *Tarantula*, seem to think that a single bite will lead to instant death.

Here's the truth: about the only way you get bit is if you leave your boots out at camp, and one crawls inside at night for a nice warm spot to sleep. The next morning, you jam your foot into the boot, almost squish the poor guy, and it bites your foot trying to save itself. It feels kind of like being stung by a wasp, and the surprise is enough for most folks to let out a "Yeeoow!"

But that's as bad as it gets.

That is not to minimize how painful a tarantula bite can be. Anybody who has been stung by a wasp will attest to this. The instant pain can cause a frightful shock, but you will get over it. As mentioned, tarantulas are not poisonous, but it is a mistake to handle them or let them crawl on you as if they were your pet hamster.

Biologists' Notes

Different species of the tarantula (*Aphonopelma* spp.) occur in many parts of the world. The ones found in North America occur in the southern and southwestern states, including the dry and warmer parts of the southern half of California. These have a body length of less than two inches and a leg span of from three to four inches. There is a wide color variation, from a soft tan to reddish brown to dark brown.

They are all quite fearsome in appearance with their long hairy legs and body covered with almost mouse-like fur. However, the chance of being bitten is so low one has little need to worry.

A tarantula is a deliberate walker, picking its steps with the greatest grace and caution. In spite of its loitering gait it can cover considerable distance in a day's time.

The tarantula does not spin a web to capture its prey, but catches it by activity and speed afoot, chasing down the bugs it eats. It feeds primarily on small insects: grasshoppers, beetles, sow bugs, and other small spiders. Upon seizing its prey, it kills it with venom. Through the wound made by the fangs it injects a fluid from its mouth that digests the victims outside the spider's body. This fluid reduces the prey to a consistency where it may be sucked in by the spider with the aid of its strong stomach muscles. It is then absorbed in the tarantula's stomach.

The tarantula prefers to live in dry, well-drained soil. If the soil is suitable, the female digs a deep burrow, which she lines with silk webbing. This helps prevent sand and dirt from trickling in. Otherwise, they hide in cracks in logs and under any loose-lying debris. In winter she covers the entrance to her home with a plug of leaves and silk and lies dormant in her "den" until the return of spring. She also uses the burrow as a safe retreat for molting and guarding her cocoon, and the newly hatched young, in its depth.

Tarantulas are naturally long-lived creatures They do not reach sexual maturity for about 10 years. During this time they undergo a series of molts,

Where to *see* tarantulas

Afton Canyon, in San Bernardino County

Devil's Punchbowl Natural Area, in Los Angeles County

Harper Lake, in San Bernardino County

New Melones Lake Recreation Area, in Tuolumne County

Pinnacles National Monument, in San Benito County

and until they reach maturity you can't tell the male from the female. The mature male is quite dark, nearly black, while the mature female is brown. The degree of coloring varies with the species and geographical location. Upon maturity the males abandon their burrows and go forth to seek a mate.

After mating, males live only a short time. It may die a natural death or be eaten by the female, sometimes even before mating can occur.

When it comes time for egg laying, the female spins a large sheet of webbing on which she deposits numerous large pearly white eggs. The eggs are covered by a second sheet of webbing, which is tightly bound at the edges. She guards this flattened egg sac or cocoon carefully for six or seven weeks until the eggs are hatched. The baby tarantulas stay in the mother's burrow for a week or so before they go out and establish dens of their own.

Some females may live as long as 20 to 25 years, but long life in the wild is rare for they have many enemies: lizards, snakes, spider-eating birds, and the deadly tarantula hawk. This large, metallic blue, green, and red wasp is the spider's fiercest and most dreaded enemy. Once it has found and paralyzed the spider with its poisonous sting, the wasp drags its victim to a prepared burrow, deposits its eggs in the spider's abdomen and seals its victim in. Upon hatching, the wasp larvae feed on the tarantula's body.

Tortoise, Desert

The desert tortoise, when alarmed, can sprint off at a top speed of about 20 feet a minute. Of course, there's no telling for how long it can keep this speed up. Even a tortoise has to rest now and then.

The truth is that tortoise don't get alarmed, even though slow and steady doesn't always win the race when confronted by criminal wildlife grabbers. After all, a tortoise can't outrun a poacher. Their biggest enemy, just like the horned lizard, are people who find them by accident and take them home as pets—or, worse, poachers who hunt them down

ANIMAL	Tortoise, Desert
SPECIES	*Gopherus agassizii*
TYPE	reptile
STATUS	Threatened

and sell them in the illegal black market at some pet shops in Southern California. The desert tortoise is listed as a threatened species under state and federal law.

When a tortoise is removed from its natural habit in the desert, it is not magically replaced by the Big Tortoise in the Sky. Tortoises can live to be ancient, one of the longest-lived air-breathing creatures in California. One lived in captivity for 152 years before it was killed accidentally, and some people believe tortoises, like the giant sea turtles, can live for hundreds of years. While there are no records of how long the desert tortoise can live in the wild, biologists estimate they live between 50 and 100 years. Turtles in general live longer than any vertebrate (creature having a spinal column), including man. Hence, when one is removed from its habitat, it is not quickly replaced.

desert tortoise

They not only can live long lives, but are slow to develop. The shells do not harden until the tortoises are three years old and remain flexible until the fifth or sixth year. Tortoises reach about three-fourths of their final size in six or seven years and continue to grow slowly after that.

The desert tortoise, when alarmed, can sprint at a speed of 20 feet per minute. They can live to be ancient; one lived in captivity for 152 years before it was killed accidentally. The tortoise has existed on earth in its present form for millions of years.

Because they don't exactly move at the speed of light, they have another means of defense. All tortoises, young and old, are masters of concealment.

I once spotted one on the edge of the Mojave Desert, just sitting there along a trail, nearly perfectly camouflaged simply from the way the shell blended into the surrounding sandy ground. In the next half hour, while taking a break for a trail lunch, I watched five different people walk right on past without a hint of detection. One of the hikers even asked me, "Seen any turtles?" They're tortoise, buddy, desert tortoise, and yeah, you're standing 10 feet away from one but I'm not going to tell you.

But that's only a start. When the desert tortoise buries itself in sand, or burrows in for winter, it is virtually impossible to see, except by complete accident.

In addition to its abilities to live so long and to conceal itself, desert tortoises are also marked by their strange and incredible eating and drinking habits. A tortoise can go without food for as much as a year, then gorge when food is available. They also can go without water for months, but here again, they are prodigious drinkers when fluid is available. In one test, a medium-sized specimen increased its weight by a little more than 40% with one long drink.

Where to see desert tortoise

DESERT TORTOISE NATURAL AREA, IN KERN COUNTY
NOTE: Be alert to the presence of the poisonous Mojave green rattlesnake, which is resident here.

DEVIL'S PUNCHBOWL NATURAL AREA, IN LOS ANGELES COUNTY

JOSHUA TREE NATIONAL PARK, IN RIVERSIDE AND SAN BERNARDINO COUNTIES

LIVING DESERT, IN RIVERSIDE COUNTY

MOJAVE NATIONAL PRESERVE, IN SAN BERNARDINO COUNTY

PROVIDENCE MOUNTAINS STATE RECREATION AREA, IN SAN BERNARDINO COUNTY

Before laws were passed giving the desert tortoise complete protection, many were picked up to be sold as tourist oddities, sold in pet shops, and taken home as pets. Away from their desert home, and without proper care, many escaped and eventually perished in the metropolitan environment. Many others died after not being cared for.

So if you visit the desert and are lucky enough to encounter a tortoise, look at it, examine it, and let it be. Remember that all this gentle, inoffensive creature asks is to be left alone.

Biologists' Notes

The desert tortoise *(Gopherus agassizii)* has existed on earth in its present form for millions of years.

The tortoise is a member of the reptile family that is composed of snakes, lizards, crocodiles, and other "chelonians," or turtles. Turtles are obviously different from other reptiles and are recognized not only by the absence of teeth but by the shell or bony box that completely covers the body. The shell is actually a part of the body. Once the shell has hardened (when the tortoise is about three years old), it protects them from nearly all enemies except man.

There are about 250 kinds of turtles living in the warm belt around the globe. Like all other reptiles, they cannot survive in permanently frozen areas. About one-quarter of the earth's turtles live in North America. Down through the ages, evolution has caused some turtles to adapt themselves to salt water, some to fresh water, and some to land. But they are all at least partially bound to the land, for their eggs cannot hatch unless they are buried in warm sand or decomposing vegetation.

Tortoise are strictly land forms, equipped with a high arched shell and stumpy hind legs. The adult tortoise may be as much as 12 inches long. The carapace, or shell, is dome shaped and marked with an attractive design caused by growth rings. Desert tortoise males average a little larger than the females, and the bottom of the male's shell is concave. The tail is short, the male's tail a little longer than that of the female. Legs are elephantoid, particularly the hind legs, much different than the flipper-like legs of turtle that have adapted to the sea.

The overall color of the tortoise ranges from a yellowish brown to a dark brown and blends well with the colors of the desert, making them difficult to observe when they are not moving.

Desert tortoises have adapted themselves well to life in the deserts of the southwest. In California they are found in northeastern Los Angeles, eastern Kern, and southeastern Inyo Counties and over most of San Bernardino, Riverside, and Imperial Counties.

Sometime between June and November the female digs a shallow nest and carefully deposits from two to six snow-white eggs. She spends a little over an hour digging and covering her eggs. Hatching has been observed from August to November.

Like other cold-blooded reptiles that cannot control their body temperatures, tortoises are sensitive to both heat and cold. Consequently, they are most active in summer between the cold mornings and the early heat of the day or on overcast or cloudy days. In October, when daytime temperatures get cold, they dig burrows for themselves and hibernate until the following March. In the spring when they appear, they take very little food. But as the days get warmer, they eat grass and the blossoms and tender parts of plants.

Trout, Golden

High in the south Sierra Nevada, the headwaters of the Kern River run down the center of a towering granite canyon, carved by glaciers eons ago. It was here where it felt as if I'd been touched by divine providence, or at least, a magic golden trout.

We were hiking the John Muir Trail, from Mount Whitney to Yosemite Valley, and it turned out I had broken my ankle on the third day near Forester Pass. At the headwaters of the Kern, my right ankle had become swollen and sore, at times feeling like it was being stabbed with an ice pick. The trip seemed over for me.

ANIMAL	Trout, Golden
SPECIES	*Oncorhynchus aguabonita whitei*
TYPE	fish
STATUS	Threatened
SEE ALSO	Salmon, Steelhead

My brother, Rambob, and I stopped for lunch next to a river pool where I soaked that ankle in the cold water to try and keep the swelling down. I would have tried anything to complete the trip.

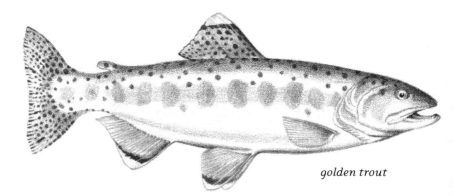

golden trout

At the end of a long, gentle waterfall, I dunked my feet into a small pool, the cold, foaming water the best treatment available for that ankle. I was gazing at the Citadel, a towering peak that watches over the Kern River, when bang!—there was a sudden jolt at the heel of my right foot.

The golden trout is native only to California and, by an act of the State Legislature in 1947, was named the official state fish.

I pulled my foot out of the water, and, incredibly, a golden trout had bitten it. When I dunked the foot again, the golden trout came back and rapped me again, exactly on the spot where it hurt.

"That trout is actually going after you!" shouted my brother.

But in the days that followed, an extraordinary situation evolved. I had a feeling that the ankle was broken, but after that golden trout bit it, the pain was never bad enough to stop me.

"It was as if that golden trout was a magic fish sent by an angel," my brother said. "It seemed that from that moment on, you were being helped over the mountains."

It turned out that my right ankle was broken so severely that it would require two surgeries to repair the damage, but, hey, I finished the trip, about 250 miles in all, including side jaunts, and had the time of my life. So golden trout have a special meaning for me.

It's true that trout sometimes bite on almost anything, even feet, in the high Sierra, where the John Muir Trail leads to hundreds of small lakes and more than a dozen pristine streams loaded with trout. It is the golden trout that can inspire anglers to pack miles over mountain passes to reach prime fishing areas. This is California's state fish, a rare species that lives only above 8,000 feet.

It is the most beautiful of all trout, with a crimson stripe and dark discs in a line along the side, bright gold along the belly, with the top of its body lightly spotted. Goldens are not usually huge, about six to eight inches is average and occasionally reaching 12 to 14 inches, but their beauty is beyond compare. Rainbow trout are also abundant throughout the range and occasionally will cross-breed with goldens, leading to a variety of strange color combinations.

The best region for golden trout is the high Sierra in the John Muir Wilderness, high country wilderness of Kings Canyon National Park, and Golden Trout Wilderness.

You will also find bubbling, crystal-pure mountain streams filled with hungry native trout. In the evening, the trout often go on a feed that can have you catching and releasing them on many consecutive casts, before you move on to the next hole for more of the same.

Just don't dangle your feet in the water too long. Or if your ankle is broken, perhaps that is exactly what you should do.

Biologists' Notes

The golden trout is native only to California and, by an act of the State Legislature in 1947, was named the official state fish.

The golden trout (Oncorhynchus aguabonita whitei, also classified as O. mykiss whitei) originally occurred only in a few of the streams in the upper reaches of the Kern River drainage in Tulare County. Stocking of wild and hatchery-reared fish has extended its range to many waters at high elevation in the Sierra Nevada, from El Dorado and Alpine Counties southward. It has also been planted in other states. However, in 1939 legislation was enacted that prohibits the transportation of the eggs and fry of golden trout out of California. The original population of Little Kern golden trout has been federally listed as a threatened species since 1978.

The golden trout thrives in California waters at elevations from 8,500 to 10,500 feet. It has been found as low as 6,300 feet. In most streams it remains small, from five to eight inches. In some lakes it may grow much larger, 12 to 18 inches. The largest golden trout documented in California weighed nine pounds, eight ounces, caught in 1952. The world's record weighed 11 pounds, caught in Wyoming in 1948.

The golden trout is brightly colored, with a medium-dark olive back, shading down through lighter olive and lemon-golden sides to a brilliant orange to cherry-red belly. There are reddish-orange stripes midway along the sides from head to tail, broken by dull-olive vertical bars or discs called

Where to see golden trout

ANSEL ADAMS WILDERNESS, INYO AND SIERRA NATIONAL FORESTS, IN MONO AND
MADERA COUNTIES

GOLDEN TROUT WILDERNESS, SOUTH FORK KERN RIVER, INYO NATIONAL FOREST,
IN TULARE COUNTY

JOHN MUIR WILDERNESS, SIERRA NATIONAL FOREST, IN INYO AND MONO
COUNTIES

parr marks. On some trout, the head, back, tail, and dark olive back fins
are marked with black dots. The other fins are bright orange, at times tipped
with white. These bright colors become even brighter when the fish are
spawning.

Unlike lake and Eastern brook trout, the goldens rarely spawn in quiet
lake waters. They spawn in streams where there is a constant flow over
gravel, burying their eggs in the gravel. Many of the rockbound lakes in
which goldens have been planted do not have tributary streams that are
suitable for spawning. These lakes need to be periodically replanted with
hatchery-reared fish.

Golden trout will interbreed with rainbow trout. In lakes where they have
been planted together, variations occur and sometimes a complete loss of
the vivid colors results.

To maintain a pure strain of golden trout, crews spawn these fish artifi-
cially at four small lakes that have a pure strain of goldens. The eggs are
then taken to a fish hatchery, where they are reared. When the baby fish
are about two inches long they are planted in suitable waters. In years past,
pack animals carried the fish to their new homes. Now an airplane is used
and the fingerlings are dropped into the lakes from the air. The department may plant some lakes in which brook trout are established, for the
brook and golden trout do not interbreed. But for the most part, goldens are
either planted in waters that contain no other trout or waters already planted with golden trout.

So far the remoteness of the areas in which goldens are found, and the
lack of roads, have kept it possible to maintain this unique trout. In 1977,
the U.S. Congress established the Golden Trout Wilderness Area to protect
the native habitat of the golden trout.

Turkey, Wild

While Ben Franklin may be the face that drives Las Vegas, he is better known in wildlife circles as the man who almost convinced George Washington and his pals to make turkey the U.S. national bird.

Can you imagine military aircraft with a turkey image painted on the nose? The great seal of the United States, with a turkey in its center? A gold turkey head atop the flag pole at every public school and military base? A turkey on the hat of a five-star general? A turkey on the back of every quarter?

The reason Ben almost won the argument, you see, is because a turkey is one smart bird, both big and wily, and, hey, it

ANIMAL	Turkey, Wild
SPECIES	*Meleagris gallopavo*
TYPE	bird
STATUS	Introduced

steals the show every Thanksgiving, right? (Actually, there was one other reason, and we'll get to that.) But the more you see turkey out and about in the wild, the more you will start to see the logic in Ben's argument. Well, it might be a very small start, but it is a start just the same.

There are a dozen wild turkeys that live on my property, and after playing tag with them many times, I have found them among the most intriguing of all creatures. They tend to travel in flocks of a half dozen to a dozen, though I have seen as many as 30 together at once at Spenceville Wildlife Area. Occasionally you will find a solo Tom (a big male, that is) walking by itself.

At first appearance, they seem friendly enough. Even as adults, they range greatly in size, typically anywhere from three to 12 pounds, with most in the five-pound range. Because they are big, they don't seem to be moving much, stopping and feeding. Yet when you watch, you will notice that they can move on and disappear as fast as they have appeared. I have seen them in many habitats, the oak woodlands of the Central Valley, along the Sacramento River downstream of Red Bluff, and they always seem to be on the move.

Then, when you try to get closer, or follow them, they will disappear so fast it is as if Scotty has beamed them off the planet.

The turkey call is more of a squeak. I have a turkey caller, which consists of a small dowel that you scrape on a rough surface, which simulates the turkey squeak. But it isn't as if you can simply squeak away, and the turkey will come flocking to your doorstep. They're too smart. If they have even the slightest clue a human is involved, and not another turkey, you don't have a chance.

Hence, to call turkeys in, you must graduate to complete stealth mode.

One pal of mine, John Higley, is an expert at this; in fact he has written a book about it. He will leave home at midnight, dressed in complete camouflage, including a camo head and face covering, then head out to his favorite turkey area, pull out a

wild turkey

little camouflaged tri-pod chair, and have a seat in the middle of a bush. From 2 a.m. to 5 a.m., he will try to sleep a little, sitting in that chair, trying not to snore, because that would spook the turkeys into the next county. The reason he is out at 2 a.m. in that bush, he explains, is because to arrive any later could tip off his presence to the turkey. After all, a big Tom is one smart feller.

Domestic turkeys cannot fly, but wild turkeys have strong wings and legs that enable them not only to fly but to outrun most humans. According to Native American lore, the turkey is one of the most virtuous and magnanimous of all creatures. It is for that reason that Benjamin Franklin proposed it as the national bird.

A half hour before sunrise, John will start to use his turkey call, not just squeaking away with it, but with a strategy. First he will merely solicit an answer, but then adding inflections, as if yearning, then pleading, and, finally, downright begging. If he gets a call back, the conversation can ensue for hours. It can take all morning to convince a big Tom to finally emerge from its own bush. According to John, this moment is among the most exciting in all the outdoors. Why else would somebody sit in a bush in the middle of nowhere at 2 a.m. dressed up in camouflage? Another friend, John Keck of the Wild Turkey Federation, swears that he lives for this moment and has traveled to every state in America to call turkey.

In Native American lore, the turkey is one of the most virtuous of all creatures, standing for magnanimous giving, to provide to others with the simple knowledge that life is sacred.

In the end, that is why Ben Franklin proposed the turkey to be the national bird, and that makes more sense than any other argument.

Biologists' Notes

Turkeys belong to the family Phasianidae, which includes the pheasant, grouse, quail, and chicken. Within the turkey group, there are two species, the ocellated turkey, *Agriocharis ocellata*, which is confined to Guatemala and Mexico, and the North American turkey, *Meleagris gallopavo*, domesticated by the American Indians as early as A.D. 1000.

Turkeys are large compared to their cousins, reaching a length of three to four feet. Their feathers contain multiple colors, including a metallic bronze with black barring. The head and neck are featherless. A loose piece of red skin called a wattle falls from the lower jaw, and at the base of the neck are red, wart-like structures called caruncles. On the adult male, or tom, a tuft of feathers hangs from the center of the breast and there is a broad and fan-shaped tail used in displays.

Wild turkeys have smaller heads and longer backs and legs than domestic turkeys. They also weigh considerably less. Domestic toms can weigh as much as 50 pounds, while a wild tom weighs from 10 to 16 pounds and wild hens from six to 10 pounds. Domestic turkeys cannot fly; wild turkeys have strong wings and legs that enable them not only to fly but to outrun most humans.

Flocks of wild turkeys inhabit open woodland, forest edges, and wooded swamps, eating berries, nuts, seeds, and insects. They roost in trees at night but build nests on the ground, primarily of dry leaves.

Hens lay an egg every day for a period of eight to 20 days during the breeding season, resulting in an average clutch of 11 eggs. Turkey eggs are twice the size of a chicken egg and are a creamy-tan color with brown speckles. The female tends the clutch throughout the 28-day incubation

Where to see wild turkey

BIDWELL PARK, IN BUTTE COUNTY

CACHE CREEK MANAGEMENT AREA, IN LAKE COUNTY

EFFIE YEAW NATURE CENTER/AMERICAN RIVER PARKWAY, IN SACRAMENTO COUNTY

LOPEZ LAKE, IN SAN LUIS OBISPO COUNTY

SHASTA LAKE/PACKERS BAY, SHASTA-TRINITY NATIONAL FOREST, IN SHASTA COUNTY

Other places to see wild turkey

BATTLE CREEK WILDLIFE AREA, IN TEHAMA COUNTY

JOSEPH D. GRANT COUNTY PARK, IN SANTA CLARA COUNTY

LAKE RED BLUFF, IN TEHAMA COUNTY

LAKE SAN ANTONIO, LOS PADRES NATIONAL FOREST, IN MONTEREY COUNTY

LAKE SOLANO COUNTY PARK, IN SOLANO COUNTY

SPENCEVILLE WILDLIFE AREA, IN YUBA AND NEVADA COUNTIES

period; the male plays no role in nesting. Baby turkeys, called poults, remain in the nest until the following spring.

The wild turkeys in California today are not native, though there is evidence of an extinct California species unearthed from the Rancho La Brea Tar Pits in Los Angeles. Scientists believe that this turkey became extinct about 10,000 years ago.

California wild turkeys were introduced in the 1870s. The first recorded release was by private ranchers onto Santa Cruz Island. Later releases were made in at least 195 locations. Wild turkeys are now present in 45 of California's 58 counties, with the largest numbers concentrated in Butte, Calaveras, El Dorado, Mendocino, Nevada, San Luis Obispo, Shasta, Tehama, and Yuba Counties.

Whales

Nobody remembers a year, and few people can recall a month. But what comes quickly to mind for everybody are moments. That is, moments in which you experience the rare and wonderful.

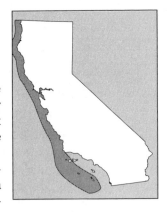

One such moment for me came in a spectacular 45-minute sequence where I saw a dozen humpback whales leaping completely out of the water in full 180-degree pirouettes. The whales landed with gigantic splashes on their backs beside our boat, perhaps trying to clean the barnacles off their skin. It happened over and over again, these giant bombers sailing through the air on the open ocean. At times a pair would even crisscross in the air in front of us like Wilkinson sword blades.

It was like nothing I'd ever seen before, being granted a privileged view into a world where few humans are allowed entry. But when it comes to whales, it seems the magical is always possible.

ANIMAL	Whales
SPECIES	Gray - *Eschrichtius robustus* Blue - *Balaenoptera musculus* Humpback - *Megaptera novaeangliae*
TYPE	mammal
STATUS	OK/Endangered
SEE ALSO	Dolphins and Porpoises

Usually all you see at first is what looks like a little puff of smoke on the ocean surface. Out of the corner of your eye you see it, and your attention becomes riveted to the spot like a magnet on iron.

A closer look and there it is again, only it quickly disappears. You watch, waiting for another sign, but the sea is quiet. A row of cormorants glides past, a dozen murres are paddling around, and for a moment you forget why you're out here on the briny blue. Then your daydreams are popped by a giant tail, the size of a lifeboat, breaking the surface of the water.

After you have seen a whale, that is, a real, live, and seemingly friendly sea monster, you will likely never again look at the ocean in quite the same way. When you see a whale, you often regain the feeling that this world of ours is still a place where great things are possible. That's because a whale is one of those things.

Some 21,000 to 24,000 gray whales swim along the California coast, cruising 50 to 100 miles per day within range of boats and many shoreline lookouts. Seeing one not only makes you feel special but can instill the kind of excitement that will stay with you for many years. Every time you look at the ocean, you will remember.

Gray whales are giant air-breathing creatures that average more than 40 feet in length and can weigh over 30 tons. They will often keep pace alongside a boat, spouting now and then, occasionally emerging to show their backs. As they gain confidence, they may fin you, give you a tail salute, and, if you're particularly lucky, come in half breach.

The gray whale migration is a 5,000-mile trip from Arctic waters to Baja, a migratory route that brings them along the Bay Area coast from December through May. Since the whales often cruise along the surface, you see the little "puffs of smoke" from their spouts, as in "Thar she blows."

Many harbors offer whalewatching tours. Some whales seem attracted to the boat and will play tag with you as they swim their migratory route. Often they will disappear and reappear several times over the course of an hour.

Another option is to try to see whales by land, driving to lookouts along the coast. The best spots are always cliff tops at significant coastal points, where your rocky perch juts well out to sea, close to the whales' migratory route. At Pigeon Point in southern San Mateo County, for instance, I have seen as many as 200 whale spouts before I stopped counting, and this has occurred several times. Binoculars and a clear day can help you home in on the whale, possibly allowing you to see a piece of its back or even a tail salute.

Gray whales are giant air-breathing creatures that average more than 40 feet in length and can weigh over 30 tons. The blue whale is the largest air-breathing creature ever to inhabit the planet, reaching a length of about 100 feet and a weight of well over 100 tons—larger than any dinosaur now known. In what is believed to be the longest migration of any animal, gray whales complete a 6,000- to 7,000-mile one-way journey from their cold water feeding grounds in the north to their warm water birthing grounds in the south.

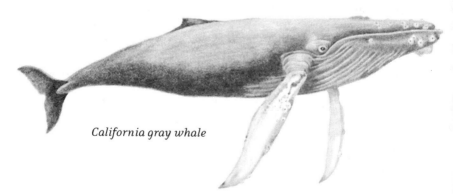

California gray whale

Humpbacks are the most spectacular, well known for their acrobatics at sea. But it can take a lucky day to see one, with their numbers relatively few compared to the more populous grays.

One of the most unique forms of whale watching is from an airplane, though obviously this is available to few people. From a low-flying airplane, I was able to follow a pod of three giant blue whales. From above, you can look straight down and see the entire body outline of the whale. Their tremendous size is awe-inspiring; after all, blue whales are the largest air-breathing creatures ever to inhabit the planet.

Seeing whales can be among the most exhilarating moments in nature. That is why I adopted a gray whale with the Oceanic Society, a whale named Spitz and identified by an unusual shaped and colored fluke. He's my boy, good ol' Spitz.

Biologists' Notes

The California gray whale *(Eschrichtius robustus)* is the best known and most often seen of any of the great whales that occur along the west coast of North America. It belongs to the family of the largest animals that ever inhabited the earth. One member of the family, the blue whale *(Balaenoptera musculus)*, reaches a length of about 100 feet and a weight of well over 100 tons. The gray whale is not as large. The female, as with all baleen whales, is several feet longer than the male. At full growth she may be nearly 50 feet long and weigh from 30 to 40 tons. The humpback whale *(Megaptera novaeangliae)* is about the same size as the gray whale, but has a small hump just before the dorsal fin and extremely long flippers. The humpback whale's throat is deeply ridged.

The gray whale is called gray because the black body is dappled with gray and is encrusted with barnacles and whitish scars. There is no dorsal fin, but there is a small distinct ridge down the back, which ends with a series of bumps. These characteristics make the gray whale easy to identify. The California gray whale spends its winters in the waters of southern and lower California and thus gets its name. Korean waters are home to another population of gray whales believed now to be very low in numbers. The two populations do not appear to mingle.

Some whales are known as toothed whales. They eat octopus, giant squid, larger fish, and some mammals. The gray whale and its relatives have no teeth. Instead they have sheets of fringed horny material hanging from their upper jaws called baleen. This material is used to strain out plankton, a sort of diluted soup of small drifting organisms. One of gray whales' favorite foods is a half-inch-long shrimp called krill. They also may feed on small fish and other crustaceans.

From late May through October, most of the gray whales feed in the shallow areas of the Bering Sea and adjacent Arctic waters along the Alaskan coastline. They literally gorge themselves all summer in these food-rich waters, for they instinctively know that for the next eight months, in order to make the 12,000- to 14,000-mile journey to and from the breeding grounds, there will be little time for feeding.

In October they start on what is believed to be the longest migration of any animal. They swim about 6,000 to 7,000 miles to the warmer waters of southern and lower Baja California, Mexico, to give birth to their calves and later to mate. They swim steadily in a constant direction parallel to the shore. Their speed is about four to six miles an hour, and they cover 70 or 80 miles in 15 to 20 hours. They do not sleep during migration but swim continuously.

During November and December, from sightseeing boats or vantage points on shore, whales can be observed moving south along the California coast. They travel close to land, sometimes within a few hundred yards of points or headlands that project into the sea, typically in groups or pods of two to five.

All whales, like other mammals, breathe air. The gray whale can hold its breath for about 10 minutes. Normally it surfaces every three to five minutes to breathe or spout three to five times. The spout of vaporized water is actually the whale's breath expelled under noisy pressure. On a clear day the spout can be seen for long distances. Sometimes, to avoid detection, it uses evasive swimming tactics in which it surfaces cautiously, exposing only the nostrils and exhaling slowly without sound or visible vapor. Otherwise, when it surfaces to breathe, the head, back, and mighty fluke or tail fin are exposed. It may breach by throwing its entire body clear of the water to crash back with a mighty splash. This violent action may be repeated several times. Occasionally a whale may raise its entire head clear of the water to look around and get its bearings, for it is believed whales find their way by vision and memory. The humpback whale, however, is mostly likely to be seen breaching and leaping out of the water. Researchers think that this behavior creates a net of bubbles that traps smalls schools of fish under the surface; the whale then swims under the net and eats the trapped fish.

Where to see whales

Dana Point Harbor, in Orange County

Patrick's Point State Park, in Humboldt County

Point Arena, in Mendocino County

Point Reyes National Seashore, in Marin County

Point St. George, north of Crescent City, in Del Norte County

Point Vicente on the Palos Verdes Peninsula

San Mateo Point, north of San Onofre State Beach, in San Diego County

The trip south to the breeding grounds in Baja California, where they spend about two months, takes approximately three months. Upon their arrival the pregnant females proceed into the warm shallow lagoons along the western shores of Baja and to other protected spots inside the Gulf of California. There they give birth to their calves. The babies are born tail first so that when the head emerges the whale can rise immediately to get its first breath of air. The calves are about 15 feet long and weigh about 1,500 pounds. They nurse by nuzzling the small nipples at the mother's side. They grow rapidly, for they must be large and strong enough by March to start their three-month journey back to the Arctic feeding grounds. The calf hugs the mother's side for the entire journey and upon arrival it is weaned, as there is abundant solid food.

In the middle of the 19th century the population of the gray whale was estimated at about 30,000. Unrestricted whaling operations reduced the population to a point that by 1890 it was no longer profitable to hunt them. In the 1920s whaling was resumed, and the gray whale numbers were again seriously reduced. In 1938 they were given complete protection by international treaty. Counting stations were established at various points on shore, and counts were made by air in the shallow breeding lagoons. These counts showed the California stock of gray whales to be increasing annually. By 1961, the whale population was estimated at 6,000. In 1970 federal laws were passed giving complete protection to eight species of whales. These regulations included banning the importation of all whale products. This ended all whaling operations in the United States. In 1994 the gray whale was considered a recovered species, though the blue whale, the humpback whale and several other whale species are still listed as endangered, and all whale populations are closely monitored.

Woodpeckers

Whenever you hike, always keep your wildlife detector turned on. That accomplished, when in the forest, tune your detector to pileated woodpecker.

They are usually heard first, seen second. The most commonly recognized sound is when they hammer their beaks like a jackhammer to drill holes in a dead or dying tree to search for insects. Another distinct sound is their call, which sounds like a "kyuck—kyuck-kyuck." It travels clearly through the quiet of an old-growth forest. When you hear one of these two sounds, the *rat-a-tat-tat* of a woodpecker undertaking a drilling operation, or its unmistakable call, you will realize that you are among woodpeckers.

Pileated woodpeckers are abundant and widely distributed throughout the state, yet they are typically seen far less often than heard. They are a beautiful bird. Unlike all other woodpeckers, both the male and female pileated woodpecker wear a red pointed crest on the crown of their heads. If there is any question, that red crest is an instant giveaway that you are looking at a pileated woodpecker. This is how the bird was named. "Pileated" means having a crest covering the pelium, the pelium being simply the top of the bird's head, from the bill to the nape. Only a scientist thinks like this, hence the name.

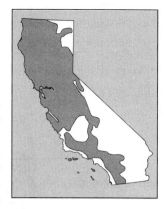

ANIMAL	Woodpeckers
SPECIES	Pileated - *Dryocopus pileatus* Acorn - *Melanerpes formicivorus*
TYPE	bird
STATUS	OK

The pileated woodpecker prefers to live and nest in the dense forests of fir and aspen, preferring old-growth, although it has been observed at lower elevations along the coast. It thrives best where there are old, dead trees both standing and rotting on the ground, for these are the source of the ants, beetles, and grubs that make up most of its diet. This is another example of how leaving dead trees either standing or downed helps create the wildlife food chain; hollowed out dead trees also provide nesting sites for many birds.

The pileated woodpecker gets its name because the word "pileated" means having a crest covering the pelium, the pelium being simply the top of the bird's head, from the bill to the nape. It also has a long, barbed tongue that can stick out five inches past the end of its bill to probe for insects.

pileated woodpecker

This woodpecker has a bill longer than its head and is so powerful that it can peck, rend, and tear its way through the thick bark of an old fir tree to find the beetles and grubs that live under the bark. It also has a long, barbed tongue. A woodpecker can stick its tongue out four or five inches past the end of its bill, which is how it uses its tongue to probe in the tunnels of wood-boring ants and fish them out with a quick flicking motion. Observing this even once is worth the price of binoculars.

Rotten logs are a favorite feeding place. One such log on my property was torn to bits in one summer by the powerful hammering of woodpeckers. I've seen other dead standing trees that had so many holes in the bark that it looked like some guy took target practice at them with a machine gun.

Biologists' Notes

The pileated woodpecker *(Dryocopus pileatus)*, the most common woodpecker in California, is the second largest member of this colorful family of North American woodpeckers. The largest is the ivory-billed woodpecker.

The entire crown and crest is a bright poppy red and was prized by the Indians in early days for feather decorations. The male is nearly as large as a crow. The largest specimens have measured as tall as 18 inches and with a wingspread of 28 inches, though most are a bit smaller.

The male and female are similar in color. The body is a dull black with contrasting stripes of white on the neck and white underparts on the wings, with a striking red crest. Woodpeckers' large size and flashing black and white color, coupled with their strident cry, make them easy to identify in flight, even at a long distance.

The pileated woodpecker is widely distributed throughout the heavily wooded portions of North America. Its gradual disappearance from some eastern areas and from parts of its former range in California is associated with logging operations, for it is rarely seen in cutover areas. In California it is found from Oregon south, down the coastal mountains to Sonoma County and from the Mt. Shasta-Lassen area south in the Sierra to the Greenhorn Mountains in Tulare County.

The male and female both work for nearly a month to chisel out a suitable nest. The entrance hole is from three to four inches across. The nest cavity is 18 inches deep and five to six inches wide at the bottom. The nest is typically about 40 or 50 feet up in an aspen or fir tree.

A covering of soft wood chips is left on the bottom of the nest. The female starts to lay her eggs in early May.

acorn woodpecker

Where to see woodpeckers

CACHUMA LAKE RECREATION AREA, IN SANTA BARBARA COUNTY

CALAVERAS BIG TREES STATE PARK, IN CALAVERAS COUNTY

CHICO GENETIC RESOURCE CENTER, IN BUTTE COUNTY

EFFIE YEAW NATURE CENTER/AMERICAN RIVER PARKWAY, IN SACRAMENTO COUNTY

TOPANGA STATE PARK, IN LOS ANGELES COUNTY

Other places to see woodpeckers

ANDREW MOLERA STATE PARK, IN MONTEREY COUNTY

BUTANO STATE PARK, IN SAN MATEO COUNTY

EMERALD BAY STATE PARK/D.L. BLISS STATE PARK, IN EL DORADO COUNTY

LAKE SAN ANTONIO, LOS PADRES NATIONAL FOREST, IN MONTEREY COUNTY

LOON LAKE/CRYSTAL BASIN RECREATION AREA, IN EL DORADO COUNTY

MCARTHUR-BURNEY FALLS STATE PARK, IN SHASTA COUNTY

MOUNT SAN JACINTO STATE PARK AND STATE WILDERNESS, IN RIVERSIDE COUNTY

PAYNES CREEK WETLANDS, IN TEHAMA COUNTY

SAND POND, PLUMAS NATIONAL FOREST, IN SIERRA COUNTY

YOSEMITE NATIONAL PARK, IN MARIPOSA COUNTY

She lays from three to six snow-white eggs. They are so smooth they look like porcelain. It takes the eggs 18 days to hatch. The young are hatched blind and without feathers, and both parents will take turns feeding, brooding, and caring for them. The young remain on or near the nest tree for several days after they leave the nest. Then they follow the parents for many weeks. They are noisy and busy learning when and how to find the choicest bugs. Parent birds may nest in the same area year after year.

The acorn woodpecker *(Melanerpes formicivorus)*, normally found in the low foothills forested with oak and pine, has a distinctive scarlet cap, a blue-black coat and black and white striped vest. They nest in dead tree cavities and peck holes in dead trees, telephone poles, and even buildings to store acorns.

Yellowtail

For fishermen, yellowtail in Southern California are the kind of fish that can get inside your mind and realign your senses. I could live year-round at Catalina Island just for the chance to get bit by yellowtail—and then enjoy the rewards.

On one trip to Catalina with my longtime compadre and fishing partner Jim Klinger, we ventured along the southwest shore of the island and started catching jacksmelt on small jigs. We then put those smelt on hooks, let them down, and started catching yellowtail. Now get this: After Klinger caught a small yellowtail, about a four-pounder, the

ANIMAL	Yellowtail
SPECIES	*Seriola lalandei*
TYPE	fish
STATUS	OK

fish was filleted out right on the spot and the meat cut into three-inch chunks. We dipped the chunks into a mix of soy sauce and wasabi in a bowl, then ate the fish raw. At sushi restaurants, yellowtail—the sweetest of all sashimi—is called hamachi and costs a fortune, and here we were in the middle of nowhere, eating all we could hold, with fish we had just caught.

It was like being transported into heaven, with the excitement of yellowtail fishing and the reward of all-you-can-eat hamachi.

yellowtail

Yellowtail can really rock you. It's nothing for them to run 60 or 70 yards and get into the rocks. With the big ones, sometimes you're playing tug-of-war and you pray your reel can take it. The big boys, the 30- and 40-pounders known as Homeguards, are usually caught right near the bottom, often so deep that landing one requires the kind of work that can make you feel like your arm is going to fall off.

Hey, maybe I *will* move to Catalina.

Biologists' Notes

The yellowtail *(Seriola lalandei)* is one of the most highly favored of near-shore saltwater fish both as food and as a game fish. They have been popular since the late 1800s.

In early April and May the warm ocean currents bring these beautiful fish north from Baja waters.

The yellowtail and jack mackerel *(Trachurus symmetricus)* are the only two members of the jack family found in abundance along our coast. They have been reported from southern Washington to as far south as Mazatlán, and north again throughout much of the Gulf of California, but are abundant primarily along the Southern California coast.

At sushi restaurants, yellowtail is called *hamachi*, the sweetest of all sashimi. A three-year-old yellowtail may contain as many as 1.5 million eggs.

Tagging and migration studies have shown there is only one population of yellowtail. They are most abundant in the Cedros Island area. The yellowtail that reach our waters only during the warmer months are just the fringe of the population, which ranges along the Baja California coast. When summer water temperatures fall below normal, a run may fail to materialize.

Yellowtail are opportunists when feeding. They gorge themselves on whatever natural foods abound in the area. In Southern California waters they feed most heavily on anchovies and squid. Farther south their diet may consist of red crabs, sardines, and the like.

The largest yellowtail believed to be recorded in the past century was an 80-pound fish caught near Guadalupe Island. However, the California state record is 62 pounds, recorded in 1953 out of La Jolla, and the official world record is 79 pounds, 4 ounces, caught in Baja. The average yellowtail caught by California anglers weigh from 6 to 10 pounds and are from two to three years old.

Many two-year-old yellowtail spawn, and all are mature at three. A three-year-old female may contain as many as 1.5 million eggs.

Where to see yellowtail

Catalina Island, offshore from Los Angeles

Dana Point Harbor, in Orange County

Oceanside Deep Sea, offshore of San Diego County

San Clemente and Coronado Islands, offshore of San Diego County

Santa Barbara Deep Sea, offshore of Santa Barbara County

Santa Monica Bay, near the rocky shore from Redondo Harbor south to Rocky Point, in Los Angeles County

Wildlife Viewing Locations

Below is a list of locations where there is excellent wildlife viewing as suggested by state wildlife biologists. The listing of primary sightings that follows the site description is merely a starting point and is keyed directly to the text. You should take advantage of the knowledge and expertise of the local rangers and guides at each of these areas to find out what else might be passing through a particular site.

If you're in the right place at the right time *and* you keep your eyes and ears open, you can see the most surprising things anywhere.

Happy trails.

A

ABALONE COVE ECOLOGICAL RESERVE, IN LOS ANGELES COUNTY
Directions: From Torrance on Highway 405, drive south about 1.5 miles. Turn right on Highway 110/Harbor Freeway and drive south about seven miles. Stay in the left lane, turn left at Gaffey Street and drive south about two miles. Turn right at 25th Street/Palos Verdes Drive and continue about four miles to the reserve on the left side. (If you reach Hawthorne Boulevard, you have gone too far).
Access/Fees: There is a per vehicle, day-use fee.
Maps: A map of the Palos Verdes Peninsula is available from the Los Angeles Chamber of Commerce, P.O. Box 513696, Los Angeles, CA 90051-1696, tel. (213) 580-7500 or fax (213) 580-7511.
Contact: Los Angeles County Lifeguards, Hermosa Beach, 1201 Strand, Hermosa Beach, CA 90254, tel. (310) 832-1179; Los Angeles County, Beaches and Harbors, 13837 Fiji Way, Marina del Rey, CA 90292, tel. (310) 305-9503 or fax (310) 821-6345.
Primary sightings: dolphins, hawks, porpoises

AFTON CANYON, in San Bernardino County
Directions: From Barstow on Interstate 15, drive east about 35 miles. Take the Afton exit and drive south on Afton Road about three miles on graded, dirt road to the parking area.
Access/Fees: Access is free.
Maps: A free recreational opportunity guide is available from the field office at the address below.
Contact: Bureau of Land Management, Barstow Field Office, 2601 Barstow Road, Barstow, CA 92311, tel. (760) 252-6000 or fax (760) 252-6099.
Primary sightings: garter snakes, horned lizards, rattlesnake, raven, roadrunner, tarantulas

AHJUMAWI LAVA SPRINGS STATE PARK, in Shasta County
Directions: From Redding on Highway 299, drive east about 83 miles. In McArthur, turn north on Main Street. The road becomes dirt. Follow signs for McArthur Swamp, turn right at the fork, crossing the canal and passing through the gate, and drive three miles to the lake.

Access/Fees: Access by private boat only. Visitors can launch at Big Lake at a PG&E public boat launch, known as "rat farm." It is reached from McArthur by turning north off Highway 299 onto Main Street, continuing past the Intermountain Fairgrounds, crossing over a canal, and proceeding three miles north on a graded dirt road.

Maps: A free map of the park is available from the McArthur-Burney State Park at the address below.

Contact: McArthur-Burney Falls Memorial State Park, 24898 Highway 89, Burney, CA 96013, tel. (530) 335-2777.

Primary sightings: osprey, swans

ANACAPA ISLAND, CHANNEL ISLANDS, offshore from Ventura County

Note: One of the Channel Islands, Anacapa is located 11 miles offshore of Oxnard. Party boats running excursions to the waters around the islands are available out of Channel Island and Port Hueneme Harbors. Island Packers, out of Ventura Harbor or Channel Islands Harbor in Oxnard, takes visitors to the islands.

Directions: To access Island Packer departure points: In Oxnard on Highway 1, exit on Channel Islands Boulevard and drive west past Victoria Avenue, over a bridge, making a left on South Harbor Boulevard. Drive about half a mile to 3600 South Harbor Boulevard at the Marine Emporium or, in Oxnard on Highway 1, exit on Channel Islands Boulevard and drive west. Channel Islands boulevard becomes Harbor Boulevard. Continue on Harbor Boulevard about six miles. Turn left on Spinnaker Drive and drive to 1867 Spinnaker Drive on the right hand side, by Channel Islands National Park.

To access party boat harbors: In Oxnard on Highway 1, exit on Victoria Avenue, make a right at the end of the off-ramp and drive 5.5 miles. Turn south and follow signs to the Channel Island and Port Hueneme Harbors.

Access/Fees: Access is free. For Island Packer reservations, phone (805) 642-1393.

Maps: Maps are available from Channel Islands National Park at the address below or on the website: www.nps.gov/chis.

Contact: Channel Islands National Park, 1901 Spinnaker Drive, Ventura, CA 93001, tel. (805) 658-5730 or fax (805) 658-5799; Island Packers, 1867 Spinnaker Drive, Ventura, CA 93001, tel. (805) 642-1393 or e-mail: ipco@isle.net, or check the website: www.islandpackers.com. Also helpful are Cisco Sportfishing, tel. (805) 985-8511 or Port Hueneme Sportfishing, tel. (805) 488-4715.

Primary sightings: anchovy, gulls

ANCIENT BRISTLECONE PINE FOREST, in Inyo County

Directions: From Big Pine on Highway 395, take Highway 168 and drive east about five miles. Turn left at the Bristlecone Pine exit and drive another five miles to the Schulman Grove visitor center.

Access/Fees: An entrance fee is charged.

Maps: A free map is available at the visitor center.

Contact: Inyo National Forest, White Mountain Ranger District, 798 North Main Street, Bishop, CA 93514, tel. (760) 873-2500 or fax (760) 873-2563.

Primary sightings: chipmunk, golden eagle, hawks, rabbits or hares, raven

ANDERSON MARSH STATE HISTORIC PARK, in Lake County

Directions: From the town of Clear Lake on Highway 53, drive south about two miles. Take the Anderson Ranch Parkway a short distance to the park entrance.

Access/Fees: There is a per vehicle, day-use fee.

Maps: A map is available for a fee at the historic Anderson Ranch House in the park.

Contact: Anderson Marsh State Historic Park, C/O Clear Lake State Park, 5300 Soda Bay Road, Kelseyville, CA 95451, tel. (707) 994-0688 (Anderson Marsh), tel. (707) 279-2267, tel. (707) 279-4293 (Clear Lake kiosk) or fax (707) 279-0401; California State Parks, Silverado District, 20 East Spain Street, Sonoma, CA 95476, tel. (707) 938-1519 or fax (707) 938-1406.

Primary sightings: bats, killdeer, mink, opossum, rattlesnake, Western meadowlark

ANDREW MOLERA STATE PARK, in Monterey County

Directions: From Carmel on Highway 1, drive 21 miles south to the park entrance on the right.

Access/Fees: There is a per vehicle, day-use fee.

Maps: A free map is available at the entrance kiosk.

Contact: Andrew Molera State Park, California State Parks, Big Sur Station Number One, Big Sur, CA 93920, tel. (831) 667-2315 or fax (831) 667-2886.

Primary sightings: foxes, garter snakes, raccoon, rattlesnake, sea otter, woodpeckers

ANNADEL STATE PARK, in Sonoma County

Directions: From Santa Rosa on US 101, take the Highway 12 exit and drive east on Highway 12 (which becomes Farmer's Lane). Turn right on Montgomery Drive and continue on Mission Drive as Montgomery merges into Mission, driving past the Spring Lake Dam. Turn right on Channel Drive and continue to the park.

Access/Fees: There is a per vehicle, day-use fee.

Maps: There is a map vending machine in the park.

Contact: Annadel State Park, 6201 Channel Drive, Santa Rosa CA 95409, tel. (707) 539-3911; California State Parks, Silverado District, 20 East Spain Street, Sonoma, CA 95476, tel. (707) 938-1519 or fax (707) 938-1406.

Primary sightings: wild pig

AÑO NUEVO STATE RESERVE, in San Mateo County

Directions: From Half Moon Bay on Highway 1, drive south 25 miles to the reserve entrance on the right.

Access/Fees: There is a per vehicle, day-use fee.

Maps: A free map is available at the visitor center.

Contact: Año Nuevo State Reserve, New Year's Creek Road, Pescadero, CA 94060, tel. (650) 879-0227 or (650) 879-2025 or fax (650) 879-2031.

Primary sightings: gulls, sea otter, sharks

ANSEL ADAMS WILDERNESS, Inyo and Sierra National Forests, in Mono and Madera Counties

Directions: From Lee Vining on US 395 southbound to the town of Mammoth Lakes, look for trailheads and roads that access trailheads.

Access/Fees: Access is free.

Maps: A map of the Ansel Adams Wilderness area is available for a fee from USDA Forest Service, Map Sales, 1323 Club Drive, Vallejo, CA 94592, tel. (707) 562-8794.

Contact: Inyo National Forest, Mammoth Lakes Ranger Station, P.O. Box 148, Mammoth Lakes, CA 93546, tel. (760) 924-5500 or fax (760) 924-5537.

Primary sightings: golden trout

ANTELOPE LAKE/INDIAN CREEK, in Plumas County

Directions: From Oroville on Highway 70, drive north about 100 miles, then north on Highway 89 about seven miles. Turn right onto County Road A22 and drive about 27 miles to Antelope Lake.

Access/Fees: Access is free.

Maps: A map is available for a fee from USDA Forest Service, Map Sales, 1323 Club Drive, Vallejo, CA 94592, tel. (707) 562-8794.

Contact: Plumas National Forest, Mt. Hough Ranger District, 39696 Highway 70, Quincy, CA 95971, tel. (530) 283-0555 or fax (530) 283-1821.

Primary sightings: beaver, Canada goose, osprey, wood duck

ANZA-BORREGO DESERT STATE PARK, in San Diego County

Directions: From San Diego on Interstate 8, exit onto Highway 67 and drive north (toward Ramona). At San Ysabel, turn left on Highway 79 and drive about 10 miles. Turn right on Highway S-2 (signed for Borrego Springs) and drive about five miles. Turn left on Highway S-22 and drive another five miles. Pass through Ranchita and drive down Montezuma Grade (a 12-mile, 8% grade) to the park visitor center.

Access/Fees: There is a per vehicle, day-use fee.

Maps: A free map is available at the visitor center.

Contact: Anza-Borrego Desert State Park, 200 Palm Canyon Drive, Borrego Springs, CA 92004, tel. (760) 767-5311 or fax (760) 767-3427.

Primary sightings: bighorn sheep, coyote, foxes, mountain lion, quail, raven

ARASTRADERO PRESERVE, in Santa Clara County

Directions: From San Francisco on Interstate 280, take the Page Mill Road exit. Turn right on Page Mill Road and drive about one-quarter mile. Turn right on Arastradero Road and drive one-half mile to the parking lot on the right.

Access/Fees: Access is free.

Maps: A free map is available at the preserve kiosk.

Contact: Foothills Park, City of Palo Alto, 3300 Page Mill Road, Los Altos Hills, CA 94022, tel. (650) 329-2434 or fax (650) 917-9647.

Primary sightings: hawks

ARCATA MARSH AND WILDLIFE SANCTUARY, in Humboldt County

Directions: In Arcata on US 101, take the Highway 255 (Samoa Boulevard) exit west and drive about two blocks. Turn left on South G Street and drive one-half mile to the Arcata Marsh Interpretive Center at 567 South G Street. To continue to the sanctuary, turn left on South I Street and drive one mile.

Access/Fees: Access is free.

Maps: A free map is available at the interpretive center.

Contact: City of Arcata, Environmental Services, 736 F Street, Arcata, CA 95521, tel. (707) 822-8184 or fax (707) 822-8018.

Primary sightings: osprey, river otter, skunks, snipe

ASH CREEK WILDLIFE AREA, in Modoc and Lassen Counties

Directions: From Redding on Interstate 5, exit on Highway 299 and drive east about 90 miles to Bieber. Continue east about three miles on Highway 299 to the Department of Fish and Game headquarters at 659-695 Highway 299 East.

Access/Fees: Access is free, though designated portions may be closed to public entry during hunting season (October through early January) and from March through mid-August to protect nesting species as necessary. Access only through six official entry points, check with headquarters.

Maps: A free map is available at the headquarters.

Contact: Department of Fish and Game, Ash Creek Wildlife Area, P.O. Box 37, Bieber, CA 96009, tel. (530) 294-5824 or (530) 225-2300 or fax (530) 294-5854.

Primary sightings: frogs, mountain lion, river otter, sage grouse

AUBURN STATE RECREATION AREA, in El Dorado and Placer Counties

Directions: From Auburn on Highway 49 southbound, drive about one mile to the park entrance.

Access/Fees: Access is free.

Maps: A map is available for a fee from the address below.

Contact: Auburn State Recreation Area, P.O. Box 3266, Auburn, CA 95604, tel. (530) 885-4527; Folsom Lake State Recreation Area, tel. (916) 988-0205.

Primary sightings: mountain lion

AUDUBON CANYON RANCH, in Marin County

Directions: In Marin County on US 101, take the Highway 1 exit and drive west 3.5 miles past Stinson Beach.

Access/Fees: Open to the public, 10 a.m. to 4 p.m., mid-March through mid-July. Access is free; donations requested.

Contact: Audubon Canyon Ranch, 4900 Highway 1, Stinson Beach, CA 94970, tel. (415) 868-9244 or fax (415) 868-1699.
Primary sightings: great blue heron, gulls, osprey, cedar waxwing, finches, magpie, mockingbird, red-winged blackbird, robin

B

BATTLE CREEK WILDLIFE AREA, in Tehama County
Directions: From Red Bluff on Interstate 5 northbound, turn east on Jellys Ferry Road and drive 14.2 miles. Turn right on Coleman Fish Hatchery Road and drive to the wildlife area, just before the hatchery.
Access/Fees: Access is free.
Maps: A free map of the wildlife area is available from the North Coast Region office, at the address below.
Contact: Department of Fish and Game, Northern California, North Coast Region, 601 Locust Street, Redding, CA 96001, tel. (530) 225-2300 or fax (530) 225-2381.
Primary sightings: deer, foxes, kingfisher, salmon, turkey

BEAVER CREEK, near McArthur, in Shasta County
Directions: From McArthur on Highway 299, drive east one mile. Turn right (south) on County Road 9S02A and drive 2.5 miles to Pittville. Turn right (south) on County Road 430 and drive 6.25 miles to Beaver Creek on the west side of the road.
Access/Fees: Access is free.
Maps: A map is available for a fee from the Alturas Field Office at the address below.
Contact: Bureau of Land Management, Alturas Field Office, 708 West 12th Street, Alturas, CA 96101, tel. (530) 233-4666 or fax (530) 233-5696.
Primary sightings: cedar waxwing, finches, magpie, mockingbird, red-winged blackbird, robin

BIDWELL PARK, in Butte County
Directions: In Chico on Highway 99, take Highway 32 and drive east about two miles. Turn left on Bruce Road (which becomes Manzanita Road) and drive 1.7 miles. Turn right on Wildwood Avenue and drive 1.5 miles to the Upper Park gate.
Access/Fees: Access is free. Gate is closed to vehicular traffic on Sunday and Monday.
Maps: A free map is available from the Chico Parks Department at the address below.
Contact: City of Chico Parks Department, P.O. Box 3420, Chico, CA 95927, tel. (530) 895-4972 or fax (530) 895-4825.
Primary sightings: foxes, opossum, raccoon, cedar waxwing, dipper, finches, magpie, mockingbird, red-winged blackbird, robin, turkey, wild pig

BIG BASIN REDWOODS STATE PARK, in Santa Cruz County
Directions: From San Francisco, take Highway 1 south to Santa Cruz. Turn east on Highway 9, then left on Highway 236 and continue to the park.
Access/Fees: There is an entrance fee.
Maps: A map is available from Sempervirens Fund, P.O. Drawer BE, Los Altos, CA 94023, tel. (650) 968-4509.
Contact: Big Basin Redwoods State Park, 21600 Big Basin Way, Boulder Creek, CA 95006, tel. (831) 338-8860 or the Rancho Del Oso outpost, tel. (831) 425-1218.

Primary sightings: killdeer, raccoon, cedar waxwing, finches, magpie, mockingbird, red-winged blackbird, robin

BIG BEAR LAKE, in San Bernardino County
Directions: From Los Angeles on Interstate 10, drive east 60 miles. Turn north on Highway 30. At Redlands, take Highway 330 north and drive 15 miles. At Running Springs, take Highway 18 east and drive 12.5 miles to Big Bear Lake.
Access/Fees: An annual or daily Adventure Pass, available at any U.S. Forest Service office or ranger station, is needed to park in the San Bernardino National Forest.
Maps: A map is available for a fee from the USDA Forest Service, Map Sales, 1323 Club Drive, Vallejo, CA 94592.
Contact: San Bernardino National Forest, Big Bear Ranger District, P.O. Box 209, Fawnskin, CA 92333; tel. (909) 866-3437 or fax (909) 866-2867.
Primary sightings: black bear

BIG MORONGO CANYON PRESERVE, in San Bernardino County
Directions: From Palms Springs on Interstate 10, drive east about three miles. Take the Highway 62 exit and drive north about 10 miles to the town of Morongo Valley. Turn right on East Drive and continue on pavement for about 200 feet. At the Y, bear left into the Big Morongo Valley Preserve.
Access/Fees: Access is free.
Maps: There is a free map available at the entrance kiosk.
Contact: U.S. Bureau of Land Management, Palm Springs/South Coast Field Office, 690 West Garnet Avenue, North Palm Springs, CA 92258, tel. (760) 251-4800 or fax (760) 251-4899.
Primary sightings: coyote, doves, jays, quail, racccoon, roadrunner

BIG SUR/VENTANA WILDERNESS, in Monterey County
See **Ventana Wilderness.**

BISCAR WILDLIFE AREA, in Lassen County
Directions: From Litchfield on Highway 395, drive north about 20 miles. Turn west on Karlo Road, and drive about six miles. Park along the road in one of several pullouts.
Access/Fees: Access is free.
Maps: A free map is available from the field office at the address below.
Contact: Bureau of Land Management, Eagle Lake Field Office, 2950 Riverside Drive, Susanville, CA 96130, tel. (530) 257-0456 or fax (530) 257-4831.
Primary sightings: chukar, raven, sage grouse

BITTER CREEK NATIONAL WILDLIFE REFUGE, in Kern County
Note: The refuge is one of the focal areas of research activities addressing recovery of the California condor. The refuge itself is closed to the public, but the area can be viewed from county roads. Watch for condors along the high ridgelines enroute to foraging and roosting areas.
Directions: From Maricopa on Highway 33, drive west to Klipstein Canyon Road, which traverses the refuge. Turn left on Cerro Noroeste Road to a scenic overlook of the refuge and the San Joaquin Valley.

Contact: Bitter Creek National Wildlife Refuge, C/O Hopper Mountain National Wildlife Refuges Complex, P.O. Box 5839, Ventura, CA 93005, tel. (805) 644-5185 or fax (805) 644-1732.

Primary sightings: California condor

BIZZ-JOHNSON TRAIL/SUSAN RIVER, in Lassen County

Note: This 25-mile trail links the towns of Susanville and Westwood, following an old railroad grade along the Susan River and passing through high desert, grasslands, oak woodlands, and fir, pine, and cedar forests.

Directions: In Susanville on Main Street/Highway 36, drive west about 1.5 miles. Turn south on South Weatherlow Street, which becomes Richmond Road, and drive one-half mile. Park at the Susanville Depot at 601 Richmond Road.

Access/Fees: Access is free.

Maps: A free map is available at the depot or write or call the Eagle Lake field office at the address below.

Contact: Bureau of Land Management, Eagle Lake Field Office, 2950 Riverside Drive, Susanville, CA 96130, tel. (530) 257-0456 or fax (530) 257-4831.

Primary sightings: bats, porcupine, raccoon

BLACK BUTTE LAKE, in Glenn and Tehama Counties

Directions: At Orland on Interstate 5, take the Highway 32 exit and drive northwest on Newville Road about eight miles to the U.S. Army Corps of Engineers headquarters and observation point.

Access/Fees: Access is fee.

Maps: A free map is available from the Black Butte Lake office at the address below.

Contact: U.S. Army Corps of Engineers, Black Butte Lake, 19225 Newville Road, Orland, CA 95963, tel. (530) 865-4781 or fax (530) 865-5283.

Primary sightings: doves

BLUE CREEK HEADWATERS, Six Rivers National Forest, in Siskiyou County

Note: During the wet season,(generally, November through May), in order to prevent contamination of the area by Port Orford Cedar Root Rot Disease, vehicles must be inspected and a free permit issued at the Orleans Ranger Station before entering the area. The station office is open 7 a.m.-5 p.m., weekdays.

Directions: From Orleans on Highway 96, turn north on Eyee Road/Forest Service Road 15N01 and drive 30 miles. Turn left on Elk Valley Road/Forest Service Road 14N03 and drive about four miles to the Orleans Ranger Station at the end of the road at the Elk Valley dispersed camping area. Stop at the station for a map and trail information before walking the portion of the Boundary Trail that passes the headwaters of Blue Creek.

Access/Fees: Access is free and does not require a permit or vehicle inspection during the dry season (generally, June through October). Use caution. There are no hiking trails that provide direct access to the headwaters of Blue Creek. Access is gained by scrambling off-trail or from dead-end logging spur roads, bushwhacking down the forested slopes of the canyon to Blue Creek. To explore the headwaters requires many river crossings and scrambling on bear trails. It is dangerous in wet weather from rising river levels and slippery shale.

Maps: A map is available for a fee from USDA Forest Service, Map Sales, 1323 Club Drive, Vallejo, CA 94592, tel. (707) 562-8794.

Contact: Six Rivers National Forest, Orleans Ranger Station, P.O. Box 410, Orleans, CA 95556, tel. (530) 627-3291 or fax (530) 627-3401.

Primary sightings: Bigfoot

BOLINAS LAGOON, in Marin County

Directions: From US 101 in Marin County, take the Sir Francis Drake Boulevard exit and drive west about 20 miles to the town of Olema. Turn left on Highway 1 and look for the lagoon on the right.

Maps: A map of Marin County is available for a fee from Tom Harrison Cartography, 2 Falmouth Cove, San Rafael, CA 94901, tel. (415) 456-7940.

Contact: Point Reyes Bird Observatory, Palomarin Field Station, 4990 Shoreline Highway, Stinson Beach, CA 94970, tel. (415) 868-1221 or fax (415) 868-1946.

Primary sightings: killdeer, kingfisher

BOLSA CHICA ECOLOGICAL RESERVE, in Orange County

Directions: From Huntington Beach on Highway 1/Pacific Coast Highway drive north about three miles to the entrance on the right.

Access/Fees: Access is free.

Maps: No maps are currently available.

Contact: Bolsa Chica Ecological Reserve, Department of Fish and Game, Long Beach Field Office, 330 Golden Shore Avenue, Suite 50, Long Beach, 90802, tel. (562) 590-5132.

Primary sightings: ducks, falcon, osprey

BOLSA CHICA STATE BEACH TO NEWPORT BAY, on the Orange County Coast

Directions: From Bolsa Chica State Beach, drive south on Highway 1/Pacific Coast Highway to Newport Bay. There are numerous wildlife observation points along the highway.

Contact: Bolsa Chica State Beach, 17851 Pacific Coast Highway, Huntington Beach, CA 92649, tel. (714) 846-3460; Orange County Newport Beach Chamber of Commerce, 1470 Jamboree Road, Newport Beach, CA 92660.

Primary sightings: falcon, great blue heron

BOULDER CREEK, Sequoia National Forest, in Fresno and Tulare Counties

Directions: From Fresno on Highway 180, drive east about 60 miles to the entrance of Kings Canyon National Park. Continue three miles beyond the entrance to a Y, bear right onto Generals Highway and drive six miles. Turn left on Big Meadow Road, drive to the Big Meadow campground on the right side and walk along Big Meadow Creek. You can also turn left at the campground and follow the signs to Boulder Creek

Access/Fees: There is an entrance fee (good for seven days).

Maps: A map is available for a fee from USDA Forest Service, Map Sales, 1323 Club Drive, Vallejo, CA 94592, tel. (707) 562-8794.

Contact: Sequoia National Forest, Hume Lake Ranger District, 35860 East Kings Canyon Road, Dunlap, CA 93621, tel. (559) 338-2251.

Primary sightings: fisher

BRANNAN ISLAND STATE RECREATION AREA, in Sacramento County

Directions: In Fairfield on Interstate 80, take the Highway 12 exit and drive 14 miles southeast to Rio Vista and continue just across the bridge at the Sacramento River to Highway 160. Turn right on Highway 160 and drive three miles to the park entrance.

Access/Fees: There is an entrance fee.

Maps: A brochure/map is available at the entrance kiosk.

Contact: Brannan Island State Park, 17645 Highway 160, Rio Vista, CA 94571, tel. (916) 777-6671 (entrance kiosk), or the Goldrush District Office, tel. (916) 445-7373.

Primary sightings: mallard, mink, striped bass, sturgeon

BUTANO STATE PARK, in San Mateo County

Directions: From Pescadero on Highway 1 northbound, turn east on Pescadero Road and drive 2.5 miles. Turn south on Cloverdale Road and drive four miles to the entrance.

Access/Fees: There is a per vehicle, day-use fee.

Maps: A free map is available at the entrance kiosk.

Contact: Butano State Park, 1500 Cloverdale Road, Pescadero, CA 94060, tel. (650) 879-2046 or (650) 879-2044; California State Parks, Bay Area District, 250 Executive Park Boulevard, Suite 4900, San Francisco, CA 94134, tel. (415) 330-6300 or fax (415) 330-6312.

Primary sightings: coyote, deer, woodpeckers

BUTTE VALLEY NATIONAL GRASSLANDS, in Siskiyou County

Directions: From Weed on Interstate 5, drive north on Highway 97 about 37 miles to the Goosenest Ranger Station for information and specific directions. Continue north on Highway 97 about two miles to Sams Neck Road on the west side and access to the Grasslands.

Access/Fees: Access is free.

Maps: A map is available for a fee from USDA Forest Service, Map Sales, 1323 Club Drive, Vallejo, CA 94592, tel. (707) 562-8794.

Contact: Klamath National Forest, Goosenest Ranger District, 37805 Highway 97, MacDoel, CA 96058, tel. (530) 398-4391 or fax (530) 398-4599.

Primary sightings: badger, hawks, rattlesnake, raven, swans

BUTTE VALLEY WILDLIFE AREA, in Siskiyou County

Directions: From Weed on Interstate 5, take Highway 97 north toward Klamath Falls about 40 miles. Turn west on Meiss Lake Road and drive 5.1 miles to the wildlife area headquarters.

Access/Fees: Access is free.

Maps: A free map is available at any of the four access points along Meiss Lake Road or at the headquarters.

Contact: Butte Valley Wildlife Area, Department of Fish and Game, P.O. Box 249, MacDoel, CA 96058, tel. (530) 398-4627 or fax (530) 398-4797.

Primary sightings: garter snakes, golden eagle

C

CABRILLO NATIONAL MONUMENT, in San Diego County

Directions: In San Diego on Interstate 5, take the Highway 209/Rosecrans exit and drive south about six miles. Turn right on Canon and drive about one mile. Turn left on Catalina Boulevard and drive to the end of the boulevard to the entrance station at the tip of Point Loma.

Access/Fees: There is a per vehicle, day-use fee (good for seven days).

Maps: A free map is available at the visitor center.

Contact: Cabrillo National Monument, National Park Service, 1800 Cabrillo Memorial Drive, San Diego, CA 92106-3601, tel. (619) 557-5450 or fax (619) 557-5469.

Primary sightings: brown pelican, dolphins, foxes, lobster, porpoises, raven

CACHE CREEK MANAGEMENT AREA, in Lake County

Directions: From Clearlake Oaks on Highway 20, drive east about eight miles to the parking area at the Redbud entrance.

Access/Fees: Access is free.

Maps: A free map is available from the Ukiah Field Office.

Contact: Bureau of Land Management, Ukiah Field Office, 2550 North State Street, Ukiah, CA 95482, tel. (707) 468-4000 or fax (707) 468-4027.

Primary sightings: raven, river otter, turkey

CACHUMA LAKE RECREATION AREA, in Santa Barbara County

Directions: From Santa Barbara on US 101, turn right on Highway 154 and drive north 20 miles to the area entrance.

Access/Fees: There is a per vehicle, day-use fee.

Maps: A free map is available from the entrance kiosk.

Contact: Cachuma Lake Recreation Area, Santa Barbara County Parks, 610 Mission Canyon Road, Santa Barbara, CA 93105, tel. (805) 686-5055 or (805) 568-2461 or fax (805) 568-2459.

Primary sightings: Canada goose, deer, golden eagle, jays, rabbits or hares, woodpeckers

CALAVERAS BIG TREES STATE PARK, in Calaveras County

Directions: From Arnold, drive four miles east on Highway 4 to the park entrance.

Access/Fees: There is a per vehicle, day-use fee.

Maps: A free map is available from the visitor center. A detailed topographical map of the park is also available at the center for a fee.

Contact: Calaveras Big Trees State Park, P.O. Box 120, Arnold, CA 95223, tel. (209) 795-2334 or fax (209) 795-7306; California State Parks, Calaveras District, 22708 Broadway, Columbia, CA 95310-9400, tel. (209) 532-0150 or fax (209) 532-5064.

Primary sightings: black bear, bobcat, mountain lion, squirrels, woodpeckers

CARMEL RIVER STATE BEACH, in Monterey County

Directions: From Carmel on Highway 1, turn west on Rio Road and drive to Santa Lucia Street. Turn left and drive about five blocks. Turn left on Carmelo Street and drive about one-quarter mile to the parking area.

Access/Fees: Access is free.

Maps: A free map is available from Point Lobos State Reserve at the address below.

Contact: Carmel River State Beach, C/O Point Lobos State Reserve, Highway 1, Box 62, Carmel, CA 93923, tel. (831) 624-4909, website: www.pointlobos.org.

Primary sightings: gulls, sea otter

CARQUINEZ STRAIT, Crockett Pier, in Conta Costa County

Directions: In Crockett on Interstate 80, take the Crockett exit to Pomona Street and drive a short distance. Turn left on Port Street, then left again on Dowrelio Road and drive to the pier.

Access/Fees: Access is free.

Maps: A free map/brochure of the Crockett area is available from the chamber of commerce at the phone number below.

Contact: Crockett Marina, P.O. Box 367, Crockett, CA 94525, (510) 787-1049. Crockett Chamber of Commerce, tel. (510) 787-1155.

Primary sightings: sturgeon

CARRIZO PLAIN NATURAL AREA, in Kern County

Directions: From Paso Robles on Highway 101, take Highway 58 and drive east about 45 miles. Turn south on Soda Lake Road and drive about about six miles to the visitor center.

Access/Fees: Access is free. Closed June through November.

Maps: A free map is available at the visitor center.

Contact: Carrizo Plain Natural Area, Bureau of Land Management, 3801 Pegasus Drive, Bakersfield, CA 93308, tel. (661) 391-6000, visitor center tel. (661) 475-2131, or fax (661) 391-6040.

Primary sightings: foxes, sandhill crane

CASTLE ROCK STATE PARK, in Santa Clara County

Directions: From Saratoga Gap on Highway 35, take the Highway 9 exit and drive south three miles to the park entrance.

Access/Fees: There is a per vehicle, day-use fee.

Maps: A free map is available at the entrance kiosk, or from the Castle Rock State Park office at the address below.

Contact: Castle Rock State Park, 15000 Skyline Boulevard, Los Gatos, CA 95033-8291, tel. (408) 867-2952; California State Parks, Santa Cruz District, 600 Ocean Street, Santa Cruz, CA 95060, tel. (831) 429-2851 or fax (831) 429-2876.

Primary sightings: band-tailed pigeon

CASWELL MEMORIAL STATE PARK, in San Joaquin County

Directions: From Manteca on Highway 99, drive south about five miles. Take Austin Road exit and drive south about five miles to the park.

Access/Fees: There is a per vehicle, day-use fee.

Maps: A free map is available at the entrance station.

Contact: Caswell Memorial State Park, 28000 South Austin Road, Ripon, CA 95366, tel. (209) 599-3810; California State Parks, Four Rivers District, 31426 Gonzaga Road, Gustine, CA 95322, tel. (209) 826-1197 or fax (209) 826-0284.

Primary sightings: coyote, opossum, raccoon, skunks, wood duck

CATALINA ISLAND, offshore from Los Angeles

Directions: From San Diego, San Pedro, Redondo Beach, Newport Beach or Long Beach, a ferry to the island towns of Avalon or Two Harbors is available.

Access/Fees: For a ferry schedule and current fee information, phone the Catalina Visitors Bureau, tel. (310) 510-1520.

Maps: A free map is available from the Catalina Visitors Bureau at the address below.

Contact: Catalina Visitors Bureau, P.O. Box 217, Avalon, CA 90704, tel. (310) 510-1520 or fax (310) 510-7606; Catalina Express, tel. (310) 519-1212; Catalina Cruises, tel. (800) 888-5939; Catalina Passenger Service, tel. (714) 673-5245.

Primary sightings: dolphins, lobster, marlin, porpoises, sharks, yellowtail

CHANNEL ISLANDS, offshore from Ventura County

Note: Excursions to the waters around the islands are available out of Channel Island and Port Hueneme Harbors. Island Packers, out of Ventura Harbor or Channel Islands Harbor in Oxnard, takes visitors to the islands.

Directions: To access Island Packer departure points: In Oxnard on Highway 1, exit on Channel Islands Boulevard and drive west past Victoria Avenue, over a bridge, making a left on South Harbor Boulevard. Drive about half a mile to 3600 South Harbor Boulevard at the Marine Emporium or, in Oxnard on Highway 1, exit on Channel Islands Boulevard and drive west. Channel Islands boulevard becomes Harbor Boulevard. Continue on Harbor Boulevard about six miles. Turn left on Spinnaker Drive and drive to 1867 Spinnaker Drive on the right hand side, by Channel Islands National Park.

To access party boat harbors: In Oxnard on Highway 1, exit on Victoria Avenue, make a right at the end of the off-ramp and drive 5.5 miles. Turn south and follow signs to the Channel Island and Port Hueneme Harbors.

Access/Fees: Access is free. For Island Packer reservations, phone (805) 642-1393.

Maps: Maps are available from Channel Islands National Park at the address below or on the website: www.nps.gov/chis.

Contact: Channel Islands National Park, 1901 Spinnaker Drive, Ventura, CA 93001, tel. (805) 658-5730 or fax (805) 658-5799; Island Packers, 1867 Spinnaker Drive, Ventura, CA 93001, tel. (805) 642-1393 or e-mail: ipco@isle.net, or check the website:

www.islandpackers.com; also helpful are Cisco Sportfishing, tel. (805) 985-8511 and Port Hueneme Sportfishing, tel. (805) 488-4715.

Primary sightings: brown pelican, dolphins, gulls, lobsters, marlin, porpoises, sea lions, sharks, swordfish

CHAW'SE INDIAN GRINDING ROCK STATE HISTORIC PARK, in Amador County

Directions: From Jackson on Highway 88, drive east about eight miles. In Pine Grove, turn left (northeast) on Pine Grove/Volcano Road and drive 1.5 miles to the park entrance.

Access/Fees: There is a per vehicle, day-use fee.

Maps: A map is available for a fee at the park visitor center.

Contact: Chaw'se Indian Grinding Rock State Historic Park, 14881 Pine Grove/Volcano Road, Pine Grove, CA 95665, tel. (209) 296-7488 or fax (209) 296-7528; California State Parks, Calaveras District, 22708 Broadway Street, Columbia, CA 95310, tel. (209) 532-3184/0150 or fax (209) 532-5064.

Primary sightings: coyote, deer, hawks, quail, rabbits or hares

CHEWS RIDGE, Los Padres National Forest, in Monterey County

Directions: From Carmel on Highway 1, drive east on Carmel Valley Road about 22 miles. Turn right (south) on Tassajara Road/County Road 5007 and drive 10 miles to the China Camp campground. A trail out of camp is routed into the Ventana Wilderness.

Access/Fees: There is a per vehicle, day-use fee in the Ventana Wilderness.

Maps: A map of Los Padres National Forest is available for a fee from Big Sur Station or from USDA Forest Service, Map Sales, 1323 Club Drive, Vallejo, CA 94592, tel. (707) 562-8794.

Contact: Ventana Wilderness, C/O Los Padres National Forest, Big Sur Station Number 1, Big Sur, CA 93920, tel. (831) 667-2423 or fax (831) 667-2886.

Primary sightings: band-tailed pigeon

CHICO GENETIC RESOURCE CENTER, in Butte County

Directions: In Chico on Highway 99, take the Skyway exit and drive east one-quarter mile. Turn right on Dominic Drive and drive two blocks. Turn left on Morrow Lane and drive about 50 yards. Turn right on Cramer Lane and continue to a fork, bear left through the gate, keep right and drive to the parking area at the center office.

Access/Fees: Access is free. The center is generally open Wednesday through Friday, 8 a.m. to 4 p.m.

Maps: A free trail map is available at the center office.

Contact: Genetic Resource Center, Mendocino National Forest, 2741 Cramer Lane, Chico, CA 95928, tel. (530) 934-3316 or fax (530) 898-8154.

Primary sightings: hawks, woodpeckers

CHILAO VISITOR CENTER, Angeles National Forest, in Los Angeles County

Directions: From Los Angeles on Interstate 2/Glendale Freeway, drive north about 3.5 miles. Turn right on Interstate 210 and drive east about three miles. Take the Highway 2/Angeles Crest Highway exit, turn left on Angeles Crest Highway and drive 27 miles. Turn left at milepost 50.65 and drive 200 yards to the center entrance.

Access/Fees: Access is free.

Maps: A free map of the four self-guided nature trails is available at the visitor center.

Contact: Chilao Visitor Center, Angeles National Forest, Los Angeles River Ranger District, Star Route 2, La Cañada, CA 91011, tel. (626) 796-5541.

Primary sightings: chipmunk, quail

CHINA FLAT/SILVER FORKS CAMPGROUNDS, El Dorado National Forest, in El Dorado County

Directions: From Pollock Pines on Highway 50, drive north about 20 miles. Turn east on Silver Fork Road and drive three miles to China Flat. Drive six miles farther to Silver Fork Campground.

Access/Fees: Access is free.

Maps: A map of El Dorado National Forest is available for a fee from the USDA Forest Service, Map Sales, 1323 Club Drive, Vallejo, CA 94592, tel. (707) 562-8794.

Contact: El Dorado National Forest, Placerville Ranger District, 4260 Eight Mile Road, Camino, CA 95709, tel. (530) 644-2324 or fax (530) 647-5311.

Primary sightings: bats, bobcats, kingfisher, mountain lion, opossum, squirrels

CLEAR CREEK HEADWATERS, SISKIYOU WILDERNESS, in Siskiyou County

Note: The Young's Valley Trail connects with the Clear Creek National Recreation Trail, which passes Wilderness Falls and continues downstream. The bedrock alternates from granite to peridotite, which gives rise to a diversity of plants and wildlife.

Directions: From Crescent City on US 101, drive north three miles, turn east on US 199 and drive 32 miles. Turn right on Forest Service Road 18N07 and drive about five miles. Continue on Forest Service Road 18N07 as it veers right and twists its way about 10 miles to Sanger Lake and beyond to the nearby trailhead. The last mile is very rough.

Maps: A map of the Klamath National Forest is available for a fee at the Happy Camp district office (see below) or from USDA Forest Service, Map Sales, 1323 Club Drive, Vallejo, CA 94592, tel. (707) 562-8794.

Contact: Klamath National Forest, Happy Camp Ranger District, P.O. Box 377, Happy Camp, CA 96039, tel. (530) 493-2243 or fax (530) 493-2212.

Primary sightings: Bigfoot

CLEAR LAKE, in Lake County

Directions: From Sacramento on Interstate 5, drive north to, turn west on Highway 20 and drive to the town of Nice.

Access/Fees: Free public boat ramps are available in Nice at H.V. Keeling County Park, Nice Community Park, and Hudson Avenue.

Maps: A free map is available from the Lake County Visitor Information Center at the address below.

Contact: Lake County Visitor Information Center, 875 Lakeport Boulevard, Lakeport, CA 95453, tel. (707) 263-9544 or (800) 525-3743; Clear Lake State Park, tel. (707) 279-4293.
Primary sightings: catfish, doves, largemouth bass, sage grouse, wood duck

CLEAR LAKE NATIONAL WILDLIFE REFUGE, in Siskiyou County
Directions: From the town of Tulelake, drive south on Highway 139 about 23 miles. Turn left on Clear Lake Road and drive east about nine miles to the Clear Lake Wildlife Refuge bordering Clear Lake Reservoir.
Access/Fees: Access is free.
Maps: A free map is available at the refuge entrance kiosk.
Contact: Clear Lake National Wildlife Refuge, C/O Klamath Basin National Wildlife Complex, Route 1, Box 74, Tulelake, California 96134, tel. (530) 667-2231.
Primary sightings: band-tailed pigeon

CLEAR LAKE STATE PARK, in Lake County
Directions: In Kelseyville on Highway 29, turn north on Gaddy Lane and drive about 2.5 miles. Turn right on Soda Lake Road and drive about one-half mile to the park.
Access/Fees: There is a per vehicle, day-use fee.
Maps: A free map is available at the visitor center.
Contact: Clear Lake State Park, 5300 Soda Bay Road, Kelseyville, CA 95451, tel. (707) 279-4293; California State Parks, Silverado District, 20 East Spain Street, Sonoma, CA 95476, tel. (707) 928-1519 or fax (707) 938-1406.
Primary sightings: golden eagle, gulls

COACHELLA VALLEY PRESERVE, in Riverside County
Directions: From Palm Springs on Interstate 10 drive east 10 miles. Turn left on Ramon Road and drive about five miles. Turn left (north) on Thousand Palms Canyon Drive and drive two miles to the entrance.
Access/Fees: Access is free.
Maps: A free map is available at the visitor center.
Contact: Nature Conservancy, P.O. Box 188, Thousand Palms, CA 92276, tel. (760) 343-2733 or (760) 342-1234 or fax (760) 343-0393; the Center for Natural Lands Management can also be helpful, tel. (760) 731-7790.
Primary sightings: bobcat, hawks, horned lizards, opossum, quail, rabbits or hares, roadrunner

COLEMAN NATIONAL FISH HATCHERY, in Shasta County
Directions: From Anderson on Interstate 5, take the Deschutes Road exit. Turn left on Deschutes Road and drive east about two miles. Turn right on Ball's Ferry Road and drive three miles. Turn left on Ash Creek Road and drive one mile. Turn right on Gover Road, drive 1.2 miles, turn left on Coleman Fish Hatchery Road and drive two miles to the hatchery.
Access/Fees: Access is free to the salmon viewing station.
Maps: A free brochure is available at the visitor center.
Contact: Coleman National Fish Hatchery, U.S. Fish and Wildlife Service, 24411 Coleman Fish Hatchery Road, Anderson, CA 96007, tel. (530) 365-8622 or fax (530) 365-0913.
Primary sightings: salmon

COLORADO RIVER, YUMA-WINTERHAVEN AREA, in Imperial County, CA and Arizona

Directions: In Winterhaven on Interstate 8 eastbound, turn north on County Road 524 or Picacho Road and continue to signed access spots.

Access/Fees: Access is free.

Maps: A free map of the area is available from the Yuma Field Office at the address below.

Contact: Bureau of Land Managment, Yuma Field Office, 2555 East Gila Ridge Road, Yuma, AZ 85365-2240, tel. (520) 317-3200 or fax (520) 317-3250.

Primary sightings: catfish

COLUSA NATIONAL WILDLIFE REFUGE, in Colusa County

Directions: From Colusa on Highway 20, drive west about one-half mile to the refuge entrance.

Access/Fees: Access is free.

Maps: A map and an interpretative, walking tour pamphlet are available at the refuge kiosk.

Contact: Colusa National Wildlife Refuge, C/O Sacramento National Wildlife Refuges Complex, 752 County Road 99W, Willow, CA 95988, tel. (530) 934-2801 or fax (530) 934-7814.

Primary sightings: pheasant

COSUMNES RIVER PRESERVE, in Sacramento County

Directions: From Sacramento on Interstate 5, drive south about 20 miles. Turn east on Twin Cities Road and drive about one mile. Turn south on Franklin Road and drive 1.5 miles to the preserve visitor center.

Access/Fees: Access is free.

Maps: A free map of the preserve is available at the visitor center. A free Willows Slough Nature Trail map is available at the trailhead.

Contact: Cosumnes River Preserve, 13501 Franklin Boulevard, Galt, CA 95632, tel. (916) 683-1700 or fax (916) 683-1702, website: www.consumnes.org, e-mail: info@ cosumnes.org.

Primary sightings: curlew, hawks, mink, river otter, sandhill crane, swans, wood duck

COTTONWOOD CREEK, in Inyo County

Directions: In Lone Pine on Highway 395, drive west on Whitney Portal Road about three miles. Turn south on Horseshoe Meadow Road and drive about 18 miles to the Horseshoe Meadow Camping Area and nearby Cottonwood Lakes Trailhead.

Access/Fees: Access is free.

Maps: A map is available for a fee from USDA Forest Service, Map Sales, 1323 Club Drive, Vallejo, CA 94592, tel. (707) 562-8794.

Contact: Humboldt-Toiyabe National Forest, Mount Whitney Ranger District, P.O. Box 8, Lone Pine, CA 93545, tel. (760) 876-6200 or fax (760) 876-6202; Los Angeles Department of Water and Power, 300 Mandich Street, Bishop, CA 93514, tel. (760) 872-1104 or fax (760) 873-0266.

Primary sightings: rabbits or hares

COYOTE HILLS REGIONAL PARK, in Alameda County

Directions: From Fremont, drive west on Highway 84 to the Paseo Padre Parkway exit. Turn right on Paseo Padre Parkway and drive to Patterson Ranch Road. Turn left and drive to the parking area. Or from Highway 880 in Fremont, take the Highway 84/Decoto Road exit, turn right on Ardenwood Boulevard, and continue to Commerce Drive. Turn left on Commerce (which becomes Patterson Ranch Road) and drive to the park entrance.

From the Peninsula, turn east on Highway 84, cross the Dumbarton Bridge, and take the Thornton Avenue exit. Turn left (the road becomes Paseo Padre Parkway) and drive north to Patterson Ranch Road. Turn left on Patterson Ranch Road and drive to the parking area.

Access: A park fee is required only when there's an attendant at the kiosk.

Maps: A map/brochure is available at the parking area.

Contact: East Bay Regional Parks District, 2950 Peralta Oaks Court, P.O. Box 5381, Oakland, CA 94605-0381, tel. (510) 635-0135, ext. 2200, or fax (510) 569-4319; Coyote Hills Regional Park, 8000 Patterson Ranch Road, Fremont, CA 94555, tel. (510) 795-9385.

Primary sightings: deer, fox

CRESCENT CITY HARBOR, in Del Norte County

Directions: In Crescent City on US 101, turn west at Citizen's Dock.

Access/Fees: Access is free.

Maps: A free map is available from the Crescent City-Del Norte Chamber of Commerce at the address below.

Contact: Crescent City-Del Norte Chamber of Commerce, 1001 Front Street, Crescent City, CA 95531, tel. (707) 464-3174.

Primary sightings: sea lions

CRYSTAL COVE STATE PARK, in Orange County

Directions: From Newport Beach on Highway 1 southbound, drive about one mile to the Pelican Point parking lot. Drive another one-quarter mile to the El Moro Canyon parking area.

Access/Fees: There is a per vehicle, day-use fee.

Maps: A free map is available at the entrance kiosk.

Contact: Crystal Cove State Park, tel. (949) 494-3539; California State Parks, Orange Coast District, 3020 Avenida Del Presidente, San Clemente, CA 92672, tel. (949) 492-0802 or fax (949) 492-8412.

Primary sightings: dolphins, osprey, porpoises, sea lions, cedar waxwing, finches, magpie, mockingbird, red-winged blackbird, robin

CUYAMACA RANCHO STATE PARK, in San Diego County

Directions: From San Diego on Highway 8, drive east about 40 miles. Turn north on Highway 79 and drive four miles to the park entrance.

Access/Fees: There is a per vehicle, day-use fee.

Maps: A map is available for a fee from the visitor center.

Contact: Cuyamaca Rancho State Park, 12551 Highway 79, Descanso, CA 91916, tel. (760) 765-0755 or fax (760) 765-3021; California State Parks, Colorado Desert District, 200 Palm Canyon Drive, Borrego Springs, CA 92004, tel. (760) 767-5311 or fax (760) 767-3427.

Primary sightings: bobcat, coyote, golden eagle, jays, mountain lion, opossum, raccoon

D

DANA POINT HARBOR, in Orange County
Directions: From Los Angeles, drive south on Interstate 5, through Mission Viejo
and San Juan Capistrano. Take the Pacific Coast Highway 1 off-ramp onto Pacific
Coast Highway and drive north about one mile to the intersection of Golden Lantern
Street. Turn left on Golden Lantern and drive about three blocks into the marina area
of the harbor.
Contact: Dana Point Chamber of Commerce, P.O. Box 12, Dana Point, CA 92629, tel.
(949) 496-1555 or fax (949) 496-5321; Dana Wharf Sportfishing, tel. (949) 496-5794.
Primary sightings: dolphins, porpoises, whales, yellowtail

DEATH VALLEY NATIONAL PARK, in Inyo County
Directions: From Baker, on Interstate 15, take Highway 127 north about 65 miles. Turn
left on Highway 178 and drive about 57 miles to the visitor center.
Access/Fees: There is a per vehicle, day-use fee.
Maps: A free map is available at the visitor center.
Contact: Death Valley National Park, P.O. Box 579, Death Valley, CA 92328, tel. (760)
786-2331.
Primary sightings: bats, bighorn sheep, chukar, rabbits or hares, raven, roadrunner

DEL VALLE RESERVOIR AND REGIONAL PARK, in Alameda County
Directions: In Livermore on Interstate 580, take the North Livermore Avenue exit. Turn
south and drive on North/South Livermore Road (which becomes Tesla Road) to
Mines Road. Turn right and drive south for three miles to Del Valle Road. Turn right
and continue for four miles to the lake entrance.
Access/Fees: There is a per vehicle, day-use fee.
Maps: A map/brochure is available at the park entrance.
Contact: East Bay Regional Parks, tel. (510) 635-0135, ext. 2200, Del Valle Regional Park,
tel. (925) 373-0332.
Primary sightings: bald eagle, catfish, deer, falcons, golden eagle, hawks, trout

DELEVAN NATIONAL WILDLIFE REFUGE, in Colusa County
Directions: From Williams on Interstate 5 northbound, drive about nine miles. Take
the Maxwell Road exit and drive east to Four Mile Road, which parallels the western
boundary of the refuge.
Access/Fees: Access is from perimeter roads and is free.
Maps: A free map is available from the Sacramento National Wildlife Refuges Complex
at the address below.
Contact: Delevan National Wildlife Refuge, C/O Sacramento National Wildlife Refuges
Complex, 752 Country Road 99W, Willows, CA 95988, tel. (530) 934-2801 or fax (530)
934-7814.
Primary sightings: ducks, swans

DESERT TORTOISE NATURAL AREA, in Kern County
Note: Be alert to the presence of the poisonous Mojave green rattlesnake, which is
resident here.
Directions: From Los Angeles on Highway 14, drive north about 85 miles, past the cities

of Palmdale and Lancaster to Mojave. Continue north on Highway 14. Turn right on California City Boulevard and drive about eight miles (past the golf course), make a sharp left and drive about six miles on a dirt road to the information kiosk (staffed only in April, May and June).

Access/Fees: Access is free.

Maps: A free map is available from the Desert Tortoise Preserve Committee at the address below.

Contact: Desert Tortoise Natural Area, C/O Desert Tortoise Preserve Committee, 4067 Mission Inn Avenue, Riverside, CA 92501, tel. (909) 683-3872 or fax (909) 583-6949, e-mail: dtpc@pacbell.net, website: www.tortoise-tracks.org.

Primary sightings: chukar, coyote, foxes, horned lizards, rattlesnake, raven, roadrunner, tortoise

DEVILS POSTPILE NATIONAL MONUMENT, in Madera County

Directions: From Mammoth Lakes on Highway 203 westbound, turn right on Minaret Road and drive 5.4 miles, passing the Mammoth Mountain Ski Area, to the entrance kiosk.

Access/Fees: Access is free, but from about mid-June to the Thursday after Labor Day (exact dates subject to weather conditions), it is necessary to take a shuttle bus, for which there is a charge, to the monument. Buses run from 7:30 a.m.-5:30 p.m. daily, from the Mammoth Inn at the ski area. The remainder of the year, the access road is subject to closure due to weather conditions. Call ahead for current access information.

Maps: A free map is available from the office at the address below.

Contact: Devils Postpile National Monument, P.O. Box 501, Mammoth Lakes, CA 93546, tel. (760) 934-2289 (summer and fall), tel. (209) 565-3134 (winter and spring). For year-round recreation information, call the Mammoth Lakes Ranger Station, tel. (760) 924-5500. For lodging information, phone (888) 466-2666.

Primary sightings: black bear

DEVIL'S PUNCHBOWL NATURAL AREA, in Los Angeles County

Directions: In Pearblossom on Highway 138, turn south on Longview Road/County Road N-6 and drive about three miles. Turn left on Fort Tejon Road and drive an eighth of a mile. Turn right on Longview Road and drive south two miles. Turn left on Tumbleweed Road/Punchbowl Road and drive east about three miles to the end of the road and the parking area.

Access/Fees: Access is free.

Maps: A free map is available at the visitor center.

Contact: Devil's Punchbowl Natural Area, County of Los Angeles, Department of Parks and Recreation, 28000 Devil's Punchbowl Road, Pearblossom, CA 93553, tel. (661) 944-2743 or fax (661) 944-6924.

Primary sightings: bobcat, garter snakes, gopher snake, hawks, horned lizards, rattlesnake, tarantulas, tortoise

D.L. BLISS STATE PARK, in El Dorado County
See **Emerald Bay State Park.**

DORST CAMP, Sequoia National Park, in Fresno County

Directions: From Fresno, drive east on Highway 180 about 55 miles to the Big Stump entrance station at Kings Canyon National Park. Continue 1.5 miles and turn right on the General's Highway, heading toward Sequoia National Park. Drive about 17 miles to the turnoff on the right for Dorst Campground.

Access/Fees: There is an entrance fee at Sequoia and Kings Canyon National Parks, good for seven days.

Maps: Free park maps are available at park entrance stations. A more detailed map is available for a fee from Tom Harrison Cartography, tel. (415) 456-7940 or from Trails Illustrated, tel. (800) 962-1643.

Contact: Sequoia and Kings Canyon National Parks, Three Rivers, CA 93271-9700, tel. (559) 565-3341 or fax (559) 565-3730.

Primary sightings: black bear

DOS PALMAS PRESERVE, in Riverside County

Directions: From Indio on Highway 111 southbound, drive about 25 miles. Turn left on Parkside Drive and drive one mile. Turn right on Desertaire Drive and continue on unpaved road about three miles to the preserve.

Access/Fees: Access is free:

Maps: A free map/brochure is available from the Palm Springs-South Coast Field Office at the address below.

Contact: Bureau of Land Management, Palm Springs-South Coast Field Office, 690 West Garnet Avenue, North Palm Springs, CA 92258, tel. (760) 251-4800 or fax (760) 251-4899.

Primary sightings: raven

DYE CREEK PRESERVE, in Tehama County

Directions: All access to Dye Creek Preserve is by reservation only through the Nature Conservancy. No walk ups. When the reservation is confirmed, the Nature Conservancy will provide directions and will provide necessary information for the day-long hike. Guided group hikes are offered in the spring and fall.

Access/Fees: A small fee is charged.

Maps: No maps are available.

Contact: Nature Conservancy, 201 Mission Street, 4th Floor, San Francisco, CA 94105, tel. (415) 777-0487.

Primary sightings: wild pig

ℰ

EAGLE AND HONEY LAKES, in Lassen County
Directions: Points near Eagle Lake: From Susanville, drive north on County Road A1 to the north end of Eagle Lake, then continue north on Highway 139. Look for pronghorn along County Road A1 and Highway 139 near Eagle Lake.
 Points near Honey Lake: From Susanville, drive south on Highway 395 about 20 miles to Honey Lake. Look for pronghorn along Highway 395 near Honey Lake.
Access/Fees: Access is free.
Maps: A free map is available from the Bureau of Land Management office at the address below.
Contact: Bureau of Land Management, Eagle Lake Resource Area, 2950 Riverside Drive, Susanville, CA 96130, tel. (530) 257-0456 or fax (530) 257-4831.
Primary sightings: pronghorn antelope

EAGLE LAKE, Lassen National Forest, in Lassen County
Directions: At Red Bluff on Interstate 5, take the Highway 36 exit and drive east about 105 miles. Turn north on County Road A1 (three miles west of Susanville) and drive 15.5 miles, continue northeast on County Road 201 to the lake.
Access/Fees: Access is free.
Maps: A map of Lassen National Forest is available for a fee from USDA Forest Service, Map Sales, 1323 Club Drive, Vallejo, CA 94592, tel. (707) 562-8794.
Contact: Lassen National Forest, Eagle Lake Ranger District, 55 South Sacramento Street, Susanville, CA 96130, tel. (530) 257-4188.
Primary sightings: bald eagle

EASTMAN LAKE, in Madera County
Directions: From Merced, drive south on Highway 99 for 15 miles to the town of Chowchilla. Take the Robertson Boulevard exit and turn east onto Avenue 26. Continue east for 17 miles to County Road 29. Turn north on and drive eight miles to the lake.
Access/Fees: There is a small fee for boat launching.
Maps: A map is available from the U.S. Army Corps of Engineers.
Contact: U.S. Army Corps of Engineers, Eastman Lake, P.O. Box 67, Raymond, CA 93653-0067, tel. (760) 689-3255 or fax (559) 689-3408.
Primary sightings: bass, bobcat, coyote, hawks

EAST WALKER WILDLIFE AREA, in Mono County
Directions: From Bridgeport on Highway 182, at the junction with Highway 395, drive north about five miles. There are pullouts along Highway 182 for about seven miles.
Access/Fees: Access is free.
Maps: A free map is available from the Bishop Field Office at the address below.
Contact: East Walker Wildlife Area, C/O Department of Fish and Game, Bishop Field Office, 417 West Line Street, Bishop, CA 93514, tel. (760) 872-1171 or fax (760) 872-1284.
Primary sightings: mink, river otter

EATON CANYON NATURAL AREA, in Los Angeles County
Directions: In Pasadena on Highway 210, turn north on Altadena Drive and drive about 1.5 miles to the park entrance.
Access/Fees: Access is free.
Maps: A free map is available at the area visitor center.
Contact: Eaton Canyon Natural Area, 1750 North Altadena Drive, Pasadena, CA 91107, tel. (626) 398-5420 or fax (626) 398-5422; County of Los Angeles, Department of Parks and Recreation, 433 South Vermont Avenue, Los Angeles, CA 90020-1975, tel. (213) 738-2961 or fax (213) 487-0380.
Primary sightings: deer, garter snakes, hawks, jays, rabbits or hares

EEL RIVER, in Humboldt County
Directions: From Eureka on US 101 southbound, drive south through Fortuna, Rio Dell, Shively, and Holmes. US 101 parellels the river along the way and provides many access points along spur roads.
Access/Fees: Access is free.
Maps: A free map is available from the Ukiah Field Office at the address below.
Contact: Bureau of Land Management, Ukiah Field Office, 2550 North State Street, Ukiah, CA 95482, tel. (707) 468-4000 or fax (707) 468-4027.
Primary sightings: salmon, steelhead

EFFIE YEAW NATURE CENTER/AMERICAN RIVER PARKWAY, in Sacramento County
Directions: From Sacramento on Interstate 5, take the Highway 50 east exit. Drive east on Highway 50 to the Watt Avenue North exit. Drive north on Watt Avenue, then northeast on Fair Oaks Blvd. Turn right on Van Alstine Avenue, then left on California Avenue. Drive one block. Turn right on Tarshes Drive and continue to the entrance to Ancil Hoffman Park. Follow the signs to the nature center.
Access/Fees: There is a parking fee.
Maps: A free map of the three nature trails are available at the center.
Contact: Effie Yeaw Nature Center, P.O. Box 579, Carmichael, CA 95609, tel. (916) 489-4918 or fax (916) 489-4983.
Primary sightings: kingfisher, raccoon, skunks, turkey, woodpeckers

EMERALD BAY STATE PARK/D.L. BLISS STATE PARK, in El Dorado County
Directions: From Tahoe City on Highway 89, drive south about 16 miles to the D.L. Bliss park entrance. Continue four miles to Emerald Bay State Park entrance.
Access/Fees: There is a per vehicle, day-use fee for each park.
Maps: A map is available for a fee from the entrance kiosks.
Contact: D.L. Bliss State Park, P.O. Box 266, Tahoma, CA 96142, tel. (530) 525-7277; California State Parks, High Sierra District, P.O. Box 266, Tahoma, CA 96142, tel. (520) 525-9535 or fax (530) 525-6730.
Primary sightings: Canada goose, chipmunk, coyote, pine marten, raven, woodpeckers

F

FARALLON NATIONAL WILDLIFE REFUGE, offshore from San Francisco

Note: The refuge is located about 30 miles offshore of San Francisco and is closed to the public, however, it is possible to view a large variety of wildlife on and near the islands via educational boat tours conducted from June through November by the Oceanic Society.

Directions: Tours depart from the Fort Mason Center. From US 101 in San Francisco, take the Marina Boulevard exit and drive on Marina Boulevard to Buchanan Street. Turn left into the Fort Mason parking area.

Access/Fees: It is recommended that reservations be made two weeks in advance. For reservations and current fees, contact Oceanic Society Expeditions, tel. (415) 474-3385.

Contact: Oceanic Society Expeditions, Fort Mason Center, Building E, San Francisco, CA 94123-1394, tel. (415) 474-3385 or fax (415) 474-3395.

Primary sightings: dolphins, gulls, porpoises, sea lions, sharks

FEATHER RIVER HATCHERY, in Butte County

Directions: In Oroville on Highway 70, take the Montgomery Street exit. Turn left on Washington Street and after crossing Green Bridge, turn right and drive to the parking area.

Access/Fees: Access is free.

Maps: A brochure/map is available from the Department of Fish and Game at the address below.

Contact: Feather River Hatchery, Department of Fish and Game, 5 Table Mountain Boulevard, Oroville, CA 95965, tel. (530) 538-2222

Primary sightings: salmon, steelhead

FISH LAKE, Six Rivers National Forest, in Humboldt County

Directions: From Redding on Interstate 5, exit on Highway 299 and drive west to the town of Willow Creek. At Willow Creek, turn north on Highway 96 drive seven miles past Weitchpec. Turn left on Fish Lake Road and drive five miles (stay to the right at the Y) to Fish Lake.

Maps: A map of the Six Rivers National Forest is available from the Orleans Ranger District (see below), or from USDA Forest Service, Map Sales, 1323 Club Drive, Vallejo, CA 94592, tel. (707) 562-8794.

Contact: Six Rivers National Forest, Orleans Ranger District, P.O. Box 410, Orleans, CA 95556, tel. (530) 627-3291 or fax (530) 627-3401.

Primary sightings: Bigfoot

FISHERMAN'S WHARF, in Monterey County

Directions: From the San Francisco Bay Area drive south on Highway 1 to Monterey and take the Pacific Grove/Del Monte Avenue exit. Travel about one mile to Figuaro Street, then turn right and continue west to Wharf No. 1.

Access/Fees: Access is free.

Maps: A map and travel guide is available from the Monterey Chamber of Commerce.

Contact: Monterey Chamber of Commerce, 380 Alvarado Street, Monterey, CA 93940, tel. (831) 648-5360.

Primary sightings: gull, pelican, sea lion

FISHERMAN'S WHARF, in San Francisco
Directions: Located off of Jefferson Street and the Embarcadero, between Taylor and Jones Streets.
Access/Fees: Access is free.
Maps: A map of San Francisco is available for a fee from Olmstead Brothers, P.O. Box 5351, Berkeley, CA 94705, tel. (510) 658-6534.
Contact: San Francisco Chamber of Commerce, 465 California Street, 9th Floor, San Francisco, CA 94104, tel. (415) 392-4520 or fax (415) 392-0485; Fisherman's Wharf Merchants Association, tel. (415) 626-7070.
Primary sightings: anchovy, brown pelican, sea lions

FOLSOM LAKE STATE RECREATION AREA, in Sacramento County
Directions: From Sacramento on Highway 50 eastbound, take the Folsom Boulevard exit. Turn left and drive about five miles, cross the American River and continue straight as Folsom Boulevard becomes Folsom-Auburn Road. Drive about 2.5 miles to Beals Point.
Access/Fees: There is a per vehicle, day-use fee.
Maps: A map is available for a fee from the entrance kiosk.
Contact: Folsom Lake State Recreation Area, 7806 Folsom-Auburn Road, Folsom, CA 95630, tel. (916) 988-0205 or fax (916) 988-9062.
Primary sightings: Canada goose, catfish, coyote, largemouth bass

FORT FUNSTON SUNSET TRAIL, in San Francisco County
Directions: In San Francisco on Geary Boulevard westbound, drive to the end of Geary Boulevard at the ocean. Turn left on the Great Highway and drive four miles to the parking area on the right.
Access/Fees: Access is free.
Maps: A free map is available from the Golden Gate National Recreation Area at the address below.
Contact: Golden Gate National Recreation Area, Fort Mason, Building 201, San Francisco, CA 94123, tel. (415) 561-4323 or (415) 556-0560, fax (415) 561-4320; Fort Funston Visitor Center/Ranger Station, tel. (415) 239-2366.
Primary sightings: brown pelican

FORT TEJON STATE HISTORIC PARK, in Kern County
Directions: From Bakersfield on Highway 99, drive south about 25 miles to the junction with Interstate 5. Drive south on Interstate 5 about 12 miles to the Fort Tejon exit and parking lot.
Access/Fees: There is an entrance fee.
Maps: A self-guided tour map is available at the visitor center.
Contact: Fort Tejon State Historic Park, P.O. Box 895, Lebec, CA 93243, tel. (661) 248-6774 or fax (661) 248-8373.
Primary sightings: deer

G

GARCIA RIVER, in Mendocino County
Directions: From the town of Point Arena on Highway 1, turn east on Eureka Hill Road and drive about five miles to a bridge over the river. The river can be accessed by foot downsteam of the bridge.
Access/Fees: Access is free.
Maps: A topographic map of the Point Arena area is available for a fee from Maps, Western Distribution Center, U.S. Geological Survey, Box 25286, Federal Center, Denver, CO 80225, tel. (303) 202-4700.
Contact: California State Parks, Mendocino District, P.O. Box 440, Mendocino, CA 95460, tel. (707) 937-5804 or fax (707) 937-2953.
Primary sightings: steelhead

GOLDEN GATE NATIONAL RECREATION AREA (HAWK HILL), in Marin County
Directions: In Marin on US 101, take the Alexander Avenue exit. Turn left and drive underneath the highway. Take the wide, paved road to the right (Conzelman, but there is no sign), and look for the Marin Headlands sign. Continue on Conzelman (bearing left at the fork with McCullough Road) and drive a short distance. Just before Conzelman becomes a one-way road, park on the shoulder.
Access/Fees: Access is free; the access road is closed each day at sunset.
Maps: A free map is available at the Marin Headlands visitor center. A more detailed map is available for a fee from Olmsted Brothers Map Company, P.O. Box 5351, Berkeley, CA 94705, tel. (510) 658-6534.
Contact: Golden Gate National Recreation Area, Marin Headlands Visitor Center, Building 948, Fort Barry, Sausalito, CA 94965, tel. (415) 331-1540 or fax (415) 331-6963.
Primary sightings: bobcat, gulls, hawks, sea lions

GOLDEN TROUT WILDERNESS, South Fork Kern River, Inyo National Forest, in Tulare County
Directions: From Olancha on US 395 northbound, access to trailheads into the wilderness is available from spur roads between Olancha and and the town of Cartago.
Access/Fees: Access is free.
Maps: A map of Inyo National Forest is available for a fee from USDA Forest Service, Map Sales, 1323 Club Drive, Vallejo, CA 94592, tel. (707) 562-8794.
Contact: Inyo National Forest, Mount Whitney Ranger District, P.O. Box 8, Lone Pine, CA 93545, tel. (760) 876-6200 or fax (760) 876-6202.
Primary sightings: golden trout

GOLETA BEACH COUNTY PARK, in Santa Barbara County
Directions: From Goleta on US 101, take the University of California, Santa Barbara/ Route 217 exit. Turn right on Sand Spit Road, and then left on Moffett Road and drive a short distance to the beach on the left.
Access/Fees: Access is free.
Maps: A free map of Santa Barbara is available from the Santa Barbara Visitor Center, P.O. Box 299, Santa Barbara, CA 93102, tel. (805) 965-3021.
Contact: Santa Barbara County Parks, 610 Mission Canyon Road, Santa Barbara, CA 93105, tel. (805) 568-2461 or fax (805) 568-2459.
Primary sightings: brown pelican

Goose Lake, near Davis Creek, in Modoc County
Directions: From Alturas, drive north on Highway 395. Just south of the town of Davis Creek, turn west on County Road 48.
Access/Fees: Access is free.
Maps: A map is available for a fee from USDA Forest Service, Map Sales, 1323 Club Drive, Vallejo, CA 94592, tel. (707) 562-8794.
Contact: Modoc National Forest Headquarters, 800 West 12th Street, Alturas, CA 96101, tel. (530) 233-5811 or fax (530) 233-8709.
Primary sightings: chukar, pronghorn antelope

Gorda Overlook, in Monterey County
Directions: At the town of Gorda, the overlook is located on the west side of Highway 1.
Access/Fees: Access is free.
Maps: A map of Los Padres National Forest is available for a fee from USDA Forest Service, Map Sales, 1323 Club Drive, Vallejo, CA 94592, tel. (707) 562-8794.
Contact: Los Padres National Forest, Monterey Ranger District, 406 South Mildred Street, King City, CA 93930, tel. (831) 385-5434 or fax (831) 385-0628.
Primary sightings: dolphins, porpoises

Grant County Park, in Santa Clara County
See **Joseph D. Grant County Park,** in Santa Clara County.

Grassland Resource Conservation District, in Merced County
Note: Public access to the private lands within the Conservation District is limited to a self-guided auto-tour on a public road, Santa Fe Grade, which traverses the grasslands area. Visitors are asked not to park along the grade. Three state wildlife areas (Volta, Salt Slough and Los Banos) and five national wildlife refuges (Merced, San Luis, Kesterson, East Bear and China Island) can be accessed from the Santa Fe Grade loop. November, February and March are peak months for waterfowl.
Directions: From Gustine on Highway 140, drive east about 7 miles. Turn right on Santa Fe Grade, a gravel road, and drive the 25 mile loop.
Access/Fees: Access is free. San Luis National Wildlife Refuge, Merced National Wildlife Refuge and East Bear National Wildlife Refuge are open to the public year-round. There is limited access to the remaining areas during hunting season (September through January).
Maps: A free map is available from the Grassland Water District at the address below.
Contact: Grassland Water District, 22759 South Mercey Springs Road, Los Banos, CA 93635, tel. (209) 826-5188 or fax (209) 826-4984; U.S. Fish and Wildlife Service, San Luis National Wildlife Refuge Complex, tel. (209) 826-3508.
Primary sightings: Canada goose, ducks, great blue heron, killdeer, pheasant, rattlesnake, swans

GRAY LODGE STATE WILDLIFE AREA, in Butte County

Directions: From Chico on Highway 99, drive south about 26 miles. Turn right (west) on Sycamore and drive 6.5 miles. Turn south (left) on Pennington Road and drive about three miles, turn right at the signed entrance on Rutherford Road.

Access/Fees: There is an entrance fee.

Maps: There is a free map and brochures at the exhibit room.

Contact: Gray Lodge State Wildlife Area, 3207 Rutherford Road, Gridley, CA 95948, tel. (530) 846-3315 or (530) 846-3481.

Primary sightings: deer, frogs, hawks, osprey, pheasant, cedar waxwing, finches, magpie, mockingbird, owls, red-winged blackbird, robin

GRIZZLY ISLAND WILDLIFE AREA, in Solano County

Note: The Grizzly Wildlife Area is generally open to the public from the third week in January through July and the last two weeks in September. This schedule is subject to change, however. Call ahead for the current schedule. Viewing is best in the early morning or after 6 PM until dark.

Access/Fees: There is an entrance fee.

Directions: From San Francisco, on Interstate 80, drive north about 40 miles. At Fairfield, take Highway 12 East and drive to the 4th stoplight, turn right on Grizzly Island Road, and drive about 10 miles to the visitor center.

Maps: A free map is available from the Grizzly Island Wildlife Area at the address below.

Contact: Grizzly Island Wildlife Area, 2548 Grizzly Island Road, Suisun City, CA 94585-9539, tel. (707) 425-3828 or fax (707) 425-1403.

Primary sightings: ducks, elk, frogs, golden eagle, mink, river otter

GROUSE LAKES AREA, in Nevada County

Directions: From Yuba Gap on Interstate 80, take the Highway 20 exit and drive to Bowman Road. Turn right on Bowman Road and note signs on the spur roads leading to a series of lakes.

Access/Fees: Access is free.

Maps: A map of Tahoe National Forest is available for a fee from USDA Forest Service, Map Sales, 1323 Club Drive, Vallejo, CA 94592, tel. (707) 562-8794.

Contact: Tahoe National Forest, Nevada City Ranger District, 631 Coyote Street, Nevada City, CA 95959-2250, tel. (530) 265-4531 or fax (530) 478-6109.

Primary sightings: chipmunk

GROVER HOT SPRINGS STATE PARK, in Alpine County

Directions: From Markleeville on Highway 89, turn west on Hot Springs Road and drive 3.5 miles to the park entrance.

Access/Fees: There is a per vehicle, day-use fee.

Maps: A map is available for a fee from the kiosk at the park entrance.

Contact: Grover Hot Springs State Park, P.O. Box 188, Markleeville, CA 96120, tel. (530) 694-2248; California State Parks, High Sierra District, P.O. Box 266, Tahoma, CA 96142, tel. (530) 525-9535 or fax (530) 565-6730.

Primary sightings: band-tailed pigeon, chipmunk, dipper, squirrels

GUALALA RIVER, in Mendocino and Sonoma Counties

Directions: From Gualala on Highway 1, turn east on Old Stage Road/County Road 501, then right on Old State Road/County Road 502 from which there is direct access to the river.

Access/Fees: Access is free.

Maps: A topographic map of the Point Arena area is available for a fee from Maps, Western Distribution Center, U.S. Geological Survey, Box 25286, Federal Center, Denver, CO 80225, tel. (303) 202-4700.

Contact: Gualala Point Regional Park, P.O. Box 95, Gualala, CA 95445, tel. (707) 785-2377 or (707) 785-3741; California State Parks, Russian River/Mendocino District, P.O. Box 440, Mendocino, CA 95460, tel. (707) 937-5804 or fax (707) 937-2953.

Primary sightings: steelhead

H

HAIWEE DEER WINTER RANGE, in Inyo County

Directions: From Olancha on Highway 395, drive south about five miles. Turn right on Sage Flat Road and drive west 1.3 miles to the viewing area.

Access/Fees: Access is free; best viewing season is December through February.

Maps: A free map of Inyo County is available from the Bishop Area Chamber of Commerce, Visitor's Bureau, 690 North Main Street, Bishop, CA 93514, tel. (760) 873-8405.

Contact: Department of Fish and Game, Bishop Field Office, 407 West Line Street, Bishop, CA 93514, tel. (760) 872-1171 or fax (760) 872-1284.

Primary sightings: deer, raven

HARPER LAKE, in San Bernardino County

Directions: From Barstow on Highway 58, drive west about 18 miles. Turn north on Harper Road and drive six miles. Turn right (east) on Lockhard Road and drive 2.2 miles to the southern edge of Harper Dry Lake.

Access/Fees: Access is free.

Maps: A free recreational opportunity guide is available from the field office at the address below.

Contact: Bureau of Land Management, Barstow Field Office, 2601 Barstow Road, Barstow, CA 92311, tel. (760) 252-6000 or fax (760) 252-6099.

Primary sightings: ducks, golden eagle, gopher snake, killdeer, tarantulas

HAWK HILL, Golden Gate National Recreation Area, in Marin County

See **Golden Gate National Recreation Area.**

HENRY W. COE STATE PARK, in Santa Clara County

Directions: At Morgan Hill on Highway 101, take the East Dunne Avenue exit and drive east about 13 miles on the steep, winding road to the park entrance.

Access/Fees: There is a per vehicle, day-use fee.

Maps: A free map is available at the visitor center.

Contact: Henry W. Coe State Park, P.O. Box 846, Morgan Hill, CA 95038, tel. (408) 779-2728 or fax (408) 848-4030.

Primary sightings: doves, gopher snake, mountain lion, quail, rabbits or hares, rattlesnake, cedar waxwing, finches, magpie, mockingbird, red-winged blackbird, robin, Western meadowlark, wild pig

HIGH SIERRA RECREATION AREA, in Fresno County
Directions: From the town of Shaver Lake on Highway 168, drive north about 20 miles to Huntington Lake Basin. Turn east on Kaiser Pass Road and drive about 12 miles to the Pineridge Ranger Station for information. Continue eight miles to reach the Jackass Nature Trail.
Access/Fees: Access is free.
Maps: A map is available for a fee from USDA Forest Service, Map Sales, 1323 Club Drive, Vallejo, CA 94592, tel. (707) 562-8794.
Contact: Sierra National Forest, Pineridge Ranger District, P.O. Box 559, Prather, CA 93651, tel. (559) 855-5355 or fax (559) 855-5375.
Primary sightings: garter snakes, osprey, rattlesnake

HIGHWAY 270, Inyo National Forest, in Mono County
See **Inyo National Forest.**

HOBO GULCH TRAIL, Shasta-Trinity National Forest, in Trinity County
Directions: From Weaverville on Highway 299, drive west to the town of Helena. Turn north on East Fork Road (County Road 421) and drive 3.9 miles. Turn left on Hobo Gulch Road (Forest Service Road 34N07Y) and drive 12 miles to the Hobo Gulch Trailhead.
Maps: A map of Shasta-Trinity National Forest is available for a fee from USDA Forest Service, Map Sales, 1323 Club Drive, Vallejo, CA 94592, tel. (707) 562-8794.
Contact: Shasta-Trinity National Forest, Big Bar Ranger Station, Star Route 1, Box 10, Big Bar, CA 96013, tel. (530) 623-6106 or fax (530) 623-6123.
Primary sightings: band-tailed pigeon

HONEY LAKE WILDLIFE AREA, in Lassen County
Directions: From Litchfield on Highway 395, drive about three miles east. Turn south on Mapes Road and drive 1.8 miles. Turn left on Fish and Game Road and drive one mile to the Fleming Unit entrance and the area headquarters.
Access/Fees: Access is free. Open to the public except Saturday, Sunday, and Wednesday during waterfowl hunting season (October through mid-January).
Maps: A free map is available at the area headquarters.
Contact: Honey Lake Wildlife Area, Department of Fish and Game, 728-600 Fish and Game Road, Wendel, CA 96136, tel. (530) 254-6644.
Primary sightings: beaver, Canada goose, swans

HOPE VALLEY WILDLIFE AREA, in Alpine County
Directions: From the town of South Lake Tahoe, drive south on US 50 about two miles to the junction with Highway 89. Continue south about 10 miles on Highway 89 to the junction with Highway 88 (Picketts Junctions). Park on the south side of the junction and follow the trail into the area.
Access/Fees: Access is free.

Maps: A free map is available from the Rancho Cordova Office at the address below.

Contact: Department of Fish and Game, Rancho Cordova Office, 1701 Nimbus Road, Suite A, Rancho Cordova, CA 95670, Region 2, tel. (916) 358-2877 or fax (916) 358-2912.

Primary sightings: blue grouse, bobcat, coyote, marmot, porcupine, snipe

HOT CREEK WETLANDS AND FISH HATCHERY, in Mono County

Directions: From the town of Mammoth Lakes, drive east on Highway 203 to the junction with Highway 395. Drive south on Highway 395 about three miles. Turn left on Hot Creek Hatchery Road and drive east about one mile to the parking area.

Access/Fees: Access is free.

Maps: A map of the Inyo National Forest, which includes the wetlands, is available for a fee from USDA Forest Service, Map Sales, 1323 Club Drive, Vallejo, CA 94592, tel. (707) 562-8794.

Contact: Hot Creek Wetlands, tel. (760) 934-2664. Department of Fish and Game, Bishop Field Office, 407 West Line Street, Bishop, CA 93514, tel. (760) 872-1171 or fax (760) 872-1284.

Primary sightings: curlew

HUENEME CANYON, offshore from Ventura County

Note: Hueneme Canyon, a massive underwater gorge, is located directly offshore of Port Hueneme in Oxnard. Boats making the trip to the canyon are available out of Ventura Harbor.

Directions: In the city of Ventura on US 101, take the Seaward exit. Turn left, then left again on Harbor Boulevard and drive 1.5 miles. Turn right on Schooner Street and drive to the end of the street. Turn right on Anchors Way and drive a short distance to the harbor on the left.

Access/Fees: Current fee and schedule information is available from Harbor Villlage Sportfishing, tel. (805) 658-1060.

Maps: A free map is available from the Ventura Visitors and Convention Bureau at the address below.

Contact: Ventura Visitors and Convention Bureau, 89 South California Street, Suite C, Ventura, CA 93001, tel. (805) 648-2075.

Primary sightings: salmon

HUMBOLDT BAY NATIONAL WILDLIFE REFUGE, in Humboldt County

Directions: From Eureka on US 101, drive south about 10 miles to Hookton Road exit. Turn right and drive a short distance to the refuge entrance:

Access/Fees: Access is free.

Maps: A free map and brochure are available at the refuge.

Contact: Humboldt Bay National Wildlife Refuge, 1020 Ranch Road, Loleta, CA 95551, tel. (707) 733-5406.

Primary sightings: brown pelican, curlew, ducks, falcon, great blue heron, killdeer, swans

HUNTINGTON LAKE, Sierra National Forest, in Fresno County

Directions: From Fresno on Highway 168, drive about 72 miles northeast to the lake.

Access/Fees: Access is free.

Maps: A map of Sierra National Forest is available for a fee from USDA Forest Service, Map Sales, 1323 Club Drive, Vallejo, CA 94592, tel. (707) 562-8794.

Contact: Sierra National Forest, Pineridge Ranger District, P.O. Box 559, Prather, CA 93651, tel. (559) 855-5360 or fax (559) 855-5375.

Primary sightings: osprey

I

INYO NATIONAL FOREST, Highway 270, in Mono County

Directions: From the Bay Area, take Highway 120 east through Yosemite and over Tioga Pass to US 395. Drive north on US 395 about 30 miles to Highway 270. Drive east on Highway 270 about 10 miles on paved road, then three miles on dirt road, to the Bodie State Historic Park entrance directly ahead.

Access/Fees: Access is free.

Maps: A map is available for a fee from USDA Forest Service, Map Sales, 1323 Club Drive, Vallejo, CA 94592, tel. (707) 562-8737.

Contact: Inyo National Forest, Mammoth Lakes Ranger Station, P.O. Box 148, Mammoth Lakes, CA 93546, tel. (760) 924-5500 or fax (760) 924-5537.

Primary sightings: pronghorn antelope

ISHI WILDERNESS, in Tehama County

Directions: From Red Bluff on Highway 36, drive east about 20 miles Take the exit onto Plum Creek Road and drive about 6 miles. Turn right on Ponderosa Way and drive about 15 miles on the dirt road to the signed Black Rock Trailhead.

Access/Fees: There is no entrance fee.

Maps: A map of the Ishi Wilderness is available for a fee from USDA Forest Service, Map Sales, 1323 Club Drive, Vallejo, CA 94592, tel. (707) 562-8794.

Contact: Lassen National Forest, Almanor Ranger District, P.O. Box 767, Chester, CA 96020, tel. (530) 258-2141 or fax (530) 258-5194.

Primary sightings: wild pig

J

JACKSON MEADOWS RESERVOIR, in Nevada County

Directions: From Truckee on Highway 89, drive north about 15 miles. Turn left on Jackson Meadows Road and continue west for 17 miles to the reservoir.

Access/Fees: Access is free.

Maps: A map of Tahoe National Forest is available for a fee from USDA Forest Service, Map Sales, 1323 Club Drive, Vallejo, CA 94592, tel. (707) 562-8794.

Contact: Tahoe National Forest, Sierraville Ranger District, P.O. Box 95, Highway 89, Sierraville, CA 96126, tel. (530) 994-3401 or fax (530) 994-3143.
Primary sightings: dipper, snipe

JENKINSON LAKE/SLY PARK RECREATION AREA, in El Dorado County
Directions: From Pollock Pines on Highway 50, turn south on Sly Park Road and drive 7.5 miles to the park entrance.
Access/Fees: There is a per vehicle, day-use fee.
Maps: A free map is available from the Sly Park Recreation Area at the address below.
Contact: Sly Park Recreation Area, C/O U.S. Bureau of Reclamation, P.O. Box 577, Pollock Pines, CA 95726, tel. (530) 644-2545.
Primary sightings: doves, frogs, osprey

JOE DOMECQ WILDLIFE AREA, in Stanislaus County
Directions: From Modesto on Highway 99, take Highway 132 east and drive about 30 miles. Turn right on Lake Road and drive one-quarter mile. Turn right at Old Basso Bridge into the parking area.
Access/Fees: Access is free. Open year-round, day-use only.
Maps: For a free map, write to Stanislaus County Parks at the address below.
Contact: Stanislaus County Parks, 3800 Cornucopia Way, Suite C, Modesto, CA 95358, tel. (209) 525-4107 or fax (209) 525-6773.
Primary sightings: beaver, deer, quail, salmon

JOHN MUIR WILDERNESS, Sierra National Forest, in Mono County
Note: Thirty of the hundreds of hike-in lakes in the John Muir Wilderness are stocked by the Department of Fish and Game with golden trout (Apollo Lake, Aweetasal Lake, Bearpaw Lake, Beartrap Lake, Big Bear Lake, Bighorn Lake, Black Bear Lake, Brown Bear Lake, Chapel Lake, Claw Lake, Coronet Lake, Den Lake, Hooper Lake, Island Lake, Neil Lake, Upper Nelson Lake, Orchid Lake, Pemmican Lake, Rose Lake, Rosebud Lake, Silver Pass Lake, Spearpoint Lake, Teddy Bear Lake, Three Island Lake, Toe Lake, Tooth Lake, Ursa Lake, Vee Lake, Virginia Lake and White Bear Lake). Other lakes, like Tamarack Lake, are home to golden trout but are not stocked.
Directions: From Fresno, drive east on US 395 or west on Highway 168. Spur roads access trailheads into the wilderness. To reach the Tamarack Lakes: From Lee Vining on US 395, drive about 40 miles south to Tom's Place and the Rock Creek Road turnoff on the right, 15 miles south of the Mammoth Lakes turnoff and 24 miles north of Bishop. Follow Rock Creek Road southwest for 8.5 miles to the east shore of Rock Creek Lake and trailhead parking for Tamarack Lakes, on the left.
Access/Fees: Fishing access is free. A wilderness permit is required for overnight stays and is available in advance for a small fee by mail, phone, or fax. Contact Wilderness Reservations, P.O. Box 430, Big Pine, CA 93513, tel. (888) 374-3773 or fax (760) 938-11137.
Maps: A map of the John Muir Wilderness is available for a fee from USDA Forest Service, Map Sales, 1323 Club Drive, Vallejo, CA 94592, tel. (707) 562-8794.
Contact: Inyo National Forest, White Mountain Ranger District, 798 North Main Street, Bishop, CA 93514, tel. (760) 873-2500 or fax (760) 873-2563; Sierra National

Forest Headquarters, 1600 Tollhouse Road, Clovis, CA 93611-0532, tel. (559) 297-0706 or fax (559) 294-4809.
Primary sightings: golden trout

JOSEPH D. GRANT COUNTY PARK, in Santa Clara County
Directions: From US 101 in San Jose, go south on Interstate 680. Drive to the Alum Rock Avenue East exit, turn right on Mount Hamilton Road, and drive eight miles east to the parking area on the left.
Access/Fees: An small entrance fee is charged daily from April to September and on weekends and holidays the rest of the year, using the honor system. A small, slotted register is posted at the parking area.
Maps: For a free trail map, contact Joseph D. Grant County Park at the address below.
Contact: Joseph D. Grant County Park, 18405 Mount Hamilton Road, San Jose, CA 95140, tel. (408) 274-6121.
Primary sightings: hawks, jay, turkey, wild pig

JOSHUA TREE NATIONAL PARK, in Riverside and San Bernardino Counties
Directions: In Twentynine Palms on Highway 62, turn right on Utah Trail and drive about one-half mile to the visitor center on the right. Continue about three miles on the Utah Trail to the park entrance.
Access/Fees: There is a per vehicle, day-use fee (good for seven days). An annual Joshua Tree pass is available for a fee.
Maps: A free map is available at the visitor center.
Contact: Joshua Tree National Park, 74485 National Park Drive, Twentynine Palms, CA 92277, tel. (760) 367-5500 or fax (760) 367-6392.
Primary sightings: bats, bighorn sheep, bobcat, doves, foxes, horned lizards, quail, rabbits or hares, rattlesnake, tortoise

JUNE LAKE, Inyo National Forest, in Mono County
Directions: From Bishop on US 395 northbound, drive about 54 miles. Take the Highway 158/June Lakes Loop Road exit. Turn left on Highway 158 and drive southwest about three miles to the lake.
Access/Fees: Access is free.
Maps: A map of Inyo National Forest is available for a fee from USDA Forest Service, Map Sales, 1323 Club Drive, Vallejo, CA 94592, tel. (707) 562-8794.
Contact: Inyo National Forest, Headquarters Office, 873 North Main Street, Bishop, CA 93514, tel. (760) 873-2400 or fax (760) 873-2458; Mono Lake Visitor Center, P.O. Box 429, Lee Vining, CA 93541 or fax (760) 647-3046.
Primary sightings: osprey

K

KALMIOPSIS WILDERNESS, in southwest Oregon.
Note: The headwaters of the Chetco and Illinois river give rise to a stunning, lush old-growth interior with plants (such as the Kalmiopsis wildflower) which are not found anywhere else in the world. Access to the wilderness trailheads requires a 4-wheel drive and/or high-clearance vehicle.

Directions: From Redding, drive north on Interstate 5 into Oregon to the last Grants Pass exit. Exit left onto Sixth Street/Highway 99 and drive through Grants Pass. Cross the Rogue River, keeping in the right hand lane. Turn right onto Redwood Highway/Highway 199 and drive 45 miles to Selma. At Selma, turn on Forest Service Road 4103 and drive to a parking lot at the end of the road and the Illinois River Trailhead. Alternate trailheads are available further south off of Highway 199. Just before the town of Kirby, turn right on County Road 5240/Forest Service Road 4201/Eight Dollar Mountain Road which ends at several trailheads (Babyfoot Lake Trail, North Kalmiopsis Rim Trail, South Kalmiopsis Rim Trail).

Maps: A map of the Kalmiopsis Wilderness is available for a fee from the Siskiyou National Forest(se below).

Contact: Siskiyou National Forest, Galice Ranger District, 200 Northeast Greenfield, P.O. Box 440, Grants Pass, OR 97526, tel. (541) 471-6500 or fax (541) 471-6514 or contact the Illinois Valley Ranger District, tel. (541) 592-2166.

Primary sightings: Bigfoot

Kelly Reservoir, in Modoc County

Directions: From Canby, take Modoc County Road 54 and drive southeast about eight miles. Turn south on an unmarked dirt road, pass through a metal gate and drive one-quarter mile. Park at the side of the road and walk 200 feet up the ridge to the reservoir.

Access/Fees: Access is free.

Maps: A free map is available from the address below.

Contact: Bureau of Land Management, Alturas Field Office, 708 West 12th Street, Alturas, CA 96101, tel. (530) 233-4666 or fax (530) 233-5696.

Primary sightings: Canada goose, chukar, golden eagle, gopher snake, sage grouse

Kern National Wildlife Refuge, in Kern County

Directions: From Delano on Highway 99, drive west on Highway 155/Garces Highway 20 miles to the refuge entrance at the end of highway.

Access/Fees: Access is free. Open daily, all seasons.

Maps: There is a free map available at the refuge kiosk.

Contact: Kern National Wildlife Refuge, P.O. Box 670, Delano, CA 93216, tel. (661) 725-2767 or fax (661) 725-6041.

Primary sightings: foxes, hawks, osprey, owls

King Range National Conservation Area, in Humboldt County

Directions: From Garberville on US 101 heading north, take the Redway exit and drive on the frontage road about 200 yards. Turn west (left) on Briceland-Thorne/Shelter Cove Road and drive about 32 miles to the King Range National Conservation Area.

Access/Fees: Access is free.

Maps: A free map is available at the Arcata Field Office at the address below.

Contact: Bureau of Land Management, Arcata Field Office, 1695 Heindon Road, Arcata, CA 95521-4573, tel. (707) 825-2300 or fax (707) 825-2301.

Primary sightings: dolphins, garter snakes, porpoises, raven

Klamath Basin National Wildlife Refuges Complex, in Oregon and Siskiyou County, California

Note: There are six areas making up the Klamath Basin Wildlife Refuges Complex (Lower Klamath, Tule Lake, Clearlake, Bear Valley, Upper Klamath and Klamath Marsh National Wildlife Refuges).

Directions: Bear Valley Viewing Site, Oregon: From Redding on Interstate 5, drive north about 70 miles. At the town of Weed, take the Highway 97 turnoff and drive about 50 miles to Dorris. Continue on Highway 97 about five miles. Turn left (west) on the Keno-Worden Road just south of Worden, in Oregon. Drive a short distance past the railroad crossing and turn left on a dirt road. Continue on this dirt road about half a mile, then park along the shoulder.

Lower Klamath auto tour: From Redding on Interstate 5, drive north about 70 miles. At Weed, take the Highway 97 turnoff and drive northeast about 50 miles through Dorris. Two miles past Dorris, turn right on Highway 161 and drive about six miles to the entrance to the interpretive, auto-tour route (a 10-mile loop). To continue to the visitor center, drive five miles past the auto-tour turnoff on Highway 161 to Hill Road. Turn right and drive four miles to the visitor center on the right.

Contact: Klamath Basin National Wildlife Refuges Complex, Route 1, Box 74, Tule Lake, CA 96134, tel. (530) 667-2231. For current sightings information, check the website: www.klamathnwr.org.

Primary sightings: bald eagle

KLAMATH RIVER, in Humboldt and Siskiyou Counties

Directions: From the town of Orleans on Highway 96, drive northeast, along the Klamath River. Direct river access is available from turnouts and short spur roads along the highway.

Access/Fees: Access is free.

Maps: A map is available for a fee from USDA Forest Service, Map Sales, 1323 Club Drive, Vallejo, CA 94592, tel. (707) 562-8794.

Contact: Six Rivers National Forest, Orleans Ranger District, P.O. Box 410, Orleans, CA 95556, tel. (530) 627-3291 or fax (530) 627-3401.

Primary sightings: steelhead

KYBURZ MARSH, in Sierra County

Directions: From Sierraville on Highway 89, drive south 10 miles. Turn (left) east on Forest Service Road/Henness Pass Road and drive two miles on the gravel road to the parking area.

Access/Fees: Access is free.

Maps: A map is available for a fee from the USDA Forest Service, Map Sales, 1323 Club Drive, Vallejo, CA 94592, tel. (707) 562-8794.

Contact: Tahoe National Forest, Sierraville Ranger District, P.O. Box 95, Sierraville, CA 96126, tel. (530) 994-3401 or fax (530) 994-3143.

Primary sightings: badger, bats, coyote, snipe

L

LAKE ALPINE, Stanislaus National Forest, in Alpine County
Directions: From Markleeville on Highway 4, drive southeast about 36 miles to the lake.
Access/Fees: Access is free.
Maps: A map of Stanislaus National Forest is available for a fee from USDA Forest Service, Map Sales, 1323 Club Drive, Vallejo, CA 94592, tel. (707) 562-8794.
Contact: Stanislaus National Forest, Calaveras Ranger District, P.O. Box 500, Hathaway Pines, CA 95323, tel. (209) 795-1381 or fax (209) 795-6849.
Primary sightings: osprey

LAKE BERRYESSA, in Napa County
Directions: From the town of Napa on Highway 128, drive north about 10 miles. Turn right on Knoxville Road and drive another five miles to the visitor center at the lake.
Access/Fees: Access is free.
Maps: A free map is available at the lake visitor center
Contact: Lake Berryessa, U.S. Bureau of Reclamation, 5520 Knoxville Road, Napa, CA 94558, tel. (707) 966-2111.
Primary sightings: hawks

LAKE CASITAS, in Ventura County
Directions: From the north end of Ventura on US 101, turn north on Highway 33 and drive 12 miles. Turn left (west) on Highway 150 and drive four miles to the lake.
Access/Fees: There is a per vehicle, day-use fee.
Contact: Lake Casitas Recreation Area, 11311 Santa Ana Road, Ventura, CA 93001, tel. (805) 649-2233.
Primary sightings: catfish, largemouth bass

LAKE CASTAIC, in Los Angeles County
Directions: From Los Angeles on Interstate 5, drive north 40 miles. Take the Hughes Road exit and drive to the lake.
Access/Fees: There is a per vehicle, day-use fee on weekends.
Contact: Lake Castaic, P.O. Box 397, Castaic, CA 91310, tel. (661) 257-4050 or fax (661) 257-3759; Lake Castaic Marina, tel. (805) 257-2049.
Primary sightings: catfish, largemouth bass

LAKE DAVIS, Plumas National Forest, in Plumas County
Directions: In Truckee on Highway 89, drive north through Sugarville to Sattley. Turn right on County Road A23 and drive 13 miles. Turn left on Highway 70 and drive one mile, then turn right on Grizzly Road and drive seven miles to an unnamed paved road (look for the sign: "Services, 1 Mile"). Turn left on that road, drive over the Davis Lake Dam to the lake.
Access/Fees: Access is free.
Maps: A map of the Plumas National Forest is available for a fee from the USDA Forest Service, Map Sales, 1323 Club Drive, Vallejo, CA 94592, tel. (707) 562-8794.
Contact: Plumas National Forest, Headquarters Office, P.O. Box 11500, Quincy, CA 95971, tel. (530) 283-2050 or fax (530) 283-4156.
Primary sightings: bats

LAKE EARL WILDLIFE AREA, in Del Norte County
Directions: In Crescent City on US 101, turn north on Northcrest Avenue (which becomes Lake Earl Drive). Turn left on Old Mill Road and drive one mile to the area office. To reach the area entrance, continue on Lake Earl Drive, turning left on Lakeview Road and drive three-quarters of a mile to the parking area.
Access/Fees: Access is free.
Maps: A free map is available from the area office on Old Mill Road.
Contact: Lake Earl Wildlife Area, P.O. Box 1934, Crescent City, CA 95531, tel. (707) 464-2523; Department Fish and Game, Eureka Field Office, 619 Second Street, Eureka, CA 95501, tel. (707) 445-6493 or fax (707) 445-6664.
Primary sightings: Canada goose, river otter, skunks

LAKE HAVASU, in San Bernardino County and Arizona
Directions: From Southern California, take Interstate 10 east to Blythe and turn north on U.S. 95. Continue to Vidal Junction at the intersection of U.S. 95 and Highway 62. Or, take Highway 62 directly east to Vidal Junction. To access the west side of the lake, turn north on U.S. 95 and drive about 28 miles to Havasu Lake Road. Turn east and continue to the lake. To reach the east side of the lake, drive east on Highway 62 to Parker, then turn north on Arizona Highway 95 (the Arizona side) or Parker Dam Road (the California side) and drive to Parker Dam. Continue north on Highway 95 to Lake Havasu City.
Access/Fees: Access is free.
Maps: A visitor guide is available from the Lake Havasu Tourism Bureau.
Contact: Lake Havasu Tourism Bureau, 314 London Bridge Road, Lake Havasu City, AZ 86403, tel. (800) 2-HAVASU (800-242-8278), fax (520) 453-3344.
Primary sightings: catfish, striped bass

LAKE HENSHAW, in San Diego County
Directions: From Escondido, turn north on Interstate 15 and drive about 15 miles to the Highway 76 exit. Turn east and drive 30 miles to the lake entrance on the left.
Access/Fees: Access is free
Contact: Lake Henshaw Resort, 26439 Highway 76, Santa Ysabel, CA 92070, tel. (760) 782-3501; Cleveland National Forest, Palomar Ranger District, 1634 Black Canyon Road, Ramona, CA 92065, tel. (760) 788-0250 or fax (760) 788-6130.
Primary sightings: great blue heron

LAKE IRVINE, in Los Angeles County
Directions: From Los Angeles on Interstate 5 eastbound, take the Highway 91 exit and drive about nine miles east. Turn south on Highway 55 and drive four miles. Turn east on Chapman Avenue (which becomes Santiago Canyon Road) and drive about nine miles to the lake.
Access/Fees: Access is free.
Maps: A topographic map of the Lake Irvine area is available for a fee from Maps, Western Distribution Center, U.S. Geological Survey, Box 25286, Federal Center, Denver, CO 80225, tel. (303) 202-4700.
Contact: Lake Irvine, 4621 Santiago Canyon Road, Silverado, CA 92676, tel. (714) 649-9111.
Primary sightings: catfish

LAKE KAWEAH, in Tulare County
Directions: From Visalia on Highway 198 drive east 20 miles to the lake.
Access/Fees: Access is free.
Maps: A free map/brochure is available from the U.S. Army Corps of Engineers at the address below.
Contact: U.S. Army Corps of Engineers, Lake Kaweah, P.O. Box 44270, Lemon Cove, CA 93244-4270, tel. (559) 597-2301 or fax (559) 597-2468.
Primary sightings: catfish

LAKE MORENA, Cleveland National Forest, in San Diego County
Directions: From San Diego, on Interstate 8, drive east for 53 miles. Turn right on County Road S1 and drive five miles. Turn right on Oak Drive and drive to the lake entrance.
Maps: A free map is available from the San Diego County Parks Department at the address below.
Contact: Lake Morena County Park, tel. (619) 478-5473; San Diego County Parks Department, 5201 Ruffin Road, Suite P, San Diego, CA 92123, tel. (858) 694-3049 (information), tel. (858) 565-3600 (reservations), or fax (858) 495-5841.
Primary sightings: band-tailed pigeon

LAKE RED BLUFF/SALMON VIEWING PLAZA, in Tehama County
Directions: At Red Bluff on Interstate 5, turn east on Highway 36/Antelope Road and drive about one-quarter mile. Turn right on Sale Lane and drive about one mile to the lake. Drive another 1.4 miles to the Salmon Viewing Plaza.
Access/Fees: Access is free.
Maps: A free brochure is available at the visitor center.
Contact: Mendocino National Forest, Grindstone Ranger District, 825 North Humboldt Avenue, Willows, CA 95588, tel. (530) 824-5196 or fax (530) 824-6034.
Primary sightings: salmon, turkey

LAKE SAN ANTONIO, Los Padres National Forest, in Monterey County
Directions: From San Luis Obispo on US 101, drive north about 47 miles. Turn west on County Road G18/Jolon Road to reach the north shore. To reach the south shore, take the 24th Street exit west and continue on County Road G14. Cross the Nacimiento Dam, turn left on Interlake Road and drive 10 miles to the lake.
Access/Fees: A day-use fee is charged.
Maps: A map of Los Padres National Forest is available for a fee from USDA Forest Service, Map Sales, 1323 Club Drive, Vallejo, CA 94592, tel. (707) 562-8794.
Contact: Lake San Antonio, tel. (805) 472-2311 or Los Padres National Forest, Monterey Ranger District, 406 South Mildred Street, King City, CA 93930, tel. (831) 385-5434 or fax (831) 667-2886.
Primary sightings: bald eagle, cedar waxwing, finches, magpie, mockingbird, red-winged blackbird, robin, turkey, wood duck, woodpeckers

LAKE SOLANO COUNTY PARK, in Solano County
Directions: From Vacaville on Highway 80, take the Highway 505 exit and drive north about 13 miles to the town of Winters. Take the Winters off-ramp onto Highway 128, drive over the freeway and through Winters and drive another three miles, turn left on County Road 89 and drive about 200 yards to the park entrance.
Access/Fees: There is a per vehicle, day-use fee.

Maps: A free map is available at the park office.

Contact: Lake Solano County Park, 8685 Pleasants Valley Road, Winters, CA 95694, tel. (530) 795-2990 or fax (530) 795-1408.

Primary sightings: band-tailed pigeon, beaver, deer, foxes, hawks, mink, raccoon, skunks, snipe, turkey, wild pig

LAKE SONOMA, in Sonoma County

Directions: From Healdsburg on US 101 heading north, turn left on Dry Creek Road and drive about 12 miles to the visitor center at the lake.

Access/Fees: Access is free.

Maps: A free map is available at the park visitor center.

Contact: U.S. Army Corps of Engineers, 3333 Skaggs Springs Road, Geyserville, CA 95441, tel. (707) 433-9483 or fax (707) 431-0313.

Primary sightings: catfish, wild pig

LAKE SONOMA RECREATION AREA, in Sonoma County

Directions: From Santa Rosa, drive north on U.S. 101 to Healdsburg. In Healdsburg, take the Dry Creek Road exit, turn left, and drive northwest for 11 miles. After crossing a small bridge, the visitor center will be on your right.

Access/Free: Access is free.

Maps: A visitor guide is available from the U.S. Army Corps of Engineers.

Contact: U.S. Army Corps of Engineers, 3333 Skaggs Springs Road, Geyserville, CA 95441, tel. (707) 433-9483, ext. 27, fax (707) 431-0313.

Primary sightings: largemouth bass, deer, squirrels, wild pig

LAKE TAHOE VISITOR CENTER AT TAYLOR CREEK, in El Dorado County

Directions: From South Lake Tahoe and the junction of highways 50 and 89, take Highway 89 north about 3.5 miles to the Lake Tahoe Visitor Center at Taylor Creek.

Access/Fees: Access is free.

Maps: A map of the Lake Tahoe area is available for a fee from the visitor center.

Contact: Lake Tahoe Basin Management Unit, 870 Emerald Bay Road, South Lake Tahoe, CA 96150, tel. (530) 573-2600 or fax (530) 573-2693.

Primary sightings: osprey

LAS GALLINAS WILDLIFE PONDS, in Marin County

Directions: From San Rafael on US 101 northbound, take the Smith Ranch Road exit. Turn east and drive one-half mile, cross the railroad tracks and turn left again, just before the

McInnis Park entrance. Drive one-half mile on the road around the treatment plant and park by the bridge.

Access/Fees: Access is free.

Maps: A free map/brochure is available from the main office at the address below.

Contact: Las Gallinas Valley Sanitary District, 300 Smith Ranch Road, San Rafael, CA 94903, tel. (415) 472-1734 or fax (415) 499-7715.

Primary sightings: killdeer

LASSEN VOLCANIC NATIONAL PARK, in Lassen County

Directions: From Red Bluff on Highway 36, drive east about 49 miles to the southwest entrance. From Redding on Interstate 5, take Highway 44 and drive east about 48 miles to the northwest entrance at Manzanita Lake.

Access/Fees: There is a per vehicle, day-use fee (good for seven days).

Maps: A free map is available at the entrance stations.

Contact: Lassen Volcanic National Park, P.O. Box 100, Mineral, CA 96063, tel. (530) 595-4444, website: www.nps.gov/lavo/

Primary sightings: black bear, Canada goose, dipper, fisher, foxes, marmot, pine marten, raven, squirrels

LAUREL PONDS, in Mono County

Directions: From Bishop on Highway 395, take the Convict Lake exit. Turn south and drive less than one-quarter mile. Turn right on Forest Service Road 4S31, a dirt road, and continue two miles to the ponds.

Access/Fees: Access is free.

Maps: A map of Inyo National Forest is available for a fee from USDA Forest Service, Map Sales, 1323 Club Drive, Vallejo, CA 94592, tel. (707) 562-8794.

Contact: Inyo National Forest, Mammoth Lakes Ranger Station, P.O. Box 148, Mammoth Lakes, CA 93546, tel. (760) 924-5500 or fax (760) 924-5537.

Primary sightings: chukar, golden eagle, sage grouse

LAVA BEDS NATIONAL MONUMENT, in Siskiyou County

Directions: From Redding on Interstate 5, drive east on Highway 299 about 133 miles. At the town of Canby, turn north on Highway 139 and drive 20 miles. Turn west on Lava Beds National Monument Road and follow signs to the entrance. Drive another 3.5 miles to the visitor center.

Access/Fees: There is an entrance fee.

Maps: A free trail map is available at the visitor center.

Contact: Lava Beds National Monument, P.O. Box 867, Tulelake, CA 96134, tel. (530) 667-2282 or fax (530) 667-2737.

Primary sightings: osprey, owls, raven

LEWISTON LAKE/TRINITY RIVER HATCHERY, in Trinity County

Directions: From Redding on Highway 299, drive west about 37 miles. Take the Trinity Dam/Lewiston Lake exit and drive north on County Road 105 about 5.5 miles. At the junction, continue on Trinity Dam Boulevard to the lake, or bear right on Deadwood Road to reach the hatchery.

Access/Fees: Access is free.

Maps: A map of Shasta-Trinity National Forest is available for a fee from USDA Forest Service, Map Sales, 1323 Club Drive, Vallejo, CA 94592, tel. (707) 562-8794.

Contact: Shasta-Trinity Naitonal Forest, Weaverville Ranger Station, P.O. Box 1190, Weaverville, CA 96093, tel. (530) 623-2121 or fax (530) 623-6010.
Primary sightings: dipper, raccoon, river otter, wood duck

LITTLE PANOCHE WILDLIFE AREA, south of Los Banos in Fresno County
Directions: From Los Banos on Highway 165, drive south about seven miles. Turn south on Interstate 5 about 25 miles. Take the Shields/Little Panoche Road exit. Turn right and drive west on little Panoche Road about seven miles to the parking lot.
Access/Fees: Access is free.
Maps: A free map is available from the Department of Fish and Game at the address below.
Contact: Department of Fish and Game, Los Banos Wildlife Area, 18110 West Henry Miller Avenue, Los Banos, 93635, tel. (209) 826-0463 or fax 826-1761.
Primary sightings: chukar, osprey, roadrunner, Western meadowlark

LIVING DESERT, in Riverside County
Directions: From Interstate 10 west of Palm Springs, drive east on Highway 111 about 15 miles. Turn right on Highway 74 and drive two miles. Turn left on Haystack Road and drive 1.5 miles. Turn right on Portola Road and look for the parking area on the left.
Access/Fees: There is an entrance fee.
Maps: A free map is available at the admissions booth.
Contact: Living Desert, 47-900 Portola Avenue, Palm Desert, CA 92260, tel. (760) 346-5694 or fax (760) 568-9685.
Primary sightings: pronghorn antelope, badger, bighorn sheep, coyote, deer, horned lizards, rattlesnake, tortoise

LOON LAKE/CRYSTAL BASIN RECREATION AREA, in El Dorado County
Directions: From Pollock Pines on Highway 50, drive east eight miles. Turn north on Ice House Road and drive 30 miles to Loon Lake in the Crystal Basin Recreation Area. To reach the El Dorado National Forest Information Center, from Pollock Pines on Highway 50, drive west about three miles. Turn left on Camino Heights Drive and continue to the center at 3070 Camino Heights Drive.
Access/Fees: Access is free.
Maps: A free map of the Crystal Basin Recreation Area is available at the information center on Camino Heights Drive. A map of the El Dorado National Forest is available for a fee from USDA Forest Service, Map Sales, 1323 Club Drive, Vallejo, CA 94592, tel. (707) 562-8794.
Contact: El Dorado National Forest, Pacific Ranger Station, 7887 Highway 50, Pollock Pines, CA 95726, tel. (530) 644-2349 or fax (530) 647-5405. El Dorado National Forest, Information Center, 3070 Camino Heights Drive, Camino, 95709, tel. (530) 644-6048 or fax (530) 295-5624.
Primary sightings: blue grouse, Canada goose, chipmunk, golden eagle, woodpeckers

LOPEZ LAKE, in San Luis Obispo County
Directions: From Arroyo Grande on Highway 101, take the Grand Avenue/Lopez Drive exit and drive east about 11 miles to the park entrance.

Access/Fees: There is a per vehicle, day-use fee.

Maps: A free map is available at the entrance kiosk.

Contact: Lopez Lake, C/O San Luis Obispo County, 6800 Lopez Drive, Arroyo Grande, CA 93420, tel. (805) 489-1122 or fax (805) 473-7181.

Primary sightings: bobcat, brown pelican, deer, foxes, rabbits or hares, turkey

LOS ANGELES DEEP SEA, offshore from Los Angeles County

Directions: There are four harbors providing deep sea access (San Pedro, Long Beach, Newport, and Dana Point). To access San Pedro Harbor: In San Pedro on Interstate 110/Harbor Freeway southbound, turn left on Gaffey Street, then left on 22nd Avenue and drive to the harbor. To access Long Beach Harbor: In Long Beach on Interstate 405 southbound, take the Seal Beach Boulevard exit. Turn west and drive to the end of the pier. To access Newport Harbor: In Newport Beach on Highway 55/Newport Boulevard southbound, drive to the end of Newport Boulevard at the foot of Newport Pier. Turn left and drive about 1.5 miles. Turn right on Palm Drive and continue to Newport Landing Sportfishing at 309 Palm Street, Suite F. To access Dana Point Harbor: From San Juan Capistrano on Interstate 5 southbound, take the Pacific Coast Highway North and drive to the second traffic light. Turn left on Dana Point Harbor Drive and continue to the harbor.

Access/Fees: For partyboat schedules and fees, contact the sportfishing operations. At San Pedro: L.A. Sportfishing, tel. (310) 547-9916 or 22nd Street Landing, tel. (310) 832-8304. At Long Beach: Seal Beach Pier Sportfishing, tel. (562) 598-8677 or Long Beach Sportfishing, tel. (562) 432-8993. At Newport: Newport Landing, tel. (949) 675-0550 or Davey's Locker, tel. (949) 673-1434. At Dana Point: Dana Wharf Sportfishing, tel. (949) 496-5794.

Maps: Free maps of the Los Angeles area are available from the chambers and visitor bureaus below.

Contact: San Pedro Chamber of Commerce, 390 West Seventh Street, San Pedro, CA 90731, tel. (310) 832-7272 or fax (310) 832-0685; Long Beach Area Convention and Visitor Bureau, 1 World Trade Center, Suite 300, Long Beach, CA 90831, tel. (562) 436-3645 or (800) 452-7829 or fax (562) 435-5653; Newport Beach Visitors Bureau, 3300 West Coast Highway, Newport Beach, CA 92663, tel. (949) 722-1611 or fax (949) 722-1612; Dana Point Chamber of Commerce, P.O. Box 12, Dana Point, CA 92629, tel. (949) 496-1555 or fax (949) 496- 5321.

Primary sightings: marlin, swordfish

LOS BANOS STATE WILDLIFE AREA, in Fresno County

Directions: From Los Banos on Highway 165, drive north about three miles. Turn east on Henry Miller Avenue, and drive one mile to the area entrance on the left.

Access/Fees: There is an entrance fee in the absence of a hunting, fishing, or trapping license, or wildlands pass. Open to the public from late January through mid-September.

Maps: For a free map, write to the address below.

Contact: Los Banos State Wildlife Area, 18110 West Henry Miller Avenue, Los Banos, CA 93635, tel. (209) 826-0463 or fax (209) 826-1761.

Primary sightings: frogs, owls

Lower Klamath National Wildlife Refuge, in Siskiyou County

Directions: From Redding on Interstate 5, drive north about 70 miles. At Weed, take the Highway 97 turnoff and drive northeast about 50 miles through Dorris. Two miles past Dorris, turn right on Highway 161 and drive about 10 miles. Turn right on Hill Road and drive four miles to the visitor center on the right.

Contact: Klamath Basin National Wildlife Refuges Complex, Route 1, Box 74, Tule Lake, CA 96134, tel. (530) 667-2231. For current sightings information, check the website: www .klamathnwr.org.

Primary sightings: pronghorn antelope, catfish, gulls, killdeer

Lower Otay Lake, in San Diego County

Directions: From San Diego, drive south on Interstate 805 to Chula Vista. Turn east on Telegraph Canyon Road and drive five miles. Turn right on Otay Lake Road and drive two miles east, then turn south on Wueste Road. The boat ramp is located off of Wueste Road on the west shore.

Access/Fees: The lake is open Wednesday, Saturday and Sunday from January through mid-October. There is a boat-launching and a fishing fee.

Contact: San Diego Water Utilities, Lake Department, 12375 Morena Avenue, Lakeside, CA 92040-1135, tel. (619) 668-2050 or fax (619) 443-7681.

Primary sightings: catfish, coyote, largemouth bass

M

Madeline Plains, in Modoc and Lassen Counties

Directions: From Likely on Highway 395, drive south through the Madeline Plains about 20 miles along the route from the town of Madeline.

Access/Fees: Access is free.

Maps: A free map is available from the Bureau of Land Management at the address below.

Contact: Bureau of Land Management, Alturas Resource Area, 708 West 12th Street, Alturas, CA 96101, tel. (530) 233-4666 or fax (530) 233-5696.

Primary sightings: pronghorn antelope

Malibu Creek State Park, in Los Angeles County

Directions: From Calabasas on US 101 westbound, take the Las Virgenes/Malibu Canyon Road exit and drive south on Las Virgenes Road about three miles to the park entrance.

Access/Fees: There is a per vehicle, day-use fee.

Maps: A map is available for a fee from the entrance kiosk.

Contact: Malibu Creek State Park, 1925 Los Virgenes Road, Calabasas, CA 91302, tel. (818) 880-0350.

Primary sightings: coyote, foxes, kingfisher, raccoon

MARBLE MOUNTAIN WILDERNESS, Klamath National Forest, in Siskiyou County

Directions: From Interstate 5 at Yreka, drive north about eight miles. Turn west on Highway 96/Klamath River Road and drive 65 miles to the town of Happy Camp. A visitor center is located on the left side at 63822 Highway 96. To continue to the wilderness, turn south on Elk Creek Road and drive 16 miles to Norcross campground. Several popular trailheads into the wilderness begin here (Ukonum Lake, Kelsey Trail, Granite Lakes Trails).

Access/Fees: Access is free.

Maps: A trail information sheet is available for a fee from the Happy Camp Ranger Station at the address below. A map is also available for a fee from the USDA Forest Service, Map Sales, 1323 Club Drive Vallejo, CA 94592, tel. (707) 562-8794.

Contact: Klamath National Forest, Happy Camp Ranger District, P.O. Box 377, Happy Camp, CA 96039-0377, tel. (530) 493-2243 or fax (530) 493-2212.

Primary sightings: fisher, squirrels

MARTINEZ REGIONAL SHORELINE, in Contra Costa County

Directions: In Martinez on Highway 680, take the Marina Vista exit. Turn left on Marina Avenue and drive west about 1.5 miles. Turn left on Ferry Street and drive about one-half mile north into the park.

Access/Fees: Access is free.

Maps: A free map is available at the entrance kiosk.

Contact: Martinez Regional Shoreline, P.O. Box 707, Martinez, CA 94553, tel. (925) 228-0112; East Bay Regional Parks District, tel. (510) 228-0112.

Primary sightings: curlew, Western meadowlark

MARTIS CREEK LAKE, in Nevada County

Directions: In Truckee on Highway 80, take the Central Truckee exit. Turn southwest on Highway 267, toward Kings Beach and drive three miles to the Martis Creek Lake turnoff. Turn left and drive about 2.5 miles to the lake.

Access/Fees: Access is free. Open May through October, weather permitting.

Maps: A free map/brochure is available from the Englebright office at the address below.

Contact: U.S. Army Corps of Engineers, Englebright Lake, P.O. Box 6, Smartville, CA 95977, tel. (530) 639-2342, website: www.spk.usace.army.mil/cespk-co/lakes/englebright.html.

Primary sightings: raccoon

MATTOLE RECREATION SITE, in Humboldt County

Directions: From Garberville on US 101, drive north about 25 miles. Take the South Fork/Honeydew exit. Turn left on Bull Creek and drive 22 miles. At the town of Honeydew, turn north on Mattole Road and drive 13.5 miles. Before crossing the river, turn west on Lighthouse Road and drive five miles to the parking area.

Access/Fees: Access is free.

Maps: A free map is available from the Arcata Field Office at the address below.

Contact: Bureau of Land Management, Arcata Field Office, 1695 Heindon Road, Arcata, CA 95521, tel. (707) 825-2300 or fax (707) 825-2301.

Primary sightings: killdeer, sea lions

MATTOLE RIVER, in Humboldt County

Directions: From the town of Honeydew, drive west on Mattole Road to Petrolia. The river parallels Mattole Road.

Access/Fees: Access is free.

Maps: A topographic map of the Mattole River area is available for a fee from Maps, Western Distribution Center, U.S. Geological Survey, Box 25286, Federal Center, Denver, CO 80225, tel. (303) 202-4700.

Contact: Bureau of Land Management, Arcata Field Office, 1695 Heindon Road, Arcata, CA 95521, tel. (707) 825-2300 or fax (707) 825-2301.

Primary sightings: steelhead

MCARTHUR-BURNEY FALLS STATE PARK, in Shasta County

Directions: From Redding on Highway 299, drive east six miles past Burney. Turn north on Highway 89 and drive six miles to the park entrance.

Access/Fees: There is a per vehicle, day-use fee.

Maps: A trail map is available for a fee at the entrance station.

Contact: McArthur-Burney Falls Memorial State Park, 24898 Highway 89, Burney, CA 96013, tel. (530) 335-2777.

Primary sightings: kingfisher, raven, woodpeckers

MCCLOUD RIVER PRESERVE, in Siskiyou County

Directions: From Redding on Interstate 5, drive north toward Mount Shasta City. Turn east on Highway 89 and drive 17 miles to the town of McCloud. Turn right on Squaw Valley Road and drive 10 miles to Lake McCloud. Turn right and take the dirt road along the right side of the lake. At Battle Creek, turn right at the signed turnoff for Ah-Di-Na Campground.

Access/Fees: Access is free.

Maps: A map of Shasta-Trinity National Forest is available for a fee from USDA Forest Service, Map Sales, 1323 Club Drive, Vallejo, CA 94592, tel. (707) 562-8794.

Contact: Shasta-Trinity National Forest, McCloud Ranger Station, P.O. Box 1620, McCloud, CA 96057, tel. (530) 964-2184 or fax (530) 964-2938.

Primary sightings: kingfisher, mink, river otter

MCGRATH STATE BEACH, in Ventura County

Directions: In Ventura on Highway 101, take the Seaward exit. Turn left, and almost immediately, left again onto Harbor Boulevard and drive four miles, past Ventura Harbor and across the Santa Clara River, to the beach entrance on the right.

Access/Fees: There is a per vehicle, day-use fee.

Maps: A free map is available at the entrance kiosk.

Contact: McGrath State Beach, 901 South San Pedro Street, Ventura, CA 93001, tel. (805) 654-4744; California State Parks, Ventura Sector, tel. (805) 648-4127.

Primary sightings: gulls

MENDOTA STATE WILDLIFE AREA, in Fresno County

Directions: From Fresno on Highway 180, drive west about 30 miles. Turn left into the signed entrance to the wildlife area.

Access/Fees: Access is free during the months of February through August. Area is closed from September through January for waterfowl hunting only.

Maps: A free map is available from the Mendota State Wildlife Area at the address below.

Contact: Mendota State Wildlife Area, P.O. Box 37, Mendota, CA 93640, tel. (559) 655-4645 or fax (559) 655-1517.

Primary sightings: osprey, owls

MERCED NATIONAL WILDLLIFE REFUGE, in Merced County

Note: There are two, self-guided auto-tours available; one of which is routed around the tule elk and another around waterfowl.

Directions: From Merced on Highway 59, drive about eight miles. Turn west on Sandy Mush Road and drive about eight miles to the main gate at the refuge.

Access/Fees: Access is free.

Maps: A free map is available at the main gate.

Contact: Merced National Wildlife Refuge, C/O San Luis National Wildlife Complex, P.O. Box 2176, Los Banjos, CA 93635, tel. (209) 826-3508 or fax (209) 826-1445.

Primary sightings: coyote, curlew, great blue heron, pheasant, sandhill crane

MIDDLE FALLS, McCloud River Loop, in Siskiyou County

Directions: From Redding on Interstate 5, drive north to the town of Mount Shasta. Turn east on Highway 89 and drive 17 miles past the town of McCloud, turn right on the Fowler's Camp access road/Forest Service Road 39N28, and follow the signs to the parking lot at Lower Falls. The trail to Middle Falls follows along the left side of the river.

Contact: Shasta-Trinity National Forest, McCloud Ranger Station, P.O. Box 1620, McCloud, CA 96057, tel. (530) 964-2184 or fax (530) 964-2938.

Primary sightings: chukar, cedar waxwing, dipper, finches, magpie, mockingbird, red-winged blackbird, robin

MILLERTON LAKE STATE RECREATION AREA, in Fresno County

Directions: In Madera on Highway 99, take Highway 145 eastbound and drive 22 miles to the lake.

Access/Fees: There is a per vehicle, day-use fee.

Maps: A free map is available at the entrance kiosk.

Contact: Millerton Lake State Recreation Area, P.O. Box 205, Friant, CA 93626, tel. (559) 822-2332 or fax (559) 822-2319.

Primary sightings: bobcat, Canada goose

MODOC NATIONAL WILDLIFE REFUGE, in Modoc County

Directions: From Alturas on U.S. 395, turn east on County Road 56 and drive a half mile to County Road 115. Turn south and drive one mile to the refuge entrance (well signed).

Access/Fees: Access is free.

Maps: A free map is available at the refuge office.

Contact: Modoc National Wildlife Refuge, P.O. Box 1610, Alturas, CA 96101, tel. (530) 233-3572 or fax (530) 233-4143.

Primary sightings: chukar, pronghorn antelope, osprey, owls, rabbits or hares, sandhill crane, skunks, swans

MOJAVE NATIONAL PRESERVE, in San Bernardino County
Directions: From Barstow on Interstate 15, drive north about 61 miles. In Baker, take the Baker Boulevard exit, and drive east about one mile to the visitor center.

Access/Fees: Access is free.

Maps: A free map is available at the visitor center.

Contact: Mojave Desert Information Center, P.O. Box 241, Baker, CA 92309, tel. (760) 733-4040, website: www.nps.gov/moja/; Mojave National Preserve, 222 East Main Street, Suite 202, Barstow, CA 92311, tel. (760) 255-8801.

Primary sightings: bighorn sheep, raven, tortoise

MONO LAKE, Inyo National Forest, in Mono County
Directions: From Lee Vining, take Highway 395 north about one-quarter mile to the visitor center.

Access/Fees: Access is free to private passenger vehicles.

Maps: A free map is available from the visitor center. A map of Inyo National Forest is available for a fee from USDA Forest Service, Map Sales, 1323 Club Drive, Vallejo, CA 94592, tel. (707) 562-8794.

Contact: Mono Lake Scenic Area Visitor Center, P.O. Box 429, Lee Vining, CA 93541, tel. (760) 647-3044 or fax (760) 647-3046.

Primary sightings: coyote, gulls, killdeer, rabbits or hares

MONTANA DE ORO STATE PARK, in San Luis Obispo County
Directions: From San Luis Obispo on Highway 1, take the Baywood exit. Turn left on South Bay Boulevard and drive south about seven miles. Tun right on Los Osos Valley Road and drive about five miles to the park entrance. Continue five miles on Los Osos Valley Road to the visitor center.

Access/Fees: Access is free.

Maps: A free map is available at the visitor center.

Contact: Montana de Oro State Park, Pecho Valley Road, Los Osos, CA 93402, tel. (805) 528-0513.

Primary sightings: bobcat, coyote, dolphins, mountain lion, porpoises, raccoon, sea lions

MONTEREY BAY, from Moss Landing to Fort Ord, in Monterey County
Directions: In Monterey on Highway 1, take the Pacific Grove/Del Monte exit and drive one mile. Turn right on Figuaro Street and drive west to Wharf No. 1. Boat ramps are located at the wharf and at the Coast Guard Headquarters.

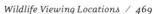

Access/Fees: Salmon are migrating through Monterey Bay in March and April. For current party boat fees and schedules, contact Monterey Sportfishing, tel. (831) 372-2203; Sam's Sportfishing, tel. (831) 372-0577; Randy's Sportfishing, tel. (831) 372-7440, or Chris' Sportfishing, tel. (831) 375-5951.

Maps: A free visitor guide/map is available from the Monterey Peninsula Chamber of Commerce at the address below.

Contact: Monterey Peninsula Chamber of Commerce, 5 Custom House Plaza, Monterey, CA 93940, tel. (831) 649-1770 or fax (831) 648-5373.

Primary sightings: brown pelican, salmon

MONTEREY BAY DEEP SEA, offshore from Monterey County

Directions: In Monterey on Highway 1 southbound, take the Pacific Grove/Del Monte Avenue exit and drive about one mile. Turn right on Figuaro Street and drive west to Wharf No. 1. Boat ramps are located at the wharf and at the Coast Guard Headquarters.

Access/Fees: For partyboat schedules and fees, contact Chris' Sportfishing, tel. (831) 375-5951; Randy's Sportfishing, tel. (831) 372-7440; Sam's Sportfishing, tel. (831) 372-0577; Monterey Sportfishing, tel. (831) 372-2203.

Maps: A free map/brochure of the Monterey Bay area is available from the Monterey Peninsula Chamber of Commerce at the address below.

Contact: Monterey Peninsula Chamber of Commerce, 5 Custom House Plaza, Monterey, CA 93940, tel. (831) 649-1770 or fax (831) 648-5373.

Primary sightings: swordfish

MORRO BAY DEEP SEA, offshore from San Luis Obispo

Directions: In Morro Bay on Highway 1 northbound, take the Main Street exit and turn right. Continue up the grade, under the freeway. Turn right on Beach Street, then right on the Embarcadero and continue to the bay.

Access/Fees: For party boat schedules and fees, contact Virg's Landing, tel. (805) 772-1222.

Maps: A free map/brochure of the Morro Bay area is available from the chamber of commerce at the address below.

Contact: Morro Bay Chamber of Commerce, 880 Main Street, Morro Bay, CA 93442, tel. (805) 772-4467 or fax (805) 772-6038.

Primary sightings: whale watching

MORRO BAY STATE PARK, in San Luis Obispo County

Directions: From San Luis Obispo on Highway 1 northbound, drive about 11.5 miles and take the Los Osos/Baywood Park exit in Morro Bay. Turn left on South Bay Boulevard and drive about 1.5 miles to the park. To reach the Museum of Natural History continue about one-half mile past the park on South Bay Boulevard.

Access/Fees: Access is free.

Maps: A free map is available at the musem, tel. (805) 772-2694.

Contact: Morro Bay State Park, State Park Road, Morro Bay, CA 93442, tel. (805) 772-7434 or fax (805) 772-5760; California State Parks, San Luis Obispo District, 3220 South Higuera Street, Suite 311, San Luis Obispo, CA 93401, tel. (805) 549-3312 or fax (805) 541-4799.

Primary sightings: ducks, falcon, killdeer, raccoon, sea lions, sea otter

MOUNT DIABLO STATE PARK, in Contra Costa County

Directions: From Interstate 680 in Danville, take the Diablo Road exit and drive east for three miles. Turn left on Mount Diablo Scenic Boulevard, which will take you right into the park.

Access/Fees: There is a day-use fee per vehicle.

Maps: Maps are available for a fee from the address below.

Contact: Mount Diablo State Park, 96 Mitchell Canyon Road, Clayton, CA 94517, tel. (925) 837-2525 or state park district headquarters, tel. (925) 673-2891.

Primary sightings: bobcat, coyote, deer, hawks, mountain lion, rabbits or hares, raccoon

MOUNT PINOS OBSERVATION POINT, in Ventura County

Directions: From Frazier Park on Interstate 5, take the Mount Pinos Recreation Area exit and drive west on Frazier Mountain Road/Cuddy Valley Road 20 miles to the parking area.

Access/Fees: There is a per vehicle, day-use fee.

Maps: A map is available for a fee from USDA Forest Service, Map Sales, 1323 Club Drive, Vallejo, CA 94592, tel. (707) 562-8794.

Contact: Los Padres National Forest, Mount Pinos Ranger District, 34580 Lockwood Valley Road, Frazier Park, CA 93225, tel. (661) 245-3731 or fax (661) 245-1526.

Primary sightings: band-tailed pigeon, California condor, quail

MOUNT SAN JACINTO STATE PARK AND STATE WILDERNESS, in Riverside County

Directions: From Palm Desert on Highway 111, take the Highway 74 exit and drive about 25 miles. Bear right on Highway 243 and drive about five miles to the park entrance. Continue less than one mile past the park entrance to the Deer Springs Trailhead, the Riverside County Nature Center, and access to the wilderness. To access the aerial tramway: From Palm Springs on Highway 111, take the Chino Canyon/Aerial Tramway Road exit. Turn west and drive 3.5 miles to the tram parking lot.

Access/Fees: There is a per vehicle, day-use fee.

Maps: A free map is available at the park.

Contact: Mount San Jacinto State Park, P.O. Box 308, Idyllwild, CA 92549, tel. (909) 659-2607 or fax (909) 659-4769; California State Parks, California Desert District, 6221 Box Springs Boulevard, Riverside, CA 92507, tel. (909) 696-5200 or fax (909) 697-5299.

Primary sightings: bats, bobcat, coyote, golden eagle, jays, mountain lion, raccoon, woodpeckers

MOUNT TAMALPAIS STATE PARK, in Marin County

Directions: In Marin County on Highway 101, take the Highway 1 exit and drive west about two miles. Turn right on Panoramic Highway and drive five miles to park headquarters at Pantoll Camp.

Access/Fees: Access is free.

Maps: A map is available for a fee from the park at the address below.

Contact: Mount Tamalpais State Park, 801 Panoramic Highway, Mill Valley, CA 94941, tel. (415) 388-2070 or fax (415) 388-2968.

Primary sightings: deer, foxes, jays, mountain lion, raccoon, raven

MUIR WILDERNESS, Sierra National Forest, in Mono County
See **John Muir Wilderness.**

N

NAPA RIVER ECOLOGICAL RESERVE, in Napa County
Directions: North of Yountville on Highway 29, turn east on Oakville Cross Road and
drive 2.5 miles. Turn right on Silverado Trail and drive 2.3 miles. Turn right on
Yountville Cross Road and drive about one mile to the reserve parking area.
Access/Fees: Access is free.
Maps: A free map is available from the Department of Fish and Game at the address
below.
Contact: Department of Fish and Game, P.O. Box 47, Napa, CA 94558, tel. (707) 944-
5500 or fax (707) 944-5563.
Primary sightings: mink, opossum, raccoon, skunks

NAVARRO RIVER, in Mendocino County
Directions: From Mendocino on Highway 1 southbound, drive 10 miles. turn left
on Highway 128 and drive east, paralleling the lower river.
Access/Fees: Access is free.
Maps: A topographical map of the Navarro River area is available for a fee from Maps,
Western Distribution Center, U.S. Geological Survey, Box 25286, Federal Center,
Denver, CO 80225, tel. (303) 202-4700.
Contact: Fort Bragg-Mendocino Chamber of Commerce, P.O. Box 1141, Fort Bragg,
CA 95437, tel. (707) 961-6300 or fax (707) 964-2056.
Primary sightings: steelhead

NEW HOGAN LAKE, in Calaveras County
Directions: From Valley Springs on Highway 26, drive south about one-half mile.
Turn left on Hogan Dam Road and drive about two miles to the park headquarters.
Access/Fees: Access is free.
Maps: A free map is available from New Hogan Lake office at the address below.
Contact: U.S. Army Corps of Engineers, New Hogan Lake Office, 2713 Hogan Dam
Road, Valley Springs, CA 95252, tel. (209) 772-1343 or fax (209) 772-9352.
Primary sightings: coyote, deer, rabbits or hares, cedar waxwing, finches, magpie,
mockingbird, red-winged blackbird, robin, striped bass, Western meadowlark
NEW MELONES LAKE RECREATION AREA, in Tuolumne County
Directions: From Sonora on Highway 49, drive north to Tuttletown. Turn left on
Reynolds Ferry Road and drive to the lake.
Access/Fees: Access is free.
Maps: A free map is available from the U.S. Bureau of Reclamation office at the
recreation area.
Contact: New Melones Lake Recreation Area, U.S. Bureau of Reclamation, 6850
Studhorse Flat Road, Sonora, CA 95370, tel. (209) 536-9094 or fax (209) 536-9652.
Primary sightings: tarantulas

NIMBUS/AMERICAN RIVER HATCHERIES, in Sacramento County
Directions: From Sacramento on Highway 50, take the Hazel Avenue exit. Turn left, cross over the freeway, turn left on Gold Country Boulevard, then immediately right into the hatcheries.
Access/Fees: Access is free.
Maps: A free brochure/map is available at the visitor center.
Contact: Department of Fish and Game, 2001 Nimbus Road, Rancho Cordova, CA 95670, tel. (916) 358-2820 or fax (916) 358-1466.
Primary sightings: steelhead

O

OCEANSIDE DEEP SEA, offshore from San Diego County
Directions: In Oceanside on Interstate 5, take the Oceanside/Harbor Drive exit. Turn west and continue to the harbor.
Access/Fees: For schedules and partyboat fees contact Helgren's Sportfishing, tel. (760) 722-2133 or Pacific Coast Bait and Tackle, tel. (760) 439-3474.
Contact: Oceanside Chamber of Commerce, 928 North Coast Highway, Oceanside, CA 92054-2136, tel. (760) 722-1534 or (760) 722-8336.
Primary sightings: marlin, yellowtail

ONION VALLEY CAMPGROUND, Inyo National Forest, in Inyo County
Directions: From US 395 in the town of Independence in Inyo County, turn west on Onion Valley Road and drive 15 miles to the campground at the road's end.
Access/Fees: Parking is free; there is a camping fee for overnighters.
Maps: A map of Inyo National Forest is available for a fee from USDA Forest Service, Map Sales, 1323 Club Drive, Vallejo, CA 94592, tel. (707) 562-8794.
Contact: Inyo National Forest, Mt. Whitney Ranger District, P.O. Box 8, Lone Pine, CA 93545, tel. (760) 876-6200 or fax (760) 876-6202.
Primary sightings: black bear

OROVILLE WILDLIFE AREA, in Butte County
Directions: From Oroville on Oro Dam Boulevard, drive west about one-third mile to the wildlife area headquarters.
Access/Fees: Access is free.
Maps: A free map is available at the area headquarters.
Contact: Oroville Wildlife Area, 945 Oro Dam West, Oroville, CA 95965, tel. (530) 538-2236. You can also contact the Department of Fish and Game, 2001 Nimbus Road, Rancho Cordova, CA 95670, tel. (916) 358-2900 or fax (916) 358-2912.
Primary sightings: beaver, Canada goose, opossum, racoon, river otter, cedar waxwing, finches, magpie, mockingbird, red-winged blackbird, robin, Western meadowlark

OWENS VALLEY, Tinemaha Reservoir, in Inyo County
Directions: From Los Angeles, drive north on Highway 14 through Lancaster, Palmdale, Mojave and Bishop. At the town of Inyokern, Highway 14 joins with Highway 395. Continue north on Highway 395 to Poverty Hills. Between Big Pine and Independence, Highway 395 becomes two lanes with a pull-off area for wildlife viewing.

Contact: Department of Water and Power, City of Los Angeles, 300 Mandich Street, Bishop, CA 93514, tel. (760) 872-1104.

Contact: Inyo National Forest, Mount Whitney Ranger Station, tel. (760) 876- 6200 or fax (760) 876-6202.

Primary sightings: elk

P

PACIFICA PIER, in San Mateo County

Directions: In Pacifica on Highway 1, exit at Paloma Avenue and drive west. Paloma Avenue becomes Beach Boulevard. Look for the pier to the right off of Beach Boulevard.

Access/Fees: Access is free.

Maps: A free map/brochure is available from the Pacifica Chamber of Commerce at the address below.

Contact: Pacifica Pier, 2100 Beach Boulevard, Pacifica, CA 94044, tel. (650) 355-0690; Pacifica Chamber of Commerce, 225 Rockaway Beach, Suite 1, Pacifica, CA 94044, tel. (650) 355-4122 or fax (650) 355-6949; Coastside No. 2 Bait and Tackle, tel. (650) 359-9790.

Primary sightings: anchovy, striped bass

PACKERS BAY, Shasta-Trinity National Forest, in Shasta County

See Shasta Lake/Packers Bay, Shasta-Trinity National Forest.

PALM TO PINES SCENIC BYWAY TOUR, in Riverside County

Directions: From Banning on Interstate 10, take Highway 243 and drive south about 25 miles to the town of Idyllwild, Continue south three miles to the junction of Highway 243 and 74 at the town of Mountain Center. Drive east about 35 miles on Highway 74 through Garner Valley to Palm Desert and finish the tour at the Living Desert wildlife park.

Access/Fees: Access to viewing sites is free; an Adventure Pass is required for recreation purposes (hiking, camping). A per vehicle, day-use fee is charged.

Maps: A map of San Bernardino National Forest is available for a fee from USDA Forest Service, Map Sales, 1323 Club Drive, Vallejo, CA 94592, tel. (707) 562-8794.

Contact: San Bernardino National Forest, San Jacinto Ranger District, P.O. Box 518, Idyllwild, CA 92549, tel. (909) 659-2117 or fax (909) 659-2107.
Primary sightings: Canada goose, golden eagle, horned lizards, jays, cedar waxwing, finches, magpie, mockingbird, red-winged blackbird, robin

PALOMAR MOUNTAIN STATE PARK, in San Diego County
Directions: From Escondido on Interstate 15, drive north about 14 miles. Take Highway 76 and drive east about 21 miles to County Road S-6. Turn north and drive seven miles. Turn left at the mountaintop intersection, and left again onto State Park Road and drive three miles to the park entrance.
Access/Fees: There is a per vehicle, day-use fee.
Maps: A map is available for a fee from the entrance kiosk.
Contact: Palomar Mountain State Park, P.O. Box 175, Palomar Mountain, CA 92060, tel. (760) 742-3462 or fax (760) 742-1092; California State Parks, Colorado Desert District,200 Palm Canyon Drive, Borrego Springs, CA 92004, tel. (760) 767-5311 or fax (760) 767-3427.
Primary sightings: deer, mountain lion, squirrels

PATRICK'S POINT STATE PARK, in Humboldt County
Directions: From Eureka, drive north on U.S. 101 for 22 miles to Trinidad. At Trinidad, continue north on U.S. 101 for 2.5 miles and take the well-signed exit. At the stop sign, turn left and drive a short distance to the park entrance.
Access/Fees: There is a day-use fee per vehicle.
Maps: A map/brochure is available at the entry kiosk.
Contact: Patrick's Point State Park, tel. (707) 677-3570 or state park district headquarters, tel. (707) 445-6547.
Primary sightings: pelicans, raccoon, whales

PAYNES CREEK WETLANDS, in Tehama County
Directions: From Red Bluff on Interstate 5, drive north about six miles to the Jelly's Ferry exit. Turn right (east) and drive 2.6 miles. Turn right on Bend Ferry Road, cross over the Sacramento River, and drive 2.6 miles to the parking area.
Access/Fees: Access is free.
Maps: A free map is available at any of the wetlands kiosks.
Contact: Bureau of Land Management, Redding Field Office, 355 Hemsted Drive, Redding, CA 96002, tel. (530) 224-2100 or fax (530) 224-2172.
Primary sightings: deer, ducks, fisher, foxes, kingfisher, mink, porcupine, raccoon, river otter, squirrels, wood duck, woodpeckers

PESCADERO MARSH, in San Mateo County
Directions: At the town of Pescadero on Highway 1, take the Pescadero exit and drive a short distance to the marsh on the eastern side of the highway.
Access/Fees: Access is free.
Maps: A free map/brochure is available from the Bay Area District office at the address below.
Contact: California State Parks, Bay Area District, 250 Executive Park Boulevard, Suite 4900, San Francisco, CA 94134, tel. (415) 330-6300 or fax (415) 330-6312.
Primary sightings: garter snakes, rabbits or hares

PICACHO STATE RECREATION AREA, on the Colorado River, in Imperial County
Directions: In Winterhaven on Interstate 8, exit at Winterhaven/Fourth Avenue. Turn left on Fourth Avenue and then right on County Road 524. Turn left on Picacho Road. Picacho Road becomes a dirt road beyond the American Canal. Continue north for 18 miles on the winding dirt road to the area entrance.
Access/Fees: There is a per vehicle, day-use fee.
Maps: A free map is available at the ranger station, just past the entrance.
Contact: Picacho State Recreation Area, P.O. Box 848, Winterhaven, CA 92283, tel. (760) 996-2963 or Salton Sea State Park, tel. (760) 393-3052 or fax (760) 393-2466. You can also access their website, www.picacho.statepark.org.
Primary sightings: bats, beaver, bobcat, coyote, frogs, golden eagle, quail

PINECREST LAKE, in Tuolumne County
Directions: From Sonora on Highway 108, drive east about 30 miles. Turn right on Pinecrest Lake Road and drive about three-quarters of a mile, keep right at the Y and drive about one-half mile around the south shore to the parking area and the trailhead for the Pinecrest Lake National Recreation Trail.
Access/Fees: Access is free.
Maps: A map of Stanislaus National Forest is available for a fee from USDA Forest Service, Map Sales, 1323 Club Drive, Vallejo, CA 94592, tel. (707) 562-8794.
Contact: Stanislaus National Forest, Summit Ranger Station, 1 Pinecrest Lake Road, Pinecrest, CA 95364, tel. (209) 965-3434 or fax (209) 965-3372
Primary sightings: band-tailed pigeon, cedar waxwing, doves, finches, magpie, mockingbird, red-winged blackbird, robin

PINNACLES NATIONAL MONUMENT, in San Benito County
Directions: From Gilroy on US 101, take Highway 25 south about 42 miles. Turn right on Highway 146 and drive five miles to the visitor center on the east side of the park. To reach the west entrance, from Soledad on US 101, take Highway 146 and drive east 12 miles to the end of the road and the visitor center at the west entrance.
Access/Fees: There is a per vehicle, day-use fee (good for seven days).
Maps: A free map is available at either of the two visitor centers.
Contact: Pinnacles National Monument, 5000 Highway 146, Paicines, CA 95043, tel. (831) 389-4485 or fax (831) 389-4489.
Primary sightings: chukar, foxes, horned lizards, raven, tarantulas, wild pig

PIRU CREEK, in Los Angeles and Ventura Counties
Directions: From Castaic on Interstate 5, take the Templin Highway exit and turn left, under the freeway and drive northwest on Templin Highway about three miles. At Old Highway 99, turn right and drive five miles to Frenchman's Flat. Park at Frenchman's Flat day-use area and walk along Piru Creek.
Access/Fees: There is a per vehicle, day-use fee.
Maps: A map of Angeles National Forest is available for a fee from USDA Forest Service, Map Sales, 1323 Club Drive, Vallejo, CA 94592, tel. (707) 562-8794.
Contact: Angeles National Forest, Saugus Ranger Station, 30800 Bouquet Canyon, Saugus, CA 91350, tel. (661) 296-9710 or fax (661) 296-5847.
Primary sightings: bobcat, California condor, kingfisher, raccoon

PISMO STATE BEACH, in San Luis Obispo County
Directions: From Pismo Beach on Highway 1 southbound, drive one mile to the beach entrance.
Access/Fees: There is a per vehicle, day-use fee.
Maps: A free map is available at the entrance kiosk.
Contact: Pismo State Beach, 555 Pier Avenue, Oceano, CA 93445, tel. (805) 489-1869 or fax (805) 489-6004; California State Parks, San Luis Obispo District, 3220 South Higuera Street, Suite 311, San Luis Obispo, CA 93401, tel. (805) 549-3312 or fax (805) 541-4799
Primary sightings: bobcat, rabbits or hares, sea otter

PLACERITA CANYON PARK, in Los Angeles County
Directions: From Sylmar on Interstate 5 northbound, take the Highway 14 exit. Turn right and drive northwest about two miles toward Palmdale/Lancaster. Turn right on Placerita Canyon Road and drive about one mile to the parking area and the entrance on the right.
Access/Fees: Access is free.
Maps: A free map is available at the nature center.
Contact: County of Los Angeles, 19152 Placerita Canyon Road, Newhall, CA 91354, tel. (661) 259-7721 or fax (661) 254-1426.
Primary sightings: gopher snake

POINT ARENA, in Mendocino County
Directions: From Santa Rosa on US 101, turn west on Highway 12, which becomes Highway 116 at Forestville, and drive to Highway 1 at Jenner. Turn north on Highway 1 and drive 55 miles to Point Arena.
Contact: Manchester State Beach, tel. (707) 937-5804 or Fort Bragg-Mendocino Chamber of Commerce, 332 North Main Street, Fort Bragg, CA 95437, tel. (800) 726-2780.
Primary sightings: whales

POINT CONCEPTION, in Santa Barbara County
Note: Great white sharks are sighted off of the point, but land access is private. Boats can be launched from Gaviota State Park, 15 miles south of Point Conception.
Directions: From Santa Barbara on US 101 northbound, drive 33 miles to Gaviota State Park on the left.
Access/Fees: There is a per vehicle, day-use fee.
Maps: There is a map available for a fee at the entrance.
Contact: Gaviota State Park, 10 Refugio Beach Road, Goleta, CA 93117, tel. (805) 968-1033.
Primary sightings: sharks

POINT LOBOS STATE RESERVE, in Monterey County
Directions: From Carmel on Highway 1, drive south about 3.5 miles to the park entrance.
Access/Fees: There is a per vehicle, day-use fee.
Maps: A free map is available at the entrance kiosk.
Contact: Point Lobos State Reserve, Highway 1, Box 62, Carmel, CA 93923, tel. (831) 624-4909, website: www.pointlobos.org.
Primary sightings: dolphins, killdeer, porpoises

POINT MUGU STATE PARK, in Los Angeles County

Directions: From Oxnard on US 1/Pacific Coast Highway, drive south 12 miles to the Thornhill Broom park entrance. The Sycamore Canyon entrance is one mile further along US 1.

Access/Fees: There is a per vehicle, day-use fee.

Maps: A free map is available at the entrance stations.

Contact: Point Mugu State Park, C/O California State Parks, Angeles District, 1925 Los Virgenes Road, Calabasas, CA 91302, tel. (818) 880-0350 or fax (818) 706-3869.

Primary sightings: bats, deer, dolphins, foxes, mountain lion, porpoises, sea lions, skunks, cedar waxwing, finches, magpie, mockingbird, red-winged blackbird, robin, sharks

POINT PINOLE REGIONAL SHORELINE, in Contra Costa County

Directions: From Richmond on Interstate 80, take the Richmond Parkway Exit. Turn left on Richmond Parkway and drive about 1.5 miles. Take the Giant Highway Exit, turn right and drive about one-quarter mile to the park entrance on the left.

Access/Fees: Access is free on weekdays; there is a per vehicle, day-use fee on weekends and holidays.

Maps: A free map is available at the park kiosk.

Contact: Point Pinole Regional Shoreline, P.O. Box 684, Pinole, CA 94564, tel. (510) 237-6896. East Bay Regional Parks, P.O. Box 5381, Oakland, CA 94605-0381, tel. (510) 635-0135, extension 2200.

Primary sightings: hawks

POINT REYES NATIONAL SEASHORE, in Marin County

Directions: From San Francisco, drive north on US 101 to the Sir Francis Drake Boulevard exit in Marin County. Drive west on Sir Francis Drake Boulevard to Olema. Turn right on Highway 1 and drive north to Bear Valley Road. Turn left on Bear Valley Road and drive one-half mile to the Point Reyes National Seashore entrance on the left.

Access/Fees: Access is free.

Maps: A free map is available at the Bear Valley Visitor Center.

Contact: Bear Valley Visitor Center, Point Reyes National Seashore, Point Reyes, CA 94956, tel. (415) 663-1092.

Primary sightings: bats, elk, mountain lion, osprey, rabbits, raccoon, sea lions, skunks, whales

POINT ST. GEORGE, north of Crescent City, in Del Norte County

Directions: From Crescent City on US 101, turn west on Front Street and drive about one-half mile. Turn right on A Street and drive about one-quarter mile. Turn left on Fifth Street and drive about one-third mile. Turn right on Pebble Beach Drive. At the T, turn left and continue on Pebble Beach Drive which ends at Point St. George.

Contact: Del Norte Chamber of Commerce, 1001 Front Street, Crescent City, CA 95531, tel. (707) 464-3174 or fax (707) 464-9676.

Primary sightings: whales

POINT VICENTE ON THE PALOS VERDES PENINSULA, in Los Angeles County

Directions: From Rancho Palos Verdes on Hawthorne Boulevard, drive south to the boulevard's end. Turn left onto Palos Verdes Drive West, and then make the next possible right and drive a short distance to the Point Vicente Interpretive Center.

Access/Fees: Access is free.

Maps: A map is available for a fee from the interpretive center at the address below.

Contact: Point Vicente Interpretive Center, 31501 Palos Verdes Drive West, Rancho Palos Verdes, CA 90275, tel. (310) 377-5370.

Primary sightings: dolphins, porpoises, whales

PRAIRIE CREEK REDWOODS STATE PARK, in Humboldt County

Directions: From Eureka on US 101, drive 41 miles to Orick. At Orick, continue north on US 101 for six miles. Exit onto Newton B. Drury Scenic Parkway and drive north one mile to the park.

Contact: Prairie Creek Redwoods State Park, Visitor Center, tel. (707) 822-7611, ext. 5300; Redwood National and State Parks, Redwood Coast Sector, tel. (707) 464-6101 or fax (707) 464-7722.

Primary sightings: elk, raven, cedar waxwing, finches, magpie, mockingbird, red-winged blackbird, robin

PROVIDENCE MOUNTAINS STATE RECREATION AREA, in San Bernardino County

Directions: From Barstow on Interstate 40, drive east about 100 miles. Turn north on Essex Road and drive 16 miles to the visitor center.

Access/Fees: There is a per vehicle, day-use fee. Visitors can also take a guided tour for a fee. Groups of 10 or more require advance reservations; call the Mojave Desert Information Center for information.

Maps: A free map is available from the visitor center.

Contact: Providence Mountains State Recreation Area, C/O California State Parks, Mojave Desert Information Center, 43779 15th Street, Lancaster, CA 93534, tel. (661) 942-0662, fax (661) 940-7327, website: calparksmojave.com. The Providence Mountains State Recreation Area can be reached directly at (760) 928-2586.

Primary sightings: bats, coyote, foxes, horned lizards, roadrunner, tortoise

R

RED BLUFF RECREATION AREA/SACRAMENTO RIVER DISCOVERY CENTER IN TEHAMA COUNTY

Directions: From Red Bluff on Interstate 5, take the Highway 36 exit toward Chico/Lassen Park. Turn east on Highway 36/Antelope Boulevard, at the first stop light, turn right on Sale Lane and drive about two miles to the recreation area gate. Continue about one-third mile to the Sacramento River Discovery Center.

Access/Fees: Access is free.

Maps: There are fee maps available at the Discovery Center.

Contact: Sacramento River Discovery Center, P.O. Box 1298, Red Bluff, CA 96080, tel. (530) 527-1196 or fax (530) 527-1312.

Primary sightings: chukar, snipe

REDONDO DEEP SEA, offshore from Los Angeles
See **Santa Monica/Redondo Deep Sea.**

REDWOOD CREEK, Redwood National Park, in Humboldt County

Directions: From Eureka on US 101 northbound, drive 42 miles to the town of Orick. Continue on US 101 north about one-half mile to creek access.

Access/Fees: Access is free.

Maps: A free map is available from the Redwood National and State Parks office at the address below.

Contact: Redwood National and State Parks, 1111 Second Street, Crescent City, CA 95531, tel. (707) 464-6101, extension 5100 or fax (707) 464-1812.

Primary sightings: steelhead

REDWOOD NATIONAL AND STATE PARKS, in Del Norte County

Note: US 101 runs through the park, about 40 miles, from Crescent City to Orick. There are well-marked access points all along the way.

Directions: FromCrescent City on US 101, drive south about 30 miles to the Redwood Information Center. Coast access points are best for viewing the peregrine falcon. Walk north along the beach to the Redwood Creek Estuary to see shorebirds and river otters.

Access/Fees: Access is free.

Maps: A free map of the parks is available from the information center.

Contact: Redwood National and State Parks, 1111 2nd Street, Crescent City, CA 95531, tel. (707) 464-6101 or fax (707) 464-1812.

Primary sightings: coyote, falcon, raven, river otter

RUSSIAN RIVER, in Sonoma County

Directions: From Santa Rosa on US 101 northbound, take the River Road/Mark West exit and drive west on River Road, which closely follows the river from east of Forestville to River's End at Jenner.

Access/Fees: Access is free.

Maps: A free map/brochure is available from the Sonoma Coast State Park at the address below.

Contact: Sonoma Coast State Park, 3095 Highway 1, Bodega Bay, CA 94923, tel. (707) 875-3483; California State Parks, Russian River/Mendocino District, P.O. Box 123, Duncans Mills, CA 95430, tel. (707) 865-2391 or fax (707) 865-2046.

Primary sightings: steelhead

RUTH LAKE, in Trinity County

Directions: From Eureka on US 101 southbound, take the Highway 36 exit and drive east for 54 miles. Turn right on County Road 501/Ruth Lake Road and drive south about 12 miles to the lake.

Access/Fees: There is a per vehicle, day-use fee.

Maps: A map of Six Rivers National Forest is available for a fee from USDA Forest Service, Map Sales, 1323 Club Drive, Vallejo, CA 94592, tel. (707) 562-8794.

Contact: Six Rivers National Forest, Mad River Ranger Station, Star Route Box 300, Bridgeville, CA 95526, tel. (707) 574-6233 or fax (707) 574-6273.

Primary sightings: osprey, river otter, wood duck

S

SACRAMENTO NATIONAL WILDLIFE REFUGES COMPLEX, in Butte, Colusa, Glenn, Sutter, and Tehama Counties

Directions: At Willows, on Interstate 5, exit onto County Road 57, drive over the overpass to the stop sign. Turn right onto County Road 99W and drive about five miles to the complex entrance on the left side.

Access/Fees: There is a per vehicle, day-use fee.

Maps: A free map is available at the entrance kiosk.

Contact: Sacramento National Wildlife Refuges Complex, 752 County Road 99W, Willows, CA 95988, tel. (530) 934-2801 or fax (530) 934-7814.

Primary sightings: Canada goose, deer, frogs, great blue heron, river otter

SACRAMENTO RIVER NATIONAL WILDLIFE REFUGE (LLANO SECO UNIT), in Butte County

Directions: From Chico on Highway 99, take Highway 32/8th Street and drive west about two miles. Turn left on Walnut Street, which in turn becomes Dayton Road. Continue on Dayton Road about 6 miles. Turn right on Durham-Dayton Road, drive through the town of Dayton and continue about 5 miles. Turn left on Seven Mile Lane (also known as Road Z) and drive about a mile to the refuge on the right.

Alternatively, from Interstate 5, take the Road 68 exit (Norman Road on most maps) and travel east on Road 68. At the intersection of Road 68 and Highway 99W, turn left (north). Continue north past the headquarters of Sacramento National Wildlife Refuge on your right, and take the next right at Road 60, between two large rice driers. Continue east on Road 60 past the intersection of Highway 45 (a 4-way stop). Road 60 will change names and will eventually become Highway 162 East. Approximately four miles past Butte City, turn north (left) on Road Z (which will change to Seven Mile Lane). The refuge is approximately 10 miles north and on the left.

Access/Fees: Access is free.

Maps: A free map is available from the Sacramento National Wildlife Refuges Complex at the address below.

Contact: Sacramento River National Wildlife Refuge, C/O Sacramento National Wildlife Refuges Complex, 752 County Road 99W, Willows, CA 95988, tel. (530) 934-2801 or fax (530) 934-7814.

Primary sightings: beaver, sandhill crane, snipe

SACRAMENTO RIVER, FROM RED BLUFF TO COLUSA, in Colusa County
Directions: From Orland on Highway 45, drive southeast to Colusa. Highway 45 parellels the river and provides multiple direct access points.

Access/Fees: Access is free.

Maps: A free brochure/map is available from the Shasta-Cascade Wonderland Association at the address below.

Contact: Shasta-Cascade Wonderland Association, 1699 Highway 273, Anderson, CA 96007, tel. (530) 365-7500 or (800) 474-2782 or fax (530) 365-1258. Department of Fish and Game, Inland Fisheries Division, P.O. Box 578, Red Bluff, CA 96080, tel. (530) 527-8892 or fax (530) 527-8674.

Primary sightings: salmon, steelhead, sturgeon

SACRAMENTO RIVER, NEAR GRIMES AND KNIGHTS LANDING, in Colusa County
Directions: From the town of Colusa on Highway 45, drive south to the town of Grimes or continue to the town of Knights Ferry. Highway 45 parallels the river and provides multiple direct access points and boat ramps, especially at Grimes and at Knights Landing.

Access/Fees: Access is free.

Maps: A free map of the Colusa area is available from the Colusa Area Chamber of Commerce at the address below.

Contact: Colusa Area Chamber of Commerce, 258 Main Street, Suite 213, Colusa, CA 95932, tel. (530) 458-5525.

Primary sightings: crayfish

SALINAS RIVER NATIONAL WILDLIFE REFUGE, in Monterey County
Directions: From Monterey on Highway 1, drive north about 11 miles. Take the Del Monte Avenue exit and drive west about three-quarters of a mile, some part of which is a dirt road, to the refuge parking lot.

Access/Fees: Access is free.

Maps: A free map is available from the refuges complex at the address below.

Contact: Salinas River National Wildlife Refuge, C/O Don Edwards San Francisco Bay National Wildlife Refuges Complex, P.O. Box 524, Newark, CA 94560-0524, tel. (510) 792-0222.

Primary sightings: falcon

SALTON SEA, in Imperial and Riverside Counties
Directions: From Indio on Interstate 10 eastbound, turn south on Highway 111, left on Highway 195, right on Old Highway 111 and drive nine miles to the Salton Sea.

Access/Fees: Access is free.

Maps: A free map is available from the Salton Sea State Recreation Area at the address below.

Contact: Salton Sea State Recreation Area, 100-225 State Park Road, North Shore, CA 92201, tel. (760) 393-3059 or fax (760) 393-1338; Salton Sea National Wildlife

Refuge, U.S. Fish and Wildlife Service, 906 West Sinclair Road, Calipatria, CA 92233, tel. (760) 348-5278 or fax (760) 348-7245.

Primary sightings: Canada goose, corvina, ducks, quail, roadrunner

SALTON SEA NATIONAL WILDLIFE REFUGE, in Imperial County

Directions: From Indio onHighway 111, drive south about 70 miles. Past the town of Niland, turn right on Sinclair Road and drive west about four miles to the end of the road and the refuge entrance.

Access/Fees: Access is free.

Maps: A free map is available at the visitor center.

Contact: Salton Sea National Wildlife Refuge, U.S. Fish and Wildlife Service, 906 West Sinclair Road, Calipatria, CA 92233, tel. (760) 348-5278 or fax (760) 348-7245.

Primary sightings: falcon, frogs

SALT POINT STATE PARK, in Mendocino County

Directions: From Jenner on Highway 1, drive north about 20 miles to the park entrances at Gerstle Cove and Woodside.

Access/Fees: There is a per vehicle, day-use fee.

Maps: A free map is available at the park visitor center.

Contact: Salt Point State Park, tel. (707) 847-3221; California State Parks, Russian River/Mendocino District, P.O. Box 123, Duncans Mills, CA 95430, tel. (707) 865-2391 or fax (707) 865-2046.

Primary sightings: bobcat

SAN CLEMENTE AND CORONADO ISLANDS, offshore from San Diego County

Note: Party boats are available at San Diego Bay harbors in Chula Vista and National City.

Directions: From San Diego on Interstate 5, take the Hawthorne Street/Airport exit. Turn west on Harbor Drive and continue to the sportfishing operations.

Contact: San Diego Visitors Bureau, 401 B Street, Suite 1400, San Diego, CA 92101, tel. (619) 232-3101; H & M Landing, tel. (619) 222-1144; Fisherman's Landing, tel. (619) 222-0391; or Point Loma Sportfishing, tel. (619) 223-1627.

Primary sightings: lobster, yellowtail

SAN DIEGO DEEP SEA, offshore from San Diego County

Directions: In the city of San Diego on Interstate 5, take the Hawthorne Street/Airport exit. Turn west on Harbor Drive and continue to the sportfishing operations. Boat ramps at the bay are available in Chula Vista and National City.

Access/Fees: For partyboat schedules and fees contact H & M Landing, tel. (619) 222-1144; Fisherman's Landing, tel. (619) 222-0391; or Point Loma Sportfishing, tel. (619) 223-1627.

Maps: A free map/brochure of the San Diego area is available from the San Diego Visitors Bureau at the address below.

Contact: San Diego Visitors Bureau, 401 B Street, Suite 1400, San Diego, CA 92101, tel. (619) 232-3101.

Primary sightings: marlin, swordfish

SAN FRANCISCO BAY, out of Emeryville, in Alameda County
Directions: In Emeryville on Interstate 90, take the Powell Street exit. Drive west to the end of Powell Street and the Emeryville Marina.
Access/Fees: For partyboat schedules and fees, contact Emeryville Sportfishing, tel. (510) 654-6040.
Maps: A free map/brochure of the Emeryville area is available from the Emeryville Chamber of Commerce, at the address below.
Contact: Emeryville Chamber of Commerce, 1900 Powell Street, Suite 1126, Emeryville, CA 94608, tel. (510) 652-5223; Emeryville Marina, 3310 Powell Street, Emeryville, CA 94608, 654-3716; City of Emeryville, tel. (510) 596-4300.
Primary sightings: striped bass

SAN JACINTO WILDLIFE AREA, in Riverside County
Directions: From Riverside on Interstate 215 drive south to the Ramona Expressway. Turn east on Ramona Expressway and drive about five miles to the town of Lakeview. Turn left on Davis Road and drive north one mile to the entrance on the right.
Access/Fees: Access is free.
Maps: A free map is available at the entrance kiosk.
Contact: San Jacinto Wildlife Area, Department of Fish and Game, Long Beach Field Office, 330 Golden Shore Avenue, Suite 50, Long Beach, 90802, tel. (562) 590-5132.
Primary sightings: pheasant, rabbits or hares, roadrunner, snipe

SAN JOAQUIN DELTA, in San Joaquin County
Directions: In Antioch on Highway 160 westbound, drive south to Eddo's Boat Harbor.
Access/Fees: Access is free.
Maps: A free map/brochure is available from the Delta Chamber of Commerce at the address below.
Contact: Delta Chamber of Commerce, P.O. Box 6, Isleton, CA 95641, tel. (707) 374-5007, website: www.californiadelta.org. Eddo's Boat Harbor, tel. (925) 757-5314.
Primary sightings: striped bass

SAN LUIS DAM AND RESERVOIR, in Merced County
Directions: From Los Banos on Highway 152, drive west about 15 miles to the park entrance.
Access/Fees: There is a per vehicle, day-use fee.
Maps: A free map is available at the entrance station on weekends or for a fee from the San Luis State Recreation Area office at the address below.
Contact: California State Parks, San Luis State Recreation Area, 31426 Gonzaga Road, Gustine, CA 95322, tel. (209) 826-1197/1196 or fax (209) 826-0284.
Primary sightings: foxes, golden eagle, gopher snake

SAN LUIS OBISPO BAY DEEP SEA, offshore from San Luis Obispo County
Directions: From San Luis Obispo on US 101 southbound, take the San Luis Drive exit. Turn west on San Luis Drive, then right on Avila Drive and continue to the parking area at the end of the street. Partyboat operations are on the third pier.
Access/Fees: For partyboat schedules and fees, contact Avila Beach Sportfishing, tel. (805) 595-7200.

Maps: A free map/brochure of the San Luis Obispo area is available from the chamber of commerce at the address below.

Contact: San Luis Obispo Chamber of Commerce, 1039 Chorro Street, San Luis Obispo, CA 93401, tel. (805) 781-2777 or fax (805) 541-8416.

Primary sightings: swordfish

SAN MATEO POINT, north of San Onofre State Beach, in San Diego County

Directions: From San Clemente on Interstate 5, drive three miles south. Take the Cristianitos exit, turn left and drive to San Mateo Point.

Access/Fees: There is a per vehicle, day-use fee.

Contact: San Onofre State Beach, tel. (949) 492-4872 or (949) 492-0802 or fax (949) 492-8412.

Primary sightings: dolphins, porpoises, whales

SAN PABLO BAY, Loch Lomond Marina, in Marin County

Directions: From US 101 in Marin County northbound, take the Central San Rafael exit. Turn right on Third Street/San Pedro Road, right again on Loch Lomond Road and continue to the marina.

Access/Fees: Access is free.

Maps: A free map of selected public areas bordering the bay is available from East Bay Regional Parks at the address below. A topographic map is available for a fee from Maps, Western Distribution Center, U.S. Geological Survey, Box 25286, Federal Center, Denver, CO 80225, tel. (303) 202-4700.

Contact: Point Pinole Regional Shoreline, P.O. Box 684, Pinole, CA 94564, tel. (510) 237-6896; East Bay Regional Parks, P.O. Box 5381, Oakland, CA 94605-0381, tel. (510) 635-0135, ext. 2200.

Primary sightings: striped bass, sturgeon

SAN PABLO BAY NATIONAL WILDLIFE REFUGE, in Contra Costa County

Directions: The public access gate is on the south shoulder of Highway 37 and must be accessed from the right lane, heading east. From Vallejo, drive west on Highway 37 to the intersection with Highway 121. Turn back onto Highway 37 and drive east about one-quarter mile. Park on the south shoulder at the public access gate. Walk the levees along the Tubbs Island Trail, which parallel the east bank of Tolay Creek, to the Lower Tubbs Island entrance.

Access/Fees: Access is free.

Maps: A free brochure with map is available from the Don Edwards San Francisco Bay National Wildlife Refuge, P.O. Box 524, Newark, CA 94560, tel. (510) 792-4275 or fax (510) 792-5828.

Contact: San Pablo Bay National Wildlife Refuge, P.O. Box 2012, Mare Island, CA 94592-0012, tel. (707) 562-3000.

Primary sightings: cedar waxwing, ducks, finches, magpie, mockingbird, red-winged blackbird, pheasant, robin, Western meadowlark

SAN PABLO RESERVOIR, in Contra Costa County

Directions: At San Pablo on Interstate 80, take the San Pablo Dam exit and drive east to the main park entrance at the reservoir.

Access/Fees: There is a per vehicle, day-use fee.

Maps: A free map is available from the San Pablo Reservoir office at the address below.

Contact: San Pablo Reservoir, 7301 San Pablo Dam Road, El Sobrante, CA 94803, tel. (510) 223-1661.

Primary sightings: catfish, sturgeon

SAN PEDRO LANDING, in Los Angeles County

Directions: From Los Angeles on Interstate 110/Harbor Freeway, drive south to San Pedro. Turn left on Gaffey Street and drive to 22nd Street. Continue on 22nd Street 4.5 blocks to the 22nd Street Landing. To reach L.A. Harbor Sportfishing, drive south on the Harbor Freeway until it dead-ends and exit left at Harbor Boulevard. Drive to #79 in the Ports O'Call Village.

Contact: San Pedro Chamber of Commerce, 390 West 7th Street. San Pedro, CA 90731, tel. (310) 832-7272 or fax (310) 832- 0685; L.A. Harbor Sportfishing, 1150 Nagoya Way, San Pedro, CA 90731, tel. (310) 547-9916.

Primary sightings: anchovy

SAN VICENTE LAKE, in San Diego County

Directions: From San Diego on Interstate 8, drive east to El Cajon. Turn north on Highway 676 and drive about 10 miles. Turn left on Morena Drive and continue to the lake.

Access/Fees: The lake is open from November through May. There is a boat-launching and a fishing fee.

Contact: San Diego Water Utilities, Lake Department, 12375 Morena Avenue, Lakeside, CA 92040-1135, tel. (619) 668-2050 or fax (619) 443-7681; San Diego City Lakes, tel. (619) 465-3474.

Primary sightings: largemouth bass

SAND POND, Tahoe National Forest, in Sierra County

Directions: From Sierra City on Highway 49, drive east about five miles. Turn left on Gold Lake Highway and drive one mile. Turn left on Sardine Lakes Road and drive about one-half mile to the pond parking area.

Access/Fees: Access is free.

Maps: A map is available for a fee from USDA Forest Service, Map Sales, 1323 Club Drive, Vallejo, CA 94592, tel. (707) 562-8794.

Contact: Tahoe National Forest, Downieville Ranger District, 15924 Highway 49, Camptonville, CA 95922, tel. (530) 288-3232 or fax (530) 288-0727.

Primary sightings: beaver, birds, woodpeckers

SANTA ANA RIVER LAKE, in San Bernardino County

Directions: At Redland on Interstate 10 take the Highway 38 exit and drive east past Angelus Oaks. Turn left on Seven Oaks Road. Access is available from the road.

Access/Fees: Access is free.

Maps: A map of San Bernardino National Forest is available for a fee from USDA Forest Service, Map Sales, 1323 Club Drive, Vallejo, CA 94592, tel. (707) 562-8794.

Contact: San Bernardino National Forest, San Gorgonio Ranger District, 34701 Mill Creek Road, Mentone, CA 92359, tel. (909) 794-1123 or fax (909) 794-1125.

Primary sightings: catfish

SANTA BARBARA DEEP SEA, offshore from Santa Barbara

Directions: In Santa Barbara on US 101, take the Cabrillo Boulevard exit and turn left at the bottom of the offramp. Drive west for 3.5 miles at which Point Cabrillo Boulevard becomes Shoreline Boulevard. Continue on Shoreline Boulevard and after the first stop sign, turn left on Harbor Way, where the sportfishing operations are located.

Access/Fees: For partyboat schedules and fees, contact Sea Landing, tel. (805) 963-3564.

Maps: A free map/brochure of the Santa Barbara area is available from the visitor bureau at the address below.

Contact: Santa Barbara Visitors Bureau, 12 East Carrillo Street, Santa Barbara, CA 93101, tel. (805) 966-9222 or fax (805) 966-1728.

Primary sightings: marlin, yellowtail

SANTA MARGARITA LAKE, in San Luis Obispo County

Directions: From Santa Margarita on US 101, turn right on Highway 58/Pozo Road (signed for Highway 58, McKittrich, and Santa Margarita Lake), and drive east about seven miles. Continue straight on Pozo Road to Santa Margarita Lake Road. Turn left and drive one mile to the entrance.

Access/Fees: There is a per vehicle, day-use fee.

Maps: A free map/brochure is available from the county office below.

Contact: Santa Margarita Lake, C/O San Luis Obispo County, 4695 Santa Margarita Lake Road, Santa Margarita, CA 93453, tel. (805) 438-5485 or fax (805) 438-4467.

Primary sightings: golden eagle, kingfisher

SANTA MONICA BAY, near the rocky shore from Redondo Harbor south to Rocky Point, in Los Angeles County

Directions: From Los Angeles, drive south on Interstate 110. Take the 190th Street exit and turn right. Continue west until the street deadends at the beach on Harbor Drive. Turn left and continue a quarter-mile to Redondo Sportfishing at 233 North Harbor Drive.

Maps: A free map/brochure is available from the chambers of commerce at the addresses below.

Contact: Santa Monica Chamber of Commerce, 501 Colorado Avenue, Suite 150, Santa Monica, CA 90401-2430, tel. (310) 393-9825 or fax (310) 394-1868; Redondo Beach Chamber of Commerce, 200 North Pacific Coast Highway, Redondo Beach, CA 90277, tel. (310) 376-6911 or fax (310) 374-7373.

Primary sightings: yellowtail

SANTA MONICA/REDONDO DEEP SEA, offshore from Los Angeles

Directions: To access the Redondo Harbor from Los Angeles on Interstate 110 southbound, take the 190th Street exit, turn right and drive west until the street deadends at the beach. Turn left on Harbor Drive and continue one-quarter mile to Redondo Sportfishing at 233 North Harbor Drive. To access the Marina del Rey boat launch from Los Angeles on Highway 1 southbound, drive past Venice and turn right on Lincoln Boulevard, then right again on Fiji Way and drive to the boat ramp.

Access/Fees: For partyboat schedules and fees, contact Redondo Sportfishing, tel. (310) 372-2111.

Maps: A free map/brochure is available from the chambers of commerce at the addresses below.

Contact: Santa Monica Chamber of Commerce, 501 Colorado Avneue, Suite 150, Santa Monica, CA 90401-2430, tel. (310) 393-9825 or fax (310) 394-1868; Redondo Beach Chamber of Commerce, 200 North Pacific Coast Highway, Redondo Beach, CA 90277, tel. (310) 376-6911 or fax (310) 374-7373.

Primary sightings: marlin

SANTA ROSA PLATEAU ECOLOGICAL RESERVE, in Riverside County

Directions: From Escondido, drive north on Interstate 15 about 35 miles. Turn left on Clinton Keith Road and drive four miles to the visitor center.

Access/Fees: There is an entrance fee.

Maps: A free map is available at the entrance kiosk or the visitor center.

Contact: Riverside County Parks, 39400 Clinton Keith Road, Murrieta, CA 92562, tel. (909) 677-6951 or fax (909) 696-5968.

Primary sightings: band-tailed pigeon, bobcat, coyote, deer, golden eagle, gulls, horned lizards, rattlesnake, roadrunner

SEQUOIA AND KINGS CANYON NATIONAL PARKS, in Tulare and Fresno Counties

Directions: From Visalia on Highway 63 heading north, drive about 20 miles. Turn right on Highway 180 and drive about 23 miles to the park entrance station.

Access/Fees: There is an entrance fee.

Maps: A map is available for a fee at the entrance station.

Contact: Sequoia and Kings Canyon National Parks, Ash Mountain, Three Rivers, CA 93271-9700, tel. (559) 565-3134 or (559) 335-2856 (Grant Grove Visitor Center) or fax (559) 565-3730.

Primary sightings: black bear, garter snakes, marmot, rattlesnake, cedar waxwing, dipper, finches, magpie, mockingbird, red-winged blackbird, robin

SEQUOIA NATIONAL FOREST, in Fresno and Tulare Counties

Directions: From Fresno on Highway 180, drive east about 60 miles to the entrance of Kings Canyon National Park. Continue three miles beyond the entrance to a Y, bear right onto Generals Highway and drive six miles. Turn left on Big Meadow Road, drive to the Big Meadow campground on the right side and walk along

Big Meadow Creek. Or turn left at the campground and follow the signs to Boulder Creek

Access/Fees: There is an entrance fee (good for seven days).

Maps: A map is available for a fee from USDA Forest Service, Map Sales, 1323 Club Drive, Vallejo, CA 94592, tel. (707) 562-8794.

Contact: Sequoia National Forest, Hume Lake Ranger District, 35860 East Kings Canyon Road, Dunlap, CA 93621, tel. (559) 338-2251.

Primary sightings: fisher

SHASTA LAKE NATIONAL RECREATION AREA, in Shasta County

Directions: From Redding, drive north on Interstate 5 for about 20 miles to the Gilman exit. Take Gilman Road (County Road 7H009) and drive northeast for 17 miles to the McCloud River Bridge.

Access/Fees: Day-use is free.

Maps: A map of Shasta-Trinity National Forest is available for a fee from USDA Forest Service, Map Sales, 1323 Club Drive, Vallejo, CA 94592, tel. (707) 562-8794.

Contact: Shasta-Trinity National Forest, Shasta Lake Ranger District, tel. (530) 275-1587 or fax (530) 275-1512.

Primary sightings: bald eagle, blue heron, deer, elk, golden eagle, jays, largemouth bass, osprey, raccoon

SHASTA LAKE, Shasta-Trinity National Forest, in Shasta County

Directions: To access Fisherman's Point at Shasta Dam, take the Shasta Dam Boulevard exit from Interstate 5 north of Redding and drive to Lake Boulevard. Turn right and follow signs to the dam. To access a public boat ramp at the Pit River Arm confluence with the Squaw Valley Creek Arm, exit Interstate 5 three miles north of Redding at Oasis Road and follow the signs to the Jones Valley ramp.

Access/Fees: Access is free.

Maps: A map of Shasta-Trinity National Forest is available for a fee from USDA Forest Service, Map Sales, 1323 Club Drive, Vallejo, CA 94592, tel. (707) 562-8794.

Contact: Shasta-Trinity National Forest, Shasta Lake Ranger Station, tel. (530) 275-1587 or fax (530) 275-1512 or Shasta-Cascade Wonderland Association, tel. (800) 474-2782 or (530) 365-7500 or fax (530) 365-1258.

Primary sightings: bald eagle, catfish, largemouth bass, osprey, quail, raccoon, river otter, sturgeon

SHASTA LAKE/PACKERS BAY, Shasta-Trinity National Forest, in Shasta County

Directions: From Redding on Interstate 5 northbound, drive about 17 miles. Take the Packers Bay exit and drive west about 1.5 miles on Packers Bay Road to the lake.

Access/Fees: Access is free.

Maps: A map of Shasta-Trinity National Forest is available for a fee from USDA Forest Service, Map Sales, 1323 Club Drive, Vallejo, CA 94592, tel. (707) 562-8794.

Contact: Shasta-Trinity National Forest, Shasta Lake Ranger Station, tel. (530) 275-1587 or fax (530) 275-1512 or Shasta-Cascade Wonderland Association, tel. (800) 474-2782 or (530) 365-7500 or fax (530) 365-1258.

Primary sightings: catfish, turkey

SHASTA VALLEY STATE WILDLIFE AREA, in Siskiyou County

Directions: From Yreka on Interstate 5, turn east on Highway 3 and drive about eight

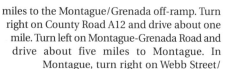

miles to the Montague/Grenada off-ramp. Turn right on County Road A12 and drive about one mile. Turn left on Montague-Grenada Road and drive about five miles to Montague. In Montague, turn right on Webb Street/ State Route 3 (which becomes Ball Mountain Road/Little Shasta Road), and drive about 1.5 miles to the signed entrance on the right. Turn right and drive another one-half mile to the area headquarters.

Access/Fees: Access is free.

Maps: A free map is available at the area headquarters.

Contact: Shasta Valley State Wildlife Area, 1724 Ball Mountain Road, Montague, CA 96064, tel. (530) 459-3926 or fax (530) 459-0346.

Primary sightings: badger, bobcat, hawks, marmot, sandhill crane, swans

SILVERWOOD LAKE STATE RECREATION AREA, in San Bernardino County
Directions: At Cajon on Interstate 15, take Highway 138 east about 12 miles to the lake.
Access/Fees: There is a per vehicle, day-use fee.
Maps: A free map is available at the park visitor center.
Contact: Silverwood Lake State Recreation Area, tel. (760) 389-2303; California State Parks, San Bernardino District, 17801 Lake Perris Drive, Perris, CA 92571, tel. (909) 657-0676 or fax (909) 657-2736.
Primary sightings: bats, coyote, golden eagle, jays, osprey, rattlesnake, squirrels

SINKYONE WILDERNESS STATE PARK, in Humboldt County
Directions: From Highway 101 near Garberville, take the Redway exit, turn west on Briceland Road and drive 17 miles to Whitehorn. From Whitehorn, drive six more miles to the four corners fork. Take the middle left fork and drive four miles on a gravel road to the Needle Rock Ranger Station.
Access/Fees: There is a per vehicle, day-use fee.
Maps: A free map is available at the Needle Rock Ranger Station.
Contact: Sinkyone Wilderness State Park, P.O. Box 245, Whitethorn Avenue, CA 95489, tel. (707) 986-7111 or 247-3318 or fax (707) 247-3300; California State Parks, North Coast Redwoods District, P.O. Box 2006, Eureka, CA 95501-0163, tel. (707) 445-6547 or fax (707) 441-5737.
Primary sightings: foxes, mountain lion, porcupine

SKYLINE RIDGE OPEN SPACE PRESERVE, in Santa Clara County
Directions: In Palo Alto on Interstate 280, turn west on Page Mill Road and drive eight miles. Turn left and drive south on Highway 35/Skyline Boulevard about one mile to the parking area.
Access/Fees: Access is free.
Maps: A free map is available at the entrance.

Contact: Midpeninsula Regional Open Space District, 330 Distel Circle, Los Altos, CA 94022, tel. (650) 691-1200 or fax (650) 691-0485.

Primary sightings: coyote, deer, cedar waxwing, finches, magpie, mockingbird, red-winged blackbird, robin

SMITH RIVER, in Del Norte County

Directions: In Crescent City at the junction of US 101 and US 199, drive east on US 199 to direct access points along the highway.

Access/Fees: Access is free.

Maps: A map of the Smith River National Recreation Area is available for a fee from USDA Forest Service, Map Sales, 1323 Club Drive, Vallejo, CA 94592, tel. (707) 562-8794.

Contact: Smith River National Recreation Area, P.O. Box 228, Gasquet, CA 95543, tel. (707) 457-3131 or fax (707) 457-3794.

Primary sightings: jays, steelhead

SMITH RIVER NATIONAL RECREATION AREA, Six Rivers National Forest, in Del Norte County

Directions: From Crescent City on US 101 northbound, drive five miles. Turn east on US 199 and drive about 17 miles to campground and trailhead access roads.

Access/Fees: Access is free.

Maps: A map is available for a fee from USDA Forest Service, Map Sales, 1323 Club Drive, Vallejo, CA 94592, tel. (707) 562-8794.

Contact: Smith River National Recreation Area, Six Rivers National Forest, P.O. Box 228, Gasquet, CA 95543, tel. (707) 457-3131 or fax (707) 457-3794.

Primary sightings: blue grouse

SONOMA COAST STATE BEACH VISTA TRAIL, in Sonoma County

Directions: From Jenner, drive seven miles north on Highway 1 to the entrance and the trailhead on the west side.

Access/Fees: Access is free.

Maps: A free map is available at the Jenner Visitor Center next to the Jenner Post Office.

Contact: Salt Point State Park, tel. (707) 847-3221; California State Parks, Russian River/Mendocino District, P.O. Box 123, Duncans Mills, CA 95430, tel. (707) 865-2391 or fax (707) 865-2046.

Primary sightings: sea lions

SONOMA STATE BEACHES/BODEGA BAY, in Sonoma County

Directions: From Jenner on Highway 1, drive south about 12 miles to the town of Bodega Bay. Look for signed beach access along Highway 1 at Goat Rock, Shell, Furlong Gulch, South Pacific View, Wrights Beach, Duncans Landing, Gleason, Portugese, Schoolhouse, Carmet, Arched Rock, Salmon Creek, and Bodega Dunes.

Access/Fees: Access is free.

Maps: A free map is available at the visitor centers in Jenner and Duncans Mills.

Contact: Salt Point State Park, tel. (707) 847-3221; California State Parks, Russian River/Mendocino District, P.O. Box 123, Duncans Mills, CA 95430, tel. (707) 865-2391 or fax (707) 865-2046.

Primary sightings: gulls, osprey

SOUTH SAN FRANCISCO BAY, Oyster Point Marina, in San Francisco
Directions: In South San Francisco on US 101, take the Oyster Point Boulevard exit. Follow Oyster Point Boulevard, turn right on Marine Boulevard and continue to the public ramp.
Access/Fees: Access is free.
Maps: A free map is available from the San Francisco Convention and Visitors Bureau, 900 Market Street, San Francisco, CA 94102, tel. (415) 391-2000.
Contact: Oyster Point Marina, 95 Harbor Master Road, Road No. 1, South San Francisco, CA 94080, tel. (650) 871-7344.
Primary sightings: sturgeon

SOUTH WARNER WILDERNESS, in Modoc County
Directions: From Alturas on US 395 southbound, drive about 18.5 miles to Likely. Turn east on Jess Valley Road, then south on South Warner Road to Patterson Campground. The Summit Trail, which traverses both sides of the Warner Ridge, is accessible from the campground.
Access/Fees: Access is free.
Maps: A map of the South Warner Wilderness is available for a fee from USDA Forest Service, Map Sales, 1323 Club Drive, Vallejo, CA 94592, tel. (707) 562-8794.
Contact: Modoc National Forest, Warner Mountain Ranger District, P.O. Box 220, Cedarville, CA 96104, tel. (530) 279-6116 or fax (530) 279-6107.
Primary sightings: blue grouse

SPENCEVILLE WILDLIFE AREA, in Yuba and Nevada Counties
Directions: From Marysville drive east on either Highway 20 or Hammonton-Smartville Road for about 15 miles to Smartville, then turn right (south) on Smartville Road. Drive 4.5 miles to Waldo Road and bear left onto the gravel road. Follow Waldo Road for 2.1 miles to Spenceville Road. Turn left and drive 2 miles to the end of the road at a blocked-off bridge. Park by the bridge and hike across.
Access/Fees: Access is free.
Maps: Free maps of Spenceville Wildlife Area are available at information signposts in the refuge.
Contact: Spenceville Wildlife Area, C/O Oroville Wildlife Area, Department of Fish and Game, 945 Oro Dam Boulevard, Oroville, CA 95965, tel. (530) 538-2236.
Primary sightings: wild turkey

STAMPEDE RESERVOIR, Tahoe National Forest, in Sierra County
Directions: From Truckee on Interstate 80 eastbound, drive about seven miles and take the Boca-Hirschdale/County Road 270 exit. Drive north on County Road 270/Stampede Meadows Road about eight miles, passing Boca Reservoir, to Stampede Reservoir.
Access/Fees: Access is free.
Contact: Tahoe National Forest, Truckee Ranger District, 10342 Highway 89 North, Truckee, CA 96161, tel. (530) 587-3558 or fax (530) 587-6914.
Primary sightings: osprey

STANISLAUS RIVER PARKS, in Stanislaus County

Directions: From Modesto on Highway 99 northbound, take Highway 108 and drive east about 30 miles to the Knights Ferry Visitor Center.

Access/Fees: Access is free.

Maps: A free map is available from the U.S. Army Corps of Engineers at the address below.

Contact: U.S. Army Corps of Engineers, Knights Ferry Information Center, P.O. Box 1229, Oakdale, CA 95361, tel. (209) 881-3517 or fax (209) 881-3203, website: www.spk .usace.army.mil/

Primary sightings: band-tailed pigeon, hawks

STONE LAKES NATIONAL WILDLIFE REFUGE, in Sacramento County

Directions: From Sacramento on Interstate 5, drive south about 20 miles. Take the Elk Grove exit, turn right at the stop sign and continue to the refuge gate.

Access/Fees: Open to the public one weekend each month. Contact the refuge office for a current date and fee schedule.

Contact: Stone Lakes National Wildlife Refuge, 2233 Watt Avenue, Suite 230, Jamaica Plaza, Sacramento, CA 95825-0509, tel. (916) 979-2085.

Primary sightings: garter snakes

SUCCESS LAKE, in Tulare County

Directions: From Visalia on Highway 99, drive south about 15 miles. Turn east on Highway 190 and drive about 25 miles to Porterville. Continue on Highway 190 about five miles past Porterville to the lake.

Access/Fees: Access is free.

Maps: A free brochure with map is available from the U.S. Army Corps of Engineers at the address below.

Contact: U.S. Army Corps of Engineers, P.O. Box 1072, Porterville, CA 93258, tel. (559) 784-0215 or fax (559) 784-5469.

Primary sightings: bobcat, catfish, deer, doves, foxes, gulls, hawks, rabbits or hares, cedar waxwing, finches, magpie, mockingbird, red-winged blackbird, robin, Western meadowlark

SUISUN BAY, MARTINEZ PIER, in Contra Costa County

Directions: In Martinez on Interstate 80, take the Highway 4 exit and drive to the Alhambra Avenue off-ramp. Drive through Martinez to the end of Ferry Street and follow the signs to the parking area and pier at Martinez Regional Shoreline Park.

Access/Fees: Access is free.

Maps: A free map is available at the entrance kiosk.

Contact: Martinez Regional Shoreline, P.O. Box 707, Martinez, CA 94553, tel. (925) 228-0112; East Bay Regional Parks District, tel. (510) 228-0112.

Primary sightings: striped bass, sturgeon

SUNBEAM LAKE/FIG LAGOON, in Imperial County

Directions: From El Centro on Interstate 8, drive west about eight miles. To reach Sunbeam Lake, turn north on Drew Road and drive one-half mile to the Lake. To reach Fig Lagoon, turn south on Drew Road and drive about 2.5 miles, then west on

Diehl Road and drive about one mile. Turn north on Derrick Road and drive about two miles to the lagoon.

Access/Fees: Access is free.

Maps: For a free map of Imperial County, write to El Centro Chamber of Commerce, 1095 South Fourth Street, El Centro, CA 92243, tel. (760) 352-3681 or fax (760) 352-3246.

Contact: County of Imperial, Imperial Irrigation District, P.O. Box 937, Imperial, CA 92251-0937, tel. (760) 339-9220; El Centro Chamber of Commerce, 1095 South Fourth Street, El Centro, CA 92243, tel. (760) 352-3681 or fax (760) 352-3246.

Primary sightings: brown pelican, curlew, quail, roadrunner

SUNOL/OHLONE REGIONAL WILDERNESS, in Alameda County

Directions: From San Jose on Interstate 680, drive north to the Highway 237/Calaveras Road turnoff. Drive west on Calaveras Road to Sunol Valley Regional Park.

Access/Fees: There is a parking fee and a pet fee.

Maps: A trail map is available at the wilderness kiosk.

Contact: Sunol Valley Regional Park, P.O. Box 82, Sunol, 94586, tel. (925) 862-2244; East Bay Regional Park District, tel. (510) 635-0135, ext. 2200.

Primary sightings: deer

SUTTER NATIONAL WILDLIFE REFUGE, in Sutter County

Note: Sutter National Wildlife Refuge is closed to the public, but wildlife can be viewed from roads bordering the refuge.

Directions: From Yuba City on Highway 99 southbound, turn right on Oswald Road and drive to the end of the road. Turn right on Schlag Road, then left on Hughes Road. Hughes Road will meet again with Oswald Road.

Access/Fees: Access is free.

Maps: Free maps are available from the Sacramento National Wildlife Refuges Complex at the address below.

Contact: Sutter National Wildlife Refuge, C/O Sacramento National Wildlife Refuges Complex, 752 County Road 99W, Willows, CA 95988, tel. (530) 934-2801 or fax (530) 934-7814.

Primary sightings: ducks

SWEETWATER MARSH NATIONAL WILDLIFE REFUGE, in San Diego County

Directions: From the city of San Diego on Interstate 5, drive south about 10 miles. Turn right on E Street and enter the parking lot. Free shuttle buses to the refuge run daily, every 25 minutes from 10:05 a.m. to 4 p.m.

Access/Fees: There is an entrance fee.

Maps: A free trail map is available at the refuge center.

Contact: Sweetwater Marsh National Wildlife Refuge, C/O San Diego National Wildlife Refuge Complex, 1000 Gunpowder Point, Chula Vista, CA 91910, tel. (619) 422-2481.

Primary sightings: brown pelican, curlew, hawks, osprey, owls, Western meadowlark

T

TEHAMA STATE WILDLIFE AREA, in Tehama County
Directions: From Red Bluff on Highway 99, drive east on Highway 36 about 20 miles. Turn right at Paynes Creek Loop and drive about one-half mile. Turn right on Plum Creek Road, drive east about 3.5 miles, turn left and drive one-half mile on a gravel road to the wildlife area headquarters at 30490 Plum Creek Road.
Access/Fees: Access is free.
Maps: A map is available at the headquarters office.
Contact: Tehama Wildlife Area, P.O. Box 188, Paynes Creek, CA 96075, 30490 Plum Creek Road, (530) 597-2201 or fax (530) 597-2109.
Primary sightings: osprey, owls, wild pig

TIJUANA SLOUGH NATIONAL WILDLIFE REFUGE, in San Diego County
Directions: From San Diego on Interstate 5, drive south past the Coronada Bridge about 12 miles to the Coronado Avenue exit at Imperial Beach. Turn right on Coronado Avenue (becomes Imperial Beach Boulevard) and drive about three miles. Turn left on Third Street and bear left on Caspian Way which deadends at the refuge parking lot. The visitor center borders the parking lot.
Access/Fees: Access is free.
Maps: A free map of the refuge and trails is available at the visitor center.
Contact: Tijuana Slough National Wildlife Refuge, 301 Caspian Way, Imperial Beach, California 91932, tel. (928) 572-2704 or phone the visitor center, tel. (928) 575-3613.
Primary sightings: brown pelican, coyote, ducks, rabbits or hares

TIMBER MOUNTAIN, Modoc National Forest, in Modoc County
Directions: From Redding on Interstate 5, take the Highway 299 exit and drive east 133 miles to Canby. Turn north on Highway 139 and drive 20 miles. Turn west on Forest Service Road 97 and drive about one mile. Turn south on County Road 97A and drive 1.5 miles. Turn south on Forest Service Road 44N19 and drive about three miles to the base of the mountain. The road continues to the summit, where there is a Forest Service lookout.

Access/Fees: Access is free.
Maps: For a map of Modoc National Forest, write to USDA Forest Service, Map Sales, 1323 Club Drive, Vallejo, CA 94592, tel. (707) 562-8794.
Contact: Modoc National Forest, Doublehead Ranger Station, P.O. Box 369, Tulelake, CA 96134, tel. (530) 667-2246 or fax (530) 667-4808.
Primary sightings: deer

TOMALES BAY STATE PARK, in Marin County

Directions: In Marin County on US 101, take the Sir Francis Drake Boulevard exit and drive west about 20 miles. Turn right on Highway 1, drive a short distance, turn let on Bear Valley Road and drive north about eight miles. (Bear Valley rejoins Sir Francis Drake Boulevard.) Turn right on Pierce Point Road and drive about one mile to the access road for Tomales Bay State Park and the park entrance on the right.

Access/Fees: There is a per vehicle, day-use fee.

Maps: There is a map available for a fee at the entrance kiosk.

Contact: Tomales Bay State Park, Star Route, Inverness, CA 94937, tel. (415) 669-1140 or fax (415) 669-1701; California State Parks, Marin District, 7665 Redwood Boulevard, Suite 150, Novato, CA 94945, tel. (415) 893-1580 or fax (415) 893-1583.

Primary sightings: sharks

TOPANGA STATE PARK, in Los Angeles County

Directions: From Santa Monica on Highway 1, drive about 5.5 miles north. Continue north about four miles on Topanga Canyon Boulevard/Highway 27. Take the Entrada exit and drive east about 500 to the entrance kiosk.

Access/Fees: There is per vehicle, day-use fee.

Maps: A map is available for a fee at the park kiosk or from Tom Harrison Cartography, 2 Falmouth Cove, San Rafael, CA 94901, tel. (415) 456-7940.

Contact: Topanga State Park, 20825 Entrada Road, Topanga, CA 90290, tel. (310) 455-2465 or (310) 573-7255; California State Parks, Angeles District, 1925 Los Virgenes, Calabasas, CA 91302, tel. (818) 880-0350 or fax (818) 880-6165.

Primary sightings: badger, coyote, deer, jays, woodpeckers

TORREY PINES STATE RESERVE/LOS PENAQUITOS MARSH, in San Diego County

Directions: From San Diego on Interstate 5 northbound, take the Carmel Valley Road exit and drive west to the end of Carmel Valley Road. Turn left on US 101 and drive south about one mile to the park entrance station on the right. To reach the marsh/lagoon, take the Carmel Valley Road exit and drive one mile. Turn left on McGonigle Road into the North Torrey Pines State Beach entrance.

Access/Fees: There is a per vehicle, day-use fee.

Maps: A free map is available from the entrance kiosk.

Contact: Torrey Pines State Reserve, C/O California State Parks, San Diego Coast District, 9609 Waples Street, Suite 200, San Diego, CA 92121, tel. (858) 755-2063 (Torrey Pines State Reserve) or (858) 642-4200 (San Diego District Office) or fax (858) 755-7114.

Primary sightings: bobcat, dolphins, killdeer, porpoises

TRINITY LAKE, Shasta-Trinity National Forest, in Trinity County

Directions: From Redding on Interstate 5, take the Highway 299 West exit and drive 52 miles to the town of Weaverville. Turn north on Highway 3/Weaverville-Scott Mountain Road and continue for 14 miles to the lake.

Access/Fees: Access is free.

Maps: A map of Shasta-Trinity National Forest is available for a fee from USDA Forest Service, Map Sales, 1323 Club Drive, Vallejo, CA 94592, tel. (707) 562-8794.

Contact: Shasta-Trinity National Forest, Weaverville Ranger Station, P.O. Box 1190, Weaverville, CA 96093, tel. (530) 623-2121 or fax (530) 623-6010.

Primary sightings: pine marten

TULE ELK STATE RESERVE, in Kern County

Directions: From Bakersfield, on Highway 99, take the Stockdale Highway exit and drive west to Morris Road. Turn left on Morris Road, which becomes Station Road. Continue on Station Road to the park entrance on the left. The park is about three miles from Interstate 5.

Access/Fees: There is a day-use fee.

Maps: A free map is available at the entrance kiosk.

Contact: Tule Elk State Reserve, 8653 Station Road, Buttonwillow, CA 93206, tel. (661) 764-6881; California State Parks, San Joaquin District, P.O. Box 205, Friant, CA 93626, tel. (559) 822-2630 or fax (559) 822-2319.

Primary sightings: coyote, elk

TULE LAKE NATIONAL WILDLIFE REFUGE, in Siskiyou County

Directions: At Weed on Interstate 5, turn north on Highway 97 and drive four miles past the town of Dorris. Turn right on Highway 161/State Line Road and drive about 20 miles to Hill Road. Turn right on Hill Road and drive 4.5 miles to the refuge headquarters on the right.

Access/Fees: There is a per vehicle, day-use fee.

Maps: A free map is available at the refuge headquarters office.

Contact: Tule Lake National Wildlife Refuge, C/O Klamath Basin National Wildlife Refuges Complex, Route 1, Box 74, Tulelake, CA 96134, tel. (530) 667-2231

Primary sightings: gulls

TULLOCH RESERVOIR, in Calaveras and Tuolumne Counties

Directions: From Manteca on Highway 120, drive east about 35 miles, past Knights Ferry. Turn north on Tulloch Road to reach the south shore, or, to reach the north shore, continue another 10 miles on Highway 120/108 and turn left on Byrnes Ferry Road.

Access/Fees: Access is free.

Maps: A free map is available from the Tri-Dam Authority at the address below.

Contact: Tri-Dam Authority, P.O. Box 1158, Pinecrest, CA 95364, tel. (209) 965-3996 or (209) 785-3838 or fax (209) 965-4235.

Primary sightings: crayfish

TUOLUMNE MEADOWS, Yosemite National Park, in Tuolumne County

Directions: From Merced on Highway 140, drive east to the El Portal entrance station at Yosemite National Park. Continue east on Highway 140 to the junction with New Big Oak Flat Road. Turn north and drive to the Highway 120/Tioga Road junction (just before entering the valley). Turn right and drive 46 miles to the Tuolumne Meadows campground on the right side of the road.

Access/Fees: There is a per vehicle, day-use fee, which is good for seven days.

Maps: A free map is available at the visitor center.

Contact: Yosemite National Park, P.O. Box 577, Yosemite National Park, CA 95389, tel. (209) 372-0265 or (209) 372-0200 for a recorded message.

Primary sightings: black bear

See also Yosemite National Park.

U

UKONOM BASIN, MARBLE MOUNTAIN WILDERNESS, in Siskiyou County

Note: The Elk Creek Trailhead at Sulphur Springs Campground initiates a 14-mile hike to Ukonom Lake in the basin. Most folks break the trip in half, overnighting at one of the Granite Meadows camps situated along the route to Green and Gold Granite Lake.

Directions: From Interstate 5 at Yreka, take the Central Yreka exit and turn right (north) on Main Street, (which becomes Highway 263/Shasta River Road). Turn left at the Klamath River Highway/Highway 96 turnoff and drive about 65 miles to the town of Happy Camp. In Happy Camp, turn left on Elk Creek Road, cross the bridge and bear to the right, continuing on Elk Creek Road about 16 miles to the Sulphur Springs campground entrance. Park here and walk across the footbridge, into Sulphur Springs campground. The Elk Creek trailhead is at the south end of the campground. Follow the trail along Elk Creek for about three miles. At the wilderness campsite, stay to the right at the fork. Do not cross the creek. Continue up the trail another mile and a quarter. At the next trail junction, near the Marble Mountain Wilderness sign, keep to the right and continue up the Granite Creek Trail about one mile. Fifty feet past the wilderness camp near Tickner Creek, cross the creek and continue up the Granite Creek Trail another three miles, past the Blue Granite Lake and the Green and Gold Granite Lake turnoffs. About one mile past the Green and Gold Granite Lake turnoff, stay to the right at the trail junction signed Ukonom Lake and hike another 1.5 miles to the lake.

Access/Fees: A free annual campfire permit is required for hikers who camp in the wilderness. Trail parking and access are free.

Maps: A trail information sheet is available from the Happy Camp Ranger Station at the address below. A map is also available for a fee from the USDA Forest Service, Map Sales, 1323 Club Drive, Vallejo, CA 94592, tel. (707) 562-8794.

Contact: Klamath National Forest, Happy Camp Ranger District, P.O. Box 377, Happy Camp, CA 96039-0377, tel. (530) 493-2243 or fax (530) 493-2212.

Primary sightings: black bear

UNDERWATER WORLD, in San Francisco

Directions: The aquarium at Underwater World is located in San Francisco at Pier 39 on the Embarcadero at Beach Street.

Access/Fees: There is an entrance fee.

Contact: Write to Underwater World, Embarcadero at Beach Street, San Francisco, California 94133, tel. (415) 623-5300.

Primary sightings: anchovy

UPPER NEWPORT BAY ECOLOGICAL RESERVE AND REGIONAL PARK, in Orange County

Directions: From Huntington Beach on Highway 1/Pacific Coast Highway drive south about six miles. Turn left onJamboree Road and drive about one-quarter mile. Turn left on Back Bay Drive and drive to the reserve entrance on the left.

Access/Fees: Access is free.

Maps: Contact the office below for current map availability.

Contact: Upper Newport Bay Ecological Reserve and Regional Park, Department of Fish and Game, Long Beach Field Office, 330 Golden Shore Avenue, Suite 50, Long Beach, 90802, tel. (562) 590-5132.

Primary sightings: snipe

V

VAN DUZEN RIVER, in Humboldt County

Directions: From Eureka on US 101 southbound, drive about 16 miles. Turn left and drive east on Highway 36. River access is available along the highway.

Access/Fees: Access is free.

Maps: A topographic map of the Van Duzen River area is available for a fee from Maps, Western Distribution Center, U.S. Geological Survey, Box 25286, Federal Center, Denver, CO 80225, tel. (303) 202-4700.

Contact: Department Fish and Game, Eureka Field Office, 619 Second Street, Eureka, CA 95501, tel. (707) 445-6493 or fax (707) 445-6664.

Primary sightings: steelhead

VENTANA WILDERNESS, in Monterey County

Directions: From Carmel on Highway 1, drive south about 26 miles to Big Sur Station and the Pine Ridge Trailhead. Hike-in 10 miles to Sykes Hot Springs. The trail continues another 19 miles and ends at either China Camp or Arroyo Seco campgrounds.

Access/Fees: There is a per vehicle, day-use fee.

Maps: A map is available for a fee from Big Sur Station or from USDA Forest Service, Map Sales, 1323 Club Drive, Vallejo, CA 94592, tel. (707) 562-8794.

Contact: Ventana Wilderness, C/O Los Padres National Forest, Big Sur Station Number 1, Big Sur, CA 93920, tel. (831) 667-2423 or fax (831) 667-2886.

Primary sightings: California condor, hawks, sea lions, sea otter

VENTURA DEEP SEA, offshore from Ventura County

Directions: In Ventura on US 101 northbound, take the Seaward exit. Turn left, then left again on Harbor Boulevard and drive 1.5 miles. Turn right on Schooner Street and drive to the deadend. Turn right on Anchors Way and drive a short distance to the harbor.

Access/Fees: For partyboat schedules and fees, contact Ventura Harbor Village Sportfishing, tel. (805) 658-1060.

Maps: A free map/brochure of the Ventura area is available from the chambers and visitor bureaus at the addresses below.

Contact: Ventura Visitor Center, 89 South California Street, Suite C, Ventura, CA 93001, tel. (805) 648-2075 or fax (805) 648-3535; Ventura Chamber of Commerce, 785 South Seaward Avenue, Ventura, CA 93001, tel. (805) 648-2875.

Primary sightings: marlin

W

WADDELL CREEK, in Santa Cruz County
Directions: From San Francisco, take Highway 1 south to Santa Cruz. Turn east on Highway 9, then left on Highway 236 and continue to Big Basin Redwoods State Park.
Access/Fees: There is an entrance fee.
Maps: A map is available for a fee from Sempervirens Fund, P.O. Drawer BE, Los Altos, CA 94023, tel. (650) 968-4509.
Contact: Big Basin Redwoods State Park, 21600 Big Basin Way, Boulder Creek, CA 95006, tel. (831) 338-8860 or the Rancho Del Oso outpost, tel. (831) 425-1218.
Primary sightings: blue heron, deer, quail, squirrel, steelhead

WHITTIER NARROWS NATURE CENTER, in Los Angeles County
Directions: From Pasadena on Highway 210, drive east about 10 miles. Turn south on Highway 605 and drive about five miles. Turn west on Highway 60/Pomona Freeway and drive about seven miles. Take the Santa Anita Avenue exit, turn left over the Highway 60 freeway, and drive one-quarter mile to the visitor center on the left at 750 South Santa Anita Avenue. To reach the nature center entrance, continue on South Santa Anita Avenue, turn left on Durfee Avenue and drive to the entrance on the right.
Access/Fees: Access is free.
Maps: A free map is available at the visitor center.
Contact: Whittier Narrows Nature Center, 750 South Santa Anita Avenue, South El Monte, CA 91733, tel. (626) 575-5526 or fax (626) 448-7308; County of Los Angeles, Department of Parks and Recreation, 433 South Vermont Avenue, Los Angeles, CA 90020-1975, tel. (213) 738-2961 or fax (213) 487-0380.
Primary sightings: rabbits or hares, raccoon, wood duck

XYZ

YOLO BYPASS WILDLIFE AREA, in Yolo County
Directions: From Sacramento on Interstate 80, drive west across the Yolo Causeway. Exit on frontage road at the west side of the causeway (first road to the right after the causeway). Turn right on County Road 32A and drive one-half mile to the west levee gate on the left side of the road. To reach Yolo Bypass Wildlife Area headquarters, continue on County Road 32A, which becomes County Road 32B, and drive about two miles to 45211 County Road 32B.
Access/Fees: Access is free. Open year-round, sunrise to sunset.
Maps: A free map is available at the area headquarters.
Contact: Yolo Bypass Wildlife Area, 45211 County Road 32B, Davis, CA 95616, tel. (530) 757-2461 or fax (530) 757-2518; Department of Fish and Game, 1701 Nimbus Road, Rancho Cordova, CA 95670, tel. (916) 358-2877 or fax (916) 358-2912.
Primary sightings: ducks, raccoon, river otter, swans

YOSEMITE NATIONAL PARK, in Mariposa and Tuolumne Counties
Directions: From Merced on Highway 140, drive east to the El Portal entrance station at Yosemite National Park. Continue east on Highway 140 to the junction with New

Big Oak Flat Road. Turn north and drive to the Highway 120/Tioga Road junction (just before entering the valley). Turn right and drive 46 miles to the Tuolumne Meadows campground on the right side of the road.

Access/Fees: There is a per vehicle, day-use fee, which is good for seven days.

Maps: A free map is available at the visitor center.

Contact: Yosemite National Park, P.O. Box 577, Yosemite National Park, CA 95389, tel. (209) 372-0265 or (209) 372-0200 for a recorded message.

Primary sightings: band-tailed pigeon, foxes, jays, raccoon, woodpeckers

See also Tuolumne Meadows.

Index

BIRDS

general discussion: 358-360, 371-372
American kestrel: 197-198, 200-203
American wigeon duck: 139-142
bald eagle: 147-151
band-tailed pigeons: 284-287
barn owl: 265-268, 270-272
belted kingfisher: 219-222
blue grouse: 183-188
brown pelican: 273-276
California quail: 297-302
canvasback duck: 126-130
cedar waxwing: 360-362
chukar: 84-87
condor: 88-92
crane: 101-104
curlew: 109-112
dipper: 362
doves: 123-126
ducks: 126-146
finch: 362-363
golden eagle: 152-156
goose: 179-183
great blue heron: 203-207
great horned owl: 265-270
green-winged teal duck: 131-132
grouse: 183-192
gulls: 192-197
hawks: 197-203
jays: 212-215
killdeer: 215-219
kingfisher: 219-222
magpies: 363-364
mallard duck: 133-135
mockingbird: 365-367
northern pintail duck: 135-136
northern shoveler duck: 137-139
osprey: 252-256
owls: 265-272
peregrine falcon: 162-165
pheasant: 277-280
pigeons: 284-287
quails: 297-303
raven: 320-323
red-tailed hawk: 197-200
red-winged blackbird: 366-367
ringed-neck pheasant: 277-280
roadrunner: 324-327
robin: 367-368
sage grouse: 188-192
snipe: 354-357
songbirds: 358-372
swans: 387-390
turkey: 406-409
western meadowlark: 369-372
wild turkey: 406-409
wood duck: 142-146
woodpeckers: 415-418

About the Author

JEFFREY PATTY

Tom Stienstra is the outdoors columnist for the *San Francisco Examiner & Chronicle* and the nation's top-selling author of outdoor guidebooks. He is an avid outdoorsman with a gift for sniffing out hidden places and wildlife, and networking with field scouts across the state. He has written 14 books, including *California Camping,* the No. 1 outdoor book in the nation in 1999, as awarded by Amazon.com. In the 1990s, he was twice named national Outdoor Writer of the Year, newspaper division, among 1,600 entrants, and three times California Outdoor Writer of the Year. He was also awarded a special commendation from the City of San Francisco for helping the San Francisco Police Department convert the therapy pool at Shriner's Children Hospital into a trout pond, then taking disabled youngsters on their first fishing trips. To complete this book, he explored all 58 counties in California—hiking, boating, driving, and flying his way across the state. He can be reached directly on the internet at www.TomStienstra.Com, where signed copies of his books are available. He lives with his wife and two sons in Northern California.

Other Books by Tom Stienstra

Epic Trips of the West
California Wildlife (with illustrator Paul Johnson)
California Camping
California Hiking (with Ann Marie Brown)
California Fishing
California Recreational Lakes & Rivers
Tom Stienstra's Outdoor Getaway Guide: Northern California
Easy Camping in Northern California
Sunshine Jobs: Career Opportunities Working Outdoors

FOGHORN ✖ OUTDOORS

Founded in 1985, Foghorn Press has quickly become one of the country's premier publishers of outdoor recreation guidebooks. Foghorn Press books are available throughout the United States in bookstores and some outdoor retailers.